Dictatorship and Information

D1264574

Dictatorship and Information

Authoritarian Regime Resilience in Communist Europe and China

MARTIN K. DIMITROV

OXFORD
UNIVERSITY PRESS

OXFORD
UNIVERSITY PRESS

Oxford University Press is a department of the University of Oxford. It furthers
the University's objective of excellence in research, scholarship, and education
by publishing worldwide. Oxford is a registered trade mark of Oxford University
Press in the UK and certain other countries.

Published in the United States of America by Oxford University Press
198 Madison Avenue, New York, NY 10016, United States of America.

Library of Congress Cataloging-in-Publication Data
Names: Dimitrov, Martin K., 1975- author.
Title: Dictatorship and information : authoritarian regime resilience in
communist Europe and China / Martin K. Dimitrov.
Description: First Edition. | New York : Oxford University Press, [2023] | Includes index.
Identifiers: LCCN 2022030798 (print) | LCCN 2022030799 (ebook) |
ISBN 9780197672938 (Paperback) | ISBN 9780197672921 (Hardback) |
ISBN 9780197672952 (epub)
Subjects: LCSH: Authoritarianism—Case studies. |
National security—Bulgaria. | National security—China. |
Intelligence service—Bulgaria. | Intelligence service—China.
Classification: LCC JC480 .D56 2023 (print) | LCC JC480 (ebook) |
DDC 320.53—dc23/eng/20220811
LC record available at https://lccn.loc.gov/2022030798
LC ebook record available at https://lccn.loc.gov/2022030799

DOI: 10.1093/oso/9780197672921.001.0001

1 3 5 7 9 8 6 4 2

Paperback printed by Sheridan Books, Inc., United States of America
Hardback printed by Bridgeport National Bindery, Inc., United States of America

For Bradin

Contents

PART V. GENERALIZABILITY OF THE THEORY

Figures and Maps

Tables

Acknowledgments

Writing this book has been an adventure, an intellectual but also a real one, that took me to several dozen research sites across Asia, Europe, Latin America, and various parts of the United States. Since 2007, I have accumulated intellectual and personal debts that I am glad to acknowledge in the lines that follow.

Several institutions provided fellowship support for this project: the Woodrow Wilson International Center for Scholars; the Notre Dame Institute for Advanced Study; the American Academy in Berlin; the Aleksanteri Institute at the University of Helsinki (which hosted me repeatedly); the Princeton Institute for International and Regional Studies; and the ATLAS program of the Louisiana Board of Regents. Further financial assistance was supplied by grants from the Rockefeller Center and the Dickey Center at Dartmouth College; by the School of Liberal Arts, the Stone Center, the Cuban and Caribbean Studies Institute, and the Office of Academic Affairs at Tulane University; by the Institute for Studies of the Recent Past in Sofia; and by the China and Inner Asia Council of the Association for Asian Studies. In addition, I want to thank several institutions that generously opened their doors to me: the Fairbank Center at Harvard; the Davis Center at Harvard; the East Asian Legal Studies Program at Harvard Law School; and the Universities Service Centre at the Chinese University of Hong Kong.

Over the years, I had the opportunity to present portions of this project at Tulane University; Harvard University; Princeton University; Cornell University; Brown University; Dartmouth College; Yale University; Columbia University; Temple University; Southern Methodist University; Louisiana State University; Emory University; the University of Wisconsin Madison; Duke University; the University of Pittsburgh; Wesleyan University; the University of Chicago; the University of Michigan; Stanford University; the University of California Berkeley; the University of California San Diego; the University of California Irvine; Miami University; the Woodrow Wilson International Center for Scholars; the University of Notre Dame; the University of Helsinki; the Finnish Center of Excellence in Russian Studies; the American Academy in Berlin; the Wissenschaftszentrum zu Berlin; the Stasi Records Archive (BStU); GIGA Hamburg; Bundesstiftung Aufarbeitung; the Maison des Sciences de l'Homme et de la Société and the Institute for Studies of the Recent Past in Sofia; the Institute for the Study of Totalitarian Regimes (ÚSTR) and NYU Prague; the University of Nottingham; the University of Melbourne; National

Chengchi University; Shanghai Jiaotong University; NYU Shanghai; East China Normal University; Zhejiang University; Renmin University of China; Beijing Union University; Shandong University; and McGill University. Presentations under the aegis of the Harvard-Yenching Institute (at Sun Yat-sen University, Fudan University, and at Harvard-Yenching) and at the Virtual Workshop on Authoritarian Regimes provided additional opportunities for engagement with thoughtful audiences. Elizabeth Perry and Valerie Bunce generously commented on seven chapters of an earlier version of the manuscript. Beatriz Magaloni, Jennifer Gandhi, Grigore Pop-Eleches, Mary Gallagher, Iza Ding, and Dimitar Gueorguiev provided feedback on a more recent draft. I am grateful to all for their constructive suggestions. I also received detailed feedback from two anonymous reviewers for Oxford University Press.

Writing this book has allowed me to get to know a number of exceptional individuals who lead institutions of academic excellence. I am grateful to all of them: Gary Smith (American Academy in Berlin); Markku Kivinen, Markku Kangaspuro, and Anna Korhonen (Aleksanteri Institute in Helsinki); Mark Beissinger (Princeton Institute for International and Regional Studies); Jan Berris (the National Committee on United States–China Relations); William Alford (East Asian Legal Studies at Harvard Law School); and Elizabeth Perry (Harvard-Yenching Institute). At Tulane, I want to acknowledge especially Nancy Maveety, Ana López, and Brian Edwards for their support.

Though I need to protect the anonymity of nearly all the individuals who agreed to participate in ninety-six interviews for this book, I am profoundly grateful that they took the time to speak with me in China, Cuba, Russia, Germany, Bulgaria, and the United States; interviews with public figures are referenced in the footnotes. I feel fortunate to be able to acknowledge explicitly the various archives in which I collected materials for this book; the major repositories are listed in Chapter 2. I want to highlight in particular the assistance of Antonia Guleva (Dossier Commission in Sofia); Pierre Landry and Celia Chan (Universities Service Centre in Hong Kong); and Nancy Hearst (Fairbank Center Library), whose care and attention also improved this book. In addition, I want to thank my research assistants Zhu Zhang (now Professor Zhang), Lumin Li, and Andres Sandoval (who constructed the two GIS maps in Chapter 6). At Oxford University Press, Dave McBride deserves special mention for seeing this book through with professionalism and efficiency.

I have been fortunate to be able to call on a group of colleagues, friends, and family over the years. For their support, counsel, and good humor, I am grateful to Carolina Caballero, Calvin Chen, Linda Cook, Nara Dillon, Iza Ding, Dimitar Gueorguiev, Nancy Hearst, Yoshiko Herrera, Sean Knowlton, Anna Korhonen, Zinaida Kurochkina, Ana López, Beatriz Magaloni, Melanie Manion, Isabela Mares, Nancy Maveety, Jean Oi, Virginia Oliveros, Elizabeth Perry, Ben Read,

Joseph Sassoon, Victor Shih, Hiroki Takeuchi, Allison Truitt, and Jeremy Wallace. In New Orleans, Norma Sandoval opened up for me the city she loves. Mary Ann Bohlke taught me a lot about good citizenship. My sister Katya Sabeva and her family have always been there for me. My mother Zlatka Kostadinova has been my rock. And Bradin, well, what is there to say.

Abbreviations

AKRDOPBGDSRSBNA	Bulgarian State Security Dossier Commission
AMVR	Archive of the Bulgarian Ministry of the Interior
ANCLA	Clandestine News Agency (Argentina)
ATA	Albanian Telegraph Agency
BBS	bulletin board service
BCP	Bulgarian Communist Party
BStU	Stasi Records Archive (Germany)
BTA	Bulgarian Telegraph Agency
CCP	Chinese Communist Party
CDR	Committee for Defense of the Revolution (Cuba)
CESPO	Center for Sociopolitical Studies and Opinion Research (Cuba)
CID	Central Investigation Department (China)
CNA	Central News Agency (Taiwan)
CNI	*Central Nacional de Informaciones* (Chile)
CoCom	Coordinating Committee for Multilateral Export Controls
COMECON	Council for Mutual Economic Assistance
CPSU	Communist Party of the Soviet Union
DGCI	Counterintelligence Directorate (Cuba)
DGI	Intelligence Directorate (Cuba)
DIER	*Departamento de Investigaciones del Ejército Rebelde* (Cuba)
DIFA	*Dirección de Inteligencia de la Fuerza Aérea* (Chile)
DIIFAR	*Departamento de Información e Investigaciones de las Fuerzas Armadas Revolucionarias* (Cuba)
DINA	*Dirección de Inteligencia Nacional* (Chile)
DINE	*Dirección de Inteligencia del Ejército* (Chile)
DPRK	Democratic People's Republic of Korea
DSE	State Security Department (Cuba)
FDI	foreign direct investment
FH	volunteer assistant (GDR Ministry of the Interior)
FOIA	Freedom of Information Act
G-2	State Security Department (Cuba)
GARF	State Archive of the Russian Federation
GDP	gross domestic product
GDR	German Democratic Republic
GIS	geographic information system
GMS	societal collaborator for security (Stasi)
GPU	State Political Directorate (Soviet Union)

GRU	Main Intelligence Directorate of the General Staff of the Armed Forces of the Soviet Union
IfM	Central Committee Institute for Opinion Research (GDR)
IKM	secret informant (GDR Ministry of the Interior)
IM	unofficial collaborator (Stasi)
IMK	unofficial collaborator for securing conspiracy (Stasi)
ISP	Internet service provider
KDNK	Committee for Control by the State and the People (Bulgaria)
KGB	Committee for State Security (USSR)
KMT	Guomindang (Taiwan)
MdI	Ministry of the Interior (GDR)
MfS (Stasi)	Ministry of State Security (GDR)
MGB	Ministry of State Security (USSR)
MINFAR	Ministry of Defense (Cuba)
MININT	Ministry of the Interior (Cuba)
MJIB	Ministry of Justice Investigation Bureau (Taiwan)
MPS	Ministry of Public Security (China)
MSS	Ministry of State Security (China)
MVD	Ministry of Internal Affairs (USSR)
NGO	nongovernmental organization
NKGB	People's Commissariat for State Security (USSR)
NKVD	People's Commissariat for Internal Affairs (USSR)
NPC	National People's Congress (China)
NT$	New Taiwan Dollar
OGI	Open Government Information Initiative (China)
OGPU	Joint State Political Directorate (USSR)
OibE	special assignment officer (Stasi)
OLS	ordinary least squares
ORI	Integrated Revolutionary Organizations (Cuba)
PAP	People's Armed Police (China)
PDB	*President's Daily Brief* (U.S.)
PLA	People's Liberation Army (China)
PNR	National Revolutionary Police (Cuba)
PPS	probability proportional to size
PRC	People's Republic of China
PRI	Institutional Revolutionary Party (Mexico)
PSB	Public Security Bureau (China)
PURSC	United Party of the Cuban Socialist Revolution
RFE	Radio Free Europe
RMB	renminbi (Chinese yuan)
ROSTA	Russian Telegraph Agency
RTsKhIDNI	Russian Center for the Preservation and Study of Documents of Most Recent History

SAPMO	Foundation Archives of the Parties and Mass Organizations of the GDR in the Federal Archives (Germany)
SED	Socialist Unity Party of Germany (GDR)
SICAR	*Servicio de Inteligencia de Carabineros* (Chile)
SIDE	*Secretaría de Inteligencia del Estado* (Argentina)
SIN	*Servicio de Inteligencia Naval* (Chile)
SMA	Shanghai Municipal Archives
SMS	short-messaging service
SOE	state-owned enterprise (China)
SR	socialist revolutionaries (*essers*)
SSR	Soviet Socialist Republic
TASS	Telegraph Agency of the Soviet Union
TsDA	Bulgarian Central State Archives
TsIAS	Central Information-Analytical Service (Bulgarian State Security)
TsKhSD	Center for Preservation of Contemporary Documentation (Russia)
TsUM	Central Department Store (Sofia)
TVE	township and village enterprise (China)
UMAP	military units to aid production (Cuba)
USSR	Union of Soviet Socialist Republics
VChK (Cheka)	All-Russian Extraordinary Commission
VOA	Voice of America
WTO	World Trade Organization
XPCC	Xinjiang Production and Construction Corps
ZAIG	Central Evaluation and Information Group (Stasi)
ZIJ	Central Youth Research Institute (GDR)

PART I
THEORY AND METHOD

This book offers a systematic theory of how autocrats assess the level of popular discontent they face and how they deploy repression and concessions in light of these assessments. Evaluating mass dissatisfaction necessitates detailed information about the willingness of individuals to engage in overt challenges to the regime and about brewing latent discontent that has not yet been visibly expressed. Both overt and latent discontent can stem from political frustrations, socioeconomic grievances, or a combination of the two. Assessing popular dissatisfaction requires the creation of institutions that can collect and transmit information that is either extracted involuntarily from citizens or is willingly transmitted by them. The richest complements of such institutions develop in single-party communist autocracies, which are also the longest-lived type of authoritarian regime. In such regimes, information about popular discontent is compiled mainly by State Security, by the party, and by journalists. It is then transmitted internally to decision makers who use it to determine the optimal mix of rewards and punishments to be deployed in order to maintain power.

This study departs from existing theories of information in autocracies in three ways. With regard to the conventional wisdom that the dictator's dilemma (which involves the uncertainty of those in power about the level of popular support they have) cannot be solved, the book demonstrates that autocrats are aware of this problem and invest substantial resources into creating institutions that generate the information needed to mitigate it. Second, although the study concurs with more recent research on the value of elections, protests, and liberalized media for indexing levels of popular discontent, it argues that as the information generated through these channels is available both to autocrats and to the general public (which can use it to coordinate antiregime collective action), autocrats actively foster other mechanisms that allow for the private transmission of information only to regime insiders. Finally, this study challenges assumptions that information can ensure the indefinite survival of dictatorships. While complex information-gathering institutions can extend the lifespan of regimes, they can do so only when autocrats are willing to use the assessments of popular discontent generated by these institutions to guide decisions about the use of force and the making of concessions. As this study demonstrates, such nimble governance is feasible only under certain conditions. Therefore, it is theoretically possible (and empirically verifiable) that autocrats may possess abundant information about discontent but prove unable to act on it.

Empirically, the focus of the book is on the origins and temporal evolution of information-gathering institutions in single-party communist autocracies. The study offers a paired comparison of one case where the mechanisms for assessing popular discontent outlasted the communist regime itself (Bulgaria, 1944–1991) and another in which the evolution of both the information-gathering institutions and of the single-party system is still ongoing (China, 1949–2022). By tracing the development of these institutions from the moment of regime creation, the book provides abundant evidence of the role of information gathering for communist state building. Yet, by showing that these information-collection channels can survive past the demise of single-party rule, the study demonstrates that the capacity of these institutions to maintain the communist regime can erode over time. This finding has implications for the future of the current Chinese political model. In addition to the extended Bulgaria–China comparison, the book provides brief empirically informed discussions of how its argument applies to other cases of both existing and collapsed communist regimes (Cuba, the German Democratic Republic, and the Soviet Union); to Leninist and non-Leninist single-party systems (Taiwan under martial law, 1949–1987, and Iraq, 1968–2003); to multiparty autocracies (Russia, 2000–2022); and to autocracies without political parties (Chile, 1973–1989, and Argentina, 1976–1983). These cases delineate the scope conditions for the argument.

Methodologically, this book argues that studies of dictatorships need to confront the problem of authoritarian opacity, which involves keeping most political processes hidden from public view. Information gathering is a crucial example of a phenomenon impacted by opacity, since most of the relevant activities occur in secret. How might we conduct research on nontransparent processes in autocracies? This study stresses that relying on publicly disseminated documents is of limited utility, as autocrats have no incentive to reveal what information on popular discontent they collect (and how they do so). Decisions to selectively permit the open circulation of information that is critical of the regime are guided by a public relations logic of carefully orchestrated responsiveness. These materials are instructive of how the autocrats want to shape public perceptions of the regime. However, they cannot be used to generate a theory of the nontransparent process of information gathering in dictatorships.

Reservations about openly circulating information raise the importance of identifying and using classified materials that are not meant for public dissemination. Such documents (produced by the party, by State Security, and by journalists writing internal reports) hold the promise of generating hypotheses about the hidden logic of information gathering in autocracies. These hypotheses can be tested through qualitative and quantitative internal data or, in rare cases, through a combination of internal sources and appropriately contextualized data meant for public dissemination (although publicly circulating materials are unlikely to reveal the logic driving information gathering, they may contain quantifiable indicators of the results of these activities).

This part of the book consists of two chapters. Chapter 1 presents the theoretical puzzle motivating the study and provides an overview of its main findings, whereas Chapter 2 makes an argument that classified materials can reveal internal government understandings of the institutions that need to be created and maintained in order to assess popular discontent. Jointly, the two chapters present a discussion of the theory and method that this study uses in approaching the question of the origins and evolution of authoritarian information states.

1

Introduction

Solving the Dictator's Dilemma

Eruptions of discontent are often unexpected. In 1953, the leaders of the German Democratic Republic (GDR) had not received sufficient warning about the worker unrest that extended to fourteen of the fifteen provinces in the country.[1] In 1959, the capital of Tibet was engulfed in an uprising that largely came as a surprise to the leadership in Beijing and to Chairman Mao, who did not believe that the discontent in other areas inhabited by Tibetans would spread to Lhasa.[2] In April 1999, 10,000 Falun Gong followers gathered outside the leadership compound in the center of Beijing to demand recognition of their right to organize. Coordination, which had been carried out via email and bulletin board services (BBS), caught the ministries of public and state security off guard.[3]

And yet there are counterexamples. One is provided by the GDR, where in 1983 the East German Ministry of State Security (Stasi) issued a forecast regarding the potential for the incipient opposition to serve as a catalyst for political destabilization.[4] According to the Stasi, most dangerous was the peace movement, which had developed under the auspices of the evangelical church. In the future, the Stasi opined, the number of opposition groups was likely to increase, with new movements emerging around environmental issues, human rights, and countercultural arts and music. Subsequent Stasi reports from 1988–1989 present powerful evidence that this 1983 forecast was exceedingly accurate—but also that the Stasi was unable to counteract the trends it had itself foreseen.[5]

---

[1] Gary Bruce, "The Prelude to Nationwide Surveillance in East Germany: Stasi Operations and Threat Perceptions, 1945–1953," *Journal of Cold War Studies* 5:2 (Spring 2003), 3–31.

[2] See Chapter 6, as well as Jian Chen, "The Tibetan Rebellion of 1959 and China's Changing Relations with India and the Soviet Union," *Journal of Cold War Studies* 8:3 (2006), 54–101, esp. 72; Xiaoyuan Liu, *The End of Revolution: The Chinese Communist Party in Tibet, 1949–1959* (New York: Columbia University Press, 2020), 252–63; and *Neibu cankao* (1958–1959).

[3] James Tong, "An Organizational Analysis of the *Falun Gong*: Structure, Communications, Financing," *The China Quarterly*, no. 171 (September 2002), 636–60; James W. Tong, *Revenge of the Forbidden City: The Suppression of the Falungong in China, 1999–2005* (New York: Oxford University Press, 2009).

[4] Archive of the Bulgarian Ministry of the Interior (AMVR) f. 1 op. 12 a. e. 501 (1983), 178.

[5] Frank Joestel, ed., *Die DDR im Blick der Stasi 1988: Die geheimen Berichte an die SED-Führung* (Göttingen: Vandenhoeck and Ruprecht, 2010); Armin Mitter and Stefan Wolle, eds., *Ich liebe euch doch alle! Befehle und Lageberichte des MfS, Januar–November 1989* (Berlin: Basis Druck Wolle, 1990); Daniela Münkel, ed., *Die DDR im Blick der Stasi: Die geheimen Berichte an die SED-Führung*

Dictatorship and Information. Martin K. Dimitrov, Oxford University Press. © Oxford University Press 2023.
DOI: 10.1093/oso/9780197672921.003.0001

Or take Bulgaria, where in the summer of 1989 the communist incumbent Todor Zhivkov was aware of widespread popular unrest and, more importantly, of a plot by members of the Politburo to oust him by staging a palace coup. Yet he was unable to avert the coup and was deposed in November 1989 (see Chapter 7). Knowledge does not always help.

Finally, at the end of April 2005, in the midst of preparations for anti-Japanese protests in Beijing, the Chinese Ministry of Public Security sent a text message to everyone with a cell phone registered in the capital to forgo joining the demonstration that was planned for May 1—thus issuing a clear signal that it was able to read the short-messaging service (SMS) communications through which the organizers had coordinated their contentious activities.[6] The protests did not go forward.

The first three vignettes document the existence of the *dictator's dilemma*, which involves an incapacity to calibrate repression and concessions due to a lack of information about the degree of popular and elite opposition to the regime.[7] The second three indicate that intelligence can be collected, and the dilemma can be solved, though having information does not mean that dictators will always be able to act on it. Collectively, the six vignettes allow us to focus on a central problem of authoritarian rule.

This study makes three interrelated arguments that jointly generate a new theory about the temporal variation in the strategies that authoritarian regimes deploy to confront the dictator's dilemma. First, the dilemma can be solved by designing institutions that collect information and transmit it to decision makers. Second, these institutional solutions vary—some are retrospective and focus mostly on repression, whereas others are anticipatory and primarily involve concessions. Typically, retrospective institutions emerge first, while the more sophisticated mechanisms that enable anticipatory rule are created later. Third, the solutions have a major limitation, namely, solving the dilemma by fostering institutions of anticipatory governance does not mean that either a dictator or his autocratic regime can persevere indefinitely. Information extends the

---

Herbst 1989 (Berlin: BStU, 2014); Mark Schiefer and Martin Stief, eds., *Die DDR im Blick der Stasi: Die geheimen Berichte an die SED-Führung 1989* (Göttingen: Vandenhoeck and Ruprecht, 2019).

[6] Personal experience. The text of the message sent on April 30, 2005 is as follows: 北京市公安局提醒您: 不信谣, 不传谣, 理性表达爱国热情, 不参加非法游行活动. 帮忙不要添乱, 爱国不要违法, 做一个遵纪守法的好公民. (The Beijing City Public Security Bureau reminds you: Do not believe rumors, do not spread rumors, express your patriotism reasonably, do not join illegal demonstrations. Do not add to the disorder, do not engage in illegal patriotic acts, be a law-abiding citizen.)

[7] The term is used in various ways by political scientists. I rely on the classic definition: "Dictators cannot know . . . whether the population genuinely worships them or worships them because they command such worship." See Ronald Wintrobe, *The Political Economy of Dictatorship* (New York: Cambridge University Press, 1998), 20.

lifespan of dictatorships only under certain conditions, as discussed in this book. When those optimal conditions are absent, even well-informed dictators may be deposed and regimes with sophisticated intelligence-gathering institutions may disappear.

1.1 The Dictator's Dilemma and Its Solutions

One of the fundamental challenges of authoritarian governance is the difficulty of obtaining reliable information about the public mood. This problem was first identified in the classic literature on dictatorship, which posited that autocrats operate in an information vacuum because they have "no way of ascertaining the common man's views."[8] Subsequent work has built on these foundational ideas, arguing that repression exacerbates this information problem because citizens in dictatorships are unwilling to reveal their true level of support for the system due to fear that criticism will be met with reprisals.[9] Instead of showing their opposition to the regime, therefore, individuals engage in preference falsification, which manifests itself as reluctant participation in ritualistic acts of public dissimulation ("as if" compliance),[10] such as compulsory mass rallies and noncompetitive elections. Preference falsification makes dictators fundamentally insecure, since they cannot know their true level of support and thus face the risk of being deposed through a revolution or a coup.[11] This produces the theoretical expectation that autocracies will be relatively short lived. However, as Table 1.1 illustrates, there is substantial variation in the lifespan of authoritarian regimes. In particular, the remarkable longevity of communist dictatorships and the relative infrequency of coups in them suggest that these regimes succeed in finding strategies that will allow them to obtain accurate information about the public mood.[12]

---

[8] Carl J. Friedrich and Zbigniew Brzezinski, *Totalitarian Dictatorship and Autocracy* (New York: Praeger, 1965), 135.

[9] Wintrobe, *The Political Economy of Dictatorship*.

[10] Timur Kuran, *Private Truths, Public Lies: The Social Consequences of Preference Falsification* (Cambridge, MA: Harvard University Press, 1995); Lisa Wedeen, *Ambiguities of Domination: Politics, Rhetoric, and Symbols in Contemporary Syria* (Chicago: University of Chicago Press, 1999).

[11] Timur Kuran "Now Out of Never: The Element of Surprise in the East European Revolution of 1989," *World Politics* 44:1 (1991), 7–48; Suzanne Lohmann, "The Dynamics of Informational Cascades: The Monday Demonstrations in Leipzig, East Germany, 1989–91," *World Politics* 47:1 (1994), 42–101.

[12] In communist regimes, palace coups are more typical than military coups. Unsuccessful military coup attempts took place in a number of countries, ranging from Bulgaria (1965) and the Soviet Union (1991) to North Korea (1956 and 2013) and China (1971); in these cases, there were preparations for a coup, but they never materialized. In contrast to military coups, palace coups occur considerably more often, as my dataset on palace and military coups reveals. As many as nineteen incumbent leaders were removed through Politburo votes in every communist regime except for Albania, North Korea, and Cuba, where leaders died in office or retired due to

Table 1.1 Average Tenure of Autocracies, 1946–2008

Regime Type	N	Tenure (years)
Parties banned	81	16.56
Multiple parties	195	15.91
Noncommunist single-party	51	29.87
Collapsed communist single-party (1991)	10	48.3
Surviving communist single-party (2022)	5	65

Sources: Benjamin Smith, "Life of the Party: The Origins of Regime Breakdown and Persistence Under Single-Party Rule," *World Politics* 57:3 (2005), 421–51; Milan W. Svolik, *The Politics of Authoritarian Rule* (New York: Cambridge University Press, 2012), esp. 184–92; author's calculations.

The literature has proposed several solutions to the information problem that assume autocrats are interested in acquiring knowledge to help them solve the dictator's dilemma. One is emblematized by Haroun al-Rashid, who "disguised himself from time to time and mingled, in the dark of night, with the people in taverns and streets to listen to their tales of woe."[13] Although inspection tours survive to this day,[14] they are not a practical way to ensure access to information. Recent research on authoritarian politics has articulated several additional solutions to the agency problems that can prevent the transmission of negative information to the top leadership. One is competitive elections, which can provide information to the regime about the level of mass support.[15] Another hinges on the capacity of protests to transmit to the leadership information about levels of discontent.[16] A third line of inquiry focuses on the content of news published

incapacitation. On coups, see especially Anne Meng, *Constraining Dictatorship: From Personalized Rule to Institutionalized Regimes* (New York: Cambridge University Press, 2020) and Barbara Geddes, Joseph Wright, and Erica Frantz, *How Dictatorships Work: Power, Personalization, and Collapse* (New York: Cambridge University Press, 2018).

[13] Friedrich and Brzezinski, *Totalitarian Dictatorship and Autocracy*, 135.

[14] Wen Jiabao, "Zai hui Xingyi yi Yaobang," *Renmin ribao* (April 15, 2010), 2.

[15] This insight is centrally associated with Beatriz Magaloni, *Voting for Autocracy: Hegemonic Party Survival and its Demise in Mexico* (New York: Cambridge University Press, 2006). See also Jason Brownlee, *Authoritarianism in an Age of Democratization* (New York: Cambridge University Press, 2007); Jennifer Gandhi, *Political Institutions under Dictatorship* (New York: Cambridge University Press, 2008); Jennifer Gandhi and Ellen Lust-Okar, "Elections Under Authoritarianism," *Annual Review of Political Science*, no. 12 (2009), 403–22; Beatriz Magaloni and Ruth Kricheli, "Political Order and One-Party Rule," *Annual Review of Political Science*, no. 13 (2010), 123–43; and Lisa Blaydes, *Elections and Distributive Politics in Mubarak's Egypt* (New York: Cambridge University Press, 2011).

[16] See Peter Lorentzen, "Regularizing Rioting: Permitting Public Protest in an Authoritarian Regime," *Quarterly Journal of Political Science* 8 (2013), 127–58. On protests, see also Kevin O'Brien and Lianjiang Li, *Rightful Resistance in Rural China* (New York: Cambridge University Press, 2006); Yongshun Cai, *Collective Resistance in China: Why Popular Protests Succeed or Fail* (Stanford,

in liberalized media as an important source of information about public discontent.[17] In addition, research on China documents how legislatures and the notice-and-comment process that accompanies some legislative proposals can generate information about popular preferences.[18]

A general problem is that the mechanisms for monitoring discontent that are emphasized in the recent literature generate information that is available to three sets of audiences: scholars, ordinary citizens, and regime insiders. By contrast, the institutions for assessing public opinion in Eastern Europe produced information that was directed only at regime insiders. This book stresses that identical institutions for generating internal information about discontent eventually emerged in China as well.[19] Much like its counterparts in Eastern Europe, the Chinese party-state has valued such internal channels for the vertical transmission of information, rather than the avenues highlighted in the literature, which enable the horizontal spread of knowledge about discontent. The existence of internal sources of information raises a question about the utility of those channels that are visible to multiple audiences. This study maintains that the main function of such channels is not to transmit information, but rather to serve as tools of authoritarian dramaturgy that allow the government to demonstrate its responsiveness to popular grievances in highly scripted public spectacles.[20]

1.2 Raw Data, Unprocessed Intelligence, and Information

To be useful to decision makers, information must be accurate, granular, and actionable. Information is data that are collected with a specific purpose and then subjected to analysis, which transforms them into a finished product that is useful to decision makers; in other words, information is actionable intelligence. Information is different from raw data and unprocessed intelligence. A question is necessary to cull unprocessed intelligence from raw data; a trained analyst can then distill information from the unprocessed intelligence. An example

CA: Stanford University Press, 2010); and Xi Chen, *Social Protest and Contentious Authoritarianism in China* (New York: Cambridge University Press, 2012).

[17] Daniela Stockmann, *Media Commercialization and Authoritarian Rule in China* (New York: Cambridge University Press, 2013).

[18] Melanie Manion, *Information for Autocrats: Representation in Chinese Local Congresses* (New York: Cambridge University Press, 2015); Rory Truex, *Making Autocracy Work: Representation and Responsiveness in Modern China* (New York: Cambridge University Press, 2016); Dimitar Gueorguiev, *Retrofitting Leninism: Participation without Democracy in Modern China* (New York: Oxford University Press, 2021).

[19] Martin K. Dimitrov, "Internal Government Assessments of the Quality of Governance in China," *Studies in Comparative International Development* 50:1 (March 2015), 50–72.

[20] Martin K. Dimitrov, "The Political Logic of Media Control in China," *Problems of Post-Communism* 64:3–4 (2017), 121–27.

might help illustrate these distinctions. Imagine that a government agency is interested in knowing whether a terrorist is on board an inbound international flight. Passport information on all passengers is routinely collected raw data. Querying that data by nationality would produce a shorter list of citizens of specific countries. If suspicious indicia are found (e.g., a citizen of a country with an elevated level of terrorism is onboard), that unprocessed intelligence can then be subjected to in-depth analysis using other sources of data (e.g., social media posts or records from classified government databases) to assess whether the individual poses a security risk. The information can be transmitted to decision makers in the form of a report that can subsequently be used to take specific action toward the suspect.

The granularity of the information that is produced depends on three factors: the precision of the question that guides collection; the capaciousness of the collection method; and the sophistication of the analysts. Questions asked by State Security usually aim to ascertain the relative density of certain categories of individuals who may threaten stability. Some categories are very broad (e.g., enemies, counterrevolutionaries, religious devotees), whereas others are much more circumscribed (e.g., persons who have engaged in terrorism, treason, or the distribution of anticommunist propaganda and agitation). Ascertaining whether individuals belong to a narrow category is meaningful but requires an elevated collection capacity. Therefore, when such capacity is constrained, more modest questions about individuals belonging to broader categories are asked. Technological advances allow for more targeted collection and analysis, but they do not obviate the need to formulate clear collection goals. The precision of the question determines the quality of the information that the regime aims to gather. For example, if the number of people who display signs of religious piety is used as a proxy for terrorist proclivities (as it has been in Xinjiang since the 1990s), the quality of the information generated would be very low.

The involuntary collection of information (which involves individuals being monitored against their will) is executed by human agents and through technology. Although it is a costly and labor-intensive method, human intelligence has persisted over the centuries; radical improvements in technology have helped clarify the specific need for human intelligence but have neither obliterated it nor made it obsolete.[21] Human collection methods are standard: spies receive guidance from agent handlers who subsequently transmit to desk analysts the collectors' field intelligence that, in turn, is converted into actionable intelligence.

---

[21] If anything, high-quality human intelligence has become scarcer, with a corresponding premium attached to expert collectors. See Joseph W. Wippl, "Observations on Successful Espionage," *International Journal of Intelligence and Counterintelligence* 29:3 (2016), 585–96.

Advances in technology enable the accumulation of vast amounts of raw data and make the generation of many kinds of unprocessed intelligence easier; however, human collection is still indispensable for the most delicate tasks (like figuring out the precise whereabouts of Osama bin Laden prior to his execution in 2011) and quite useful for generating insights that are needed to place putative regime enemies into more meaningful and more precisely defined categories of oppositional activity. Humans are also essential for the analytical process that converts unprocessed intelligence into actionable information (with or without the aid of machines and algorithms).

Several constraints impact the accuracy of information that is collected involuntarily. One is agency problems, which may involve shirking and deception by collectors and analysts; enhanced monitoring and appropriate incentives can help mitigate these concerns. Cross-checking and triangulation can increase certainty in the analysis; this necessitates redundant information streams. A second concern is the poor quality of collection and analysis, which calls for improved recruitment, investment in training spies and analysts, as well as technological upgrading. The final challenge is also the most unwieldy, namely, attempts to escape surveillance by those who are subject to involuntary monitoring, with minorities being the limit case. Standard solutions involve increasing the density of collection networks and using advanced surveillance technology.

The voluntary provision of information starts with citizens willingly revealing their grievances to the regime, preferably in the form of complaints. This raw data can then produce concrete insights about specific types of concerns (e.g., welfare, services, environmental problems, official corruption). Once this unprocessed intelligence is subjected to in-depth analysis, it can yield actionable information about the levels of regime support. The limitation of the system is responsiveness, which hinges on material resources and bureaucratic quality (state capacity). If citizens perceive that their complaints will be ineffective, they will not complain, which, in turn, compromises the voluntary transmission of information (and concurrently sends a signal to regime insiders that popular trust has eroded).

Archives reveal the questions guiding information gathering (what regime insiders want to know); the method through which information is collected (how they go about finding out); and the constraints to information gathering. Collection cannot proceed unless it is guided by a question that will be answered once the intelligence is present (otherwise, what we have is raw data). Intelligence-collection questions are typically driven by categories that are highly specific and that may be limiting (e.g., assessing the density of fascists or foreign spies)—nonetheless, indexing these categories can provide useful insights on the internal information-gathering priorities of the regime.

1.3 The Communist Difference in Information Collection

Although all states need information, only some compile it systematically on a national scale. Mechanisms for intelligence gathering have been documented in settings as diverse as those of ancient China,[22] ancient Rome,[23] early modern Europe,[24] colonial India,[25] and Qing China.[26] Regardless, the aspiration to systematically collect nationwide information is a relatively recent development that rests on the adoption of the quantificatory episteme (the notion that everything can be counted and measured) and the introduction of statistical thinking into the calculus of governance.[27] Statistics, Michel Foucault tells us, is "the knowledge of the state about itself."[28] Once gathered, statistical information can be used to enumerate and categorize citizens and to thus make them "legible" and more easily administered.[29] Modern states aim to develop a panoptical vision of their populations,[30] collecting a wide array of data on their subjects in order to carry out basic functions, such as taxation, conscription, public health supervision, political surveillance, and food distribution.[31]

---

[22] Lu Zongli, *Handai de yaoyan* (Hangzhou: Zhejiang Daxue Chubanshe, 2011).

[23] Anna Maria Liberati and Enrico Silverio, *Servizi segreti in Roma antica: Informazioni e sicurezza dagli initia Urbis all'impero universale* (Roma: "L'Erma" di Bretschneider, 2010).

[24] Markus Friedrich, *Der lange Arm Roms? Globale Verwaltung und Kommunikation im Jesuitenorden 1540–1773* (Frankfurt am Main: Campus Verlag, 2011); Edward Higgs, *The Information State in England: The Central Collection of Information on Citizens, 1500–2000* (New York: Palgrave Macmillan, 2004).

[25] C. A. Bayly, *Empire and Information: Intelligence Gathering and Social Communication in India, 1780–1870* (Cambridge, UK: Cambridge University Press, 1996); Martin J. Bayly, *Taming the Imperial Imagination: Colonial Knowledge, International Relations, and the Anglo–Afghan Encounter, 1808–1878* (Cambridge, UK: Cambridge University Press, 2016).

[26] Silas H. L. Wu, *Communication and Imperial Control: The Evolution of the Palace Memorial System, 1693–1735* (Cambridge, MA: Harvard University Press, 1970); Thomas A. Metzger, *The Internal Organization of the Ch'ing Bureaucracy: Legal, Normative, and Communication Aspects* (Cambridge, MA: Harvard University Press, 1973).

[27] Theodore M. Porter, *Trust in Numbers: The Pursuit of Objectivity in Science and Public Life* (Princeton, NJ: Princeton University Press, 1995); Ian Hacking, *The Taming of Chance* (Cambridge, UK: Cambridge University Press, 1990); Talal Asad, "Ethnographic Representations, Statistics, and Modern Power," in Brian Keith Axel, ed., *From the Margins: Historical Anthropology and Its Future* (Durham, NC: Duke University Press, 2002), 66–91; U. Kalpagam, *Rule by Numbers: Governmentality in Colonial India* (Lanham, MD: Lexington Books, 2014), esp. 10.

[28] Original quote: "La statistique, c'est le savoir de l'État sur l'État." See Michel Foucault, *Sécurité, territoire, population: Cours au Collège de France, 1977–1978* (Paris: Seuil, 2004), 323.

[29] Michel Foucault, "Governmentality," in Graham Burchell, Colin Gordon, and Peter Miller, eds., *The Foucault Effect: Studies in Governmentality: With Two Lectures by and an Interview with Michel Foucault* (Chicago: University of Chicago Press, 1991), 87–104; James C. Scott, *Seeing Like a State: How Certain Schemes to Improve the Human Condition Have Failed* (New Haven, CT: Yale University Press, 1998).

[30] Michel Foucault, *Discipline and Punish: The Birth of the Prison* (New York: Vintage Books, 1979). On technologies of "seeing," see Priya Satia, *Spies in Arabia: The Great War and the Cultural Foundation of Britain's Covert Empire in the Middle East* (New York: Oxford University Press, 2008) and Martin Thomas, *Empires of Intelligence: Security Services and the Colonial Disorder after 1914* (Berkeley: University of California Press, 2008).

[31] Scott, *Seeing Like a State*.

There is no better illustration of the obstacles to acquiring this panoptical vision than a census, which is the most basic manifestation of the capacity of a state to collect nationwide information. Censuses require both trained personnel and the cooperation of those who are to be counted. Neither can be taken for granted, which was a key reason for designating the police as the lead agency in charge of the first all-Russian census in 1897.[32] Those who were counted resisted the epistemic violence of categories (e.g., caste);[33] the granularity of the census (enumeration at the individual, rather than the household or *baojia* level);[34] and the universalistic and uniform categories that counted everyone the same regardless of ethnic or religious identity.[35] Concerns about the use of the information ranged from the stealing of souls (to be put at the foundations of bridges and railways) and personal astrological information in China, to the more ominous fears harbored by minorities in Russia that the census data would be utilized in campaigns to Russify them.[36] The combined effect of low state capacity and popular resistance to being counted meant that China could not implement its first nationwide census until 1953. In sum, even a data-gathering undertaking as rudimentary as conducting a census is marked by complexity.

Beyond the specific case of the census, numerous deficiencies characterize the collection of basic socioeconomic information. Some have to do with agency problems ("juking the stats" and other forms of statistical manipulation),[37] whereas others reflect epistemic differences about the most appropriate method for gathering information: in China, such differences involved the Soviet technique of exhaustive enumeration versus Western random sampling and the Maoist typical survey.[38]

The gathering of sociopolitical intelligence is incommensurately more complicated than the collection of socioeconomic indicators, especially in

---

[32] Juliette Cadiot, *Le laboratoire imperial Russie-URSS 1870–1940* (Paris: CNRS Editions, 2007), esp. 39–40.

[33] Arjun Appudarai, "Number in the Colonial Imagination," in Carol A. Breckenridge and Peter van der Veer, eds., *Orientalism and the Postcolonial Predicament: Perspectives on South Asia* (Philadelphia: University of Pennsylvania Press, 1993), 314–39.

[34] On these concerns during the unsuccessful 1909–1910 Qing census in China, see Tong Lam, *A Passion for Facts: Social Surveys and the Construction of the Chinese Nation-State, 1900–1949* (Stanford, CA: Stanford University Press, 2011), 39, 68, 86–87.

[35] Cadiot, *Le laboratoire imperial*, 50–52, 58–60.

[36] Lam, *A Passion for Facts*, 74–78; Cadiot, *Le laboratoire imperial*, 46–50.

[37] Jeremy Wallace, *Seeking Truth and Hiding Facts: Information, Ideology, and Authoritarian Rule in China* (New York: Oxford University Press, 2022); Jeremy Wallace, "Juking the Stats? Authoritarian Information Problems in China," *British Journal of Political Science* 46:1 (January 2016), 11–29; Carsten A. Holz, "'Fast, Clear, and Accurate': How Reliable are Chinese Output and Economic Growth Statistics?" *The China Quarterly*, no. 173 (March 2003), 122–63.

[38] Arunabh Ghosh, *Making It Count: Statistics and Statecraft in the Early People's Republic of China* (Princeton, NJ: Princeton University Press, 2020).

an authoritarian setting. Sociopolitical intelligence (political information) involves collecting military and foreign intelligence; monitoring elites; and assessing the mood of the masses. Most states acquire military and foreign intelligence and develop mechanisms for monitoring elites, as demonstrated by the existence of state security services and other coup-proofing institutions throughout the world. Differences emerge in the capacity to monitor the masses. This problem is especially acute in authoritarian settings, where citizens might engage in preference falsification and conceal their attitudes toward the regime. Nevertheless, communist regimes excel at this task and over time develop sophisticated systems for monitoring the popular mood.

The primary focus of this study is the origins, evolution, and decay of the apparatus that collects information about popular discontent as one type of political information. From the perspective of an authoritarian regime, this is technically the most challenging type of intelligence to gather, because of the required bureaucratic capacity and because of the unwillingness of citizens to reveal their actual level of discontent. In discussing the information-gathering institutions of authoritarian regimes, this study also examines those that have already received attention from scholars: elections, protests, and liberalized media. Although these channels are important in noncommunist autocracies, their utility as sources of information on popular discontent in communist regimes is limited by their potential to facilitate the horizontal dissemination of information.[39] The focus of this study is on a subject that has not previously received sustained scholarly attention, namely, the confidential channels that enable the vertical transmission of intelligence in communist regimes. The communist difference lies in the range of such channels that are developed both to incentivize voluntary provision and to enable the involuntary extraction of information about popular discontent. Acquiring and skillfully using such information are both essential for regime survival and long-term resilience.

---

[39] Elsewhere, I discuss why a communist regime may allow critical letters to be published in the media. My argument is that by appearing responsive to the grievances outlined in such letters, the communist party can incentivize citizens to provide information by sending in more complaints, the vast majority of which will never be published. What this points to is that various phenomena in autocracies may have a hidden logic: in this case, the function of printing selected critical letters is not to reveal to the regime information about popular discontent, but rather to allow for many letters to be sent to the media so that they can subsequently be analyzed by the readers' mail departments in order to transmit to the regime information about popular grievances. See Martin K. Dimitrov, "Informing the Party: The Functions of Letters to the Editor in Reform-Era Cuba," *Latin American Research Review* 54:1 (2019), 1–15 and Martin K. Dimitrov, "Socialist Social Contracts and Accountability," in Scott Morgenstern and Jorge Pérez-López, eds., *Reforming Communism: Cuba in Comparative Perspective* (Pittsburgh: University of Pittsburgh Press, 2018), 135–56.

1.4 The Argument in Brief

Communist regimes develop an extraordinary awareness of the importance of collecting information about external and domestic threats to their rule. Foreign intelligence collection is straightforward and thus not treated extensively in this book. Domestically, the three main threats to the regime are elites, the masses and, in ethnically heterogenous countries, minorities. Because compactly settled ethnoreligious minorities prove impenetrable,[40] the strategy is to proceed with ethnic assimilation once the elite and the mass constraints have been solved, as occurred in Eastern Europe in the 1980s and in China in the 2010s. The main task of information collection is to foster techniques that allow for sufficient intelligence to be gathered about the elites and the masses. In practice, monitoring elites (who are numerically small) does not present a serious logistical challenge. Therefore, most energy is devoted to assessing levels of mass discontent. For this reason, although the book engages with elites and minorities, its primary focus is on the information-collection ecosystem that is established by communist states as they attempt to monitor mass discontent among the ethnic majority.

Regardless of whether they emerge through a revolution or not,[41] communist regimes develop the same complement of institutions for assessing domestic threats to their rule, namely, the triumvirate of State Security, the party, and internal journalistic reporting that is not meant for official publication. As regime origins are always violent (revolution or war), the military may also be part of the ecosystem during the initial period of communist rule,[42] but it is expeditiously sidelined from monitoring the popular mood by the triumvirate. State Security, the party, and the internal media supply the leadership with a range of classified reporting on domestic discontent. When necessary, they call on various branches of the party-state and, in contemporary China, on social media companies to assist with the collection, aggregation, and transmission of information to the leadership. Initially, the goal of information collection is retrospective,

---

[40] This is not a problem unique to communist regimes. On the penetration of Arab-Israelis, see Ami Pedahzur, *The Israeli Secret Services and the Struggle Against Terrorism* (New York: Columbia University Press, 2009).

[41] Jean Lachapelle, Steven Levitsky, Lucan A. Way, and Adam E. Casey, "Social Revolution and Authoritarian Durability," *World Politics* 72:4 (October 2020), 557–600.

[42] Scholars working on noncommunist regimes have argued that a fragmented security apparatus is necessary for coup-proofing: James Quinlivan, "Coup Proofing," *International Security* 24:2 (1999), 131–65; Sheena Chestnut Greitens, *Dictators and Their Secret Police: Coercive Institutions and State Violence* (New York: Cambridge University Press, 2016). In the communist world, the obverse is true: the number of intelligence agencies is reduced during periods of elevated coup threats. Eliminating the military (which poses the greatest coup threat) from domestic counterintelligence collection is a relevant example. Another is the merging of intelligence agencies during periods of elevated coup threats, as occurred in the USSR in 1933–1943 and 1953–1954 and in the GDR in 1953–1955.

centering on detecting discontent that has already been expressed. Over time, however, when specific conditions are met, intelligence collection may move in the direction of forecasting the expected occurrence of discontent.

An important distinction exists between the involuntary extraction of intelligence and the voluntary provision of information. Involuntary extraction relies on a variety of channels, ranging from the surveillance of communications to the monitoring of rumors, jokes, and even dreams. Information is collected against individuals' will by full-time operatives, by part-time informants, and by technical means. Involuntary collection, which is initially crude, enables ex-post (retrospective) governance that results in a high volume of poorly targeted repression. After the techniques for involuntary extraction evolve, allowing it to become more precise, the improved quality of information enables more selective repression. A drop in repression is essential for transitioning from ex-post to ex-ante governance, as it incentivizes citizens to complain, especially when levels of responsiveness are high. In turn, state capacity determines how responsive a regime will be to citizen grievances. When levels of fear are low and responsiveness is high, regimes can switch to a different type of governance mode—ex-ante (anticipatory) governance, which is a stable system of selective repression and generous redistribution that aims to identify and satisfy popular grievances articulated through the complaints system while they are still at their latent stage. The system operates well unless the underlying parameters change, as they did in Eastern Europe when the economic crisis of the 1980s led to widespread dissatisfaction that transformed latent into overt discontent.

Although structural constraints like economic resources and state capacity may preclude the transition from ex-post to ex-ante governance, another factor preventing such a transition is the lack of an external stimulus in the form of an ideological threat. In Eastern Europe, concerns about a physical invasion by the West were greatly reduced by the end of the 1950s and were replaced by an ideological battle. East–West competition generated intense rivalry between the communist and noncommunist economic and political models. A three-pronged response was hence developed in the Eastern Bloc: selective repression of ideologically unstable individuals; massive redistributive spending (a socialist welfare state); and extensive support for indigenous cultural production with the aim of distracting publics from being co-opted into an anticommunist worldview through the consumption of Western cultural products. A different process unfolded in China, which pursued an autarkic development model from the late 1950s to the late 1970s, thus shielding the country from Western influence. When the Ministry of State Security was created in 1983 and tasked with combating hostile ideology, the strategy was two-pronged: selective repression and cultural security, which involved the promotion of indigenous culture (though we should note that Chinese exposure to Western ideological influence never reached Eastern European levels).[43] Missing from the Chinese model was a promise of matching Western standards of living, the reason being that China's per capita GDP at the end of the 1970s was 1/100th that of the United States,[44] in contrast to a gap of 2.5 times between the Eastern Bloc and Western Europe when East–West competition intensified at the end of the 1950s.[45] Thus, despite their common origins, Eastern Europe and China subsequently diverged in the direction of two different models: a socialist market economy in China (from the late 1970s onward) and bread and circuses in Eastern Europe. These two models had implications for the subsequent regime trajectories.

The Eastern European welfare model featured a gradual transition to a low-fear high-redistribution equilibrium in the 1960s. A central planning system gave extraordinary discretion to the top leadership to allocate resources for material and cultural consumption. A high volume of voluntarily transmitted information allowed for the deployment of anticipatory institutions of rule that underpinned the stability characterizing the decades during which the socialist social contract operated. However, the model had a major weakness, namely, low levels of fear meant that the regime could not secure its position through a systematic use of brute force in case it reneged on its commitment to ensure a continuous improvement in the standards of living. In addition, from the second half of the 1970s onward, the Helsinki Accords greatly facilitated the free movement of ideas and people, thus rendering futile the strategy of counteracting Western influence through indigenous cultural production. By the second half of the 1980s, incumbents had abundant warnings about the transformation of latent into overt discontent due to mounting economic and political grievances— moreover, they even had information about elite splits and preparations for a palace coup. Being well-informed, however, did not allow incumbents to retain their positions in 1989.

China never made the transition to a low-fear high-redistribution model. Levels of fear began to decline in the 1980s, but this was also the decade when the narrow urban welfare state (which extended benefits that were quite modest by Eastern European standards) began to be dismantled. In the 1990s, China moved

---

[43] In 2018, which was a peak year for Western media penetration in China, the audience for U.S. media reached 6.2 percent of the adult population, up from 0.3 percent in 2015 (U.S. Agency for Global Media, *Audience and Impact: Overview for 2019* [Washington, DC: U.S. Agency for Global Media, 2018], 15); the average share of the adult population that listened to Western radio exceeded 50 percent during the Cold War in several Eastern European countries (*Cold War Broadcasting Impact* [Stanford, CA: Hoover Institution, 2005], 45–47).

[44] In 1977, per capita GDP (in constant 2010 U.S. dollars) was $279.6 in China and $27,161.4 in the United States, which represented a 97-fold difference (World Development Indicators database).

[45] Calculated from Angus Maddison, *The World Economy: A Millennial Perspective* (Paris: OECD, 2006), 185. On the economic aspects of the competition, see Herbert Obinger and Carina Schmitt, "Guns and Butter? Regime Competition and the Welfare State during the Cold War," *World Politics* 63:2 (April 2011), 246–70.

to a moderate-repression moderate-redistribution market-economy model. Levels of voluntary provision of information through the complaints system were low and declined even further in the 2000s because the decentralized political system could not ensure a rate of responsiveness comparable to that which was possible under central planning in Eastern Europe. Routine protests rather than complaints have functioned as the dominant mode for the voluntary transmission of information about the failures of the market social contract. In contrast to complaints, which reveal latent dissatisfaction, protests index overt discontent and thus heighten regime insecurity and elevate stability maintenance into an overarching concern. The Chinese model continued to upgrade technologies for the involuntary collection of intelligence (and for blocking access to outside information), surpassing the sophistication of the Eastern European regimes. Today, China has the most advanced systems of surveillance of any authoritarian regime ever extant. But even those systems do not help penetrate compact minorities like the Tibetans and the Uyghurs, as evidenced by the assimilation campaigns that are currently underway against them. It remains to be seen whether the backlash from these campaigns will contribute to regime instability, similar to the effort to assimilate the Turks in Bulgaria in the 1980s. It is also unclear how the imperative of preventing the occurrence of both minority and nonminority protests will impact the already very limited voluntary provision of information in China through complaints.

The argument is based on a paired comparison of an Eastern European regime (Bulgaria) and China. Additional process-tracing evidence is provided by other communist regimes (the Soviet Union, the GDR, and Cuba), as well as by Leninist single-party systems (Taiwan prior to 1987), by single-party autocracies (Iraq under the Ba'th), by multiparty regimes (Russia since 2000), and by regimes without any political parties (Argentina and Chile under military rule). These additional cases specify the scope conditions for the theory: a communist party is essential for developing the complex information-gathering ecosystem discussed in this book. The party collects intelligence, coordinates the information-gathering activities of other agencies, and is the ultimate consumer of the intelligence products generated by the information-collection ecosystem. Moreover, although complaints systems can be found throughout the universe of autocracies, a high volume of voluntary provision of information through complaints that enables the deployment of anticipatory rule is most likely to emerge under the low-fear high-redistribution equilibrium that existed under central planning. Market social contracts develop as well, but they are less redistributive and thus less burdensome for autocrats—yet they are also less informative about levels of latent dissatisfaction before its transformation into regime-destabilizing overt discontent.

1.5 Contributions of the Study

Information gathering in autocracies is a hidden activity. When confronting nontransparent phenomena, scholars have three options: ignore them; study them through officially released materials or secondary sources; or approach them by analyzing internal documents not meant for public dissemination. This study favors the last research strategy because of its methodological advantages, chief among which is the potential to reveal the logic of information gathering. By conducting archival ethnography (see Chapter 2), we can develop a sense of the internal understandings of phenomena that are central to information collection. One example concerns the function of prices as mechanisms for ensuring social stability rather than as signals of supply and demand. Another is the synonymous use of the terms "ideological police" and "political police," which is indicative of the primacy assigned to preventing harmful foreign ideas (ideological subversion) from disrupting social stability. A third is the notion of cultural consumption, which is promoted jointly with material consumption as a response to external ideological influence. Most important are the distinctions between overt and latent discontent; the notion that the regime is bound by a social contract and failure to fulfill its commitments will result in overt expressions of discontent; and, finally, that any type of protest may threaten social stability. The cumulative effect of these internal sources is to provide insights into the conceptual frames that autocrats develop as they confront the problem of assessing and responding to popular discontent.

Another methodological advantage of internal materials is that they reveal the epistemic anxieties of regime insiders. Internal materials allow us to understand what autocrats want to know. A key insight is that information gatherers devote substantial efforts to assessing the threat they face from internal enemies (among members of the elite, the masses, and minorities) and from foreign countries, which in the understandings of regime insiders, gradually abandon plans for an armed invasion and promote instead ideological subversion through vectors that include high standards of living and attractive cultural products; minorities, intellectuals, religious devotees, and the youth are considered to be susceptible and therefore are subject to monitoring by State Security. As the document-generation process is not driven by the expectation that these materials will be seen by anyone beyond regime insiders, we can be confident that they provide an authentic representation of the fears of regime insiders.

A final methodological insight concerns the internal rank-ordering of information channels. Although they are fascinating to study, mechanisms like the monitoring of rumors, jokes, and dreams do not yield information that is accurate, granular, and actionable and thus they are much less useful to autocrats than channels like surveillance (in-person or technologically enabled), internal media reporting, and the analysis of citizen complaints. Awareness of the rank-ordering of information channels allows us to know what methods of information gathering are understood to be especially valuable internally. The cumulative methodological contribution of this study therefore is to open the black box of information gathering in autocracies by reading the same documents that regime insiders consult—rather than the materials that they might want scholars to see.

Empirically, this study makes three main contributions. The first is to map the ecosystem of information-gathering institutions in communist regimes and their evolution over time. Some of these institutions are relatively new to students of autocracies: the informational utility of monitoring jokes,[46] public statements (usually made while queueing up),[47] and especially of dreams has not been systematically documented through direct sources.[48] Other mechanisms are familiar but only for a certain period within a specific regime: for instance, the existence of internal journalistic reporting in China under Mao is known, though there is considerable uncertainty whether internal reporting survived after Mao (it did) and whether the system is unique to China (it is not). Regardless of whether or not the existence of a specific channel has been documented for a certain communist regime, the operation of the system as a whole has not been discussed. This study thus presents the logic guiding the formation of the information-collection ecosystem, the tradeoffs between different channels for involuntary collection and voluntary provision of information, and the fact that the system is redundant by design (to allow decision makers to cross-check intelligence).

The second empirical contribution is to shed light on the process of building communist information states. The study demonstrates that despite variation in precommunist state capacity, all communist regimes eventually develop the same institutional complements for the involuntary collection of information: State Security, the party, and the internal media. Low state capacity does not impede

---

[46] Bodo Müller, ed., *Lachen gegen Ohnmacht: DDR-Witze im Visier der Stasi* (Berlin: Ch. Links, 2015); Hans-Hermann Hertle and Hans-Wilhelm Saure, eds., *Ausgelacht: DDR-Witze aus den Geheimakten des BND* (Berlin: Ch. Links, 2015).

[47] In Mexico, *orejas* reported on criticisms against the current government that could be heard in public (*diversas críticas que se oyen en la vía pública en contra del actual régimen de gobierno*). See Louise E. Walker, "Spying at the Drycleaners: Anonymous Gossip in 1973 Mexico City," *Journal of Iberian and Latin American Research* 19:1 (2013), 52–61.

[48] Although there has been no direct evidence yet that dreams were studied in autocracies, discussions of fears of hypothetical punishment for transgressive dreams expressed by patients undergoing psychoanalysis in Nazi Germany and anecdotal evidence that such punishment may have been meted out against a Syrian soldier do exist in the literature. See Charlotte Beradt, *The Third Reich of Dreams* (Chicago: Quadrangle Books, 1968) and Lisa Wedeen, *Ambiguities of Domination: Politics, Rhetoric, and Symbols in Contemporary Syria* (Chicago: University of Chicago Press, 1999), esp. 68.

the creation of institutions, but it does impact how well they operate by, for example, slowing down the completion of an information-gathering network that covers the full territorial expanse of the state. Precommunist state capacity is also a factor explaining whether regimes will make a prompt transition to anticipatory (ex-ante) governance, which relies on low levels of fear and high rates of responsiveness to incentivize citizens to voluntarily transmit information through the complaints system; maintaining responsiveness creates extraordinary bureaucratic demands, which cannot be met by regimes with low state capacity. What is perhaps most remarkable about the dynamics of building information states is that they are not impacted by regime origins: no matter whether communist autocracies emerge after a revolution or following a war, they eventually develop the same institutional complements.

The final empirical contribution is to comparative thinking about information-gathering institutions in autocracies. This book uses direct sources (classified documents generated internally for regime insiders) to document the institutions that are established to collect information on popular discontent in a range of autocracies: regimes without parties; multiparty regimes; non-Leninist single-party regimes; Leninist noncommunist regimes; and both revolutionary and nonrevolutionary communist regimes. Several findings emerge from these comparisons. First, although all regimes rely on State Security for surveillance, parties are essential for providing nuanced assessments of popular dissatisfaction. On a related note, Leninist parties have a distinct organizational advantage in collecting information due to their large size and capacity to penetrate deep at the grassroots level. Second, internal media emerge only in Leninist regimes, with the full complement developing exclusively in communist Leninist regimes (as noncommunist Leninist regimes establish incomplete control over the media). Third, although petitioning institutions exist in every autocracy, high volumes of voluntary provision of information through complaints emerged only in communist regimes under central planning, thus enabling a sufficient level of responsiveness to citizen demands. In sum, these empirical investigations allow us to think systematically about institutional variation across autocracies.

These methodological and empirical insights have several theoretical implications. The most important is that the dictator's dilemma can be solved, except with regard to compactly settled ethnoreligious minorities. The solution provided by the extensive systems for involuntary extraction of information is suboptimal, as there is a nonnegligible probability that citizens suspect that they are under surveillance and thus self-censor to some extent. However, under specific conditions outlined in this book, dictatorships can develop techniques that allow them to overcome the unwillingness of citizens to reveal their actual level of discontent and to elicit the routine transfer of information that does not suffer from preference falsification, as occurred in Eastern Europe where privately transmitted petitions formed the wellspring of anticipatory governance. China provides a different model, in which public acts of offline and online contention are gradually displacing private petitioning, thus compromising the adoption of ex-ante rule.

Neither the Eastern European nor the Chinese model guarantees the permanence of either the incumbent or the regime. In Bulgaria, anticipatory (ex-ante) governance functioned very well from the early 1960s to the mid-1980s, but economic difficulties in the late 1980s led to the government reneging on the socialist social contract, thus resulting in the alienation of the ethnic majority at a time when the Turkish minority was being subjected to ethnic assimilation. The nationwide economic and political discontent was used by elites as a cue for staging a palace coup against the incumbent, who had full knowledge of his impending ouster but could not prevent it. Time will tell whether the Xi era Chinese model of deploying AI policing (and an informant corps with the highest rate of saturation in the communist world) to counteract the now permanent state of protest-induced crisis will prove more durable than the Bulgarian model of basing decades-long social stability and high-quality governance on politically expedient but economically ruinous elevated budget expenditures to subsidize mass consumption.

Another theoretical implication concerns how we should conceptualize the events of 1989–1991 in Eastern Europe, which are typically described as collapse driven by a lack of information. As this book amply demonstrates, there was abundant intelligence that allowed the Bulgarian incumbent to anticipate both the widespread protests and his own ouster. The relevant question is why he did not react to this information. The reason is that the incumbent was not exclusively in possession of the intelligence about popular discontent. A feature of sophisticated systems of anticipatory rule is that the circle of recipients of classified reporting about popular dissatisfaction must be fairly broad (a few dozen to perhaps a couple hundred people) so that the requisite response can be mounted to prevent latent discontent from being transformed into overt acts of opposition to the regime. Thus, it is precisely the circulation of information that enabled the removal of incumbents like Zhivkov in 1989. The coup-plotters in 1989 could not foresee that their actions would lead to the definitive ouster of the communist party from power after two rounds of competitive elections in 1990 and 1991. What they aimed for was to extend the lifespan of the regime by sacrificing the incumbent. Rather than collapse, the elite soft-liners sought to unleash a process of democratization similar to that undertaken in Taiwan, though at a different pace: in Taiwan, the first competitive elections occurred nine years after the initiation of democratization (vs. seven months in Bulgaria) and the second took place four years later in 2000 (vs. sixteen months later in Bulgaria).[49]

[49] On Taiwan, see Dan Slater and Joseph Wong, "The Strength to Concede: Ruling Parties and Democratization in Developmental Asia," *Perspectives on Politics* 11:3 (September 2013), 717–33.

Democratization moves at a more rapid speed when it also involves the politically destabilizing process of simultaneous property transformation.

The final theoretical implication concerns the general problem that the institutions for monitoring discontent that have been emphasized in the literature (protests, elections, and liberalized media) generate information that is available to ordinary citizens and to regime insiders. By contrast, communist party-states value internal channels for the vertical transmission of information rather than avenues that enable the horizontal spread of knowledge about discontent. When information about dissatisfaction is deliberately released on platforms that are visible to ordinary citizens, this is done for a public relations purpose to allow the government to demonstrate its responsiveness to popular grievances.[50] We should keep in mind that Gorbachev, widely perceived to be a champion of investigative journalism, maintained a long list of taboo topics, and as late as October 1989, he instructed the press to tone down its negative coverage.[51] Curated public information about discontent should be distinguished from classified internal intelligence about dissatisfaction.

1.6 Choice of Cases

This study provides a theory of the monitoring of popular discontent in autocracies. As communist regimes have the most complex apparatus for assessing discontent and enjoy the longest average lifespan, they are the primary focus. The theory is developed by a paired comparison of Bulgaria and China, with scope conditions elucidated by analyzing additional cases of autocracies (single-party communist, noncommunist Leninist, single-party noncommunist, multiparty, and regimes without parties). The choice of the two primary cases is driven by a matching design logic. For the purposes of this study, the relevant criteria are the following: communist rule was not maintained by a foreign power, thus heightening the importance of information collection; a unitary state existed that was ethnically heterogeneous, with compact masses of ethnic minorities making up about 10 percent of the population, thus creating a barrier for information collection among minorities, though not precluding successful penetration of the majority; and the regime experienced a period of declining repression that facilitated the collection of information. To achieve greater inferential leverage by

[50] Dimitrov, "Informing the Party"; Iza Ding, "Performative Governance," *World Politics* 72:4 (October 2020), 525–56.
[51] Off-limits issues included Afghanistan (Center for Preservation of Contemporary Documentation [TsKhSD] f. 89 per. 11 d. 103 [July 22, 1985]), crime (TsKhSD f. 89 per. 11 d. 44 [September 20, 1987]), the results of elections (TsKhSD f. 89 per. 11 d. 130 [June 15, 1987]), and natural disasters and industrial accidents (TsKhSD f. 89 per. 9 d. 24 [August 25, 1989]). On the October 1989 instructions, see N. S. Leonov, *Likholetie* (Moscow: Russkii dom, 2003), 293.

tracing the evolution of information-gathering institutions throughout the life-span of a communist regime, China had to be paired with one of the ten communist autocracies that existed in Eastern Europe and Mongolia until 1989–1991, rather than with one of the four regimes that persist to the current day and in which institutional development is still ongoing (Vietnam, Laos, North Korea, and Cuba). Some of the previously extant regimes are excluded because they had Soviet troops on their soil (East Germany, Hungary, Czechoslovakia, Poland, and Mongolia), because they were ethnically homogeneous (Albania, Poland, and East Germany), or because they were federal states with a minority share of the population significantly above 10 percent (the Soviet Union, Czechoslovakia, and Yugoslavia). This leaves Romania and Bulgaria as candidates for comparison with China; Romania is excluded because it did not undergo a decline in repression similar to the one that enabled the development of information-gathering institutions in Bulgaria.[52] Therefore, the theory is generated primarily using the cases of Bulgaria and China. The two countries are similar in terms of the absence of Soviet troops; the minority share of the population (about 10 percent); and the eventual decline of repression (though this decline was slower and less extensive in China). The two are different in terms of their origins (one emerged after a war and the other after a revolution) and their precommunist levels of state capacity.

1.6.1 Precommunist State Capacity Index

Weak state capacity impacts the quality of information collection and can lead to significant delays in the transition from ex-post (reactive) to ex-ante (anticipatory) governance. It is therefore important to develop an index of precommunist state capacity, which will serve as a benchmark for the likelihood that a speedy transition to anticipatory rule will take place shortly after establishment of the regime. Although no such index exists, prior research has produced findings that can be leveraged when developing one.

Several indicators are useful for constructing the index. First, though essential for information collection, complete territorial penetration may be constrained by size and topography, which lead to an uneven state reach,[53] thus limiting the state's infrastructural capacity.[54] Scholars have pointed out that small size and

---

[52] *Raport final* (Bucureşti: Comisia Prezidenţială pentru Analiza Dictaturii Comuniste din România, 2006).

[53] Catherine Boone, "Territorial Politics and the Reach of the State: Unevenness by Design," *Revista de Ciencia Política* 32:3 (2012), 623–41.

[54] Michael Mann, "The Autonomous Power of the State: Its Origins, Mechanisms and Results," *European Journal of Sociology* 25:2 (1984), 185–213.

nonrugged terrain enable the central state to project power throughout the territory more efficiently.[55] From an information-gathering standpoint, rugged terrain creates incomplete territorial control, resulting in "brown areas" of limited state presence.[56] Complete territorial penetration is essential to enable the panoptical gaze of authoritarian states.[57] Extending these insights, this study emphasizes that the systematic collection of information on popular discontent is more challenging in regimes that are large in size and have a rugged terrain.

Another constraint to information gathering arises from ethnolinguistic heterogeneity. Communist autocracies pursue with exceptional determination the goal of achieving complete penetration of all social groups. The abundant archival materials that have emerged from various communist regimes indicate that such efforts were successful, except for one major hurdle: ethnolinguistic heterogeneity.[58] What made penetration of minorities considerably more difficult than any other group was language (more so than ethnicity or religion), as demonstrated by the capacity of communist regimes to collect information from ethnic or religious groups that shared the language of the majority. The limited fluency of information gatherers in minority languages created a problem of legibility that proved very difficult to surmount.

An essential proxy for state capacity is the level of illiteracy that exists at the time when the regime is established. Although this indicator is crude, it is nevertheless highly revealing. It would be unrealistic to expect that a modern country with an elevated level of illiteracy might have a competent bureaucracy.

These four proxies are given different weight: small size, favorable topography, and ethnic homogeneity are scored from 0 to 10, while high literacy is scored from 0 to 20. The composite score is then validated through an outcome measure of state capacity, namely, the experience of having conducted a census, which is scored from 0 to 50. The composite score of the four proxies is correlated with the census variable at 0.8087, thus giving us high confidence that the precommunist state capacity index presented in Table 1.2 is a valid measure of

---

[55] Jeffrey Herbst, *States and Power in Africa: Comparative Lessons in Authority and Control* (Princeton, NJ: Princeton University Press, 2014), 171; Catherine Boone, *Political Topographies of the African State: Territorial Authority and Institutional Choice* (New York: Cambridge University Press, 2003); James C. Scott, *Against the Grain: A Deep History of the Earliest States* (New Haven, CT: Yale University Press, 2017); James Fearon and David Laitin, "Ethnicity, Insurgency, and Civil War," *American Political Science Review* 97:1 (2003), 75–90.

[56] Guillermo O'Donnell, "On the State, Democratization and Some Conceptual Problems: A Latin American View with Glances at Some Post-Communist Countries," *World Development* 21:8 (1993), 1355–69.

[57] Scott, *Seeing Like a State*.

[58] Martin K. Dimitrov and Joseph Sassoon, "State Security, Information, and Repression: A Comparison of Communist Bulgaria and Ba'thist Iraq," *Journal of Cold War Studies* 16:2 (Spring 2014), 4–31.

Table 1.2 Composite Score of Bureaucratic Capacity at Regime Inception

Regime (years of initial establishment) and Mode of Establishment (R= postrevolution or W= postwar)	Small Size	Flat Terrain	Ethnic Homogeneity	High Literacy	Prior Census	TOTAL	Composite Capacity
Laos (1975) R	7.5	2.5	5	5	0	20	Low
China (1949–1953) R	2.5	5	7.5	0	10	25	Low
Soviet Union (1917–1928) R	0	7.5	2.5	10	20	40	Low
Mongolia (1924–1928) R	5	7.5	5	0	30	47.5	Medium
Vietnam (1954–1975) R	7.5	5	7.5	10	20	50	Medium
North Korea (1948–1953) R	10	2.5	10	5	40	67.5	Medium
Yugoslavia (1943–1948) R	7.5	5	0	15	40	67.5	Medium
Albania (1944–1948) R	10	0	10	15	40	75	Medium
Romania (1944–1948) W	7.5	7.5	5	15	50	85	High
Poland (1945–1948) W	7.5	10	10	20	40	87.5	High
Bulgaria (1944–1949) W	10	7.5	7.5	15	50	90	High
Czechoslovakia (1946–1949) W	10	7.5	5	20	50	92.5	High

Cuba (1959–1962) R	10	10	10	15	50	95	High
Hungary (1944–1948) W	10	10	7.5	20	50	97.5	High
GDR (1945–1949) W	10	10	10	20	50	100	High

Sources: **Size, terrain, and ethnic heterogeneity:** Author's dataset, based primarily on the replication dataset for James Fearon and David Laitin, "Ethnicity, Insurgency, and Civil War," *American Political Science Review* 97:1 (2003), 75–90 and on the ruggedness dataset of Nathan Nunn and Diego Puga, https://diegopuga.org/data/rugged/ (accessed April 1, 2018) (the coding of multiple cases diverges across the two datasets; errors corrected and missing country data calculated by the author); **Literacy:** Author's dataset, based primarily on UNESCO literacy data; **Census:** Author's dataset, based primarily on replication data for Evan Lieberman and Prerna Singh, "Census Enumeration and Group Conflict," *World Politics* 69:1 (2017), 1–53 (missing country values added by the author).

Coding Rules: a) Regime establishment: Martin K. Dimitrov, ed., *Why Communism Did Not Collapse: Understanding Authoritarian Regime Resilience in Asia and Europe* (New York: Cambridge University Press, 2013), 14; b) Small size: Scored 0–10, as follows: 0: territory over 10,000,000 km²; 2.5: territory 2,000,001–10,000,000 km²; 5: territory 500,001–2,000,000 km²; 7.5: territory 200,001–500,000 km²; 10: territory under 200,000 km². Range of raw values: 28,748 km² (Albania)–22,402,000 km² (Soviet Union); c) Flat terrain: Scored 0–10, as follows: 0: rugged terrain over 60 percent; 2.5: rugged terrain 41 percent–60 percent; 5: rugged terrain 21 percent–40 percent; 7.5: rugged terrain 11 percent–20 percent; 10: rugged terrain 10 percent or less. Range of raw values: 0.9 percent (Hungary)–62.1 percent (Albania); d) Ethnic homogeneity: Scored 0–10, as follows: 0: largest ethnic group below 50 percent; 2.5: largest ethnic group 51 percent–60 percent; 5: largest ethnic group 61 percent–85 percent; 7.5: largest ethnic group 86 percent–95 percent; 10: largest ethnic group 96 percent or more. Range of raw values: 36.2 percent (Yugoslavia)–99.9 percent (North Korea); e) High literacy: Scored 0–20 for the closest available year to regime establishment, as follows: 0: illiteracy over 80 percent; 5: illiteracy 51 percent–80 percent; 10: illiteracy 31 percent–50 percent; 15: illiteracy 21 percent–30 percent; 20: illiteracy 20 percent or less. Range: 1 percent (GDR)–97 percent (Mongolia); f) Prior census: Scored 0–50, as follows: 0: no census conducted; 10: attempted census; 20: completed census of an entity comprising more than 50 percent of the territory of the new state; 30: one census completed less than ten years prior to the establishment of the regime; 40: multiple censuses completed, with the first census more than twenty years prior to the establishment of the regime; 50: history of censuses going back at least fifty years prior to regime establishment (for Czechoslovakia, the history of the Czech and Slovak censuses was used). Range of raw values: first census was conducted 142 years prior to regime establishment (Cuba) to ten years after regime establishment (Laos). The first Chinese census was conducted in 1953 (the 1909–1910 census was unsuccessful). The first all-Soviet census took place in 1926 (the first all-Russian census was carried out in 1897).

bureaucratic quality at the time of regime inception. A paired comparison of a country with a relatively high capacity to collect information and a country where information-gathering capacity was low allows us to highlight the importance of tempo in our explanations: thus, we can expect that China will attempt to transition from ex-post to ex-ante governance at a substantially slower speed than a state that had a high precommunist capacity—a case in point is the GDR, which was both the country with the highest bureaucratic capacity in the communist world and the first to adopt ex-ante governance in 1953. Because its capacity was not as high as that of the GDR, Bulgaria did not make a transition until the late 1950s. In China, the transition began in the 1980s but was not completed.

1.7 Sources and Methods

A key obstacle to theory generation in the study of autocracy is that nondemocratic polities are characterized by opacity. Theories of authoritarian rule are usually generated on the basis of readily observable indicators.[59] Though this approach has led to major advances in the study of electoral authoritarianism,[60] focusing on observable indicators cannot shed light on a hidden activity like information gathering. For this reason, the book relies on regime-generated materials prepared for insiders. The empirical core of the study is an archival corpus of State Security, communist party, and internal media documents from Bulgaria, China, the Soviet Union, the GDR, and Cuba; these documents are supplemented with primary sources from Taiwan and with a variety of materials from Russia, Iraq, Argentina, and Chile. Because they were not meant to reach the hands of scholars, regime-generated materials hold a promise to reveal how autocrats themselves understand the information problem. They also allow political scientists to benefit from the new method of archival ethnography. When used in conjunction with more traditional social scientific tools of analysis,

---

[59] Bruce Bueno de Mesquita, Alastair Smith, Randolph M. Siverson, and James D. Morrow, *The Logic of Political Survival* (Cambridge, MA: MIT Press, 2003); Gandhi, *Political Institutions under Dictatorship*; Svolik, *The Politics of Authoritarian Rule*.

[60] Magaloni, *Voting for Autocracy*; Kenneth F. Greene, *Why Dominant Parties Lose: Mexico's Democratization in Comparative Perspective* (New York: Cambridge University Press, 2007); Alberto Simpser, *Why Governments and Parties Manipulate Elections: Theory, Practice, and Implications* (New York: Cambridge University Press, 2013); Andreas Schedler, *The Politics of Uncertainty: Sustaining and Subverting Electoral Authoritarianism* (New York: Oxford University Press, 2013); Michael K. Miller, "Elections, Information, and Policy Responsiveness in Autocratic Regimes," *Comparative Political Studies* 48:6 (2015), 691–727.

archival immersion can produce rich insights into the internal logic of author-itarian rule.

Two sources that this study uses judiciously are memoirs and interviews.[61] Writing this book has involved carefully reading over 100 memoirs by intelli-gence operatives and leading political figures in Bulgaria, East Germany, the Soviet Union, and China, and conducting 96 interviews with information gatherers and recipients in China, the former GDR, Bulgaria, Cuba, and the former Soviet Union. The dangers in using such sources are two-fold: memo-ries of past events are subject to the twin problems of strategic forgetfulness and opportunistic invention of facts to suit the current political environment;[62] in addition, the complexity of information collection, transfer, and usage makes it exceedingly difficult to locate individuals who can knowledgeably discuss the is-sues theorized in this book. For these reasons, although memoir and interview evidence is not employed to generate or test the major hypotheses in this study, it is occasionally used when discussing certain aspects of information gath-ering and reception (especially when it is possible to corroborate such evidence through government-generated materials).

1.8 Organization of the Study

This book consists of ten chapters organized in five parts. Part I serves as an introduction to the theory and method used in the study. Parts II, III, and IV present paired comparisons of the parallel origins of the information states in Bulgaria and China in the 1940s–1950s; of their divergent evolution in the 1960s–1970s and convergence in the crisis year of 1989; and of their separate paths in the aftermath of 1989. Part V engages with the generaliz-ability of the theory by presenting a chapter on scope conditions and a con-cluding reflection on information and authoritarian regime resilience. Table 1.3 provides an overview of the study by specifying the chapters in which the main channels for the collection of information and the entities managing them are discussed.

---

[61] For examples of memoir-based studies, see Joseph Sassoon, *Anatomy of Authoritarianism in the Arab Republics* (New York: Cambridge University Press, 2016) and Xuezhi Guo, *China's Security State: Philosophy, Evolution, and Politics* (New York: Cambridge University Press, 2012).

[62] *12:08 East of Bucharest* (A fost sau n-a fost?), director Corneliu Poromboiu (Bucharest: 42 Km Film, 2006).

Table 1.3 Overview of the Study: Main Channels for the Collection of Information and Entities Managing These Channels

Collection Channel	Discussed in Chapter	Entities Managing the Channel
Monitoring correspondence	3, 4, 6, 7, 8, 9	State Security
Phone tapping	3, 4, 7, 8, 9	State Security
Surveillance (in-person or technological)	3, 4, 5, 6, 7, 8, 9	State Security
Monitoring dreams	3	State Security
Monitoring public conversations	3, 5, 9	Party, State Security, and journalists writing internal reports
Monitoring offline rumors	3, 4, 5, 6, 8	Party, State Security, and journalists writing internal reports
Monitoring offline jokes	5	Party, State Security, and journalists writing internal reports
Monitoring antiregime propaganda (e.g., graffiti), sabotage, and protests	3, 4, 5, 6, 7, 8, 9	Party, State Security, and journalists writing internal reports
Analyzing anonymous denunciations (submitted by mail and, since the 1990s, on websites)	3, 4, 6, 8	Party (aided by Internet Service Providers [ISPs] since the 1990s), State Security, and journalists writing internal reports
Analyzing real-name complaints (mail or email)	3, 4, 5, 6, 7, 8, 9	Party-state and journalists writing internal reports
Opinion polling	5, 6, 7, 8, 9	Party and journalists writing internal reports, pollsters
Monitoring real-name social media posts	8	Party, Internet service providers, State Security, and journalists writing internal reports
Monitoring anonymous social media posts	8	Party, Internet service providers, State Security, and journalists writing internal reports
Email/chat monitoring	8	State Security

2

Studying Government Perceptions of Popular Discontent in Autocracies

Opacity is a fundamental feature of nondemocratic politics that confronts scholars when they consider what type of evidence to collect for their research. The classic studies of autocracies are based on a stylized fact, namely, that dictatorships are repressive regimes in which fear is widespread.[1] In turn, fear gives rise to two distinct pathologies. The first is agency problems, where bureaucrats are afraid of transmitting negative news to their superiors. The central insight here is that accurate information can be collected locally, but officials will either distort it prior to transmission or block it from being transferred to the higher levels.[2] The second issue is preference falsification, which involves citizens publicly declaring their support for the system, even though they are privately opposed to it.[3] In contrast to the agency problem approach, a preference falsification framework excludes the possibility that accurate information can be collected. The preference falsification concept has given rise to the influential notion of the dictator's dilemma, where dictators are insecure because they cannot know what level of support they have from society.[4]

Recent research on autocracies has been based on empirical indicators rather than on stylized facts. Scholars have made powerful arguments stating that elections,[5] protests,[6] and liberalized media generate information on levels of opposition to the regime and can therefore serve to mitigate the dictator's dilemma.[7]

---

[1] Hannah Arendt, *The Origins of Totalitarianism* (New York: Harcourt, Brace and Company, 1951).

[2] Carl J. Friedrich and Zhigniew K. Brzezinski, *Totalitarian Dictatorship and Autocracy* (Cambridge, MA: Harvard University Press, 1965), 135.

[3] Václav Havel, *Moc bezmocných* (London: Londýnské listy, 1979); Timur Kuran, "Now Out of Never: The Element of Surprise in the East European Revolution of 1989," *World Politics* 44:1 (1991), 7–48; Timur Kuran, *Private Truths, Public Lies: The Social Consequences of Preference Falsification* (Cambridge, MA: Harvard University Press, 1995); Lisa Wedeen, *Ambiguities of Domination: Politics, Rhetoric, and Symbols in Contemporary Syria* (Chicago: University of Chicago Press, 1999).

[4] Ronald Wintrobe, *The Political Economy of Dictatorship* (New York: Cambridge University Press, 1998).

[5] Beatriz Magaloni, *Voting for Autocracy: Hegemonic Party Survival and Its Demise in Mexico* (New York: Cambridge University Press, 2006).

[6] Peter Lorentzen, "Regularizing Rioting: Permitting Public Protest in an Authoritarian Regime," *Quarterly Journal of Political Science* 8:2 (2013), 127–58.

[7] Georgy Egorov, Sergei Guriev, and Konstantin Sonin, "Why Resource-Poor Dictators Allow Freer Media: A Theory and Evidence from Panel Data," *American Political Science Review* 103:3 (November 2009), 645–68; Daniela Stockmann, *Media Commercialization and Authoritarian Rule*

Dictatorship and Information. Martin K. Dimitrov, Oxford University Press. © Oxford University Press 2023.
DOI: 10.1093/oso/9780197672921.003.0002

This book does not contest the insights generated by either the classic or the recent research on authoritarianism. Agency problems and preference falsification certainly exist in autocracies. Furthermore, elections, protests, and liberalized media undoubtedly have the dual effects of overcoming agency problems and providing valuable indicia of discontent that can reduce the dictators' uncertainty about their level of support. The problem is that these indicators are visible not only to regime insiders but also to the general public and may therefore facilitate collective action. Channels that allow for the confidential internal transmission of information on latent discontent have considerably greater utility from the perspective of regime insiders, as they may reveal popular preferences to regime insiders and thus serve as a solution to the dictator's dilemma but without simultaneously enabling horizontal dissemination, as elections, protests, and liberalized media do.

What might these internal channels be? This book maps out the entire system of confidential information collection and transmission in communist autocracies that is centered on the three key institutions tasked with assessing the popular mood: the party, State Security, and the internal journalism system. These institutions (which are sometimes assisted by the army, by other branches of the party-state, and since the 1990s, by Internet service providers [ISPs]) develop numerous mechanisms for assessing dissatisfaction, ranging from phone tapping to the monitoring of active opposition to the system. These mechanisms, in turn, allow for various indicia of discontent to be recorded and monitored. Information gatherers distinguish between signs of overt dissatisfaction and indicators of latent discontent. Over time, their primary goal becomes assessing dissent while it is still at a latent stage. Seen through this framework, the value of elections, protests, and liberalized media (all of which are tracked by information collectors) is limited: they are widely circulating indicia of overt dissatisfaction. Monitoring overt dissent is needed for reactive (ex-post) governance. By contrast, assessing latent discontent enables anticipatory (ex-ante) governance. Although both types of discontent have to be monitored, autocrats eventually place more value on information-collection mechanisms that enable anticipatory governance.

Information gathering in dictatorships is nontransparent by design. In China, for instance, compendia on the development and evolution of government bureaucracies do not provide any information on the Ministry of Public Security, the Ministry of State Security, the State Secrets Administration, or the Ministry of Supervision: these entities are listed as omitted (*lüe*

in China (New York: Cambridge University Press, 2013); and Peter Lorentzen, "China's Strategic Censorship," *American Journal of Political Science* 58:2 (April 2014), 402–14. On media manipulation and the popularity of incumbents, see Sergei Guriev and Daniel Treisman, "The Popularity of Authoritarian Leaders: A Cross-National Investigation," *World Politics* 72:4 (October 2020), 601–38.

略).[8] This creates a fundamental dilemma for scholars, namely, how can they study something that is not readily observed? One approach has been to focus on what can be seen (elections, protests, or liberalized media) and to then make inferences about its informational function in autocracies. A parallel strategy has been to develop theories from public artifacts,[9] such as official photographs, speeches, ceremonies, interviews, and specific legislation and policies.[10] Both approaches rely on information that either cannot be suppressed or is purposefully disclosed. Yet, as researchers have noted, public artifacts are indirect sources that produce equivocal evidence.[11] The danger is that we may end up studying surface phenomena rather than deep politics.[12] Understanding the mechanisms of autocratic rule requires piercing the veil of authoritarian secrecy by utilizing direct sources that are generated internally for regime insiders rather than for public distribution.

The present chapter engages with two central questions that arise when working with internal government materials. The first is definitional: What are these direct sources? Where are they located? And how have they been constituted? The second is methodological: How do we approach documents of this kind? This chapter argues that archival ethnography is the most effective technique for engaging with direct sources. This methodological approach yields both empirical and theoretical insights about information gathering in communist autocracies that are presented in the remainder of this chapter. The chapter ends with Appendix A1 that illustrates how direct sources enrich our understandings of an issue as complex as estimating the size of the informant corps in autocracies.

2.1 Types of Archives

When drawing on archival sources to study autocracies, distinctions should be made among the various entities that generated the materials, the repositories where these materials are held, the type of materials, and the media on which

---

[8] Guojia Xingzheng Xueyuan, *Zhonghua renmin gongheguo zhengfu jigou wushi nian* (Beijing: Dangjian Duwu Chubanshe, 2000), 94–95.

[9] Robert Barros, "On the Outside Looking In: Secrecy and the Study of Authoritarian Regimes," *Social Science Quarterly* 97:4 (December 2016), 953–73.

[10] On photographs, see Roderick MacFarquhar, "On Photographs," *The China Quarterly*, no. 46 (April–June 1971), 289–307.

[11] Barros, "On the Outside Looking In"; David Art, "Archivists and Adventurers: Research Strategies for Authoritarian Regimes of the Past and Present," *Social Science Quarterly* 97:4 (December 2016), 974–90.

[12] Thomas Pepinsky, "The Institutional Turn in Comparative Authoritarianism," *British Journal of Political Science* 44:3 (July 2014), 631–53; Jennifer Gandhi, Ben Noble, and Milan Svolik, "Legislatures and Legislative Politics without Democracy," *Comparative Political Studies* 53:9 (2020), 1359–79.

these materials are encoded. These are not arcane questions. Rather, they allow us to critically assess the value of the materials on which the research is based and to be fully cognizant of their potential for elucidating questions that have empirical, methodological, and theoretical relevance for scholarship on authoritarian politics.

2.1.1   Entities Generating Materials

For a study of the internal regime understandings of popular discontent in communist autocracies (by "internal regime understandings," we mean the knowledge or awareness of regime insiders), the agencies that can generate directly relevant original content are limited to the party, the state security apparatus, and the internal media.[13] These entities produce materials for internal use that can elucidate to scholars the mechanics of monitoring discontent. Often, the archive of one information gatherer contains materials produced by the other collection agencies; in general, the party archive is the richest in this regard, as copies of many State Security documents can be found there; sometimes, other archives facilitate unexpected discoveries—for example, the Bulgarian State Security Archive contains communist party documents from the 1989–1990 period that were never deposited in the Central State Archives and were considered to have been lost as a consequence of a fire in the Central Committee headquarters in 1990.[14]

Occasionally, other parts of the government, such as the Ministry of Environment and Ecology in China (which tracks contentious episodes stemming from pollution), may publicly disseminate information that sheds light on the incidence of discontent.[15] Similarly, when combined with the appropriate internal materials, crowd-sourced data such as Wickedonna's raw reports on 65,317 protests in 2013–2016 can be used, as demonstrated in Chapter 8, to generate some insights about the government's willingness to suppress protests. But these are exceptions. In general, only information produced for internal use within the regime can reliably reveal how insiders perceive discontent and how they go about managing it.

Scholars of contemporary China may point out that the Open Government Information (OGI) Initiative has made available substantial amounts of data from the 2000s and 2010s, thus apparently rendering a search for internal

---

[13] Memoirs and interviews are likely to be impacted by a retrospective fallacy and should therefore be used with the utmost caution.

[14] These documents are analyzed in Chapter 7.

[15] See, for instance, *Zhongguo huanjing nianjian 2016* (Beijing: Zhongguo Huanjng Bao She, 2016), 791.

materials unnecessary. Closer inspection reveals, however, that most of what has been publicized through OGI is limited to issues like power lists, procurement notices, budgets, and government regulations.[16] Curated citizen complaints also appear on "mayors' mailboxes" and similar websites.[17] But it would be naïve to think that the Chinese government feels compelled to publicize its inner operations because of OGI. All of the key information collectors analyzed in this book have remained nontransparent. OGI has not improved openness for bureaucracies considered sensitive: for instance, the National Public Complaints and Proposals Administration (*guojia xinfang ju* 国家信访局) granted only 3.8 percent of the 444 OGI requests it received in 2018–2020.[18] Successful requests demanded the disclosure of regulations, not the decisions in specific cases or statistics about the caseload of the Complaints and Proposals Administration. This example from China, which presents the limit case of openness, highlights the importance of locating the internal government documents that are read by regime insiders and are not meant for public distribution.

2.1.2 Location and Access

Ascertaining where archival materials are held and securing access to them is far from trivial. In the most straightforward scenario, the entity that produced the documents also maintains archival copies and allows researchers to consult relevant finding aids and the documents themselves. This situation is exceedingly rare: in the process of writing this book, I encountered only one information gatherer (the Bulgarian Telegraph Agency) that granted me unimpeded access to its proprietary archive.

It is more common to have to confront a closed proprietary archive (e.g., of the Committee for State Security [KGB]), from which documents are released at the discretion of current employees of the entity that produced the original materials.[19] While valuable (and used in Chapter 9),[20] such sources need to

---

[16] Jonathan R. Stromseth, Edmund J. Malesky, and Dimitar Gueorguiev, *China's Governance Puzzle: Enabling Transparency and Participation in a Single-Party State* (New York: Cambridge University Press, 2017), esp. 81.

[17] Greg Distelhorst and Yue Hou, "Constituency Service under Non-Democratic Rule: Evidence from China," *The Journal of Politics* 79:3 (2017), 1024–40.

[18] Calculated from annual reports that were available on www.gjxfj.gov.cn through March 2021, but appeared to be inaccessible on April 19, 2022.

[19] Closed archives exist in democracies as well. In the United States, systematic declassification rules do not extend to CIA documents, which are typically released at the discretion of CIA archivists in redacted form following Freedom of Information (FOIA) requests. Similarly, systematic access to unredacted MI5 and MI6 files is not possible in the United Kingdom.

[20] The primary set of KGB archival materials is the ten-volume collection *"Sovershenno sekretno": Lubianka–Stalinu o polozhenii v strane (1922–1934 gg)* (Moscow: Institute of Russian History of the Russian Academy of Sciences, 2000–2017).

be evaluated with a view to understanding the selection principles involved in decisions to make certain sensitive documents publicly available. Sometimes proprietary archives are partially opened. For example, documents produced prior to the 1950s were easily accessible at the Guomindang (KMT) Archive in Taiwan in the 2010s; in contrast to these documents, which can also be consulted at the Hoover Institution, the KMT Archive made very few files from the 1950s or 1960s available to scholars. Materials produced during the later decades of the KMT's rule were completely unavailable.[21]

A third type of situation, the most typical, involves the administration of documents by an entity different from the one that created them. There are several possible permutations here. One involves the expatriation of documents away from their country of origin, with the expectation that they may eventually be repatriated to the place where they were created.[22] Documents may also be transferred in-country to a new entity expressly established to administer them, as occurred in several Eastern European states that set up special archives for safeguarding State Security files. Access to these materials may be temporarily or permanently restricted due to privacy considerations, as in the case of the Stasi files. Another possibility is to have documents transferred to a general repository (usually the national archive). This took place in most Eastern European states after 1989, when communist party materials were absorbed into the holdings of the central state archives. This may also happen in Taiwan, where since its creation in 2018 the Transitional Justice Commission has demanded the systematic transfer of various party (KMT) and intelligence agency files to the National Archives Administration.

The general concern when documents are administered by an entity different from the one that created them is whether the entirety of the original records was transferred;[23] when the transfer is selective, awareness of the principles

[22] Others have referred to such materials as "displaced" or "captured" (see James Lowry, ed., *Displaced Archives* [London: Routledge, 2017] and Robert Wolfe, ed., *Captured German and Related Records: A National Archives Conference* [Athens, OH: Ohio University Press, 1974]). Some materials were indeed captured: the Smolensk Archive (seized by the Nazis and then transported to the United States); the Nazi papers acquired by Allied troops during World War II; and the Iraqi materials collected by the U.S. government and the Iraq Memory Foundation. But other materials, such as the Rosenholz and Mitrokhin collections, were not captured (on Rosenholz, see Robert Gerald Livingston, "An Operation Called 'Rosenholz'—How the CIA Bought the Stasi Files for $75,000," *The Atlantic Times* [March 2006]; on Mitrokhin, see https://digitalarchive.wilsoncenter.org/collect ion/52/mitrokhin-archive [accessed April 19, 2022] and Christopher M. Andrew, *The Sword and the Shield: The Mitrokhin Archive and the Secret History of the KGB* [New York: Basic Books, 1999]). Finally, some materials were willingly placed in overseas depositories such as the Library of Congress (the Rubinov Collection of citizen letters to *Literaturnaia gazeta* and the Volkogonov Papers, which contain KGB and communist party archival documents). Thus, "expatriated" is a more precise descriptor.

[23] This proviso also applies to microfilm collections, such as those that were produced by an agreement between the Hoover Institution and various post-Soviet archives. While extraordinarily useful (in part because on occasion the original documents have been reclassified in their country of

of selection is important for evaluating the available documents, namely, who chose these materials and with what purpose. For example, the captured Ba'th Party documents have been split between the Hoover Institution (11 million pages) and the Conflict Records Research Center in Washington, D.C. (100 million pages); the guidelines that determined how the materials would be divided remain unknown. Another concern is whether the new entity administering the documents will grant scholars unimpeded access. For example, although the U.S. army transported to Washington, D.C., and digitized 100 million pages of Iraqi documents, scholars were granted access to only 0.143 percent of these materials (143,000 pages). It is not clear what procedures were followed to determine which documents should be declassified and which should remain confidential. These caveats notwithstanding, expatriated documents can have high value for research on autocracies where archival access is impossible, as powerfully illustrated by the numerous studies based on the Smolensk Archive and on the seized Ba'th Party materials.[24]

Finally, we should draw a distinction between partial collections and entire archives. Expatriated collections are always partial, whereas archives in situ are entire. In order to determine the size of these collections, we need a metric. European archives report their holdings in linear kilometers, whereas the collections expatriated to the United States are measured in pages. The page-to-meter conversion is straightforward: 1,000 pages of paper with standard thickness equal 10 centimeters; 10,000 pages constitute 1 meter; and 10 million pages make up 1 linear kilometer. This conversion system allows us to compare the Stasi Archive (111 kilometers) with the Smolensk Archive (0.02 kilometers),[25] the Ba'th Regional Command Collection at the Hoover Institution (1.1 kilometers), and the classified Iraqi loot inaccessible to researchers (10 kilometers and 2,000

origin and thus made unavailable to researchers), these collections often skip over files that exist in the archives but remain classified and therefore were not microfilmed. There are multiple examples of such missing files in the Fond 89 and the Lithuanian KGB microfilm collections at the Hoover Institution.

[24] On the Smolensk Archive, see Merle Fainsod, *Smolensk under Soviet Rule* (Cambridge, MA: Harvard University Press, 1958). For studies produced on the basis of the expatriated Iraqi materials, see Kevin M. Woods, David D. Palkki, and Mark E. Stout, eds., *The Saddam Tapes: The Inner Workings of a Tyrant's Regime, 1978–2001* (New York: Cambridge University Press, 2011); Joseph Sassoon, *Saddam Hussein's Ba'th Party: Inside an Authoritarian Regime* (New York: Cambridge University Press, 2012); Dina Rizk Khoury, *Iraq in Wartime: Soldiering, Martyrdom, and Remembrance* (New York: Cambridge University Press, 2013); Martin K. Dimitrov and Joseph Sassoon, "State Security, Information, and Repression: A Comparison of Communist Bulgaria and Ba'thist Iraq," *Journal of Cold War Studies* 16:2 (Spring 2014), 4–31; Aaron M. Faust, *The Ba'thication of Iraq: Saddam Hussein's Totalitarianism* (Austin: University of Texas Press, 2015); and Lisa Blaydes, *State of Repression: Iraq under Saddam Hussein* (Princeton, NJ: Princeton University Press, 2018).

[25] Fainsod, *Smolensk under Soviet Rule*, provides information (pp. 3, 456) that allows us to calculate that the size of the Smolensk Archive is 20 meters (0.02 kilometers), as it consists of 536 files that total about 200,000 pages.

hours of tape, 14.3 meters and 200 hours of which were selectively declassified and made available to scholars at the now defunct Conflict Records Research Center).[26] As is clear, in all of these cases, the expatriated archives equal less than one-tenth of the size of a single Eastern European archive in situ. Discussions based on partial archives require more provisos than those informed by research in entire archives.

2.1.3 Current Operational Records versus Archival Material

There exists a difference between current operational records and archival material. The decision to archive a current record means that the case is closed and that instead of discarding the files as useless, they must be preserved because of their potential future value. There is no assumption that all operational records should be preserved. The culling that takes place during the archiving of operational records is different from archival cleansing (which is routine and is conducted at specific intervals with the aim of determining which archival files need to be discarded) and from the willful destruction of archives. The only operational records used in this book are the two leaked Propaganda Department datasets from Jiangxi (the Zhanggong dataset and the Jiujiang dataset), which are discussed in Chapter 8.[27]

2.1.4 Deliberate Destruction of Archival Material

Archives evolve and are incomplete by design: documents are damaged or destroyed (which is why, in 1337 the city of Siena purchased a cat to guard its archive against mice),[28] misfiled or lost, or thrown out as insignificant. Pristine and complete archives in which every document is preserved do not (and cannot)

[26] Currently, neither the declassified nor the classified materials are readily available to scholars. The originals have been returned to Iraq, the Conflict Records Research Center closed definitively in 2015, and the digital copies can only be obtained through FOIA requests filed with the National Archives and Records Administration. See Bruce P. Montgomery, *The Seizure of Saddam Hussein's Archive of Atrocity* (Lanham, MD: Lexington Books, 2019); Bruce P. Montgomery and Michael P. Brill, "The Ghosts of the Past Live on in a Crucial Archive," *War on the Rocks*, September 11, 2019, https://warontherocks.com/2019/09/the-ghosts-of-past-wars-live-on-in-a-critical-archive/ (accessed April 19, 2022); and Michael R. Gordon, "Archive of Captured Enemy Documents Closes," *The New York Times*, June 22, 2015, A5, https://www.nytimes.com/2015/06/22/world/middleeast/archive-of-captured-terrorist-qaeda-hussein-documents-shuts-down.html (accessed April 19, 2022).
[27] When using leaked materials, we need to be mindful of their provenance: see Christopher Darnton, "The Provenance Problem: Research Methods and Ethics in the Age of Wikileaks," *American Political Science Review* (2021): 1–16, doi: 10.1017/S0003055421001374.
[28] Randolph C. Head, *Making Archives in Early Modern Europe: Proof, Information, and Political Record-Keeping, 1400–1700* (New York: Cambridge University Press, 2019), 1.

exist. Normal losses should be differentiated from the deliberate destruction of documents during political transitions (including through staged looting and fires, as happened in the German Democratic Republic [GDR] and Bulgaria in 1989–1990) and from the removal of documents as a form of political insurance (this occurred most notably with the files displaced from the archives by Polish Interior Minister Czesław Kiszczak to facilitate blackmailing opposition leader Lech Wałęsa, whose political career would have been compromised should his collaboration with State Security have become public knowledge).[29] In some cases, theft seems to be motivated exclusively by pecuniary needs, as occurred with the Rosenholz data that were removed from the Stasi archive under unspecified circumstances and subsequently purchased by the CIA.[30] Scholars should be mindful of the types of materials that were deliberately withheld from the archive as it came to be constituted and the bureaucratic logic that governed decisions regarding which documents might be made available to researchers.

2.1.5 Types of Archival Materials: Personal Files versus Summary Reports

Among the wealth of diverse sources that are housed in the archives, personal files and summary reports are most likely to reveal the techniques deployed to monitor popular discontent. Personal files are created on the basis of material supplied *by* individuals (when citizens gather intelligence consistent with their duties as State Security agents or provide information voluntarily by contacting the authorities through letters, emails, phone calls, and in-person visits) or collected *about* individuals who have become objects of State Security surveillance, party monitoring, or corruption investigations. Summary reports originate with the party, State Security, or the internal media and aim to produce general descriptions of the sources and types of discontent; when individuals are mentioned in such digests, it is done for illustrative purposes, in contrast to the personal files, which focus squarely on the actions of specific citizens. Though referred to in a variety of ways (brief, digest, information, and of course "report"), these summary materials are typically daily, weekly, monthly, quarterly, or yearly overviews of some type of problem or issue related to popular discontent. As discussed below, personal files and summary reports generate quite different kinds of evidence.

---

[29] https://ipn.gov.pl/en/news/899,Information-on-the-experts-opinion-on-the-secret-collaborator-Boleks-files.html (accessed April 19, 2022).

[30] Livingston, "An Operation Called 'Rosenholz.'"

Personal files are vivid and often gripping documents that make for fascinating reading, as evidenced, for example, by the public intellectuals and scholars who have used such files to write books about their own experience of being placed under surveillance by State Security.[31] Sordid tales of wives informing on their husbands have inspired screenplays for award-winning films.[32] Though less shocking in terms of their content, collections of citizen letters have been published as well;[33] such curated compendia make palpable the daily life struggles of ordinary citizens in autocracies.

A scholar working with personal files confronts the twin problems of authenticity and representativeness. In nearly every high-profile case, the authenticity of the files has been disputed. Illustrative examples include the familiar names of German writer Christa Wolf, Czech-French novelist Milan Kundera, and of course, Poland's former president Lech Wałęsa. Bulgaria's most controversial case involves a determination in 2018 by the Dossier Commission that the highly decorated Bulgarian-French intellectual Julia Kristeva had served as a State Security informant in the 1960s–1970s.[34] Can we generalize from such cases and cast doubt on the authenticity of all personal files? Systematic data are useful to address this question. For example, between 2007 and 2017 the Bulgarian Dossier Commission disclosed the names of 12,404 individuals who had had an affiliation with State Security during the communist period;[35] 380 people (3.1 percent of the total) disputed the commission's determinations through the court system.[36] It deserves to be noted that, in most of these cases, the Dossier Commission won against the challengers, thus instilling confidence in the validity of its assessments, which often are made on the basis of fragmentary evidence, due to politically motivated and willful destruction of archival materials that took place in 1989–1990. In sum, concerns about authenticity

---

[31] Timothy Garton Ash, *The File: A Personal History* (New York: Random House, 1997); Katherine Verdery, *My Life as a Spy: Investigations in a Secret Police File* (Durham, NC: Duke University Press, 2018); Vera Wollenberger, *Virus der Heuchler: Innenansicht aus Stasi-Akten* (Berlin: Elefantenpress, 1992).

[32] *Das Leben der Anderen*, director Florian Henckel von Donnersmark (München: Buena Vista Home Entertainment, 2006); *Zift*, director Iavor Gurdev (Sofia: Alexandra Films, 2008).

[33] Monika Deutz-Schroeder and Jochen Staadt, eds., *Teurer Genosse! Briefe an Erich Honecker* (Berlin: Transit, 1994); Siegfried Suckutt, ed., *Volkes Stimmen: "Ehrlich, aber deutlich"—Privatbriefe an die DDR-Regierung* (München: DTV, 2016); Henrik Eberle, *Mit sozialistischem Gruß: Eingaben, Briefe und Mitteilungen an die DDR-Regierung* (Berlin: Berolina, 2016); G. V. Gorskaia, M. S. Astakhova, V. Denningkhaus, E. E. Kirillova, A. S. Kochetova, comps., *Poslednie pis'ma Stalinu 1952–1953: Rekonstruktsiia dokumental'nogo kompleksa* (Moscow: Rosspen, 2015).

[34] Jennifer Schuessler and Boryana Dzhambazova, "Bulgaria Says French Thinker Was a Secret Agent. She Calls It a 'Barefaced Lie,'" *The New York Times*, April 1, 2018, https://www.nytimes.com/2018/04/01/arts/julia-kristeva-bulgaria-communist-spy.html (accessed April 19, 2022).

[35] This is not equivalent to the number of informants. The law stipulates that only the names of those running for office or holding certain leadership positions must be disclosed.

[36] Dossier Commission, *Activity Report* (July–December 2007), 12 and Dossier Commission, *Stocktaking 2007–2017* (2017), 34.

arise infrequently, are generally limited to high-profile public figures, and remain overwhelmingly unsubstantiated.

More serious is the threat to representativeness that is presented by the nonsystematic preservation of personal files. This applies to both letters and State Security dossiers. Individual letters (and the paperwork generated in the process of responding to and following up on them) are ephemeral documents that are typically culled during the periodic purging of current operational records; for such materials to enter a permanent archive, especially at the central level, they must be unusual in some way: addressed to the general secretary, for instance, or presenting a case that is highly atypical and thus worthy of being preserved. When it comes to State Security materials, we possess unmistakable evidence that because of their current affairs value, personal files were most likely to be destroyed by the archivists during the transition period, when evidence of collaboration with the security services could damage the careers of anticommunist politicians. As the destruction orders were not executed fully, some files were spared—but the logic guiding decisions about preservation is unclear. It is very difficult to use personal files systematically as they present the challenge of generalizing about typical behavior from anecdotal case-specific evidence that has survived nonsystematically.

The main shortcoming of personal files is that although they may document the existence of a certain phenomenon (e.g., the use of abductions or assassinations by State Security),[37] they cannot reliably reveal its frequency. We can only determine how typical a phenomenon is by consulting the appropriate summary documents. In contrast to the personal files, which were heavily politicized, these drier records were protected from public attention during the transition; the archival rosters indicate that they survived virtually intact the deliberate destruction that affected personal files. We should also note that there are no squabbles about the authenticity of summary reports. These documents present the types of evidence in which this study is interested. They reveal generalizable patterns in the methods used to collect information on dissent and illuminate their temporal evolution.

2.1.6 Media Formats for Encoding Documents

The medium on which archival materials are encoded impacts the ease of reproduction and subsequent circulation of the original. Prior to the fall of the

---

[37] Khristo Khristov, *Durzhavna sigurnost sreshtu bulgarskata emigratsiia* (Sofia: Ivan Vazov, 2000); Khristo Khristov, *Ubiite "Skitnik": Bulgarskata i britanskata durzhavna politika po sluchaia Georgi Markov* (Sofia: Ciela, 2006).

Berlin Wall, most party and government documents were typewritten rather than computer-generated (in China, handwritten documents were quite common throughout the Mao years). Although archival materials were initially encoded on paper, existing technology allows them to be photocopied, microfilmed, or scanned; digitized copies can then be stored on various devices or platforms. Beyond paper, additional media formats for encoding original documents include audiotapes, videotapes, email inboxes, and social media accounts. The challenges these types of media present to researchers who want to access and systematically extract information from them vary, though none are insurmountable. Original paper records that have not been photocopied, microfilmed, or digitized are least likely to circulate. For this reason, they tend to be the most closely guarded, and accessing them requires, at the very least, a visit to the specific repository where they are kept. This study is based primarily on such original paper documents (located in archives holding Chinese, Bulgarian, Soviet, East German, Cuban, and Taiwanese materials), which are supplemented by Soviet and East German microfilm, two Jiangxi email datasets (with document attachments), and a protest dataset constructed from Wickedonna's social media posts.

2.1.7 Summing Up

Knowledge of the provenance of archival documents and the decision processes that led to their inclusion in specific repositories is important for understanding the inferential limitations of arguments based on internal sources. Such concerns are elevated when using expatriated materials, personal files, and published compendia of archival documents. Scholars must also be mindful of situations in which finding aids are missing, thus making it difficult to get a sense of the size and organization of the archive. Direct sources provide invaluable insight into the internal logic of information gathering in autocracies—but they need to be approached with a set of queries about the purposes for which the documents were created, who were their intended recipients, and how those individuals reacted to the intelligence contained in them. To address these questions, we turn to the principles of archival ethnography.

2.2 Methodological Contributions: Archival Ethnography

As awareness of the value of using internal documents is in the process of emerging in mainstream political science, we do not yet have commonly accepted procedures for conducting research on autocracies using direct sources. This study argues that direct sources allow scholars to practice archival ethnography. Its logic and methodological contributions are presented below. This section also discusses some caveats about the sources of bias in archival materials.

2.2.1 Archival Ethnography

Traditional ethnography involves the study of people in their own environment through face-to-face interviews or participant observation. Students of political ethnography describe these practices as immersion, though they allow for immersion to take forms of intensive engagement that are not limited to interviews and participant observation.[38] Political ethnographers also highlight the importance of a higher-order ethnographic sensibility, which involves caring to understand the meaning that the subjects of the study ascribe to social and political phenomena. While this sensibility typically emerges from immersion, it may also develop through other pathways that allow for deep engagement with a subject.[39] In short, ethnography is a flexible concept, centered around immersion (which typically involves cumulative time) and understanding (which often arises as the result of past immersive experiences).[40]

Archival ethnography, as employed in this project, rests on immersion in regime documents with the goal of identifying the network of mechanisms created to gather and process intelligence. Specifically, this study focuses on the collection, transfer, and use of information about popular discontent in autocracies. Because archival sources are primarily textual, they yield rich and easily quantifiable data. Yet, approaching these materials with an ethnographic sensibility means treating them not simply as sources of machine-readable data but rather analyzing who produced them, how, and for which audience.[41] The answers to these questions allow us to reconstruct a system of information flow. If the archive is at a sufficiently high level (a central-level party, State Security, or media repository), we can obtain a top-down view of the entire system. Because the circulation of information is among the most secretive aspects of authoritarian politics, the analytic payoffs from reconstructing it are significant: we can document what dictators know. If we accept that there is no political power without

---

[38] Edward Schatz, ed., *Political Ethnography: What Immersion Contributes to the Study of Power* (Chicago: University of Chicago Press, 2009), 5.

[39] Schatz, *Political Ethnography*, 5–6.

[40] Lorraine Bayard de Volo and Edward Schatz, "From the Inside Out: Ethnographic Methods in Political Research," *PS* 37:2 (April 2004), 267–71.

[41] Stephanie Decker and Alan MacKinlay, "Archival Ethnography," in Raza Mir and Anne-Laure Fayard, eds., *The Routledge Companion to Politics and Business* (New York: Routledge, 2020), 17–33.

control of the archive and that modern states are archive-states,[42] access to archival materials gives us the key to understanding how such power is projected.

Reading archival materials with an ethnographic sensibility provides a second payoff, as it exposes us to the language that state actors themselves use to describe to one another the social and political realities they are observing. The concepts and categories that emerge from the documents reveal how bureaucrats see the world. Moreover, it is these categories that guide the scope and method of information collection. Ultimately, these concepts shape how information will be used to preserve regime stability, which is the express goal of bureaucrats. Some of the understandings that emerge from the documents may appear counterintuitive to scholars. For instance, industrial accidents are seen as acts of sabotage;[43] minority unrest as incited by hostile foreign forces;[44] and protests as threats to state security.[45] The meta-point is that these schemas reflect the view of regime insiders that domestic and foreign enemies abound but can be counteracted once information about them is collected. There is also a second meta-point: not every act that the regime tracks is seen as a sign of hostile intent—complaints, for instance, are understood as an index of citizen trust in the regime, which has to be nurtured through responsiveness.[46] In sum, archives are a way of seeing, and in order to see like a state (and understand its epistemic anxieties), we need to read its archives.[47]

As we try to understand how information collectors make sense of the world, we discover their various misperceptions and lacunae. Their sense-making may be imperfect and in real time, thus exposing us to the contingency of history (a

[42] Jacques Derrida, *Archive Fever: A Freudian Impression* (Chicago: University of Chicago Press, 1996), 4.

[43] *Durzhavna sigurnost i bulgarskata energetika (1944–1991)* (Sofia: Dossier Commission, 2016); Cynthia V. Hooper, "Participation and Coercion in Soviet Power, 1924–1964" (Ph.D. Dissertation, Princeton University, Department of History, 2003), 179.

[44] Qin Weidong, *Xizang wenti beiwanglu* (Lanzhou: Lanzhou Junqu Zhengzhibu Lianluobu, 1990), esp. 1–59; Renzhen Luose, Xie Gangzheng, and Chen Zhichun, *Suowei 'Xizang wenti' de lishi yu xianzhuan* (Chengdu: Sichuan Zangxue Yanjiusuo, 2001).

[45] Xinjiang Shengchan Jianshe Bingtuan Gong'an Zhi and Xinjiang Shengchan Jianshe Bingtuan Difang Zhi Bangongshi, *Xinjiang shengchan jianshe bingtuan gong'an zhi* (Urumqi: Xinjiang Shengchan Jianshe Bingtuan Gong'an Zhi and Xinjiang Shengchan Jianshe Bingtuan Difang Zhi Bangongshi, 1999), 186–89.

[46] Martin K. Dimitrov, "What the Party Wanted to Know: Citizen Complaints as a 'Barometer of Public Opinion' in Communist Bulgaria," *East European Politics and Societies and Cultures* 28:2 (May 2014), 271–95.

[47] Ann Laura Stoler, *Along the Archival Grain: Epistemic Anxieties and Colonial Common Sense* (Princeton, NJ: Princeton University Press, 2009); James C. Scott, *Seeing Like a State: How Certain Schemes to Improve the Human Condition Have Failed* (New Haven, CT: Yale University Press, 1998); Nicholas B. Dirks, "Annals of the Archive: Ethnographic Notes on the Sources of History," in Brian Keith Axel, ed., *From the Margins: Historical Anthropology and Its Future* (Durham, NC: Duke University Press, 2002), 47–65.

history in the subjunctive)—information collectors do not know the outcome, unlike researchers with the benefit of hindsight.[48]

Archival ethnography can be fruitfully combined with other field methods. This project, which is based on three years of immersive work in thirty in- and out-of-country archival repositories and special collections in 2007–2021 (see Table 2.1), also relies on standard ethnographic techniques, such as intensive interviews (96 interviews, with country coverage as follows—Bulgaria: 22; China: 21; Cuba: 26; the GDR: 24; and the Soviet Union: 3). Archival ethnography does not impose a single method of inquiry: thick description is one option, but this project offers an analytic narrative that contains abundant quantitative data that are analyzed through standard statistical approaches. Archival ethnography also enables process tracing.[49] In short, the ethnographic sensibility to understand and interpret meaning lends itself to a variety of subsequent analytic approaches.

Classical ethnography cannot be replicated: a researcher observes a community at a specific point in time and interprets what they see through their own analytic lens.[50] An observation by another scholar will yield different results because the community has changed, the analytic procedures have been amended, or simply as a result of the perspective that the new researcher brings with them. By contrast, archival ethnography is replicable. This book is explicit about the multisite archival repositories it has used, thus providing a guide to those who want to embark on the same journey of immersion, discovery, and understanding. It also refers to individual documents to back up specific conclusions. Consulting these documents allows for fact checking, though it will likely prove insufficient for reconstituting the immersion and sensibility that are constitutive of the ethnographic experience—not to mention the triumphant feeling of serendipitous discovery that occurs regularly in the detective-like ethnographic research process.

Conducting archival ethnography in autocracies presents special challenges. One obvious constraint is access: it is difficult to obtain direct sources on dictatorships that are still extant. Although the availability of materials is generally enhanced when dealing with autocracies that have undergone regime change, research on historical cases presents a different problem, namely, scholars may experience pressure to take a stance in debates regarding the character of the previous regime. An apt illustration is provided by Russia, where the communist party was put on trial by Boris Yeltsin in 1991. Two decades later, Vladimir

---

[48] Roger Hillman, "*Goodbye, Lenin* (2003): History in the Subjunctive," *Rethinking History: The Journal of Theory and Practice* 10:2 (2006), 221–37.

[49] Derek Beach and Rasmus Brun Pedersen, *Process-Tracing Methods: Foundations and Guidelines* (Ann Arbor: University of Michigan Press, 2013).

[50] Wedeen, *Ambiguities of Domination*.

Table 2.1 Archives and Special Collections and Their Locations

Provenance and Time Period Covered	In-Country Location	Out-of-Country Location
Argentina (1976–1983)	• Museo Sitio de Memoria ESMA	
Bulgaria (1944–1991)	• Archives: Central State Archives (party documents); Ministry of the Interior Archive (State Security materials); Dossier Commission (State Security materials); Bulgarian Telegraph Agency Archive (classified bulletins) • Special collections: Bulgarian National Library	
China (1949–present)	• Archives: Shanghai Municipal Archives • *Neibu* collections: Universities Service Centre (Chinese University of Hong Kong); Shanghai Municipal Library; National Library of China	• Archive: Hoover Institution Zhongguo Gong Chan Dang Issuances Collection • Special collections: C. V. Starr Library (UC Berkeley); Fung Library (Harvard); Harvard-Yenching Library; International Legal Studies Collection (Harvard Law School); China Library (George Washington University); Gest Library (Princeton); Staatsbibliothek zu Berlin • Leaked data: Wickedonna (protests); Jiujiang (Propaganda Department); Zhanggong (Propaganda Department)
Cuba (1959–present)	• Archives: *Memorial de la Denuncia* (State Security documents) • Special collections: National Library of Cuba	• Archive: Bulgarian Dossier Commission (Cuban-Bulgarian State Security consultations) • Special collections: Ibero-Amerikanisches Institut (Berlin); Latin American Library (Tulane University)
German Democratic Republic (1949–1989)	• Archives: Foundation Archives of the Parties and Mass Organizations of the GDR in the Federal Archives (SAPMO) (party and government materials); Stasi Records Archive (BStU) (Stasi documents)	• Special collections: Staatsbibliothek zu Berlin

Table 2.1 Continued

Provenance and Time Period Covered	In-Country Location	Out-of-Country Location
Soviet Union (1922–1991)	• Archives: Gorbachev Fund; Russian State Archive (GARF)	• Archives: Hoover Institution (Fond 89 and Lithuanian KGB Archives); Lamont Library (Harvard) (Fond 89 and other archival collections); Regenstein Library (University of Chicago) (Fond 89); Library of Congress (Rubinov Collection and Volkogonov Papers)
Taiwan (1949–1987)	• Archives: KMT Archives; National Archives Administration • Special collections: National Library	

Putin aimed to whitewash the abuses of the Soviet period through his campaign against the "falsification of history." Heated arguments about how to deal with the past (*Vergangenheitsbewältigung*) have unfolded in other formerly communist regimes as well.[51] Although politically motivated pressures to condemn or extol a political system are orthogonal to the research program of understanding the mechanisms that allow a regime to operate, scholars seeking knowledge of the inner logic of dictatorships are in danger of being labeled apologists, especially if they are interested in mechanisms of regime maintenance that go beyond repression and that include tools such as mass co-optation, acquiescence (*Anpassung*), and genuine or conditional support.[52] We should of course note that understanding does not mean uncritical acceptance: researchers bring their outside observer (etic) perspectives as they uncover internal actor (emic) understandings.[53]

---

[51] Carola S. Rudnick, *Die andere Hälfte der Erinnerung: Die DDR in der deutschen Geschichtspolitik nach 1989* (Bielefeld: Transcript, 2011).

[52] Detlev Peukert, *Volksgenossen und Gemeinschaftsfremde: Anpassung, Ausmerze und Aufbegehren unter dem Nationalsozialismus* (Köln: Bund-Verlag, 1982); Mary Fulbrook, *The People's State: East German Society from Hitler to Honecker* (New Haven, CT: Yale University Press, 2005).

[53] Carlo Ginzburg, "Our Words, and Theirs—A Reflection on the Historian's Craft, Today," in Susanna Fellman and Marjatta Rihikainen, eds., *Historical Knowledge: In Quest of Theory, Method, and Evidence* (Cambridge, UK: Cambridge Scholars Publishing, 2012), 97–119.

2.2.2 Caveats: Agency Problems, Segmented Provision, and Content Bias

When conducting archival ethnography, we need to be mindful of archival biases. The content of some documents may be skewed away from reporting popular dissatisfaction with the regime. In a chapter in his book on Zaire, Michael Schatzberg discusses the political police (nontransparently named the *Centre National de Documentation*) and argues that it provided symbolic reassurance to leaders that all was well in the countryside by producing reports stating that "the situation is calm"—just as things were getting out of control.[54] Although materials meant for public dissemination may contain panegyrics for the leader and paeans of popular support for the regime,[55] willful misrepresentation in documents intended for internal consumption is the bête noire of autocrats. It reflects agency problems, where lower-level bureaucrats may try to withhold information that reflects negatively on their locality. This problem is familiar, and its solutions are well known—heightened monitoring; bypassing the reporting chain by going directly to the source;[56] and redundancy (multiplying the number of entities that generate information). As Chapters 3–9 demonstrate, redundancy emerges as the dominant solution to the agency problem in communist regimes.

Agency problems should be differentiated from the segmented provision of information: only relevant intelligence should be sent to higher levels. Certain reports meant for the top leadership are so sensitive that numerical data sometimes are added by hand, to prevent passing on the information to the typist (see Figure 2.1); if a sanitized version of a report is allowed to circulate to lower-level insiders, the numbers may be erased or crossed out (see Figure 2.2). We cannot expect that top decision makers should receive detailed reports about all problems in the country. Some studies make the assumption that all information should be passed on from the grassroots to higher levels;[57] such assumptions are unwarranted, as certain types of events are of no interest to higher-ups. In practice, it is very difficult to convincingly demonstrate that some information existed and should have been passed along but was not. What we can show is that information transfer is sometimes delayed. This occurred in Bulgaria in 1989, probably contributing to the slowing down of Zhivkov's reactions to domestic

---

[54] Michael G. Schatzberg, *The Dialectics of Oppression in Zaire* (Bloomington: Indiana University Press, 1988), esp. 47–48.

[55] On letters published in the Dominican Republic under Trujillo, see Lipe Collado, *El Foro Público en la Era de Trujillo: De cómo el chisme fue elevado a la categoría de asunto de Estado* (Santo Domingo: Editora Collado, 2000) and Lauren Derby, *The Dictator's Seduction: Politics and the Popular Imagination in the Era of Trujillo* (Durham, NC: Duke University Press, 2009), 135–72.

[56] Jie Gao, "'Bypass the Lying Mouths': How Does the CCP Tackle Information Distortion at Local Levels?" *The China Quarterly*, no. 228 (December 2016), 950–69.

[57] Jennifer Pan and Kaiping Chen, "Concealing Corruption: How Chinese Officials Distort Upward Reporting of Online Grievances," *American Political Science Review* 112:3 (2018), 602–20.

В комплексе мер, принятых в интересах более успешного решения контрразведывательных задач, важное место занимали мероприятия по укреплению агентурного аппарата. В 1967 году органами КГБ было завербовано *24952* агента, что составляет около *15* % всего агентурного аппарата, численность которого с учетом исключенной из него агентуры в течение года существенно не изменилась. Наряду с этим совершенствовались формы и методы использования наружного наблюдения и оперативной техники. Особое внимание при этом обращалось на

Figure 2.1 KGB 1967 annual report, with number of spies added by hand.
Source: Center for Preservation of Contemporary Documentation (TsKhSD) f. 89 per. 51 d. 3 (May 6, 1968), 7.

局，重在质量"的原则，制定物建指标和特情管理使用规定，从使用管理、教育培训、档案管理、考核办法及经费保障等方面制定具体细则。2003 年 8 月、9 月和 10 月分别举办了三期秘密力量建设培训班，提高了民警对特情工作的业务知识和管理水平。在秘密力量的使用上，实行管理考核、奖励惩罚、吐故纳新相结合的工作机制，对长期不起作用或失去工作条件的特情进行清洗整顿，及时物建质量较高、有培养价值、真心向我的特情。到 2003 年底，全地区共新建调整特情×××名，其中尖子特情××名，特情总人数达到×××名，建成了一支有一定数量、较高质量、布局合理、能发挥作用的秘密力量队伍，超额完成了省厅《十五期间全市国内安全保卫秘密力量重点建设方案》要求的年度物建指标。

Figure 2.2 Chinese police almanac information on spies in Changchun in 2003, with numbers deleted.
Source: Changchun Shi Gong'an Ju, *Changchun gong'an nianjian 2001–2003* (Changchun: Changchun Gong'an Ju, 2004), 130.

discontent and, in light of the intelligence about foreign developments, which was passed on instantaneously (see Chapter 7), increasing his propensity to resign. Zhivkov was aware of this delay and wrote a letter to State Security in September 1989 demanding the speedy transfer of domestic intelligence.[58] But delay is different from withholding and it only occurred in the final few months of the communist regime.

Content bias is different from agency problems: content bias is not malevolent, whereas agency problems are. In order to become sophisticated consumers of information, regime insiders must learn about the content biases of the various entities generating information. In the Soviet Union in the 1930s, for example, party reporting tended to cover successes in party building, and for this reason it focused on expressions of enthusiastic popular support for the regime, whereas

[58] Kostadin Chakarov, *Ot vtoriia etazh do nashestvieto na demokratite* (Sofia: Trud, 2001), 158–59.

State Security briefs overwhelmingly analyzed opposition to the regime; leaders read both types of documents but paid more attention to the reporting by the secret police. Scholars who have analyzed the Soviet State Security documents criticize them for being exceedingly negative and thus one-sided—but not for being too rosy (see Chapter 9). From a practical point of view, the solution to content biases is triangulation and redundancy; this is what Haile Selassie practiced by maintaining several different groups of palace spies.[59]

2.2.3 General Insights Generated by the Categorical Concepts Guiding Information Collection

Information gathering is guided by the Manichean friend–enemy categorical constructs used by the agents of surveillance. Communist archival materials abound in inflammatory language, with the meta-category of "enemy" impacting political analysis and evaluation in all countries and persisting until the very end of communist rule. The dichotomous friend–enemy thinking (*Freund-Feind-Denken*) was ingrained in the worldview of information gatherers.[60] In Bulgaria. the notion was so fundamental to how security services operated that they had to be issued the following instructions during the transition period: "The concept of 'us and them' should disappear from our terminology. The notion of 'enemies' should disappear from our thinking."[61] What was subsumed under the category of enemy varied from country to country and changed over time. The specific lists of enemies were frequently revised and updated. An early indicator of such a process of evolution comes from China, where Zhou Enlai wrote a letter to Xinhua News Agency in 1952 stating that its use of inflammatory language ("bandit" *feilei* 匪类, "imperialist" *diguo zhuyi* 帝国主义, "devil" *emo* 恶魔, "fascist" *faxisi* 法西斯) in overseas broadcasts and official announcements should stop; news for domestic publication should also avoid using inflammatory words (*cijixing de ciyu* 刺激性的词语).[62] These categories gradually disappeared from internal Xinhua reporting as well, only to be replaced by counterrevolutionaries, spies, and hostile elements. Extreme linguistic formulas persist today in public

---

[59] Ryszard Kapuscinski, *The Emperor* (New York: Vintage, 1989), esp. 7–11.

[60] On the friend–enemy thinking of the Stasi, see Karin Hartewig, "'Bilder vom Feind': Die DDR-Opposition in den Fotografien des Ministeriums für Staatssicherheit," in Alf Lüdtke, Herbert Reinke, and Michael Sturm, eds., *Polizei, Gewalt und Staat im 20. Jahrhundert* (Wiesbaden: VS Verlag, 2011), 169–86 and Mark Schiefer and Martin Stief, eds., *Die DDR im Blick der Stasi 1989* (Göttingen: Vandenhoeck and Ruprecht, 2019), 57. More generally, see Lev Gudkov, ed., *Obraz vraga* (Moscow: OGI, 2005).

[61] Remark by Bulgarian Minister of the Interior Semerdzhiev during a meeting of the Collegium of the Ministry of the Interior, Archive of the Bulgarian Ministry of the Interior (AMVR) f. 1 op. 12 a. e. 971 (February 5, 1990), also referenced in Khristov, *Ubiite "Skitnik,"* 490.

[62] *Xinhua she dashiji (1931–2001)*, vol. 2 (Beijing: Xinhua She, 2002), 14–15.

discourse in China, where counteracting hostile foreign forces forms part of the official national security strategy of the regime (see Chapter 8).

These categories reveal the epistemic anxieties of communist regime insiders.[63] By reconstructing the rosters of regime enemies, we can document what the leadership wanted to know. Information gatherers were instructed to enumerate and neutralize the different types of enemies that presented a threat to the regime at various points in its development. Therefore, the value of these categories is that they provide direct evidence about the dictator's dilemma. The numerical details compiled about the different subcategories of enemies constitute direct proof that autocrats were aware of the value of information and deployed substantial resources to assess the size of the enemy corps. This was a crucial step prior to solving the dictator's dilemma, which involves decisions about targeting repression and concessions. The value of categories for a study of information is therefore paramount: they not only reveal how regime insiders understand the challenge of governing, but also highlight the concrete steps taken to solve the dictator's dilemma by collecting more detailed information on their real and perceived enemies.

We might be concerned about the impact of the categorical concepts used by information gatherers on objectivity. Leading historians of science have provided illuminating accounts of the exceedingly difficult task of achieving objectivity in the study of nature, in which, given the deficiencies of mechanical objectivity, trained judgment has emerged as the method for interpreting the natural world.[64] Another insight produced by historians of science is that the method we use to observe something changes both what we see and the conclusions we might draw from the observation.[65] The challenge of achieving objectivity is immeasurably greater when we are dealing with the social world.[66] Ultimately, the value of categorical concepts is that they allow us to understand what information gatherers are searching for, which, in turn, determines what they discover: one finds enemies when looking for them. Therefore, the ultimate payoff of categorical concepts is to help us see the world through the particular lens

---

[63] On epistemic anxieties, see Stoler, *Along the Archival Grain*.

[64] Initially, scientists sought to achieve truth-to-nature, where they searched for representative types rather than individual examples of species; in trying to locate the universal, many individual characteristics had to be erased. It was this loss of specificity that led to the rise of mechanical objectivity, where the attempt was to capture individual particularity with as little intervention as possible. But mechanical objectivity led to overwhelming complexity, which required the use of trained judgment, where the scientist would "subjectively" smooth the data. See Lorraine Daston and Peter Gallison, *Objectivity* (New York: Zone Books, 2010), esp. 17–53.

[65] Lorraine Daston and Elizabeth Lunbeck, eds., *Histories of Scientific Observation* (Chicago: University of Chicago Press, 2011), esp. 1–9.

[66] Yoshiko M. Herrera, *Imagined Economies: The Sources of Russian Regionalism* (New York: Cambridge University Press, 2005); Yoshiko M. Herrera, *Mirrors of the Economy: National Accounts and International Norms in Russia and Beyond* (Ithaca, NY: Cornell University Press, 2013).

used by the bureaucrats who collect intelligence in communist autocracies. This is, in essence, the main methodological contribution of archival ethnography.

2.3 Empirical Insights

Archives reveal the internal logic of the information-gathering system. The queries are straightforward: Who? What? How? Why? Though simple, these fundamental questions necessitate evidence-based answers. In turn, gathering such evidence requires opening up the black box of the internal understandings of information collection, transfer, and use in autocracies.

2.3.1 Who Collects Information about Popular Discontent in Autocracies?

Archival materials provide direct evidence to address this question. They reveal that in mature communist regimes, there emerge three main collectors of information: the party; the state security apparatus; and the media, which produce classified reports for distribution to regime insiders. Although noncommunist regimes might also mobilize some of these systems to generate assessments of popular discontent, the full institutional complement develops only in single-party communist autocracies. The party coordinates all collection activities and may require other entities (e.g., government bureaucracies, opinion polling outfits, or ISPs) to assist by joining the team of information gatherers. As already noted, the party is both a producer and the ultimate consumer of information. Therefore, information collection is guided by its needs and priorities.

Building the institutions of an information state does not follow a standard sequence across communist regimes. What these autocracies have in common is that initially the party does not play a leading role in information collection. This may appear counterintuitive, but it stems from the fact that the party is ill equipped to meet the early challenges of communist governance, which include the twin tasks of establishing full territorial control and eliminating individual and organized elite and mass opposition. Realizing these goals requires the involvement of the security services, which collect information on hostile activities and mete out repression against regime enemies. One source of variation is whether the army joins the police and State Security to produce its own assessments of popular discontent. The general pattern is that sidelining the army is essential for allowing State Security to take control over information gathering during this initial period. Another source of variation concerns how actively the print media and the telegraph agency are engaged in monitoring dissent; more substantial initial involvement reflects the corresponding weakness of State Security. The third way in which regimes differ concerns how quickly the party develops the capacity to collect the necessary information, which allows it to transition from being a mere coordinator of information collection to playing a central role in the information-gathering ecosystem.

There exist tradeoffs to different sequencing patterns of institution building. When bureaucratic weakness prevents State Security and the party from getting immediately involved in information collection, the telegraph agency and the army become primary suppliers of information on popular discontent. However, their capacity to compile granular indicia of discontent is limited. This is a task that can only be fulfilled once State Security and the party join the information-collection ecosystem. Overall, as documented in Chapters 3–9, the sequencing of institution building and the speed with which various actors enter the information-collection system (or exit it, as occurs with the army, when party-appointed political commissars take over the task of monitoring the political mood of soldiers) have specific implications for the frequency, severity, and indiscriminacy of repression meted out in the country.

2.3.2 What Information Is Collected?

The archives reveal the extremely broad range of behaviors that were systematically monitored in communist regimes in order to assess popular dissatisfaction. There are different ways to classify them.

Types of Discontent: Overt versus Latent and Individual versus Group
One distinction concerns whether discontent is publicly expressed or privately held: throwing paint at the portrait of a leader is an index of overt discontent, whereas writing a private letter to the authorities to report a personal grievance reveals latent discontent. As overt expressions of discontent are publicly observable and send a signal to others that there is dissatisfaction with the regime, they raise a higher level of alarm among collectors than does latent discontent. This explains why the regime prefers to detect and handle discontent while it is still at its latent phase.[67]

A second way to classify the information concerns whether the grievances are expressed by an individual or by a group. To illustrate the difference, we can contrast a letter of complaint written by a single person with a collective petition.

---

[67] Tracking latent discontent is akin to a police patrol: Mathew McCubbins and Thomas Schwartz, "Congressional Oversight Overlooked: Police Patrols versus Fire Alarms," *American Journal of Political Science* 28:1 (1984), 165–79.

Table 2.2 Types of Discontent

	Overt	Latent
Individual	Writing antiregime graffiti	Personal complaint
Group	Human rights demonstration	Collective petition

Group grievances have the potential to lead to systemwide instability and are thus handled with a greater sense of urgency by the collectors. A summary of these two ways of classifying information and specific examples are presented in Table 2.2.

Political Demands versus Material Frustrations

Collectors draw a distinction between material frustrations and demands for human rights and civil liberties. Least worrisome are private petitions about consumption, welfare, and the protection of property rights over housing or land (we will collectively refer to these as material frustrations). At the other extreme are collective demands for human rights. A central insight that emerges from the archives concerns the internal regime understandings about the links among different types of discontent. The most straightforward connection is between latent and overt welfare demands: when not met at their latent stage, these frustrations are publicly expressed.[68] Less intuitive is the concern that welfare grievances may be transformed into calls for the protection of human rights and civil liberties. The reasoning here is that citizens will be willing to hold political demands in abeyance only in exchange for satisfying their material concerns.[69] This logic has several implications. One is that stability can be ensured through responsiveness to welfare demands.[70] Moreover, appropriately managed latent welfare dissatisfaction is seen as regime-supportive, as citizens and the government enter into a bargain (described as a social contract) that involves exchanging quiescence for the satisfaction of consumer needs.[71] The second implication is that any type of overt discontent is seen as a potential or a real threat.[72] A summary of these ways of classifying discontent and specific examples are presented in Table 2.3.

---

[68] AMVR f. 1 op. 1 a. e. 802 (July 27, 1951), 1–12.
[69] AMVR f. 1 op. 1 a. e. 61 (1959), 1–32; AMVR f. 44 op. 3 a. e. 41 (April 1974), 16–24.
[70] Bulgarian Central State Archives (TsDA) f. 1B op. 34 a. e. 52 (March 23, 1967), 1–112.
[71] Linda Cook and Martin K. Dimitrov, "The Social Contract Revisited: Evidence from Communist and State Capitalist Economies," *Europe–Asia Studies* 69:1 (2017), 8–26.
[72] TsDA f. 1B op. 6 a. e. 345 (July 13, 1971), 1–32.

Table 2.3 Political Demands versus Material Frustrations

	Overt	Latent
Political	Human rights demonstration: *Highly threatening*	Plan to boycott elections: *Potentially threatening*
Material	Protest about prices or salaries: *Moderately to highly threatening*	Housing petitions: *Regime supportive, when responsiveness is sufficiently high*

Mode of Collection: Involuntary Extraction versus Voluntary Provision

A final distinction concerns the mode of collection, which can be involuntary or voluntary, coerced or noncoerced. Involuntary gathering is coerced because information is collected from individuals against their will and, in theory, without their knowledge. By contrast, voluntary provision is noncoerced because individuals willingly supply information to the regime. The distinction in mode of collection is important because it has implications for how reliable the information is. There is a slight paradox here. It might seem that, as an answer to preference falsification, information gathered involuntarily will be most reliable. Regimes recognize, however, that, should individuals suspect that they are under surveillance, involuntarily collected information then becomes massively compromised. This is a logistical complexity in collection that always entails the need for careful interpretation, even if it does not rule out the possibility of using involuntary collection to solve the dictator's dilemma, by, for example, employing redundancy to cross-check reports arriving through different channels. In contrast, as argued throughout this study, the voluntary or noncoerced provision of information does not suffer from preference falsification. But here the regime faces two other problems that may limit the utility of this mode of transmission. Even where an individual provides information only vertically, the regime may find that it is insufficiently granular to be useful, as, for example, in ballot spoiling. Where voluntarily provided information is sufficiently granular to be useful, a second problem will emerge if the information is transmitted both vertically and horizontally, the horizontal transmission being per se corrosive of political stability.

In view of these complexities, the status of protests in relation to the transmission of information becomes clear. Like defacing ballots or scrawling anti-government graffiti, protests are unquestionably a form of voluntary provision and do transmit accurate information about political discontent. In contrast to complaints, however, protests are neither solicited nor welcomed by the regime,

Table 2.4 Involuntary Extraction versus Voluntary Provision of Information

	Involuntary (coerced) Extraction	Voluntary (noncoerced) Provision
Individual Dissent	Phone tapping; secret surveillance; *monitoring of public conversations*	Petition; *self-immolation*; *graffiti*; defacing ballots
Group Dissatisfaction	Monitoring of coup plotting	*Participation in protests*; *Charter 77*; *Charter 08*

NB: Italics used for activities that have the potential to disseminate information about discontent both vertically and horizontally.

even though officials must of course respond post factum to contentious episodes that have emerged. The logic here is straightforward. Since protests showcase an overt dissatisfaction that is transmissible horizontally, regime insiders actively discourage them, in favor of promoting channels, like complaints, that allow for a strictly vertical transmission of granular information. Protests cannot *safely* provide information about popular dissatisfaction. Although they may well be granular enough to enable retrospective (ex-post) governance, they do not facilitate the anticipatory (ex-ante) rule of the kind made possible by evaluations of latent discontent through the analysis of complaints. A summary of modes of collection in relation to the classification of discontent and with illustrative examples is presented in Table 2.4.

Indicia of Discontent

Table 2.5 presents the vast array of information that is collected in communist autocracies in efforts to assess popular discontent. Not all of these channels emerge simultaneously. Yet, remarkably, there is a gradual convergence around monitoring identical indicia of discontent across regimes. For instance, despite having many differences, as of 1989, Bulgaria and China relied on a very similar complement of mechanisms to assess dissatisfaction (though the relative emphasis placed on individual channels varied). As technology evolved, new mechanisms developed: monitoring Internet activity did not emerge until the 1990s and it only truly expanded in the 2000s and 2010s. It is worth noting that digital surveillance did not displace analog information-collection mechanisms. Although digital surveillance is only associated with communist autocracies that are currently extant, it is beyond doubt that had the Eastern European communist regimes survived, they would have embraced digital authoritarianism: after all, their state security services integrated computers into the management of

Table 2.5 Main Mechanisms for Assessing Discontent

Collection Channel	Discussed Chapter	Monitoring Entities	Difficulty of Collection/ Analysis	Specificity/ Utility of Information	Political or Material Grievances
Monitoring correspondence	3, 4, 6, 7, 8, 9	State Security	High	Medium	Political
Phone tapping	3, 4, 7, 8, 9	State Security	High	Medium	Political
Surveillance (in-person or technological)	3, 4, 5, 6, 7, 8, 9	State Security	High	Medium	Political
Monitoring dreams	3	State Security	High	Low	Either
Monitoring public conversations	3, 5, 9	Party, State Security, journalists	High	Medium	Either
Monitoring offline rumors	3, 4, 5, 6, 8	Party, State Security, journalists	High	Low	Either
Monitoring offline jokes	5	Party, State Security, journalists	High	Low	Either
Monitoring antiregime propaganda (e.g., graffiti), sabotage, and protests	3, 4, 5, 6, 7, 8, 9	Party, State Security, journalists	Low	High	Either
Analyzing anonymous denunciations (mail or website)	3, 4, 6, 8	Party, aided by ISPs, State Security, journalists	Low	Medium	Either
Analyzing real-name complaints (mail or email)	3, 4, 5, 6, 7, 8, 9	Party-state, journalists	Medium	High	Material
Opinion polling	5, 6, 7, 8, 9	Party, journalists, pollsters	Low	Low	Either

(*continued*)

Table 2.5 Continued

Collection Channel	Discussed Chapter	Monitoring Entities	Difficulty of Collection/ Analysis	Specificity/ Utility of Information	Political or Material Grievances
Monitoring real-name social media posts	8	Party, ISPs, State Security, journalists	Low	Low	Either
Monitoring anonymous social media posts	8	Party, ISPs, State Security, journalists	Low	Low	Either
Monitoring email/chat	8	State Security	Medium	Medium	Political

dissent as early as the 1960s,[73] and technology was systematically upgraded in the subsequent decades.

Empirical details on the operation of these mechanisms and the information they generate are supplied in Chapters 3–9. We can highlight the main findings here. Some channels are used only by State Security to monitor individuals who pose a political threat, though a more typical arrangement is to have all three main information collectors utilize the same mechanism to assess public support for the regime. The rise of the Internet has introduced ISPs to the information-collection ecosystem; however, ISPs operate under strict party and State Security supervision.[74] The party remains the ultimate arbiter of what information should be collected and how it will be used.

Information collectors are interested in determining the identities of individuals who express dissatisfaction with the regime. For this reason, almost all channels for information collection violate the expectation of privacy. This expectation is waived only when citizens use their real names to lodge complaints or to post on social media. Opinion polling presents a special case, as it is anonymous by design, yet citizens traditionally have had low confidence that their

---

[73] Angel Solakov, *Predsedateliat na KDS razkazva* (Sofia: Teximreklama, 1993), 72.

[74] Lotus Ruan, Masashi Crete-Nishihata, Jeffrey Knockel, Ruohan Xiong, and Jakub Dalek, "The Intermingling of State and Private Companies: Analyzing Censorship of the 19th Congress of the Chinese Communist Party on WeChat," *The China Quarterly*, no. 246 (June 2021), 497–526; Mary Gallagher and Blake Miller, "Who Not What: The Logic of China's Information Control Strategy," *The China Quarterly*, no. 248 (December 2021), 1011–36.

answers cannot be used to identify specific respondents.[75] Violating the expectation of privacy means that the information is involuntarily extracted, thus raising questions about its reliability. A further concern relevant to reliability was produced by sociological research on the fear of participating in opinion polling in Poland in the early 1980s.[76] As demonstrated in Chapters 5, 7, and 9, this fear declined over time and by the late 1980s, opinion polling became more accurate in Eastern Europe. A similar process took place in China in the 2010s (see Chapter 8). These temporal shifts in the reliability of opinion polling should be taken into account when using polling data as an evidentiary basis for arguments about popular support for the regime.

Finally, as we can see from Table 2.5, most channels do not yield information that has high specificity and utility. There are two exceptions: real-name citizen complaints and the monitoring of antiregime propaganda and agitation, acts of sabotage, and protests. The latter group of activities is easy to detect, though the identity of the individuals who engage in these antigovernment behaviors is often difficult to ascertain. Even without full individual-level data on the participants, the very occurrence of these overt acts of discontent sends important signals to the regime. However, the information is available to both regime insiders and to other dissatisfied citizens, thus presenting a potential opportunity for antiregime coordination. Citizen complaints are a superior avenue for information collection: they contain voluntarily transmitted grievances, thus alleviating concerns about falsifying support for the regime; they are private, therefore limiting the opportunity for coordination; they allow for discontent to be detected and managed at its latent stage prior to being transformed into overt expressions of dissatisfaction; and, most importantly, in the view of regime insiders, petitioning indexes trust in the system—and drops in the number of complaints under worsening economic conditions signal an erosion of trust and a transformation of latent into overt discontent.[77] Thus, complaints have a very high informational value.

---

[75] Based on the recollections of sociologists conducting opinion polls in Bulgaria in the 1970s (Iuri Aslanov interview, June 29, 2009, Sofia) and youth research in the GDR in the 1970s (Dieter Wiedemann interview, June 8, 2012, Potsdam-Babelsberg). Concerns about confidentiality and beliefs that opinion polling is conducted by the government (rather than by private companies) persisted into the 2010s in Bulgaria (Bulgaria interview, May 17, 2017).

[76] Anthony Sułek, "Systemic Transformation and the Reliability of Survey Research: Evidence from Poland," *Polish Sociological Review*, no. 106 (1994), 85–100.

[77] Based on a comment that Todor Zhivkov made to his chief-of-staff, reported in Georgi Chukrin, *Zapiski ot totalitarnoto vreme: Kraiat* (Sofia: Iztok–Zapad, 2007), 85. See also Dimitrov, "What the Party Wanted to Know." On China, see Xi Zhongxun's comments reported in Diao Jiecheng, *Renmin xinfang shilüe, 1949–1995* (Beijing: Beijing Jingji Xueyuan Chubanshe, 1996), 158. See also Martin K. Dimitrov, "Internal Government Assessments of the Quality of Governance in China," *Studies in Comparative International Development* 50:1 (March 2015), 50–72.

2.3.3 How Is Information Collected?

On some level, there is no particular surprise in what the archival materials reveal in terms of how information is collected. It involves technology; part-time informants; and full-time staff working at the various entities that constitute the information-gathering ecosystem. Still, there are specific empirical regularities about the operation of the three main collectors that are unexpected. We will illustrate this by focusing on State Security.

A major misconception about State Security is that its main task is to suppress dissent. Although State Security and the political police are used synonymously, they are not identical. Apart from counteracting political dissent, State Security has very broad external intelligence, domestic counterintelligence, military counterintelligence, and economic protection portfolios. A few statistics from the GDR help demonstrate this. The Stasi division most closely associated with managing political dissent was Directorate XX (*Hauptabteilung XX*), which was in charge of supervising high-level state corruption, the block parties, mass organizations (the trade union, the women's federation, and the youth league), the churches, the media, various other cultural institutions, and underground activities. Remarkably, despite this broad purview, Directorate XX had fewer personnel at the Stasi headquarters than did the sports club Dynamo, one-third of whose managerial staff were full-time Stasi employees: as of 1989, the respective manpower allocation at headquarters was 461 versus 464.[78] This powerfully demonstrates that counteracting dissent was one among various priorities for the Stasi.

The case of the Stasi also helps us illustrate some of the empirical insights about part-time informants. Again, the received wisdom is that the vast number of Stasi agents were chiefly involved in spying on other citizens. Yet, statistics reveal that Directorate XX relied on fewer informants than did the foreign intelligence, military counterintelligence, or economic security divisions.[79] This empirical fact helps us grasp the broad range of activities that state security services carry out. Further discussion of the complex issue of who was an informant is provided in Appendix A1 to this chapter.

Another empirical question concerns the motivations for joining the ranks of informants. A stylized fact is that most citizens agreed to collaborate with State Security due to blackmail.[80] Internal discussions paint a different picture,

---

[78] https://www.bstu.de/mfs-lexikon/detail/hauptabteilung-xx-staatsapparat-kultur-kirchen-untergrundha-xx/ (accessed April 19, 2022); http://www.argus.bstu.bundesarchiv.de/BStU_MfS_B dZL-SV-Dyn_SG/index.htm (accessed April 19, 2022).

[79] Calculated from Helmut Müller-Enbergs, *Inoffizielle Mitarbeiter des Ministeriums für Staatssicherheit: Teil 3: Statistiken* (Berlin: Ch. Links, 2008).

[80] For a cinematic representation, see *Das Leben der Anderen* (2006).

namely, blackmail was the least effective recruitment technique, as it resulted in low-quality intelligence.[81] Those who volunteered to join the ranks similarly provided poor information. According to State Security, the optimal recruitment methods were ideological conviction and monetary incentives.[82] Archival findings of this type demonstrate that the security services possessed a degree of introspection that is not usually accorded to them.

Finally, the archives yield some surprising insights about the use of technology. We tend to forget that technological surveillance existed decades before the arrival of digital authoritarianism. The Bulgarian archives provide evidence of the deployment of audio surveillance that goes back to the 1940s.[83] By the 1960s, video surveillance was in use throughout the Eastern Bloc.[84] Infrared photography was adopted in the 1970s.[85] This was also the decade when computers were widely integrated into the arsenal of State Security technology throughout Eastern Europe. Efforts to catalog the entire population and to obtain biological samples from them are nothing new: they go back at least to the East German plans to collect scent specimens,[86] which offer a 1970s preview of the DNA sample collection that the Chinese police was carrying out in Xinjiang in the 2010s and Tibet in the 2020s. Attempts at mass surveillance began before the advent of cheap cameras and software that can scrape data from social media. Likewise, concern about the quality of the collected data existed in the age of analog phone tapping just as it does under grid policing in China today: raw intelligence collected through technology ultimately requires humans to separate the noise from the nuggets of granular information that can indicate intent to engage in antigovernment activity.

2.3.4 Why Is Information Collected?

Once collected, intelligence is systematized and transferred to decision makers, with the goal of enabling ex-ante (anticipatory) governance, which involves detecting and responding to discontent when it is still at its latent disorganized stage. This sophisticated understanding emerges at a fairly late point

---

[81] Bulgarian State Security Dossier Commission (AKRDOPBGDSRSBNA-M) f. 1 op. 1 a. e. 219 (September 7, 1946), 1–7, at 2.

[82] AKRDOPBGDSRSBNA-M f. 1 op. 11 a. e. 49 (June 20, 1962), 60–81, at 66. On the GDR, see Leslie Colitt, *Spymaster: The Real-Life Karla, His Moles, and the East German Secret Police* (Reading, MA: Addison-Wesley, 1995), 59, 266.

[83] AMVR f. 1 op. 1 a. e. 835 (August 11, 1949), 2–17.

[84] AKRDOPBGDSRSBNA-M f. 1 op. 11 a. e. 48 (May 26, 1962), 224–39.

[85] Łukasz Kamiński, Krzysztof Persak, and Jens Gieseke, eds., *Handbuch der kommunistischen Geheimdienste in Osteuropa 1944–1991* (Göttingen: Vandenhoeck and Ruprecht, 2009), 511.

[86] "Geheimdienste: Schnüffeln, im Wortsinne," *Der Spiegel*, no. 32/1990, http://www.spiegel.de/spiegel/print/d-13499696.html (accessed April 19, 2022).

in the development of communist regimes, when the full complement of information-collection institutions is present and there exists a low-repression high-redistribution equilibrium. Under conditions of high repression and low redistribution, information is used for ex-post (retrospective) governance, which involves reacting to discontent that has already occurred. As responding to overt discontent requires high levels of the use of force, ex-post rule is considerably more repressive than ex-ante governance.

2.3.5 Summing Up

By design, long-lived autocracies foster multiple channels for compiling information about dissatisfaction. The archives generate systematic evidence on the internal organization and size of the systems for the collection of intelligence; on the sequencing in their creation and the tradeoffs among the systems; on the types of insights produced by different channels; and, finally, on the upward transmission of reports to regime insiders who make governance decisions. By understanding those nuts-and-bolts issues, we can make informed comparisons across autocratic regimes.

2.4 Theoretical Insights

Archival ethnography generates a number of theoretical insights about the capacity of authoritarian regimes to solve their information problems and about the contribution of information on popular discontent to authoritarian durability.

2.4.1 Solving the Dictator's Dilemma

Internal documents demonstrate that communist autocracies gradually develop a near-obsession with collecting information. The challenge is not to assess the mood of elites (who, as already noted, are numerically small and thus easy to monitor), but to engineer mechanisms for measuring levels of popular discontent. As this study shows, the party, the secret police, and the internal media successfully develop strategies for evaluating the popular mood. Although these mechanisms privilege involuntary extraction, avenues for voluntary provision exist as well. The extraordinarily high volume of critical information that is generated for the top leadership powerfully demonstrates that communist regimes are able to solve the dictator's dilemma and to produce nuanced assessments of dissatisfaction with the system. Of course, obstacles to complete territorial penetration exist, especially in states with regionally concentrated ethnolinguistic minorities, which prove to be imperfectly legible. This variation notwithstanding, in general communist autocracies are unusually capable of collecting the information they need to evaluate levels of opposition to the dictator.

2.4.2 Agency Problems

Information collection and transmission are subject to agency problems in any political setting. The general concern is that no negative news will reach the top leadership. This may occur for several reasons. One kind of pathology involves lower-level bureaucrats blocking the transmission of reports that reflect negatively on their performance. Alternatively, intelligence gets passed up the chain but is manipulated to present a rosy picture, either to shield bureaucrats from repercussions for corruption or because the top leader is not interested in reading negative news. Although agency problems are endemic in any bureaucracy, communist regimes develop strategies to mitigate them. Redundancy emerges as the preferred solution to information-transfer pathologies: even though it involves duplicative efforts (and numerous reports about the same issue), it does allow for the cross-checking of intelligence and minimizes the likelihood that certain events will not be reported at all. Redundancy also explains why some information-collection channels are suspended when they have outlived their utility. With regard to rosy reporting, a different strategy is developed, namely, incentivizing bureaucrats to report negative news through detailed requirements specifying the range of hostile behavior that should be covered in operational briefs. The final, and most effective, mechanism for incentivizing the transfer of negative news is the interest of the dictator in receiving such news. Most theorizing of dictatorial attitudes toward information is driven by the case of Nazi Germany,[87] where Hitler did not want to receive regular reports on domestic discontent, and this type of reporting ended altogether a year before the collapse of the Third Reich.[88] Communist dictators ranging from Stalin to Zhivkov to Honecker approached intelligence very differently, as illustrated through specific

---

[87] For archival materials, see Heinz Boberach, ed., *Meldungen aus dem Reich, 1938–1945: Die geheimen Lageberichte des Sicherheitsdienstes der SS*, 17 vols. (Herrsching: Pawlak, 1984); Martin Broszat, Elke Fröhlich, and Falk Wiesemann, eds., *Bayern in der NS-Zeit*, 6 vols. (Munich: Oldenbourg, 1977–1983).

[88] Friedrich and Brzezinski, *Totalitarian Dictatorship and Autocracy*, 136; Ian Kershaw, "Consensus, Coercion, and Popular Opinion in the Third Reich: Some Reflections," in Paul Corner, ed., *Popular Opinion in Totalitarian Regimes: Fascism, Nazism, Communism* (New York: Oxford University Press, 2009), 33–46; Peukert, *Volksgenossen und Gemeinschaftsfremde*. On information circulation in Fascist Italy, see Friedrich and Brzezinski, *Totalitarian Dictatorship and Autocracy*, 136–37.

evidence in Chapters 3–9 about the transfer of negative news to them.[89] Thus, agency problems characterize information transfer to a much smaller extent than is conventionally assumed in stylized accounts of communist dictatorships.

2.4.3   Acting on the Available Information

Acting on the intelligence received is theoretically and analytically distinct from collection and transfer. Leaders may ignore reporting in any setting.[90] In communist regimes, the optimal conditions for acting on information exist when intelligence is abundant (all three collectors operate), diverse in terms of the ways in which it is acquired (voluntary vs. involuntary), and the issues with which it engages (overt vs. latent discontent); levels of fear are moderately low; and economic resources at the disposal of the center are plentiful. Under this set of conditions, repression is limited, and welfare is efficiently allocated. When any of these parameters shifts, changes in repression and redistribution occur. When the amount of information is limited and it comes from a restricted number of sources, crude responses are likely, such as reprisals against broadly defined groups (indiscriminate repression) or universal redistribution (e.g., in the Gulf states). When fear is too low, repression cannot be used. When fear is high, redistribution is limited. When economic resources are constrained, effective redistribution cannot occur. Thus, solving the dictator's dilemma is not always sufficient to ensure regime survival: a second condition, which has not been examined in the existing literature, is the capacity of incumbents to act on the available information.

2.4.4   Revolutionary Cascades

The conventional wisdom is that revolutions occur because dictators lack information.[91] This book shows that it is both theoretically plausible and empirically demonstrable that incumbents have a high level of information but are unable to act on it; this leads to a very different interpretation of how some revolutionary cascades emerge—namely, it is the incapacity to act by deploying repression and

---

[89] Determining that negative news is transferred is analytically different from assuming that all the negative news should be transferred (see Chapter 8).

[90] On the reception of the President's Daily Brief (PDB), see David Priess, *The President's Book of Secrets: The Untold Story of Intelligence Briefings to America's Presidents from Kennedy to Obama* (New York: Public Affairs, 2016). On Stalin, see David E. Murphy, *What Stalin Knew: The Enigma of Barbarossa* (New Haven, CT: Yale University Press, 2005).

[91] Kuran, "Now Out of Never"; Susanne Lohmann, "The Dynamics of Informational Cascades: The Monday Demonstrations in Leipzig, East Germany, 1989–91," *World Politics* 47:1 (1994), 42–101.

concessions despite the availability of information, rather than the incapacity to act due to the lack of information (an unsolved dictator's dilemma).

2.4.5 Institutional Persistence

Institutions may outlive the regimes they are created to serve. This challenges the intuitive understanding of how regime breakdown occurs (the assumption is that it must have happened because there were either no institutions for collecting information, or they ceased to operate). Although vital institutions may be discontinued (as occurred with the *Meldungen aus dem Reich* report series after July 1944 in Nazi Germany, the dissolution of the Stasi in the final months of the GDR, and the banning of the Communist Party of the Soviet Union after the August 1991 coup), this does not routinely take place in communist regimes. The volume of reporting may diminish: for example, the voluntary provision of information may decline prior to regime breakdown and thus send a valuable signal to elite insiders about the erosion of public trust, yet it does not cease—and other systems beyond voluntary provision might also indicate the erosion of citizen trust. In other words, diminished reporting is not the same as the demise of institutions. Moreover, those institutions often persist after the transition begins. In Bulgaria, for instance, having forecast the emergence of widespread discontent against the single-party regime, these institutions survived once a transition to a multiparty system had occurred (see Chapter 7). Their task was to supply the party with information that could prevent the opposition from coming to power.

2.4.6 Summing Up

Prior research has centered on identifying individual mechanisms that have an informational function in autocracies. Internal sources provide a view of the entire system of information collection, not only of the discrete individual mechanisms that may reveal popular opposition to the regime. These sources also present the internal logic of the system, its temporal evolution, and the extent of the contribution of information to maintaining regime resilience.

2.5 Conclusion: Evidence, Theory, and Method in the Study of Autocracies

Scholars have three methodological choices for developing theories of authoritarian politics: they can proceed from stylized facts; they can turn to publicly available materials; or they can use internal documents. These methodological choices have implications for the resulting theories. As this chapter shows, evidence produced by analyzing direct sources does not support the most prominent theory derived from stylized facts, namely, that the dictator's dilemma is unsolvable. With regard to the dominant arguments based on publicly observable indicia, internal documents demonstrate that elections, protests, and liberalized media do indeed transmit information about popular discontent, but they do not do so efficiently, as both regime insiders and the general public become aware of this discontent. Internal sources reveal the existence of numerous channels that allow for the confidential vertical transmission of intelligence to regime insiders. These mechanisms are privileged in autocracies over channels like elections, protests, and liberalized media, which can allow for antiregime coordination by horizontally disseminating information about popular grievances. Autocracies encourage confidential vertical transmission and discourage horizontal transmission. Thus, the primary function of allowing critical content to appear in channels like the publicly accessible media is not information collection but the projection of responsiveness to popular grievances.[92]

This chapter has presented a method for studying direct sources from dictatorships. Although we need to approach them carefully and be aware of their limitations, archives not only reveal to us how information circulates in autocracies but also provide a lens onto the higher-order question of the desiderata and conceptual frameworks that drive information collection and use. Archival ethnography presents us with an unparalleled opportunity to see through the eyes of regime insiders. The remainder of this book details the empirical and theoretical insights that emerge from this methodological approach.

Appendix A1
An Empirical Example: Estimating the Number of Informants

Estimating the number of informants should be one of the most straightforward questions in the study of autocracies. This extended empirical example, which primarily references the widely discussed case of the GDR, shows that there exist various empirical, theoretical, and methodological questions that must be answered prior to producing a numerical estimate of the size of the informant corps. First, there is the issue of how many entities are recruiting informants. Second, we need to distinguish between covert and overt informants. Last, we should be mindful of some special categories of associates and should carefully consider whether they can be classified as informants.

---

[92] Martin K. Dimitrov, "The Functions of Letters to the Editor in Reform-Era Cuba," *Latin American Research Review* 54:1 (2019), 1–15.

A.1.1 Divided State Security Portfolio

Of the fifteen countries that constitute the universe of communist regimes, only four had separate bureaucracies for handling state and public security: the Soviet Union (except in 1933–1943 and 1953–1954), the GDR (except in 1953–1955), North Korea (since 1973), and China (since 1983). The Soviet KGB was unique in terms of its complete control over domestic antistate activity;[93] in the other three countries, this portfolio was divided between the two ministries.

Scholars working on noncommunist regimes argue that a unified state security apparatus exists when regimes prioritize internal security and a divided structure develops when coup-proofing is a priority.[94] But this argument does not extend to communist regimes,[95] in which separate state and public security agencies were unified during periods of elevated coup threats: this occurred in the Soviet Union in 1933–1943 and 1953–1954 and in the GDR in 1953–1955. Similarly, the counterintelligence mandate of the army was acquired by the Ministry of the Interior in Bulgaria due to an elevated coup threat in 1944–1947 (see Chapter 3). When both internal security and coup-proofing were priorities for communist regimes, these desiderata were achieved through different institutional configurations, with the typical one being a single ministry of the interior handling both public and state security.[96] Although the existence of separate ministries has no bearing on achieving the twin goals of coup-proofing and internal security in the communist world, it does impact the question that motivates this Appendix: specifically, it increases the potential number of informants.

A.1.2 Covert and Overt Informants

We are accustomed to thinking of informants as secret collaborators. However, this is factually inaccurate, as there exist both covert and overt informants. To take an example from the United States, we can point to the difference between visible Neighborhood Watch volunteers and undercover FBI informants.[97] In communist regimes, both visible and secret informants collect intelligence relevant for managing domestic dissent and both are

---

[93] See Decree of the Supreme Soviet "On Granting the Right to Conduct Preliminary Investigation to the Organs for the Protection of Public Order" (June 8, 1963), which delineates the areas in which the KGB had exclusive investigative jurisdiction. The foreign espionage portfolio was split between State Security (the KGB) and military intelligence (the Main Intelligence Directorate of the General Staff of the Armed Forces of the Soviet Union or simply the GRU), as it is in all other communist regimes.

[94] James Quinlivan, "Coup Proofing," *International Security* 24:2 (1999), 131–65; Sheena Chestnut Greitens, *Dictators and Their Secret Police: Coercive Institutions and State Violence* (New York: Cambridge University Press, 2016).

[95] Greitens, in *Dictators and their Secret Police*, 301, states that the GDR fits her argument and that only China and North Korea do not. This is based on a miscoding of the GDR as having a single state security agency (the Stasi) (Greitens, *Dictators and Their Secret Police*, 8 and 277–82).

[96] We should note that having State Security under the control of the Ministry of the Interior does not mean that there was a single ministry in charge of information collection: the Ministry of Defense always managed foreign military intelligence and the Ministry of Foreign Affairs typically had certain foreign-intelligence functions as well. However, counterintelligence, even within the army, was the domain of the State Security divisions of the Ministry of the Interior.

[97] Joshua Reeves, *Citizen Spies: The Long Rise of America's Surveillance State* (New York: New York University Press, 2017).

subject to enumeration by the security bureaucracies. The existence of these two types of informants raises theoretical, methodological, and empirical questions. The theoretical puzzle centers on the respective utility of deploying covert and overt informants for the optimal monitoring of different types of dissent. The methodological concern involves the tripartite problem of who should be counted as an informant; on the basis of collaboration with which specific agency; and at what precise point in time. Once we have made these methodological choices, we can address the empirical query of the rate of saturation with informants in communist societies. We will illustrate these empirical, methodological, and theoretical challenges through the specific example of the GDR.

In the GDR, the monitoring of political dissent was the shared responsibility of the Ministry of State Security (*Ministerium für Staatssicherheit*, or MfS, known colloquially as the Stasi) and the police, which was part of Ministry of the Interior (*Ministerium des Innern*, or MdI). Both the Stasi and the police used covert and overt informants. The nomenclature of Stasi collaborators is complex but can be pared down to secret counterintelligence informants (IM);[98] secret foreign intelligence agents; citizens secretly facilitating the transmission of information;[99] and visible associates,[100] who were expected to appear in public and take aggressive steps to protect security and resolve grievances in the workplace, in neighborhoods, and in social organizations.[101] In turn, the Ministry of the Interior also employed secret informants (*inoffizielle kriminalpolizeiliche Mitarbeiter*, or IKM) and visible associates (*freiwillige Helfer*, or FH).

This complex landscape raises the question of precisely who should be considered an informant. We cannot count those individuals who were not subject to internal accounting. This applies to various "contact persons" (*Kontaktpersonen* or *kriminalpolizeiliche Kontaktpersonen*) and "trusted people" (*V-Leute*) who were used by the Stasi and by the police as liaisons but were never subjected to any systematic enumeration. The Stasi itself classified only counterintelligence assets as IMs, but not visible associates, citizens secretly facilitating the transmission of information, and secret foreign intelligence agents.[102] This indicates that internally only those covertly collecting counterintelligence information were considered informants. The approach favored by this book is that all categories of Stasi collaborators should be counted as informants, except citizens secretly facilitating the transmission of information, who did not collect intelligence. Similarly,

[98] This abbreviation IM stands for *inoffizieller Mitarbeiter*, or unofficial collaborator, which was subdivided into several additional categories, depending on the specific tasks they were responsible for.

[99] The general category was IMK (*inoffizieller Mitarbeiter zur Sicherung der Konspiration und des Verbindungswesens*, or unofficial collaborator for securing communication and secrecy), which was subdivided into *IM konspirative Wohnung* (safe house unofficial collaborator) and *IM konspiratives Objekt* (cover object unofficial collaborator). The cover object could be a cover address (*Deckadresse*) or a cover telephone (*Decktelefon*).

[100] GMS (*gesellschaftlicher Mitarbeiter für Sicherheit*, or societal collaborator for security). The existence of GMS supports the statement of a German researcher that "regular reporting came from employees and cadres who cooperated *officially* with the Stasi to a greater or lesser extent" (emphasis added). See Bernd Florath, "Die inoffiziellen Mitarbeiter," in Daniela Münkel, ed., *Staatssicherheit: Ein Lesebuch zur DDR-Geheimpolizei* (Berlin: BStU, 2014), 40–52, at 42.

[101] "Richtlinie 1/68 für die Zusammenarbeit mit Gesellschaftlichen Mitarbeitern für Sicherheit und Inoffiziellen Mitarbeitern im Gesamtsystem der Sicherung der Deutschen Demokratischen Republik," BStU ZA DSt 101126 (January 1968). GMS were not encouraged to use secret methods in their work or to have clandestine interactions with MfS handlers in safe houses.

[102] Helmut Müller-Enbergs, *Inoffizielle Mitarbeiter des Ministeriums für Staatssicherheit: Teil 1: Richtlinien und Durchführungsbestimmungen*, 4th ed. (Berlin: Ch. Links, 2010), 59.

both overt (FH) and covert (IKM) Ministry of the Interior collaborators should be included. Ultimately, this means that we should count the secret and visible associates who routinely *supplied* information, rather than those who facilitated the transmission of information for the Stasi (safehouse owners and those providing cover addresses or cover telephones) or came across information accidentally (the various categories of trusted persons in the GDR; in Bulgaria and the Soviet Union, trusted persons had functions akin to those of the visible associates of the Stasi and were therefore typically included in the total agent network count).

How many informants existed? One answer is provided by a speech that the minister of the interior delivered to the legislature to justify the need for passage of the 1968 Law on the Tasks and Powers of the People's Police. In this widely publicized address, Minister Dickel mentioned that 1.9 million adult citizens and youth collaborated with the police, as "voluntary helpers" (*freiwillige Helfer*) and in other ways;[103] this number is very similar to the assertion in the English-language literature that there were 2 million informants in the GDR.[104] Are such estimates plausible? To answer this question, we need to know who was included in this group. The English-language literature provides no useful guidance on this issue. German sources allow us to ascertain that the voluntary helpers highlighted in the minister of the interior's speech were indeed informants—yet they constituted considerably fewer than one-tenth of the 1.9 million citizens mentioned. Then who were these 1.9 million police collaborators? And was every collaborator an informant?

Academic research in German has unearthed that, besides the voluntary helpers (*freiwillige Helfer*), the police managed the following groups of associates: the Society for Sports and Engineering, whose 670,000 members learned marksmanship, among other skills; the Fighting Groups, whose 400,000 members could support the army, if needed; the Youth Order Maintenance Groups (64,000 members); the Fire Protection Volunteers (470,000 members); the Youth Fire Brigades (39,000 members); the Traffic Safety Collectives in enterprises (280,000 members); the Society of Young Traffic Assistants (45,000 members); and the Student Navigators (9,000 members).[105] This long list makes clear that there was substantial overlap across these groups of police associates. More importantly, it casts doubt on whether the officially announced figure of 1.9 million adult collaborators should be understood as a useful indicator of the rate of saturation with police informants in the GDR. This statistic was publicized in order to demonstrate the close links between the police and citizens,[106] not to apprise the public of the number of informants.

Most police informants in the GDR were similar to the visible social-order protection volunteers in China (*zhibaohui huiyuan* 治保会会员), who are discussed in Chapters 4, 6, and 8. Technically, they were known as volunteer assistants of the police (*freiwillige Helfer der Deutschen Volkspolizei*, or FH) and, like their Chinese counterparts, usually wore red armbands that publicly identified their affiliation with the police. Their number rapidly

[103] The speech is included in various editions of the *Gesetz über die Aufgaben and Befugnisse der Deutschen Volkspolizei* (Berlin: Ministerium des Innern, 1971, 1976).

[104] Andrea Kendell-Taylor, Erica Frantz, and Joseph Wright, "The Digital Dictators: How Technology Strengthens Autocracy," *Foreign Affairs* (March–April 2020), 103–15, at 103.

[105] Matthias Judt, ed., *DDR-Geschichte in Dokumenten: Beschlüsse, Berichte, interne Materialien und Alltagszeugnisse* (Berlin: Ch. Links, 1998), 440–42.

[106] As stated by the minister of the interior in his speech: "die enge Verbundenheit der Polizei mit der Bevölkerung" (*Gesetz über die Aufgaben* [1971], 40).

expanded from 27,285 in 1952 to 88,364 in 1956;[107] in parallel with the relatively static size of the police in the following decades, the volunteer assistant corps did not exceed 100,000 in 1989.[108] Although they often focused on mundane matters like social order, the responsibility of these individuals also extended to issues that were handled by the KGB in the USSR, namely, detecting oral or written expressions of antistate propaganda and agitation.[109] Moreover, a subset of these informants had the right to inspect household registers and to highlight suspicious irregularities therein.[110] Thus, there is no doubt that the volunteer assistants acted as informants.

In addition to the visible collaborators, the police used secret informants (IKM), who either joined voluntarily or were recruited through blackmail or intimidation. Most of these secret informants were managed by Department K-1 of the People's Police (*Abteilung K1 der Deutschen Volkspolizei*), whose mandate to fight antistate crimes was equivalent to that of the State Security (*guobao* 国保) division of the Ministry of Public Security in China. The social composition of the police informant corps was different from that of the Stasi because it included a higher proportion of former criminals.[111] This presents a parallel to China, where the Ministry of Public Security (MPS) recruited agents from among ex-convicts.[112] Though we lack time-series statistics on the number of these secret police informants during the initial decades of communist rule, we know that in 1989 the IKM amounted to 15,000;[113] this is equivalent to less than one-tenth of the Stasi informant corps at the time.

The number of Stasi informants is disputed. By one estimate, 620,000 individuals served as informants at some point between 1950 and 1989.[114] However, such aggregate statistics reveal little about the more meaningful issue of the size of the informant corps at specific points in time. Well-publicized data on the yearly number of MfS informants between 1950 and 1989 exist, both in German and English. They inevitably reference the same scholarly source (Helmut Müller-Enbergs' multivolume study),[115] but rarely acknowledge that Müller-Enbergs provides an estimate rather than hard-and-fast numbers.

[107] Thomas Lindenberger, *Volkspolizei: Herrschaftspraxis und öffentliche Ordnung im SED-Staat 1952–1968* (Cologne: Böhlau, 2003), 276.

[108] Calculation based on an October 6, 1989, report from Bezirk Neubrandenburg listing 1,103 police and 1,026 voluntary assistants (*freiwillige Helfer*) (report reproduced in Georg Herbstritt, ed., *Die Lageberichte der Deutschen Volkspolizei im Herbst 89: Eine Chronik der Wende im Bezirk Neubrandenburg*, Second Revised Edition [Schwerin: Die Landesbeauftragte für die Unterlagen des Staatssicherheitsdienstes der ehemaligen Deutschen Demokratischen Republik, 2009], 22–24). The GDR as a whole had 88,000 police at the time (Herbstritt, *Die Lageberichte der Deutschen Volkspolizei im Herbst 89*, 264), thus making 100,000 *freiwillige Helfer* a very generous estimate for 1989.

[109] *Merkbuch für freiwillige Helfer der Deutschen Volkspolizei* (Berlin: Ministerium des Innern, 1976), 57–59.

[110] *Merkbuch für freiwillige Helfer*, 55–56.

[111] Klaus Richter, *Arbeitsgebiet I der Kriminalpolizei: Aufgaben, Struktur und Verhältnis zum Ministerium für Staatssicherheit* (Berlin: BStU, 1994), 16.

[112] "Gong'an bu guanyu yinfa 'Zhi'an ermu jianshe zanxing guiding' de tongzhi" (October 20, 1984).

[113] Herbstritt, *Die Lageberichte der Deutschen Volkspolizei im Herbst 89*, 254.

[114] Helmut Müller-Enbergs, *Inoffizielle Mitarbeiter des Ministeriums für Staatsicherheit: Teil 3: Statistiken* (Berlin: Ch. Links, 2008), 216.

[115] Müller-Enbergs, *Inoffizielle Mitarbeiter des Ministeriums für Staatsicherheit: Teil 1*; Helmut Müller-Enbergs, *Inoffizielle Mitarbeiter des Ministeriums für Staatsicherheit: Teil 2: Anleitungen für die Arbeit mit Agenten, Kundschaftern und Spionen in der Bundesrepublik Deutschland*, 3rd ed. (Berlin: Ch. Links, 2011); Müller-Enbergs, *Inoffizielle Mitarbeiter des Ministeriums für Staatsicherheit: Teil 3*.

Time-series statistics on the number of informants in 1950–1989 are imputed by Müller-Enbergs from subnational data from several provinces (*Bezirke*) representing 4.2 percent–18.2 percent of the GDR population in 1950–1989.[116] The imputed time-series data were cross-checked by Müller-Enbergs against the known nationwide totals for 1983–1985 and 1988. Yet these nationwide totals, which only include what the Stasi itself considered unofficial collaborators (*inoffizielle Mitarbeiter*, or IM), amounted to 109,281 IM for 1988. Müller-Enbergs imputed 108,000 IM for 1989; to these IM, he added an estimated 33,000 citizens secretly facilitating the transmission of information and an estimated 33,000 visible associates to generate the universally known grand total of 174,000 counterintelligence collaborators.[117] Subsequently, the estimate was revised upward by incorporating 14,950 foreign intelligence assets. This produced a grand total of 189,000 estimated Stasi collaborators in 1989 (one for every eighty-seven citizens).[118] The imputed total of 174,000 was accepted as the official number of informants by the German government in the 1990s. The currently used statistic is the higher estimate of 189,000, which is equivalent to almost 1.2 percent of the GDR population in 1989.[119]

Even if we assume that there is no overlap whatsoever between Stasi and police collaborators, no more than 2 percent of the population would have carried out informant duties in the peak year of 1989: this involves using the highest existing estimate of 189,000 Stasi collaborators, 100,000 police FH, and 15,000 police IKM, producing a grand total of 304,000 individuals (1.9 percent of the GDR population). A more restrictive approach, excluding Stasi associates secretly facilitating the transmission of information and foreign intelligence agents, nets 255,000 domestic counterintelligence informants in 1989 (1.6 percent of the population), slightly more than one-half of whom were visible police and Stasi collaborators. Despite the stylized fact that the GDR was the most deeply penetrated communist regime, this is significantly lower than the comparable statistics for China at several points between 1951 and 2017, as demonstrated in Chapters 4, 6, and 8. Nevertheless, the GDR had a highly saturated network of individuals who supplied information that was used to keep the leadership apprised of popular discontent (though, of course, we should bear in mind that the functions of informants were not limited to the monitoring of discontent).

The theoretical payoff of thinking about both types of informants is to highlight the tradeoffs between quality and quantity: though numerous, visible informants were somewhat less effective than secret collaborators; and yet visible informants played an important role, as they identified antistate acts, such as the dissemination of hostile propaganda

---

[116] Müller-Enbergs, *Inoffizielle Mitarbeiter des Ministeriums für Staatssicherheit: Teil 3*, 35–36.

[117] Müller-Enbergs, *Inoffizielle Mitarbeiter des Ministeriums für Staatssicherheit: Teil 1*, 59.

[118] Müller-Enbergs, *Inoffizielle Mitarbeiter des Ministeriums für Staatssicherheit: Teil 3*, 216.

[119] A heated debate has unfolded on whether the active Stasi informants in 1989 amounted to 0.7 percent of the population or to 1.2 percent. For the low estimate, see Ilko-Sascha Kowalczuk, *Stasi konkret: Überwachung und Repression in der DDR* (Munich: C. H. Beck, 2013), esp. 222–33; for the high estimate, see Müller-Enbergs, *Inoffizielle Mitarbeiter des Ministeriums für Staatsicherheit: Teil 1* and Müller-Enbergs, *Inoffizielle Mitarbeiter des Ministeriums für Staatsicherheit: Teil 3*. The disagreement stems from the fact that the high estimate includes informants working overseas, GMS (whose identity as State Security collaborators was publicly known), and IMK (who allowed the Stasi to use their apartments for meetings with agents but did not provide any information themselves). The disagreement has been politicized: those who argue in favor of the low estimate are accused of being pro-communist sympathizers aiming to whitewash the cruelty of the communist regime (see Christian Booß, "Der IM, der keiner war," *Der Tagespiegel*, March 13, 2013, https://www.tagesspiegel.de/politik/streit-um-stasi-forschung-der-im-der-keiner-war/7921198.html [accessed April 19, 2022]).

and agitation, and might even detect the individuals who engaged in them; discovering the root causes of such behavior, however, typically required using covert informants. The existence of the two types of collaborators demonstrates that not all information-gathering activities in communist regimes are clandestine: the monitoring of political dissent was executed by deploying citizens both as covert operatives (for sensitive tasks) and as crude overt collectors in less delicate domains (we should note that the intelligence collected by those latter informants was still confidential—only their status as informants was publicly known).

A.1.3 Summary Evaluation

The purpose of empirical Appendix A1 is to illustrate what insights are produced through archival methods about a question that is of central importance in any study of autocracies, yet eludes easy answers. Specific statistics on the saturation rate of the agent network in different countries at various points in time are supplied in Chapters 3–9. What is important to state here is that methodological decisions about who should be counted as an informant must be driven by theoretical considerations and an understanding of the empirical record, rather than by reproducing widely circulated stylized estimates without questioning the assumptions that are built into generating these assessments.

PART II

PARALLEL ORIGINS
OF COMMUNIST
INFORMATION STATES

Part II is made up of two chapters on the parallel origins of communist information states in Bulgaria (1944–1958) and China (1949–1958). Although the two regimes came to power in different ways (a gradual takeover in Bulgaria in 1944–1949 and as the result of a revolution that concluded in 1949 in China), their initial state-building tasks were remarkably similar. Three domestic groups had to be monitored: elites; the masses; and members of the ethnic minorities. In both regimes, the information that was necessary to assess discontent within these groups was collected through the same complement of institutions: the state security apparatus, the party, and the internal media. The emphasis was on involuntary extraction instead of voluntary provision of information. The dominant governance mechanism was repression, rather than welfare provision. Minorities remained poorly penetrated in both countries. Considering the variation in precommunist state capacity, the commonalities in the institutional solutions to the information problem that emerged during the initial decade of communist rule in Bulgaria and China are nothing short of remarkable, reflecting the relationship between regime type and information-collection mechanisms.

As there was very little voluntarily transmitted information during the initial period of regime establishment and consolidation, the focus of this part is on analyzing involuntary extraction. Once pre-existing channels are repurposed or information-gathering institutions are created anew, they need to be tasked with collection targets and appropriately staffed. The two chapters find unexpected parallels between Bulgaria and China in this regard. In both countries, staffing involved developing full-time personnel and part-time informants. The nomenclature of informants, the methods of their recruitment, and the information they provided were quite similar in the two settings; one difference is that China compensated the shortage of full-time state security staff with the rapid build-up of visible community informants, whereas covert agents were more typical in Bulgaria. The types of targets were also largely identical and consisted of political and economic elites, landlords, members of religious groups and sects, foreign spies, and small armed groups and individuals. Differences in emphasis existed (elites were a bigger threat in Bulgaria and sects, in particular secret societies, were more prominent in China), but the commonalities are nevertheless striking. As this part argues, these commonalities reflect the similar state-building goals pursued by the two regimes in the decade of initial establishment and consolidation.

During this period, attention to welfare was limited to efforts to supply food to the population (both countries experienced famine prior to 1959) and to provide for the basic living needs of urban workers. Initially, information was used primarily to guide decisions about the meting out of repression, which involved physical elimination, imprisonment, and being sent to a labor camp. These decisions were crude and affected larger groups of individuals. As the information became more granular, repression started to be more targeted. By the second half of the 1950s, with further improvements in the quality of information, both countries began to move toward a system of widespread surveillance and selective punishment of a subset of the individuals who would have been harshly repressed in the initial months and years of communist rule. Complaints started to inform decisions about welfare redistribution.

The two chapters here produce several theoretically relevant insights about information gathering. The first concerns the tradeoff between information quality and the selectiveness of repression. An awareness that more abundant information allows for more selective repression emerged in the 1950s in both countries. Another tradeoff is between the size and the quality of the informant corps. In Bulgaria, the information collectors developed a keen sense that a numerically smaller cadre of high-quality informants is preferable to having a high number of low-quality informants. In China, efforts to assess the quality of informants can be traced back to the initial decade of communist rule. The final tradeoff is between monitoring and responding to political and welfare discontent, with overt expressions of consumer-driven dissatisfaction in the 1950s resulting in concessions in Bulgaria that paved the way for the adoption of a social contract and the transition to ex-ante rule in the 1960s.

Collectively, these two chapters allow us to trace the establishment of the information states in the two regimes. Importantly, this process was not impacted by regime origins: China and Bulgaria show that no matter whether communist autocracies emerge after a revolution or following a war, they eventually develop the same institutional complements. Despite the numerous similarities, a relevant difference is precommunist state capacity: although low state capacity does not prevent the creation of institutions for information collection that parallel those in countries with higher state capacity, it does slow down the speed with which the transition from ex-post to ex-ante governance may occur.

3

Monitoring and Counteracting Dissent
in Bulgaria, 1944–1958

This chapter provides a theoretical discussion of the challenges that the Bulgarian communist regime faced as it created systems for tracking popular discontent. One important feature of communist rule in Bulgaria is that it was established gradually over several years, in contrast to the faster revolutionary takeover of power in China. In practical terms, this means that, in comparison with China, Bulgaria faced a more formidable elite threat at the moment of regime inception. In Bulgaria, the communist party was initially part of a coalition government that came to power as a result of a coup on September 9, 1944. The communists held only four of the sixteen ministerial seats. Although they controlled two crucial ministries (Interior and Justice), gaining and maintaining full command of the government was a nontrivial task. The steps involved abolishing the monarchy (which existed until 1946), organizing and manipulating competitive elections (in 1945, 1946, and 1947), banning the main opposition party and then executing its leader (in 1947), and making sure that the remaining opposition parties would either merge with the communist party or be dissolved (in 1948–1949).[1] The communists needed to deploy a system of party-appointed political commissars in order to establish control over the Ministry of Defense, which was initially headed by a noncommunist.[2] Once illegal army organizations were neutralized and the multiparty system had been eliminated,[3] the communist leadership tackled threats within the party through wide-ranging purges of elites and ordinary party members (1949–1950).[4] The urgency of solving elite threats

---

[1] For more details on this process, see Mito Isusov, *Politicheskiiat zhivot v Bulgariia 1944–1948* (Sofia: Akademichno Izdatelstvo "Prof. Marin Drinov" and Universitetstko Izdatelstvo "Sv. Kliment Okhridski," 2000) and Liubomir Ognianov, *Durzhavno-politicheskata sistema na Bulgariia 1944–1948* (Sofia: Standart, 2007).

[2] The political commissars were technically known as "assistant commanders" and were managed by the Organization Department of the Central Committee of the Bulgarian Communist Party. These individuals were assigned to army units a mere two weeks after the September 9, 1944, coup, and by 1946 they numbered 462. See Aleksandur Vezenkov, *9 septemvri 1944 g.* (Sofia: Ciela, 2014), 308–9.

[3] After the merger of the Bulgarian Worker Social-Democratic Party (BRSDP) with the communist party in 1948 and the dissolution of the Zveno Popular Movement and the Radical Party in 1949, a second party technically remained in place (the Bulgarian Agricultural National Union), but it had adopted socialist positions and functioned as a docile block party that never presented a meaningful challenge to the system until the very end of communist rule.

[4] Liubomir Ognianov, *Politicheskata sistema v Bulgariia 1949–1956* (Sofia: Standart, 2008).

Dictatorship and Information. Martin K. Dimitrov, Oxford University Press. © Oxford University Press 2023.
DOI: 10.1093/oso/9780197672921.003.0003

meant that the party did not develop the capacity to begin tracking popular discontent until the 1950s.

The main concern from 1951 until the early 1980s was how to solve the mass threat. This chapter discusses only the period up to the late 1950s, as this is when the mechanisms for assessing public dissatisfaction were being established. Chapter 5 focuses on how the institutions for assessing latent discontent operated in 1958–1988, when repression declined, the active search for enemies stopped, and the information collectors were gradually orienting themselves toward tracking latent discontent among the masses. Chapter 5 also discusses how, once it believed that it had solved both the elite and mass threat in the early 1980s, the regime deployed a systematic response to the separatist threat presented by one segment of the masses, namely, the Turkish minority. Chapter 7 analyzes how the failure to solve the minority threat, along with the reemergence of the mass threat and the rise of elite threats in 1988–1989, contributed to the end of communist rule in Bulgaria. Regime transformation occurred because available information clearly indicated that preserving single-party rule through repression was not a viable option; political liberalization constituted a strategically deployed concession that aimed to extend the lifespan of the system by allowing the party to maintain a dominant position in a more pluralistic environment.

The current chapter is organized as follows. Section 3.1 analyzes the structural constraints to information gathering in Bulgaria. Section 3.2 discusses the main tasks that the Bulgarian communist regime faced during the initial decade of its existence. Section 3.3 describes the institutions that were created in Bulgaria to collect information, with an emphasis on involuntary collection. Section 3.4 reviews decision making based on information about individual and organized overt discontent, whereas Section 3.5 discusses the tracking of latent discontent through the voluntary provision of information in the form of citizen complaints. Section 3.6 focuses on the key obstacle to information gathering in Bulgaria, namely, the incapacity of the regime to penetrate large and compactly settled ethnoreligious minorities. Section 3.7 concludes by reviewing the main chapter's findings about the logic of ad hoc crisis-driven governance during the initial decade of communist rule in Bulgaria.

3.1 Structural Constraints

Bulgaria experienced moderate structural constraints to information gathering. Although the regime was established during the final stages of World War II, the war did not destroy the bureaucratic sinews of the state. The fact that the communist party seized power only gradually over a five-year period (1944–1949) tempered the destructive impulse to create a governance tabula rasa. Many of the pre-existing institutions that were preserved (key among them being the State Security Directorate of the Ministry of the Interior) were re-oriented toward collecting information that met the needs of the communist party. The party's control of the ministries of interior and justice allowed it to selectively direct its members toward staffing these crucial parts of the coercive apparatus. Overall, bureaucratic quality was relatively high, as demonstrated by the existence of nine precommunist censuses (conducted in 1881, 1887, 1892, 1900, 1905, 1910, 1920, 1926, and 1934) and substantial levels of literacy (74 percent as of 1946). Information gathering was aided further by the small size of the country and its relatively hospitable topography (combined with an extensive rail network that existed prior to the establishment of the communist regime). These factors allowed the center to penetrate the entire territory of the state.

In contrast to China, there was no shortage of personnel. In part, this reflected the considerably larger size of the communist party in Bulgaria, whose members constituted 3.7 percent of the population at the time of the establishment of the regime (compared with 0.8 percent in China).[5] The gradual takeover of power by the party and the limited number of ministries that initially had to be staffed meant that the available resources could be efficiently allocated. The Ministry of the Interior emerged as a crucial target—the party was able to promptly direct 17,000 communists and loyal allies there in the four months between September and December 1944.[6] Contrast this with the situation in China, where the party was only able to allocate 1,302 party members and loyal allies to the Beijing police during the first four months after the communist takeover (January–April 1949), despite the central importance of the city to the newly established regime.[7] On a per capita basis, the number of party members allocated to the Beijing police was 3.6 times less than that in Bulgaria.[8] This statistic highlights how personnel shortages constrained bureaucratic capacity in China.

The main hurdle, which was never successfully overcome during the entire lifespan of the regime, was the systematic collection of information about latent discontent among sizable territorially concentrated ethnoreligious minorities, in particular the Bulgarian Turks. However, we should stress that, with the

---

[5] As of March 1, 1945, the party had 254,140 members (Stoian Tsvetanski, *Organizatsionno razvitie na BKP, 1944–1986: Istoriko-statisticheski analiz* [Sofia: Institut po Istoriia na BKP pri TsK na BKP, 1988], 29); the population of Bulgaria at the time was 6,936,000 (www.nsi.bg [accessed April 19, 2022]). In China, the party had 4,488,080 members at the end of 1949 (Zhonggong Zhongyang Zuzhi Bu, *Zhongguo gongchandang dangnei tongji ziliao huibian, 1921–2010* [Beijing: Dangjian Duwu Chubanshe, 2011], 7), and the population stood at 541,670,000 (www.stats.gov.cn [accessed April 19, 2022]).

[6] Archive of the Bulgarian Ministry of the Interior (AMVR) f. 44 op. 4 a. e. 45 (1967), 5.

[7] Beijing Shi Difang Zhi Bianzuan Weiyuanhui, *Beijing zhi: Zhengfa juan: Gong'an zhi* (Beijing: Beijing Chubanshe, 2003), 59.

[8] Calculated from data in *Beijing zhi: Zhengfa juan*, 362. Beijing had a registered population of 1,918,200 as of 1948.

exception of the Turkish minority, the Bulgarian state did not experience debilitating structural constraints to information gathering at the time of regime establishment.

3.2 Tasks

Like all autocracies, the communist regime in Bulgaria faced two types of domestic threats at the time of regime establishment: an elite threat and a mass threat. The elite threat had two components. One was the members of the old elite and the other was inner-party opposition; of the two, neutralizing the old elite was a more pressing concern than dealing with dissent within the party. It is important to keep in mind that here there are two differences with China. First, China did not experience a comparable problem with the old elite, who escaped virtually en masse following the 1949 communist takeover of power. Second, in contrast to Bulgaria, although the All-China People's Political Consultative Conference was established in 1949 and the National People's Congress in 1954, there were no competitive parliamentary elections in China. With regard to the mass threat, in Bulgaria it consisted of overt acts of opposition to the regime and a build-up of latent discontent. Both overt opposition and latent discontent could result from either political dissatisfaction or consumer frustrations (or a combination of the two), although political dissatisfaction tended to be the motor of overt displays of opposition, whereas latent discontent primarily reflected consumption problems.

Neutralizing both elite and mass threats required information. As the elite was numerically smaller and more easily identifiable than the masses, gathering intelligence on it did not prove to be a challenge for the party and State Security. With regard to the masses, information collection was more difficult because of the larger number of individuals who had to be catalogued. Both threats could be handled either through positive inducements (co-optation) or through repression. The relationship between information and the use of co-optation and repression was complex, as discussed in the lines that follow.

3.2.1 Managing Elite Threats

The old elite was the *crème de la crème* of the *ancien régime* that included the Council of Regents (which ruled on behalf of the underage king until the monarchy was abolished in 1946); former government ministers; leaders of the opposition parties (which remained legal until 1947); bank owners, large industrialists and major landowners; publishers of independent media; the top echelon of the army officer corps; and the high clergy. Some of these individuals were subjected to immediate repression by the People's Court (Bulgaria's equivalent of the Nuremberg Trials), which was organized by the communist-controlled Ministry of Justice between December 1944 and April 1945. The People's Court trials led to the arrest of 28,630 individuals, of whom 11,122 were indicted and, of those who were indicted, 2,730 were sentenced to death for exhibiting pro-fascist sympathies.[9] Altogether, between 8,000 and 30,000 citizens fell victim to brutal executions in the first months of communist rule.[10] Those who were not targets of repression were initially co-opted with positions in the coalition government, the army, or the National Assembly. Yet, co-optation did not mean trust: members of the old elite remained under the close watch of State Security.[11]

The policies of co-optation were short-lived. One example is provided by the fate of Minister of Defense Damian Velchev, who represented the opposition group "Zveno" that was a member of the coalition government formed after the September 1944 coup. General Velchev irked the communist party in November 1944 when he issued an order that aimed to stop the abduction of active-duty officers by the communist-controlled police (per this order, officers were given permission to use arms to resist arrest).[12] Although he continued to serve as minister of defense, General Velchev was placed under State Security surveillance. He was fortunate to be sent as ambassador to Switzerland in the fall of 1946. Other members of the old elite were executed (most notably Nikola Petkov, the undisputed leader of the opposition since 1945), sent to the camps (which existed intermittently until 1962), or interned (as occurred in the cases of both Exarch Stefan, who had been head of the Bulgarian Orthodox Church until 1948, and Venelin Ganev, who had been a member of the Council of Regents from the time of the communist coup until abolition of the monarchy in 1946).[13]

Once the old elite was neutralized by the end of 1948, the party turned inward and conducted a series of purges in 1949–1950.[14] The most notable elite victims were Traicho Kostov (Prime-Minister Georgi Dimitrov's putative successor, who was executed after a show trial in December 1949) and General Dobri Terpeshev (a Politburo member whose decision to inform the Politburo of widespread popular discontent with the economic policies of the government in 1948 eventually

[9] Polia Meshkova and Diniu Sharlanov, *Bulgarskata gilotina: Tainite mekhanizmi na Narodniia sud* (Sofia: Agentsiia "Demokratsiia," 1994).

[10] Diniu Sharlanov, *Tiraniiata: Zhertvi i palachi* (Sofia: Strelets, 1997), 10; Iskra Baeva and Evgeniia Kalinova, *Bulgarskite prekhodi* (Sofia: Paradigma, 2006), 55.

[11] See archival materials collected in *Durzhavna sigurnost i promenite v Bulgariia (septemvri 1944– dekemvri 1947)* (Sofia: Dossier Commission, 2010).

[12] Bulgarian State Security Dossier Commission (AKRDOPBGDSRSBNA-M) f. 10 (TK) op. A25 a. e. 3 (November 18, 1944), 2.

[13] Isusov, *Politicheskiiat zhivot v Bulgariia*; Ognianov, *Durzhavno-politicheskata sistema na Bulgariia*.

[14] *Borbi i chistki v BKP (1948–1953)* (Sofia: Bulgarian State Archives, 2001).

led to his removal from this body in 1950).[15] The search for "enemies with a party ID" extended beyond the elite: as many as 170,000 individuals, equivalent to one-third of all party members, were expelled from the party.[16] Although there were purges during the initial decade of communist rule in China as well, they were smaller in scale. In contrast to Bulgaria, party size continuously *increased* in China in 1951–1958.[17]

The purges ended in the early 1950s and the subsequent decades brought relative calm. Prior to the 1980s, the only serious threats to the regime in the 1956–1968 period came from party insiders rather than from regime enemies outside the party: one was the Kufardzhiev-Varon letter to the Central Committee in 1960,[18] another was Gorunia's attempted pro-Maoist coup in 1965,[19] and a third was Doktorov's "second center" in the struggle against Zhivkov.[20] All three conspiracies were promptly dealt with. Importantly, these were internal party splits that reflected the rise of factionalism, not broader social opposition to the regime.

Assessing the mood of the elite was not especially complicated from a logistical point of view. Because the leaders of the old elite had high visibility, constructing a roster of surveillance targets was a simple task.[21] This meant personnel could be immediately assigned by State Security to monitor these individuals. For inner-party dissent, the Control and Revision Commission (equivalent to the Discipline Inspection Commission in China) was exclusively in charge of identifying elite dissenters until the mid-1960s; from the mid-1960s onward, it was assisted in its work by six employees of State Security, who were in charge of investigating illegal behavior among the party elite.[22] Contrary to theoretical expectations, the problem with the old elite was promptly solved by 1948 and inner-party divisions appeared fully manageable after the purges of 1949–1950. This meant that State Security could redirect the bulk of its resources toward monitoring the mass threat.

[15] See Terpeshev's letter in the Bulgarian Central State Archives (TsDA) f. 1B op. 6 a. e. 545 (September 11, 1948), 11–12. The Politburo's initial harsh response is documented in TsDA f. 1B op. 6 a. e. 545 (September 23, 1948), 1–3.

[16] Tsvetanski, *Organizatsionno razvitie na BKP*, 29–31.

[17] *Zhongguo gongchandang dangnei tongji ziliao huibian, 1921–2010*, 8.

[18] On the handling of the case, see the Central Committee letter to provincial, city, district, county, and basic party organizations, TsDA f. 1B op. 5 a. e. 445 (March 3, 1961), 69–86.

[19] Tsviatko Anev, *Spomeni i razmisli na edin "gorunevets"* (Sofia: Geo Press, 1996).

[20] Dimitar Ivanov, *Politicheskoto protivopostaviane v Bulgariia 1956–1989 g.* (Sofia: Ares Press, 1994), 10–44; Mikhail Doktorov, *V skhvatka s oktopoda: "Vtoriiat tsentur" v borbata sreshtu zhivkovistite, 1965–1968 g.* (Sofia: Ares Press, 1993).

[21] See documents in *Durzhavna sigurnost i promenite v Bulgariia*.

[22] Dimitar Ivanov, *Shesti otdel* (Sofia: Trud, 2004).

3.2.2 Managing the Mass Threat

Assessing the mass threat was a much more complicated undertaking than monitoring the elite, as it involved cataloging the political attitudes of a considerably larger number of individuals. That said, from the point of view of State Security and the party, identifying overt mass discontent was remarkably easier than detecting brewing latent popular dissatisfaction.

Overt discontent could stem either from political frustrations or from consumer dissatisfaction. The most innocuous expression of discontent involved the distribution of anticommunist leaflets and slogans. Although leaflets were being spread throughout the lifespan of the communist regime,[23] their circulation reached a peak in 1953–1956, when they provided information about the upheavals in the Eastern Bloc and urged Bulgarians to follow the example of their Czechoslovak, East German, and Polish brethren.[24] A more serious threat was presented by armed resistance groups (*goriani*), which persisted until 1955.[25] These groups organized acts of sabotage aimed at destabilizing the communist regime. Finally, overt discontent could be expressed as protests or mass resistance driven by broadly defined consumption concerns. In villages these events came in response to land collectivization (particularly in 1951–1952) and in urban areas they were linked to shortages, unemployment, and inadequate compensation (especially in 1953).[26]

There were varying responses to these types of discontent. Overt resistance linked to consumption matters was sporadic and always unanticipated. The reaction involved some type of consumer concessions (slowdown in the pace of collectivization; lowering of prices; increase in salaries; efforts to improve the availability of consumer goods). Other instances of discontent were met with repression: short-term imprisonment for those distributing leaflets and longer sentences for participants in armed resistance groups. In general, overt discontent could be easily identified and efficiently responded to.

By contrast, tracking latent discontent presented a major logistical challenge. State Security and the party had to identify individuals who harbored latent dissatisfaction for political reasons and distinguish them from those who were frustrated as a result of consumer difficulties. This was necessary because even if both

---

[23] AMVR f. 1 op. 1 a. e. 646 (November 3, 1948), 1–3; AKRDOPBGDSRSBNA-M f. 1 op. 10 a. e. 398 (1967), 4–6; AMVR f. 1 op. 12 a. e. 599 (September 11–16, 1984), 47.

[24] TsDA f. 1B op. 24 a. e. 125 (1953); TsDA f. 1B op. 24 a. e. 126 (1953); TsDA f. 1B op. 24 a. e. 159 (1954); TsDA f. 1B op. 24 a. e. 162 (1954); TsDA f. 1B op. 24 a. e. 221 (1956).

[25] See documents reproduced in *Gorianite: Sbornik dokumenti, 1944–1949*, vol. 1 (Sofia: Central State Archives, 2001) and *Gorianite: Sbornik dokumenti, 1949–1956*, vol. 2 (Sofia: Central State Archives, 2010).

[26] See documents reproduced in *Durzhavna sigurnost i kolektivizatsiiata (1944–1959): Dokumentalen sbornik* (Sofia: Dossier Commission, 2015).

groups were deemed hostile during the initial decades of communist rule, those expressing consumer dissatisfaction were considered to be grumblers, whereas individuals who harbored latent discontent on political grounds were subject to entry onto the "enemy contingent" roster, which resulted in long-term monitoring and repression. Identifying individuals who harbored latent discontent was a labor-intensive and time-consuming process, especially because it relied overwhelmingly on involuntarily extracted intelligence (voluntarily provided information in the form of citizen complaints was very useful for evaluating consumption-based latent discontent, but, as discussed in Section 3.5, such information was scarce until the late 1960s, due to widespread fear resulting from high levels of repression). Practically, the ability of State Security and the party to track consumption preferences through the involuntary collection of information in the 1950s was limited to monitoring rumors and hostile statements made in public (often in queues). The techniques that were used to track latent political discontent were crude but effective: driven by the logic that those who sympathized with the old regime were more likely to be opposed to the new system, State Security developed lists of likely regime opponents that included former members of fascist organizations; former members of army organizations; former members of previously legal opposition parties; former kulaks; and those who had previously been punished for antiregime activity. The cumulative number of individuals on the lists constituted at least one-tenth of the population (in the estimation of State Security, the youth fascist organization *Brannik* alone had 300,000 members, or 4.3 percent of the population prior to the establishment of communist rule),[27] so monitoring all of them was impractical. Instead, a pared down enemy contingent roster was compiled that consisted of individuals who had provided a concrete reason to suspect that they might be harboring hostile attitudes toward the regime. Citizens on that list were then monitored by State Security, which took repressive measures as needed.

In sum, the tasks of information gathering involved managing elite and mass threats, with mass threats rapidly becoming the primary concern within the first decade of the establishment of communist rule. Initially, the emphasis was on detecting organized challenges to the regime. As organized resistance slowly declined, by the mid-1950s a new two-pronged approach relied on counteracting the rare acts of individual overt discontent and, more consequentially, on tracking latent discontent stemming from consumption difficulties or from external ideological influences. These conceptual understandings of the vectors of discontent persisted until the end of communist rule.

---

[27] AKRDOPBGDSRSBNA-M VI-L-765 vol. 1 pt. 1 (May 15, 1967), 132–48, at 132.

3.3 Institutions for the Involuntary Collection of Information

This book identifies three main channels through which communist regimes collect information on popular discontent: State Security, the communist party, and internal journalistic reporting. We will review their respective operations during the initial decade of communist rule in the lines that follow. Reflecting the importance that the power holders attached to identifying and neutralizing overt expressions of discontent, State Security became the key provider of information during this period. Assuming the lead position was not straightforward, as it involved acquiring most of the portfolio of a fourth collector of information, namely, the army.

3.3.1 The Party

Like State Security, the party relied on full-time cadres and part-time informants to track discontent through regular reports on the popular mood. Shortly after establishment of the regime, the Central Committee issued an "Instruction on Raising Party Vigilance," which required party members to "immediately report to the nearest State Security office or the People's Militia and to apprise the party leadership of any information they have acquired or of hostile elements they have encountered that are planning, preparing, or have commenced carrying out acts against the people."[28] Though never fully realized, this ambitious instruction effectively aimed to turn every party member into an unofficial State Security collaborator. Another technique, introduced after the unexpected protests of 1953 and 1956, was personal inspection tours conducted by high-level cadres, who would then inform the Central Committee about their findings upon returning to the capital.[29]

One important discovery that emerges from the archives is that the impetus for hierarchically organized reporting on the popular mood on a fixed schedule came in response to unanticipated public outbursts of discontent in March 1951, when peasant protests against collectivization led to a decision by the Central Committee to require provincial party committees and State Security to issue daily reports on popular unrest.[30] The content of this decision was reiterated in April 1951, when provincial, prefectural, city and district party committees were instructed "to provide continuous, accurate, and timely information to the

[28] TsDA f. 1B op. 6 a. e. 525 (October 7, 1948), 11.
[29] TsDA f. 378B op. 1 a. e. 493 (June 1953); TsDA f. 1B op. 7 a. e. 1778 (November 15–19, 1956).
[30] Vladimir Migev, *Kolektivizatsiiata na bulgarskoto selo (1948–1958)* (Sofia: Universitetsko Izdatelstvo "Stopanstvo," 1995), 124.

Central Committee."[31] In noncrisis situations, this meant that lower-level party offices had to send weekly reports analyzing the popular mood and enumerating instances of excessive violence.[32] As we will discuss in Chapter 4, the emergence of regularized party reporting was also an important benchmark in the development of the communist information state in China.

3.3.2   Internal Media Reporting

Internal media reporting exists in all communist autocracies. During the period examined in this chapter, the Bulgarian Telegraph Agency produced classified bulletins based on its monitoring of foreign wire services, which rarely discussed any domestic political developments in Bulgaria.[33] Because it reported to the minister of foreign affairs (who was not a communist), the telegraph agency could not be entrusted with the delicate task of monitoring domestic discontent after the 1944 coup; in the initial months and years after the establishment of communist rule, this was the prerogative of the party, State Security, and especially of Military Intelligence, which functioned as the key entity that monitored both newsprint and radio broadcasts.

In the 1940s and 1950s, internal reporting by print media played a minor role in informing the leadership, mostly due to the party's mistrust of journalists at the time. Consequently, the period was marked by an effort to place the propaganda system under complete communist control. The main obstacle to realizing that goal was created by the remaining independent news outlets and publishing houses. Therefore, the Print Directorate of the communist-controlled Ministry of the Interior was tasked with producing regular reports on the circulation and content of all media in 1944–1946.[34] In 1947, all independent domestic media and printing houses were closed down.

In the early years of communist rule, print media that carried critical content were penalized. In 1951, the editor-in-chief of *Vecherni novini* (Evening News) was dismissed following a letter from General Secretary Valko Chervenkov that detailed a long list of grievances against the paper.[35] In particular, the general secretary was displeased by news stories about long queues outside food stores; about the shortage of coal for winter heating; and about the scarcity of

---

[31] TsDA f. 1B op. 5 a. e. 94 (April 23, 1951), ix–xiv.

[32] Migev, *Kolektivizatsiiata na bulgarskoto selo*, 163.

[33] For an example from the 1940s, see a bulletin reporting Reuters coverage of opposition leader Nikola Petkov (AKRDOPBGDSRSBNA-M f. 1 op. 1 a. e. 104 [1945], 1). For an illustration of the content of the top-secret international information bulletin (*strogo poveritelen biuletin "Mezhdunarodna informatsiia"*) from the 1950s, see TsDA f. 378B op. 1 a. e. 1014 (1959).

[34] AKRDOPBGDSRSBNA-M f. 1 op. 1 a. e. 100 (1945–1946).

[35] TsDA f. 28 op. 9 a. e. 11 (October 6, 1951), 29–31.

public housing. Even typos were suspect: for example, the general secretary wondered whether an article willfully mentioned the "nontriumph of the ideas of Marx, Engels, Lenin, and Stalin."[36] The letter concluded by rhetorically asking who benefited from reading such content—and it responded that it was only enemies of the state who welcomed "findings" and "information" of this kind.[37] Identical language was used to describe overseas radio programs, which were seen as sources of harmful rumors and hostile propaganda.[38] Therefore, critical media, both domestic and foreign, were understood to serve the goals of regime enemies.

The party drew a distinction between constructive criticism (which was to be encouraged) and publicizing sensational hearsay about shortcomings that provided fodder for regime opponents.[39] As the line between allowable and proscribed criticism was not clear, in 1959 the editorial staff of the satirical weekly *Sturshel* (Gadfly) requested a meeting with the Central Committee to solicit guidance on the boundaries of permissible criticism.[40] The newspaper, which was published by the Central Committee and by design was supposed to be critical, had previously been penalized for printing "materials that present a perverted picture of our reality and contain spiteful antiparty criticism (*nepartiina kritika*) against leading state organs."[41] Although at their meeting with the Central Committee the editors were told that all criticism except that of the party line was allowed,[42] in 1961 the editor-in-chief was replaced by a more pliable individual who then toned down the critical content of the newspaper. In sum, throughout the 1950s, distrust of the media precluded the party from grasping the value of encouraging critical journalism in the publicly disseminated press and in internal classified publications.

State Security also sought to block the importation of politically subversive print material from abroad and to physically destroy the "hostile" Hristo Botev Radio and Radio Gorianin, both of which were broadcasting from the same Athenian suburb.[43] Transcripts of radio broadcasts were sent to the leadership and were referenced in closed-door speeches that the general secretary delivered

---

[36] For a parallel instance in China, see the Chinese government's March 2016 reaction to a misprint calling Xi Jinping the "last" leader (最后 vs. 最高): https://www.bbc.com/news/world-asia-china-35800437 (accessed April 19, 2022).

[37] TsDA f. 28 op. 9 a. e. 11 (October 6, 1951), 29–31.

[38] AKRDOPBGDSRSBNA-R f. 4 op. 9 a. e. 37 (1959), 143–47; AKRDOPBGDSRSBNA-M f. 2 op. 1 a. e. 771 (1959–1961), 225–52.

[39] For examples of encouraged criticism, see TsDA f. 1B op. 15 a. e. 683 (October 6, 1956), 1–14. For reader opposition to critical content published in *Sturshel*, see AMVR f. 1 op. 1 a. e. 2779 (September 15, 1953), 55–59.

[40] TsDA f. 1B op. 15 a. e. 734 (November 20, 1959), 1–10.

[41] TsDA f. 1B op. 15 a. e. 702 (May 4, 1957), 33–42.

[42] TsDA f. 1B op. 15 a. e. 734 (November 20, 1959), 1–10.

[43] AKRDOPBGDSRSBNA-M f. 1 op. 1 a. e. 318 (1946); AKRDOPBGDSRSBNA-R f. 4 op. 9 a. e. 39 (1958–1962).

to party activists.[44] The monitoring of foreign radio by State Security gradually sensitized the leadership to the value of internal journalism. Eventually, the telegraph agency assumed a greater role in informing the leadership about discontent in 1967, when it took over from State Security the task of transcribing Bulgarian-language broadcasts of these "hostile" foreign radio stations.[45]

3.3.3 Hollowing Out the Military Intelligence Portfolio

Although State Security emerged as the main collector of information in the 1950s, its prospects for assuming that role in the 1940s had been impeded by Military Intelligence, which possessed a formidable portfolio. Organized into four divisions, Military Intelligence had the following functional responsibilities: overseas military espionage; army counterespionage; domestic counterespionage; and the monitoring of print media, radio transmissions, and correspondence (this mandate was duplicated by the Print Directorate of the Ministry of the Interior).[46] The Bulgarian Communist Party felt threatened by the existence of a fragmented state security apparatus. The fear was that Military Intelligence could use the information in its possession to stage a coup against the communist party.[47] In contrast to theories about the organization of State Security in noncommunist regimes,[48] coup-proofing in Bulgaria involved a series of steps that were aimed at limiting the power of Military Intelligence by narrowing its mandate. First, by December 1944 communist Petar Vranchev was put in charge of Military Intelligence. Second, by 1946 noncommunist Minister of Defense Damian Velchev was replaced by a communist. Third, the portfolio of Military Intelligence was gradually reduced, and by 1950, its only remaining functions involved overseas military espionage.[49] The important responsibilities of army counterintelligence, domestic counterintelligence, and control of the press and communications were transferred to State Security.[50] The plan stopped short of the desired merger of State Security and Military Intelligence,

---

[44] For transcripts, see AKRDOPBGDSRSBNA-M f. 2 op. 1 a. e. 787 (May 11, 1955), 7–8 and AKRDOPBGDSRSBNA-M f. 2 op. 1 a. e. 877 (1960), 41–45. For a reference to a broadcast, see Sofia State Archive (DA-Sofia) f. 1V op. 23 a. e. 26 (November 2, 1956), 133–51.

[45] On the genesis of the decision to shift responsibilities for monitoring these broadcasts from State Security to the telegraph agency, see AKRDOPBGDSRSBNA-M VI-L chart 1 (1967), 7–8.

[46] AKRDOPBGDSRSBNA-M f. 3 op. 3 a. e. 158 (1952), 3–3A.

[47] Stancho Stanchev, Rumen Nikolov, and Iordan Baev, *Istoriia na bulgarskoto razuznavane*, vol. 1 (Sofia: Iztok–Zapad, 2017), 159.

[48] James Quinlivan, "Coup Proofing," *International Security* 24:2 (1999), 131–65; Sheena Chestnut Greitens, *Dictators and Their Secret Police: Coercive Institutions and State Violence* (New York: Cambridge University Press, 2016).

[49] TsDA f. 1B op. 64 a. e. 78 (April 12, 1950), 1–3.

[50] TsDA f. 1B op. 6 a. e. 520 (July 21, 1948); TsDA f. 1B op. 6 a. e. 933 (June 21, 1950), 1–7.

but it did involve the hostile takeover of the entire domestic portfolio of Military Intelligence by State Security with the express purpose of coup-proofing. The capacity of the Ministry of Defense to preserve exclusive jurisdiction over its foreign military espionage portfolio is not surprising—though not appreciated by existing theories, there is no case in the communist world where Military Intelligence is not a bureaucracy that is entirely separate from State Security.

It is noteworthy that as the wholesale merger of the two spy agencies was being attempted, the communist placed in charge of Military Intelligence presented the utility of redundancy as an argument for preserving Military Intelligence as an independent information collector with all its four divisions.[51] This book argues that redundancy is desirable, as it allows for the cross-checking of sensitive information. In the late 1960s, when elite threats had been neutralized, the top party leadership was itself promoting the idea of the value of redundancy.[52] But in the mid-1940s, when the likelihood of a coup was high, the informational benefit that might ensue from having a fragmented intelligence apparatus was not seen as a sufficient reason to allow the Ministry of Defense to pose a threat to the party by maintaining the crucial domestic counterintelligence mandates of three of the four divisions of Military Intelligence.

3.3.4 State Security

In all communist regimes, State Security was subordinate to the party. It is therefore not surprising that in Bulgaria in 1954 State Security was characterized as "the eyes and ears of the party" by Prime Minister Valko Chervenkov.[53] This parallels China, where informants are also known as eyes and ears (ermu 耳目). However, one difference is that whereas the Chinese Ministry of Public Security initially was not centralized,[54] a Bulgarian Politburo meeting on June 12, 1945, promptly decided that State Security would be organized in a centralized fashion, thus making it easier to ensure that lower levels would implement central directives.[55]

State Security relied on its corps of full-time employees, numerous secret informants, and surprisingly sophisticated technical means to collect information that allowed it to assess and counteract threats to regime stability. During the period examined in this chapter (1944–1958), the main focus of State Security

---

[51] AKRDOPBGDSRSBNA-M f. 10 (TK) op. 25 a. e. 1 vol. 4 (June 2, 1949), 191–204, at 194.

[52] See Chapter 5. For a similar understanding in the Soviet Union, see Chapter 9.

[53] AKRDOPBGDSRSBNA-M f. 1 op. 5 a. e. 133 (April 17, 1954), 2–11B.

[54] Suzanne Scoggins, *Policing China: Street-Level Cops in the Shadow of Protest* (Ithaca, NY: Cornell University Press, 2021).

[55] AMVR f. 44 op. 4 a. e. 45 (1967), 9.

shifted from monitoring elite threats in the mid- to late 1940s to registering overt mass discontent in the early to mid-1950s; it was not until the late 1950s that attention shifted to producing assessments of latent discontent. Although none of these tasks could be accomplished without information, collection of the necessary intelligence became progressively more difficult as State Security moved from monitoring the small and highly visible contingent of elite regime opponents (or the equally uncomplicated task of registering and counteracting overt discontent) to the complex challenge of developing indicators of latent discontent, using those indicators to monitor individuals, and acting on the information collected. Monitoring latent discontent required high-quality information. How could it be obtained? The tradeoff between the use of repression and the quality of information was already evident in the 1950s, when State Security realized that a decline in the frequency and severity of repression made possible the collection of more abundant and more fine-grained information, which, in turn, enabled the more selective and targeted use of repression.[56]

Institution Building

Rather than creating an institution anew, the communist party refashioned the pre-existing secret police apparatus so that it would serve its own goals. Prior to 1944, Division A of the Police Directorate carried out the functions of a political police. Organized in three sections and two groups, the division was in charge of identifying communists and their sympathizers and helpers (Section 1); collecting information on noncommunist parties and social organizations (Section 2); assessing and countering Soviet influence operations (Section 3); ensuring the personal safety of cabinet members and protecting the legislature and the main Orthodox cathedral (Guards Group); and conducting surveillance of the top communist leadership (Targets Group).[57] When the communist party assumed control over the Ministry of the Interior in 1944, it allowed Division A to retain its name and most of its portfolio; the most fundamental change was that instead of focusing on communists, Division A was tasked with identifying fascists and their sympathizers and helpers—which also meant that it could no longer work against the Soviet Union. The Bulgarian example indicates that, in newly established regimes, institutional takeover often precedes the more complicated task of institution building.

Institution building began by purging sympathizers of the old regime from the full-time police staff and developing an informant corps that was loyal to the communist party. This led to an initial contraction in the number of State

---

[56] Martin K. Dimitrov and Joseph Sassoon, "State Security, Information, and Repression: A Comparison of Communist Bulgaria and Ba'thist Iraq," *Journal of Cold War Studies* 16:2 (Spring 2014), 4–31.

[57] *Durzhavna sigurnost: Politicheska politsiia* (Sofia: Dossier Commission, 2011), 519.

Security employees and informants in late 1944–1945, followed by an expansion that unfolded throughout 1946. By September 1946, Division A had 400 full-time staff and nearly 4,000 agents and informants in the capital and the provincial police directorates.[58] The mandate of State Security involved surveillance of the political elite of the *ancien régime*; the monitoring of former policemen, army officers, and members of the clergy; and the collection of information on the activities of all noncommunist political parties. Even though Bulgaria still had a multiparty system, control over the Ministry of the Interior allowed the communist party to swiftly begin remaking State Security into an instrument that served its goals of establishing a single-party dictatorship.

The next step in institution building involved re-organizing State Security. In 1947, new specialized groups were created that focused on political banditry, on intellectuals and youth, and on ethnic minorities (the existing divisions handling noncommunist political parties, fascist sympathizers, the clergy, and the political and military elite of the *ancien régime* were maintained).[59] This internal structure reveals the broad spectrum of the threat perceptions of the communist party at the time. Following the September 1946 referendum to abolish the monarchy, the party moved aggressively to establish a full monopoly on power by forcing all opposition parties out of existence in 1947–1948. As legal opposition parties were being outlawed, State Security prioritized the task of developing a roster of the "enemy contingent" (*vrazheski kontingent*),[60] and using full-time staff, part-time informants, and technical surveillance to manage these enemies.

Full-Time Staff

The main tasks of full-time staff were to develop a list of targets that were to be watched; to recruit informants and deploy the technical means necessary to monitor these targets; and to execute appropriate actions against such targets in light of the evidence produced through surveillance. The quality of the full-time employees of State Security had a major impact on the successful execution of these tasks. Initially, political reliability trumped competence when recruiting State Security staff, sometimes resulting in the hiring of unqualified personnel, especially in faraway provincial outposts.[61] Gradually, staff qualifications improved: by 1951, the share of full-time State Security employees who possessed only a primary school education had declined to 4.7 percent (we should stress that even this level of minimal schooling provides literacy in Bulgarian, whereas more extensive training is necessary to achieve basic literacy in Chinese).[62] The

---

[58] Calculated from AKRDOPBGDSRSBNA-M f. 13 op. 1 a. e. 32 (1946), 1–8.
[59] *Durzhavna sigurnost: Politicheska politsiia*, 521.
[60] This was equivalent to the targeted population roster in China, discussed in Chapters 4, 6, and 8.
[61] AMVR f. 1 op. 8 a. e. 110 (1945), 30.
[62] Calculated from AKRDOPBGDSRSBNA-M f. 1 op. 5 a. e. 5 (1951), 254.

quality of the staff improved further by using the specialized training opportunities presented by the police academy and by introducing foreign-language
instruction.

Informants

No state security system can rely simply on full-time staff. Thus, the Bulgarian
political police attracted informants, who were to infiltrate families or personal circles of citizens placed under surveillance (elites, enemies of the people,
and ideologically suspect individuals). They also penetrated armed resistance
groups.[63] State Security reached the conclusion that the quality of the information provided increased when the informants belonged to the same social milieu
as the targets of surveillance.[64]

Agency problems emerged early on. Quality was negatively impacted by the
method of recruiting informants. Because informing in exchange for regular
payments was rare during the initial decade of communist rule,[65] blackmail and
voluntary cooperation constituted the main channels for recruiting agents. The
archives reveal that State Security was aware that those recruited through blackmail supplied information only reluctantly.[66] A concern about overreliance on
blackmail was expressed as early as 1946; for example, one State Security report
stated: "We need to learn how to recruit through more flexible methods . . . open
blackmail is naturally not always an effective approach."[67] Nevertheless, an assessment of the informant network in 1950 indicates that 54 percent of its
members had still been recruited through blackmail.[68] Efforts to increase voluntary cooperation continued throughout the 1950s; most effective in this regard
were instructions to use blackmail only in exceptional cases.[69]

Another concern was the number of informants. In 1949, the secret informant
network stood at 20,000 people, but that was still considered insufficient, and
State Security reached a determination that the network had to be improved
both quantitatively and qualitatively.[70] As a result, the number of informants
grew rapidly, reaching 55,000 by 1953.[71] Analysis revealed that this vast network
was of poor quality, leading to a Politburo decision to put an end to the practice of indiscriminate recruitment of informants and to reduce the size of the

---

[63] AMVR f. III raz. 1713 vol. 3 (1949), 1.

[64] AKRDOPBGDSRSBNA-M f. 13 op. 1 a. e. 842 (1952), 11; TsDA f. 1B op. 64 a. e. 185 (November
8, 1953), 11–87.

[65] It was first mentioned in a 1962 recruitment instruction, AKRDOPBGDSRSBNA-M f. 1 op. 11
a. e. 49 (June 20, 1962), 60–81, at 66.

[66] AKRDOPBGDSRSBNA-M f. 1 op. 11 a. e. 31 (January 13, 1957), 11–27, at 16–17.

[67] AKRDOPBGDSRSBNA-M f. 1 op. 1 a. e. 219 (September 7, 1946), 1–7, at 2.

[68] AKRDOPBGDSRSBNA-M f. 13 op. 1 a. e. 616 (January 11, 1951), 2–20, at 13.

[69] AKRDOPBGDSRSBNA-M f. 1 op. 11 a. e. 49 (June 20, 1962), 60–81, at 66.

[70] AMVR f. 1 op. 1 a. e. 835 (August 11, 1949), 2–17.

[71] TsDA f. 1B op. 64 a. e. 185 (November 8, 1953), 11–87.

network by one-third.[72] Emphasis was placed on terminating agents whose work was unsatisfactory and on more careful and targeted recruitment of new secret collaborators.

Technical Surveillance

Archival materials reveal that from the very beginning of communist rule State Security used surprisingly sophisticated means of technical surveillance. For example, as early as 1944, information within the State Security system was transmitted through telephonograms.[73] Another unexpected discovery is that by 1948, State Security conducted audio surveillance by microphone.[74] The systematic efforts to use technical surveillance relied on the fifty-one employees of the Second Division of the Sixth Department, who were in charge of phone tapping and audio surveillance as well as the tape recording of relevant conversations.[75] Like other communist regimes,[76] Bulgaria engaged in systematic mail inspection.[77] Finally, indicative of the wide scope of its monitoring capacity, by the early 1960s State Security could carry out video surveillance.[78]

Using the Available Information

The work of State Security was guided by the concept of "the enemy contingent" (*vrazheski kontingent*), whose members were cataloged by detecting "hostile elements" (*vrazheski elementi*).[79] Those who initially entered the enemy contingent were the political, military, intellectual, and industrial elite of the *ancien régime* as well as individuals who engaged in overt displays of opposition to the system by participating in organized resistance groups, by spreading antiregime pamphlets, or by organizing strikes. Although the process of systematically cataloging different groups of high-profile and overt opponents began as early as 1947,[80] identifying ordinary citizens who might be harboring latent discontent proceeded more slowly.

---

[72] TsDA f. 1B op. 64 a. e. 185 (November 21, 1953), 1–10.

[73] For examples of telephonograms, see AMVR f. 1 op. 8 a. e. 1–240 (1944–1959). On the use of the telephone in the Chinese bureaucracy, see Michel Oksenberg, "Methods of Communication within the Chinese Bureaucracy," *The China Quarterly*, no. 57 (January–March 1974), 1–39.

[74] AMVR f. 1 op. 1 a. e. 835 (August 11, 1949), 2–17; AKRDOPBGDSRSBNA-M f. 10 op. A1 a. e. 19 t. 2 (March 8, 1951), 76–78; AKRDOPBGDSRSBNA-M f. 1 op. 11 a. e. 22 (February 7, 1955), 383–93.

[75] AMVR f. 1 op. 1 a. e. 835 (August 11, 1949), 2–17.

[76] Joachim Kallinich and Sylvia de Pascuale, *Ein offenes Geheimnis: Post- und Telefonkontrolle in der DDR* (Heildelberg: Braus, 2002).

[77] AKRDOPBGDSRSBNA-M f. 1 op. 11 a. e. 31 (May 6, 1957), 274–95; AKRDOPBGDSRSBNA-M f. 1 op. 11 a. e. 31 (February 19, 1957), 165–73.

[78] AKRDOPBGDSRSBNA-M f. 1 op. 11 a. e. 48 (May 26, 1962), 224–39.

[79] AKRDOPBGDSRSBNA-M f. 13 op. 1 a. e. 842 (1951), 39–105.

[80] AKRDOPBGDSRSBNA-M f. 1 op. 1 a. e. 377 (1947), 137–39; AKRDOPBGDSRSBNA-M f. 13 op. 1 a. e. 795 (March 12, 1951), 1–15, at 1.

In the 1950s, the approach to latent discontent was to look for sympathizers of the old regime; members of the formerly legal political parties; tsarist military officers and members of illegal army organizations; members of fascist organizations (including for youth); anarchists and followers of Trotsky and the purged Politburo member Traicho Kostov; and individuals who had already been punished for espionage or subversion.[81] This broad spectrum of potential enemies bears a resemblance to the wide range of groups included on the targeted population roster in China in the 1950s. As in China, it had the effect of excessively inflating the list of individuals who were seen as posing a potential threat to the regime. Yet, in contrast to China, where lists were maintained in a decentralized fashion in certain urban areas, the Bulgarian roster was hierarchically organized, with the most dangerous enemies monitored at the central level and the less threatening individuals being placed on provincial- and city-level lists.

The archives provide us with some numerical indicators of the size of the enemy contingent and of the agents who were used to monitor it and to collect other information of operational interest. At the end of 1951, the central-level enemy contingent roster included 10,395 individuals, who were managed by 120 full-time staff and 915 agents.[82] A subset of those on the enemy roster (877 individuals) were subjected to enhanced surveillance that aimed to ascertain whether they engaged in antistate activities; the evidence collected was used eventually to arrest one-third of those surveilled (264 individuals). At the subnational level, the number of agents reached 18,054 in 1951, with various types of surveillance deployed against 10,789 individuals;[83] the evidence collected led to 2,324 arrests. By 1951, the enemy contingent roster had become the main tool for managing political dissent. Updating it on a regular basis was a key task for State Security throughout the remainder of communist rule.

The enemy contingent and the agent network grew so rapidly in the early 1950s that the leadership of State Security expressed concerns about the roster becoming unwieldy (and thus less useful) and about the declining quality of the newly recruited agents. To redress this situation, the Ministry of the Interior issued Order No. 276 in November 1953, which mandated the use of stricter standards when assigning individuals to the enemy contingent.[84] By its own admission, State Security had relied on arbitrary criteria and it had rounded numbers upward in the late 1940s, which led to an initial estimate of an enemy contingent of 800,000 (subsequently halved to 400,000 individuals).[85] Following

---

[81] AMVR f. 1 op. 1 a. e. 1739 (1951), 1–26.
[82] AMVR f. 1 op. 1 a. e. 1739 (1951), 1–26.
[83] Using the ratio of individuals placed under surveillance to the total number of people on the central enemy roster, we can estimate that the subnational roster included at least 100,000 names.
[84] AMVR f. 1 op. 5 a. e. 40 (1955).
[85] AMVR f. 13 op. 1 a. e. 1162 (1955), 1–11.

the stricter accounting rules mandated by Order No. 276, the enemy contingent was reduced to 32,300 individuals (equivalent to 0.4 percent of the population in 1954). The personal information of those included in the enemy contingent was entered into the operational-reporting system, which subjected them to surveillance aimed at preventing overt expressions of discontent.

Simultaneously with reducing the size of the enemy contingent, State Security registered a decline in the incidence of political crime. This trend began in 1952 and persisted throughout the decade, despite temporary increases in antistate activity in 1953 and 1956.[86] When he was retrospectively assessing the reasons for this decline at the end of the 1950s, the minister of the interior concluded that there were three causes: increased satisfaction as a result of the enhanced standards of living; better monitoring of the enemy contingent; and, in turn, more selective and precise use of punishment.[87] In the 1950s, State Security had already come to realize that, aside from punishment, other methods could be used, such as warnings and political work aimed at the decomposition of hostile groups.[88] This new philosophy resulted in a change in the work of State Security, which adopted preventive prophylaxis instead of repression—or, to quote from a document: "In its practical activities, State Security increasingly more skillfully combines the method of coercion with the method of persuasion and reeducation."[89] In 1967, the size of the enemy contingent had declined nine-fold compared with that in 1955, with three times fewer informants. This is evidence of a major reduction in threat perceptions.

Information Quality and Repression

A major discovery that emerges from the Bulgarian archives is that the low quality of the informant network had a direct impact on the way in which dissent was handled. State Security reports indicate that, when information was of insufficient quality, mass repression was used. Although this approach was favored in the 1940s, by the early 1950s there was a growing awareness that mass coercive measures were not as effective for handling dissent as targeted repression. The logic is simple: mass repression was conducted without sufficient information, which meant that many of those who were arrested would eventually have to be released because of lack of evidence of a crime (Type I error).[90] Mass repression also affected the wrong group of citizens: workers, who occupied a privileged

---

[86] AMVR f. 13 op. 1 a. e. 1162 (1955), 1–11; AMVR f. 1 op. 1 a. e. 62 (1959), 1–32; ARPDOPBGDSRSBNA-M f. 1 op. 2 a. e. 320 (June 30, 1957), 1–3.

[87] AMVR f. 1 op. 1 a. e. 62 (1959), 1–32.

[88] AMVR f. 1 op. 1 a. e. 62 (1959), 1–32.

[89] AMVR f. 1 op. 1 a. e. 62 (1959), 1–32.

[90] TsDA f. 1B op. 64 a. e. 185 (November 8, 1953), reproduced in Veselin Angelov, comp., *Strogo sekretno! Dokumenti za deinostta na Durzhavna sigurnost (1944–1958)* (Sofia: Simolini, 2007), 229–38, at 235.

ideological space, would be targeted as "enemies of the people," thus under-mining the fragile social basis of the dictatorship.[91] Archival documents from Bulgaria reveal that as early as 1952, State Security already realized that resorting to mass arrests underscored the weakness of its informant network.[92] Thus, State Security interpreted the decline in arrests to be directly related to the enhanced quality of the informant network; to quote from a top-secret report: "Due to the improving agent-operative and investigative work, unnecessary arrests have been greatly reduced."[93] The relationship between information quality and the incidence of repression helps us to understand the subsequent changes that took place not only in Bulgaria but in all post-Stalinist regimes where repression declined in favor of surveillance.[94]

A relaxation of repression favors better information gathering. Although the general 1953–1955 trend points toward such a relaxation (demonstrated, among other indicia, by the closing of some labor camps and of eleven of the nineteen prisons in the country),[95] the Polish and Hungarian upheavals of 1956 provided a welcome pretext for a domestic crackdown on dissent in Bulgaria.[96] State Security used the 1956 events to justify expansion of the size of the enemy contingent to include Roma and vagrants (*lumpeni*) and to focus on members of the intelligentsia, youth, and students.[97] Yet, harsh re-pression gradually declined in the second half of the 1950s. One statistic is revealing: only 14.2 percent of the 23,531 individuals who were sent to labor camps in 1944–1962 were interned during the 1956–1962 period (we should note that those who were sent to the camps were not exclusively incarcerated for political reasons).[98] Although arrests were still carried out (e.g., against so-called hooligans in 1958),[99] State Security was re-orienting itself toward sur-veillance and selective repression.

[91] TsDA f. 1B op. 64 a. e. 185 (November 8, 1953), reproduced in Angelov, comp., *Strogo sekretno!* 229–38, at 235–36.

[92] AMVR f. 1 op. 5 a. e. 30 (1953), reproduced in Angelov, comp., *Strogo sekretno!* 221–25, at 222.

[93] TsDA f. 1B op. 64 a. e. 185 (November 8, 1953), reproduced in Angelov, comp., *Strogo sekretno!* 229–38, at 235.

[94] On this process in the GDR, see Gary Bruce, "The Prelude to Nationwide Surveillance in East Germany: Stasi Operations and Threat Perceptions, 1945–1953," *Journal of Cold War Studies* 5:2 (Spring 2003), 3–31.

[95] Ognianov, *Politicheskata sistema v Bulgariia*, 189–90.

[96] Sofia State Archive (DA-Sofia) f. 3B op. 13 a. e. 2 (1957), 92–96.

[97] AKRDOPBGDSRSBNA-M f. 1 op. 2 a. e. 312 (1957), 21–26.

[98] Penka Stoianova and Emil Iliev, *Politicheski opasni litsa: Vudvoriavaniia, trudova mobilizatsiia, izselvaniia v Bulgariia sled 1944 g.* (Sofia: Universitetsko Izdatelstvo "Sv. Kliment Okhridski," 1991), 101.

[99] The January 21, 1958, Politburo decision authorizing State Security to conduct arrests of "hooligans" is reprinted in Stoianova and Iliev, *Politicheski opasni litsa*, 155.

3.3.5 Summary Assessment

In the fifteen years between 1944 and 1958, the regime developed two main channels for involuntary extraction of information about overt and latent discontent: party monitoring and State Security monitoring. Internal journalistic reporting played an insignificant role because the regime had started off with a distrust of the media. After it had sidelined the army, State Security emerged as the key supplier of information on popular discontent during the years of regime establishment and consolidation. The party would not assume greater prominence until the 1960s, when a stronger awareness of the importance of monitoring latent discontent emerged.

3.4 Mood Reports on Overt Discontent

One of the central distinctions in the theory of information advanced in this book is between overt and latent discontent. This section focuses specifically on how the party-state tracked manifestations of overt discontent (hostile acts of opposition; electoral disobedience; consumer protests; and subversive dreams) and how information about such behaviors impacted leadership decision making during the initial decades of communist rule. When thinking about overt discontent, we need to differentiate between acts of dissent that the regime understood to be hostile (this involved both organized and individual opposition to communist rule) and dissatisfaction that was seen as neutral. The distinction is meaningful because hostile acts were treated harshly, whereas reactions to regime-neutral overt discontent were more lenient and might even involve concessions.

3.4.1. Monitoring Hostile Acts of Opposition

Intelligence collectors systematically tracked hostile acts of opposition. Evaluating the allegiance of the army top brass was essential for coup-proofing, but it was complicated, because military officers were circumspect and rarely expressed their views publicly.[100] Though the Ministry of Defense was not controlled by the communists until 1946, assessments of the loyalty of officers were handled by Military Intelligence, which was led by a communist party member beginning from 1944—General Vranchev had established a network of informants who gathered information on the political orientation of officers, on their participation in anticommunist military associations, and on

---

[100] AKRDOPBGDSRSBNA-M f. 1 op. 1 a. e. 42 (December 5, 1944), 23.

coup-plotting.[101] Informants were also essential for tracking leaders of the opposition parties. As early as September 1946, State Security was boasting that it had penetrated the leadership of both the opposition parties and the coalition partners of the communists in the Fatherland Front, an umbrella political organization whose functions are parallel to those of the United Front in China.[102] Multiple narrative reports on the daily activities and public pronouncements of all key political leaders remain in the archives, revealing the degree to which all parties were infiltrated by secret-police informants.[103] Thus, State Security was essential to manage organized threats to communist party rule.

In contrast to eliminating high-profile leaders of the organized opposition, identifying small groups of anticommunist resisters and individual dissenters posed a greater challenge for the party and the secret police. There were three main targets. One was the indigenous armed resistance (*goriani*) movement, which comprised both small groups (*cheti*) and individual guerrillas. Various estimates of the size of the movement exist, ranging from 3,500 to 7,000 *goriani* and up to 20,000 helpers (*iatatsi*).[104] The indigenous movement persisted throughout the 1945–1955 period, but it was most active prior to the second half of 1953.[105] Another threat arose from the imported armed resistance groups sent by political émigrés in Greece, Turkey, Yugoslavia, Italy, and France to infiltrate several border regions in Bulgaria. These groups had as many as 2,685 members,[106] some of whom joined the *goriani* movement, whereas others aimed to destabilize the regime by distributing leaflets and by engaging in various acts of sabotage. The third threat was peasant resistance to collectivization, which was expressed through either individual or group displays of violent discontent.[107] Importantly, by the mid-1950s, all types of armed resistance were under control. As we will see in Chapters 4 and 9, this parallels the speed with which similar challenges were handled in China, the Soviet Union, and Cuba.

---

[101] AKRDOPBGDSRSBNA-M f. 1 op. 1 a. e. 159 (June 8, 1945), 71; AKRDOPBGDSRSBNA-M f. 1 op. 1 a. e. 295 (August 4, 1946), 1–4.

[102] AKRDOPBGDSRSBNA-M f. 1 op. 1 a. e. 219 (September 7, 1946), 1–7.

[103] These are periodic (daily, weekly, monthly, quarterly, and yearly) reports. See AKRDOPBGDSRSBNA-M f. 1 op. 1 a. e. 286 (January 17, 1946), 23–24; AKRDOPBGDSRSBNA-M f. 1 op. 1 a. e. 159 (January 29, 1946), 6; AKRDOPBGDSRSBNA-M f. 1 op. 1 a. e. 264 (April 2, 1946); AKRDOPBGDSRSBNA-M f. 1 op. 1 a. e. 355 (October 14, 1946), 4–5; AKRDOPBGDSRSBNA-M f. 13 op. 1 a. e. 228 (August 1946–May 1947), 4–6; AKRDOPBGDSRSBNA-M f. 1 op. 1 a. e. 728 (January 1, 1948), 1–3.

[104] The low estimate is from Diniu Sharlanov, *Istoriia na komunizma v Bulgariia*, vol. 2 (Sofia: Ciela, 2009), 134. The high estimate is from Marian Giaurski and Konstantin Kasabov, "Vuoruzhena suprotiva sreshtu komunisticheskiia rezhim v Bulgariia—gorianskoto dvizhenie (1944–1955 g.)," in Ivailo Znepolski, ed., *Da poznaem komunizma: Izsledvaniia* (Sofia: Ciela, 2012), 9–57, at 19.

[105] Sharlanov, *Istoriia na komunizma v Bulgariia*, vol. 2, 139; *Gorianite: Sbornik dokumenti*, vol. 2 (1949–1956).

[106] Sharlanov, *Istoriia na komunizma v Bulgariia*, vol. 2, 265.

[107] See documents in *Durzhavna sigurnost i kolektivizatsiiata*.

3.4.2 Elections: Monitoring and Responding to Low Support for the Party

A second area of concern for State Security was the link between economic diffi-culties and low support for the communist party, which became apparent as early as 1946, when opposition parties still existed.[108] A report on the outcome of the elections in Khaskovo prefecture states: "For the opposition voted all fascist reac-tionaries and a small part of the people who are dissatisfied mainly because of the disorder in the economic sphere."[109] State Security and the party continued to monitor the public mood before elections even after opposition parties were banned and dissolved. During the municipal polling of May 1949, when voters had only two binary choices (to vote or not to vote; and if they voted, to vote for the Fatherland Front party coalition or not), reports from all 106 electoral precincts revealed the wide variability in turnout (from 90.2 to 100 percent) and the even more surprising range of invalid ballots (from 0.1 to 31 percent).[110] This prompted further analysis, which highlighted thirteen precincts in which in-dividual counties registered less than 50 percent of the vote for the Fatherland Front.[111] One step below in the administrative hierarchy, seventeen counties were identified as having at least one village registering a vote of less than 50 per-cent.[112] What might explain these results? This was a question of great interest to the regime, as indicated by the document referenced above, in which precincts with low turnouts and with a low share of the vote for the Fatherland Front were underlined.[113] An even more meaningful signal of concern was the con-vening in June 1949 of a Central Committee plenum to discuss the results of the elections.[114]

We can provide our own answer to a question that consumed the Central Committee. Although it was not used by the party at the time, OLS statistical analysis reveals several patterns. One is that protest votes were higher in non-urban areas, as indicated by the larger number of invalid ballots in rural electoral precincts (see Model 1 in Table 3.1). The second is that lower voter turnout facil-itated the casting of protest votes (as revealed by Model 2 in Table 3.1). An ex-ample might help illustrate the link between turnout and pro–Fatherland Front voting: only the army reported 100 percent turnout and 99.8 percent votes for the

[108] Such links are discussed in influential research on the function of elections in autocracies: see Victor Zaslavsky and Robert J. Brym, "The Functions of Elections in the USSR," *Soviet Studies* 30:3 (July 1978), 362–71 and Beatriz Magaloni, *Voting for Autocracy: Hegemonic Party Survival and its Demise in Mexico* (New York: Cambridge University Press, 2006).

[109] AMVR f. 1 op. 8 a. e. 110 (November 4, 1946), 57.

[110] TsDA f. 146 op. 4 a. e. 1871 (May 16, 1949).

[111] TsDA f. 1B op. 6 a. e. 606 (June 8, 1949).

[112] TsDA f. 1B op. 6 a. e. 606 (June 8, 1949).

[113] TsDA f. 1B op. 6 a. e. 606 (June 8, 1949).

[114] TsDA f. 1B op. 5 a. e. 35 (June 11, 1949).

Table 3.1 Determinants of the Percentage of Invalid Votes in the 1949 Bulgarian Elections

	M1 Bivariate	M2 Turnout	M3 Rural	M4 Controls
Urban prefecture	−5.10***	−5.16***		
	(1.92)	(1.54)		
Turnout (%)		−1.82	−2.30***	−2.34***
		(24)***	(0.35)	(0.35)
Kulak opposition party member (%)			21.2***	20.8***
			(5.97)	(5.87)
Eligible voters total				−0.0000296
				(0.0000184)
Constant	8.62	185.42	229.7	234.9
	(0.696)	(23.41)	(34.3)	(33.81)
N	106	106	44	44
R-squared	0.06	0.40	0.56	0.58

Source: Author's dataset.

Significance levels: * = 0.1; ** = 0.05; *** = 0.01.

Fatherland Front, providing evidence of the remarkable mobilizational capacity of the political commissars in the military. To explore further what was driving the protest vote in nonurban precincts, we can truncate the sample and run regressions only on the rural precincts (Models 3 and 4 in Table 3.1). The regression results indicate that the share of invalid votes is strongly correlated with a lower turnout and with a higher proportion of voters, who had been members of the opposition parties that had been legal through 1947 (those voters were designated as kulaks by State Security). In sum, just as they did elsewhere throughout the Eastern Bloc, noncompetitive elections in Bulgaria provided valuable information about the levels of opposition to the regime.[115]

In response, the communist party adopted the practical solution of redistricting the counties and villages so that areas with a high number of invalid votes would be merged with communist strongholds.[116] Redistricting was successful: when the legislative elections were held in December 1949, despite numerous election-day displays of overt opposition to the regime registered by State Security (slogans, provocative public statements, and destruction of ballots or

---

[115] Hans Michael Kloth, *Vom "Zettelfalten" bis zum freien Wählen: Die Demokratisierung der DDR 1989/90 und die "Wahlfrage"* (Berlin: Ch. Links Verlag, 2000).

[116] TsDA f. 1B op. 6 a. e. 606 (June 8, 1949).

offensive statements written on the ballots),[117] turnout in each of the fifteen electoral precincts was 97.5 percent or higher and support for the Fatherland Front
was 95 percent or higher.[118] Ensuring similar levels of turnout and voting results
in future polls required continuous pre-electoral monitoring and election-day
vigilance. The fervor of State Security led to some unexpected outcomes, such
as statements by members of reactionary circles that they planned to cast their
votes in public (not inside the voting booths), in order to preempt any suspicions
of disloyalty.[119]

3.4.3 Tracking Consumer Discontent and Making Concessions

Beyond hostile opposition and electoral disobedience, the information
collectors also tracked consumer dissatisfaction. The political vacuum created
by the death of Stalin on March 5, 1953, resulted in a wave of worker strikes
throughout the Eastern Bloc. In Bulgaria, laid-off tobacco workers in Plovdiv
went on strike on May 3–4, 1953, to protest unemployment.[120] There were also
work stoppages organized by textile workers in Khaskovo and preparations for a
strike in the Maritsa textile plant in Plovdiv later in 1953.[121] In Czechoslovakia, a
strike wave began when, on June 1, 1953, thousands of workers in the Škoda factory in Plzeň protested the higher food prices that had resulted from a currency
redenomination.[122] Furthermore, additional strikes took place in various cities
in Bohemia and Moravia.[123] Largest in scale, the East German strike wave started
on June 17, 1953, in Berlin and engulfed fourteen of the fifteen provinces of the
German Democratic Republic (GDR). Up to 1 million East German workers
protested the increase in prices for staples, which was announced at the same
time when higher work norms and lower pay for industrial workers were introduced.[124] The uprising was quelled with the help of Soviet troops, which led to
the killing of hundreds of protesters.

These instances of unrest had several commonalities. One is that in the GDR
and Bulgaria contention came as a surprise to the party and to State Security,

---

[117] AMVR f. 1 op. 1 a. e. 1151 (December 19, 1949), 88–95.
[118] TsDA f. 117 op. 9 a. e. 75 (December 19, 1949), 2–3.
[119] AKRDOPBGDSRSBNA-M f. 13 op. 1 a. e. 1024 (December 16, 1953), 136–38.
[120] AMVR f. 1 op. 1 a. e. 2922 (1953), 5.
[121] AKRDOPBGDSRSBNA-M f. 13 op. 3 a. e. 579 (1953), 6.
[122] Muriel Blaive, *Une déstalinisation manquée: Tchécoslovaquie 1956* (Bruxelles: Éditions
Complexe, 2005), 90–93.
[123] Ivan Pfaff, "Weg mit der Partei!" *Die Zeit*, May 22, 2003, http://www.zeit.de/2003/22/S_86_Vors
pann_Pilsen (accessed April 19, 2022).
[124] Christian F. Ostermann, ed., *Uprising in East Germany, 1953: The Cold War, the German
Question, and the First Major Upheaval Behind the Iron Curtain* (New York: Central European
University Press, 2001).

both of which lacked the sophisticated institutions needed to evaluate the popular mood and to produce accurate warnings about trends in latent discontent that had the potential of leading to the rise of overt discontent.[125] A second parallel is that, lacking such institutions of anticipatory governance, the Eastern European regimes reacted to the surprise eruptions of discontent in the same way, namely, by deploying brute and sometimes deadly force. The final similarity is that the response of the power holders to these episodes of regime crisis consisted of a two-pronged strategy of consumer concessions and the establishment of institutions to help detect latent dissatisfaction prior to its being expressed as overt discontent. These institutions (most effective of which was the analysis of citizen complaints) allowed for the routinized collection of information on popular grievances and for stable anticipatory governance (in contrast to the ad hoc retrospective governance that was needed following surprise mass eruptions of discontent such as the ones that occurred in the GDR or Bulgaria in 1953). The time-consuming process of building these institutions of anticipatory governance could not begin until the regimes had made concessions.

Consumer concessions were expressed primarily through a lowering of prices in the weeks and months following the strikes. In Bulgaria, the initial concessions comprised forgiveness for unfulfilled procurement targets for various agricultural goods as well as improvement in the quality and a lowering of the price of bread.[126] Both of these measures were consistent with popular expectations, as revealed in rumors registered by the party in the summer of 1953.[127] Other policies involved the payment of compensation to owners of small businesses whose property had been nationalized in 1947–1950 and a reduction of the tax burden imposed on craftsmen and itinerant peddlers.[128] The remaining concessions that came in response to the protests of 1953 were unveiled in early 1954, when the leadership announced its goals for the second five-year plan. In January, General Secretary of the Bulgarian Communist Party Valko Chervenkov proclaimed that the chief task for the second five-year plan was a rapid improvement in the standard of living for workers. Specifically, as in all the other countries in the Eastern Bloc, starting with the Soviet Union under Malenkov, this included higher salaries, price reductions, and increases in the quality and variety of

---

[125] AMVR f. 1 op. 1 a. e. 2811 (1954); Armin Mitter, "Die Ereignisse im Juni und Juli 1953 in der DDR," *Aus Politik und Zeitgeschichte*, no. 5 (1991), 31–41.

[126] Migev, *Kolektivizatsiiata na bulgarskoto selo*, 163–65; Vladimir Migev, "Nasiliia, reformi i kompromisi: Kum vuprosa za otrazhenieto v Bulgariia na krizisnite protsesi v suvetskiia blok (1953–1981 g.)," in Vitka Toshkova, Vasilka Tankova, Nikolai Poppetrov, eds., *Istoriiata—profesiia i sudba: Sbornik v chest na 60-godishninata na chlen-korespondent d. ist. n. Georgi Markov* (Sofia: Tangra TanNakRa, 2008), 549–59, at 550.

[127] TsDA f. 1B op. 15 a. e. 585 (July 17, 1953), 2–7.

[128] Vladimir Migev, "Za Aprilskiia plenum—1956 godina i za liberalizatsiiata na rezhima v Bulgariia prez 50-te i 60-te godini na XX vek (Opit za istoricheska eseistika)," *Istoricheski pregled* LXV:1–2 (2009), 187–99, at 193.

consumer goods.[129] Details about these promises were further clarified in the draft directive of the Sixth Party Congress, which took place in March 1954. This document outlined ambitious targets for improving the well-being of ordinary citizens by raising the quality and variety of food products, shoes, and apparel, as well as by increasing the amount of housing stock and enhancing the quality of municipal services.[130]

Another round of policies aimed at raising living standards was unveiled in 1956. At the April Plenum, the party initially announced a lowering of prices and an increase in salaries and pensions, as well as a two-hour reduction of the Saturday workday.[131] Further details on the increase in salaries were provided in December 1956, following the events in Poland and Hungary earlier that year.[132] By the end of 1956, Bulgaria had instituted pensions for members of collective farms (this did not occur in the Soviet Union until 1964), had limited the state procurement targets and raised the procurement prices for agricultural goods, had increased the amount of monthly child subsidies, and had lowered the price of food in workplace canteens.[133] These policies were consistent with popular concerns, as communicated to the leadership through anonymous leaflets,[134] citizen letters,[135] and a brief prepared by Khristo Radevski, who at the time was chief secretary of the Union of Bulgarian Writers.[136] A report by Prime Minister Anton Iugov explicitly acknowledged the role of the Polish and Hungarian events in stimulating regime efforts to improve the standard of living and to eliminate unemployment.[137] The cumulative result of the policies implemented in 1953–1956 was to send a strong signal that the party took the consumption preferences of the population seriously; this stood in marked contrast to the situation in China, where strikes in the 1950s did not have a similar systemwide welfare-enhancing effect.

These measures reflected a new understanding that popular discontent was directly linked to frustrated consumption preferences, as revealed by an October 1956 instruction sent to the heads of the provincial offices of the Ministry of the Interior, with the aim of drawing their attention to the activation of the enemy contingent, whose members called for antiregime activities similar to those in Poland

---

[129] TsDA f. 1B op. 5 a. e. 131 (January 19, 1954), 51–58.
[130] TsDA f. 1B op. 5 a. e. 131 (February 25–March 4, 1954), 25–50.
[131] Kalinova and Baeva, *Bulgarskite prekhodi*, 133.
[132] TsDA f. 1B op. 5 a. e. 239 (December 4, 1956); Valentin Aleksandrov, *Ungarskata revoliutsiia 1956: Vutreshnopoliticheski i mezhdunarodni aspekti* (Sofia: Voenno Izdatelstvo, 2007), 164.
[133] Migev, "Nasiliia, reformi i kompromisi," 552–53.
[134] TsDA f. 378B op. 1 a. e. 757 (November 9, 1956).
[135] TsDA f. 378B op. 1 a. e. 748 (November 10, 1956); TsDA f. 378B op. 1 a. e. 748 (November 17, 1956).
[136] TsDA f. 1B op. 7 a. e. 1778 (November 15, 1956), 1–2.
[137] TsDA f. 317B op. 1 a. e. 135 (December 7, 1956), 4–34.

and Hungary due to "certain difficulties in the provision of bread."[138] Western diplomats arrived at identical conclusions about the connection between consumption and discontent. According to an August 1957 report by British Ambassador Richard Speaight, the new policies reflected decisive government efforts to deflect calls for political liberalization by granting material concessions.[139]

The available evidence indicates that, at least as far as the big cities are concerned, there was a rapid improvement in the quality and variety of consumer goods immediately after 1956.[140] The opening of Sofia's Central Department Store (*Tsentralen universalen magazin*, or TsUM) in 1957 stood as a concrete physical manifestation of the new emphasis on consumption. Western diplomats noted the relative abundance of goods in the capital. In an August 1957 report to the Foreign Office, Ambassador Speaight observed that the availability and variety of goods in stores had improved since the previous year.[141] Speaight's successor, Ambassador Lincoln, noted more generally that communist rule had led to an increase in the standard of living.[142]

Quite atypically, State Security and Western diplomats reached identical assessments of the political effects of improved access to consumer goods. According to State Security, regime efforts to enhance the quality of food served in worker canteens, to raise salaries, and to increase the number of paid vacation days were very popular.[143] State Security opined that the cumulative effect of these policies was increased loyalty to the regime, which made it more difficult for foreign intelligence services to recruit informants in Bulgaria.[144] British Consul Mark Heath similarly remarked in a diplomatic dispatch that the increase in consumer goods had reduced the level of popular discontent.[145] The agreement between British diplomats and Bulgarian State Security analysts about the regime-sustaining effects of policies aimed at promoting consumption is remarkable. As Chapter 5 demonstrates, in the 1960s State Security gradually came to see consumer dissatisfaction as regime-neutral rather than as regime-hostile. This paved the way for the socialist social contract, whereby citizens rewarded the regime with quiescence in exchange for their welfare demands being met.[146]

---

[138] AKRDOPBGDSRSBNA-M f. 1 op. 1 a. e. 3780 (October 29, 1956), 1–3.

[139] Dimitar Dimitrov, *Suvetska Bulgariia prez tri britanski mandata (1956–1963): Iz arkhiva na Foreign Office za subitiia i lichnosti v Bulgariia* (London: BBC, 1994), 19.

[140] Elitsa Stanoeva, "Organizirane na sotsialisticheskata turgoviia v Bulgariia (1954–1963): doktrinalni protivorechiia i mezhduinstitutsionalni naprezheniia," *Sotsiologicheski problemi* XLVII:1–2 (2015), 111–33.

[141] Dimitrov, *Suvetska Bulgariia prez tri britanski mandata*, 17–18.

[142] Dimitrov, *Suvetska Bulgariia prez tri britanski mandata*, 76.

[143] AMVR f. 1 op. 1 a. e. 61 (June 23, 1959), 1–31.

[144] AMVR f. 1 op. 1 a. e. 61 (June 23, 1959), 1–31.

[145] Dimitrov, *Suvetska Bulgariia prez tri britanski mandata*, 120.

[146] Linda Cook and Martin K. Dimitrov, "The Social Contract Revisited: Evidence from Communist and State Capitalist Economies," *Europe–Asia Studies* 69:1 (2017), 8–26.

3.4.4 Dream Monitoring

The final type of mood reporting was the most unusual. The archives reveal at least one instance in which State Security recorded dreams: in 1957, a report, prepared for the chief of the political police (the Third Department of the Sofia Provincial Directorate of State Security), focused on religious dreams (and rumors of such dreams) in villages surrounding Bulgaria's biggest Orthodox monastery that was named after St. Ivan of Rila.[147] Just as peasants were being forced to transfer all their cattle to the collective farms, they publicly discussed dreaming that cows had to be offered to the monks in the Rila Monastery as a token of religious piety.[148] The report is notable for its rarity. Thus far, no other document has been found demonstrating that an authoritarian state sought to catalog the dreams of its citizens.

What can we make of this document, which records dreams that were politically transgressive in the context of a communist state committed to suppressing religiosity? We have no evidence how the information was used, so we do not know whether any individuals were punished for their dreams.[149] All we can say is that State Security did track dreams, at least in the case of Bulgaria. However, the extreme scarcity of such documents, along with the fact that in the above report dreams are interspersed with rumors, attests to the difficulties that the authorities had in using such a source of information.

But a discussion on the tracking of rumors may shed additional light on the limitations of dream monitoring. Rumor reports appear considerably more frequently in the archives. For example, the secret bulletin *Neibu cankao* (内 部参考), aimed at the Chinese leadership, featured 517 reports of rumors and superstitions between 1949 and 1964.[150] Yet, a feature of these rumor reports from the earliest years of communist rule in China suggests the limitations of dream reporting: the Chinese narratives about rumors, similar to the Bulgarian dream report from 1957, were presented at random, without any effort to contextualize them or to show whether they were representative of general trends. An important shift that occurs over time in rumor monitoring is that the information-collection agencies began to orient their reporting toward "typical," or "representative," rumors, which are more useful to regime insiders as their goal is to obtain systematic knowledge about popular dissent (see Chapter 5). In

---

[147] AKRDOPBGDSRSBNA-M f. 13 op. 1 a. e. 567 (1957).

[148] Martin K. Dimitrov, "Dream Reporting," *Cabinet Magazine*, no. 67 (2020), 97–98.

[149] On the fear of such punishment, see Charlotte Beradt, *The Third Reich of Dreams* (Chicago: Quadrangle Books, 1968) and Lisa Wedeen, *Ambiguities of Domination: Politics, Rhetoric, and Symbols in Contemporary Syria* (Chicago: University of Chicago Press, 1999), esp. 68.

[150] Martin K. Dimitrov, "The Political Logic of Media Control in China," *Problems of Post-Communism* 64: 3–4 (May 2017), 121–27.

the end, dreams formed only a small part of the complex array of information that was collected to assist the party-state in its pursuit of omniscience.

3.4.5 Information Transmission and Leadership Decision Making

One of the biggest challenges that a study of information faces is to demonstrate that the leadership makes its decisions in light of reports on dissent that are transmitted to it.[151] In part, the problem reflects deeply entrenched assumptions that leaders are ignorant of, or willfully disregard, all intelligence they receive. Although this is doubtlessly true for some leaders (in both democratic and authoritarian contexts),[152] others actively seek out information and use it when making governance decisions.

We are in the unusually fortunate position of possessing access to the personal archives of Bulgaria's leaders, in particular those of Georgi Dimitrov (who was prime minister in 1946–1949) and of Todor Zhivkov (who stood at the helm of the party-state from 1954 until 1989). This allows us to document the type of intelligence they received. For example, a special daily information bulletin was prepared for Dimitrov. When opposition parties existed, the bulletin focused primarily on their activities.[153] After the opposition was neutralized, the bulletin had a relatively standard structure: briefs produced by the party; intelligence collected by State Security; press highlights; information gathered through the agent network; and a summary of major incidents, including along the border.[154] It is important to stress that Dimitrov was receiving this bulletin even as he was on his deathbed at the Barvikha sanitarium on the outskirts of Moscow—the information was wired from Sofia and then transcribed and transmitted to Dimitrov by his personal assistant.[155] Dimitrov also received a classified Bulletin of Party Information (*Biuletin "Partiina informatsiia"*).[156] A sizable portion of this bulletin focused on the popular mood (*Nastroeniia sred naroda*), examining

---

[151] These reports may be incomplete or inaccurate even in democracies. See Robert Jervis, *Why Intelligence Fails: Lessons from the Iranian Revolution and the Iraq War* (Ithaca, NY: Cornell University Press, 2010) and Thomas Fingar, *Reducing Uncertainty: Intelligence Analysis and National Security* (Stanford, CA: Stanford University Press, 2011).

[152] On democracies, see Joshua Rovner, *Fixing the Facts: National Security and the Politics of Intelligence* (Ithaca, NY: Cornell University Press, 2011) and Amy B. Segart, *Spying Bling: The CIA, the FBI, and the Origins of 9/11* (Princeton, NJ: Princeton University Press, 2009). On autocracies, see Frank Dikötter, *Mao's Great Famine: The History of China's Most Devastating Catastrophe, 1958–1962* (New York: Walker and Company, 2010) and David E. Murphy, *What Stalin Knew: The Enigma of Barbarossa* (New Haven, CT: Yale University Press, 2005).

[153] AVMR f. 1 op. 1 a. e. 267 (1946), 148–84.

[154] TsDA f. 146B op. 4 a. e. 1871 (1949).

[155] See the information on transmission and transcription in TsDA f. 146B op. 4 a. e. 1871 (1949).

[156] TsDA f. 146B op. 2 a. e. 402 (December 4, 1948), 55–56.

issues such as the attitudes of religious devotees and reactions to purges among university professors.[157] The death of Dimitrov did not end the production of these reports.[158] His successor, Valko Chervenkov, received both regular general bulletins as well as specialized briefs on specific problems prepared by State Security. Chervenkov also showed an avid interest in citizen complaints: he demanded daily summaries of letters and periodic reports on recurrent problems raised in petitions.[159]

Zhivkov's personal papers and the archive of his chief-of-staff, which have recently become available at the Central State Archives in Sofia,[160] allow us to reconstruct the types of information that reached the general secretary. Like his predecessors, Zhivkov received regular updates from State Security (weekly digests in normal times; daily reports during periods of crisis), as well as specialized briefs on topics ranging from external intelligence and domestic counter-intelligence to the state of major industrial plants and the incidence of political dissent. The reports were delivered to Zhivkov with the approval of the minister of the interior. But this created agency problems, which might explain why there was frequent turnover among the ministers of the interior in the 1960s. To deal with this issue, there emerged another kind of State Security reporting stream, which bypassed the minister of the interior: the Sixth Department of the Sixth Directorate of State Security transmitted the so-called leadership report directly to the general secretary; as this department monitored extremely sensitive elite targets, such as former general secretaries, former ministers of the interior, and members of the family of the general secretary, its reports were highly valued.[161] Zhivkov also received digests from the Telegraph Agency; prior to the 1970s, the content of these digests focused overwhelmingly on international news.[162] The Ministry of Foreign Affairs supplied him with updates on relevant international developments.[163] The minister of defense dispatched monthly reports on incidents, accidents, and the political mood in the army.[164] But the party was the provider of the most abundant information: provincial party committees sent regular updates on the political mood in the localities (often focusing on rumors

[157] TsDA f. 146B op. 5 a. e. 404 (January 13, 1949), 125–26.
[158] AMVR f. 1 op. 1 a. e. 1118 (1949).
[159] Vasil Ivanov, Valentina Ganchovska, and Krum Vasilev, comps., *Valko Chervenkov prez pogleda na negovite suvremennitsi* (Sofia: Evropresa, 2000), 43, 90–91, 151–53.
[160] TsDA f. 378B and TsDA ChP 174B.
[161] The actual reports have not been preserved. For evidence that Zhivkov read them, see Kostadin Chakarov, *Vtoriia etazh* [sic] (Sofia: n.p., 1990), 101–2; Kostadin Chakarov, *Vtoriiat etazh* (Sofia: Plamuk, 1990), 64; Kostadin Chakarov, *Ot vtoriia etazh do nashestvieto na demokratite* (Sofia: Trud, 2001), 95–96, 104–6. For examples of the content of these reports, see Ivanov, *Shesti otdel*, 212–58, 390–95.
[162] TsDA f. 378B op. 1 a. e. 1084 (1959).
[163] For an example, see TsDA f. 378B op. 1 a. e. 977 (July 19, 1969), 60–70.
[164] TsDA f. 378B op. 1 a. e. 976 (1969–1973); TsDA f. 378B op. 1 a. e. 959 (1973–1975).

about price increases);[165] the Organization Department prepared an overview of the political situation in each province;[166] and the Information-Sociological Group apprised the general secretary of the scope and incidence of popular discontent.[167]

It is difficult to assess systematically to what extent routine decisions were guided by the information that was received because the archival records are incomplete. However, marginal comments on various reports allow us to document how the leadership reacted to the information it received. State Security took very seriously the task of tracking these instructions, given their importance in guiding policy. For example, the State Security Archive contains 162 archival holdings of resolutions by Politburo members, issued between 1947 and 1963, in response to reports about the popular mood, incidents, and public statements.[168] As just one of these documents is 162 pages long,[169] the combined length of the archival holdings containing reports about popular discontent that resulted in reactions from Politburo members in 1947–1963 significantly exceeds 10,000 pages. The communist party took great pains to preserve documents with marginal comments or resolutions (this is the Bulgarian equivalent to *pishi* 批示, which are discussed in the China chapters), thus providing us with evidence of leadership reactions to the information received.

When it comes to major decisions that are relevant to the discussions in this book, we can document that many such decisions were taken in light of the intelligence that was made available to the leadership. For example, the 1953 Politburo instruction to reduce the size of the State Security agent network by one-third was issued in response to a report by the minister of the interior that recommended that such a measure would improve the quality of the informant corps.[170] We also have abundant evidence that attention to consumer frustrations after unexpected eruptions of overt mass discontent was driven by information about consumer dissatisfaction[171]—this was explicitly acknowledged in Politburo discussions and speeches to the Central Committee,[172] in

---

[165] For an example from the province of Smolian, see TsDA f. 378B op. 1 a. e. 1050 (1969).

[166] TsDA f. 378B op. 1 a. e. 1111 (1968).

[167] TsDA f. 378B op. 1 a. e. 1114 (1969).

[168] AMVR f. 1 op. 1 a. e. 1–162 (1947–1963).

[169] AMVR f. 1 op. 5 a. e. 69 (1958).

[170] See the report and the recommendation in TsDA f. 1B op. 64 a. e. 185 (November 8, 1953), 11–87 and the Politburo decision in TsDA f. 1B op. 64 a. e. 185 (November 21, 1953), 1–10.

[171] For examples of such reports issued by the party, see TsDA f. 1B op. 15 a. e. 585 (July 17, 1953), 2–7; for a State Security report, see AKRDOPBGDSRSBNA-M f. 1 op. 1 a. e. 2811 (January 7, 1954); for a personal inspection report, see TsDA f. 1B op. 7 a. e. 1778 (November 15, 1956), 1–2.

[172] TsDA f. 317B op. 1 a. e. 133 (October 31, 1956), 1–16; TsDA f. 317B op. 1 a. e. 135 (December 7, 1956), 4–34.

circulars sent to subnational party committees and State Security offices,[173] and in meetings with small groups of party activists.[174]

In May 1956, Bulgarian State Security engaged in introspection in light of the Twentieth Congress of the Communist Party of the Soviet Union (CPSU) and found that the cult of personality had impacted its practice of intelligence transfer. In response, it decided that it needed to expand the circle of recipients of the information that it previously provided only to the general secretary to include other members of the Politburo; the assumption that, when a report was sent to the general secretary, it would subsequently be shared with the Politburo had proven erroneous.[175] Analysis of the list of recipients of information bulletins produced by State Security reveals that this error was quickly rectified and the group of recipients was expanded in the late 1950s.[176] As we will discuss in Chapter 7, in 1989 the wide distribution of classified information among the top leadership sensitized coup-plotters to economic and political discontent, thus giving them confidence about the likely success of their plan to remove Zhivkov from power.

Overall, then, it is beyond doubt that the leaders of the Bulgarian regime sought information and aimed to reach decisions about repression and concessions in light of the intelligence that was made available to them.

3.5 Voluntary Provision of Information

This book argues that citizen complaints functioned as the main channel for evaluating consumption-driven latent discontent under central planning in communist societies. The unanticipated eruptions of overt discontent as a result of frustrated consumption expectations both domestically and elsewhere in the Eastern Bloc demonstrated to the Bulgarian regime the importance of assessing and addressing this type of discontent when it was still in a latent phase. Citizen complaints provided direct indicators of latent discontent, in contrast to the proxies monitored by State Security (rumors, jokes, and dreams).

In Bulgaria, complaining had received legal sanction with the promulgation of the 1947 Constitution, whose Article 91 stipulates that citizens have the

---

[173] AKRDOPBGDSRSBNA-M f. 1 op. 1 a. e. 3780 (October 29, 1956), 1–3.

[174] Sofia State Archive (DA-Sofia) f. 1V op. 23 a. e. 26 (November 2, 1956); Sofia State Archive (DA-Sofia) f. 3V op. 13 a. e. 2 (March 13, 1957), 92–96.

[175] AKRDOPBGDSRSBNA-M f. 1 op. 2 a. e. 208 (May 3, 1956), 1–23.

[176] See AMVR f. 1 op. 5 a. e. 69 (1958) for a list of Politburo and Central Committee recipients of twenty-five State Security information reports; AMVR f. 1 op. 10 a. e. 206 (1966), 166–67 for a list of the recipients of the Information Bulletin of the Ministry of the Interior; AMVR f. 1 op. 10 a. e. 698 (1968) for a list of Politburo recipients of Information No. 701 to Information No. 800 from the Committee for State Security.

right to make requests, lodge complaints, and file petitions. Yet, legal guarantees are insufficient to incentivize citizens to complain, especially under conditions of harsh terror. In a similar vein, scholars of petitioning under Stalinism and Nazism have emphasized that the majority of complaints were denunciatory.[177] Therefore, in light of the existing literature, we would expect that if we were to find information on complaints in Bulgaria during the initial years of repressive communist rule, these complaints would be denunciatory as well. Moreover, as denunciations, especially under conditions of terror, can transmit false or exaggerated information, they would not be useful to the regime as a tool for providing accurate assessments of latent discontent.

Zhivkov's personal archive produces a major surprise that contradicts expectations created by the literature, namely, citizens not only wrote nondenunciatory letters, but also it was information about such letters, rather than summaries of denunciatory complaints, that was systematized and transmitted to the top leadership. For example, in November 1956, as repression was being unleashed in Bulgaria in order to preclude a reprise of the Hungarian events, Todor Zhivkov was presented with a digest prepared by the Office of Personal Letters of the Central Committee.[178] The digest distilled the content of noteworthy letters into three categories: twenty-seven suggestions for improving the material and cultural standard of living of the workers; twenty-seven characteristic statements; and nine questions about problems of rural life (eight letters raised issues of no import and three anonymous hostile letters contained offensive antiregime language like "greetings, thick necks").[179] Of the twenty-seven suggestions, twenty-four concerned welfare and benefits. Of the twenty-seven characteristic statements, twenty were complaints about low salaries, the process of land collectivization, the luxurious lives of the leaders, and the difficult lot of ordinary people. Finally, all nine questions about conditions in villages focused on the low quality of life, excessive procurement, and insufficient compensation. In short, citizen letters, at least those that were communicated to the top leadership by the Central Committee, overwhelmingly centered on consumer frustrations rather than denunciations (the digest noted a mere six letters denouncing cadre corruption in the pile of eighty letters analyzed; as discussed in Chapter 4, the share of denunciations in Bulgaria in the 1950s was significantly lower than that in China).

The letters were surprisingly frank. One dated November 29, 1956, asks: "How long will you keep thinking that if you are doing well, the people are also doing

[177] Sheila Fitzpatrick and Robert Gellately, "Introduction to the Practices of Denunciation in Modern European History," *The Journal of Modern History* 68:4 (December 1996), 747–67.

[178] TsDA f. 378B op. 1 a. e. 803 (December 1, 1956), 175–80.

[179] TsDA f. 378B op. 1 a. e. 804 (November 11, 1956), 149.

well? The situation of the people is difficult. We have become destitute."[180] Another states: "Tell the comrades in the Central Committee that the people are embittered toward the people's government. Demagoguery should stop and life should be improved quickly."[181] Letters alerted the leadership about the shortages of bread and the miserable existence of ordinary citizens.[182] An anonymous communication dated November 12, 1956, and signed "from the entire Bulgarian people" plainly asks: "Don't you see that people are mired in misery and the peasants dress like beggars? Everything people produce is taken away from them by force, land collectivization is carried out by beatings, etc."[183] The letter concludes by asserting: "Workers cannot live on those wages."[184] The need to raise compensation and lower prices are recurrent tropes in such communications.

One noteworthy feature of the letters digest is the explicit link that complainants drew between latent and overt discontent. One letter warns that "[w]hen the voice of the people is not heard, then we get to the Hungarian mess."[185] Another states that "[p]eople are so anxious that they will rise up with their sticks as soon as someone claps his hands."[186] A candidate party member implores power holders to "[r]aise the salaries of all workers now, unless you want to only raise them once things become the same as in Hungary and Poland and you have lost the people—and party members, nonmembers, and everyone else rises against us [the party], as occurred in Hungary."[187] One citizen concludes matter-of-factly: "[c]onsidering the high level of unemployment, measures need to be taken to avoid a Hungarian scenario."[188] Noteworthy is an ultimatum "from the entire Bulgarian people" dated November 1, 1956, that states: "Popular discontent has already boiled over; to avoid victims, we have conditions: . . . stop the formation of agricultural cooperatives; . . . raise low salaries; . . . conduct general free and secret elections that include the banned parties."[189] Finally, an anonymous letter deemed hostile and thus forwarded to State Security issues a warning: "Comrade Secretary, The contagious disease from Hungary and Poland is also coming to Bulgaria. . . . Your only salve [sic] would be to hit the road to the Urals."[190] These letters, along with State Security reporting on consumer discontent, guided decisions to increase the availability of consumer goods and reduce prices.

[180] TsDA f. 378B op. 1 a. e. 803 (1956), 29.
[181] TsDA f. 378B op. 1 a. e. 803 (1956), 47.
[182] TsDA f. 378B op. 1 a. e. 804 (1956), 138–139B.
[183] TsDA f. 378B op. 1 a. e. 804 (1956), 156–156B.
[184] TsDA f. 378B op. 1 a. e. 804 (1956), 156–156B.
[185] TsDA f. 378B op. 1 a. e. 803 (1956), 177.
[186] TsDA f. 378B op. 1 a. e. 803 (1956), 179.
[187] TsDA f. 378B op. 1 a. e. 803 (1956), 50B.
[188] TsDA f. 378B op. 1 a. e. 804 (1956), 75.
[189] TsDA f. 378B op. 1 a. e. 804 (1956), 148–148B.
[190] TsDA f. 378B op. 1 a. e. 804 (1956), 154.

Because these letters were read so closely, it is not surprising that the regime understood the link that the citizens themselves had highlighted between frustrated consumption preferences and the transformation of latent popular discontent into potentially destabilizing overt political dissent. Although the regime reacted to unanticipated public eruptions of dissatisfaction with increased social-spending commitments, those one-off responses were inefficient. Gradually, an awareness of the utility of ongoing assessments of latent discontent through systematic analysis of citizen complaints emerged. The problem was two-fold—how to encourage citizens to complain, and once complaints were lodged, how to make sure that they were analyzed not only at the Office of Personal Letters at the Central Committee but also at all levels of the party-state. As we will discuss in Chapter 5, these problems were resolved in the 1960s, thus giving regime insiders extraordinary insight into latent discontent.

3.6 Information Gathering among Minorities

Ethnic minorities constituted nearly 15 percent of the population of Bulgaria in 1946, thus presenting significant penetration obstacles. The main minorities at the time of the establishment of communist rule were Turks (9.6 percent); Bulgarian-speaking Muslims, or *pomaks* (1.8 percent); Roma (2.4 percent); Armenians (0.3 percent); and Jews (0.8 percent). The communist leadership deployed varying policies toward these different ethnoreligious groups. Beyond co-optation, minorities could be managed through exclusion, assimilation, or accommodation.[191]

3.6.1 Techniques of Co-Optation: Elite Recruitment, Job Assignments, and Selective Rewards

Like all autocracies, communist regimes used elite recruitment, elite job assignments, and the selective granting of rewards as strategies for ensuring compliance by minorities. We can collect data that allow us to measure the use of techniques of co-optation in communist Bulgaria. But before we discuss what the data reveal, we should define the above three concepts explicitly and provide empirical examples of their use.

Policies of elite recruitment included training that allowed members of the minority groups to eventually assume positions within the leading echelons of the

[191] Harris Mylonas, *The Politics of Nation-Building: Making Co-Nationals, Refugees, and Minorities* (New York: Cambridge University Press, 2012).

party-state. The main mechanism for providing such training was inclusion on the roster of party members who had been approved to enroll at elite party academies, most prestigious of which was the Central Party School. Cadres groomed for high-level work were dispatched to party institutes in the Soviet Union. Those who had no chance of being assigned to elite positions were directed to provincial party schools or to party academies for minorities. This applied especially to the Turks. If they were sent to the Central Party School, they were either enrolled in brief training courses or assigned to the Agricultural Division; neither path positioned them for a career in the top echelons of power.[192] The party exhibited distrust of the Turks, especially when compared to the Jews and the Armenians who had proved their bona fides during the guerrilla warfare of the precommunist period.

Elite job assignments involved being granted a coveted spot on the central *nomenklatura* list, such as an employee of a Central Committee department; a member of the editorial board of one of the central media outlets; directorship of a large state firm, an economic association, or an industrial committee; a posting in the foreign service; or placement in a leadership position on a provincial party committee. These posts were desirable because they conferred high status, which meant not only superior compensation but also, more importantly under the planned economy, nonmonetary benefits that were only available to the top *nomenklatura*, such as access to high-end housing, special shops, and luxurious vacation homes. Moreover, unscrupulous members of the *nomenklatura* could use their positions to extort additional material benefits in the form of bribes for facilitating some kind of favor.

The internal hierarchy of rewards in autocracies has not been discussed in the literature. In Bulgaria, these were typically administered in the form of medals, appointments as a delegate to a party congress, or a representative at the National Assembly. These honorifics constituted public acknowledgment of the value that the regime placed on individual members of the various minorities. The privileges bestowed on the recipient and her family varied. Some rewards were more prestigious than others: individuals who were decorated for assisting the party in the fight against Nazism had considerably higher status than those who received medals for achievements in agricultural productivity (say, in growing potatoes, as occurred in 1956 when two such medals were awarded to Bulgarian Muslims from the village of Arda in the Smolian region).[193] Positions as a party congress delegate or a National Assembly representative also conferred high prestige. Because many different types of rewards existed, they functioned as a

---

[192] For a roster of Turks assigned to short-term training courses, see TsDA f. 1B op. 8 a. e. 6510 (January 18, 1964), 1. For a roster of Turks assigned to the Agricultural Section of the Central Party School, see TsDA f. 312B op. 1 a. e. 315 (March 26, 1962), 1, 4.

[193] TsDA f. 1B op. 6 a. e. 2942 (August 8, 1956).

Table 3.2 Elite Recruitment, Elite Job Assignments, and Selective Rewards
for Minorities in Bulgaria, 1945–1970 (per 1,000 members of the minority)

Minority	Recruitment	Job Assignments	Rewards
Jewish	18.06	11.7	61.8
Armenian	1.2	0.23	3.6
Bulgarian Muslim	0.83	0.023	2.2
Turkish	0.85	0.06	0.66
Roma	0.006	0.006	0.006

Source: Calculated by the author on the basis of a large corpus of TsDA and AKRDOPBGDSRSBNA files.

somewhat broader tool of minority management than elite recruitment or job
assignments.

Table 3.2 presents statistical data on the recruitment, job assignments, and rewarding of minorities during the initial decades of communist rule in Bulgaria
(1945–1970). The statistics were calculated on the basis of information extracted
by the author from 312 decisions of the Secretariat and the Politburo of the
Central Committee of the Bulgarian Communist Party that were made between
1945 and 1970 (all files are from the Bulgarian Central State Archives [TsDA]).
Normalizing the raw data involved taking into account the size of each minority
and reporting values per 1,000 members of each of the main minority groups.
Minority size, which was calculated as of 1946, remained relatively stable during
this period, as a result of emigration, intermarriage, and the recording of some
members of the minority as Bulgarians, except for the Jewish minority, whose
size declined by 89 percent shortly after the establishment of the communist regime due to emigration to Israel in 1944–1948; for this reason, 1950 population
data are used in the case of the Bulgarian Jews.[194]

As Table 3.2 reveals, the Turks were especially disadvantaged by comparison
with the Jews and the Armenians with regard to co-optation through recruitment, job assignments, and rewards. The Bulgarian Muslims were in a comparable situation to the Turks (and the Roma were even worse), but the relevant
comparison groups for the Turks were the Jews and the Armenians, who both
had kin abroad and external homelands.[195] As resources were limited and neither the Bulgarian Muslims nor the Roma presented an imminent threat, the
party ignored them. This decision was rational. The logic driving the treatment

---

[194] Population data from AKRDOPBGDSRSBNA-M f. 2 op. 1 a. e. 1832 (1950), 2–6 and
AKRDOPBGDSRSBNA-M f. 2 op. 1 a. e. 1740 (1951), 4.

[195] On the importance of kin and external homelands, see Mylonas, *The Politics of Nation-Building.*

of the Turks was less clear-cut. For this reason, the remainder of this section will discuss the Turkish minority.

3.6.2 Policies toward the Turkish Minority, 1944–1952

From the very beginning of communist rule, the party was unsure about how to approach the Turkish minority. In February 1945, Georgi Dimitrov instructed the Central Committee: "Minorities should be given full rights, but we need to be careful with the Turks."[196] The following year, when evaluating the elections that had just concluded in the province of Ruse, State Security produced a perceptive assessment that stated: "In the past, reflecting the pressure and the empty promises of those in power, the Turks overwhelmingly voted for the government. Similarly, in the current election, the vast majority of them voted for the communist party. Support for the party from the Turks in this province helped us avoid a catastrophic electoral outcome. Their vote for the party should not, however, be understood as a 'government dowry'; rather, it was a conscious decision. The explanatory work conducted among them by the party was very significant. Our party was the first and remains the only one to have sent to them female Turkish canvassers and canvassing groups consisting of Turkish youth. The result of this canvassing work, as well as the genuinely equal treatment of the Turkish minority by the government and the party, generated their support during the election."[197]

The initial decade of communist rule produced major fluctuations in the approach toward the Turks. The period during which opposition parties existed (1944–1948) was characterized by relative tolerance of the Turkish minority. Policies of accommodation included special radio broadcasts in Turkish;[198] allowing members of the minority to enroll at Sofia University and at the State Polytechnic without sitting for entrance exams;[199] and the printing of a newspaper and various brochures in Turkish.[200] Efforts were made to develop plans for co-opting those Turks who were communist party members.[201] These policies changed abruptly in 1948–1949, when the Central Committee adopted the position that the Turkish minority was a foreign entity ("a non-Bulgarian population that constitutes a persistent ulcer for our country," in the formulation of Prime Minister Georgi Dimitrov) and should therefore be encouraged to

---

[196] TsDA f. 1B op. 6 a. e. 32 (February 6, 1945), 5.
[197] AMVR f. 1 op. 8 a. e. 110 (October 29, 1946), 41–42.
[198] TsDA f. 1B op. 7 a. e. 460 (1945), 2.
[199] TsDA f. 136 op. 1 a. e. 442 (1947).
[200] TsDA f. 1B op. 15 a. e. 207 (1947), 1.
[201] TsDA f. 1B op. 25 a. e. 66 (1945), 1–120; TsDA f. 146B op. 4 a. e. 727 (1945), 1–2.

emigrate to Turkey;[202] Bulgarians were to settle in the depopulated border areas previously inhabited by Turks.[203] Perhaps unsurprisingly, mood reports produced by the party registered low enthusiasm among the Turkish minority for participation in the compulsory National Day parades in 1950.[204] This apathy was displayed in the midst of a campaign in 1949–1951 to encourage emigration so as to reduce the size of the minority by one-fifth.[205]

In March 1951, a delegation from Azerbaijan (a Turkic-speaking Soviet republic) visited Bulgaria and remarked on the underrepresentation of the Bulgarian Turks in the higher echelons of the party-state. The Azeri delegation produced a data-rich report, highlighting that even in regions with a heavy concentration of Turks, minority cadres were either completely absent from the provincial party committees or else they were only nominally represented. Turkish cadres were not recruited for elite positions, as demonstrated by the presence of only one Turkish student at the Central Party School. Consequently, Turks were seriously underrepresented among Central Committee staff; in the leadership of the trade unions; and on the editorial boards of the central media. The delegation concluded that neglect of the task of training and assigning Turkish cadres to leading positions in the party-state and within firms and industrial associations represented a "serious political error by the party organizations in Bulgaria."[206] The report sent alarm bells to the top leadership. In response, the Central Committee Department for Work Among the Turkish Population was promptly established in April 1951; in addition, similar departments were created in three provinces with a high concentration of Turks.[207] In 1952, the decision was made to allow Turks (and representatives of other minorities) to serve in the army, thus sending a signal that members of the minorities should not be presumed to be fifth columns of foreign countries.[208]

3.6.3 Monitoring of the Turkish Minority

Efforts to penetrate the Turks were postponed during the initial years of communist rule. However, a 1951 report revealed that although the Turkish minority

[202] TsDA f. 1B op. 5 a. e. 19 (January 4, 1948), 17.

[203] TsDA f. 1B op. 6 a. e. 653 (August 18, 1949), 4–5.

[204] Daniel Vachkov, *Avarii i katastrofi: Khronika na sotsialisticheskata industriia* (Sofia: Ciela, 2017), 49.

[205] On encouraging emigration, see TsDA f. 1B op. 6 a. e. 983 (August 3, 1950), 5–7 and TsDA f. 1B op. 5 a. e. 79 (1950), 39–44.

[206] Document reproduced in *Politicheska istoriia na suvremenna Bulgariia: Sbornik dokumenti*, vol. 2 (Sofia: Central State Archives, 2018), 496–503, at 500.

[207] TsDA f. 1B op. 6 a. e. 1298 (1951), 37–43. In 1958, the department was renamed the Department for Work Among National Minorities; in 1962, it was dissolved.

[208] TsDA f. 1B op. 6 a. e. 1590 (1952), 110.

constituted 8.3 percent of the population of the country, its members made up only 0.6 percent of the enemy contingent registered in the State Security operational-reporting system; this was understood not as a sign that very few Turks harbored hostility toward the communist regime but rather as evidence of the poor legibility of the minority for the secret police.[209]

The first obstacle was linguistic. Among Bulgaria's minorities, only the Turks and the Roma were linguistically impenetrable, but the dispersed settlement of the Roma (along with the absence of an external homeland) limited the urgency of developing an extensive agent network to monitor them. Specific evidence of the party's lack of interest in penetrating the Roma is provided by a report that reveals that, as of 1950, State Security relied on only two agents to keep track of the minority's 167,481 members.[210] But no such lackadaisical attitude could be maintained toward the Turks. Thus, State Security made a decision in 1952 to activate its agent work among the Turkish minority.[211] Nonetheless, when evaluating its informant network in 1959, the secret police determined that "the number of agents in the operational-reporting system is not small, but considering that the majority of agents are semi-literate and unable to write in Bulgarian, there are great difficulties in accepting their reports."[212]

Apart from language, religion created a second line of impenetrability. One of the main findings of the 1951 Azeri report was that the imams were enjoying extraordinary sway over the Turkish community. In the ensuing decade, the party-state proved incapable of limiting the influence of Muslim clerics. In the evaluation of State Security, the majority of the muftis and a sizable proportion of the imams were hostile to the communist regime as of 1958.[213] The main indicator of the impact of the clerics was the high degree of religiosity among members of the minority. The party regarded imams as harmful, as they prevented it from penetrating the Turks. For example, claiming that bumper tobacco crops reflected the benevolence of Allah rather than advances in agricultural techniques, the imams would organize collective prayers of gratitude to Allah that were attended even by party members.[214] Another sign of the impact of religiosity was the adoption of customs that marked individuals as followers of Islam. One example is male circumcision, which was universally practiced

---

[209] Percentages calculated by the author from raw data in AKRDOPBGDSRSBNA-M f. 1 op. 5 a. e. 5 (1951), 248–82.

[210] AKRDOPBGDSRSBNA-M f. 13 op. 1 a. e. 759 (1950), 66–67.

[211] AKRDOPBGDSRSBNA-M f. 13 op. 1 a. e. 970 (1952), 5–7.

[212] AKRDOPBGDSRSBNA-M f. 2 op. 1 a. e. 2057 (1959), 8–11, at 9–10.

[213] A 1958 report stipulates that 12 of the 18 muftis (and 1,085 of the 2,798 imams) had hostile attitudes toward the regime. See AKRDOPBGDSRSBNA-M f. 13 op. 1 a. e. 1685 (1958), 15–21, at 15.

[214] As stated in a report on the activities of imams, which was prepared by the National Minorities Department of the Central Committee of the Bulgarian Communist Party. See TsDA f. 1B op. 91 a. e. 1394 (1958), 1–5.

by Muslims in Bulgaria and was understood by the party as a manifestation of Turkish national identity.[215] Veiling was seen as a further instance of a religiously inflected custom. Although State Security boasted about its successes in limiting the incidence of veiling in preparation for celebration of the fifteenth anniversary of the establishment of communist rule in 1959,[216] the practice proved impossible to eradicate and it was a persistent irritant for the regime well past the 1950s.[217] The minority remained as illegible and as distinct from the ethnic majority as it had been at the time of the establishment of the communist regime. In the eyes of the party leadership, this situation called for a radical solution, which will be discussed in Chapter 5.

3.7 Conclusion: From Crisis-Driven Governance to Anticipatory Rule

The focus of this chapter has been on the creation of the institutions of a communist information state and the rise of an initial awareness of the need to monitor latent discontent. Two distinct subperiods can be identified during the 1944–1958 timespan. The initial one, which lasted from 1944 to 1953, was a time of intense violence, when all available information-gathering resources were directed toward identifying and eliminating various regime enemies. A confluence of domestic and international crises in the first half of 1953 forced the party-state to shift its focus to placating unrest by satisfying the consumption preferences of the population. The period from the second half of 1953 until the late 1950s was characterized by an increased awareness (strengthened by the 1956 crises in Hungary and Poland) that assessing and satisfying popular consumption preferences were both important for regime stability. It marked the end of de-Stalinization and the definitive transition to a low-repression equilibrium that enabled the creation of the institutions needed for the systematic collection of information on popular discontent. These institutions enabled the transition to anticipatory rule, which will be analyzed in Chapter 5.

---

[215] Since the 1950s, the party-state sought to limit the prevalence of circumcision. As part of these efforts, the Grand Mufti's Office was required to issue a circular to the provincial mufti offices stipulating that circumcision could only be performed by qualified doctors in clinics (AKRDOPBGDSRSBNA-M f. 1 op. 2 a. e. 212 [1960], 17–17A). However, the circular was not effective in reducing the rates of circumcision.

[216] AKRDOPBGDSRSBNA-M f. 1 op. 1 a. e. 4365 (1959), 4–7 and AKRDOPBGDSRSBNA-M f. 2 op. 1 a. e. 2101 (1959), 1–4.

[217] AKRDOPBGDSRSBNA-M f. 1 op. 12 a. e. 414 (1982), 150–52.

4

Monitoring and Counteracting Dissent in China, 1949–1958

This chapter uses the case of China to extend the main arguments of this book about the origins and evolution of systems for the involuntary extraction and the voluntary provision of information developed in Chapters 1–3. Although differences between Eastern Europe and China exist, they are of degree, not of kind. Most consequential is that China experienced the highest structural constraints of any communist regime, except Laos. This means that its capacity to develop institutions that enabled the systematic nationwide involuntary extraction of information on popular discontent was limited. Notwithstanding, China faced similar problems of intelligence gathering during regime inception and succeeded in establishing mechanisms for the involuntary extraction of information that were nearly identical to those created in Eastern Europe. However, structural constraints impacted the operation of these institutions. In particular, responsiveness to citizen complaints requires high state capacity. Thus, one notable difference between the two models is that responsiveness in China was extremely limited during the initial decade of communist rule and, consequently, the amount of voluntary transfer of information through citizen complaints was exceptionally low. Another effect of low state capacity was that minority legibility was lower in China than it was in Eastern Europe.

The survival of all autocracies depends on their capacity to eliminate opponents (by meting out repression) and to co-opt supporters (by demonstrating responsiveness to their needs). Communist party-states are no exception. These twin goals are pursued throughout the lifespan of communist autocracies, although the emphasis varies, with most energy devoted to the violent elimination of opponents during the stage of regime establishment and consolidation and the emphasis gradually shifting toward the co-optation of increasingly wider segments of the population during the stage of regime maturation. The pursuit of both goals requires detailed information, which allows repression and responsiveness to be more efficiently deployed. The lack of information means that repression will be indiscriminate (targeting entire social or ethnic groups, rather than individuals within these groups) and that responsiveness will be limited. Although information shortages occur during regime establishment in all autocracies, they are particularly pronounced in communist party-states, where state

Dictatorship and Information. Martin K. Dimitrov, Oxford University Press. © Oxford University Press 2023.
DOI: 10.1093/oso/9780197672921.003.0004

building is complicated by violent regime origins through war or revolution. Structural constraints further exacerbate these shortages, although they can be mitigated by sui generis pre-existing institutional legacies.

This chapter is organized as follows. Section 4.1 reviews the extraordinary structural constraints to be overcome in China when creating institutions for the collection of information. This section also investigates the extent to which historical legacies of information gathering might mitigate these constraints. Sections 4.2 and 4.3, respectively, focus on how enemies were identified and sub-sequently repressed. Section 4.4 explores the extent to which the Chinese party-state succeeded in assessing and satisfying the welfare needs of the population during its first decade of existence, and it finds that voluntary transmission and efforts to respond to consumer needs were limited, though not entirely absent. Section 4.5 is dedicated to the question of the blind spot of minority penetration, which is analyzed based on the case of Tibet prior to the 1959 Uprising. The concluding Section 4.6 argues that a general trend toward rationalization and creating functioning institutions of an information state was underway during the initial decade of communist rule—but progress was disrupted by subsequent calamities such as the Great Leap Forward and the Cultural Revolution, whose impact on information gathering will be discussed in Chapter 6.

4.1 Structural Constraints to Information Gathering

China faced severe structural constraints at the time of regime establishment. Size, topography, ethnolinguistic heterogeneity, low bureaucratic quality (measured by levels of illiteracy and experience with organizing a census), and shortage of ad-ministrative personnel all negatively impacted information gathering. The sec-tion reviews these deficiencies and discusses the extent to which prerevolutionary institutional legacies mitigated structural impediments and helped enhance the capacity of the Chinese state to collect information on popular discontent.

4.1.1 Size and Topography

With a territory of 9.6 million square kilometers, China has the second-largest landmass of any communist state in history (the size of the Soviet Union was 22.4 million square kilometers). Following the liberation of Tibet in 1951, the Chinese Communist Party (CCP) assumed control over the entirety of this terri-tory. A revolutionary party that only had experience governing on a small scale in the base areas now had to project power over a landmass that was approximately 100 times the size of the most successful soviets (Jiangxi and Yan'an) that it had administered prior to 1949. Forbidding topographical features—high mountains, deserts, and permafrost—complicated the task of penetrating the entire territory of the state, especially when taking into account the poor pre-existing infrastructure. One Western source reports that as of 1945, China possessed only 27,000 kilometers of railways, 13,000 of which were in Manchuria.[1] Official Chinese statistics paint an even more dispiriting picture: in 1949, there were 21,800 kilometers of railways.[2] As a result, reaching outlying areas was especially challenging: it is worth noting that Beijing was not connected to Tibet by rail until 2006.

4.1.2 Low Bureaucratic Quality

The new regime had to confront significant limitations when trying to scale up to a national level the local governance practices that it had pioneered in the base areas. This book argues that we can evaluate bureaucratic quality at the time of regime establishment by assessing whether a country fulfills two minimum requirements for administrative competence: a record of a census conducted prior to communist takeover and a moderate level of illiteracy (below 25 percent). Despite efforts dating back to the Qing dynasty to count the population, the first nationwide census (with a barebones four questions) was not carried out until 1953, with Soviet assistance.[3] Reliable assessments of the levels of illiteracy at the time of regime establishment are difficult to find, in part because of the lack of a pre-existing nationwide census. However, both Chinese and Western estimates place illiteracy in 1949 at about 80 percent.[4] Levels of illiteracy declined to below 25 percent either in 1982 (according to Chinese sources) or in 1990 (according to UNESCO).[5] In other words, China did not reach a level of illiteracy comparable to that of Bulgaria at the time of regime inception until the fourth decade of communist governance.

Classified materials further attest that improvements in literacy were difficult to achieve. Statistical data indicate that a full decade after establishment of the regime, urban workers (a higher-status group than rural residents, and thus more

---

[1] Norton S. Ginsburg, "Manchurian Railway Development," *Far Eastern Quarterly* 8:4 (August 1949), 398–411. For comparison purposes, China had 2.8 kilometers of railways per 1,000 square kilometers of territory in 1945; Bulgaria had 33.6 kilometers in 1946; and Czechoslovakia 102.3 kilometers in 1946 (Brian R. Mitchell, *International Historical Statistics: Europe 1750–1993* [London: Macmillan Reference, 1998], 678).

[2] Li Xiaojun, ed., *Shudu Zhongguo 60 nian (1949–2009)* (Beijing: Shehui Kexue Wenxian Chubanshe, 2009), 7.

[3] Arunabh Ghosh, *Making It Count: Statistics and Statecraft in the Early People's Republic of China* (Princeton, NJ: Princeton University Press, 2020).

[4] The Chinese estimate is 80 percent. See Li, *Shudu Zhongguo 60 nian*, 181. The Western estimate is 80.6 percent. See UNESCO Division of Statistics, "Adult Illiteracy in China," *Statistical Issues*, STE-14 (January 1994), 2.

[5] In 1982, 22.8 percent according to Li, *Shudu Zhongguo 60 nian*, 181. In 1990, 22.2 percent according to UNESCO, "Adult Illiteracy in China," 2.

likely to be literate) remained at a low cultural level (*wenhua chengdu* 文化程度): as revealed by a classified report for the leadership, among the 20 million workers in twenty-one provinces and cities who were evaluated in November 1959, as many as 21.75 percent were illiterate; 50.55 percent had a beginner's cultural level (*chuji* 初级); and only 1.41 percent had the cultural level of someone with an associate's degree (*dazhuan* 大专).[6]

We possess no longitudinal data to assess reductions over time of levels of illiteracy in the Chinese bureaucracy. However, taking into account the extraordinarily low rates of overall literacy in China at the time of communist takeover and the fact that communist loyalists were more likely to be rural residents (and thus illiterate), we cannot assume universal literacy in the Chinese bureaucracies at the time of regime establishment. Classified reports to the leadership indicate that levels of illiteracy in November 1959 stood at between 1.9 percent and 40 percent in fourteen ministerial *xitong* (系统), which included the ministry itself and its subordinate enterprises (see Table 4.1). Although the data do not

Table 4.1 Levels of Illiteracy in Chinese Ministerial *xitong*, 1959

Ministry	Level of Illiteracy
Coal	40%
Agriculture	33.52%
Forestry	27.7%
Construction	26.91%
Textile	24%
Metallurgy	21.7%
Transportation	19.94%
Light industry	15.9%
Chemical industry	13%
Railways	12.3%
Geology	4.91%
Hydropower	4.48%
Petroleum	2.5%
Post office	1.9%

Source: Neibu cankao, no. 2955 (January 8, 1960), 15.

---

[6] *Neibu cankao*, no. 2955 (January 8, 1960), 15.

distinguish between bureaucrats and regular workers, such elevated levels of illiteracy in these ministerial *xitong* do not inspire confidence in the general bureaucratic capacity of the Chinese state.

Perhaps most revealing are statistics on illiteracy in the CCP itself. In 1949, only 0.92 percent of party members had a high school diploma or higher—and fully 69 percent were illiterate. By 1958, illiteracy had declined to 16.51 percent, but the share of those with high school and university degrees still stood at a low 4.12 percent.[7] These statistics indicate the limited capacity of the CCP to staff the bureaucracy with high-quality personnel during the initial decade of communist governance.

4.1.3 Shortage of Bureaucratic Personnel

China also experienced a problem that is common to all autocracies at the time of regime establishment: a difficulty finding a sufficient number of loyalists to staff the numerous branches of the bureaucratic apparatus necessary for effective governance. In communist regimes, a basic choice following the takeover of power involves the extent to which existing personnel can be purged from the bureaucracy without completely hollowing it out. This calculus is driven at least in part by the stock of available sympathizers, which was exceedingly low in China.

One way to measure the shortage of personnel is to assess communist party membership. This is a reasonable proxy because party members, as opposed to nonmembers, are more likely to be recruited into bureaucratic positions. The severity of the problem is illustrated by internal data on party membership in Beijing. Although their ranks increased 10-fold from 1945, a mere 3,376 underground CCP members existed on the eve of the takeover at the end of 1948 in what would become the capital of the communist state.[8] The size of the party in Beijing was paltry even if we add the corps of 5,000 youth sympathizers (*waiwei zuzhi* 外围组织).[9] The situation was dispiriting in China as a whole as well, with only 4.2 million party members when the new communist state was declared on October 1, 1949 (0.7 percent of the population).[10] Although by the end of 1949, the CCP claimed 4.49 million members (0.8 percent of the population),[11]

---

[7] Calculations based on Zhonggong Zhongyang Zuzhi Bu, *Zhongguo gongchandang dangnei tongji ziliao huibian, 1921–2000* (Beijing: Zhonggong Zhongyang Zuzhi Bu Xinxi Guanli Zhongxin, 2002), 50–51.

[8] Beijing Shi Difang Zhi Bianzuan Weiyuanhui, *Beijing zhi: Gongchandang juan: Gongchandang zhi* (Beijing: Beijing Chubanshe, 2012), 7.

[9] *Beijing zhi: Gongchandang juan*, 7.

[10] Calculated from *Zhongguo gongchandang dangnei tongji ziliao huibian, 1921–2000*, 72–73.

[11] Zhonggong Zhongyang Zuzhi Bu, *Zhongguo gongchandang dangnei tongji ziliao huibian, 1921–2010* (Beijing: Dangjian Duwu Chubanshe, 2011), 7.

this still proved woefully inadequate for staffing the bureaucracies of the new communist state. A relevant comparison is the size of the communist party in Bulgaria, which was equivalent to 3.7 percent of the population in 1945 (when the communists were still members of a coalition government) and grew to 7.1 percent of the population in 1949, when the opposition parties were banned and the communists were ready to practice single-party rule.[12]

The shortage of personnel required tough decisions in terms of limiting the purges of Guomindang (KMT) staff. For example, the CCP found only 671 cadres to staff the Beijing police upon the takeover of the city in January 1949.[13] Although another 631 cadres were added between February and April 1949,[14] the available manpower was highly insufficient to operate the Beijing police, which had a personnel allocation (*bianzhi* 编制) of 13,890 as of December 1946.[15] These shortages necessitated the retention of 5,000 former KMT police (*jiu jing* 旧警) as of December 1949.[16]

The personnel shortage in Beijing was symptomatic of a nationwide problem. Namely, although the Ministry of Public Security (MPS) received a personnel allocation of 190,000, the shortfall was two-thirds of its allotted *bianzhi* in June 1950.[17] Moreover, of the 72,684 officers employed by the MPS at the end of 1950, only 1,636 were party cadres.[18] These statistics highlight the extraordinary governance challenges faced by the CCP at the time of regime establishment.

4.1.4 Prerevolutionary Institutional Endowments

The constraints to building a communist information state presented by size, topography, and bureaucratic quality were relaxed to a certain extent by the positive legacies of other prerevolutionary institutions. Some of these institutions had emerged many centuries before communist rule. In the area of voluntary provision, for example, routinized petitioning has a long history that dates back at least to the Tang dynasty (618–907).[19] Another example is the *baojia* (保甲) system for community supervision, which can be traced to the Song dynasty

---

[12] Calculations based on Stoian Tsvetanski, *Organizatsionno razvitie na BKP, 1944–1986: Istoriko-statisticheski analiz* (Sofia: Institut po Istoriia na BKP pri TsK na BKP, 1988), 29.

[13] Beijing Shi Difang Zhi Bianzuan Weiyuanhui, *Beijing zhi: Zhengfa juan: Gong'an zhi* (Beijing: Beijing Chubanshe, 2003), 59.

[14] *Beijing zhi: Zhengfa juan*, 59.

[15] *Beijing zhi: Zhengfa juan*, 53.

[16] *Beijing zhi: Zhengfa juan*, 59.

[17] *Zhongguo renmin gong'an shigao* (Beijing: Jingguan Jiaoyu Chubanshe, 1997), 247.

[18] Michael Dutton, *Policing Chinese Politics: A History* (Durham, NC: Duke University Press, 2005), 144.

[19] Qiang Fang, *Chinese Complaint Systems: Natural Resistance* (New York: Routledge, 2013), 13.

(960–1279).[20] The CCP was able to appropriate these traditional institutions for its needs shortly after seizing power. The party also borrowed from the KMT police, which had developed a system of card registers (*kapian* 卡片) for households and individuals.[21] These catalogs served as the basis for constructing CCP registers that proved to be especially valuable to monitor the population. In addition to the noncommunist institutional legacies, there were two information-collection mechanisms that were expressly developed by the CCP prior to 1949: the state security apparatus and the telegraph agency.

The origins of the Chinese intelligence system can be traced back to the creation of the Special Section of the CCP (*zhongyang teke* 中央特科) in November 1927, which was transformed into the Political Security Department (*zhengzhi baowei chu* 政治保卫处) in January 1931 and eventually into the State Political Security Bureau (*guojia zhengzhi baowei ju* 国家政治保卫局) of the Jiangxi Soviet in November 1931.[22] The Political Security Bureau was organized along the hierarchical model of the USSR's People's Commissariat for Internal Affairs (NKVD), in which the center had vertical command over lower-level bureaus. Alongside the Political Security Bureau, another entity with policing responsibility was the Internal Affairs Department (*neiwu bu* 内务部), which was created in 1931; tasked with managing social order, it consisted of a militia (*minjing ju* 民警局) and a criminal investigation division (*xingshi zhencha ju* 刑事侦察局).[23] Political Security and Internal Affairs formed the core of the prerevolutionary state security apparatus.

Important changes to the system were made in 1939, when the State Political Security Bureau was renamed the Social Affairs Department (*shehui bu* 社会部) and re-organized as a decentralized entity, with local branches receiving instructions both from the central Social Affairs Department and from local party committees.[24] The department had separate divisions focusing on intelligence, investigation, protection, and communication. Its paramount task was to identify enemies and traitors by using various methods such as penetration agents (*neixian* 内线).[25] The other change that took place in 1939 involved transforming the Internal Affairs Department into the Public Security Department, with the following general structure: confidential office; social

---

[20] Kung-chuan Hsiao, *Rural China: Imperial Control in the Nineteenth Century* (Seattle: University of Washington Press, 1960), 27. On the *baojia* system under the Qing, see Zhang Houan and Bai Yihua, *Zhongguo nongcun jiceng jianzhi de lishi yanbian* (Chengdu: Sichuan Renmin Chubanshe, 1992), 73–77.

[21] Household registries predate the Nationalist era. The introduction of card catalogs, which made it easier to consult the registers, was a KMT innovation.

[22] *Zhongguo renmin gong'an shigao*, 20–32.

[23] *Zhongguo renmin gong'an shigao*, 34.

[24] Xuezhi Guo, *China's Security State: Philosophy, Evolution, and Politics* (New York: Cambridge University Press, 2012), 332.

[25] *Zhongguo renmin jingcha jianshi* (Beijing: Jingguan Jiaoyu Chubanshe, 1989), 52–53.

affairs section (intelligence, investigation); education section; police team (*jingwei dadui* 警卫大队); and reformatory (*ganhua yuan* 感化院) in charge of reeducating traitors.[26] In some places, Public Security and Social Affairs worked under a two-nameplate principle: externally Public Security but internally Social Affairs. Even when they were separate entities, they both belonged to the core of the state security apparatus. The value of these policing structures was that they allowed the CCP to test various methods for involuntary information gathering that were subsequently adopted by the intelligence agencies of the newly formed revolutionary state.

The party also created a telegraph agency, which served as a source of classified intelligence for the leadership. The origins of Xinhua extend back to the Red China News Agency, which was established in November 1931 and then transformed into Xinhua News Agency in January 1937.[27] From its beginnings, Xinhua supplied top leaders and high-level officials in the communist base areas with confidential news bulletins. In 1937, for example, *Cankao xiaoxi* (参考消息) was issued in 400 copies and dispatched to a select group of recipients.[28] In the lead-up to the establishment of CCP rule throughout China, Xinhua rapidly extended its geographic reach. In 1946, it had 12 regional offices and 124 personnel at headquarters.[29] By October 1948, its head count had reached 839 staff at headquarters.[30] New internal publications continued to appear: *Dangnei ziliao* (党内资料) began being issued as needed in 1948 and *Neibu cankao* (内部参考) started regular publication on September 22, 1949.[31] Initially, the focus of *Neibu cankao* was on international news, such as hostile reactions and criticisms of the CCP that were deemed too sensitive for publication in *Cankao xiaoxi*. Beginning in May 1950, dispatches written by domestic correspondents were included. From then on, *Neibu cankao* focused primarily on internal domestic reporting.[32] Such reporting was an extremely valuable prerevolutionary institution that could be mobilized by the leadership to build the communist information state. Importantly, as a party organ that predated 1949, Xinhua could be trusted after the revolution. This stood in contrast to the Ministry of Public Security, where the CCP had to graft its cadres onto the distrusted policing infrastructure left by the KMT.

[26] *Zhongguo renmin jingcha*, 53–54.
[27] *Xinhua she dashiji (1931–2001)*, vol. 1 (Beijing: Xinhua She, 2002), 1, 10.
[28] *Xinhua she dashiji*, vol. 1, 12.
[29] *Xinhua she dashiji*, vol. 1, 50.
[30] *Xinhua she dashiji*, vol. 1, 79.
[31] *Xinhua she dashiji*, vol. 1, 75.
[32] *Xinhua she dashiji*, vol. 1, 96.

One point that should be clearly stated is that, except for petitioning, the pre-existing institutions helped with involuntary extraction, not the voluntary transmission of information.

4.1.5 Ethnolinguistic Heterogeneity

The final constraint was presented by ethnic diversity. Although China has only a medium level of ethnolinguistic heterogeneity, several characteristics of its minorities foster imperfect legibility. From the point of view of the central state, minorities that are most difficult to penetrate are those that have a separate language and religion, constitute a majority in the region they inhabit, and occupy distant peripheral regions. In practice, this means that Uyghurs and especially Tibetans presented the greatest barrier to legibility for the party-state. The obstacle was so substantial that the central authorities initially decided to allow Tibet a limited degree of autonomy (which, as explained in Section 4.5, rendered the center unable to collect information in the autonomous region and thus incapable of anticipating the 1959 Uprising). As this chapter and Chapters 6 and 8 argue, the CCP has never succeeded in effectively penetrating these minorities despite the rapid increase in the size of party membership in both regions since the 1959 Tibetan Uprising and the post-2008 use of technologically sophisticated grid policing (*wanggehua guanli* 网格化管理) in both Tibet and Xinjiang. Efforts to involuntarily extract information have had limited success and attempts to incentivize the population to voluntarily transmit information through citizen complaints have also been a dismal failure due to these minorities' lack of trust in the party-state.

4.1.6 Summary Assessment

The structural constraints discussed in this section impaired the capacity of the CCP to establish those institutions that were necessary to systematically collect information about popular discontent. The paucity of intelligence in the initial years after the seizure of power resulted in elevated levels of violence and low rates of responsiveness, which, in turn, compromised the effective deployment of institutions for the voluntary transmission of information on popular discontent during most of the 1949–1958 period. This weakness notwithstanding, the regime was able to develop mechanisms for involuntary extraction in the Han-dominated areas, in part relying on sui generis prerevolutionary institutional legacies. This demonstrates that structural constraints have the greatest impact in terms of inhibiting the operation of the institutions needed for minority penetration and for the voluntary provision of information.

4.2 The Problem of Identifying Enemies

Apart from the structural constraints discussed in the previous section, another impediment to information collection is the lack of a clear set of surveillance targets. This section analyzes how the police, the party, and the media identified and collected information about them so that they could be individually enumerated and managed. The discussion complements the examination of the Bulgarian enemy contingent roster in Chapter 3.

4.2.1 Developing a Roster of Regime Enemies

There are two approaches to monitoring discontent: registering it once it occurs and aiming to detect it at an early stage prior to its transformation into acts of overt opposition. Early detection requires surveillance of the entire population for signs of dissatisfaction. Because few regimes have such a capacity at the time of inception, a more practical approach during the period of initial regime establishment is to monitor those who are most likely to be hostile. In order for these enemies to be identified, a roster listing the types of individuals who pose a threat to the regime needs to be created. After these categories are articulated, the intelligence required to locate and enumerate those who belong to them can be collected. In the understanding of the Chinese police, once enemies are identified, they should be registered and managed via arrests (*bu* 捕), executions (*sha* 杀), imprisonment (*guan* 关), and social surveillance (*guan* 管).[33] Thus, at the most fundamental level, the difficulty of identifying regime enemies stems from a lack of information. A detailed categorization of the potential types of enemies in a roster guides the collection of the necessary intelligence.

We can reconstruct the process of developing an increasingly sophisticated list of regime enemies by consulting classified police histories, almanacs, gazetteers, and yearbooks. This study draws on a corpus of such national-level and subnational materials covering all thirty-one Chinese provinces, the Xinjiang Production and Construction Corps, and eleven cities and counties (Dalian, Jilin city, Changchun, Ji'nan, Nanjing, Chengdu, Guiyang, Urumqi city,

---

[33] Guangxi Zhuangzu Zizhiqu Difangzhi Bianzuan Weiyuanhui, *Guangxi tongzhi: Gong'an zhi* (Nanning: Guangxiqu Zhengfu Yinshuachang, 2002), 246–63.

Urumqi county in Xinjiang, Lincang county in Yunnan, and Aksu prefecture in Xinjiang); these sources are supplemented by classified national and provincial police journals.

The corpus of classified police materials reveals that in 1949, when the Ministry of Public Security was being created, it was given the broad but very general mandate to suppress internal and external enemies.[34] Within a year, a more specific set of categories had been created. In urban areas, the main targets included: the mainstays of the reactionary parties and groups like the KMT and its youth league; religious followers, especially of certain Christian apostolic organizations such as the Legion of Mary (*shengmujun* 圣母军); and enemy and Japanese puppet party, government, police, and gendarmerie members (*diwei dangzheng jingxian* 敌伪党政警宪).[35] In rural areas, attention focused primarily on bandits, tyrants, and chiefs of reactionary secret societies, such as the White Lotus, Green Gang, and Yiguandao.[36] In both rural and urban areas, catch-all categories like counterrevolutionaries (*fangemingfenzi* 反革命分子) and spies (*tewu* 特务) were also used to identify enemies of the regime.[37] In contrast to Eastern Europe, no centralized roster existed in China: lists were kept locally, primarily in those cities that had population card catalogs. Enumerating these individuals required collection of information by the police, the party, and the media.

4.2.2 Tools for Identification: Full-Time Police Staff and Technical Surveillance

Although informants constituted the primary mechanism for identifying enemies of the people, some rudimentary technical surveillance measures were utilized as well. Available materials on this issue are not abundant, but internal police sources reveal that as early as 1954, the MPS issued regulations on communications security, stressing the importance of relying on vigilant citizens and postal employees to protect secrets transmitted through the mail and to prevent spies from using the postal system.[38] In various parts of the country, full-time police staff were also occasionally tasked with tailing targets (*genzong* 跟踪). In contrast to Bulgaria, which used clandestine audio-recording in the 1940s (see

---

[34] *Jianguo yilai gong'an gongzuo dashi yaolan (1949–2000)* (Beijing: Qunzhong Chubanshe, 2003), 2–3.

[35] *Jianguo yilai gong'an gongzuo*, 38; *Zhongguo renmin jingcha jianshi*, 104; Dalian Shi Shizhi Bangongshi, *Dalian shizhi: Gong'an zhi* (Beijing: Fangzhi Chubanshe, 2004), 253.

[36] *Guangxi tongzhi: Gong'an zhi*, 258–59.

[37] *Zhongguo renmin gong'an shigao*, 244.

[38] *Jianguo yilai gong'an gongzuo*, 67.

Chapter 3),[39] China did not implement technical surveillance measures like clandestine photography (*mimi paizhao* 秘密拍照) or clandestine audio-recording (*mimi luyin* 秘密录音) during the initial decade of communist governance.[40] It is important to keep in mind that both full-time staff and the technical capabilities of the police were extremely limited in the 1950s. A solution to this problem was found by fostering a corps of both secret and visible police informants.

4.2.3 Tools for Identification: Secret and Visible Police Informants

Of greatest utility to the MPS, both in urban and rural areas, was the use of informants, referred to by a variety of names: agents (*teqing* 特情), eyes and ears (*ermu* 耳目), secret forces (*mimi liliang* 秘密力量), social-order protection committee members (*zhibao hui huiyuan* 治保会会员), social-order protection small-group members (*zhibao xiaozu huiyuan* 治保小组会员), and social-order protection liaisons (*zhibao lianluo yuan* 治保联络员).[41] There were three methods to recruit informants: patriotic conviction, monetary rewards, and blackmail. In practice, these methods often intersected, and individuals joined the ranks for complex and hybrid reasons. In terms of budgetary allocations, funds for managing and rewarding informants were provided locally by the public security bureaus (PSBs) that counted on these individuals to supply leads about counterrevolutionary and other illegal activities.

As in other communist regimes, there is a distinction between visible and secret police informants. The visible informants often wore armbands and were referred to as social-order protection committee members, social-order protection small-group members, or social-order protection liaisons. Although social-order protection committees began to be formed in Beijing and elsewhere as early as 1949, their tasks were not formally outlined until May 1951, when Chairman Mao said that "in the great struggle to suppress counterrevolutionaries, all parts of the country must organize mass social-order protection committees" (全国各地必须在此次镇压反革命的伟大斗争中普遍地组织群众的治安保卫委员会), which have a "responsibility to assist the people's government in eliminating counterrevolutionaries, preventing treason and conspiracies, and protecting

[39] On technical surveillance in China in comparison with that in Eastern Europe, see *Zhongguo renmin jingcha jianshi*, 157.

[40] Yu Botao, *Mimi zhencha wenti yanjiu* (Beijing: Zhongguo Jiancha Chubanshe, 2008).

[41] See, for example, discussions of this nomenclature in internal police serials like *Heilongjiang gong'an* (1980–1988) and *Gong'an jianshe* (1980–1988). On *teqing*, see also Michael Schoenhals, "Recruiting Agents in Industry and Trade: Lifting the Veil on Early People's Republic of China Operational Work," *Modern Asian Studies* 45:5 (2011), 1345–69 and Michael Schoenhals, *Spying for the People: Mao's Secret Agents, 1949–1967* (New York: Cambridge University Press, 2013).

the country and social order" (担负协助人民政府肃清反革命, 防奸, 防谋, 保卫国家和公众治安的责任).[42] In August 1952, the MPS issued temporary regulations on the organization of social-order protection committees (治安保卫委员会暂行组织条例), which largely reiterated Chairman Mao's dictum: in addition to denouncing counterrevolutionaries and other criminals (揭发检举反革命和其他刑事犯罪分子), the committees were tasked with preventing spying, theft, fires, and public security accidents (防特, 防盗, 防火, 防治安灾害事故).[43] These committees were supposed to consist of three to eleven people under a director and vice-director. They were to be located in cities, rural areas, and within agencies (*jiguan*机关).[44]

In contrast to the visible social-order informants, there were many fewer secret collaborators who were more carefully chosen. Internally, they were described as secret forces, or more concretely as agents and eyes and ears. Agents (*teqing*) were recruited to investigate suspicious individuals; to maintain the technical security of sensitive locations and to prevent their operational secrets from being stolen; and to carry out secret investigations aimed at collecting enemy intelligence, assessing the reactions of all social classes, monitoring reactionary factions, and detecting irregularities in production facilities, special occupations, and sensitive locations.[45] *Teqing* were also needed to control the activities of imperialist agents.[46] The identity, tradecraft, and operational reports of the *teqing* were to be kept confidential.[47] In the 1950s, eyes and ears (*ermu*) were second-grade secret informants, who received less training than the *teqing* in undercover work and who primarily engaged in straightforward covert surveillance rather than in enemy penetration or other complex clandestine activities. Individuals on the targeted population roster could be recruited as *ermu* and then tasked with spying on other members of the targeted population.[48] *Ermu* were also recruited from among former prisoners, reeducation-through-labor inmates, and individuals who had committed minor infractions that were insufficient for formal punishment but nevertheless gave the police reason to blackmail them.

The existing literature does not provide an estimate of the size of either visible social-order protection committee members or of the secret informants. But we are in the extremely fortunate position of being able to estimate the size of the social-order protection committees by consulting police gazetteers that

---

[42] Heilongjiang Sheng Difang Zhi Bianzuan Weiyuanhui, *Heilongjiang shengzhi: Gong'an zhi* (Harbin: Heilongjiang Renmin Chubanshe, 2001), 316.

[43] *Jianguo yilai gong'an gongzuo*, 49.

[44] Shandong Sheng Difang Shizhi Bianzuan Weiyuanhui, *Shandong shengzhi: Gong'an zhi* (Ji'nan: Shandong Renmin Chubanshe, 1995), 316.

[45] *Gong'an jianshe*, no. 132 (July 16, 1955), 12-15.

[46] *Gong'an jianshe*, no. 154 (March 30, 1956), 8.

[47] *Renmin gong'an*, no. 11 (1956), 24.

[48] See Article 13.2 of the 1956 MPS "Temporary Regulation on Managing the Targeted Population," *Gong'an jianshe*, no. 178 (October 30, 1956), 16.

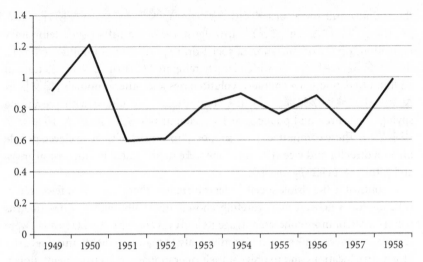

Figure 4.1 Rate of saturation with social-order informants in China, 1949–1958 (as a percentage of the population).
Source: Author's dataset.

contain data on individual Chinese provinces. Although the process of obtaining the complete set of provincial gazetteers and of identifying, extracting, and standardizing the relevant data is labor-intensive, the empirical, methodological, and theoretical payoffs are highly significant: simply put, such data allow us to gain direct insights into an aspect of Chinese politics that is shrouded in secrecy. The police materials reveal that in 1949–1958, up to 1 percent of the population functioned as visible informants (see Figure 4.1). As social-order protection work did not officially commence until 1951, the figures for 1949–1950 may represent some initial overzealous recruitment efforts that were subsequently tempered and regularized.

Although statistics on the number of *teqing* are exceedingly difficult to obtain,[49] the unusually rich subnational data from Guangxi allow us to compile some numerical indicators for the initial decade of postrevolutionary governance. The Guangxi materials reveal that separate recruitment targets existed for political and criminal *teqing*. Guangxi's goal was to reach 1,800 political *teqing* (*zhengzhi teqing* 政治特情) in 1958. This would allow for three secret informants to be deployed to each enemy agent special case; complex counterrevolutionary cases (*fangeming jiuhe an* 反革命纠合案) were allotted two *teqing*. The plans called for recruiting a further 1,100 criminal *teqing* (*xingshi teqing* 刑事特情) in

---

[49] For example, in his path-breaking study of *teqing* in 1949–1966, Schoenhals, *Spying for the People*, provides no empirical details about their numbers.

1958. Agents were evaluated based on the quality of their work: in 1958, the target was for at least 80 percent of the *teqing* to be effective (*qi zuoyong* 起作用).[50] Guangxi is also one of very few provinces to release statistics on the number of *ermu* in the later decades of communist rule (further details will be provided in Chapters 6 and 8). To the extent that Guangxi can be a guide for the rest of China, the ratio of social-order protection members to *teqing* was 32:1 (1957–1958) and of social-order protection members to *ermu* was 12:1 (1988). These ratios allow us to conclude that when identifying and counteracting discontent the Chinese MPS, much like the East German Ministry of the Interior, relied primarily on visible informants.[51]

4.2.4 Identification of Enemies by the Party and State through Denunciations

Beyond the police, party and government agencies also identified enemies. They did so on the basis of information that was provided to them voluntarily through letters and in-person visits (*xinfang* 信访). Complaints were directed both to the local party and government offices and to the central authorities. A portion of these complaints were denunciatory (*jubao* 举报), consisting of reports, accusations, and criticisms (*jianju konggao piping xinfang* 检举控告批评信访).[52] Within the CCP, the Discipline Inspection Commission and the Organization Department functioned as internal watchdogs that received complaints either directly addressed to them or forwarded from the CCP General Office and from government agencies.

Available statistics indicate that the share of denunciations in citizen complaints varied depending on the recipient. For example, in 1951–1954, reports and accusations made up 18 percent of the complaints received by central government agencies; 15.5 percent of the letters and visits to the Government Administration Council (*zhengwuyuan* 政务院), a predecessor of the State Council; 26 percent of the postbag in six major cities and provinces; and 20 percent–25 percent of the visits and mail handled by the CCP General Office.[53] Only a third of these accusatory complaints were judged to be false

---

[50] *Gong'an jianshe*, no. 266 (August 5, 1958), 18.

[51] Like China, the German Democratic Republic (GDR) had a separate Ministry of State Security (Stasi), which had its own informants. See Appendix A1 in Chapter 2 and Chapter 9.

[52] Diao Jiecheng, *Renmin xinfang shilüe 1949–1995* (Beijing: Beijing Jingji Xueyuan Chubanshe, 1996), 56.

[53] Diao, *Renmin xinfang shilüe*, 56–57. The six major cities and provinces included Tianjin, Shanghai, and Hebei. These cities may not represent dynamics across China as a whole. For example, a detailed coding of the 29,365 letters and visits received by the party, government, enterprises, the Youth League, and the Women's Federation in Gansu in 1954 reveals that only 2,305 (9 percent) were denunciatory. See *Gansu xinfang zhi 1949–1989* (Lanzhou: Gansu Minzu Chubanshe, 1991), 5.

(*bushi* 不实).[54] Although in later periods such denunciations focused on corruption, in the 1950s citizens were encouraged to report counterrevolutionaries, bad elements, and religious devotees.[55] Therefore, citizen signals of this type had a high informational value for identifying regime enemies.[56]

The volume of denunciations was manageable. For example, a district party office in Shanghai received only a handful of accusations in 1954.[57] Similarly, the party discipline inspection departments in large cities such as Beijing and Shanghai handled 1,000–1,500 cases per year in 1953–1954.[58] At the central party headquarters, discipline inspection letters and visits rarely exceeded 10,000 per year. Denunciations peaked in 1957, as those who had been encouraged to criticize the party during the Hundred Flowers Campaign in the first half of the year were subject to persecution during the Anti-Rightist Campaign in the second half of the year. Thus, even though the Central Discipline Inspection Commission handled 15,875 letters and visits in 1957, the volume rapidly declined to under 10,000 per year during the Great Leap Forward.[59] Accusatory complaints were investigated and party members were punished via various disciplinary sanctions that included expulsion from the CCP.[60] Similar procedures were applied by the Communist Youth League, whose Organization Department identified and punished counterrevolutionaries and other enemies in its ranks.[61] In sum, denunciations were essential for party and government agencies to identify and manage regime opponents.

4.2.5 The Contribution of the Internal Media to Identifying Enemies

Unlike the police and the party, which aimed to identify latent regime enemies, the internal media, published primarily by Xinhua News Agency, focused on documenting expressions of overt opposition to the regime. Xinhua enjoyed considerable latitude prior to the Great Leap Forward. Mao opined: "We cannot

---

[54]   Diao, *Renmin xinfang shilüe*, 55. These statistics are based on the examination of letters and visits received by the Government Administration Council.

[55]   Based on the categories listed in a form for recording denunciations. See Shanghai Municipal Archives (SMA) A49_1_218_185 (1955).

[56]   This stands in sharp contrast to Bulgaria, where voluntary denunciations were extremely rare and discouraged.

[57]   SMA A80_2_100_5 (1954). The district in question is Shuishang (水上区), which existed from 1954 to 1956.

[58]   Shanghai handled 1,614 discipline inspection letters in 1954 (SMA A80_2_2 [1954]), whereas Beijing received 1,334 in 1954 (*Beijing zhi: Gongchandang juan*, 435).

[59]   Diao, *Renmin xinfang shilüe*, 118.

[60]   See SMA A80_2_100_5 (1954); SMA A48_1_301 (1955); and SMA A80_2_166_17 (1955).

[61]   SMA C21_1_239_47 (1953).

live without Xinhua, as our eyes and ears will no longer work."[62] Various intelligence bulletins were produced, with *Neibu cankao* having very restricted circulation.[63] Classified as secret (*jimi* 机密), this daily intelligence brief was dispatched solely to central and provincial leading cadres from its inception in September 1949 until the end of January 1960.[64] The bulletin is especially valuable prior to February 1960, when the list of recipients expanded to prefectural-level cadres (*diwei changwei* 地委常委), with a corresponding change in content (the articles became shorter and their tone less critical and analytical).

Neibu cankao was guided by instructions that came from the very top of the party-state. In 1953, the Central Committee issued guidelines to journalists on how to carry out internal reporting. This gives us a sense of the type of coverage leaders expected from the internal media during the initial years of communist governance.[65] The journalists were generally instructed to collect information on notable events not suitable for the open media and to provide objective, factual reporting. Specifically, this included the political attitudes of the population and the views of various social strata about important domestic and international events. In addition, *Neibu cankao* contributors were expected to track the opinions of people from various strata about life and work problems as well as to monitor their dispositions toward the leading party and government organs. Finally, *Neibu cankao* was to cover natural disasters and counterrevolutionary activities.[66] In sum, it was entrusted with a very broad mandate to report on negative news.

A detailed coding of the frequency of coverage of various sensitive items in the 2,596 issues of *Neibu cankao* that were published between 1949 and 1958 reveals that the top leadership was apprised of a number of negative phenomena, such as episodes of hunger; shortages of goods; and the incidence of corruption, theft, and waste. It is also noteworthy that there were reports of ethnic and religious minority unrest. In addition, *Neibu cankao* tracked various antiregime and enemy activities, such as the creation of counterrevolutionary organizations or the infiltration of various parts of China by foreign spies. Most frequent were reports on hostile reactions, opinions, and views, which also occasionally included dispatches on superstitious rumors.[67] A specific breakdown of a range of sensitive news items appearing in *Neibu cankao* is provided in Table 4.2.

---

[62] *Xinhua she dashiji (1931–2001)*, vol. 2 (Beijing: Xinhua She, 2002), 32.

[63] *Xinhua she dashiji*, vol. 2, 21.

[64] *Neibu cankao*, no. 2968 (February 1, 1960), 24.

[65] "Zhonggong zhongyang guanyu Xinhua jizhe caixie neibu cankao ziliao de guiding" (July 1953).

[66] "Zhonggong zhongyang guanyu Xinhua jizhe caixie neibu cankao ziliao de guiding" (July 1953).

[67] On rumors and superstitions in *Neibu cankao*, see S. A. Smith, "Talking Toads and Chinless Ghosts: The Politics of 'Superstitious' Rumors in the People's Republic of China, 1961–1965," *American Historical Review* 111:2 (2006), 405–27. We should note that in the 1950s and 1960s, rumors in China differed from those in Eastern Europe, where they focused on consumption rather than on superstition.

Table 4.2 Coverage of Some Sensitive News Items in *Neibu cankao*, 1949–1958

Issue	Number of Reports
Famine	64
Minoriies and religion	265
Corruption, theft, and waste	365
Markets, quality, and supply of goods	727
Enemies, spies, and enemy/antiregime activity	1,136
Reactions, opinions, views, superstitions, and rumors	1,603

Source: Author's calculations based on hand-coding of article titles.

The quality of these reports varied. One revealing metric is the reactions of people from all walks of life (*shehui ge jieceng renshi* 社会各阶层人士). *Neibu cankao* published 139 such reports in 1949–1958. They usually focused on specific urban localities and synthesized the views of various segments of the population on party and government policies, ranging from changes in currency denomination to reforms in industry and agriculture. Reactions to major international events were also assessed.[68] In theory, reporting of this type could be highly useful to evaluate popular attitudes. In practice, its informational utility was diminished by the great variability in the content of the articles. In Shanghai, for instance, the roster was comprehensive: the attitudes of workers, cadres, associate-degree students, democratic party members, and the industrial and commercial circles were assessed.[69] But a shorter list was much more typical: thus, in a remote and poor city like Guiyang, all walks of life meant nothing more than the residents of the urban districts; residents of the rural suburbs; and capitalists.[70] Variation in bureaucratic capacity impacted the quality of reporting.

The main shortcoming of the internal media was that, as a consequence of low information-gathering capacity, China simply did not have enough bureaucrats to span the entire country and collect systematic information from every province. One index of that problem is the rarity of reports that are nationally comprehensive: there were only five such news items published in the bulletin in 1949–1958; of these, one report was about food. It focused on grain procurement in 1953.[71] However, even that report—whose title claimed that it

---

[68] *Neibu cankao*, no. 2369 (November 28, 1957), 10–11; *Neibu cankao*, no. 225 (September 30, 1952), 449–50.

[69] *Neibu cankao*, no. 2477 (May 12, 1958), 3–15.

[70] *Neibu cankao*, no. 2 (January 4, 1954), 24–26.

[71] *Neibu cankao*, no. 283 (December 3, 1953), 39–63.

covered the whole country (*quanguo gedi* 全国各地)—only discussed fifteen of the forty-five provinces, provincial-level cities, and ethnic autonomous regions that existed at that time; this is hardly nationally comprehensive. Only two instances of reporting that actually covered every existing Chinese province could be located: one is on reactions to the death of Stalin and the other on steel production.[72] These rare exceptions notwithstanding, reports from the 1950s and early 1960s were geographically specific, discussing events in a single large city (Beijing, Shanghai, Tianjin, Chongqing, Chengdu, Wuhan, Nanjing, Guangzhou, or Nanning), part of a province (Southern Jiangsu), a single province, or at the highest level of aggregation, a macro-region consisting of several provinces (the Southwestern Region; North China; or Northeast China). It is impossible to get a sense of systematic subnational variation from these reports. In the GDR, by contrast, in the immediate aftermath of the June 1953 Worker Uprising, the Stasi sought to provide leaders with mood assessments for each of the fifteen provinces (*Bezirke*).[73]

The orientation of the internal media toward reporting on what had already occurred (rather than anticipating future events), alongside their geographically limited coverage, diminished their potential to function as a central source of information on popular discontent. When combined with police and party reporting, however, the internal media helped reduce uncertainty among top decision makers.[74]

4.2.6 Contemporaneous and Retrospective Evaluations of the Enemy Contingent

Police and party gazetteers published since the 1980s present us with some striking and detailed statistics on the size of the enemy contingent in the early years of the People's Republic of China (PRC). They reveal that at liberation, there were 1 million armed remnants of the collapsed (*kuisan* 溃散) KMT, 2 million bandits, 600,000 spies, and 600,000 mainstays of the reactionary parties.[75] There were also evil bullies in the countryside and reactionary forces in the cities,

---

[72] Reports on reactions to the death of Stalin appeared throughout March 1953 and have been analyzed in Hua-yu Li "Reactions of Chinese Citizens to the Death of Stalin: Internal Communist Party Reports," *Journal of Cold War Studies* 11:2 (Spring 2009), 70–88. The steel production reports appeared on October 18, 1958, and October 20, 1958, and covered every Chinese province except Tibet.

[73] Stasi Records Archive (BStU MfS) SdM 249 Bl. 102–107 (Meldung Nr. 7/53) (1953).

[74] This is the main function of intelligence in any context. See Thomas Fingar, *Reducing Uncertainty: Intelligence Analysis and National Security* (Stanford, CA: Stanford University Press, 2011).

[75] *Zhongguo renmin gong'an shigao*, 244; Zhongguo Jianyu Xuehui, *Zhonghua Renmin Gongheguo jianyu shi 1949–2000* (Beijing: Zhongguo Jianyu Xuehui, 2004), 66.

consisting of feudal heads (*fengjian batou* 封建把头), gang heads (*banghui touzi* 帮会头子), and rogues (*dipi liumang* 地痞流氓).[76] Secret societies were an especially serious problem,[77] with the White Lotus (*hongbang* 洪帮) and Green Gang (*qingbang* 青帮) having the widest reach. Core members (*gugan fenzi* 骨干分子) often included landlords, tyrants, hoodlums, traitors, and spies. These counter-revolutionary elements organized violent attacks on cadres and citizens, manufactured political rumors, and spread mystical ideas and philosophies.[78] Internal police sources reveal that at liberation, China had over 300 kinds of secret societies, with 820,000 core members and 13 million followers.[79] This is alarming when we take into account that the CCP claimed only 4.49 million members at the end of 1949.[80] It is clear that regime enemies greatly outnumbered party members at the time of establishment of communist rule.

Statistics that are currently available also document the wide variability in the threat posed by regime opponents throughout the country. In Beijing, for instance, there were over 16,000 enemies when the city was liberated in January 1949. In addition to 10,000 spies and conspirators led by the more than 100 foreign organizations operating in the capital, the group of enemies comprised 6,000 mainstays of the reactionary parties, such as the KMT, the KMT Youth League (*sanqingtuan* 三青团), the China Democratic Socialist Party (*Zhongguo minzhu shehui dang* 中国民主社会党), and the Youth Party (*qingniandang* 青年党).[81] The enemies were equivalent to 1 percent of the population of the city, thus greatly outnumbering CCP members, who stood at 0.2 percent at the time of liberation.[82] Though the Beijing statistics may appear alarming, other provinces had considerably larger enemy contingents. A look at Henan reveals that at the time of liberation, there were 63,000 leaders (*daoshou* 道首) and 1,060,000 followers (*daotu* 道徒) of at least 46 different secret societies.[83] Thus, the secret-society members alone were equivalent to 2.7 percent of Henan's population in 1949. It was not until 1965 that Henan's 1.098 million CCP members came close to matching the number of secret-society members that the province had had in 1949.[84] In Beijing, by the end of 1950 the ranks of party members exceeded the

---

[76] *Zhongguo renmin jingcha jianshi*, 104.

[77] Kenneth Lieberthal, "The Suppression of Secret Societies in Post-Liberation Tientsin," *The China Quarterly*, no. 54 (April–June 1973), 242–66; Elizabeth J. Perry, *Rebels and Revolutionaries in North China, 1845–1945* (Stanford, CA: Stanford University Press, 1980); Brian G. Martin, "The Green Gang and the Guomindang State: Du Yuesheng and the Politics of Shanghai, 1927–37," *Journal of Asian Studies* 54:1 (1995), 64–92.

[78] Xinjiang Weiwuer Zizhiqu Difang Zhi Bianzuan Weiyuanhui, *Xinjiang tongzhi: Gong'an zhi* (Urumqi: Xinjiang Renmin Chubanshe, 2004), 311.

[79] *Xinjiang tongzhi: Gong'an zhi*, 311.

[80] *Zhongguo gongchandang dangnei tongji ziliao huibian, 1921–2010*, 7.

[81] *Beijing zhi: Zhengfa juan*, 115.

[82] At the time, the Beijing CCP had 3,376 members. See *Beijing zhi: Gongchandang juan*, 196.

[83] Henan Sheng Difang Shizhi Bianzuan Weiyuanhui, *Henan shengzhi: Gong'an zhi* (Zhengzhou: Henan Renmin Chubanshe, 1994), 53–56.

[84] *Zhongguo gongchandang dangnei tongji ziliao huibian, 1921–2010*, 12.

size of the January 1949 enemy contingent.[85] In short, regime enemies posed a serious threat to the CCP that varied in its intensity geographically and it was strongest in places where the CCP had the fewest members.[86]

However, these detailed statistics, which may create the impression of an all-seeing state, were compiled post-factum. The CCP did not have a good grasp of the exact size of the opposition at the time of regime establishment. A roster of the groups to be monitored was gradually established and a clearer sense of the size of the enemy contingent emerged over time.[87] Yet, repression could not be deferred until the enemy contingent had been fully identified and enumerated. Therefore, in the initial years of the PRC, we find elevated levels of poorly targeted repression: entire groups were eliminated rather than specific individuals within groups. A capability to collect fine-grained information that would have allowed precise individual-level targeting of selective repression was absent in China in the early 1950s, when violence was most brutal. Yet by the mid-1950s, the various systems for information collection by the police, the party, and the media gradually began to yield more granular insights about the size of the enemy contingent. As information quality improved, a decision was made in 1958 to kill less, arrest less, and use supervision more.[88]

In contrast to Bulgaria, where significant elite threats existed during the initial assumption of power by the communist party in 1944–1949 and where one-third of party members were purged in the 1940s, the Chinese model of revolutionary takeover featured more manageable elite challenges (due to the exit option to Taiwan) and less inner-party opposition during the initial decade of rule. This meant that, from the very beginning of its existence, the regime could focus on nonelites.

4.3 Repression of Regime Enemies

Critical differences can be observed between repression in China in 1949–1953 and in 1954–1958. These have to do primarily with the increased availability of information on the enemy contingent, which enabled more precise and less frequent deployment of repression in the second half of the first decade of postrevolutionary governance.

---

[85] *Beijing zhi: Gongchandang juan*, 201.

[86] On variation in the size of the CCP, see Daniel Koss, *Where the Party Rules: The Rank and File of China's Communist State* (New York: Cambridge University Press, 2018).

[87] Yang Kuisong, "Reconsidering the Campaign to Suppress Counterrevolutionaries," *The China Quarterly*, no. 193 (March 2008), 102–21, at 104.

[88] *Zhongguo renmin jingcha jianshi*, 148.

4.3.1 Initial Years of Communist Rule, 1949–1953

In March 1950, the Ministry of Public Security (MPS) informed the Politburo that there were ongoing counterrevolutionary revolts and mass riots in rural areas; these were not random instances but rather planned acts of sabotage by spies and bandits who had joined evil bullies and landlords. As the report noted, the riots had a considerable mass scale.[89] In the same month, the CCP Central Committee issued instructions on suppressing counterrevolutionaries to guide the work of the MPS. By November 1950, 1.8 million bandits had been annihilated (*jiaomie* 剿灭).[90] This was followed by the Campaign to Eliminate Counterrevolutionaries, which began officially in 1951 and concluded by the end of 1953. A quota mechanism of 0.5–1.5 executions per thousand residents was imposed; the range depended on location (cities were tasked with eliminating a smaller share of their populations than rural areas) and on the magnitude of the problem, with localities that had a higher density of counterrevolutionaries being asked to kill more.[91] Exact numbers have not become available, but one estimate indicates that 712,000 were executed (0.12 percent of the population), 1.29 million were imprisoned, and 1.2 million subjected to control.[92] Other sources cite higher figures.[93] The low estimate of executions in November 1950–October 1953 is comparable to the low estimate of victims in Bulgaria during the worst period of red terror, which took place in the fall of 1944. The high estimate for Bulgaria is a near exact match of the high estimate for China once we add the pre-November 1950 Chinese victims.[94]

Subnational data allow us to document the precise magnitude of repression in some localities. Table 4.3 presents detailed data from Guangxi for the period from November 1950 through October 1953. One observation is that the rate of executions was very high (2.35 per thousand, thus significantly exceeding the national quota of 0.5–1.5 per thousand).[95] Rates of arrest were also very high (1.44 percent of the population, compared with a national average of 0.46 percent [2.62 million] of the population of 574 million).[96] Additional research is

[89] *Jianguo yilai gong'an gongzuo*, 8.

[90] *Jianguo yilai gong'an gongzuo*, 19.

[91] Felix Wemheuer, *A Social History of Maoist China: Conflict and Change, 1949–1976* (New York: Cambridge University Press, 2019), 67; Julia C. Strauss, *State Formation in China and Taiwan: Bureaucracy, Campaign, and Performance* (New York: Cambridge University Press, 2020), 101.

[92] Yang, "Reconsidering the Campaign," 120.

[93] Strauss, *State Formation in China and Taiwan*, 101.

[94] In Bulgaria, estimates vary from 8,000 to 30,000 executions, or 0.12 percent–0.46 percent of the population (see Chapter 3). In China, if we add the pre-November 1950 victims, 0.44 percent of the population was executed during the high tide of repression in 1949–1953.

[95] Calculated on the basis of Guangxi's 1953 population of 19.76 million.

[96] On the national average, see Yang, "Reconsidering the Campaign," 120.

Table 4.3 Suppression of Counterrevolutionaries in Guangxi, 1950–1953

	Bandits	Tyrants	Spies	Mainstays of Reactionary Parties and Groups	Leaders of Reactionary Secret Societies	Other	Total
Arrest	218,058	36,129	16,741	1,851	892	12,002	285,673
Execution	34,048	8,314	3,119	187	20	590	46,278
Imprisonment	69,412	14,483	8,458	1,057	502	8,733	102,645
Surveillance	35,439	14,914	3,203	3,954	279	3,125	60,914

Source: Guangxi Zhuangzu Zizhiqu Difangzhi Bianzuan Weiyuanhui, *Guangxi tongzhi: Gong'an zhi* (Nanning: Guangxiqu Zhengfu Yinshuachang, 2002), 259–60.

necessary to understand the factors that drove this geographical variation in the volume of repression.[97]

4.3.2 Detecting Counterrevolutionaries after 1953

The successful suppression of counterrevolutionaries, coupled with improvements in information-collection capacity, meant that a more sophisticated approach toward state security policing could gradually begin to be adopted. From 1953 on, the emphasis was on the detection (*zhenpo* 侦破) of individual counterrevolutionary cases rather than on campaign-style violent suppression of large groups of people labeled counterrevolutionaries.[98] National-level indicators support this conclusion: for example, *Neibu cankao* printed thirty-one exposés on eliminating groups of bandits in 1949–1953, but only four articles on this issue in the next decade (1954–1964).[99] Subnational data indicate that the main tasks during the post-1953 period were to identify spies dispatched (*paiqian tewu* 派遣特务); to locate the authors of slogans, leaflets, and reactionary correspondence; to prevent acts of sabotage (*fangeming xingdong pohuai* 反革命行动破坏); and to uncover counterrevolutionary organizations.[100] *Neibu cankao* provides evidence of similar trends nationwide: although it printed only one report on leaflets (*chuandan* 传单) in 1949–1953,

---

[97] For a community-based account applied to a later period, see Yang Su, *Collective Killings in Rural China during the Cultural Revolution* (New York: Cambridge University Press, 2011).

[98] *Guangxi tongzhi: Gong'an zhi*, 264–72; *Beijing zhi: Zhengfa juan*, 142–43.

[99] Calculated by hand-coding the contents of all 3,612 issues of *Neibu cankao*, 1949–1964.

[100] *Guangxi tongzhi: Gong'an zhi*, 264–72.

twenty-one such articles appeared in 1954–1964.[101] Needless to say, the police rightly understood that the distribution of leaflets was an act of individual (or small-group) dissent rather than an indicator of organized activity by large classes of counterrevolutionaries.

An ongoing focus involved striking against and destroying reactionary secret societies. What might explain this pre-occupation? The police gazetteers stress that these entities spread rumors, aided and abetted bandits, and engaged in harmful and fraudulent activities. Yet, precisely what these organized groups did might have been less important than their number of followers. Tellingly, secret societies were so popular in Guangxi that as late as March 1953, they still had more members than the Chinese Communist Party.[102] The implications were clear and alarming, necessitating firm action.

As more detailed information became available, rates of repression decreased. Imprisonment for counterrevolutionary crimes declined after the end of the Campaign to Suppress Counterrevolutionaries in 1953, which was initially reflected in a slower increase of the slope of the total number of individuals incarcerated for counterrevolutionary activity, followed by an eventual decrease in 1956–1957 (see Figure 4.2). Correspondingly, the share of prisoners held for counterrevolutionary crimes peaked in 1954 at 54.89 percent, but it dropped thereafter (see Figure 4.3).

As the quantity and quality of information improved, it was possible to adopt a less violent approach to enemies of the regime: identification (detection), enumeration, registration (via the targeted population roster), and management (not only by execution or imprisonment but also by surveillance). Although registration began as early as 1949 in Beijing and in a few developed northeastern and coastal provinces,[103] it was not until the mid-1950s that it became a reality throughout China.

---

[101] Calculated by hand-coding the contents of all 3,612 issues of *Neibu cankao*, 1949–1964.

[102] Reactionary secret societies had 45,820 members as of the end of March 1953 (*Guangxi tongzhi: Gong'an zhi*, 273). CCP membership stood at 34,980 at the end of 1952 and rose to 46,565 at the end of 1953 (*Zhongguo gongchandang Guangxi zhuangzu zizhiqu zuzhi shi ziliao 1925–1987* [Nanning: Zhonggong Guangxi Zhuangzu Zizhiqu Zuzhi Bu, March 1995], 416). Thus, although we lack statistics about CCP membership precisely at the end of March 1953, it is reasonable to assume that the party ranks could not have exceeded the number of secret-society members at the time. I want to thank Daniel Koss for generously sharing materials on CCP size in Guangxi in 1953.

[103] *Beijing zhi: Zhengfa juan*, 118; Liaoning Sheng Difang Zhi Bianzuan Weiyuanhui Bangongshi, *Liaoning shengzhi: Gong'an zhi* (Shenyang: Liaoning Kexue Jishu Chubanshe, 1999), 83; Zhejiang Sheng Gong'an Zhi Bianzuan Weiyuanhui, *Zhejiang renmin gong'an zhi* (Beijing: Zhonghua Shuju, 2000), 83. In Jiangsu, registration began in 1950: see Jiangsu Sheng Difang Zhi Bianzuan Weiyuanhui, *Jiangsu sheng zhi: Gong'an zhi* (Beijing: Qunzhong Chubanshe, 2000), 106.

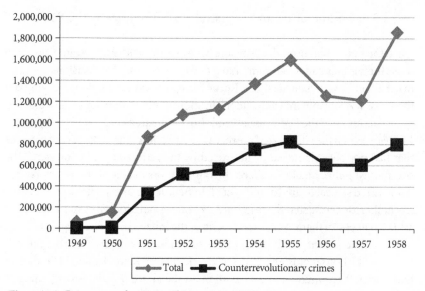

Figure 4.2 Prison population in China, 1949–1958.

Source: Author's dataset, based on Sifa Bu Jianyu Guanli Ju, *Dangdai Zhongguo jianyu tongji ziliao (1949–1989)* (Beijing: Sifa Bu Jianyu Guanli Ju, November 1998).

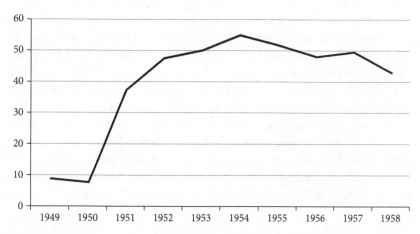

Figure 4.3 Share of prisoners incarcerated for counterrevolutionary crimes in China, 1949–1958.

Source: Author's dataset, based on Sifa Bu, *Dangdai Zhongguo jianyu tongji ziliao.*

4.3.3   Enumeration and Registration of Enemies by the Police

Once the police had used the available information to identify regime enemies, those individuals had to be enumerated and registered so that decisions could be made about how to manage them. Record-keeping was essential for carrying out these tasks. A key tool that aided identification, enumeration, and registration in urban settings was the KMT police catalog of population cards (*renkou kapian* 人口卡片). When the CCP seized power in the cities, it acquired those card catalogs that had not been damaged or destroyed by the retreating KMT forces.[104] The communist police quickly realized the informational value of these rosters, and it organized special teams to study them. In Beijing, for example, the public security authorities evaluated the existing 3,372,000 population cards in 1950 and set aside 2,000,000 of them.[105] An assessment of the inhabitants of Beijing conducted by the public security authorities in the summer of 1949 revealed that the city had 448,141 households and 2,004,807 residents.[106] Remarkably, this indicates that the CCP acquired basic information on the entire population of Beijing as well as on that of certain other cities whose residents had been catalogued by the KMT. The population card catalog explains how an otherwise under-resourced police force was able to issue lists of category C households (*bingzhong hukou* 丙种户口) in places like Ji'nan, Shanghai, and Beijing as early as 1949.[107] Category C households were the precursor of the targeted population (*zhongdian renkou* 重点人口), consisting of enemies and questionable people; precise tallies of both groups were produced in cities with good records. In Liaoning, for instance, the categories of individuals on the targeted population roster included KMT army and government members; professional spies; secret-society leaders; and bandits.[108] The targeted population roster was continuously updated in light of the intelligence collected by informants and full-time police staff.

The share of the urban population covered by these catalogs varied throughout the country. For example, in the city of Jilin, which is located in an industrially developed province, as many as 82 percent of the inhabitants of six urban districts had been entered into the card catalog by 1956.[109] In the much less prosperous province of Guangxi,[110] only 65.15 percent of the residents of the four

---

[104] *Zhongguo renmin gong'an shigao*, 162.

[105] *Beijing zhi: Zhengfa juan*, 364.

[106] *Beijing zhi: Zhengfa juan*, 364.

[107] Fei-Ling Wang, *Organizing Through Division and Exclusion: China's Hukou System* (Stanford, CA: Stanford University Press, 2005), 43–44.

[108] *Liaoning shengzhi: Gong'an zhi*, 250.

[109] Jilin Shi Difang Zhi Bianzuan Weiyuanhui, *Jilin shizhi: Gong'an zhi* (Changchun: Jilin Wenshi Chubanshe, 1992), 130.

[110] Guangxi remained a province until 1958, when it became the Guangxi Zhuang Autonomous Region.

largest cities (Nanning, Liuzhou, Guilin, and Wuzhou) were cataloged by the conclusion of the campaign to expand registration in 1956–1957.[111]

For these general population rosters to be useful for monitoring regime enemies, the files of ordinary urban residents had to be clearly separated from those of individuals who were problematic. A technical innovation was useful here: by 1958, the population cards of those who had been freed from prison, subjected to surveillance, or on the targeted population roster (刑满释放, 管制人员, 重点人口) were marked with the appropriate characters (刑, 管, 重) to distinguish them more easily from the cards of others with the same name.[112] The police consulted the cards in the course of various campaigns to identify counterrevolutionaries, as well as during routine investigations of political or criminal cases.[113] By the start of the Great Leap Forward, the card catalog was functioning as a formidable tool for enumerating enemies among urban residents in many parts of China.[114]

4.4 Welfare during the Initial Decade of Communist Rule

No autocracy can survive through repression alone. This makes it imperative to assess the extent to which the Chinese communist regime responded to the welfare frustrations articulated by citizens during the initial decade of its existence. These concerns were expressed primarily through information transmitted voluntarily via complaints and strikes. Another indicator of party-state responsiveness to the welfare needs of the population is provided by food-supply monitoring, which is also discussed in this section.

4.4.1 Strikes

Welfare frustrations resulted in strikes.[115,116] In 1956, there was a wave of worker and student unrest in China, with 29 strikes and 57 collective petitions by workers (each with more than 10,000 participants) and 30 student strikes (each with more than 10,000 participants). Worker contention stemmed from dissatisfaction with production norms, job training, work conditions, living

---

[111] *Guangxi tongzhi: Gong'an zhi*, 515.

[112] Anhui Sheng Difang Zhi Bianzuan Weiyuanhui, *Anhui shengzhi: Gong'an zhi* (Hefei: Anhui Renmin Chubanshe, 1993), 355.

[113] *Jilin shizhi: Gong'an zhi*, 133.

[114] At the time, the urbanization rate stood at 16.25 percent. See Li, *Shudu Zhongguo 60 nian*, 25.

[115] Unless otherwise indicated, this paragraph is based on *Gong'an jianshe*, no. 5/187 (April 10, 1957), 2–25.

[116] Elizabeth J. Perry, *Challenging the Mandate of Heaven: Social Protest and State Power in China* (Armonk, NY: M.E. Sharpe, 2002), 275–308; *Neibu cankao*, no. 2098 (January 7, 1957), 127–30.

arrangements, and levels of compensation. Students protested about the organization and content of instruction, low stipends, poor food and dorm hygiene,
and shortcomings of the job assignment system. These strikes were seen as un-
desirable, and in March 1957 the MPS drafted a report with clear instructions to
the local police authorities on how to prevent such occurrences in the future.[117]
In contrast to routinized individual complaining through the letters-and-visits
system, strikes were infrequent events, thus limiting their utility as a source to
systematically assess the welfare concerns of the population.

4.4.2 Complaints

Citizen petitions are the primary avenue for the voluntary transmission of information in communist regimes. China has a long tradition of complaints, and a
rich literature in Chinese and English has emerged on petitioning during both
the imperial and Republican periods.[118] The more modest research on Maoist
China has noted the importance of complaints as a means of political participation,[119] but it has not examined their aggregate volume; their content (what
people were concerned with); and the responsiveness of the regime. One obstacle in analyzing complaints in China is the limited scope of Chinese archival
documents. In contrast to several Eastern European regimes, the central communist party and State Security archives in China remain closed to researchers.
Nevertheless, other sources have now become available. Provincial archives have
declassified certain party and government files up to the early 1980s. This section
draws, in particular, on materials on citizen complaints gathered at the Shanghai
Municipal Archives (SMA). In addition, classified internal circulation (*neibu*)
materials and non-*neibu* publications, such as provincial yearbooks, scholarly
works, and media reports, contain information on citizen petitions, allowing us
to assess the extent to which the party-state focused on the welfare preferences of
the population.

We have evidence that complaints began to be tracked shortly after the establishment of the regime. In Beijing, for instance, the party formed a petitions team
as early as 1949. Although the volume of complaints was initially small (a mere

[117] *Gong'an jianshe*, no. 5/187 (April 10, 1957), 2–25.

[118] See, for example, Li Qiuxue, *Zhongguo xinfang shilun* (Beijing: Zhongguo Shehui Kexue
Chubanshe, 2009). Also see Jonathan K. Ocko, "I'll Take It All the Way to Beijing: Capital Appeals
in the Qing," *Journal of Asian Studies* 47:2 (May 1988), 291–315 and Qiang Fang, "A Hot Potato: The
Chinese Complaint System from Early Times to the Present" (Ph.D. Dissertation, SUNY Buffalo,
Department of History, 2006).

[119] James R. Townsend, *Political Participation in Communist China* (Berkeley: University
of California Press, 1967), 177–79; Tianjian Shi, *Political Participation in Beijing* (Cambridge,
MA: Harvard University Press, 1997), esp. 60–66.

sixty-six letters arrived between January and August 1951),[120] the authorities received regular reports on petitions handled by the Beijing offices of the CCP. By 1952, a Beijing CCP bulletin had been established under the title *Renmin laixin jianbao* (人民来信简报), which was transformed into the monthly *Renmin laixin meiyue jianbao* (人民来信每月简报) in 1953.[121]

The bulk of citizen letters and visits focused on welfare.[122] Technically, these were requests for help with work or study, preferential treatment, relief, or other difficult issues (要求解决工作, 学习, 优抚, 救济及其他困难问题的来信来访). Such petitions increased steadily among the letters and visits directed to the State Council, from 38.4 percent in 1954 to 71.86 percent in 1956.[123] A similar trend can be noted with regard to requests sent to party central: by 1956, as many as 55–60 percent of those petitions to the CCP General Office were asking for help with life difficulties.[124] Data from Shanghai indicate that subnational complaints also focused primarily on welfare. For example, one of the departments of the Shanghai City Government reported that 91.7 percent of the letters it handled in 1957 concerned job and life difficulties; passenger and cargo transportation; and public utilities.[125] Similarly, letters sent to the Jiangsu Provincial Party Committee in August 1957 stressed welfare concerns, such as the lack of food, the desire to leave cooperatives, and employment assistance.[126]

This welfare orientation notwithstanding, complaints work in China suffered from several shortcomings, main among which was the very low frequency of complaining. In the German Democratic Republic, for example, one in twenty-two citizens was complaining in 1956.[127] The available statistics for China are incomplete, but there is no reason to believe that the number of complaints exceeded 1 per 1,000 citizens in 1956, which was the last "normal" year before the peak in letter writing that occurred during the 1957 Hundred Flowers Campaign, when complaints may have reached a high of 1 per 500 citizens.[128] Subsequently, complaints declined three-fold in 1958–1960.[129] Separate from the precipitous drop in the overall volume of letters and visits, the share of both welfare complaints and denunciations decreased after 1957 as well.[130] Thus, citizens

---

[120] *Beijing zhi: Gongchandang juan*, 573.

[121] *Beijing zhi: Gongchandang juan*, 583.

[122] As discussed in Section 4.2, up to one-quarter of the complaints prior to the Great Leap Forward were denunciatory.

[123] Diao, *Renmin xinfang shilüe*, 80.

[124] Diao, *Renmin xinfang shilüe*, 80.

[125] SMA B7_2_268_5 (1958).

[126] These letters also highlighted cadre corruption. See *Neibu cankao*, no. 2323 (September 29, 1957), 8–10.

[127] Calculated from Felix Mühlberg, *Bürger, Bitten und Behörden: Geschichte der Eingabe in der DDR* (Berlin: Karl Dietz Verlag 2004), 173–87.

[128] Imputed from data in Diao, *Renmin xinfang shilüe*, 76–78, 118.

[129] Diao, *Renmin xinfang shilüe*, 118.

[130] Diao, *Renmin xinfang shilüe*, 123.

were contacting the authorities even less often during the Great Leap Forward than they had in the mid-1950s, and most letters and visits were suggestions, inventions, and rationalizations (*jianyi faming chuangzao* 建议发明创造) aimed at improvements in productivity or efficiency, not welfare requests.[131] In general, there was a lack of trust in the complaints system, as also indicated by the rapid increase in the share of anonymous complaints.[132]

Another challenge stemmed from the extreme variability in human resources devoted to handling citizen complaints. At the central level, 30 people at the State Council and 300 in 50 different ministries and commissions were tasked with receiving letters and visits in 1957.[133] A subnational survey of twenty-two provinces reveals a wide range of bureaucratic endowments allocated to complaints work by provincial governments in 1957: Shanghai had fourteen people handling this portfolio; eleven provinces reported a dedicated staff of eight; another nine provinces had designated two to four people; and Hunan had assigned a single person to this task.[134] What human resources existed in the remaining provinces or below the provincial level is unknown. But during the period prior to the Great Leap Forward, petitioning was an urban phenomenon,[135] thus making it unlikely that expert personnel would be located at the grassroots level or in rural settings.

Related to the unequal bureaucratic endowments devoted to handling letters and visits, there was also patchiness in the collection of complaints information. The internal media were not useful in this regard: most of the thirty-five reports on citizen communications published in *Neibu cankao* in 1949–1958 focus on an exemplary letter or, at most, on the post received in a single province or by a specific news outlet. The most complete available tally provides statistics on complaints to the government in twenty-one provinces in 1956 (containing 81.1 percent of China's population of 620 million at the time).[136] Data on central-level complaints to the CCP General Office, CCP Discipline Inspection Commission, the State Council, the National People's Congress, the Supreme People's Court, and thirteen (out of fifty) other government agencies exist for 1957–1960.[137] Such incompleteness in the data does not bode well for

---

[131] Diao, *Renmin xinfang shilüe*, 123.

[132] Anonymous letters (*niming xin* 匿名性) increased in 1958–1960. The respective share of such letters was 23 percent for complaints to the Discipline Inspection Commission; 18.4 percent for the Beijing city government; 15 percent for the Beijing CCP; 9.26 percent for the State Council; and 10.1 percent for the Ministry of Public Security. There were also letters with false names (*shujiaming* 署假名), whose precise number has not been ascertained (Diao, *Renmin xinfang shilüe*, 119).

[133] Diao, *Renmin xinfang shilüe*, 82.

[134] Diao, *Renmin xinfang shilüe*, 83.

[135] Although they collectively constituted 1.85 percent of China's population at the time, Shanghai, Beijing, and Tianjin accounted for 36.6 percent of the 137,069 letters and visits received in 21 provinces in 1956 (Diao, *Renmin xinfang shilüe*, 76).

[136] Diao, *Renmin xinfang shilüe*, 76–78.

[137] Diao, *Renmin xinfang shilüe*, 118. Some data are only available for 1958–1960.

the regime's capacity to make systematic use of the information about welfare needs transmitted through citizen complaints.

4.4.3   Responsiveness to Welfare Concerns: Origins of the Food Supply Monitoring System

One of the difficulties when evaluating the effectiveness of complaints is locating specific proof of either individual-level responsiveness or of major policy change. Although the available materials do not yield systematic evidence about individual responsiveness, we are in the fortunate position of having access to two sources that elucidate how the party-state monitored the food supply, which was a major source of popular dissatisfaction in the 1950s. The first is *Neibu cankao*. The second source is a top-secret (*juemi* 绝密) compendium of 320 documents on price policies, which was prepared by the Price Department of the Ministry of Commerce in June 1959 in order to provide leaders with reference materials on pricing during the first decade of the PRC.[138]

Neibu cankao reveals that Chinese leaders were apprised of a wide variety of food distribution problems, ranging from price fluctuations and the persistence of black-market activities to poor quality and ongoing shortages;[139] most distressing are reports of spring and summer hunger, famine, malnutrition-induced medical conditions, and even cannibalism.[140] A frequent refrain in the reports is discontent due to the short supply of food. This stood in marked contrast to the experience of central leaders: in Beijing, as in the capitals of other communist regimes, special stores catered to the needs of the leadership. These stores, only selling first-grade (*yiji* 一级) meat, allowed top-level cadres and their family members to purchase as much pork as they wanted; two such special stores in Beijing accounted for 16 percent of pork consumption in the capital.[141] Thus, central leaders needed to be sensitized to the difficulties of daily life, particularly outside the capital city. This is precisely what was achieved through a report on widespread dissatisfaction with the poor quality of grain rations (which included coarse grains like maize, barley, oats, and millet) among migrant workers engaged in road construction and pit digging in the Qaidam Basin.[142] Reports of

---

[138] Zhonghua Renmin Gongheguo Shangye Bu Wujia Ju, *Wujia zhengce zhongyao wenjian huibian (1949–1958)* (Beijing: Zhonghua Renmin Gongheguo Shangye Bu Wujia Ju, June 1959).

[139] The underground markets specialized in the sale of specific commodities: grain; meat (especially pork); and, in at least one case, peanuts (in Nanjing, over 10,000 *jin* of peanuts were sold daily on the black market—see *Neibu cankao*, no. 2091 [December 29, 1956], 679–80).

[140] On seventeen cases of cannibalism in Gansu and other provinces, see *Neibu cankao*, no. 3032 (April 14, 1960), 25–26.

[141] *Neibu cankao*, no. 2102 (January 11, 1957), 214–215.

[142] *Neibu cankao*, no. 1923 (July 3, 1956), 25–26. Located in Qinghai province, the arid inhospitable environment of Qaidam Basin is considered to be a Martian analogue by China's Mars Program.

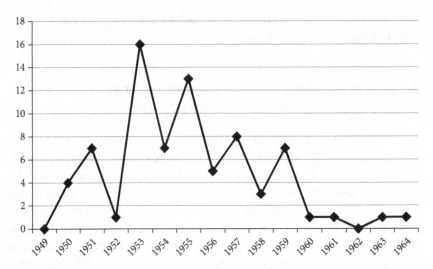

Figure 4.4 Total number of reports on hunger and famine in *Neibu cankao*, 1949–1964.

Source: Author's calculations.

famine, appearing regularly through 1959, were even more graphic (see Figure 4.4). Their frequency declined in 1960, when the number of recipients of *Neibu cankao* was expanded and statistics on deaths from starvation were too sensitive for inclusion in this classified bulletin. This deterioration in the quality of reporting in *Neibu cankao* occurred at the height of the Great Leap Forward when information distortion was widespread. As Chapter 6 discusses, a statistical introspection took place after the conclusion of the leap in the early 1960s.

How was the available intelligence used? Efforts were made to alleviate shortages through price adjustments. However, when procurement prices were revised upward (e.g., to incentivize peasants to sell pork to the state rather than to slaughter it for personal use or to sell it on the black market), there was discontent in the cities because of the sharp increases in prices. The leadership was apprised of the sensitivity of price changes by publications about Poland, where in the assessment of Xinhua journalists, price volatility (*wujia bodong* 物价波动) was a major contributor to instability.[143]

The dilemma of how to price food was compounded by an incapacity to collect systematic nationwide pricing information, as revealed by the compendium of documents on pricing policies, in which the typical report focuses on the value of several items in a geographically limited part of China. In 1958, the Central

---

[143] *Neibu cankao*, no. 1945 (July 28, 1956), 591–604.

Committee and the State Council issued a joint regulation giving control over most pricing decisions to subnational governments. The center only regulated the procurement prices for grain, cotton, oil, tobacco, live hogs, and timber, as well as the retail prices for a dozen commodities (grain, cooking oil, pork, table salt, wrist watches, etc.) sold in important markets throughout the country.[144] This regulation, which revealed the incapacity of the central government to control prices throughout the country, was followed up by a notice that required subnational governments to send information to the Ministry of Commerce about the price adjustments they had implemented.[145] It is not known how well this policy was enforced, though the fact that it was issued after the start of the Great Leap Forward suggests that compliance was most likely suboptimal.

In general, bureaucratic capacity to collect information relevant to satisfying welfare concerns was limited. This is illustrated by a classified statistical report from the Ministry of Finance on the peasant burden in 1949–1957.[146] This document allows us to assess the limitations of the collection of economic statistics during the initial decade of communist governance. Namely, although it contains provincial-level indicators on the fulfillment of agricultural production plans and the level of the peasant burden in all provinces except Tibet, its coverage of natural disasters (which were clearly one reason for the under-fulfillment of production plans) is limited to twenty-two provinces in the 1955–1957 period (and there is no coverage prior to that).[147] Curiously, this report also attempts to provide data on the population of counties that had had prerevolutionary soviets (*laosuqu* 老苏区) in eighteen provinces, but it only supplies this information for twelve provinces.[148] It is no surprise that a bureaucratic apparatus, which proved incapable of collecting data on natural disasters and population statistics, could not accomplish the more sophisticated task of generating nationally comprehensive information on levels of overt and latent discontent, whether they stemmed from frustrated welfare expectations or not.

4.5 The Scotoma of Minority Penetration

Successful penetration of ethnoreligious minorities is challenging for any communist regime. Unsurprisingly, China experienced problems in this area as

---

[144] CCP Central Committee and the State Council, "Guanyu shichang wujia fenji guanli guiding" (October 18, 1958).

[145] Zhonghua Renmin Gongheguo Shangye Bu, "Guanyu shangqing baogao wenti de tongzhi" (November 7, 1958).

[146] Caizheng Bu Nongyeshui Si, *Quanguo nongmin fudan tongji ziliao* (Beijing: Caizheng Bu Nongyeshui Si, December 1957).

[147] *Quanguo nongmin fudan tongji ziliao.*

[148] *Quanguo nongmin fudan tongji ziliao.*

well. More unexpected is the variation among minority groups. As this section demonstrates, there were considerable differences in the penetration capacity in Tibet and Xinjiang, both of which had compact masses of non-Han populations in the 1950s. The contrasting cases of Tibet and Xinjiang point to the importance of deploying a two-pronged strategy to penetrate minority regions: establishing well-policed settler communities and recruiting a substantial share of minority police outside the settler areas. This strategy was successfully implemented in Xinjiang, though not in Tibet, which remained a terra incognita for Beijing throughout the 1950s. Given its modest penetration capacity, the center was incapable of anticipating the regionwide 1959 Uprising.

4.5.1 The Failure of Minority Penetration in Tibet

We possess various indicators about the limited vision of the central state in Tibet in the 1950s. Perhaps most revealing is the fact that although *Neibu cankao* reported from Tibet, this occurred infrequently. Table 4.4 contains statistics on the Xinhua reports filed from Tibet and from three other provinces in the ten-year period preceding the uprising (1949–1958). It is remarkable that this intelligence bulletin, which was tasked with monitoring domestic news, contained more coverage about Yugoslavia, Poland, and Hungary than it did about Tibet. The structural constraints to information gathering were so forbidding that Xinhua published little original reporting from Tibet, with predictable outcomes in terms of keeping leaders apprised of the popular mood.

Another indicator of poor legibility is the low number of party members in Tibet. The party can function as a formidable collector of information on popular discontent, provided that several conditions are fulfilled, namely, that it has

Table 4.4 Number of Reports from Selected Chinese Provinces and from Yugoslavia in *Neibu cankao*, 1949–1958

Tibet	50
Xinjiang	82
Inner Mongolia	262
Hebei	272
Yugoslavia	96

Source: Author's calculations, based on hand-coding the titles of *Neibu cankao* articles.

deeply penetrated the area under surveillance; that it has developed a cadre of party members who can act as intelligence providers; and, finally, that information is systematically transferred up the party chain of command. The CCP did poorly on all these counts during its initial decade of governing Tibet.

When it came to developing a grassroots infrastructural presence, the party could not demonstrate any great achievements during the 1950s. As it lacked an underground organization in Tibet prior to the establishment of the PRC,[149] progress in setting up party branches was slow throughout the 1950s. Thus, an internal gazetteer on the CCP organizational history in Tibet reveals that a mere sixty-six party branches existed throughout the region as of 1953. Of these, five were located at schools, nine at enterprises, and the rest at various military and government outfits.[150] By 1955, there were 63 grassroots and 10 city party organizations (branches, general branches, and committees) in Tibet, whereas nationwide the CCP had already established 514,812 grassroots branches.[151] Considering that Tibet constituted one-tenth of the territory of China (even if its 1.27 million residents made up only 0.25 percent of China's population at the time), the existing party branches hardly offer evidence of deep saturation of the region.

Perhaps unsurprisingly in light of these indicators of incomplete territorial penetration, recruitment of party members could not be described as successful. Statistics began to be kept in 1952, when the party had 877 members and candidate-members in Tibet. By 1953, the roster had grown to 897, of which 57 were candidate-members. Over one-third of the members were based in Lhasa. A breakdown by occupation showcases a motley crew of workers, hired farmhands, peasants (poor, middle, and rich), apprentices, office workers, students, independent professionals, traders, former members of the KMT army, peddlers, and even vagrants (*youmin* 游民).[152] We should note that this lack of discrimination reveals that the party was exceptionally determined to fill its ranks. Although such efforts led to a quintupling of party size within five years (4,186 members by the end of 1958), party building in Tibet still lagged far behind that in other parts of the country. For example, there were 251,190 CCP members in Beijing in 1958, a rate that was 26 times higher per million residents than that in Tibet.[153] Such a low rate of party member saturation had

---

[149] *Zhonggong Xizang difang zuzhishi zhigao 1950–1999* (Lasa: Zhonggong Xizang Zuzhibu, 2000), 696.

[150] *Zhonggong Xizang difang zuzhishi zhigao*, 256.

[151] *Zhongguo gongchandang dangnei tongji ziliao huibian, 1921–2000*, 169, 177.

[152] *Zhonggong Xizang difang zuzhishi zhigao*, 249. Article 12 of the Seventeen-Point Agreement (Agreement of the Central People's Government and the Local Government of Tibet on Measures for the Peaceful Liberation of Tibet, signed in 1951) allowed erstwhile pro-imperialist and pro-KMT officials to hold office, provided that they had severed their former relations and had not engaged in sabotage or resistance. Similarly broad criteria seem to have been applied to party membership.

[153] *Beijing zhi: Gongchandang juan*, 201.

clear negative implications for the capacity of the CCP to engage in intelligence collection in Tibet.

Even more consequential from an information-gathering perspective was the low proportion of Tibetans among party members in the region. For example, Tibetans constituted only 7.3 percent of the 301 CCP members newly recruited in the second half of 1956. Tellingly, a mere 1,190 Tibetans joined the party during the entire eight-year period from 1951 to the end of 1958.[154] To put this in perspective, with its 110,000 monks and nuns (nearly all of whom were Tibetan), Tibet had almost 100 times more Tibetan religious workers than CCP members.[155] This did not bode well for the capacity of the party to rely on its members to collect the information needed to assess levels of discontent among the non-Han living in Tibet.

Beyond the internal media and the party, a third indicator of incomplete penetration is provided by the weakness of the security apparatus, which consisted of the People's Liberation Army (PLA), the Public Security Bureau (PSB), and the People's Armed Police (PAP). The main information gatherer was the Liaison Department of the PLA, which is also sometimes described as the PLA intelligence department. A rare top-secret manual produced by the Liaison Department in November 1952 sheds valuable light on what information was collected, through what methods, and with what limitations.

The manual, which is modestly entitled "Introduction to Persons from Tibet" (*Xizang renwu jieshao* 西藏人物介绍), is organized into four sections including information on 419 individuals: the Dalai Lama and his entourage ruling the region centering around Lhasa and Shannan/Lhoka (*Qianzang* 前藏); the Panchen Lama and his entourage governing the region centering around Shigatse (*Houzang* 后藏); elites and religious leaders from other parts of Tibet; and persons of various other nationalities living in Tibet (*lüju Xizang de geminzu renwu* 旅居西藏的各民族人物). Individuals are introduced with varying amounts of detail. Unsurprisingly, the Dalai Lama and his family members, as well as the Panchen Lama, receive the most extensive coverage, including background information on their social ties and political attitudes. At times, a person may be discussed extremely briefly, as in the case of a certain Yuan Bin ("a monk of Han nationality, from Sichuan, living at the Drepung monastery in Lhasa").[156] A typical description, even when short, includes more extensive biographical details (e.g., age) and explicitly states the reason for inclusion in the compendium. This is especially important for individuals placed in the nondescript category of "persons of various other nationalities living in Tibet," which includes mostly the

---

[154] *Zhonggong Xizang difang zuzhishi zhigao*, 250.

[155] *Zhonggong Xizang difang zuzhishi zhigao*, introduction, p. 4.

[156] Zhonggong Zhongyang Junwei Lianluo Bu, *Xizang renwu jieshao* (Lasa: Zhonggong Zhongyang Junwei Lianluo Bu Ziliao Shi, 1952), 272.

odd Han monk and Han traders whose close links with the Tibetan nobility generated suspicions that they were spying on behalf of the Tibetan elites.

Overall, this compendium focuses on tracking the most highly visible Tibetan elites and a small number of Han living in Tibet. The biographies of about 100 of the 419 people are based on extensive intelligence collected in Tibet; the remaining individuals are discussed using evidence extracted from Mongolian and Tibetan Affairs former KMT officials or gleaned from public records.[157] Missing is coverage of the political views of ordinary Tibetans. Compiling this type of information exceeded the capacity of the PLA Liaison Department.

The available evidence does not indicate whether either the PSB or the PAP was able to collect intelligence on latent discontent during the first decade of CCP rule in Tibet.[158] Internal sources reveal that both arms of the security apparatus focused on detecting foreign spies (who were supported by the Central Intelligence Agency, the KMT, and the British and Indian governments) and counteracting small guerrilla insurgencies and individual acts of dissent.[159] The focus was overwhelmingly on tracking overt dissent. There was no capacity to assess levels of latent discontent prior to the 1959 Uprising among any of the three agencies making up the Tibet security apparatus.

The weakness of the security apparatus is also demonstrated by the fact that agents were recruited from among exiles in Kalimpong in India rather than within Tibet proper. These spies provided intelligence for numerous reports (*Qingbao jianxun* 情报简讯) issued by the Central Investigation Department in the spring and summer of 1958 on armed rebels crossing from India into Tibet. In June 1958, when reading about the Tibetan Uprisings in Qinghai, Mao opined that a comprehensive rebellion could also take place in Tibet—and if that were to occur, it would be welcome, as it would hasten national liberation by the PLA troops. However, as of mid-February 1959, despite twenty clashes between armed rebels and the PLA in Tibet since 1958 (and a Xinhua report on a comprehensive rebellion, in addition to a PLA report that Tibet would serve as a haven for rebels), Mao did not foresee an imminent uprising—he stayed true to his January 1959 position that armed clashes between rebels and the PLA would be beneficial for mobilizing the masses and they could very well continue for another five to six or even seven to eight years.[160]

---

[157] *Xizang renwu jieshao*, unpaginated introduction.

[158] The PAP presence was established in 1956. See Zhongguo Renmin Wuzhuang Jingcha Budui Xizang Zizhiqu Zongdui, *Zhonghua renmin wuzhuang jingcha budui Xizang zizhiqu zongdui zuzhi shi ziliao (January 1950–October 1987)* (Lasa: Zhongguo Renmin Wuzhuang Jingcha Budui Xizang Zizhiqu Zongdui Zuzhi Shi Bianzuan Lingdao Xiaozu, 1991), 5.

[159] Xizang Zizhiqu Gong'an Ting, *Xizang gong'an dashiji, 1950–1995* (Lasa: Xizang Zizhiqu Gong'an Ting, 1999); Gong'an Bu, *Gong'an shi ziliao*, no. 23 (January 1992), 323–34; *Zhonghua renmin wuzhuang jingcha*.

[160] Paragraph based on Xiaoyuan Liu, *The End of Revolution: The Chinese Communist Party in Tibet, 1949–1959* (New York: Columbia University Press, 2020), 252–63.

In sum, all three entities in charge of involuntary extraction in Tibet (the internal media, the party, and the police) were underdeveloped in the 1950s. Voluntary provision was also limited: In 1957, when Tibet received 93 discipline letters and visits, the Beijing city Discipline Inspection Commission handled 979 complaints. When we adjust for the differences in population, Tibet received 73.2 complaints per million residents, whereas Beijing handled five times more (360.3 per million residents).[161] In light of the limited amount of voluntarily provided and involuntarily extracted information, it is not surprising that Tibet was a blind spot for the central government in the 1950s, with the corresponding implication that both the March 1959 Uprising and especially its regionwide scope were not anticipated by the central government.

4.5.2 Deeper Penetration in Xinjiang

A different approach was applied to Xinjiang. On the one hand, Han settlements were established via the Xinjiang Production and Construction Corps (XPCC),[162] a paramilitary organization that had its own police, which managed dissent so efficiently that in 1958 close to 90 percent of all cases of counterrevolutionary criminal activity were resolved;[163] the police personnel endowments of the XPCC were generous, thus necessitating less reliance on social-order informants than in the rest of the autonomous region (1.2 percent of the population for the XPCC in 1957 vs. 1.9 percent in the rest of Xinjiang in 1956).[164] The second strategy involved recruiting co-ethnics to serve as police in the Uyghur-dominated regions of Xinjiang.[165] Most important, the share of minorities in the political-protection police was higher than in the police overall: in 1953 there were twenty-nine political police in Urumqi, ten of whom (34.5 percent) were minority; in the Urumqi PSB overall, the share of minorities in 1953 was 9.3 percent (see Table 4.5).[166] In southern Xinjiang, the share of minorities

---

[161] Calculated from *Beijing zhi: Zhengfa juan*, 435 and *Zhonggong Xizang difang zuzhishi zhigao*, 517. The population of Beijing in 1957 was 2.717 million (https://populationstat.com/china/beijing [accessed April 19, 2022]); Tibet's population in 1957 was 1.27 million (see Leo A. Orleans, "A Note on Tibet's Population," *The China Quarterly*, no. 27 [July–September 1966], 120–22, at 120).

[162] This followed earlier practices of Han settlement, which dated back to the Qing: Zhang Anfu, *Qingdai yilai Xinjiang tunken yu guojia anquan* (Beijing: Zhongguo Nongye Chubanshe, 2011).

[163] Xinjiang Shengchan Jianshe Bingtuan Gong'an Zhi and Xinjiang Shengchan Jianshe Bingtuan Difang Zhi Bangongshi, *Xinjiang shengchan jianshe bingtuan gong'an zhi* (Urumqi: Xinjiang Shengchan Jianshe Bingtuan Gong'an Zhi and Xinjiang Shengchan Jianshe Bingtuan Difang Zhi Bangongshi, 1999), 185–86.

[164] *Xinjiang shengchan jianshe bingtuan gong'an zhi*, 205–6, 255–68; Wulumuqi Shi Gong'an Ju, *Wulumuqi gong'an zhi* (Urumqi: Xinjiang Renmin Chubanshe, 1998), 372.

[165] On a similar strategy applied to a different context, see Ami Pedahzur, *The Israeli Secret Services and the Struggle Against Terrorism* (New York: Columbia University Press, 2009).

[166] *Wulumuqi gong'an zhi*, 139.

Table 4.5 Minority Members of the Police in Urumqi, 1949–1958

	Total Number of Police	Minority	% Minority
1950	417	16	3.8%
1951	401	16	4%
1952	412	13	3.1%
1953	399	37	9.3%
1954	408	24	5.9%
1955	405	35	8.6%
1956	397	50	12.6%
1957	386	49	12.7%
1958	439	53	12.1%

Source: Wulumuqi gong'an zhi, 135–37.

was even higher. Take Aksu (阿克苏) prefecture as an example: in 1953, it had forty-nine detectives, 82 percent of whom were minorities.[167] Using investigation techniques that included phone tapping, in 1954 the Aksu PSB identified 1,513 enemies.[168] This was a remarkable accomplishment of societal legibility in comparison with the incapacity of the state to penetrate Tibet. A crucial difference between the two regions also involves the density of CCP membership: in 1958, there was a 26:1 ratio of minority party members to religious workers in Xinjiang (contrast this with the 1:92 ratio in Tibet).[169] The elevated capacity for penetration explains why the level of repression in Xinjiang remained below the national average throughout the 1950s (see Table 4.6).

A final relevant indicator of penetration capacity is the size of the party, which was much larger in Xinjiang than in Tibet. For example, 1.04 percent of those living in Xinjiang were party members in 1955. Although this was lower than the national average of 1.53 percent (not to mention the 3.25 percent rate in Beijing), it was nearly nine times higher than the 0.12 percent registered in Tibet.[170] Similarly, Xinjiang had 3,431 grassroots party organizations (branches, general

[167] Akesu Diqu Gong'an Chu Shizhi Bianji Shi, *Akesu gong'an zhi* (Aksu: Akesu Diqu Gong'an Chu, 1994), 168.

[168] *Akesu gong'an zhi*, 172–74.

[169] There were 55,472 CCP members who were minorities and 2,102 religious workers (*zongjiao zhiyezhe* 宗教职业者) in Xinjiang in 1958. See Guojia Minwei Bangongting, *Quanguo shaoshu minzu qingkuang tongji ziliao* (Beijing: Guojia Minwei Bangongting, February 1960), 115, 119 and *Zhonggong Xizang difang zuzhishi zhigao*, 250.

[170] *Zhongguo gongchandang dangnei tongji ziliao huibian, 1921–2000*, 4.

Table 4.6 Political Prisoners in Xinjiang and in China Overall, 1951–1958

	Individuals Imprisoned for Counter-revolutionary Crimes (national level)	As % of All Prisoners (national level)	Individuals Imprisoned for Counter-revolutionary Crimes (Xinjiang)	As % of all Prisoners (Xinjiang)	National: Xinjiang Ratio
1951	326,497	37.40	ND	ND	
1952	512,252	47.47	1,996	43.16	1.1:1
1953	565,280	50.02	3,446	40.16	1.24:1
1956	604,532	48.05	3,741	40.91	1.17:1
1957	602,241	49.48	4,244	43.97	1.12:1
1958	800,027	42.96	4,818	27.24	1.58:1

Source: Author's dataset, based on Sifa Bu, *Dangdai Zhongguo jianyu tongji ziliao.*

branches, and committees) in 1955, which was fifty-four times more than the sixty-three grassroots organizations that existed in Tibet at the time.[171] In sum, the strategies deployed in Xinjiang ensured superior visibility by comparison with Tibet in the 1950s. However, as we will see in Chapters 6 and 8, their effectiveness eroded over time.

4.6 Conclusion

The most notable feature of the first decade of communist rule in China is the country's progress in building institutions for the collection of information. This is especially remarkable in light of the unusual structural constraints that the regime faced at its inception. The communist leaders harnessed some of the pre-existing information-gathering institutions and in short order were able to set in motion mechanisms for the involuntary collection of information on regime enemies, thus generating increasingly granular intelligence to guide decisions about the use of repression. Naturally, structural constraints had implications, especially in terms of the voluntary provision of information relevant for assessing and satisfying consumption preferences and the monitoring of minorities. Similar problems (though of a smaller magnitude) can be noted during the initial period of communist rule in Bulgaria as well. Most surprising is that,

[171] *Zhongguo gongchandang dangnei tongji ziliao huibian, 1921–2000,* 169, 177.

within a decade of seizing power, the CCP had created a functioning system for monitoring overt dissent among members of the ethnic majority, thus laying the foundations for a communist information state. As Chapter 6 discusses, the speed of state building slowed down during the Great Leap Forward and the Cultural Revolution, though the wholesale destruction of existing information-gathering institutions was rare. During subsequent decades, it was difficult to deviate from the initial path of institutional development that had been established in the 1950s.

PART III
DIVERGENT EVOLUTION
OF COMMUNIST
INFORMATION STATES

Part III focuses on the major divergence in the trajectories of Bulgaria and China after 1958. Driven by an understanding that higher standards of living and the appeal of Western cultural products were vectors of ideological subversion, the Bulgarian regime built a classic socialist welfare state that aimed to prevent the rise of overt discontent by satisfying the material and cultural consumption needs of the population. Anticipatory governance relied on a high volume of information transmitted voluntarily through the citizen complaints system, which operated efficiently due to diminished levels of fear and high responsiveness. In turn, responsiveness required financial resources and an elevated state capacity. The system was stable for decades and had solved the mass constraint, thus convincing regime insiders that they could move to tackle the problem of the impenetrability of minorities through an ethnic assimilation campaign unleashed in the 1980s. By contrast, China pursued a path of autarkic development after 1958, which staved off concerns about ideological subversion until the 1980s, when the Ministry of State Security was established. A very narrow welfare regime emerged that was limited to urban residents, who constituted 10–20 percent of the population during the Mao period. Information was gathered primarily involuntarily, as voluntary provision was disrupted by the turbulent upheavals of the Great Leap Forward (1958–1962) and the Cultural Revolution (1966–1976), which eroded state capacity. Counterintuitively, considering this divergence, both countries were heading to a crisis point in the second half of the 1980s that would feature similar combinations of minority unrest, dissent driven by material frustrations stemming from plans to dismantle the socialist social contract, and political protests. The one consequential difference is that the crisis in China was limited to urban areas (and to Tibet), whereas in Bulgaria it was nationwide, thus calling for different responses.

The two chapters here show the limits of information. Under ideal conditions, abundant involuntarily collected and voluntarily provided information can be used to fine-tune selective repression and targeted redistribution, leading to a high level of social stability. Deviations from this equilibrium can occur, however. Decisions about brute repression can be undertaken under limited information, provided that indicators of overt discontent have been detected. Another deviation involves having abundant information but being unable to act because the funds for redistribution are not available and levels of fear are very low, thus making both redistribution and repression infeasible. Information can help improve the quality of governance and contribute to regime resilience, but this only occurs when specific conditions are met, as discussed in this book.

Chapters 5 and 6 produce several additional theoretically relevant insights. One concerns the divergence between China and Bulgaria with regard to the voluntary transmission of information. Although both countries developed similar information-gathering institutions (and those institutions survived despite the Great Leap Forward and the Cultural Revolution in China), complaints were infrequent in China both under Mao and during the initial decade of reforms. This had clear implications for the rise of anticipatory governance. Whereas Bulgaria made maximal use of all available channels for involuntary extraction and voluntary provision to collect high-quality nationally comprehensive information and use it to engage in ex-ante rule featuring extensive redistribution and selective repression, low levels of responsiveness and relatively high levels of fear in China precluded citizens from using the complaints system at a rate comparable to that in Eastern Europe. As a result, China was unable to adopt ex-ante rule.

Another relevant finding concerns the value of redundancy. Substantial overlap existed in the reporting streams of State Security, the party, and the internal media. This duplication was desired by decision makers, as it allowed them to cross-check intelligence and to mitigate the information-gathering pathologies that develop when relying exclusively on a single information-collection channel.

A final theoretically relevant insight that emerges from the two chapters concerns the ideological threat to communist regimes. Gradually, fears of a physical invasion were replaced by anxiety about the danger of ideological infiltration. As the case of Eastern Europe demonstrates, failure to counteract external ideological influences can have deleterious effects on stability, especially when combined with a malfunctioning of the system for redistributive spending.

5

Bread and Circuses

Consumption and Stability in Bulgaria, 1959–1988

By the late 1950s, all preconditions for a radical revision of threat perceptions were present in Bulgaria: the elite challenges had been neutralized; organized mass discontent had been extinguished; and individual acts of overt opposition to the system were declining. This allowed the information-gathering institutions to gradually re-orient from engaging in reactive ex-post governance (which involved responding to overt dissatisfaction) to practicing anticipatory (ex-ante) rule, which focused on assessing and counteracting latent popular discontent prior to its transformation into overt challenges to the regime. Anticipatory governance was premised on a novel conceptualization of external ideological subversion as the main vector that stimulated changes in the level of latent discontent. According to internal regime understandings, ideological subversion aimed to destabilize the party-state by promoting foreign culture and high standards of living. In less than two decades of communist rule, threat perceptions underwent an extraordinary evolution: instead of focusing primarily on domestic factors (elite opposition and organized mass resistance), the regime shifted its gaze to external forces that fueled latent popular dissatisfaction.

Counteracting ideological subversion necessitated a coordinated strategy that relied on three pillars: repression, bread, and circuses (the latter two are referred to internally as "satisfying the material and cultural needs of the people"). The repressive organs sought to jam foreign radio broadcasts and to block the importation of cultural products. They also monitored groups susceptible to ideological influence, such as intellectuals, the youth, ethnoreligious minorities, and followers of the banned counterrevolutionary parties. However, in contrast to the late 1940s and early 1950s, repression beginning in the late 1950s was selective. The management of latent discontent relied on collecting extensive information about individuals who were likely to engage in antiregime activity, yet this intelligence was used for prophylaxis rather than for harsh repression. The second pillar was material concessions, which involved maintaining responsiveness to information about welfare needs that was voluntarily transmitted through

Dictatorship and Information. Martin K. Dimitrov, Oxford University Press. © Oxford University Press 2023. DOI: 10.1093/oso/9780197672921.003.0005

complaints. Such responsiveness was the core of the socialist social contract, whereby citizens exchanged quiescence for the provision of welfare. Complaints were understood both to provide insights about latent discontent and to index the general level of popular trust in the system. The final pillar was the promotion of indigenous cultural consumption. The basic goal was to distract citizens from seeking foreign cultural products. A more ambitious long-term objective was to counteract Western influence through grandiose spectacles that stimulated patriotic national pride.

The strategy of co-optation failed for the ethnoreligious minorities, whose levels of well-being remained lower than those of the ethnic majority. Moreover, the minorities were excluded from cultural consumption, which catered to the needs of the ethnic majority. Faced with its inability to penetrate the Turkish minority but feeling secure that it had resolved both the popular and the elite threat, the leadership unleashed an assimilation campaign against the Turks in 1984–1985. The timing proved inauspicious, as the economic situation deteriorated rapidly beginning in 1985. Thus, on the eve of 1989, the regime was faced with the double whammy of both minority and majority unrest, neither of which could be counteracted through repression or redistributive concessions. The stage was set for the fundamental regime transformation that unfolded in 1989–1991.

This chapter on anticipatory governance in Bulgaria is organized as follows. Section 5.1 focuses on the security apparatus, which adopted prophylaxis and selective repression as the dominant techniques for managing latent discontent. State Security articulated the understanding that satisfying consumption preferences can help prevent the rise of overt discontent and that ideological subversion is more likely when citizens experience welfare frustrations. These conceptual shifts were at the core of the strategy for protecting state security in the 1970s and 1980s. Section 5.2 introduces the welfare commitments made by the regime under the socialist social contract, and Section 5.3 presents the wide range of institutions that were created to monitor specific consumption preferences. Section 5.4 provides a discussion of responsiveness to these preferences. The chapter then turns to ideological subversion (Section 5.5), examining in particular how patriotic pride, spectacles, and indigenous entertainment were deployed to counteract foreign influence (Section 5.6). Section 5.7 analyzes the ongoing incapacity of the regime to penetrate the Bulgarian Turks, their further alienation as a result of the patriotic campaigns of the 1970s, and the decision to initiate an assimilation campaign in 1984–1985. Section 5.8 focuses on the economic crisis that began in 1985 and the increasing disenchantment of the elite and the masses in 1985–1988. Section 5.9 concludes the chapter, laying the groundwork for the discussion of regime transformation in Chapter 7.

5.1 Managing Latent Discontent through Selective Repression and Prophylaxis

The communist party in Bulgaria faced both elite and mass threats during the first decade of communist rule. The elite threat stemmed from opposition parties (which were not fully eliminated until 1949); inner-party factions; the military; and prominent intellectuals, industrialists, religious leaders, and politicians who were loyal to the *ancien régime*. The popular threat was associated with armed resistance groups, organized protests, and individual acts of dissent. Cumulatively, these were formidable challenges. Nonetheless, the elite threat was neutralized by the end of the 1940s.[1] Furthermore, armed resistance (referenced internally as "political banditry") and organized protests were fully extinguished by the mid-1950s.[2] Individual acts of opposition persisted, but these were rare and limited to anticommunist propaganda and agitation (scrawling graffiti and spreading leaflets) and agricultural or industrial sabotage (arson, the poisoning of collective farm livestock, and the disabling of manufacturing equipment).[3] Within a decade of the establishment of communist rule, the party found itself in a much more secure position than it had occupied when it initiated the seizure of power in 1944. A qualitative shift in the threats facing the regime was underway.

Though the initial signs of this shift could be detected by 1953–1955,[4] the events of 1956 delayed the unveiling of the new state security doctrine, which was systematically articulated in 1959 and consolidated by the late 1960s.[5] As elite threats were easily manageable with minimal resources, the bulk of the attention focused on handling the popular threat. The new strategy involved a radical re-orientation from the monitoring of overt discontent to the detection of latent dissatisfaction. This required developing an understanding of the sources of latent discontent and devising a counterstrategy.

5.1.1 Ideological Subversion and Latent Discontent

In the late 1950s, State Security updated its conceptualization of external threats. The novel argument was that the West no longer planned to destabilize the communist regimes in Eastern Europe by invasion or by supporting an armed

---

[1] See archival documents in *Borbi i chistki v BKP (1948–1953)* (Sofia: Central State Archives, 2001).

[2] See documents reproduced in *Gorianite: Sbornik dokumenti, 1944–1949*, vol. 1 (Sofia: Central State Archives, 2001) and *Gorianite: Sbornik dokumenti, 1949–1956*, vol. 2 (Sofia: Central State Archives, 2010).

[3] Archive of Bulgarian Ministry of the Interior (AMVR) f. 1 op. 1 a. e. 3498 (1955), 1–20; AMVR f. 1 op. 1 a. e. 59 (February 4, 1956), 1–34.

[4] AMVR f. 13 op. 1 a. e. 1162 (1955), 1–11.

[5] AMVR f. 1 op. 1 a. e. 61 (1959), 1–32; AMVR f. 1 op. 1 a. e. 62 (November 23, 1959), 1–23.

insurrection.[6] Rather, the West had re-oriented itself toward ideological subversion, which aimed to build up antigovernment sentiments among morally and politically vulnerable groups (primarily the youth) by promoting Western culture and high standards of living.[7] This new understanding, which had crystallized by the mid-1960s, guided the 1967 transformation of the Political Police Department of State Security into a directorate charged primarily with monitoring ideological subversion (thus interchangeably referred to as the political or the ideological police).[8] The threat of ideological subversion would intensify in the 1970s, a decade that witnessed the entry into force of the 1975 Helsinki Final Act (enabling the free movement of ideas and people) and the flourishing of Bulgarian émigré associations in Western Europe and the Americas. A strategy that involved both inducements and punishments was deployed to counteract such ideological subversion.

On the punitive side, State Security aimed to control the impact of ideology by curtailing the vectors for the spread of foreign ideas and by monitoring those who were likely to fall prey to their influence. The vectors included visits to the country by Westerners (and travel to the West by Bulgarians), radio broadcasts, and the importation of cultural products (newsprint, books, movies, records, cassette tapes, and by the 1980s, videotapes). Restrictions were imposed on tourism and the importation of cultural products. In addition, the broadcasts of "hostile" radio stations (the British Broadcasting Corporation [BBC], Radio Free Europe [RFE], the Voice of America [VOA], and Deutsche Welle) were jammed. And yet such restrictions were not absolute, and censorship was porous (listenership reached 50 percent of the population despite the jamming), thus necessitating the deployment of a second repressive strategy, namely, monitoring those most likely to be influenced by external ideology. The targeted groups included intellectuals, supporters of counterrevolutionary parties, the youth, and ethnoreligious minorities. We should note that in contrast to the handling of overt discontent, which necessitated harsh and swift action, latent discontent required time-consuming and labor-intensive processes. State Security relied on maintaining lists of individuals who would be subjected to surveillance (similar to the targeted population roster in China).[9] Indiscriminate arrests were no

---

[6] AMVR f. 1 op. 1 a. e. 61 (1959), 1–32.

[7] AMVR f. 1 op. 1 a. e. 62 (November 23, 1959), 1–23. On the susceptibility of the youth, see also AMVR f. 1 op. 5 a. e. 40 (March 30, 1955); AMVR f. 1 op. 1 a. e. 3498 (1955), 1–20; AMVR f. 1 op. 1 a. e. 59 (February 4, 1956), 1–34; and Bulgarian Central State Archives (TsDA) f. 1B op. 34 a. e. 52 (March 23, 1967), 1–112.

[8] TsDA f. 1B op. 34 a. e. 52 (March 23, 1967), 1–112.

[9] AMVR f. 13 op. 1 a. e. 1162 (1955), 1–11; AMVR f. 1 op. 5 a. e. 40 (March 30, 1955); TsDA f. 1B op. 34 a. e. 52 (March 23, 1967), 1–112.

longer practiced.[10] Instead, prophylaxis was the preferred method of handling latent discontent.[11] Repression was selective and infrequent. Overall, a relatively mild approach to dissent was in place beginning in the late 1950s.

5.1.2 Political Repression

A notable decline in the frequency and severity of repression occurred after 1958. Several indicators allow us to document this trend. One is the August 1959 Politburo decision to close down the labor camps, which were officially designated as "reeducation-through-labor communal residence facilities" (*trudovo-vuzpitatelni obshtezhitiia*).[12] Although some inmates stayed in two remaining labor camps until 1962 (the camp in Lovech and the new camp for female detainees near Skravena), the symbolic force of the message was high. As the camps were notorious for brutal working conditions and the sadistic attitude of the guards who tortured and killed many inmates, the decision to eliminate these detention centers sent a signal that repression was declining in severity.

A second trend has to do with the overall frequency of repression. Between 1944 and 1962, a total of 23,531 citizens were sent to the camps (62.2 percent for political reasons).[13] However, whereas between 1944 and 1948 political internees constituted 75.3 percent of the 8,160 camp detainees, their share had fallen to 20.8 percent of the 3,363 inmates in 1958–1962 (the rest of the camp population consisted of criminals and "amoral" individuals, such as prostitutes, pimps, and gay men).[14] Finally, the number of arrests for antistate crimes declined,[15] as did the overall population of political prisoners due to both reduced intakes of new inmates and reduced sentences. In 1961, the total number of those imprisoned for counterrevolutionary activity stood at 1,277 (an incarceration rate of 0.015 percent of the population, which was not matched by China until 1978),[16]

---

[10] TsDA f. 1B op. 34 a. e. 52 (March 23, 1967), 1–112. Earlier calls to limit indiscriminate arrests were issued in 1946 (AMVR f. 1 op. 1 a. e. 394 [November 1946], 1–4), 1952 (AMVR f. 1 op. 5 a. e. 30 [1952], 1–32), and the spring of 1956 (AMVR f. 1 op. 1 a. e. 59 [February 4, 1956], 1–34).

[11] AMVR f. 1 op. 1 a. e. 62 (November 23, 1959), 1–23.

[12] Penka Stoianova and Emil Iliev, *Politicheski opasni litsa: Vudvoriavaniia, trudova mobilizatsiia, izselvaniia v Bulgariia sled 1944 g.* (Sofia: Universitetsko Izdatelstvo "Sv. Kliment Okhridski," 1991), 157.

[13] Bulgarian State Security Dossier Commission (AKRDOPBGDSRSBNA-M) f. 23 op. 1 a. e. 92 (May 1990), 1–20, at 14.

[14] AKRDOPBGDSRSBNA-M f. 23 op. 1 a. e. 92 (May 1990), 1–20, at 14. On the population of the Lovech camp in 1962, see AKRDOPBGDSRSBNA-M f. 23 op. 1 a. e. 111 (March 13, 1962), 18.

[15] For yearly data beginning from 1959, see *Prestupleniia i osudeni litsa, 1969–1990* (Sofia: Durzhavno Upravlenie za Informatsiia pri Ministerskiia Suvet, 1969–1990).

[16] China had imprisoned 148,930 individuals for counterrevolutionary crimes in 1978 (0.0156 percent of the population). See Sifa Bu Jianyu Guanli Ju, *Dangdai Zhongguo jianyu tongji ziliao (1949–1989)* (Beijing: Sifa Bu Jianyu Guanli Ju, November 1998), 74.

with the main categories being 400 youth who had attempted to flee the country and 250 former members of the banned opposition parties.[17] Overall, Bulgaria was entering a new period with regard to the deployment of repression in response to political dissent.

5.1.3   Decline in Overt Dissent

The remaining camps were closed down in 1962. In the early 1960s, a transition from mass repression to surveillance and targeted repression was underway. State Security was aware of the size of the so-called enemy contingent, and it was confident in its ability to establish control over these "enemies." The only serious threats to the regime in the 1956–1968 period came from insiders, reflecting party factionalism rather than broader social opposition to the regime.[18] This means that State Security had successfully neutralized the opposition through continuous surveillance and selective repression.

In the mature post-Stalinist system, massive arrests and imprisonment were used infrequently. As Minister of the Interior Angel Solakov reported at a Central Committee plenum in 1967: "Changes in the ranks of the working class, among the members of cooperative farms and the people's intelligentsia, alongside increases in the material and cultural level of workers, have consolidated further the moral-political unity of the people. As a result, political crime is constantly decreasing."[19] This conclusion is confirmed by a classified report documenting the rapid decline in the number of political crimes that were investigated by State Security (see Table 5.1).

Perhaps the most unusual indicator of the reduction in repression is the number of individuals prosecuted for spreading jokes. Antiregime jokes were tracked primarily by the secret police, which could prosecute individuals under Article 108 of the Penal Code (antistate agitation and propaganda) or Article 273 of the Penal Code (the spreading of false information). Although the State Security archives do not provide us with time-series data on the volume of antiregime jokes, a scholar has compiled and dated the jokes with the widest circulation in Bulgaria in 1957–1989; his research indicates that the number of antiregime jokes rose significantly in the 1970s and 1980s.[20] Importantly, this increase in the volume of antiregime jokes was accompanied by declines in the

---

[17] AKRDOPBGDSRSBNA-M f. 13 op. 1 a. e. 1965 (May 26, 1961), 4–6, at 4.

[18] Dimitar Ivanov, *Politicheskoto protivopostaviane v Bulgariia 1956–1989 g.* (Sofia: Ares Press, 1994), 10–44; Mikhail Doktorov, *V skhvatka s oktopoda: "Vtoriiat tsentur" v borbata sreshtu zhivkovistite, 1965–1968 g.* (Sofia: Ares Press, 1993).

[19] TsDA f. 1B op. 34 a. e. 52 (1967), 1–112.

[20] Kiril Vasilev, *45 godini vitsove: Smekhut sreshtu nasilieto* (Sofia: Universitetsko Izdatelstvo "Kliment Okhridski," 1990).

Table 5.1 Political Crimes Investigated in Bulgaria, 1952 and 1965

Crime	1952	1965
Espionage	416	1
Terrorism and sabotage	530	3
Illegal organizations	1,316	12
Hostile propaganda		23
Illegal border crossing	422	309
Other	524	88
Total number of individuals investigated	3,208	436

Source: AKRDOPBGDSRSBNA-M f. 6 op. 3 a. e. 6 (1966), 152–57.

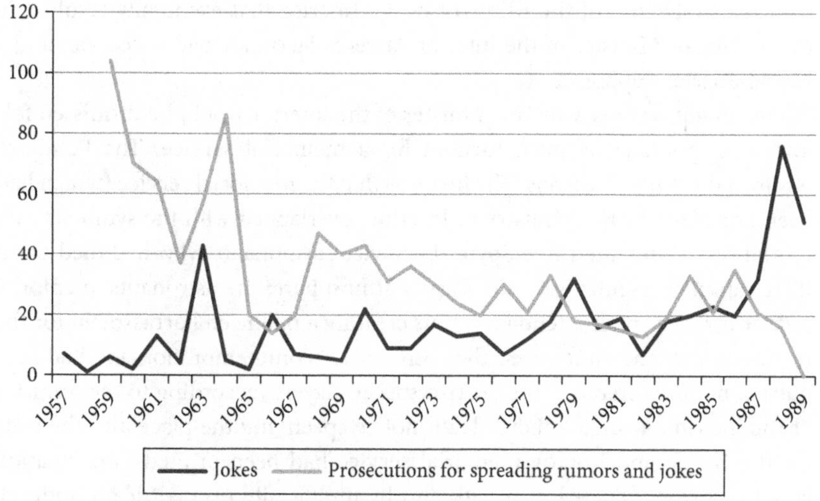

Figure 5.1 Number of jokes and prosecutions for spreading rumors and jokes in Bulgaria, 1957–1989.

Sources: Vasilev, *45 godini vitsove*; *Prestupleniia i osudeni litsa, 1969–1990* (Sofia: Durzhavno Upravlenie za Informatsiia pri Ministerskiia Suvet, 1969–1990).

number of individuals subjected to persecution for spreading antiregime jokes and rumors (see Figure 5.1).[21] This suggests that the government gradually

---

[21] *Prestupleniia i osudeni litsa, 1969–1990.* Even though prosecutions declined over time (especially after the 1975 Helsinki Accords), State Security continued to regard political jokes as a form of mild ideological subversion (AMVR f. 22 op. 1 a. e. 257 [1976], 25).

started to treat jokes as a crude indicator of the popular mood rather than as a grave political threat.

5.1.4 Sporadic Mass Incidents

A key indicator of the rarity of overt discontent was the absence of mass incidents. The most serious mass incident in 1959–1988 was the unplanned gathering of a large number of individuals in Sofia in 1971 for the memorial service for the two most charismatic soccer players of the time: Georgi Asparukhov-Gundi and Nikola Kotkov, who played for one of the two best sports teams (Levski-Spartak), which belonged to the Ministry of the Interior. Gundi and Kotkov had died in a car crash. The memorial service was attended by as many as 150,000–200,000 people. This was an unprecedented turnout, equivalent to one-fifth of the population of the capital at the time. The incident led to a meeting of the Politburo with the Collegium of the Ministry of the Interior that eventually resulted in the sacking of Minister of the Interior Angel Solakov, an avid soccer fan and a Levski-Spartak supporter.

One might wonder why the minister of the interior would be dismissed following a spontaneous mass turnout for a memorial service. The Politburo outlined three main reasons. The first was that the memorial service (which had been organized by the Ministry of Interior) overlapped with the symbolic memorial service for the three Soyuz-11 Soviet cosmonauts who had died upon their capsule's re-entry into the Earth's atmosphere; the astronauts' memorial service had very poor attendance, thus creating a public embarrassment for the regime, which had announced the cosmonauts' commemoration and had kept quiet about the ceremony for the two soccer players (according to the minister of the interior, a single official death notice specifying the place and the time for the Gundi and Kotkov memorial service had been printed—information about it spread by word of mouth and by unofficially printed death notices). Second, more people attended the Gundi and Kotkov memorial service than had attended Dimitrov's state funeral in 1949, thus dealing a further blow to the regime's confidence in its capacity to mobilize the masses. Third, and most significant, was the potential for disruption of social order when so many people assembled. The minister of the interior acknowledged this himself, by admitting to the Politburo that there existed a potential for a provocation, especially if the event were to have taken place in the downtown area instead of the suburban stadium where it had been moved.

Most remarkable about this incident is that nothing happened. As the minister of the interior stated: "The militia could not establish control over the people. Hundreds of thousands of people, tens of thousands of them crying, kilometers' worth of flowers and wreaths—and all of that entirely spontaneously. . . . We did not expect or plan for this and, in practice, were unable to maintain the necessary control over the situation."[22] This indicates that what most bothered the regime was the spontaneity of the gathering and the potential for the disruption of social order when large groups of people assemble without extensive prior planning. Given that the memory of the Prague Spring was still fresh in the minds of the leadership, one can understand its nervousness about an unprompted massive public display. We should stress that no mass gathering in the ensuing eighteen years (until the start of democratization in 1989) came close to matching the number of mourners at the Gundi and Kotkov memorial service. Mass incidents were extremely infrequent.

5.1.5 The Rise of Selective Repression and Prophylaxis

The decline in the incidence of overt discontent and political crime in the 1960s led to an important change: when a new Criminal Code was promulgated on March 15, 1968, it no longer listed neutralizing enemies of the people as a goal of criminal punishment.[23] As Figure 5.2 demonstrates, over time, there was a general softening of repression. This was not coincidental. Rather, it reflected the increased confidence of State Security that it had the information it needed to efficiently target and strategically deploy selective repression. As the minister of the interior stated: "We consider that the main criterion for assessing the work of State Security should not be the elevated number of arrested, prosecuted, and sentenced Bulgarian citizens or the number of those engaging in enemy activity who are under our control, but rather mainly the number of individuals saved from political and moral downfall."[24]

It is remarkable that by the 1970s most individuals engaging in antiregime activity were receiving warnings and reprimands, rather than prison sentences. Statistics on political prisoners are illustrative. In 1975–1976, those incarcerated for antistate crimes constituted 1.3 percent of the prison population.[25]

---

[22] TsDA f. 1B op. 6 a. e. 345 (July 13, 1971), 1–32.

[23] Martin Kanushev, "Postoianen nadzor i infranakazatelnost: Bulgarskoto nakazatelno pravo prez perioda 1957–1969 godina," *Sotsiologicheski problemi* XLI:3–4 (2009), 175–99.

[24] TsDA f. 1B op. 34 a. e. 52 (March 21, 1967), 1–112.

[25] AKRDOPBGDSRSBNA-M f. 38 op. 1 a. e. 72 (1976), 89–98, at 90. Levels of incarceration in Bulgaria stood at 0.13 percent of the population in 1975–1976, which is comparable to the 0.11 percent of China's population (1,047,157 people) who were being held in prisons and labor camps at that time. The difference is that in 1975, as many as 29.9 percent of the prisoners in China were jailed for counterrevolutionary crimes, which is exactly twenty-three times higher than the proportion of political prisoners in Bulgaria (*Dangdai Zhongguo jianyu tongji ziliao 1949–1989* [Beijing: Sifa Bu Jianyu Guanli Ju, November 1998], 6–7). It was not until 1984 that the proportion of political detainees in China declined to 1.3 percent.

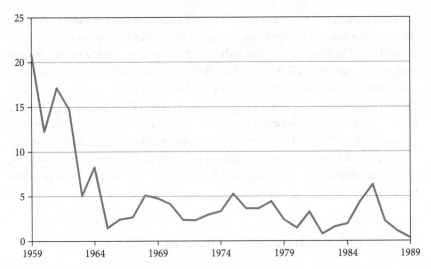

Figure 5.2 Number of individuals prosecuted for antistate crimes in Bulgaria, 1959–1989 (per million people).
Source: Prestupleniia i osudeni litsa, 1969–1990.

Punishments such as forced resettlement (which remained an option for handling dissent even after the camps were closed) continued, though at an extremely low frequency. For example, in 1975 the number of individuals subjected to forced resettlement stood at forty-nine.[26] This compares favorably with the forty-five people sentenced for antistate crimes in the same year (5 per million people).[27] These low levels of repression remained constant until the mid-1980s, when the share of political prisoners came to 1.2 percent of the prison population.[28]

These statistics reflect the information-gathering function of the secret police: It was interested in using monitoring to anticipate and prevent political crime. Instead of repression, most forms of dissent were handled through prophylaxis; ideologically unsound elements were subjected to an escalating series of warnings and threats, which were aimed at dissuading them from engaging in subversive activities. In this regard, the operation of the Bulgarian State Security parallels that of the Soviet KGB under Brezhnev, when prophylaxis rather than heavy-handed repression and imprisonment was the dominant approach toward

[26] AKRDOPBGDSRSBNA-M f. 22 op. 2 a. e. 1 (1976), 55–57.
[27] *Prestupleniia i osudeni litsa* (1976).
[28] AKRDOPBGDSRSBNA-M f. 1 op. 12 a. e. 725 (1986), 3–11, at 4–5.

dissent.[29] In Bulgaria, as in the Soviet Union and the German Democratic Republic (GDR), the network of full-time State Security employees and part-time informants was expanding, yet levels of repression were declining.[30] With access to higher-quality information, the regime did not have to resort to massive violence: targeted, strategically deployed, and infrequent repression was used to ensure regime survival.

5.1.6 Trends in Overt Discontent: Fewer Antistate Crimes, More People Fleeing

State Security faced a dilemma in the 1970s. On the one hand, levels of overt discontent, measured as instances of antistate crimes (treason, sabotage, espionage, subversion, and other crimes against the people's republic), were factors of magnitude lower than they had been in the late 1940s, and they were continuing to decline further. At the same time, the number of individuals fleeing the republic (or making preparations to do so) was increasing at a rapid pace (see Figure 5.3). Both antistate crimes and fleeing the republic were manifestations of overt discontent. In the understanding of State Security, both had resulted from foreign ideological subversion. It was not clear what could be done to counteract this trend. Even before the 1975 Helsinki Final Act, prophylaxis rather than brute repression had emerged as the preferred method for dealing with dissent. For example, 3,260 of the 4,000 tips on enemy activity received by the Sixth Directorate of State Security in 1972–1974 focused on preparations to flee the country. Yet these tips led to the sentencing and imprisonment of only 76 individuals; another 57 were forcefully resettled throughout the country; 274 were entered into the operational-reporting system; and 1,572 were subjected to prophylactic "filtration," which aimed to determine whether they had been recruited by foreign intelligence services.[31] The Helsinki Final Act further impressed upon State Security that prophylaxis rather than imprisonment should remain the dominant approach toward the rare instances of overt dissent that were registered during the 1970s.[32] Latent political discontent, however, called for a more complex response.

---

[29] See, for example, "O nekotorykh itogakh predupreditel'no-profilakticheskoi raboty organov gosbezopasnosti," Library of Congress, Volkogonov Papers, Box 28 (October 31, 1975).

[30] On the Soviet Union, see Martin K. Dimitrov, "Tracking Public Opinion under Authoritarianism: The Case of the Soviet Union under Brezhnev," *Russian History* 41:3 (2014), 329–53.

[31] AMVR f. 22 op. 1 a. e. 23 (1975), 8.

[32] AMVR f. 1 op. 12 a. e. 424A (1977), 2.

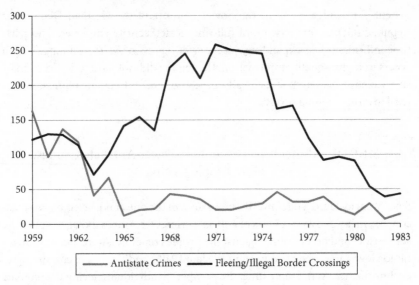

Figure 5.3 Number of individuals imprisoned for crimes against the state and for fleeing the republic or illegal border crossings in Bulgaria, 1959–1983.

Source: Prestupleniia i osudeni litsa, 1969–1990.

NB: The statistics in this table are more comprehensive than those reported in AMVR f. 22 op. 1 a. e. 23 (1975), 8. Note that AMVR f. 22 op. 1 a. e. 23 (1975) reports only cases handled by the Sixth Directorate of State Security. Figure 5.3 includes data on all cases handled by the Ministry of the Interior.

5.1.7 The Sixth Directorate and the Fight against Political Dissent

State Security took a major step in terms of institutional upgrading when it created the Sixth Directorate in 1967. The directorate represented an expansion of the earlier political police structures that had targeted counterrevolutionary crimes in 1944–1967 (Division A, the First Department, and the Third Directorate). The main mandate of the Sixth Directorate was to counteract the political dissent that stemmed from harmful ideological influence. Specifically, five operational divisions handled these tasks: Division One monitored the intelligentsia (which included artists, journalists, engineers, and doctors); Division Two tracked students and youth; Division Three was chiefly responsible for the Orthodox clergy and Christian sects; Division Four focused on religious expressions of Turkish nationalism; and Division Five concentrated on terrorism,[33] prison

---

[33] A separate terrorism division was eventually established in the early 1980s to handle expressions of discontent among the Turkish minority.

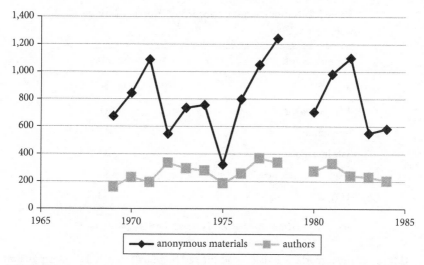

Figure 5.4 Anonymous materials and their authors in Bulgaria, 1969–1984.

Source: Petar Stoianov, *Shesto upravlenie: Moiata istina*, vol. 1 (Sofia: Daniela Ubenova, 2009), 39, 42, 47.

NB: Data for 1979 are missing.

work, and especially counterrevolutionary propaganda and agitation—this last part of the portfolio of Division Five involved not only detecting the circulation of anonymous counterrevolutionary materials (graffiti, leaflets, slogans) but also identifying their authors (see Figure 5.4). The desiderata of the authors and of State Security diverged: while those who scrawled graffiti and spread leaflets wanted their visible expressions of discontent to remain anonymous, the secret police deployed its toolkit to pierce the veil of anonymity and involuntarily pinpoint those who engaged in public acts of ideological subversion.

In addition to these five departments, a sixth division had the sensitive mandate of handling major antistate crimes and grand corruption among the party elite; this unit reported directly to the general secretary and maintained exclusive control over the information that it generated through full-time staff and agents whose identity was unknown to any State Security employees working outside the Sixth Department.[34] The number of full-time staff of the Sixth Directorate at the central level fluctuated between 200 and 300 until the mid-1980s,[35] when the

---

[34] Dimitar Ivanov, *Shesti otdel* (Sofia: Trud, 2004).

[35] AMVR f. 10 op. 6 a. e. 6 (1969), the personnel allocation of the Sixth Department at the central level in 1968 was 201 employees. AMVR f. 10 op. 6 a. e. 523 (1982) shows a planned personnel allocation of 274 for 1982 (30.4 per million people). This compares favorably with the 1982 personnel allocation of the counterpart Department XX of the Stasi, which had 400 staff at headquarters (24 per million people) (calculated from Thomas Auerbach, Matthias Braun, Bernd Eisenfeld, Gesine von Prittwitz, and Clemens Vollnhals, *Hauptabteilung XX: Staatsapparat, Blockparteien, Kirchen, Kultur,*

Table 5.2 Nationwide State Security Agent Network
in Bulgaria, 1986

Type of Agent	Number
Agent	25,628
Trusted person	24,611
Resident	840
Safe house owner	9,983
Deep cover safe house owner	80
TOTAL	61,142

Source: AKRDOPBGDSRSBNA-M f. 8 op. 2 a. e. 1102 (1986), 1–31.

addition of the terrorism division and the red beret battalion led to an expansion of the ranks to 539.[36] Full-time staff at the subnational level also came to 200–300 police officers. One question that emerges is how the ideological police were able to establish control over political dissent in a country of 9 million people with such limited staff.[37]

The management of dissent rested on three pillars: a detailed roster of the enemy contingent; a corps of strategically recruited agents (see Table 5.2); and selective prosecution of those found guilty of crimes against the state. The roster was continuously updated, with individuals included or excluded based on recent evidence of suspicious behavior. Although the general tendency was for gradual growth in the 1960s and 1970s, the roster was not particularly large: for example, it stood at 19,254 names nationwide in 1977.[38] Equivalent to 0.22 percent of the population,[39] this appears manageable—especially when we consider

---

"politischer Untergrund" [Berlin: BStU, 2008], 36). The Stasi was assisted by the GDR Ministry of the Interior Department K1, which mainly focused on economic and general criminality, though some of its 2,300 full-time employees engaged in sporadic efforts to handle political protection through working groups on border control, youth, and certain types of religious activity. See Klaus Richter, *Arbeitsgebiet I der Kriminalpolizei: Aufgaben, Struktur und Verhältnis zum Ministerium für Staatssicherheit* (Berlin: BStU, 1994), 9.

[36] AMVR f. 10 op. 6 a. e. 524 (1986).

[37] For comparison purposes, in the 1980s the Fifth Department of the Soviet KGB had 2,500 employees (9 per million people) (see O. M. Khlobustov, "Fenomen Andropova," in V. K. Bylinin, ed., *Trudy Obshchestva isuzheniia istorii otechestvennykh spetssluzhb*, vol. 1, 192–202, at 197). In China, the Political Protection Department of the Guangxi Public Security Bureau (*zhengbao ju* 政保局) had a personnel allocation of 515 in 1987 (12.7 per million people) (see *Guangxi gong'an nianjian 1987* [Guangxi Zhuangzu Zizhiqu Gong'an Bangongshi, October 1989], 307).

[38] AKRDOPBGDSRSBNA-M f. 22 op. 1 a. e. 57 (February 24, 1977), 1–67, at 45.

[39] For comparison purposes, the targeted population roster in Zouping county in China was 0.23 percent in 2009. Calculated from *Zouping nianjian 2004–2009* (Zouping: Zouping Xian Shizhi Bangongshi, 2010), 194.

that it included all individuals who had a history of expressing dissent. The roster was organized by category: intellectuals; youth and sports; individuals impacted by overseas ideological centers; reactionary clergy; nationalistic elements; counterrevolutionary elements; and individuals who had engaged in terrorism and in attempts to flee the country.[40] These categories were identical to the portfolios of the individual departments of the Sixth Directorate.

The roster was managed by full-time staff and part-time agents. Table 5.2 presents a comprehensive view of all domestic State Security agents,[41] who were equivalent to 0.68 percent of the 1986 population of 8.95 million. The density of clandestine informants was lower than the informant saturation rates in both the GDR and China at the time (see Chapters 2 and 6).[42] Only a subset of those clandestine agents in Bulgaria collected intelligence for the ideological police (the Sixth Directorate): The number of agents who were recruited and managed by individual departments within the Sixth Directorate grew steadily in the second half of the 1970s and by 1980 it had reached 762 at the central level (a 50 percent increase over the 514 agents that existed in 1961) and 5,628 at the subnational level (0.08 percent of the population, which is comparable to the situation in the GDR).[43] These ideological police agents, who constituted a fraction of the total State Security informant network, were essential to mete out selective repression against members of the enemy contingent and in cases where noncatalogued individuals engaged in acts of dissent.[44] In 1977, agents were deployed to spy on 65 percent of the enemy contingent.[45]

How was information used by the ideological police? In 1976, the Sixth Directorate received a total of 2,182 reports of counterrevolutionary activity.[46] But only 2.5 reports of those signals resulted in individuals being charged with

[40] AKRDOPBGDSRSBNA-M f. 22 op. 1 a. e. 57 (February 24, 1977).

[41] The agent network of the First Directorate (external intelligence) is not included in these numbers.

[42] As in China and the GDR, there also existed visible informants in Bulgaria. However, the archival materials clearly indicate that the visible informants did not have functions crossing over from the maintenance of public law and order into state security protection (TsDA f. 136 op. 64 a. e. 51 [1977]; TsDA f. 136 op. 24 a. e. 194 [1978]; TsDA f. 136 op. 77 a. e. 24 [1984]). This stands in contrast to the situation in China and the GDR (see Chapters 2, 4, 6, 8, and 9). The Bulgarian model featured strict delineation of the portfolios of State Security informants and visible police informants, which parallels the Soviet setup (see Chapter 9). Also, trusted persons were counted in the agent network in both Bulgaria and the Soviet Union, in contrast to the GDR.

[43] Calculated from AKRDOPBGDSRSBNA-M f. 8 op. 2 a. e. 1083 (March 19, 1980), 1–59, at 1–2 and 11–12, and AKRDOPBGDSRSBNA-M f. 13 op. 1 a. e. 1946 (1961), 1–10, at 8. The figures for the GDR are fragmentary, but the most detailed statistical compendium on Stasi informants gives no reason to think that the informants of Department XX of the Stasi exceeded 0.08 percent of the population in the 1980s: see Helmut Müller-Enbergs, Inoffizielle Mitarbeiter des Ministeriums für Staatssicherheit: Teil 3: Statistiken (Berlin: Ch. Links, 2008).

[44] AKRDOPBGDSRSBNA-M f. 22 op. 1 a. e. 54 (1976), 1–5, 6–12.

[45] AKRDOPBGDSRSBNA-M f. 22 op. 1 a. e. 54 (1976), 1–5, 6–12.

[46] AKRDOPBGDSRSBNA-M f. 22 op. 1 a. e. 57 (February 24, 1977), 1–67, at 51.

crimes against the state.[47] The reason is that additional evidence had to be collected before suspects could be arrested. The standard procedure was to open an operational-surveillance file and, in rare cases, to upgrade the case into a full-fledged investigation or (less typically) into a clandestine operation targeting a group or a specific individual. The typical outcome of State Security surveillance was prophylaxis, which involved warning individuals to cease and desist from participating in counterrevolutionary activities.[48] Most revealing of the change in repressive tactics is that by the 1970s someone who engaged in antistate activities had a 67 percent higher probability of being recruited to serve as an agent than of being sent to prison.[49]

5.1.8 Summing Up

With the 1967 re-organization of State Security, the handling of both overt and latent political dissent was the prerogative of the Sixth Directorate. Most notable about this re-orientation is that the vast majority of those belonging to the former "enemy contingent" were purged from the roster. Those who replaced the sympathizers of the old regime in the new "enemy contingent" roster were overwhelmingly victims of foreign ideological influence, be it Western, pan-Turkic (which targeted the Bulgarian Turks), or Maoist (considered a threat after the Sino–Soviet split). The roster was smaller and the strategy of prophylactic surveillance replaced brute repression. This re-orientation meant that State Security could also redirect some resources to tracking and addressing latent consumption-driven discontent.

5.2 The Socialist Social Contract: Promises of Increased Consumption

To a considerable extent, stability in the mature communist regime in Bulgaria rested on satisfying the material and cultural consumption needs of the population. The 1960s are notable for the explicit regime promises to increase the standard of living of the average citizen. At the Eighth Party Congress in 1962, Todor Zhivkov declared: "Our party, whose main concern is to take care of people and their well-being, needs to constantly take into account the growing

---

[47] *Prestupleniia i osudeni litsa.*
[48] AKRDOPBGDSRSBNA-M f. 22 op. 1 a. e. 57 (February 24, 1977), 1–67, at 54.
[49] Calculated from statistics on the share of agents recruited on the basis of compromising material contained in AKRDOPBGDSRSBNA-M f. 8 op. 2 a. e. 1083 (March 19, 1980), 1–59. Incarceration statistics compiled from *Prestupleniia i osudeni litsa.*

material and cultural needs of the population and aim to increasingly satisfy them more completely."[50] This was an explicit promise that the party-state would supply both bread and circuses. Investment in cultural consumption (book production, film releases, theater productions) was taken as seriously as subsidizing material consumption—both were key pillars of regime stability in Bulgaria.

The 1962 leadership report noted that an increase in personal income and in the consumption of rice, meat and meat products, sugar, cheese, milk, fresh vegetables, textiles, shoes, and furniture had occurred during the previous decade.[51] The party congress promised a further increase in incomes as well as improvements in the provision of municipal services and the availability of consumer goods. A key goal was to elevate expenditures of the social consumption funds (*obshtestveni fondove za potreblenie*), which were used to underwrite free medical care, kindergartens and nurseries, free education, stipends for students, old-age pensions, annual leaves, and rest packages.[52] These plans were reiterated at the Ninth Party Congress in 1966. The party made a commitment to avoid raising prices (and to lower them whenever possible), to improve the availability of durable goods (TVs, washing machines, refrigerators, vacuum cleaners, furniture, and cars), to increase expenditures of the social consumption funds, and to speed up housing construction.[53] Another key commitment was to gradually transition to a five-day workweek.[54]

The next round of policies aimed at improving consumption was announced in 1968. The timing of these measures was not random. Although some of the relevant decrees had been drafted prior to 1968, the events in Czechoslovakia accelerated their official promulgation.[55] The Prague Spring and the subsequent August 1968 Warsaw Pact invasion demonstrated the fragility of the socialist regimes, thus elevating the importance of securing popular support through increased consumption. Some of these policies targeted specific groups. For example, the party aimed to improve the standard of living of students by raising their stipends, increasing the number of spots in student dormitories, decreasing the price of meals in student canteens, and constructing new rest and recreation facilities for students.[56] In addition, social pensions for individuals over the age

---

[50] *Osmi kongres na Bulgarskata komunisticheska partiia (5 noemvri–14 noemvri 1962 g.) (Stenografski protokol)* (Sofia: Izdatelstvo na Bulgarskata Komunisticheska Partiia, 1963), 72–73. Emphasis added.

[51] *Osmi kongres*, 71–72.

[52] *Osmi kongres*, 73–74.

[53] *Deveti kongres na Bulgarskata komunisticheska partiia (14 noemvri–19 noemvri 1966 g.) (Stenografski protokol)* (Sofia: Izdatelstvo na Bulgarskata Komunisticheska Partiia, 1967), 74–81.

[54] *Deveti kongres*, 80.

[55] Vladimir Migev, *Prazhkata prolet '68 i Bulgariia* (Sofia: Iztok–Zapad, 2005), 285.

[56] Migev, *Prazhkata prolet*, 255.

of 70 without labor service (*trudov stazh*) were introduced.[57] Efforts were also made to placate the general population by decreasing the prices of some food items (poultry, cheese, fresh fish), limiting the exportation of eggs and wheat, and increasing the volume of imported meat, canned fish, olives, and coffee.[58] The final package of pro-consumer policies was adopted in November 1968, when the Central Committee instructed the organs of government to devote significant efforts to increasing the availability of repair services (even if that meant they had to be provided by private craftsmen), to supply logistical support for the construction of new housing, to improve the quality of municipal services (transportation, postal services, and various public utilities), to control the quality of services provided in stores, and to facilitate raising the standard of healthcare and education.[59]

Extensive details on the increase in consumption were provided in December 1972, when the Central Committee dedicated a three-day plenum to developing concrete targets for elevating the standard of living of the population during the coming decade, later known as the "December Program."[60] One goal was to increase real incomes (*realni dokhodi*) by raising salaries, lowering certain retail prices, expanding the size of the social consumption funds, and reducing the tax burden. Among the prices to be lowered were those of poultry, certain kinds of cloth and clothing, household appliances, building materials, personal hygiene items, food and clothing for children, and selected services.[61] There were also specific strategies for alleviating the urban housing crisis; concrete plans for expanding the availability of municipal services; and logistics for adopting a reduced workweek.

The most surprising part of the December Program was that it featured a public acknowledgment of the existence of shortages and provided a detailed plan for rectifying the imbalance between the supply and demand of consumer goods. In the understanding of the Central Committee, this problem was not simply economic, but also political, ideological, and social.[62]

---

[57] Nina Dimitrova, "Rolia na sotsialnite uslugi v Bulgariia v perioda 1944–1989 g.: Trudoviiat kolektiv kato razshireno sotsialistichesko semeistvo," in Ivailo Znepolski, ed., *Da poznaem komunizma: Izsledvaniia* (Sofia: Ciela, 2012), 227–68, at 255.

[58] Migev, *Prazhkata prolet*, 262–63.

[59] *Miastoto i roliata na narodnite suveti v sistemata na sotsialnoto upravlenie (reshenie na Tsentralniia komitet na Bulgarskata komunisticheska partiia, 27 noemvri 1968 g.)* (Sofia: Izdatelstvo na Bulgarskata Komunishticheska Partiia, 1968), 9–17.

[60] Todor Zhivkov, *Za posledovatelno izpulnenie na resheniiata na Desetiia kongres na BKP za povishavane zhiznenoto ravnishte na naroda (doklad pred plenuma na Tsentralniia komitet na Bulgarskata komunisticheska partiia, sustoial se na 11, 12 i 13 dekemvri 1972 g.)* (Sofia: Partizdat, 1972), 11.

[61] Zhivkov, *Za posledovatelno izpulnenie*, 39–40.

[62] Zhivkov, *Za posledovatelno izpulnenie*, 57.

Apart from the provision of consumer goods, the party devoted significant attention to the question of meeting the needs of women. Efforts in this area predated the 1970s. One of the very first acts of the new regime had been to implement an executive order (*naredba-zakon*) that gave equal rights to both genders.[63] Next, Article 72 of the 1947 Constitution guaranteed men and women equal rights in the area of employment, compensation, rest, social insurance, pensions, and education. Apart from access to employment, which was implemented immediately, most notable improvements in women's rights occurred after the first decade of communist rule.[64] In the 1960s, the number of nurseries and daycare centers increased, as did the length of maternity leaves and the size of monthly allowances for children. In 1968, the Central Committee instructed the organs of government (*narodni suveti*) to pay particular attention to relieving women from household labor by improving access to daycare centers and by expanding the number of municipal laundry facilities, dry cleaners, tailoring shops, and hygiene establishments.[65] In 1969, an anonymous poll by the monthly *Zhenata dnes* of 16,060 readers revealed that although women wanted to have more children, they were discouraged from doing so due to the difficulties in arranging childcare and the amount of time they had to devote to household duties.[66] The results of the poll, which were presented to Todor Zhivkov, informed future policies that aimed to improve the lives of Bulgarian women.[67] The Tenth Congress of the Bulgarian Communist Party in 1971 highlighted the importance of providing women with more free time and enhancing incentives for bearing and raising children.[68]

The December Program paved the way for the introduction of a five-day workweek and promised to increase the speed of development of municipal services, which would free women from household chores.[69] The March 1973 Decision outlined a comprehensive set of policies aimed at redressing existing inequities in employment and compensation and providing women with more free time and improved opportunities for childcare, including extended maternity leaves, increased one-time childbirth bonuses, higher monthly allowances for childcare, and better quality of the food served in school canteens.[70] In 1983, maternity

[63] "Naredba-zakon za izravniavane pravata na litsata ot dvata pola," *Durzhaven vestnik*, October 14, 1944.

[64] Dimitrova, "Rolia na sotsialnite uslugi."

[65] *Miastoto i roliata na narodnite suveti*, 11–12.

[66] Kristen Ghodsee, "Pressuring the Politburo: The Committee of the Bulgarian Women's Movement and State Socialist Feminism," *Slavic Review* 73:3 (Fall 2014), 538–62.

[67] Ghodsee, "Pressuring the Politburo."

[68] *Deseti kongres na Bulgarskata komunisticheska partiia (20 april–25 april 1971 g.) (Stenografski protokol)* (Sofia: Partizdat, 1971), 96–97.

[69] Zhivkov, *Za posledovatelno izpulnenie*, 123.

[70] *Za izdigane roliata na zhenata v izgrazhdaneto na razvitoto sotsialistichesko obshtestvo (Reshenie na Politbiuro na TsK na BKP ot 6 mart 1973)* (Sofia: Partizdat, 1977).

leaves were extended to three years; universal access to kindergartens was guaranteed; and child allowances became means-tested (thus benefiting those with lower incomes).[71] Cumulatively, implementing these policies required elevated expenditures on consumption.

In sum, a comprehensive set of policies that created increased consumption expectations was implemented in the early 1970s. In contrast to most other documents referenced in this book, the materials reviewed in this section are public and were circulated broadly in Bulgaria, thus making widely known the scope of regime commitments under the socialist social contract. Typically, the documents appeared as booklets with print-runs of at least 100,000 copies; they were also often published in *Rabotnichesko delo* and the other central newspapers, either in full or in excerpted form. In addition, they were reviewed in lengthy exposés on the radio and on TV. The systematic fulfillment of the consumption expectations they created necessitated the adept use of the information on consumer discontent that was generated by the party, State Security, and the media.

5.3 Collecting and Analyzing Information on Consumer Discontent

Aside from the communist party, three separate channels supplied power holders with reports on the popular mood in general and on consumer frustrations in particular: State Security; the telegraph agency; and the Committee for Control by the State and the People. Among these collection agencies, the party had the broadest access to information because it was the ultimate recipient of the reporting produced through all channels—yet, in addition, it also had its own internal intelligence-collection mechanisms.

Before we discuss these institutions, we need to note three related developments in the 1960s that impacted information circulation. One was the desire to multiply available sources for the collection of intelligence; redundancy was deliberately pursued as a strategy for mitigating the agency problems that could affect any single channel. At the same time, in order to prevent massive information overload, the center facilitated the creation of clearinghouses within the party and State Security. The party established the Information-Sociological Center in 1970, which was tasked both with producing original research and with systematizing existing intelligence on popular discontent. Within State Security, the equivalent entity was the Central Information-Analytical Service (*Tsentralna informatsionno-analitichna sluzhba*, or TsIAS), which was created in

---

[71] *Za po-natatushno izpulnenie na Dekemvriiskata programa za povishavane na zhiznenoto ravnishte na naroda v suotvetstvie s resheniiata na XII kongres na BKP* (Sofia: Partizdat, 1983).

1967 with the mandate to aggregate information that was collected from several types of sources. The third and final change focused on the broadening of the circulation of classified information. Although the list of recipients of military intelligence and briefs on discontent among the elite could be kept truly exclusive, confidential reports on the popular mood necessitated a wider circle of addressees, sometimes reaching up to 160 central- and provincial-level leading cadres.[72] The reason for this was that the problem of popular dissatisfaction was complex, and to address its root causes meant that a relatively wide group needed to be apprised of its existence.

5.3.1 State Security Reporting on the Popular Mood

The decline in repression in the 1960s allowed State Security to re-orient some of its vast information-gathering resources toward assessing and responding to consumer discontent. The frequency of briefs about popular dissatisfaction that resulted from consumer frustrations increased.[73] The issues were familiar from previous reporting during moments of crisis: in the cities, securing an apartment was a major source of discontent;[74] in the rural areas and small towns, shortages of various staples (and even of bread) occurred into the early 1960s.[75] Most remarkable about the reports from the 1960s is that they were produced during normal times, thus signaling that the monitoring of consumer discontent was becoming a routine task for State Security. As early as 1966, State Security sought to alleviate consumption problems through industrial espionage involving the acquisition by Scientific-Technical Intelligence personnel of the formulae for chemical and pharmaceutical inventions.[76]

The evolution of State Security reporting on the popular mood was nothing short of remarkable. Whereas in the early 1970s overt displays of consumer frustrations were still regarded as a sign of enemy activity, by the early 1980s such dissatisfaction was no longer evaluated as evidence of hostility to the regime.[77] This new attitude was reflected in State Security briefs about the discontent following the Polish events of 1980–1981, which indicated that workers were frustrated with their low pay and with poor work conditions and they often sought to form illegal trade unions; in contrast to State Security reporting from the 1950s,

---

[72] For a complaint-analysis distribution list, see TsDA f. 1B op. 55 a. e. 945 (1986).

[73] AMVR f. 1 op. 5 a. e. 80 (1963) is representative of this trend.

[74] TsDA f. 1B op. 15 a. e. 702 (May 4, 1957), 33–42.

[75] AMVR f. 1 op. 5 a. e. 79 (September 26, 1962), 12–13.

[76] Martin K. Dimitrov, *Politicheskata logika na sotsialisticheskoto potreblenie* (Sofia: Ciela, 2018), 155–58.

[77] On the 1970s, see AMVR f. 22 op. 1 a. e. 3 (1972). On the 1980s, see AMVR f. 1 op. 10 a. e. 500 (1983).

actions of this type in the 1980s were presented in a matter-of-fact way that was largely devoid of inflammatory rhetoric.[78] Perhaps most indicative of the new attitude toward consumption is a 1983 brief on bottlenecks in the production and distribution of bread and high-end confections (*fini sladkarski izdeliia*).[79] This document demonstrates that State Security had to accept its new responsibility for monitoring food production because consumer shortages were an important source of latent discontent. State Security adopted a practical attitude toward the strategies for alleviating these shortages—for example, it learned to tolerate small-scale private bars and restaurants, which were permitted to operate in the resorts along the Black Sea coast, in a public admission of the incapacity of the state to meet the demand for such services through government-owned catering outlets.[80]

Led by an understanding that the frequency of hostile antiregime public comments increases proportionally with the severity of consumer goods shortages, State Security devoted part of its monitoring capacity to assessing whether the material needs of the population were satisfied.[81] This issue assumed special prominence around the time of party congresses, elections, and national holidays.[82] For example, secret police reporting on the pre-election situation in 1983 noted rumors of imminent price increases and mentioned calls for boycotting the elections to protest the failure to build major municipal services outlets, but State Security did not characterize such behavior as stemming from hostile attitudes toward the regime.[83] The logic was simple: shortages could increase tensions and lead to public incidents. In turn, open displays of discontent could escalate more easily during public holidays, when more people were free to join protests.[84] This was to be expected. In sum, the secret police developed a realistic assessment of the sources and the political consequences of consumer discontent.

5.3.2 Party Assessments of the Popular Mood Prior to the 1970s

In the 1960s, the party devoted extensive resources to monitoring the popular mood in general and consumer discontent in particular. In 1965, the Central

---

[78] AMVR f. 1 op. 12 a. e. 406A (1981); AMVR f. 1 op. 12 a. e. 417A (1981); AMVR f. 1 op. 12 a. e. 418A (1981); AMVR f. 1 op. 12 a. e. 421A (1982).

[79] AMVR f. 1 op. 10 a. e. 500 (1983), 193–94.

[80] AMVR f. 1 op. 12 a. e. 417 (August 2–8, 1982), 64.

[81] AMVR f. 1 op. 12 a. e. 417 (July 19–25, 1982), 28.

[82] AMVR f. 1 op. 12 a. e. 413 (September 1982), 202; AMVR f. 1 op. 12 a. e. 499 (April 27, 1983), 93; AMVR f. 1 op. 12 a. e. 500 (November 30, 1983), 237.

[83] AMVR f. 1 op. 10 a. e. 500 (1983), 236–38.

[84] AMVR f. 1 op. 12 a. e. 499 (April 27, 1983), 99.

Committee Department of Trade and Food Industry informed the Politburo about problems in the production of household necessities (ranging from glassware to toys and haberdashery) and the provision of various services.[85] In the same year, Politburo members received copies of a report on the political mood prepared by the Sofia City Party Committee, indicating significant dissatisfaction stemming from problems in the allocation of housing, the poor quality of transportation, and periodic food shortages in the stores in outlying suburbs.[86] Residents of the capital also complained about air pollution.[87] In 1967, the Organization Department of the Central Committee issued a report on the political mood that documented citizen dissatisfaction with the poor quality of durable goods and meat shortages.[88] Frustration about the scarcity of spring lamb was especially severe, as reflected in a widespread rumor that the available lamb was being exported to Greece and Italy.[89] In 1969, Politburo members received a report from the Industrial-Economic Department of the Central Committee on the remaining unresolved problems in the provision of municipal services.[90] These examples evidence the attention that the party was paying to tracking and responding to popular consumption preferences. In comparison to the 1950s, when widespread consumer dissatisfaction led to large strikes and numerous riots, consumer discontent in the 1960s appeared more limited in scope and thus more manageable.

The party-state made it officially known that it welcomed citizen petitions, which gave it enhanced access to information. In this vein, the 1960s saw an emphasis on the importance of complaints for assessing and satisfying citizen consumption preferences. At the Eighth Party Congress in 1962, the head of the Central Control and Audit Commission reported that most complaints were about housing and job allocations, although citizens also highlighted problems in transportation, trade, the supply of utilities, and the provision of welfare assistance.[91] At the Ninth Party Congress in 1966, the Central Control and Audit Commission reiterated that complaints allowed the party to monitor the political mood of citizens, thus mandating a timely response.[92] In 1968, municipal councils were instructed to radically improve their complaints work. The party issued an express prohibition that complaints should be adjudicated by the authorities against whom citizens were complaining.[93] Overall, the regime

[85] TsDA f. 1B op. 91 a. e. 1060 (1965).
[86] TsDA f. 1B op. 91 a. e. 1431 (1965), 1–11, at 7–11
[87] TsDA f. 1B op. 91 a. e. 1431 (1965).
[88] TsDA f. 1B op. 91 a. e. 1437 (1967), 6–10.
[89] TsDA f. 1B op. 91 a. e. 1437 (1967), 6.
[90] TsDA f. 1B op. 91 a. e. 1118 (1969).
[91] *Osmi kongres*, 175–79.
[92] *Deveti kongres*, 126.
[93] *Miastoto i roliata na narodnite suveti*, 17.

tried to reassure citizens that they should not fear any retaliation because of their complaints.[94]

The July 1968 Plenum of the Central Committee reiterated the importance of taking complaints work seriously. A report by the Committee for Control by the State and the People highlighted various challenges in complaints work by state organs (ministries, central commissions, and provincial organs of the government) throughout 1969.[95] Of concern was that these entities received 171,982 complaints in 1969, which was 9,054 fewer than they had processed in 1968.[96] As Zhivkov himself opined, one of the shortcomings of complaints work was the lack of a central entity that would collect, systematize, and analyze information about petitions that had been sent to all organs of power.[97] Due to the lack of such a center, information from complaints could not be fully used to improve governance.

5.3.3 Creating the Information-Sociological Center of the Central Committee

In the 1960s, several entities were established with the explicit goal of assessing popular preferences. One was the Sociological Group at the Central Committee (*Sotsiologicheska grupa kum TsK*), which dated back to 1967. Another was the Center for Sociological Youth Research (*Tsentur za sotsiologicheski izsledvaniia na mladezhta*), which was created by the Komsomol in 1968. In addition, various newspapers (*Rabotnichesko delo* [Workers' Deed], *Sturshel* [Gadfly]) and magazines (*Mladezh* [Youth], *Zhenata dnes* [Contemporary Woman]) conducted surveys of their readers.[98]

By the end of the decade, the leadership had a clear sense of the importance of coordination and control of the multiple intelligence-collection streams. The Information-Sociological Center of the Central Committee of the Bulgarian Communist Party was established in March 1970 to carry out these functions.[99] As Todor Zhivkov announced to the Central Committee, the Information-Sociological Center would be granted access to all reporting streams and would serve as an intelligence provider to the Central Committee and the Politburo; it

---

[94] For more on this point, see Martin K. Dimitrov, "Zhalbite na grazhdanite v komunisticheska Bulgariia," in Znepolski, ed., *Da poznaem komunizma* (2012), 167–226; Martin K. Dimitrov, "What the Party Wanted to Know: Citizen Complaints as a 'Barometer of Public Opinion' in Communist Bulgaria," *East European Politics and Societies and Cultures* 28:2 (May 2014), 271–95.

[95] TsDA f. 378B op. 1 a. e. 985 (1970).

[96] TsDA f. 378B op. 1 a. e. 985 (1970), 2.

[97] TsDA f. 378B op. 1 a. e. 985 (1970), 4.

[98] Stoian Mikhailov, *Sotsiologiiata v Bulgariia sled Vtorata svetovna voina* (Sofia: M8M, 2003), 44–47; Migev, *Prazhkata prolet*, 276–77; Ghodsee, "Pressuring the Politburo," 549.

[99] TsDA f. 1B op. 35 a. e. 1246 (1970).

would have an unimpeded capacity to transmit information to the top leadership.[100] But one concern that accompanied the creation of a new intelligence-gathering entity was information overload. For this reason, the Secretariat of the Central Committee, at a meeting convened to discuss information flow, decided that reports transmitted to the Central Committee and the Politburo should not exceed eight to ten pages in length and, if they did, they should be accompanied by a brief summary.[101] From 1970 onward, the Information-Sociological Center played a central role in transmitting intelligence about the popular mood to the top leadership. The goal was to ensure the authenticity (*dostovernost*) of the information collected.[102]

5.3.4 Reports of the Information-Sociological Center

The Information-Sociological Center monitored public opinion through six types of reports: mood assessments; rumor digests; opinion polling; overviews of critical media publications; analytical reports on hot-button issues; and regular briefs on the volume and thematic distribution of citizen complaints. These materials were sent to a small circle of recipients (typically members of the Politburo, the Central Committee Secretariat, and about 100 leading cadres) to apprise them of trends in popular discontent. A leitmotif was consumption-related dissatisfaction.

Mood Assessments
The Information-Sociological Center prepared regular mood overviews that were based on: reports from the provincial information-sociological groups; classified dispatches from the electronic (radio and TV) and print media, as well as from telegraph agency correspondents; citizen letters; and intelligence that was collected directly by its associates through opinion polling and by talking to ordinary citizens (given persistent shortages and widespread queuing, lining up was an excellent way to learn about popular grievances). To coordinate information streams, quarterly political mood reports were prepared for the general secretary jointly by the Organization Department, the Propaganda Department, and the Information-Sociological Center.[103] Separate weekly mood reports continued to be generated by the Information-Sociological Center, the Organization

---

[100] TsDA f. 378B op. 1 a. e. 761 (1971).

[101] AKRDOPBGDSRSBNA-M f. 1 op. 10 a. e. 1483 (March 12, 1970), 71–72.

[102] Iancho Georgiev, Mincho Draganov, Boris Chakalov, Pavel Pavlov, and Shtiliiana Chakalova, *Problemi na informatsionno-sotsiologicheskoto obsluzhvane na partiinite organi* (Sofia: Partizdat, 1984), 39, 96, 124.

[103] TsDA f. 1B op. 101 a. e. 595 (1981); TsDA f. 1B op. 101 a. e. 1138 (1984); TsDA f. 1B op. 101 a. e. 2081 (1988).

Department, the Propaganda Department, and the General Department until the end of single-party rule.[104]

Party reports prepared for the top leadership often identified consumption problems as one of the main sources of social discontent (*sotsialno nedovolstvo*). There were also concerns about insufficient wage increases;[105] about the quality of a wide range of services;[106] and, above all, about shortages of goods, ranging from staples to expensive imported lingerie and TV sets.[107] In addition, the party reports also noted shortages of certain medicines and sanitary supplies such as cotton, thermometers, and menstrual pads.[108] Sometimes goods were available, but were of poor quality: "The spinach on offer is nonstandard—muddy and wilted, thus resulting in a lack of enthusiasm on the part of citizens to buy it."[109] Another problem was that the market share of luxury consumption goods was increasing, whereas the volume of economically priced items was declining.[110]

These reports unequivocally demonstrated that shortages were a source of latent social discontent. But overt hostile statements, indicating readiness to engage in antiregime activity, were also recorded. Notable is the following comment overheard in a conversation between peasants in the village of Kulata in the Blagoevgrad region: "We went on a trip to the GDR, Poland, Hungary, etc.—there was plenty of meat there, but these countries have had upheavals. If the masses rebel a little, the stores in Bulgaria will also fill up with meat."[111] Similarly, a report to Todor Zhivkov on consumption stated: "In Kiustendil province the difficulties in the supply of goods are used by individuals from the enemy contingent, who make tendentious commentaries and draw conclusions about the economic and social policies of the party."[112] These instances of consumer-good shortages giving rise to individual hostile antiregime comments helped to impress upon the top leadership the importance of satisfying consumption grievances prior to their transformation into collective acts of opposition to the system.

Reports on Rumors

Consumption rumors were monitored primarily by the Information-Sociological Center and the General Department of the Central Committee, whereas State Security focused on identifying rumors about political dissent

---

[104] TsDA f. 1B op. 11 a. e. 9 (1988); TsDA f. 1B op. 55 a. e. 956 (1988); TsDA f. 1B op. 55 a. e. 1223 (1989).

[105] On discontent among teachers and medical professionals, see TsDA f. 1B op. 91 a. e. 1482 (1973), 5–7.

[106] TsDA f. 1B op. 91 a. e. 1375 (1973).

[107] TsDA f. 1B op. 55 a. e. 1204 (1971); TsDA f. 1B op. 55 a. e. 1209 (1974).

[108] TsDA f. 1B op. 50 a. e. 80 (1977); TsDA f. 1B op. 102 a. e. 621 (1981).

[109] TsDA f. 1B op. 102 a. e. 559 (1981), 3.

[110] TsDA f. 1B op. 101 a. e. 595 (1981), 9.

[111] TsDA f. 1B op. 55 a. e. 1207 (1974).

[112] TsDA f. 1B op. 101 a. e. 595 (1981), 9.

and minority rights. The utility of monitoring rumors for tracking latent discontent is encapsulated in the following quote from a document prepared by the Information-Sociological Center, which shows a sophisticated understanding of anticipatory governance:

> Rumors in the month of July of this year: Registration of this stage in the formation of public opinion was done primarily in order to detect its future manifestations and the possibility of the rise of unhealthy moods. In the stage of "it is rumored that . . . "—this earliest, intimate, and unorganized state in the formation of public opinion—there is typically an incremental consolidation of positions, meaning that timely intervention can turn out to be greatly beneficial.[113]

With regard to consumption, most rumors in the 1970s revealed the fear of a decline in living standards. This was expressed specifically in widespread rumors about price increases, a currency redenomination, devaluation of bank deposits, the elimination of private farming (and the imposition of a tax on draft animals like donkeys), and the introduction of rationing for essentials such as sugar, bread, and paprika.[114] Other rumors were related to welfare. The most widely circulating was that the retirement age would be increased from 60 to 65 years for men and from 55 to 60 years for women.[115] According to an assessment of the Information-Sociological Center, rumors formed "an unhealthy mood among the population."[116] In order to address and respond to these rumors during their incipient stage, power holders needed to have systematic knowledge about their content.

Opinion Polling

The most fundamental challenge to the validity and reliability of opinion polling was preference falsification.[117] According to an employee of the Information-Sociological Center, the main obstacle that sociologists had to confront was the fears of respondents who did not believe that surveys were truly anonymous.[118] These fears resulted both in high levels of noncompletion of questionnaires and in "people hiding their true feelings and registering very high levels of agreement

---

[113] TsDA f. 1B op. 55 a. e. 1203 (1971), 7.

[114] TsDA f. 1B op. 55 a. e. 1203 (1971); TsDA f. 1B op. 55 a. e. 1207 (1972).

[115] TsDA f. 1B op. 55 a. e. 1207 (1972). The retirement age was never raised during communist rule.

[116] TsDA f. 1B op. 55 a. e. 1207 (1972), 1.

[117] On preference falsification, see Timur Kuran, "Now Out of Never: The Element of Surprise in the East European Revolution of 1989," *World Politics* 44:1 (1991), 7–48.

[118] Personal interview with Iuri Aslanov, June 29, 2009 (Sofia).

with official policy, up to 90–92 percent. We told the powers that be that this can't be true, and they knew it."[119]

In contrast to questions about support for the system, to which answers were unreliable in the 1960s–1970s, surveys systematically documented consumer grievances in the early 1970s. Opinion polling revealed that citizens were frustrated mainly by the poor quality of services; the key concerns centered around the provision of utilities and municipal services (*komunalno-bitovi uslugi*), transportation, retail customer services (*turgovsko obsluzhvane*), and medical services.[120] In addition, polls indicated that discontent arose from poor workplace conditions and difficulties in obtaining housing.[121] Opinion polling also revealed that the experimental adoption of a five-day workweek in the city of Stara Zagora increased stress levels because the production targets designed for a six-day workweek still had to be fulfilled, often forcing employees to continue to work on a sixth day.[122]

Reports on Critical Publications in the Mass Media

Prior to the 1970s, newspaper editors-in-chief briefed various Central Committee departments on an individual basis about reactions to critical publications in media outlets. Once the Information-Sociological Center was created, this activity was streamlined. The center prepared regular overviews of critical publications in the mass media (*biuletin "Kritichni materiali v sredstvata za masova informatsiia"*). We can illustrate the range of materials that were reviewed in this bulletin by focusing on a single sample issue, namely, the annual report on the critical publications that were excerpted in the bulletin throughout 1981. The report was sent to an unusually diverse list of addressees; in total, there were 149 recipients of this document, including members and candidate-members of the Politburo, secretaries of the Central Committee, heads of all Central Committee departments, members of the Council of Ministers, all provincial party secretaries, and editors-in-chief of the main print and electronic media.[123] The list of addressees makes it clear that this document was dispatched to the most powerful individuals in the country.

The annual report indicates that 631 critical publications had been summarized in the 77 installments of the bulletin that appeared throughout 1981. These materials were published in the central print media (provincial media were not monitored by the Information-Sociological Center), broadcast on radio or TV,

---

[119] Iuri Aslanov interview in Vera Mutafchieva, comp., *Istoriiata, naselena s khora*, vol. 1 (Sofia: Gutenberg, 2005), 776–89, at 784.

[120] TsDA f. 1B op. 55 a. e. 1203 (1971).

[121] TsDA f. 1B op. 55 a. e. 1203 (1971).

[122] TsDA f. 1B op. 55 a. e. 1204 (1971), 3.

[123] TsDA f. 1B op. 55 a. e. 868 (1982), 2–5.

or shown as newsreels (*kinokhronika*). Mass media were ranked in terms of the absolute number of critical publications they generated. An unexpected finding is that although the party daily *Rabotnichesko delo* printed the highest absolute number of critical pieces, adjusting for the frequency of publication reveals that more critical articles appeared in each issue of the satirical weekly *Sturshel*.[124]

At least one-quarter of the materials reviewed in the 1981 bulletin related to con-sumption problems, welfare, and services: 2.7 percent of the critical publications highlighted concerns about healthcare services, another 2.7 percent focused on education, and 9.8 percent centered on the quality of other services. Critical publications also discussed problems in the harvesting and storage of fruit and vegetables (3.4 percent), the regulation of personal and auxiliary land plots (3.6 per-cent), and bottlenecks in the construction of housing (2.9 percent).[125]

How effective were these critical publications? This question pre-occupied the attention of the Information-Sociological Center, which answered it by collecting data on the proportion of articles that were sent to the criticized entities for a re-sponse (90.4 percent), what these entities were, and how many of them provided a response (80.9 percent).[126] To enhance the effectiveness of critical publications, copies of such articles were also dispatched to the relevant Central Committee departments overseeing the work of the criticized entities. This signaled the seri-ousness of the party's attitude to critical publications.

Information Provided through *Zlobodnevni Problemi*

This top-secret (*strogo poveritelen*) bulletin on "pressing problems," prepared by the Information-Sociological Center, reveals that a wide array of popular concerns were made known to the top leadership in Bulgaria. The list of issues that were discussed in the bulletin was closely aligned with the commitments to improving the standard of living that were articulated in numerous party documents in the early 1970s. One was the quality of various services pro-vided to the population, such as telephone services,[127] residential elevator ser-vice,[128] taxicab services,[129] general transportation services,[130] dental care,[131] and healthcare.[132] The bulletin also alerted the leadership about the quality of food served in student and worker canteens,[133] as well as the quality of organized

[124] TsDA f. 1B op. 55 a. e. 868 (1982), 19–20.

[125] TsDA f. 1B op. 55 a. e. 868 (1982), 9–13.

[126] TsDA f. 1B op. 55 a. e. 868 (1982), 19–20, 26–27.

[127] TsDA f. 1B op. 55 a. e. 485, *Zlobodnevni problemi*, no. 1/1977 (January 1977).

[128] TsDA f. 1B op. 55 a. e. 485, *Zlobodnevni problemi*, no. 1/1977 (January 1977).

[129] TsDA f. 1B op. 55 a. e. 486, *Zlobodnevni problemi*, no. 2/1977 (March 1977).

[130] TsDA f. 1B op. 55 a. e. 507, *Zlobodnevni problemi*, no. 6/1980 (December 30, 1980).

[131] TsDA f. 1B op. 55 a. e. 529, *Zlobodnevni problemi*, no. 2/1986 (March 1986).

[132] TsDA f. 1B op. 55 a. e. 497, *Zlobodnevni problemi*, no. 1/1979 (April 10, 1979).

[133] TsDA f. 1B op. 55 a. e. 487, *Zlobodnevni problemi*, no. 3/1977 (April 1977); TsDA f. 1B op. 55 a. e. 496, *Zlobodnevni problemi*, no. 5/1978 (November 1978).

vacation packages offered to workers.[134] Regardless of how trivial the problem, *Zlobodnevni problemi* would note if it was already a source of popular discontent, and would point out that, if the issue were to be left unaddressed, it would have larger political consequences, such as creating doubt among the population regarding the governing capacity of the communist party. For example, a report on housing repair services stressed that "the weaknesses and shortcomings in the maintenance and repair of the housing stock" have "political consequences," namely, "discontent among citizens"; the report warned that "if no decisive measures for improving this situation are taken, the issue of the maintenance and repair of housing stock will turn from a purely mundane problem into a political question."[135] Finally, a brief about the poor quality of customer service provided in government offices highlighted the "political consequences" of this problem: "People form a negative opinion about the capabilities not only of the government offices but also of the governing capacity of the state as a whole."[136] Consumption under central planning had a clear political meaning.

Zlobodnevni problemi also discussed shortages, ranging from essential items like bread and car gasoline[137] to medicines, sanitary materials, and household medical devices.[138] The Information-Sociological Center saw such shortages as having potential economic, social, or political consequences. For example, the shortage of mass-consumption goods, such as spades, axes, hoes, adzes, pitchforks, wheelbarrows, metal buckets, electric pumps, stoves, door and window hinges, nails, forks, and spoons, was considered to have unfavorable economic, social, and political consequences: "The economic consequences involve a slowdown in GDP growth; the social consequences include the creation of unnecessary obstacles for the consistent and full implementation of the December Program; politically, it gives rise to discontent and prompts expressions of public criticism."[139]

Even when goods were not in short supply, the Information-Sociological Center worried about their off-putting packaging and design.[140] Reports to the leadership identified "ideological consequences" of poor industrial design, which "fosters bad taste among consumers; creates conditions for idolatry of Western goods and fashion; not infrequently forms the impression that our economy is unable to create beautiful products, which has a negative impact on the stability of views, especially among the young generation."[141] The production

---

[134] TsDA f. 1B op. 55 a. e. 512, *Zlobodnevni problemi*, no. 2/1982 (March 5, 1982).

[135] TsDA f. 1B op. 55 a. e. 502, *Zlobodnevni problemi*, no. 1/1980 (April 8, 1980), 16.

[136] TsDA f. 1B op. 55 a. e. 515, *Zlobodnevni problemi*, no. 5/1982 (November 25, 1982), 17.

[137] TsDA f. 1B op. 55 a. e. 506, *Zlobodnevni problemi*, no. 5/1980 (September 22, 1980); TsDA f. 1B op. 55 a. e. 489, *Zlobodnevni problemi*, no. 5/1977 (June 1977).

[138] TsDA f. 1B op. 55 a. e. 508, *Zlobodnevni problemi*, no. 1/1981 (June 24, 1981).

[139] TsDA f. 1B op. 55 a. e. 501, *Zlobodnevni problemi*, no. 5/1979 (December 29, 1979), 10.

[140] TsDA f. 1B op. 55 a. e. 521, *Zlobodnevni problemi*, no. 2/1984 (March 1984).

[141] TsDA f. 1B op. 55 a. e. 490, *Zlobodnevni problemi*, no. 6/1977 (September 1977), 10.

of low-quality goods also had "ideological aspects," since "part of the population forms a negative impression of the capabilities of our industry, about the organization and management of trade, about the extent of our meeting the demands of the working population."[142] Even the poor quality and lack of variety of children's clothes had ideological consequences, such as "discontent, criticism, and forming an impression that our industry is unable to supply the market with sorely needed children's clothing and shoes of high quality and variety. . . . This upsets and discourages people. Often, they form negative opinions not only about these specific industrial branches, but also about the economy as a whole, about the ambitious goals of our social policy and their incomplete realization. We should also add that inferior-quality clothing and shoes lower the aesthetic criteria of citizens, their idea of comfort and beauty (especially among children), and create obstacles for the formation and consolidation of their sense of national pride in the existing achievements [of socialism]."[143] Because the leadership had made a promise to meet the universal consumption needs of the people, any type of shortage or deficiency in the quality of goods could directly impact the regime's ideological legitimacy. This was the internal understanding of the function of consumption as revealed by the classified materials.

Reports on Citizen Complaints

As early as 1972, Todor Zhivkov articulated the importance of collecting accurate intelligence ("The need has grown to create such a system of information from the top to the bottom in which public opinion is not falsified or varnished").[144] The party-state leadership understood citizen complaints were an important source of social information that revealed the popular mood. For that reason, it aimed to incentivize citizens to complain more often.[145] In 1977, the Politburo issued a decision, distributed to all party and government offices, on improving the handling of citizen complaints, and in 1980 a special Law on Suggestions, Signals, Complaints, and Requests was promulgated.[146] The utility of complaints from the point of view of the regime was that they constituted a channel for the voluntary transmission of information ("Spontaneously, without any special organizing, on their own initiative, they [the workers] raise important personal and social problems that have to be solved").[147] Once the raw complaints were received, they were analyzed and information about them was presented

---

[142] TsDA f. 1B op. 55 a. e. 486, *Zlobodnevni problemi*, no. 2/1977 (March 1977), 8.
[143] TsDA f. 1B op. 55 a. e. 531, *Zlobodnevni problemi*, no. 2/1987 (June 1987), 14–15.
[144] TsDA f. 1B op. 55 a. e. 935 (1979), 5.
[145] TsDA f. 1B op. 55 a. e. 935 (1979), 5.
[146] See TsDA f. 1B op. 55 a. e. 933 (1977) and *Durzhaven vestnik*, no. 52 (July 4, 1980). Prior to the promulgation of the 1980 law, the handling of complaints was based on decrees going back to 1951.
[147] TsDA f. 1B op. 55 a. e. 935 (1979), 4.

Table 5.3 Issues Raised in Citizen Complaints in Bulgaria, 1982

Issue	Percent of Complaints
Housing	18.2
Negative interactions with the authorities	13.2
Land and construction disputes	11.6
Labor disputes	5.4
Social insurance	5.2
Agriculture	4.3
Transportation, communications, utilities	3.8
Retail trade and dining outlets	3.3
Others	35.0

Source: TsDA f. 1b op. 55 a. e. 940 (1983), 14.

to the leadership through periodic reports. These reports allowed for nuanced assessments of popular consumption preferences.

Although the top leadership benefited from regular updates on trends in citizen complaints from several Central Committee departments, the reports of the Information-Sociological Center were the most comprehensive, as they systematized data on all complaints received by the party, by the government, by the Committee for Control by the State and the People, by the trade unions and other parastatal organizations, and by the mass media. These aggregate reports, which do not have parallels in other communist regimes, indicated that what most people complained about were daily-life manifestations of problems with the social contract: lack of proper housing and the legally murky regulation of personally built countryside homes; job difficulties; the low quality of transportation; the shortages of consumer goods; and the abysmal quality of customer services. There were also requests for social assistance from citizens who were sick or disabled, as well as pleas for an increase in pensions.[148] Throughout the 1970s and early 1980s, the most frequent concern articulated in citizen complaints was the difficulty of obtaining housing.[149] This is demonstrated in Table 5.3, which

[148] TsDA f. 136 op. 72 a. e. 139 (1980); TsDA f. 1B op. 55 a. e. 942 (1984), 37.
[149] TsDA f. 1B op. 82 a. e. 790 (1975); TsDA f. 1B op. 55 a. e. 935 (1979); TsDA f. 1B op. 55 a. e. 936 (1980). Numerous letters about this problem were addressed to the Central Committee and personally to Todor Zhivkov (TsDA f. 224 op. 2 a. e. 648 [1982]; TsDA f. 1B op. 102 a. e. 972 [1983]). Notably, 80 percent of the requests for housing were judged to be justified (TsDA f. 1B op. 102 a. e. 800 [1982], 3).

contains a detailed breakdown of complaints in 1982. Complaint reports were read carefully because they allowed the power holders to "take the pulse" of public opinion.[150]

5.3.5 Receiving and Responding to Complaints by the Committee for Control by the State and the People (*Komitet za durzhaven i naroden kontrol*)

Beyond the party, complaints were also monitored by the *Komitet za durzhaven i naroden kontrol* (KDNK, equivalent to the Ministry of Supervision in China— *jiancha bu* 监察部).[151] The committee, created in 1948, existed throughout the communist period. With the rank of a government ministry, it was charged with monitoring state employees working in government agencies, state firms, and cooperatives. The role of the committee was to ensure that government decisions were carried out promptly; that state funds were not wasted or misappropriated; and that state employees did not engage in undisciplined behavior, bureaucratism (*biurokratizum*), indolence, or attempts to unnecessarily expand government agencies. As the reach of the communist state deepened and widened, the committee's gargantuan task of controlling state employees in all sectors of the economy required the cooperation of a large number of individuals. By 1977, the committee was relying on over 240,000 part-time and volunteer controllers (thus fulfilling its "control by the people" mandate), who constituted about 4 percent of the adult population of Bulgaria.[152] The system of control committees was hierarchically organized, with offices at the central, provincial, and county levels. Below the county level, there were smaller commissions and groups for control by the state and the people; in addition, large enterprises had their own control committees.[153] This comprehensive network allowed for a very deep reach of the committees for control by the state and the people.

Although the committees could conduct control checks on their own initiative, investigations were typically prompted by citizen complaints (the volume of which remained relatively constant at about 30,000 letters per year in the 1970s and early 1980s) or by critical media reporting.[154] Petitions and critical media publications were taken seriously primarily based on party-state instructions

[150] TsDA f. 1B op. 55 a. e. 942 (1984), 44.

[151] The Chinese Ministry of Supervision worked jointly with the Central Commission for Discipline Inspection until 2018, when it was merged into the National Supervisory Commission.

[152] TsDA f. 375 op. 30 a. e. 5 (1977), 2.

[153] TsDA f. 375 op. 33 a. e. 165 (1984).

[154] TsDA f. 375 op. 30 a. e. 5 (1977), 61; TsDA f. 375 op. 31 a. e. 2 (1978), 103; TsDA f. 375 op. 32 a. e. 3 (1979–1980), 54, 97–98; TsDA f. 375 op. 33 a. e. 13 (1983), 28; TsDA f. 375 op. 33 a. e. 161 (1984), 31.

to all party departments and government agencies.[155] An elaborate system for tracking, analyzing, and responding to citizen complaints was implemented in the second half of the 1970s. The following quote encapsulates how the committee viewed the role of petitions: "The suggestions, signals, complaints, and requests of citizens are one of the most important sources for assessing the state of public opinion and the political mood of the workers. They contain valuable information about the issues that concern citizens."[156] Other internal documents from the 1980s indicate that petitions were understood by the committee to be a prized source of "social information," because they allowed the authorities to "take the pulse of public opinion."[157] More broadly, complaints revealed "the state of public opinion and the political attitudes of the working class,"[158] provided feedback about shortcomings in the operation of government organs and, most importantly, gave the government knowledge of brewing social discontent, which could be addressed before it evolved into a full-blown crisis.[159] Therefore, in the understanding of the committee, complaints were to be used to track latent discontent.

After systematic analysis, the information extracted from complaints could be employed to improve the quality of governance (*efektivnostta na sotsialnoto upravlenie*).[160] Citizen complaints typically focused on shortages and the poor quality of services.[161] One issue that repeatedly surfaced in the annual reports of the committee was the behavior of unscrupulous food-store employees, who would cheat customers regarding the price or the weight of food items; would provide rude service; and would hide goods that were in short supply, in order to offer them to friends and relatives, often in exchange for bribes. There was also significant dissatisfaction with the quality of housing construction and repair as well as with the enforcement of zoning regulations, which made it difficult to legalize countryside homes that were often built in violation of zoning rules. Not surprisingly, there were complaints about shortcomings in the areas of transportation and telecommunications as well. The low quality of car- and TV-repair services was also a source of dissatisfaction. In addition, citizens complained about job assignments, wrongful terminations, and workplace conflicts. Finally, there were numerous reports of shortages, ranging from bread and agricultural products (fruit and vegetables) to soft drinks and meat.

---

[155] TsDA f. 1B op. 55 a. e. 933 (December 6, 1977). See also "Law on Suggestions, Signals, Complaints, and Requests," *Durzhaven vestnik*, no. 52 (July 4, 1980).

[156] TsDA f. 375 op. 33 a. e. 161 (1984), 1–2.

[157] TsDA f. 375 op. 34 a. e. 168 (1988), 81A.

[158] TsDA f. 375 op. 33 a. e. 161 (1984), 21–21A.

[159] TsDA f. 375 op. 34 a. e. 125 (1987), 27–28.

[160] TsDA f. 375 op. 34 a. e. 125 (1987), 28.

[161] Paragraph based on the following documents: TsDA f. 375 op. 30 a. e. 5 (1977); TsDA f. 375 op. 31 a. e. 21 (1978); TsDA f. 375 op. 32 a. e. 3 (1979); TsDA f. 375 op. 33 a. e. 13 (1983).

This wide spectrum of complaints was made known to the top policy makers through regular briefs from the committee. These reports estimated that up to 60 percent of complaints were justified and emphasized the importance of addressing the underlying problems that resulted in dissatisfaction.[162] The reasoning is simple but powerful: "These systematic violations create discontent among citizens and a negative popular mood."[163]

5.3.6 The Bulgarian Telegraph Agency

Beyond State Security, the party, and the Committee for Control by the State and the People, the Bulgarian Telegraph Agency (BTA) issued a range of classified bulletins compiled from translations of international newswires; from transcriptions of "hostile" foreign radio broadcasts aimed at Bulgaria; and from dispatches by BTA correspondents stationed abroad. This content was not fit for print in the public outlets because it concerned critical coverage of Bulgaria in the foreign media. In contrast to China, where Xinhua had produced domestic investigative reporting since the very beginning of the regime, reports from BTA domestic correspondents found their way into secret bulletins only during the later decades of communist rule. This divergence reflects the fact that the BTA arose as a collector of foreign intelligence for the king during the precommunist period (its first classified bulletin on foreign news dates back to 1898, when it was a department of the Foreign Ministry). In the 1950s and 1960s, domestic investigative reporting was carried out by the party, by State Security, and by the print media. This began to change in the 1970s, when BTA domestic correspondents were encouraged to report on instances of corruption, criminal negligence, and the waste of resources. Thus, in the 1970s and 1980s, BTA briefs supplemented the existing classified domestic reporting streams.

The Content of Secret and Top-Secret Bulletins

These bulletins were distributed to editors-in-chief, provincial leaders, and directors of the main enterprises. Printed twice daily, *Key International News* featured content not meant for official public dissemination that was derived from Western newswires and from dispatches of BTA correspondents stationed abroad.[164] Published five times a week, *Foreign Anti-Bulgarian Propaganda* provided a summary of Bulgarian broadcasts by stations such as the BBC, Deutsche Welle, Radio Free Europe, Voice of America, Radio Yugoslavia, Radio Skopje,

---

[162] TsDA f. 375 op. 30 a. e. 5 (1977), 62.
[163] TsDA f. 375 op. 31 a. e. 21 (1978), 20.
[164] BTA Archive, *Spetsialen biuletin "Po-vazhni suobshteniia ot chuzhbina"* (January 1, 1979).

and Radio Vatican. In addition, BTA correspondents in Belgrade, Athens, and Ankara closely monitored the Yugoslav, Greek, and Turkish press for coverage of Bulgaria. *Foreign Anti-Bulgarian Propaganda* also included occasional translations of Bulgaria-related articles printed in Western news outlets, as well as reporting by the Albanian Telegraph Agency (ATA) and Xinhua coverage of Bulgaria.[165] All content was deemed sensitive and thus not fit for public dissemination because it focused on issues such as the lack of political enthusiasm among schoolchildren;[166] delays in the adoption of a five-day workweek;[167] and the ideologically problematic need to rely on private repair shops to meet the demand for services.[168] The monitoring of "hostile" radio stations exposed the leadership to the content of the ideologically subversive messages that reached ordinary citizens and impressed upon the elite that countermeasures were needed.

The three special addenda (secret S-1 and top-secret S-2 and S-3) were the most exclusive BTA bulletins. Regardless of the level of classification, each issue of an addendum focused on a single problem, thus allowing for in-depth analysis of sensitive news items. The length varied (as short as one page and as long as sixty-six pages), as did frequency: the less exclusive S-1 and S-2 were published as needed up to twice a day, whereas S-3 was issued several times a month. All three bulletins used the same sources to produce in-depth analyses: foreign newswire reports, monitoring of foreign broadcasts, and original reporting from BTA foreign and domestic correspondents.

We are not in possession of documents clarifying what selection principles guided the placement of material into S-1, S-2, and S-3. Hand-coding of the content of 159 issues of S-1, S-2, and S-3 indicates that information about Bulgarian politics generated through investigative reporting by domestic correspondents was relatively rare.[169] A total of nine domestic reports appear in the sample. Simple signals of inefficiency or waste were placed in S-1 (eight reports). A more sensitive alert about a criminally negligent enterprise director was printed in S-2.[170]

---

[165] For a report on Xinhua's views of Soviet-Bulgarian relations, see BTA Archive, *Chuzhdata propaganda protiv Bulgariia*, no. 34 (February 10, 1975), 5.

[166] BTA Archive, *Chuzhdata propaganda protiv Bulgariia*, no. 34 (February 15, 1980), 10–12; BTA Archive, *Chuzhdata propaganda protiv Bulgariia*, no. 34 (February 15, 1980), 2–6, 7–9.

[167] BTA Archive, *Chuzhdata propaganda protiv Bulgariia*, no. 50 (February 28, 1975), 2–4.

[168] BTA Archive, *Chuzhdata propaganda protiv Bulgariia*, no. 139 (July 14, 1977), 7–8.

[169] The sample includes forty-nine S-1 bulletins issued in 1978, fifty-eight S-1 bulletins issued in 1980, twenty S-1 and S-2 bulletins issued between 1976 and 1983, and all thirty-two S-3 bulletins issued in 1981.

[170] The S-1 reports are: S-1 Report No. 9 (February 2, 1978); S-1 Report No. 10 (February 7, 1978); S-1 Report No. 1 (January 7, 1980); S-1 Report No. 3 (January 16, 1980); S-1 Report No. 15 (January 29, 1980); S-1 Report No. 17 (January 31, 1980); S-1 Report No. 21 (February 6, 1980); and S-1 Report No. 46 (March 20, 1980). The S-2 report is S-2 Report No. 414 (August 9, 1977).

Table 5.4 Issues Covered in the Bulgarian Telegraph Agency Special Addendum S-3 Reports, 1981

Issues Covered	Number of Reports	Countries Referenced
Consumer discontent, protests, and strikes	16	Soviet Union (8 reports) Romania (7 reports) Bulgaria (1 report)
NGOs	4	Poland (3 reports) Soviet Union (1 report)
Elite politics (assassinations, health of leaders, cult of personality, gerontocracy, and ossification in the Politburo)	9	Soviet Union (5 reports) Bulgaria (3 reports) Romania (1 report)
Other	3	Bulgaria (2 reports) Romania (1 report)
TOTAL	32	**Soviet Union (14 reports)** **Romania (9 reports)** **Bulgaria (6 reports)** **Poland (3 reports)**

Source: BTA Archive, *Special Addendum S-3* (1981). Coded by the author.

As the BTA bulletin with the highest level of classification, *Addendum S-3* necessitates closer attention. S-3 was exclusively based on analysis of foreign news coverage, and it did not contain any domestic investigative reporting. Dispatched only to Politburo members, this bulletin was printed irregularly as needed: for example, in 1981 there were thirty-two installments. Each issue contained a single report on a specific topic. These reports varied in length between one and twelve pages, with the average being three pages. The most frequent issue reflected in S-3 was consumer discontent and protests and strikes resulting from such discontent (see Table 5.4). A brief on discontent in Bulgaria in 1981 (a sensitive party congress year) based on a report from Reuters deserves further note, as it contained the following assessment:

> The party congress was preceded by an unprecedented wave of officially encouraged criticism in the newspapers and in radio broadcasts, focusing mainly on the shortage of housing, the irregular supply of foodstuffs, the shortfalls in the provision of public transportation, and the "bubbling up" of bureaucracy.
>
> Western diplomats say that this type of criticism was encouraged in recent years, but they add that it has probably been allowed to intensify after the Polish events, in order to create a guarantee that Bulgarian leaders will not repeat the

mistakes of the leadership in Warsaw and lose touch with the average person and his grievances.

However, diplomats state, the power holders face a risk of elevating public expectations to a level whereby it will be difficult to satisfy them.[171]

This Western assessment identifies the main dilemma of communist governance in the 1970s and 1980s and, in hindsight, it turned out to be prophetic about a key factor that ultimately contributed to the unraveling of the regime.

In sum, the BTA supplied the leadership with an extraordinary array of information about international news; external views of Bulgarian foreign policy; domestic political problems; and, from the 1970s onward, briefs on waste and corruption throughout the country based on investigative reporting by BTA domestic correspondents. Resolute efforts by the minister of the interior to prevent access to these bulletins by individuals who were not their intended recipients (on the grounds that knowledge of the intelligence contained in them "could be used as a basis for negative public comments or the spread of tendentious rumors") attests to the value they had for the leadership.[172] The bulletins helped elucidate two lessons: the first is that consumer frustrations could lead to overt discontent and the second is that the ideological subversion propagated by hostile foreign media required a response. Beyond jamming, the response had both a material component (satisfying welfare expectations) and an ideological dimension (promoting indigenous cultural consumption).

5.4 Responsiveness to the Information about Material Consumption Preferences

The social contract is not meaningful unless we can demonstrate that the leadership took seriously the consumption preferences of ordinary citizens. This section traces how the leadership responded to information about the material needs of the population during normal times and also during periods of crisis. As had occurred previously (in 1953, 1956, and 1968) this crisis was external—the events in Poland in 1980–1981 provided a reminder of the imperative to satisfy the consumption needs of the population (and the explosive nature of decisions to raise the prices of consumer goods).[173] The leadership heeded the Polish lesson, placing a greater emphasis on tracking the levels of responsiveness

---

[171] BTA Archive, *Prilozhenie S-3*, no. 10 (April 18, 1981), 3–4.

[172] AMVR f. 1 op. 12 a. e. 415 (June 17, 1982), 209.

[173] AMVR f. 1 op. 12 a. e. 420A (January 6, 1982), 9; AMVR f. 1 op. 12 a. e. 420A (January 8, 1982), 40; AMVR f. 1 op. 12 a. e. 420A (January 19, 1982), 76.

through computer-based systems and other mechanisms that would issue periodic reminders about unresolved complaints.[174] Yet, the early 1980s were also a time when the socialist redistributive model was reaching the limits of its capacity to ensure a steady improvement in standards of living, thus foreshadowing the economic crisis that would be unleashed in the mid-1980s and would signal that the regime was no longer able to maintain its side of the social contract.

5.4.1 Leadership Responsiveness to Consumption Needs in Normal Times

How engaged were leaders with the reports they received? Sometimes, the general secretary himself was involved in the resolution of a complaint. For example, a letter from General Secretary Todor Zhivkov to the Ministry of Communications following a high volume of complaints plainly states: "Comrades, for many years the quality of public post and telephone services has been a source of a social evil and of a lowering of the prestige of the people's government (*narodnata vlast*)."[175] We also have archival evidence that Zhivkov received briefs that identified scarcities of consumer goods and that follow-up reports were delivered to him specifying what measures were taken to resolve these problems.[176] One level below the general secretary, both the periodic petitioning digests and the issues raised in *Zlobodnevni problemi* were read and discussed by the Politburo. One example involves the Council of Ministers contemplating how to alleviate the shortage of table salt.[177] Another concerns a decision by the Committee on Industrial Coordination (*Komitet za stopanska koordinatsiia*) to improve the industrial design of mass consumption goods; the general secretary was apprised of this decision.[178] A third involves cataloging and responding to socially relevant (*obshtestveno znachimi*) consumption suggestions made by party members.[179] Such seemingly irrational use of the time of top leaders makes sense when we take into account that communist regimes were bound by a social contract (elaborated upon in party programs and at party congresses) and had to attempt to respond to the needs of the people, even when those needs included mundane

---

[174] For precursors, see TsDA f. 378B op. 1 a. e. 1021 (1974). See also TsDA f. 1B op. 101 a. e. 597 (1981); TsDA f. 1B op. 11 a. e. 10 (1981); TsDA f. 1B op. 11 a. e. 7 (1988); TsDA f. 1B op. 11 a. e. 12 (1989).

[175] TsDA f. 1B op. 101 a. e. 1337 (1985), 1.

[176] See TsDA f. 1B op. 102 a. e. 595 (1981) for an example of an original report and TsDA f. 1B op. 102 a. e. 597 (1981) for an example of a follow-up report.

[177] TsDA f. 375 op. 32 a. e. 5 (1979).

[178] TsDA f. 136 op. 52 a. e. 530 (1971).

[179] TsDA f. 1b op. 11 a. e. 10 (1982).

items like salt. Thus, analyses of complaints transmitted by the Information-Sociological Center became an important vehicle for alerting the leadership about the scope of latent discontent.

The regime took several steps to improve its responsiveness by increasing the rate of favorable resolution of petitions and the prosecution of corrupt officials. The reports of the Information-Sociological Center indicate that these initiatives were successful in increasing the proportion of favorably resolved cases from 20–30 percent in the mid-1970s to as high as 45 percent in the early 1980s.[180] In terms of disciplining corrupt cadres, by the early 1980s as many as one in two corruption complaints resulted in the punishment of officials by the Central Control and Audit Commission, the anticorruption body within the Communist Party.[181] There is no baseline to determine whether these rates are high or low. But internal reports demonstrate that the party regarded the continuing increases in the volume of complaints as an indicator that the rate of responsiveness was sufficiently high to provide incentives for participation in the system of citizen petitioning.[182]

The Bulgarian archives reveal that the roll-out of expansive packages of social benefits was consistent with citizen preferences, as expressed in complaint letters and through other channels. The government provided a generous extension of maternity leaves, rapidly expanded the housing stock, and legally sanctioned the private construction and ownership of countryside homes. The response to consumer preferences also featured a further increase in salaries; support for families (child supplements and subsidies for mothers); attempts to augment the variety of goods offered in stores and improve the availability of imported items; an increase in the volume and variety of services; and commitments to provide superior healthcare, education, and vacation packages in state-owned rest homes. As the regime itself had stated: "The resolute improvement in the quality of all activities, production, and services is to become the main task in our future socioeconomic and cultural development; the fulfillment of this task has enormous political, ideological, economic, and social importance for every work unit, for every working person."[183] Attempts were also made to import a sufficient number of automobiles, and to thus satisfy the third leg of the socialist consumer dream: an apartment, a villa, and a car. In addition, in the wake of a growing number of complaints from retirees, pensions were raised.

---

[180] See TsDA f. 1B op. 55 a. e. 934 (1977) and TsDA f. 1B op. 55 a. e. 937 (1981), 19.
[181] Calculated from TsDA f. 1B op. 55 a. e. 942 (1984) and TsDA f. 224 op. 2 a. e. 686 (1984), 78.
[182] TsDA f. 1B op. 55 a. e. 937 (1981).
[183] *Za po-natatushno izpulnenie na Dekemvriiskata programa*, 13.

5.4.2 Responsiveness during Times of Crisis: Learning from the Events in Poland, 1980–1981

The Polish events in 1980–1981, which largely arose from frustrated consumption expectations, proved to have profound domestic implications in Bulgaria. This was the last external crisis prior to 1989 that resulted in increased efforts to satisfy the consumption preferences of the population. The Central Committee met in November 1980, ostensibly to discuss "some current problems related to preparations for the upcoming party congress." This was not, however, a routine conclave. It came after two Politburo meetings earlier in the fall that had analyzed the same issue, namely, the reasons for the Polish crisis and the steps to take so that Bulgaria would avoid a similar turn of events.[184]

The Politburo concluded that the root cause of the crisis was the sharp decrease in trust in the party among workers. Although there were several reasons for the erosion of trust, the serious economic difficulties that Poland had experienced were key. Todor Zhivkov's report to the Central Committee stated that even though Poland had its specificities, a replay of such events in Bulgaria was possible. Yet, it could be avoided by improving living standards, which meant increasing the access to goods and services. Specifically, this would involve focusing on the supply of bread; the quality of food offered in workers' canteens; the availability of housing; worker safety; the waste of time to obtain goods and services; and the lot of pensioners.[185] A series of concrete measures were taken to alleviate the problems identified in Zhivkov's report. In the run-up to the 1981 party congress, of crucial importance was to encourage household agriculture and private production of small wares. Other policies included improving the quality of services; constructing a sufficient number of apartments to house 1 million citizens (over one-tenth of the country's population); and increasing the volume of consumer goods by 8–9 percent. The long-desired goal of securing a more rapid growth in the volume of consumer goods than the rise of salaries became a reality in 1981.[186]

Consumption issues understandably took center stage at the 1981 party congress, which articulated a series of specific commitments to elevate the living standards of the population by improving the supply of goods and services. Yet, the party congress is also notable for its official statement that the social consumption funds would increase at a slower pace in the future.[187] This constituted

[184] Vladimir Migev, *Polskata kriza, "Solidarnost," i Bulgariia (1980–1983)* (Sofia: Universitetsko Izdatelstvo "Sv. Kliment Okhridski," 2008), 150–57.

[185] TsDA f. 1B op. 65 a. e. 36 (November 4–5, 1980).

[186] TsDA f. 1B op. 65 a. e. 36 (November 4–5, 1980).

[187] *Dvanadeseti kongres na Bulgarskata komunisticheska partiia (31 mart–4 april 1981 g.) (Stenografski protokoli—chast purva)* (Sofia: Partizdat, 1981), 63.

public acknowledgment of an inability to continue to satisfy consumption preferences at the same rate as previously. Although the Decision on the Further Fulfillment of the December Program was passed in February 1983, its goals with regard to improved consumption remained largely unrealized. From 1984 onward, the regime was unable to satisfy the consumption preferences of the population, thus reneging on its commitments under the socialist social contract and undermining the citizens' remaining conditional loyalty to the system.

5.5 The Threat of Ideological Subversion

This section discusses ideological subversion, whose effects could negate all party-state efforts to secure compliance through redistributive policies. By the late 1960s, there was a shared understanding among information gatherers that ideological subversion from abroad constituted the main external threat to regime stability. This was supported by the results of a 1970 opinion poll, demonstrating that citizens lacked an appreciation for the ideological superiority of the communist regime and they were interested in Western ways of life.[188] In a similar vein, the Institute of Contemporary Social Theories transmitted an alert to Todor Zhivkov about the heightened attention to Western radio broadcasts because of the inclusion of the outcomes of British and Italian soccer matches in the Bulgarian sports lottery, which was played weekly by 100,000 individuals; eager to learn the results of the soccer matches quickly, lottery players would tune into Western radio stations. Thus, concluded the report, the lottery organizers artificially inflated interest in hostile radio broadcasting that was spreading anti-Bulgarian propaganda.[189] An important task, therefore, was to identify the main channels that enabled this subversion and to develop strategies to counteract it.

In the 1970s, State Security reached an understanding that the principal tactic of the enemy was to foment a "quiet revolution" through ideological subversion, which involved the promotion of minority self-determination, support for opposition groups, and encouragement of acts of resistance to the party-state by extremist individuals.[190] The specific vectors for subversion included contacts with the people and the ideological products of the countries that represented the enemy. State Security expressed fear that youth were particularly susceptible to the harmful ideological influence of foreigners, which could lead them to engage in provocations or attempts to flee the country.[191] For this reason, the regime sought to limit physical travel outside Bulgaria as well as to restrict the number

---

[188] TsDA f. 1B op. 36 a. e. 1021 (1970).
[189] TsDA f. 378B op. 1 a. e. 1001 (1972).
[190] AMVR f. 44 op. 3 a. e. 41 (April 1974), 16–24.
[191] AMVR f. 1 op. 12 a. e. 417 (July 19–25, 1982), 29.

of foreign citizens who were allowed to visit the country. Hostile radio stations were jammed and the voices of Bulgarian journalists who worked for them were silenced.[192] Nevertheless, it was impossible to eliminate the vectors that enabled this ideological subversion, and the Helsinki Accords exacerbated this problem.

5.5.1 The Helsinki Effect

The literature documents how the Helsinki Accords of 1975 constrained the use of repression during demonstrations and encouraged the rise of informal NGOs in the Soviet Union.[193] In fact, the Helsinki Accords had an effect throughout the Eastern Bloc.[194] In Bulgaria, the regime needed to reckon with problematic youth, who were spreading political rumors about the death of Soviet leaders.[195] Even more concerning, there were reports of neofascist organizations in the capital,[196] in addition to a documented attempt to organize a youth demonstration in Sofia.[197] State Security registered political jokes about shortages;[198] rumors about impending leadership changes;[199] and the circulation of death announcements with negative political content.[200] Despite these reports, discontent seemed manageable.

In Bulgaria, in its internal reports State Security expressed concerns about the constraints imposed by the Helsinki Accords, which promoted the free exchange of people, information, and ideas; needless to say, these principles directly challenged the secret police.[201] There were several types of effects. One was that the Ministry of the Interior received a large number of freedom-of-movement requests to allow relatives of defectors to travel to the West.[202] The second consequence was increased pressure on Bulgaria from Western diplomats. State

---

[192] The most famous case was the poisoned-tip umbrella assassination in 1978 of journalist Georgi Markov, who worked for the BBC, Radio Free Europe, and Deutsche Welle (see Khristo Khristov, *Ubiite "Skitnik": Bulgarskata i britanskata durzhavna politika po sluchaia Georgi Markov* [Sofia: Ciela, 2006]). Also in 1978, there was an unsuccessful attempt on the life of Vladimir Kostov, a Bulgarian intelligence officer originally dispatched to Paris under the cover of a journalist, who defected in 1977 and was subsequently employed by Radio Free Europe (see Vladimir Kostov, *Le parapluie bulgare* [Paris: Stock, 1986]).

[193] Daniel C. Thomas, *The Helsinki Effect: International Norms, Human Rights, and the Demise of Communism* (Princeton, NJ: Princeton University Press, 2001).

[194] Jonathan Bolton, *Worlds of Dissent: Charter 77, the Plastic People of the Universe, and Czech Culture under Communism* (Cambridge, MA: Harvard University Press, 2012).

[195] AKRDOPBGDSRSBNA-M f. 22 op. 1 a. e. 85 (1980), 163–70.

[196] AKRDOPBGDSRSBNA-M f. 1 op. 12 a. e. 409 (1981), 4–13.

[197] AKRDOPBGDSRSBNA-M f. 1 op. 12 a. e. 409A (1981), 12–15.

[198] AKRDOPBGDSRSBNA-M-VI-L a. e. 533 (1977), 230–31.

[199] AKRDOPBGDSRSBNA-M-VI-L a. e. 533 (1977), 234–35.

[200] AKRDOPBGDSRSBNA-M f. 22 op. 1 a. e. 192 (1983), 62–65.

[201] AMVR f. 22 op. 1 a. e. 51 (November 5, 1976); AMVR f. 22 op. 1 a. e. 57 (February 24, 1977).

[202] AMVR f. 1 op. 12 a. e. 427A (1977), 3.

Security reported that military attachés were using their right to freedom of movement within the country to view military installations and that cultural attachés were instigating ideological subversion by enticing students with scholarships for study abroad.[203] Ultimately, State Security asserted, the goal of Western diplomats was to promote a dissident movement in Bulgaria.[204] The final effect of the Helsinki Accords was that Bulgaria's human rights record became subject to regular evaluation by Amnesty International.[205] In sum, Helsinki posed a serious challenge to State Security to develop a pragmatic nonrepressive response to ideological subversion.

5.6 Cultural Consumption in Response to Ideological Subversion

The 1960s and 1970s were a period when the top leadership was focusing on circuses, both literally (Todor Zhivkov was presented with a lengthy report on "Problems in the Circus Arts")[206] and figuratively, when grand spectacles that aimed to build patriotic pride were organized at extraordinary expense.[207] These grand performances included staging the 1968 World Youth Festival, the launching of the International Children's Peace Assembly in 1979 (reconvened in 1982, 1985, and 1988),[208] the organization of the World Rhythmic Gymnastics Championship (in 1969 and 1987), and the hosting of the biannual International Ballet Competition beginning in 1964. Spectacles also extended to winning a sufficient number of medals to secure a place among the top ten countries in the Summer Olympics in 1972, 1976, 1980, and 1988. Beyond the world of sports, Bulgarians were regaled with sights of sending two men in space—Georgi Ivanov in 1979 and Alexander Alexandrov in 1988. But the most important spectacle, which will be discussed in this section, was the celebration of the 1300th anniversary of the founding of the Bulgarian state. It took over a decade's worth of work by the party, and, perhaps surprisingly, by State Security, to organize this celebration.

---

[203] AMVR f. 1 op. 12 a. e. 426A (1977), 38; AMVR f. 1 op. 12 a. e. 422A (1977).

[204] AMVR f. 1 op. 12 a. e. 425A (1977), 51.

[205] AMVR f. 1 op. 12 a. e. 426A (1977), 1.

[206] TsDA f. 378B op. 1 a. e. 975 (1969).

[207] Theodora K. Dragostinova, *The Cold War from the Margins: A Small Socialist State on the Global Cultural Scene* (Ithaca, NY: Cornell University Press, 2021).

[208] The International Children's Peace Assembly was monitored by State Security—see AMVR f. 1 op. 12 a. e. 417 (August 9–15, 1982), 79.

5.6.1 Spies and Patriotic Pride: The Ideological Tasks of Cultural-Historical Intelligence

At first glance, the existence of a special division of the External Intelligence Directorate of State Security that was tasked with cultural-historical intelligence might seem baffling. A review of the activities of this division may raise even more questions. Cultural-Historical Intelligence (also known as Department XIV), which was established in 1972, had three chief tasks.[209] One was to collect information about the main cultural centers and historical research institutes in hostile Western countries and in the neighboring Balkan states that were working against Bulgaria. Another was to identify and acquire valuable documents and artifacts linked with the country's cultural and historical past. Third, Cultural-Historical Intelligence deployed "active measures" (*aktivni meropriiatiia*) to assist the party's cultural policy abroad. In its activities, the department relied on full-time staff; on part-time Bulgarian associates (who were either scholars or cultural figures);[210] and on agents recruited overseas. Carrying out its mandate required infiltrating research institutes, museums, and monasteries; purchasing or stealing documents and artifacts;[211] and contracting with foreigners to promote the official party views on history, including the country's complicated past relations with its neighbors in the Balkans. Ultimately, this department was called on to assist with the consolidation of the officially promoted historical narrative,[212] which required securing the documents and artifacts necessary for writing a ten-volume history of Bulgaria, whose table of contents had been approved by the Politburo in 1968.[213]

The operations of Cultural-Historical Intelligence received support from the highest level: Liudmila Zhivkova, the daughter of the dictator and a Politburo member herself, directed its work.[214] Ultimately, this department was supposed to boost patriotic pride by staging spectacular displays, such as the Thracian gold exhibits abroad and the celebrations of the 1300th anniversary of the founding of the Bulgarian state at home in 1981.[215] The department also served the nefarious

---

[209] See the documents in *DS i kulturno-istoricheskoto razuznavane 1970–1989* (Sofia: Dossier Commission, 2014).

[210] Bozhidar Dimitrov, *Za kozhata na edno chenge* (Sofia: Unicart, 2015).

[211] Khristo Khristov, *Operatsiia "Maraton": Istinata za krazhbata na Paisievata istoriia ot Durzhavna sigurnost v "Zograf"* (Sofia: Ciela, 2012).

[212] AKRDOPBGDSRSBNA-M f. 1 op. 10 a. e. 178 (November 18, 1980), 34–44.

[213] TsDA f. 1B op. 35 a. e. 199 (May 21, 1968), 8–12.

[214] Zhivkova was a complex figure: she exhibited significant tolerance for cultural and artistic experimentation and even hosted intellectual salons at her home; she also had an interest in the occult and met regularly with Baba Vanga, the country's most influential fortune-teller; and she practiced meditation and yoga, both seen as suspect in Bulgaria at the time. Zhivkova died in July 1981 at the age of 39 under circumstances that have not been fully clarified.

[215] Secretariat of the Central Committee, Decision No. 477 (June 3, 1976).

goals of the Regenerative Process (1984–1989) by dispatching historians to the Turkish archives in search of evidence that the Bulgarian Turks were forcibly Islamized Christians and thus justifying the renaming process that involved "giving them back" their original Bulgarian names.

The rationale for spectacles in response to ideological subversion in a mature communist regime may not be immediately obvious. The literature focuses on mass rallies,[216] in which citizens declare public loyalty to the regime, even though they might privately be opposed (coerced participation helps create an image of the invincibility of the leader). But the spectacles discussed in this chapter had a different function: they were used as a tool in the ideological battle against the West, with the guiding principle being that by fostering pride in the Bulgarian nation, the regime would preclude disillusionment and alienation, which, in turn, would prevent ideological defection and subversion. The spectacles were a form of cultural consumption aimed at displacing interest in Western culture.

Beyond the spectacles, national pride was built in more routine ways: through patriotic education for students; by publishing historical fiction that was consistent with the official Politburo-approved outline of Bulgarian history; and through cinematic and creative artistic productions aimed at the mass consumer. In the view of the party, historical nihilism made citizens susceptible to foreign ideological influence. The counterstrategy of building national pride was a complex and costly undertaking.

5.6.2 The Ideological Functions of Indigenous Entertainment

In the eyes of the cadres at the Propaganda Department of the Central Committee, one function of indigenous entertainment was to distract citizens from searching for Western entertainment. Very popular series on State Security (*Na vseki kilometer*—At Every Milestone) and on the people's militia (*Siniata lampa*—The Blue Lamp) were broadcast on TV in 1969–1971 and 1974.[217] Beyond TV spy series, Bulgarian audiences were introduced to the previously unfamiliar format of the live talk show, with the most popular programs being *Panorama* (for international news analysis) and *Vsiaka nedelia* (Every Sunday), which covered a wide spectrum of international and domestic political and cultural developments. A *Jeopardy*-style quiz show called *Minuta e mnogo* (One Minute Is Too Long)

---

[216] Lisa Wedeen, *Ambiguities of Domination: Politics, Rhetoric, and Symbols in Contemporary Syria* (Chicago: University of Chicago Press, 1999); Karen Petrone, *Life Has Become More Joyous, Comrades: Celebrations in the Time of Stalin* (Bloomington: Indiana University Press, 2000); Malte Rolf, *Soviet Mass Festivals, 1917–1991* (Pittsburgh: University of Pittsburgh Press, 2013).

[217] The two series are comparable to TV productions in the GDR, where *Das Unsichtbare Visier* (1973–1979) focused on the Stasi and *Polizeiruf 110* (1971–1990) centered on the Ministry of the Interior.

appeared in the late 1970s. On radio, the favorite was *Pulsirashti noti* (Pulsating Notes), which sought to limit listening to hostile radio stations by featuring substantial Western musical content.

Another type of entertainment that received the support of the party was humor and satire. A special weekly newspaper called *Sturshel* was designated as the main outlet for satirical writing. Even though it was an organ of the Central Committee, the paper was wildly popular.[218] This did not mean that *Sturshel* could criticize as it saw fit. Newspapers were chastised for printing materials that contradicted party policy.[219] *Sturshel* was no exception, as demonstrated by a complaint from a provincial party committee against the newspaper that went straight to Todor Zhivkov's desk.[220] At the same time, as mentioned in Section 5.3, when adjusting for the frequency of publication, this satirical weekly featured the most critical articles of any news outlet in Bulgaria. Exposing small-scale corruption was permissible. Going after the party elite was dangerous.

To entertain the masses, the party had to maintain its vigilance. A battle that proved impossible to win was the effort to change the "acoustic environment" by promoting indigenous entertainment, as, in the assessment of State Security, popular music was becoming more Westernized.[221] The top leadership received multiple reports on the harmful effects of discotheques and their music (punk and heavy-metal rock).[222] As State Security communicated in a report to Todor Zhivkov, discotheques provided a forum for telling political jokes, for glorifying Western lifestyles, and for conducting antistate propaganda and agitation.[223] Insufficient control meant incapacity to counteract the ideological influence of the West.

In the end, neither the party nor State Security were successful in opposing Western culture. There are numerous indicators that support this conclusion. In the area of consumption and underground trade, polling revealed widespread adoration of Western goods (*xenomania*), including everything from Western food to Western fashions.[224] In the realm of popular culture, fascination with Western film and music trumped demand for Bulgarian cultural products. The regime grudgingly acknowledged these needs: Western film and TV series were broadcast on Bulgarian television; discotheques were tolerated (even though they were closely monitored by State Security, in part as a strategy for recruiting and managing informants); and Western music was played on national radio. Countercultural groups arose (neo-fascists, punks, Jehovah's Witnesses) who

---

[218] TsDA f. 551 op. 4 a. e. 16 (April 2, 1974), 37.

[219] AKRDOPBGDSRSBNA-M f. 38 op. 1 a. e. 84 (1975), 23–28.

[220] TsDA f. 378B op. 1 a. e. 1047 (May 15, 1979), 26–38.

[221] AKRDOPBGDSRSBNA-M-VI-L a. e. 533 t. 1 (1980), 145–146B.

[222] AKRDOPBGDSRSBNA-M f. 22 op. 1 a. e. 164 (1982), 12–15.

[223] AMVR f. 1 op. 12 a. e. 417 (September 13, 1982), 110.

[224] TsDA f. 1B op. 55 a. e. 710 (March 1985), 21–27.

proved resilient to irresolute State Security effort to disband them.[225] Finally, recent technology in the form of cassette tape recorders and VCRs, which found their way into the country in the early 1980s, allowed for the dissemination of countercultural music and videos. Regulating these new media effectively proved to be next to impossible. State Security and the party were losing the ideological battle with the West that was being waged through the increasingly unsuccessful counterstrategies of promoting material consumption and satisfying the aesthetic needs of the population with indigenous cultural products.

5.7 The Turkish Minority: The Ongoing Failure of Co-Optation

The emphasis in this book is on mass co-optation, largely because elite co-optation was only a problem for the party at the time of regime establishment in the 1940s and during the period of democratization (1987–1991). Yet, neither elite nor mass co-optation was successfully implemented in the case of the Turkish minority, which remained as illegible throughout the period discussed in this chapter as it had been during the initial decade of communist rule. This called for a radical solution to erase ethnic differences, similar to the policies that had been systematically applied to other minorities in the 1960s–early 1980s. As the most problematic group (due to the presence of an external kin state), the Turks were spared until 1984, when the so-called Regenerative Process (*Vuzroditelen protses*) was launched.

5.7.1 The Precursors of the Decision to Assimilate the Turkish Minority

The leadership gradually came to see the Turkish minority as illegible and thus impenetrable. There had been signs at the end of the 1950s that atheistic propaganda, a central goal of the regime with regard to all citizens, had been failing among the Turks.[226] This conclusion was powerfully reinforced by a 1967 nationwide survey, indicating that 46.79 percent of Turks believed that God created the world, in contrast to only 11.34 percent of Bulgarians.[227] The inability of the official propaganda to reach members of this minority was highlighted by the fact that only 43.86 percent of the Turks were able to read, speak, and write in

---

[225] AKRDOPBGDSRSBNA-M f. 22 op. 1 a. e. 70 (1979), 186–90; AMVR f. 1 op. 12 a. e. 417 (July 26–August 1, 1982), 52.
[226] TsDA f. 1B op. 91 a. e. 1406 (1959), 6–7.
[227] TsDA f. 1B op. 55 a. e. 1313 (1967).

Bulgarian.[228] Although a million books were printed in Turkish annually, along with Turkish newspapers and radio broadcasts,[229] the party concluded that the Turks were politically apathetic, as demonstrated by the fact that 64.19 percent did not read any newspapers at all and, crucially, that only 4.93 percent were members of the communist party (compared with 11.23 percent of Bulgarians and 6.82 percent of Bulgarian Muslims).[230] Rumors of an imminent decision to re-authorize emigration circulated in the 1960s,[231] thus creating additional difficulties to bind Turks to the party. These diverse indicators all signaled the failure of co-optation.

In 1967, the Politburo decided to gradually implement assimilation,[232] pursuing a goal of "integration and eventual fusion of this population with the Bulgarian nation."[233] Zhivkov emphasized his concern that "if the trend of declining [Bulgarian] fertility continues, sooner or later we will inevitably witness the creation of autonomous Turkish provinces, an autonomous republic, a state within the state."[234] Furthermore, the general secretary feared that "Turkish would become an official language in places where there was a compact Turkish population," that "Turkish national and religious fanaticism would be revived," and that the "Turkish government could lay claims to purely Bulgarian territory."[235] Thus, a decision to proceed with assimilation was forged.

The new policies were formalized in the February 1969 Politburo "Decision on Improving Work Among the Turkish Population and Its Complete Inclusion Within the Bulgarian People."[236] The decision called for a three-pronged approach to the problem: heavy social spending in regions where there was a high concentration of Turks; attempts to increase the number of Turkish youth entering the Komsomol and the communist party, with the goal of eventually creating a Turk cadre of Bulgarian-speaking intelligentsia; and enhanced propaganda efforts (consisting of changes to the educational system that involved teaching all Turkish children Bulgarian; augmenting the volume of publications aimed at the minority, while simultaneously printing fewer copies in Turkish; and eradicating "the religious-conservative remnants of feudalism in daily

[228] TsDA f. 1B op. 55 a. e. 1313 (1967).

[229] TsDA f. 1B op. 91 a. e. 1196 (1958), 1–8.

[230] According to the results from a nationwide survey broken down by nationality, TsDA f. 1B op. 55 a. e. 1313 (1967).

[231] TsDA f. 1B op. 15 a. e. 879 (1963), 13–15; TsDA f. 1B op. 15 a. e. 879 (1963), 16–19.

[232] TsDA f. 378B op. 1 a. e. 757 (1967).

[233] TsDA f. 1B op. 34 a. e. 89 (1967), 86–90.

[234] TsDA f. 1B op. 34 a. e. 89 (1967), 86–90. Subsequent data on the growth of the Turkish minority appear to validate the concerns about its higher level of fertility: although the overall population increase in the country during the 1965–1970 period was 5.2/1,000 among Bulgarians, it stood at 20/1,000 among the Turks (calculated from data in TsDA f. 1B op. 55 a. e. 1316 [1972], 2–34, at 15).

[235] TsDA f. 1B op. 34 a. e. 89 (1967), 86–90.

[236] TsDA f. 1B op. 35 a. e. 558 (1969).

life," namely, male circumcision and female veiling). The explicit ambition was to achieve the "fusion" (*slivane*) of the Turkish minority with the Bulgarian nation—or, to adapt a well-known metaphor, to make Turks into Bulgarians.[237] What remained unclear was the precise timeline for implementing this decision.

Strategies of elite and mass co-optation continued to be unsuccessful in the 1970s. With regard to the elites, a 1972 report poignantly reveals how exceptionally underrepresented the Turkish minority was in comparison with the Bulgarian majority among *nomenklatura* cadres. At the Central Committee, there were a mere 8 Turkish cadres out of a total of 1,215 staff (0.66 percent);[238] at the level of provincial party committees, the situation was slightly better— 216 Turks out of a total of 9,153 cadres (2.4 percent);[239] and at the city party committees, there were only 74 Turkish cadres out of a total of 16,156 cadres (0.46 percent),[240] reflecting the fact that most Turks resided in the rural areas. However, taking into account that the minority constituted 8–9 percent of the population throughout the communist period, its representation among the party leadership was inadequate.[241] To the extent that party cadres also functioned as trusted gatherers of information, the low number of Turks in the communist elites meant that the party had insufficient knowledge of the popular mood among the Turkish minority.

In terms of the masses, a low level of complaints indexed the erosion of trust in the regime in those provinces with a high Turkish population. A report from the Personal Letters Department of the Central Committee that was sent to Todor Zhivkov reveals that the fewest petitions to party central per capita came from the province of Kurdzhali, with 0.9 complaints per 1,000 people in 1974, as opposed to the national average of 2.77 complaints per 1,000 people.[242] A relevant characteristic of Kurdzhali is that it had the highest share of Turkish residents of any province in Bulgaria.[243] One explanation for the low volume of complaints is that the Turks were satisfied and thus did not need to communicate any grievances to the authorities. A more plausible interpretation is that the Turkish residents did not trust the authorities. This argument is supported by statistics indicating

---

[237] Eugen Weber, *Peasants into Frenchmen: The Modernization of Rural France, 1870–1914* (Stanford, CA: Stanford University Press, 1976).

[238] TsDA f. 1B op. 55 a. e. 1315 (1970–1972).

[239] TsDA f. 1B op. 55 a. e. 1315 (1970–1972).

[240] TsDA f. 1B op. 55 a. e. 1315 (1970–1972).

[241] TsDA f. 1B op. 55 a. e. 1315 (1970–1972).

[242] Calculated from raw data in TsDA f. 378B f. 1 a. e. 1152 (January 24, 1975), 16. Nationwide, there were 24,158 complaints to the Central Committee, 246 of which came from the province of Kurdzhali. The population of Bulgaria at the time was 8.7 million, whereas that of Kurdzhali was 273,000.

[243] According to the 1965 census, the Turkish population of Kurdzhali province was 72.59 percent. See http://demografia.free.bg/BT.htm (accessed April 19, 2022).

that the number of complaints declined by 60 percent in the Kurdzhali region in 1985, the year when the unpopular forced renaming of the Turks began.[244]

The monitoring of rumors provided further indicia of the failure to co-opt the Turks. Rather than inspiring a sense of belonging to the nation, the grandiose spectacles meant to mark the 1300th anniversary of the Bulgarian state led to rumors about plans for the slaughter of 1,300 Turkish children.[245] State Security also registered a rumor that the anniversary would be marked by an impending name change for all Turks.[246] Overall, the circulation of these rumors reveals that, as the descendants of former colonizers (Bulgaria was founded as an independent state in 680–681 but was part of the Ottoman Empire in 1396–1878), the Turks felt excluded from the grand celebrations of the 1300th anniversary. Instead of generating patriotic pride, these celebrations produced alienation among the minority.

Another failure involved informant penetration. The network was not sufficiently saturated: for example, State Security had 24 agents among the 564 imams in the country.[247] Although it is difficult to know what the appropriate number of informants should have been, the secret police were concerned because their associates had declined by one-sixth over the course of one year (from twenty-nine to twenty-four agents); because many informants betrayed State Security by adopting minority nationalist positions or by leaving the country; and because several provinces with compact masses of Turkish residents did not have a single imam-informant (and several had only one or two).[248] The general incapacity of State Security to recruit agents of influence among the minority signaled a crisis in fostering high-quality informants.[249] State Security was further concerned that the Helsinki Accords empowered the minority to resist the arbitrary use of state power.[250]

By 1984, the Turks remained the only Muslims who had been able to retain their Turkish names: other groups had been renamed in 1962 (certain categories of Roma, Tatars, and Bulgarian Muslims);[251] the 1970s (the remaining

[244] TsDA f. 1B op. 55 a. e. 1527 (1986).

[245] AMVR f. 22 op. 1 a. e. 119 (January 12, 1981), 1–4, 9–15; AMVR f. 22 op. 2 a. e. 231 (January 1984), 48–59. A counter-rumor that 1,300 Bulgarian children would be eliminated by Turks as revenge for not being allowed to emigrate was also recorded (see AMVR f. 1 op. 12 a. e. 499 [April 27, 1983], 98).

[246] AMVR f. 22 op. 1 a. e. 119 (January 12, 1981), 1–4, 9–15; AMVR f. 1 op. 12 a. e. 322 (May 29, 1981), 75–77; AMVR f. 22 op. 1 a. e. 171 (January 7, 1983), 8–15.

[247] AMVR f. 22 op. 1 a. e. 121 (June 25, 1980), 12–21.

[248] AMVR f. 22 op. 1 a. e. 121 (June 25, 1980), 12–21.

[249] AMVR f. 22 op. 1 a. e. 121 (November 11, 1980), 29–30. The shortage of such agents was so serious that State Security authorized recruitment through blackmail and material incentives, both of which had been abandoned in the 1960s in favor of recruiting agents on the basis of ideological conviction; see AMVR f. 22 op. 1 a. e. 141 (January 7, 1981), 50–62.

[250] AMVR f. 22 op. 1 a. e. 171 (August 23, 1982), 46–59.

[251] AKRDOPBGDSRSBNA-M f. 1 op. 11 a. e. 49 (June 15, 1962), 54–55.

Bulgarian-speaking Muslims, or *pomaks*); and the early 1980s (the remaining Turkish-leaning Roma).[252] Opposition notwithstanding (expressed in the form of protests, petitions, and anonymous complaints, one of which threatened terrorist activity, stating that both President Reagan and Radio Free Europe would be alerted to the plight of the Roma),[253] the renaming process was completed by the summer of 1982, when 219,591 of the 221,454 Roma with Turkish-Arabic names had been assigned new Slavic-Bulgarian names.[254] The regime then turned to giving Slavic names to Bulgarian Muslims in marriages with Turks and to all newborn children in mixed families. By 1984, it was the Turks' turn to be subjected to a systematic Bulgarification campaign.

5.7.2 Why 1984?

Considering all the indicia of an impending assimilation campaign, it is surprising that the campaign was postponed until 1984. The reason is that the regime did not believe it had the support of the majority. But an endorsement was bought with redistributive policies throughout the 1970s and the early 1980s. Elite and mass constraints had to be addressed before the regime could undertake policies of ethnic assimilation for the large compactly settled minority.

The key factors that led regime insiders to believe that 1984 was an auspicious year for proceeding with the renaming of the Bulgarian Turks were domestic. In particular, there were no indications of an elite threat, and the popular threat, at least as far as the ethnic majority was concerned, had been resolved: 1984 was the year with the most citizen complaints (indicating citizen trust in the system) since comprehensive accounting had been introduced in 1978. Internationally, the situation appeared favorable as well: Bulgaria had brought down its external debt to $2.9 billion, which was its lowest level since 1980. The Soviet Union experienced a leadership change from Andropov to Chernenko, but there was no reason to think that the new Soviet general secretary would look disapprovingly on a campaign to change the names of the Bulgarian Turks. The final factor was that 1984 marked the fortieth anniversary of the September 9 coup that had set in motion the process that would result in the establishment of single-party rule in Bulgaria by 1949. The general celebratory mood of 1984 helped convince the leadership that it could tackle the last remaining major threat to its rule, namely, the Turkish minority.

[252] AMVR f. 1 op. 12 a. e. 413 (January 24, 1982), 31.
[253] AMVR f. 1 op. 12 a. e. 417 (July 26–August 1, 1982), 51.
[254] AMVR f. 1 op. 12 a. e. 413 (August 1982), 187.

The fact that the minority remained impenetrable helped seal its fate. The Sixth Directorate was reporting that the number of informants stayed flat, despite efforts to recruit more agents of influence among intellectuals and community and religious leaders. This deficit of intelligence created uncertainty among secret police analysts. In 1983 (the year when the Turkish Republic of Northern Cyprus was proclaimed), State Security registered a rumor that there would soon be a third Turkish republic, this time in Bulgaria.[255] Willingness to emigrate to Turkey was seen as treason to the socialist motherland. Minority fertility remained extremely high. The party was also concerned about the steadily increasing number of villages that did not have a single Bulgarian resident. These trends strengthened the conviction of the leadership that radical measures were necessary to solve the problem.

5.7.3 The Regenerative Process and Its Consequences

The Regenerative Process was put in motion with a Politburo decision that cannot be located in the archives, but that, if it were to be found, would be numbered Politburo Decision Number 47 and would be dated late October or early November 1984.[256] Although the actual document has disappeared, confidential Ministry of the Interior briefs from late November 1984 reference that decision and allow us to glean that the essence of the Regenerative Process was the forceful replacement of Turkish-Arabic names with Slavic-Bulgarian names. Executing such measures for one-tenth of the population of Bulgaria required an extraordinary administrative effort, as a series of new documents (birth certificates, passports, marriage certificates) would have to be reissued and duly entered into various registries. Even the deceased would not be exempt from such changes, which meant that new death certificates had to be created. In some cases, zealous local officials insisted that tombstones also had to be re-inscribed with the new names. In addition to administrative capacity, given the widespread resistance to assimilation, the renaming process required a coercive capacity. Both the army (Ministry of Defense) and the militia (Ministry of the Interior) were engaged in forcing individuals to submit to the name change. The renaming was completed in 1985, attesting to the formidable capacity of the regime to implement policy.

In addition to the changing of names, the Regenerative Process involved measures that were aimed at suppressing overt markers of ethnic and religious differences. Specifically, the authorities limited access to mosques; banned the

---

[255] AMVR f. 1 op. 12 a. e. 504 (November 14–20, 1983), 91.

[256] The archival record for the top-secret Politburo decisions for Fall 1984 skips from No. 46 to No. 48.

use of the Turkish language in public; prohibited veiling and the wearing of Turkish-style pants (*shalvari*) by women; sought to eliminate ritual circumcision of boys (*sünnet*); and banned Islamic-style burials. Policing the daily-life activities of the Turks required ongoing vigilance and a strong network of informants. This was, as we might expect, the weak spot of the party-state.

The impact of the Regenerative Process on information gathering among the minority is of crucial importance. During the 1982 campaign to change the names of those in mixed marriages, the secret police reports noted that informants were simply unwilling to continue to collaborate once they were subjected to renaming.[257] Consistent with the argument about the tradeoff between repression and the quality of information,[258] once the brutal Regenerative Process was put into motion, the quality of information collected from the minority declined even further.

The problem of an insufficient quantity and quality of the agent network was so serious that the minister of the interior himself was involved in discussions with the Collegium of the ministry about how to solve it. In his understanding, there were several concerns. One was the inadequate number of agents—roughly 1 informant for every 200 Turks of working age.[259] Second, too few imams were informants. Coupled with the pre-existing problem of an inadequate number of agents of influence, these shortcomings in the informant network meant that State Security faced challenges in detecting and defusing latent discontent prior to its transformation into acts of overt resistance to the regime. The response to this criticism was to recruit collaborators as quickly as possible by resorting to methods such as blackmail and monetary incentives, which had been deemed ineffective in the decades prior to the mid-1980s.[260] The result was an expanded informant network, but one that did not provide high-quality information. State Security noted with alarm that some agents were unwilling to supply any intelligence at all.[261]

The inferior quality of the informant network among the Turks meant that State Security had to resort to repression to deal with discontent. Both short-term detention (in the reopened Belene labor camp) and imprisonment were used, depending on the severity of the threat. Although the total number of

[257] AMVR f. 22 op. 1 a. e. 171 (August 23, 1982), 46–59.

[258] Stathis N. Kalyvas, *The Logic of Violence in Civil War* (New York: Cambridge University Press, 2006); Martin K. Dimitrov and Joseph Sassoon, "State Security, Information, and Repression: A Comparison of Communist Bulgaria and Ba'thist Iraq," *Journal of Cold War Studies* 16:2 (Spring 2014), 4–31; Sheena Chestnut Greitens, *Dictators and Their Secret Police: Coercive Institutions and State Violence* (New York: Cambridge University Press, 2016).

[259] AMVR f. 1 op. 12 a. e. 656 (April 17, 1985), 3.

[260] As of 1980, only 10 percent of agents of the Sixth Directorate were recruited through blackmail; monetary incentives were used only for foreigners, with 20 percent of foreign agents recruited on such a basis.

[261] AMVR f. 1 op. 12 a. e. 815 (October 13, 1987), 23.

Table 5.5 Prison Population of Operational Interest to State Security in Bulgaria, 1986

Inmate Category	Number	Percent
Political prisoners	179	4.9%
Individuals who had attempted to flee the country	102	2.8%
Foreign citizens	123	3.3%
Draftees and army officers	617	16.8%
Members of the Turkish minority	1,859	50.5%
Individuals who had attempted acts of minor terrorism	800	21.7%
TOTAL	3,680	100%

Source: AKRDOPBGDSRSBNA-M f. 1 op. 12 a. e. 725 (1986), 3–11, at 5.

individuals who were subject to detention and imprisonment was relatively small (several thousand people), this was a major departure from the low-repression equilibrium that had been practiced in Bulgaria since the late 1950s.

Even when selective repression was employed, finding a sufficient number of prison informants (*kamerni agenti*) was challenging, thus diminishing the effectiveness of politically motivated imprisonment (the purpose of prison informants was to allow State Security to uncover entire organized groups rather than isolated individuals who engaged in antistate crimes).[262] This problem became considerably worse with the adoption of large-scale repression in the 1980s.[263] Although a network of 194 secret police associates existed in the jails (when the number of inmates sentenced for crimes against the state stood at 179),[264] the problem was that the political prisoners constituted only a small subset of the individuals who were of operational interest to State Security. Other groups that had to be monitored included individuals sentenced for attempts to flee the country (this had been a political crime in earlier decades but not in 1986); foreign citizens; drafted soldiers and army officers; inmates sentenced for minor acts of terrorism; and, especially, members of the Turkish minority (see Table 5.5). In the second half of the 1980s, the available State Security collaborators were insufficient to monitor a population of interest that outnumbered the agents nearly twenty-fold. Unsurprisingly, State Security complained about an

[262] Such agents existed in China as well (*yunei teqing* [狱内特情], discussed in Chapter 8) and the Soviet Union (see Chapter 9).

[263] AKRDOPBGDSRSBNA-M f. 1 op. 12 a. e. 725 (1986), 3–11.

[264] The network consisted of 113 agents, 67 trusted persons, and 14 residents. See AKRDOPBGDSRSBNA-M f. 1 op. 12 a. e. 725 (1986), 3–11, at 7.

insufficient number of prison informants, thus further reducing the effectiveness of repression. Cumulatively, the harsh repression only exacerbated the alienation of the minority and made information gathering considerably more complicated due to the loss of any remnants of trust in the regime among the Turks.

Members of the minority were stigmatized and, in effect, prevented from communicating with relatives abroad. Phone connections to Turkey were completely cut off during the renaming process and, thereafter, they were limited under various pretexts, in order to avoid potential terrorist activities organized under the auspices of an external power. In the rare cases when phone calls were possible, the lines were tapped. Letter writing remained an option, though State Security analyzed all correspondence with Turkey, and there was no certainty that the letters would reach their intended recipients.

Overall, the Regenerative Process was a failure, as it generated significant levels of new grievances among the minority. There were rare but powerful instances of overt discontent expressed in the form of explosions, abductions, and industrial sabotage. State Security also reported on isolated instances in which leaflets and anonymous letters opposing the Regenerative Process were seized by the secret police. In addition, pro-Turkish slogans occasionally appeared in public spaces. But much more widespread were milder acts of resistance, such as the circulation of antiregime rumors; the refusal to speak Bulgarian in public or to respond when addressed by one's new Slavic name; the ongoing practice of circumcision; and the adoption of "silent weddings" in response to the prohibition to play Turkish music at marriage celebrations.[265]

Until early 1989, this discontent seemed manageable through a mixed strategy of repression, the planting of counter-rumors by State Security, and substantial social spending in the areas inhabited by Turks.[266] However, with the changed international environment in the spring of 1989 the situation began spinning out of control.

Thus, the Regenerative Process contributed to the political liberalization. Fundamentally, the failure of the renaming campaign weakened the regime by leading to agenda overload, which made it difficult to provide optimal responses to the popular threat and the elite threat, both of which resurfaced after 1984 due to changes in the domestic and international environment. Thus, the failed Regenerative Process facilitated democratization by spurring the growth of NGOs and by giving members of the minority a valuable opportunity to organize a protest movement.

---

[265] TsDA f. 1b op. 63 a. e. 89 (1986), 1–4; TsDA f. 1b op. 99 a. e. 20 (1987), 1–5; TsDA f. 1b op. 63 a. e. 40 (1988), 1–12.
[266] See the documents reproduced in Veselin Angelov, comp., *Strogo poveritelno: Asimilatorskata kampaniia sreshtu turskoto natsionalno maltsinstvo v Bulgariia (1984–1989): Dokumenti* (Sofia: Simolini, 2008).

5.8 Alienating the Ethnic Majority

This section examines the question of how regime policies led to the alienation of the ethnic majority. Redistributive social spending and mass entertainment were successfully deployed from the late 1950s onward to defuse latent discontent and prevent it from escalating into overt discontent. Bread and circuses delivered stability, but only when they were supplied concurrently. The system experienced disequilibrium in the mid-1980s, as pervasive shortages demonstrated the incapacity of the regime to deliver on its social-spending commitments. Although the provision of entertainment continued, it was insufficient to stem the search for forbidden sources of information. State Security could not prevent associational activity: prior to the consumer goods crisis, some apolitical groups had been formed. The crisis, which coincided with glasnost, led to the creation of organizations with a clear political agenda. Citizens withdrew from the complaints system and joined these political entities. The regime had reneged on its commitments under the socialist social contract, which meant that the masses no longer felt obliged to reward it with compliance. In sum, circuses proved insufficient on their own to ensure mass support.

5.8.1 Moving toward a Consumer Goods Crisis

The contrast between 1984 and 1985 in terms of the provision of consumer goods was stark. After quieting down, rumors of price increases for consumer goods, building materials, and housing surfaced anew in 1984.[267] On the eve of National Day, State Security also registered hostile comments that the improved supply of goods was temporary and would immediately worsen after the holiday and that the salary increases would be followed by higher prices.[268] And yet these anxieties remained at the level of rumors in 1984. By 1985, however, the situation had changed: pervasive electricity blackouts and consumer-goods price increases led to widespread open expressions of discontent that were registered by State Security. Despite the higher prices, there still was a shortage of fuel and staple foods. This foreshadowed a crisis that would become progressively worse beyond 1985.

The economic difficulties meant that the leadership could not fulfill its obligations under the socialist social contract, and citizens responded by withdrawing their conditional loyalty. Although there were various indicators of this development, revealing are the trends in citizen petitions. In 1985, the number

[267] AMVR f. 1 op. 12 a. e. 599 (1984), 109–10.
[268] AMVR f. 1 op. 12 a. e. 600 (September 8, 1984), 92–93.

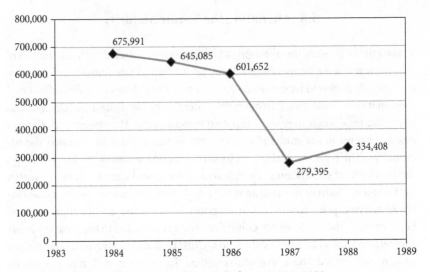

Figure 5.5 Volume of citizen complaints in Bulgaria, 1984–1988.

Sources: 1984: TsDA f. 1B op. 55 a. e. 943 (1985), 8; 1985: TsDA f. 1B op. 55 a. e. 944 (1985), 31; 1986: TsDA f. 1B op. 55 a. e. 949 (1987), 30; 1987: TsDA f. 1B op. 55 a. e. 951 (1988), 21; 1988: TsDA f. 1B op. 55 a. e. 953 (1989), 3.

of complaints dropped to 645,085, from a high of 675,991 in the previous year. In 1986, the Thirteenth Congress of the Bulgarian Communist Party was held—petitions typically increase in such "congress" years—but that year complaints dropped by another 6 percent to 601,652. However, it was not until 1987 that the full magnitude of the change became apparent: only 279,395 petitions were registered in that year, which was equivalent to 41.3 percent of the complaints received in 1984.[269] Although the number of petitions increased by 20 percent in 1988 (to 334,408), the trend is unmistakable: individuals were a lot less willing to complain to the authorities (see Figure 5.5).[270] This occurred under conditions of worsening shortages, a time when we would expect people to complain more rather than less.

How can we interpret the decline in complaints? An anecdote that Todor Zhivkov shared with his chief-of-staff in 1989 encapsulates his view of the role of petitions:

---

[269] Regional party committees did not report data on complaints in 1987, but they most certainly received them. Therefore, the true number of petitions in 1987 is probably about 330,000 (a figure produced by averaging the number of complaints to regional party committees for 1986 and 1988 and imputing that average of 50,872 for petitions to the regional party committees in 1987).

[270] The last full year for which we have information on the number of complaints is 1988.

I was told a story about a provincial leader. During the day that he was to receive the public, not a single person came to complain. He wondered what would explain this, and then said to his aide: "We have either solved all the problems that people have, or *else they no longer believe in us*, and hence they do not come to us to complain and look for help."[271]

Zhivkov was a shrewd politician and he understood better than anyone the importance of petitioning to maintain regime legitimacy: as long as people complain through the officially approved channels, they are showing their willingness to participate in the system.[272]

5.8.2 When Circuses Are Not Enough

Even when the capacity of the regime to provide redistributive spending wavered, it continued to deliver patriotic spectacles and mass entertainment, with the aim of distracting citizens from seeking foreign cultural products. By comparison with the celebration of the 1300th anniversary of the founding of the Bulgarian state in 1981, patriotic spectacles in the mid-1980s were subdued. Nevertheless, the regime sought to build national pride by sending a second Bulgarian into space in 1988 and, especially, by promoting sports. Extraordinary financial resources were devoted to fostering elite sports. The country was most successful in rhythmic gymnastics, winning four of the five world championships in the 1980s (in 1981, 1983, 1985, and 1987) and placing second in the fifth (in 1989). Even more impressive was that Bulgaria finished seventh in the 1988 Seoul Olympics in terms of total medal count. Its two unsuccessful bids to host the Winter Olympics (in 1986 and 1988) and the defection of weightlifter Naim Süleymanoğlu to Turkey in 1986 dented some of the luster of these achievements, but nonetheless sports provided a spectacle that could build national pride.[273]

In the area of pure entertainment, the regime used books, film, and especially TV for mass distraction; needless to say, the state had a monopoly on the production and distribution of all cultural products. Book publishing in the 1980s featured popular genres such as sci-fi and crime. In some cases, publications that had previously been deemed suspect (like, e.g., *Gone with the Wind*, which had last been printed in 1945) could be reissued in new translations both because of

---

[271] As reported in Georgi Chukrin, *Zapiski ot totalitarnoto vreme: Kraiat* (Sofia: Iztok–Zapad, 2007), 85. Emphasis added.

[272] On Zhivkov's interest in letters, see the recollections of his aide, academician Niko Iakhiel (who was a sociologist by training): Niko Iakhiel, *Todor Zhivkov i lichnata vlast* (Sofia: M8M, 1997), 433.

[273] For a similar argument in a different context, see Natalie Koch, "Sport and Soft Authoritarian Nation-Building," *Political Geography* 32 (January 2013), 42–51.

the massive consumer demand (reflected in the fact that the black market price of the book was equivalent to a minimum monthly salary) and as a sound commercial decision (the Propaganda Department of the Central Committee reported that the book's massive print-run of 100,000 copies would sell out despite being priced considerably above the cost of production).[274] Analysis of the catalogs of the major publishing houses in Bulgaria in the 1980s reveals that, outside the taboo areas of anticommunist and pornographic literature, a surprisingly wide range of both high- and low-brow Western fiction was translated. The same variety of entertainment (with similar taboo zones) can be observed by analyzing the cinema schedules from the 1980s. Officially sanctioned cultural consumption had expanded in scope.

But the most important source of entertainment was the importation of Western TV series. There were only two channels and nearly every household had a TV set, thus ensuring universal penetration of any content that was broadcast by the state-owned TV. In the mid- to late 1980s, Bulgarian TV viewers were exposed to *The Thorn Birds* and *Shogun*; to the French *Châteauvallon*; to the German *Das Erbe der Guldenburgs* (The Legacy of the Guldenburgs); to the Brazilian soap *Escrava Isaura* (Isaura the Slave); and to the wildly successful Italian miniseries *La Piovra* (Octopus), which focused on the activities of police inspector Corrado Cattani against the Italian mafia. Saturday night programming ended with the police procedurals of *Studio X* and Thursday evenings featured *Deseta muza* (The Tenth Muse), which exposed Bulgarian audiences to arthouse cinema ranging from Bergman to Almodóvar. Such programming provided some respite from the stultifying Soviet, Eastern European, and Bulgarian productions, which formed the mainstay of television under late socialism in Bulgaria.

Although TV became much more satisfying in the 1980s, both State Security and the party understood that the population wanted additional entertainment that either fell into a gray zone or that was expressly prohibited. Despite jamming, citizens continued to listen to "hostile" radio stations. The rapid spread of semi-legal cassette and videotape copying businesses and the availability of cassette-tape players and VCRs in the underground economy meant that citizens had access to entertainment that was different from what was officially provided by the regime. Those who did not have personal cassette or video players could consume such entertainment in discotheques and video bars (*videoteki*).[275] A decree by the Council of Ministers that sought to "improve the musical environment, as well as sound- and video programming" failed—an inspection

---

[274] TsDA f. 1B op. 101 a. e. 1516 (1986).

[275] These existed throughout the Eastern Bloc. See Constantin Parvulescu and Emanuel Copilas, "Hollywood Peeks: The Rise and Fall of Videotheques in 1980s Romania," *East European Politics and Societies and Cultures* 27:2 (2013), 241–59.

of twenty-four entertainment outlets revealed numerous instances of programming of low ideological and aesthetic quality.[276] State Security noted the subversive effect of video businesses, but it was unable to stem their spread.[277]

There was also demand for forbidden books. State Security reported that the black market price of a copy of *Fascism* (an academic study emphasizing the parallels between the Nazi and Communist regimes, published in 1982 and immediately withdrawn from circulation) reached 80–100 leva, equivalent to a minimum monthly salary.[278] In addition, State Security detected xeroxed copies of *In Absentia Reports* (written by Georgi Markov, an émigré who was killed with a poison-tipped umbrella on Waterloo Bridge in 1978) and of Solzhenitsyn's *The Gulag Archipelago*.[279] Once glasnost emerged, Bulgarians were also able to access Soviet perestroika literature, either by visiting the chain of Soviet bookstores in the country or by subscribing to the "thick journals" (*tolstye zhurnaly*) that were publishing previously dissident authors. In short, citizens were consuming cultural products that worked at cross-purposes with regime-provided entertainment that aimed to foster national pride and to distract the public from thinking about the legitimacy of the political system.

5.8.3 Organized Nonpolitical Groups

According to State Security, the increasing number of organized groups were yet another manifestation of the incapacity to establish complete ideological control over the population. Even nonpolitical groups were regarded as threatening. For instance, a top-secret report on the spread of yoga noted that it is a type of Western [*sic*] ideological penetration that has a negative impact on socialist countries.[280] Even sci-fi clubs were suspect, as they had grown into a powerful organized movement; in addition to holding meetings and discussions, they also published their own samizdat newspapers, bulletins, and collections of essays. The central issue, State Security concluded, was that there were no restrictions on membership—anyone could join, including religious devotees, fortune-tellers, and astrology aficionados.[281] State Security also informed Todor Zhivkov of a "secret society" composed of individuals who translated occult and astrological literature from English and German and who were hoping to emigrate from Bulgaria.[282]

[276] AMVR f. 1 op. 12 a. e. 686 (January 28–February 3, 1985), 54.
[277] AKRDOPBGDSRSBNA-M f. 22 op. 1 a. e. 226 (1985), 24.
[278] AMVR f. 1 op. 12 a. e. 598 (July 2–8, 1984), 59–60.
[279] AMVR f. 1 op. 12 a. e. 598 (June 11–17, 1984), 19.
[280] AKRDOPBGDSRSBNA-M f. 22 op. 1 a. e. 163 (1982), 1–17.
[281] AKRDOPBGDSRSBNA-M f. 22 op. 1 a. e. 223 (1984), 10–15B.
[282] AMVR f. 1 op. 12 a. e. 691 (August 5–11, 1985), 115.

Another concern was with youth groups promoting neofascism, religion, and "degenerate" music such as punk or hard rock.[283] General distrust of organized youth groups spread to something even as anodyne as the rapidly growing number of fan clubs of Bulgarian music stars.[284] As they attracted hundreds and occasionally thousands of members,[285] these youth groups presented a twofold danger according to State Security. First, they competed directly with the Komsomol for the energy and enthusiasm of the latter's card-carrying and fee-paying members. Second, to the extent that they promoted Western lifestyles, they facilitated ideological subversion. For this reason, such groups were infiltrated by State Security and their members were subjected to prophylaxis.[286] The threat seemed manageable, as illustrated by the assessment of the size of the youth enemy contingent, which in 1984 consisted of 349 individuals, a number that did not appear alarming.[287]

5.8.4 Instances of Overt Discontent

In 1984, State Security registered several noteworthy instances of overt expressions of discontent. These involved locating five copies of "Long live, Reagan!" leaflets;[288] detecting swastika signs and scrawls on bus seats stating, "We Will Come Back to Power" and "Communism Will Not Become a Reality";[289] and the tearing down of two portraits of newly elected Politburo members in Sofia.[290] The most serious transgression was the publication of the acrostic "Down with Todor Zhivkov" in the weekly *Puls* (Pulse) in 1985.[291] These manifestations of discontent were reported to the leadership but were deemed fully manageable because, in contrast to the organized acts of resistance by the Turkish minority, expressions of overt discontent by the Bulgarian majority were isolated and sporadic until the fall of 1987, when organized political NGOs appeared. As we will discuss in Chapter 7, these NGOs were anything but anodyne.

[283] AKRDOPBGDSRSBNA-M f. 22 op. 1 a. e. 226 (1985), 17–39.
[284] AMVR f. 1 op. 12 a. e. 600 (1984), 55–59.
[285] AMVR f. 1 op. 12 a. e. 599 (1984), 57–58.
[286] AMVR f. 1 op. 12 a. e. 599 (October 8–14, 1984), 88.
[287] AKRDOPBGDSRSBNA-M f. 22 op. 1 a. e. 226 (1985), 34–35.
[288] AMVR f. 1 op. 12 a. e. 599 (September 11–16, 1984), 47.
[289] AMVR f. 1 op. 12 a. e. 598 (July 24, 1984), 130–31.
[290] AMVR f. 1 op. 12 a. e. 594 (March 12–18, 1984), 155.
[291] AKRDOPBGDSRSBNA-M f. 22 op. 1 a. e. 1693 (1985), 15–15A.

5.9 Conclusion

The 1959–1988 period involved minimal elite threats and extremely low levels of overt popular discontent. The major threat was ideological subversion that could fuel latent popular discontent. To counteract it, the party-state deployed selective repression (through State Security) and soft strategies that aimed to increase satisfaction with the standards of living and to distract from the consumption of Western culture by offering indigenous cultural products and by enhancing national pride. Given its high state capacity, the communist regime successfully established a complex set of institutions needed to monitor popular opinion and to generate information that could be used to assess the level of latent discontent. Responsiveness to complaints undergirded the socialist social contract, whereby citizens exchanged quiescence for the provision of welfare. The top leadership was supplied with extensive reporting on complaints, which were understood both to provide insight into latent discontent and to index the general level of citizen trust of the system.

The strategy failed for the ethnoreligious minorities, who had lower levels of economic well-being than the ethnic majority. Moreover, the minorities were excluded from the national pride project, which was presented in a heavily ethnicized Bulgarian form. Facing its inability to penetrate the Turkish minority but feeling secure that it had resolved both the popular and the elite threat, the leadership unleashed an assimilation campaign against the Turks in 1984–1985. The timing proved to be highly inauspicious, as beginning in 1985 the economic situation was deteriorating rapidly. Thus, on the eve of 1989, the regime faced the double whammy of both minority and majority unrest, neither of which could be counteracted through repression or redistributive concessions.

6

Continuity and Change

Information Gathering in China, 1959–1988

The three decades that separate 1959 from 1988 allow us to analyze how periods of profound stress impacted the information-gathering infrastructure in China. In contrast to the case of Bulgaria, which experienced thirty years of relative domestic calm that lasted until the spring of 1989, China went through radical upheavals like the Great Leap Forward and the Cultural Revolution. Following the death of Mao, the momentous decision to launch reforms was undertaken, thus putting an additional strain on the political system. It is beyond doubt that the monitoring of popular discontent took place under challenging circumstances throughout the 1959–1988 period.

These decades present us with a two-fold question: Did information collection cease during the chaotic upheavals under Mao? And did institution building take place during the initial decade of reforms? The answers to both questions are counterintuitive. First, information collection was very challenging, but it did not stop during the Great Leap Forward and the Cultural Revolution. Second, institution building did take place in the 1980s, but the emphasis remained on developing new mechanisms for involuntary extraction, such as the creation of the Ministry of State Security (MSS) and the introduction of opinion polling. Voluntary provision remained very limited due to the lack of European-style welfare commitments on the part of the state. Nevertheless, as this chapter demonstrates, the meting out of violence became more discriminate as a result of the improved quality of information about regime enemies. Reductions in frequency and severity, however, never brought repression to levels as low as those in Eastern Europe, further disincentivizing voluntary provision through welfare-related letters and visits. Parallel with Eastern Europe, in the lead-up to Tiananmen, voluntary information provision declined further from an already very low base, thus sending a signal to the leadership that urban residents were dissatisfied with the prospect that the limited urban welfare state was coming undone by the reforms.

Perhaps most surprising is that China and Bulgaria began these three decades in a roughly similar place in terms of their information-gathering institutions— and then followed very different paths, only to converge again by experiencing welfare frustrations of different magnitudes in the lead-up to 1989. Despite vast

Dictatorship and Information. Martin K. Dimitrov, Oxford University Press. © Oxford University Press 2023.
DOI: 10.1093/oso/9780197672921.003.0006

differences between the two settings, China and Eastern Europe had common institutional complements that led to regime crisis in 1989.

The chapter is organized as follows. Section 6.1 focuses on the Great Leap Forward. Section 6.2 discusses the Cultural Revolution. Section 6.3 examines state building after the death of Mao, paying particular attention to concerns about ideological subversion (paralleling those in Eastern Europe) that motivated the creation of the Ministry of State Security. Section 6.4 documents the rise of selective repression in China. Section 6.5 examines the voluntary provision of information. Section 6.6 analyzes the ongoing challenges of minority penetration during the three-decade period under analysis. Section 6.7 concludes the chapter.

6.1 Information Gathering during the Great Leap Forward and Its Aftermath, 1958–1966

The Great Leap Forward, which forged ahead at full speed in the fall of 1958 and concluded by the end of 1961, was a profoundly disruptive event that led to tens of millions of excess deaths. As we might expect, it also impacted the systems for information gathering. However, that effect was limited mostly to voluntary transmission through complaints, whose volume declined greatly in 1958–1960 before returning to its pre–Great Leap level by 1962. Surprisingly, involuntary extraction continued apace throughout this period, with the number of informants actually rising and thus partially compensating for the information deficit that resulted from the decline in voluntarily provided information.

The Great Leap led to dismal economic failures, which resulted in an introspective effort to improve the quality of economic statistics that began in 1961. This initiative was orthogonal to the monitoring of popular dissatisfaction and did not effect any changes in the techniques used to assess discontent. Nonetheless, it did impact information transfer indirectly, because the elevated attention to the collection of statistics of all kinds led to a general streamlining of the systems for party and government reporting. Thus, by the mid-1960s, regular reports were being produced not only by Xinhua News Agency, but also by the party and the police. A trend toward the routinization of information gathering was in place on the eve of the Cultural Revolution.

6.1.1 Monitoring Dissent through Involuntary Extraction

There was remarkable continuity in the targets of repression and the tactics deployed to identify, enumerate, register, and manage them. A roster of counterrevolutionaries from 1960 reveals that the categories of regime enemies during the Great Leap Forward remained nearly identical to those included on lists developed during the initial decade of communist rule: former and currently active counterrevolutionaries; landlords; rich peasants; rightists; four elements; antisocialist elements; reactionary KMT elements (army, government, police, and gendarmerie); and the families of counterrevolutionaries and dangerous criminals.[1] Systematic statistics on the size of the enemy contingent throughout China are not readily available, but internal sources allow us to document that in Jiangsu, for example, there were 2,218,000 politically problematic individuals in 1960, which was equivalent to 5.17 percent of the province's population at that time.[2] This is a comparatively high level: in Bulgaria, the enemy contingent was reduced from 11.5 percent to 5.6 percent of the population in the second half of the 1940s; due to the introduction of more stringent criteria in the following years, the roster shrank to 0.4 percent of the population in 1954 (see Chapter 3). This comparison shows that, well into the second decade of communist rule, China remained uncertain about its capacity to identify enemies with precision, thus maintaining a large targeted-population list.

Identification techniques did not change either: social-order protection committees and small groups (*zhibao hui, zhibao xiaozu* 治保会, 治保小组), eyes and ears (*ermu* 耳目), and agents (*teqing* 特情) were all deployed alongside full-time police personnel. Committee and small-group members were volunteers who did not receive any material support for their assistance in providing enemy and social intelligence. Statistics compiled from police almanacs indicate that the number of individuals engaged in social-order protection committees and small groups grew between 1958 and 1959 from 1 percent of the population to nearly 1.5 percent. There was significant cross-provincial variation: whereas social-order protection committee members constituted 0.31 percent of the population in Qinghai in 1959, they made up 2.66 percent in Heilongjiang and 3.44 percent in Guizhou during the same year. There was also variation within provinces, with cities having a higher concentration of informants than rural areas. In Zhejiang, for example, the city of Hangzhou boasted 100,291 social-order committee members in 1962 (10.4 percent of the population), whereas in the same year the province as a whole had an informant penetration rate of 1.85 percent. Beijing also had a highly saturated network of social-order committees: in 1963, its members were equivalent to 7 percent of the adult population of the capital city.

Once identified, enemies were enumerated and placed on the targeted population roster so that they could be subjected to imprisonment, reeducation-through-labor, or surveillance. As we can calculate from the raw numbers in

---

[1] *Gong'an jianshe*, no. 73/400 (November 7, 1960), 6–7.
[2] *Gong'an jianshe*, no. 73/400 (November 7, 1960), 6–7.

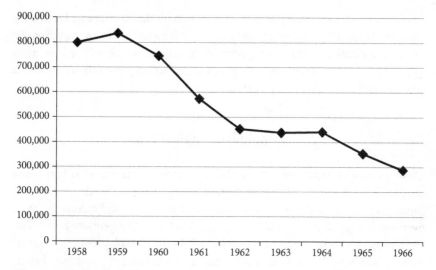

Figure 6.1 Individuals imprisoned for counterrevolutionary crimes in China, 1958-1966.

Source: Author's dataset.

Figure 6.1, the share of political prisoners peaked in 1959 to 0.13 percent of the population but dropped continuously afterward, reaching 0.07 percent in 1962. In terms of reeducation-through-labor, the peak occurred in 1960 (0.09 percent of the population), followed by a similar subsequent steady decline to 0.07 percent by 1962.[3] This substantial drop notwithstanding, repression remained high in comparative terms: Bulgaria held a grand total of 0.01 percent of its population in labor camps for political reasons in 1956-1962 and annually sent 0.005 percent to the regular prisons for crimes against the republic, for spreading harmful rumors, and for revealing state secrets in 1959-1962.[4]

Although the frequency of repression remained high by comparison with that in Eastern Europe, a notable feature of the Great Leap Forward in terms of the handling of dissent in China is that it ushered in a period of a gradual decline in imprisonment and reeducation-through-labor for those who engaged in

---

[3] As Chinese labor camp statistics do not disaggregate political from nonpolitical detainees, we cannot know the exact percentage of reeducation-through-labor inmates who were judged to be counterrevolutionary.

[4] State Security archival sources indicate that there were a total 701 political labor camp inmates in 1956-1962: see Penka Stoianova and Emil Iliev, *Politicheski opasni litsa: Vudvoriavaniia, trudova mobilizatsiia, izselvaniia v Bulgariia sled 1944 g.* (Sofia: Universitetsko Izdatelstvo "Sv. Kliment Okhridski," 1991), 101. The number of individuals subject to prison sentences for political reasons is calculated from an internal reference compendium: *Prestupleniia i osudeni litsa* (Sofia: Durzhavno Upravlenie za Informatsiia pri Ministerskiia Suvet, 1969).

counterrevolutionary activities. The chief reason for this development is that the ubiquitous surveillance during the Great Leap Forward led to an improvement in the information-collection capacity of the regime, which allowed for more precise targeting of repression. This was not a temporary shift, as it persisted well after the end of the Great Leap Forward.

6.1.2 Continuities in Cultural Protection

Another area of continuity with the initial decade of communist rule is found in the deployment of cultural protection as a technique for identifying enemies. As in Eastern Europe, the foundational notion behind cultural security was that foreign ideas and ideology constitute a threat. The primary goal of cultural protection was to assess the political reliability of employees in the cultural sphere, which included areas like science and technology; education; health; print and publications; media; the arts; and sports.[5] Another important task was the ferreting out of spies and ensuring secrecy protection, especially for units that had links with foreigners, who were understood to function as the primary vector for exercising ideological influence.[6] Police publications clarify that the more specialized mandate of cultural protection had to be separated from the general task of political protection within public security bureaus (PSBs), in order to ensure more effective operation. In addition, some key and complex units had to task special personnel with cultural protection.[7] In terms of tradecraft, police materials leave no doubt that cultural protection required the use of investigation techniques and reliance on specially designated secret informants in the form of *teqing*.[8] Concerns about cultural protection persisted in subsequent decades: they guided the formation of the Ministry of State Security in 1983 and formed a central part of China's state security doctrine in the twenty-first century.

6.1.3 Changes in Voluntary Provision

In contrast to the continuities in involuntary extraction mentioned in this section, there were changes in voluntary provision. Namely, although the data on complaints are incomplete, we have abundant evidence that the volume of letters and visits received by party and state organs decreased precipitously during

---

[5] *Gong'an jianshe*, no. 63/390 (September 6, 1960), 8–9.
[6] *Gong'an jianshe*, no. 131 (June 25, 1955), 10–16.
[7] *Gong'an jianshe*, no. 25/312 (September 20, 1959), 21–23.
[8] *Gong'an jianshe*, no. 131 (June 25, 1955), 10–16.

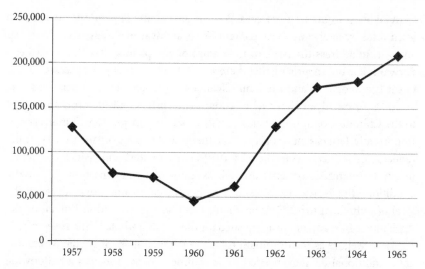

Figure 6.2 Letters and visits to the State Council in China, 1957–1965.
Source: Diao, *Renmin xinfang shilüe*, 118, 168.

the Great Leap Forward.[9] Figure 6.2 illustrates this drop with regard to petitions received by the State Council, which experienced a nearly three-fold reduction in letters and visits (*xinfang* 信访) between 1957 and 1960. The decline in complaints was accompanied by an increase in anonymous letters,[10] indicating an erosion of trust in the authorities during the most extreme period of the Great Leap Forward. As the Leap was coming to a close, letters and visits began to rise in 1961. This upward trend continued, and by 1962 the volume of complaints was greater than it had been in the peak year of 1957, when an avalanche of letters was produced during the Hundred Flowers Campaign (see Chapter 4). The increase was met with official approval, as is made clear in the 1961 statement by Vice-Premier Xi Zhongxun: "Is it better to have more letters and visits or fewer? Of course, it is better to have more. This means that the masses support us, love us, and trust us."[11] Although the top leadership welcomed complaints, it did not want petitioners to engage in appeals at the capital: therefore, officials were encouraged to resolve citizen grievances locally and to limit visits to Beijing.[12]

[9] Diao Jiecheng, *Renmin xinfang shilüe, 1949–1995* (Beijing: Beijing Jingji Xueyuan Chubanshe, 1996), 118.

[10] Diao, *Renmin xinfang shilüe*, 119.

[11] Cited in Diao, *Renmin xinfang shilüe*, 158.

[12] Li Hongbo, *Fazhi xiandaihua jincheng zhong de renmin xinfang* (Beijing: Qinghua Daxue Chubanshe, 2007), 61; Diao, *Renmin xinfang shilüe*, 177–82.

In addition to examining fluctuations in the volume of petitions, we can also learn a lot by analyzing their content. Rich archival materials from Shanghai allow us to address the issue of the nature of complaints after the Great Leap Forward. It is not surprising that there were letters criticizing the excesses of the Great Leap Forward and the Four Cleanups.[13] Predictably, denunciations survived,[14] but mostly at the level of certain enterprises and in communications to the Chinese Communist Party (CCP) Discipline Inspection Commission.[15] Importantly, letters sent to party departments and to state organs were typically requests for services. As in the mid-1950s, citizen letters and visits focused primarily on material concerns like job assignments, compensation, and living conditions; this is true regardless of whether the complaints are analyzed at the level of individual firms,[16] departments (such as the Education Bureau or the Agriculture Bureau), or are aggregated for the city as a whole.[17] The speed of this return to welfare as the dominant theme of complaints in Shanghai is remarkable. Additional data are needed to determine whether this was a nationwide trend, though there is no reason to suspect that citizens of other provinces would shy away from articulating material grievances in the relatively "normal" years immediately before the Cultural Revolution.

We must assess the general trend of an increase in letters and visits after the conclusion of the Great Leap Forward as a positive development. Yet, the average frequency of complaining remained very low by comparison with that in Eastern Europe. In the German Democratic Republic (GDR), for instance, citizens sent 101,823 letters of complaint to the State Council (5,962 per million people) in 1961. In the same year, the Chinese State Council received 62,212 letters and visits (94 per million people);[18] although by 1965 the frequency of complaining had increased to 293 per million people, this was still factors of magnitude lower than that in Eastern Europe. The implication is that, despite the important progress made in the first half of the 1960s, the voluntary transfer of information through citizen complaints remained underdeveloped in China on the eve of the Cultural Revolution. The reason for that is three-fold: high repression; rudimentary welfare commitments; and skeletal bureaucratic capacity.

---

[13] On the Great Leap Forward, see Shanghai Municipal Archives (SMA) B180_1_41_15 (April 14, 1965), 2. On the Four Cleanups, see SMA B123_6_919_76 (April 27, 1966). The Four Cleanups movement, which began in 1963, focused on cleaning up politics, the economy, organization, and ideology.

[14] SMA B150_1_231_34 (1965).

[15] For evidence from a Shanghai concrete factory, see SMA B162_2_216 (1965).

[16] SMA B202_2_284 (January 3, 1966).

[17] On education, see SMA B243_1_246_86 (May 16, 1963). On agriculture, see SMA B180_1_41_15 (April 14, 1965). See also SMA B127_1_164_51 (October 7, 1964).

[18] Felix Mühlberg, *Bürger, Bitten und Behörden: Geschichte der Eingabe in der DDR* (Berlin: Karl Dietz Verlag 2004), 177.

6.1.4 Statistical Introspection

The Great Leap Forward led to some important changes in terms of thinking about data. The early 1960s were a period of soul-searching for information-gatherers in China. Intelligence collection was fragmentary: The most comprehensive report about hunger during the Great Leap Forward that has become available thus far includes only sixteen provinces,[19] about three-fifths of China's twenty-eight provinces, provincial-level municipalities, and ethnic autonomous regions at the time. This might explain why, when confronted with evidence of hunger in some provinces, Chairman Mao reportedly interjected that the situation was better in other provinces.[20] Given the fragmented nature of information-gathering institutions in China, it is doubtful that even Mao had complete information on the spread of overt discontent.

In the midst of the devastating hunger that enveloped the country in 1959–1962, *Neibu cankao* (内部参考) published several reports in 1961 on how best to do statistical work.[21] The tension was between Maoist methods of the typical survey (*dianxing diaocha* 典型调查) and techniques that could produce more representative information. The method of the typical survey involved gathering materials by assembling a group of experienced people for a survey meeting, with from three to five up to seven to eight people.[22] The typical survey focused on one problem in one administrative village, one district, one county, one city, one township, one army, one battalion, one factory, one shop or one school—and from that one location extrapolated to the rest of the country.[23] Pioneered by Mao Zedong during the period of guerrilla warfare, this technique might have made sense given the limited territorial reach of the state and its low bureaucratic capacity at that time. It was not, however, a practical method for making governance decisions impacting all of China in the 1960s. Unfortunately, the political turmoil of the 1960s and 1970s meant that the adoption of modern statistical techniques for assessing whether data were representative could not occur until

---

[19] Zhou Xun, ed., *The Great Famine in China, 1958–1962: A Documentary History* (New Haven, CT: Yale University Press, 2012), 10–16.

[20] Frank Dikötter, *Mao's Great Famine: The History of China's Most Devastating Catastrophe, 1958–1962* (New York: Walker & Co., 2010), 89, 335.

[21] See, for example, *Neibu cankao*, no. 3188 (March 17, 1961), 23–26; *Neibu cankao*, no. 3200 (April 13, 1961), 2–7; *Neibu cankao*, no. 3204 (April 21, 1961), 2–3; *Neibu cankao*, no. 3207 (April 26, 1961), 11–13; *Neibu cankao*, no 3210 (May 3, 1961), 20–24; *Neibu cankao*, no. 3229 (June 9, 1961), 9–12; and *Neibu cankao*, no. 3503 (May 28, 1963), 8–9.

[22] I am indebted to Anthony Garnaut for drawing my attention to the importance of the typical survey both under Mao and in contemporary China.

[23] Anthony Garnaut, "Hard Facts and Half-Truths: The New Archival History of China's Great Famine," *China Information* 27:2 (2013), 223–46, at 239.

after the end of the Cultural Revolution and the death of Mao. Before then, revolutionary statistics were the norm.[24]

6.1.5 The Rise of Regularized Reporting

Concurrent with attention to improving statistics, there emerged an emphasis on regularized bureaucratic reporting by the three main collectors of information: the internal media, the police, and the party. Xinhua News Agency had been producing such digests for decades. Although the frequency declined during the Great Leap Forward (see Figure 6.3), such reports did not cease. However, their survival should not be taken for granted: After the March 1959 Uprising, journalists in the Tibet bureau were instructed to do a lot but to report little on the progress of the highly unpopular democratic reforms, in order to avoid giving the impression to the Tibetan public that reforms would proceed immediately.[25] Perhaps the most consequential decision made in 1959 was to put Xinhua journalists under the jurisdiction of the provincial party committees.[26] This led

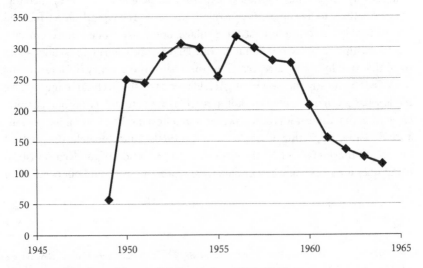

Figure 6.3 Number of issues of *Neibu cankao*, 1949–1964.
Source: Author's calculations.

---

[24] On revolutionary statistics, see Arunabh Ghosh, *Making It Count: Statistics and Statecraft in the Early People's Republic of China* (Princeton, NJ: Princeton University Press, 2020).
[25] *Xinhua she dashiji (1931–2001)*, vol. 2 (Beijing: Xinhua She, 2002), 55.
[26] *Xinhua she dashiji*, vol. 2, 65.

to inaccurate and exaggerated reporting even in internal publications,[27] thus explaining the 1962 decision of the Central Committee to place Xinhua bureaus under dual jurisdiction, with Xinhua having primary control. Most importantly, the bureaus' budgetary needs were to be met by headquarters rather than by the provincial party committees.[28] These changes helped restore a critical element in Xinhua reporting. A sign of normalization is that by 1964, the news agency had more employees in its internal reference department than it had in the division handling domestic news for public dissemination.[29]

The police also produced regular reports. One example is from Tianjin, where a secret (*jimi* 机密) public security brief (*Tianjin gong'an jianbao* 天津公安简报) started weekday publication in 1960.[30] A similar bulletin began to appear in Hebei in 1963 (*Hebei gong'an tongbao* 河北公安通报).[31] These general police bulletins were supplemented by more specialized classified serials, such as the top-secret (*juemi* 绝密) Four-Cleanups Brief (*siqing jianbao* 四清简报), issues of which have survived for the fall of 1963.[32] Thus, regular police reporting emerged no later than the early 1960s, with internal police journals and occasional reports dating back to the 1950s.

Party reporting began to be produced at regular intervals as well, although there was significant regional variation in terms of when such bulletins emerged. In Beijing, the party started to publish a regular internal brief on trends in citizen complaints as early as 1952, but it did not compile its general classified newsletter entitled *Beijing tongxun* (北京通讯) until 1973, preferring to generate internal reports as needed.[33] Compare this with Tibet, where situation reports were produced between 1960 and 1965,[34] including by the Social Affairs Department (*shehui bu* 社会部), which was tasked with documenting enemy activities and popular sentiment.[35] However, prior to 1965, these reports were generated and sent to local leaders only as needed, at highly irregular intervals. In 1965, the party in Tibet began issuing a regular bulletin. What might explain this counterintuitive empirical finding, which places Tibet ahead of Beijing in terms of the development of regularized party reporting? The most plausible

---

[27] *Xinhua she dashiji*, vol. 2, 64.

[28] *Xinhua she dashiji*, vol. 2, 65.

[29] *Xinhua she dashiji*, vol. 2, 72–73.

[30] Multiple issues from 1963 on file with the author.

[31] An issue from 1963 on file with the author.

[32] Over twenty issues from the fall of 1963 on file with the author.

[33] Beijing Shi Difang Zhi Bianzuan Weiyuanhui, *Beijing zhi: Gongchandang juan: Gongchandang zhi* (Beijing: Beijing Chubanshe, 2012), 583.

[34] See, for example, *Huiwai fanying* (1964); *Xizang gongwei dianbao zhi* (1962, 1964, 1965); and *Xizang siqing jianbao* (1965).

[35] *Zhonggong Xizang difang zuzhishi zhigao 1950–1999* (Lasa: Zhonggong Xizang Zuzhibu, 2000), 685.

explanation is that the 1959 Tibetan Uprising, which generally caught the leadership off guard, sensitized the party to the value of systematic monitoring of the popular mood and the general situation in the region (see Section 6.6 of this chapter).

Another important change was the decision to regularly compile statistics on complaints work.[36] Systematic reporting on petitions began to emerge in a number of provinces immediately after the Great Leap Forward.

In sum, the most important finding of this section is that the Great Leap Forward did not undo the existing institutions for information gathering established during the initial decade of communist rule. This does not mean that the institutions provided high-quality nationally comprehensive information: as we saw in Chapter 4, reports on the incidence of hunger in *Neibu cankao* declined during the Great Leap Forward and were replaced by occasional stories about food substitutes and cannibalism. As this section argues, the decline in the quality of information during the Great Leap Forward was not lost on regime insiders, which prompted a statistical introspection. Overall, we can say that the survival of the sinews of the communist information state and their capacity to rapidly recover from the shocks of the Great Leap Forward is surprising. Remarkably, on the eve of the Cultural Revolution, China was making progress toward the routinized collection and transfer of information on popular discontent.

6.2 Institutional Hiatus and Continuity during the Cultural Revolution, 1966–1976

The Cultural Revolution was marked by a suspension of operation of most channels for voluntary and involuntary collection of information. We should note, however, that not all institutions were on hiatus: Xinhua News Agency continued to generate classified reporting even during the most destructive initial phase of the Cultural Revolution (1966–1969). There is also evidence that analysis of voluntarily transmitted information persisted in at least some parts of China during the initial years of the Cultural Revolution. Lastly, we should stress that a gradual resumption of the work of all information-collection agencies began in 1970 and was largely completed before the end of the Cultural Revolution in 1976. Overall, though destabilizing, the tumultuous events of 1966–1976 did not lead to full-scale institutional destruction.

---

[36] Diao, *Renmin xinfang shilüe*, 182–87.

6.2.1 Disruptions of Involuntary Collection

Both secret and visible informants were put on hiatus in the initial years of the Cultural Revolution. Who were these individuals? Whereas members of the social-order protection committees and small groups had a known identity as informants, others designated as secret forces (*mimi liliang* 秘密力量) were collecting intelligence confidentially. In the 1950s and early 1960s, the secret forces were referred to as agents (*teqing*) and occasionally as eyes and ears (*ermu*). In contrast to the all-purpose MPS street-level informants, secret forces received specific tasks to collect evidence on political opposition or criminal activity that was being carried out individually or in small groups.

For reasons that remain unclear, the use of agents was discontinued in some provinces during the Four Cleanups, with Heilongjiang ceasing to rely on special investigation forces as early as 1964.[37] By 1965, Vice-Minister of Public Security Yu Sang had declared that agent work should cease nationwide.[38] As the literature has established, the MPS stopped using domestic agents in December 1967.[39] Safehouses (*mimi judian* 秘密据点) were closed down and agents were investigated for whether "they had done something bad."[40] These policies stopped the secret MPS information-gathering work. Police almanacs indicate that the operation of the visible social-order protection groups was also suspended in 1967–1969, when no province reported any activity to protect social order. The hiatus was brief, however: the visible informant groups began to be reconstituted as early as 1970 in seven cities in Shaanxi province.[41] By 1971, the social-order protection committees and small groups had been restored in another four provinces. Altogether, nine provinces reported statistics on the resumption of social-order protection work before the end of the Cultural Revolution.[42]

6.2.2 Problems with Voluntary Transfer

The institutional hiatus impacted the voluntary transfer of information as well. Systematic analysis of citizen complaints ceased in the second half of 1966 and

---

[37] *Heilongjiang gong'an*, no. 7 (1980), 9.

[38] *Gong'an jianshe*, no. 11 (1965), 15.

[39] Michael Schoenhals, *Spying for the People: Mao's Secret Agents, 1949–1967* (New York: Cambridge University Press, 2013). Agent use was declared a Soviet "OGPU revisionist line" (Michael Schoenhals, "Recruiting Agents in Industry and Trade: Lifting the Veil on Early People's Republic of China Operational Work," *Modern Asian Studies* 45:5 [2011], 1345–69, at 1368).

[40] *Jianguo yilai gong'an gongzuo dashi yaolan (1949–2000)* (Beijing: Qunzhong Chubanshe, 2003), 319.

[41] Shaanxi Sheng Zhi Gong'an Bianzuan Weiyuanhui, *Shaanxi sheng zhi: Gong'an zhi* (Xi'an: Shaanxi Renmin Chubanshe, 2011), 394.

[42] Author's collection of provincial police gazetteers.

did not resume until at least 1970. However, this was not a nationwide suspension. In Beijing, information on complaints continued to be transmitted to decision makers even during the Cultural Revolution in the form of a letters-and-visits digest (*xinfang zhaibao* 信访摘报) and a bulletin (*xinfang jianbao* 信访简报).[43] There is archival evidence that complaints also continued to be analyzed in Shanghai during 1967–1968 and that a Letters-and-Visits Department apprised the leadership of their content through regular bulletins (*laixin jianbao* 来信简报).[44] This analysis produced some unexpected findings. For example, the Shanghai Education Department reported that fully one-half of the letters it received during the last quarter of 1967 focused on the revolution in education (*jiaoyu geming* 教育革命). Less predictably, the other half concentrated on daily life and material concerns like job assignments, employment, and compensation; demands for the rectification of errors that had emerged in the initial year of the Cultural Revolution were also raised, and questions about a timeline for the resumption of classes were posed.[45] Although encountering denunciations in the archives is not surprising,[46] the persistence of welfare concerns is an unexpected finding.[47] Complaints work survived in some form in 1967–1968 in places as varied in terms of their levels of development as the capital,[48] the city of Shanghai,[49] Gansu province,[50] and Fengxin county (奉新县) in Jiangxi.[51] The fact that such letters were read and systematically analyzed is revealing of ongoing attention to voluntary information transfer.

By the early 1970s, the disruptions to complaints work that existed in the initial years of the Cultural Revolution had largely disappeared.[52] In 1972, Zhou Enlai issued an instruction that letters-and-visits work should be strengthened. Following this top-level endorsement, there ensued a rapid increase in the number of complaints that reached the State Council.[53] Similar changes can be observed at the subnational level: in Tianjin, for example, complaints doubled between 1971 and 1974.[54] Such heightened attention to letters and visits

[43] *Beijing zhi: Gongchandang juan*, 584.

[44] SMA B257_2_2 (1967).

[45] SMA B105_4_157_42 (March 6, 1968), 2.

[46] For denunciations at a Shanghai smelting factory, see SMA B246_2_554_169 (May 29, 1970).

[47] Welfare concerns were expressed but not necessarily favorably received. See Shanghai Labor Bureau response to worker requests to return to Shanghai: SMA B172_3_18_5 (February 28, 1968).

[48] *Beijing zhi! Gongchandang juan*, 584.

[49] SMA B105_4_157_42 (March 6, 1968); SMA B50_3_11_39 (1968).

[50] *Gansu xinfang zhi 1949–1989* (Lanzhou: Gansu Minzu Chubanshe, 1991), 19–20.

[51] *Fengxin xian xinfang zhi* (Fengxin: Fengxin Xian Xinfang Zhi Bianzuan Weiyuanhui, May 1994), 42.

[52] On measures to improve complaints work, see SMA B257_2_579_16 (May 14, 1971).

[53] Letters and visits rose from 130,000 in 1971 to 340,000 in 1973. See Diao, *Renmin xinfang shilüe*, 213.

[54] In the first ten months of 1971, a total of 10,609 complaints reached the joint party–government letters-and-visits office; the number in the first ten months of 1974 was 20,822. See Tianjin Shi

also meant that regular digests, entitled *laixin zhaibao* (来信摘报) or *xinfang qingkuang* (信访情况), were prepared and sent to the leadership in various parts of China.[55] Sometimes, instead of discussing the total volume of complaints, reports focused on a single letter that was worthy of note: for instance, one of the bulletins produced by the Shanghai Labor Bureau analyzes a signal about gender discrimination in heavy industrial production, which was considered to be unsuitable for women (*nü tongzhi nannong* 女同志难弄).[56] Such preferences for hiring male workers are incompatible with the idea that women hold up half the sky, the report notes.

6.2.3 Citizen Complaints and Local Investigative Reporting

One of the most surprising innovations of the Cultural Revolution is the rise of local internal investigative reporting based on citizen letters. Although central-level outlets like *Neibu cankao* occasionally published stories informed by citizen complaints, these were not directly useful to local leaders, as they described problems in a jurisdiction different from theirs. What has been preserved in the Shanghai archives is different: raw classified reports generated by newspapers prior to a decision to publish in either the internal or the publicly accessible media. We should note that occasional brief summaries of letters were generated in the 1950s and 1960s as well. However, the reports that began to emerge in the early 1970s were longer and more analytical. Produced by the Shanghai papers of record like *Wenhui bao* (文汇报) and *Jiefang ribao* (解放日报), these reports had a standard structure of identifying the problem, highlighting its negative effects, and offering a potential solution. They have survived in the archives because they generated a bureaucratic response in the form of a *pishi* (批示 instruction) to take actions to redress the problem. Once written, these reports were forwarded to the entities mentioned in the complaint, with instructions to investigate and respond to the newspaper; to investigate and respond to the reader, informing the newspaper of the response; to investigate and respond just to the reader; or to respond to the reader without investigation.[57]

Some of the issues highlighted in these reports centered around inefficiencies in the planned economy: a clothing production factory complained that

---

Difang Zhi Bianxiu Weiyuanhui, *Tianjin tongzhi: Xinfang zhi* (Tianjin: Tianjin Shehui Kexueyuan Chubanshe, 1997), 188.

[55] On Shanghai, see SMA B250_2_769_14 (1974). See also *Gansu xinfang zhi 1949–1989* (1991), 21. Other possible titles of these reports are *xinfang dongtai* (信访动态) and *xinfang fanying* (信访反映).

[56] SMA B246_2_1209_75 (January 16, 1975).

[57] See *Jiefang ribao*'s instructions sheet: SMA B326_2_35_201 (November 22, 1975).

the import-export company was artificially suppressing the price of exports and was unreasonably delaying payment for finished goods.[58] This impacted the capacity of the clothing factory to fulfill its production plans. Other letters focused on shortages: of all things, of disinfectant (this could be easily addressed by ordering chemical plants and light-industry factories to produce more, the brief concludes).[59] There were also reports on the flourishing of illegal transportation by tricycles and motorized vehicles.[60] This could be solved by cracking down on those who were violating the law and by providing more buses to run the routes.[61] The final type of report stressed environmental protection concerns like air pollution, water pollution, and excessive noise in Shanghai. The electroplating and quenching shop floors of the Shanghai Electrical Appliance factory, for example, were emitting noxious gases that led to acute bronchitis and other respiratory diseases among humans and the wilting of gardens in the alleys just off Yuyuan Road.[62] Though solving the problems identified in this particular report was not easy (half a dozen polluting factories were named in the investigative piece), the document indicates that consultations with the offending producers had begun.[63]

In general, the existence of these materials is remarkable for several reasons. First, they date back to a time when the Cultural Revolution was still ongoing. Welfare concerns were nevertheless articulated and taken seriously at the time, at least in Shanghai. Second, they allow us to assess how the government responded to the problems outlined in them. Finally, in terms of their structure, reception, and effect, these documents are nearly identical to the investigative internal reports on citizen letters that were produced by major newspapers in Eastern European countries like the Soviet Union and Bulgaria.[64] Genres of bureaucratic reporting, including internal investigative journalism based on citizen letters, were quite similar in both Shanghai and Eastern Europe in the 1970s. This reflects the shared institutional foundations of communist information states.

---

[58] For the report and the government's response to it, see SMA B252_1_109_58 (September 30, 1975).

[59] For the report and the government's response to it, see SMA B246_3_134_62 (June 26, 1976).

[60] For the report and the government's response to it, see SMA B246_2_940_40 (August 16, 1973).

[61] SMA B246_2_940_40 (August 16, 1973).

[62] For the report and the government's response to it, see SMA B246_2_944_83 (August 3, 1973).

[63] SMA B246_2_944_83 (August 3, 1973).

[64] On internal reports on citizen letters received by *Literaturnaia gazeta*, see Martin K. Dimitrov, "Tracking Public Opinion Under Authoritarianism: The Case of the Soviet Union under Brezhnev," *Russian History* 41:3 (2014), 329–53. On newspaper internal reporting in Bulgaria, see Martin K. Dimitrov, "What the Party Wanted to Know: Citizen Complaints as a 'Barometer of Public Opinion' in Communist Bulgaria," *East European Politics and Societies and Cultures* 28:2 (May 2014), 271–95.

6.2.4 Internal Reporting by Xinhua during the Cultural Revolution

One of the few entities that successfully evaded a hiatus was Xinhua News Agency. This occurred despite the tremendous pressure placed on Xinhua to suspend its internal reporting. Although Vice-Premier Chen Yi had opined in August 1966 that "[w]e cannot stop publishing *Cankao ziliao* (参考资料) as it is our daily bread (每日的食粮)—we cannot work without it,"[65] requests were mounting to discontinue internal publications, which were labeled "black materials" by orthodox supporters of the Cultural Revolution due to their "poisonous content."[66] Action was needed to safeguard Xinhua from the Red Guards by bringing in the People's Liberation Army (PLA). To avoid a complete takeover by the military, in April 1967 the Central Committee issued an instruction for the domestic Xinhua bureaus, specifying that their internal reporting should not be sent to the provincial party or PLA authorities; moreover, the document clarified that PLA representatives at the bureaus had no right to examine reports meant for the top leadership; finally, the Central Committee mandated that in order to be able to protect their right to gather materials and transmit reports, Xinhua journalists should not be subject to restrictions.[67] This instruction helped save internal reporting. Remarkably, most of the Xinhua publications that survived during the Cultural Revolution were internal rather than public: in November 1970, of the twenty-two existing Xinhua publications, twelve were internal reference bulletins.[68] Top leaders followed these classified news digests so closely that in 1974 Zhou Enlai issued an instruction to Xinhua statitng that copies of *Cankao ziliao* and *Meiri yaowen* should be sent over as soon as they were printed, as Mao and Zhou wanted to read them every evening after 9:00 p,m.[69]

6.2.5 The Recovery of Information Collection

The most important insight from this section is that all channels for information gathering resumed normal operations prior to the end of the Cultural Revolution. The CCP never lost control over the repressive organs, as illustrated by the punishments imposed on high-ranking cadres by the Central Case Examination Group (*zhongyang zhuan'an shencha xiaozu* 中央专案审查小组),

---

[65] *Xinhua she dashiji (1931–2001)*, vol. 2 (2002), 88.
[66] *Xinhua she dashiji*, vol. 2, 88–89.
[67] *Xinhua she dashiji*, vol. 2, 91.
[68] *Xinhua she dashiji*, vol. 2, 101.
[69] *Xinhua she dashiji*, vol. 2, 112.

which was directly subordinate to the Politburo and guided by Zhou Enlai.[70] Continuity was also evident in the use of secret forces for intelligence work. As the Cultural Revolution proceeded, Zhou Enlai proved to be the most ardent elite supporter of the intelligence apparatus. His advocacy helped save the CCP Central Investigation Department (*zhongyang diaocha bu* 中央调查部) from permanent absorption by the PLA General Staff.[71] Zhou was also the motor behind the idea of resuming agent work. He secured Politburo approval for a March 1971 MPS notice on restarting secret investigative work.[72] Following a November 1972 recommendation from Zhou,[73] in January 1973 the MPS mandated the development of plans for reactivating (or recruiting de novo) eyes and ears.[74] Although these efforts took off in earnest after 1976, it is important that the hiatus in intelligence work had ended before the Cultural Revolution itself had run its full course. We should also note that classified bureaucratic reporting continued throughout the Cultural Revolution, as evidenced by Xinhua bulletins, party and government reports (Shanghai),[75] and police digests (Heilongjiang) discussed in this section.[76] Overall, we can conclude that the damage suffered by the information-gathering institutions in 1966–1976 was neither totalistic nor irreparable. The sinews of the communist information state survived the onslaught of both the Great Leap Forward and the Cultural Revolution.

6.3 Institutional Change and Continuity in Involuntary Collection: The Ministry of State Security and the Ministry of Public Security

Information gathering slowly changed after the death of Mao. Involuntary collection by the party and the media was gradually re-oriented toward the monitoring of latent discontent. One early example is provided by a November 1976 investigation report commissioned by the Shanghai Municipal Party Committee on citizen reactions to a proposed change in the system of pork rationing (because pork plays a central role in the Chinese diet, its retail price is monitored by

---

[70] Michael Schoenhals, "The Central Case Examination Group, 1966–1979," *The China Quarterly*, no. 145 (March 1996), 97–111.

[71] Peter Mattis and Matthew Brazil, *Chinese Communist Espionage: An Intelligence Primer* (Annapolis, MD: Naval Institute Press, 2019), 43–50.

[72] *Jianguo yilai gong'an gongzuo*, 335.

[73] *Zhongguo renmin jingcha jianshi* (Beijing: Jingguan Jiaoyu Chubanshe, 1989), 193.

[74] *Jianguo yilai gong'an gongzuo*, 349.

[75] Reports on secrecy work in the midst of the Cultural Revolution are especially noteworthy. See SMA B252_1_3 (November 3, 1970) and SMA B252_1_3_25 (May 18, 1971).

[76] The Heilongjiang PSB (黑龙江省革命委员会人民保卫部) started to produce a secret (*jimi*) daily situation briefing (*Qingkuang jianbao* 情况简报) in 1969. Various issues of this publication are available for 1970–1971.

the government as a bellwether of inflation; in 2019, the increase in pork prices was among the top five most controversial Internet public-opinion items).[77] A second area that experienced significant change was the content of the secret bulletins prepared for the Chinese leadership. Although coverage remained region-specific (rather than presenting comprehensive nationwide information), by 1980 both *Qingkuang huibian* (情况汇编) and *Neibu cankao* had started to print longer, more in-depth reports that focused on important issues of broad significance. In contrast to earlier styles of reporting in such bulletins, in the post-Mao period, efforts were made to contextualize each incident and to showcase how it might be representative of general trends; coverage of official corruption and of retaliation against petitioners are examples of this new tendency.[78] Finally, the introduction of opinion polling in the mid-1980s further extended the ability of the state to eventually make a successful transition toward having full-fledged systems for the involuntary extraction of information about latent discontent.[79]

The most significant institutional innovation in the realm of involuntary extraction during the initial post-Mao years was the creation of the Ministry of State Security (MSS) in 1983. Annual work summaries produced by the MSS reveal that the origins of the ministry are linked to concerns about foreign ideological influence, which also justified successively the launching of the Campaign Against Spiritual Pollution and the Campaign Against Bourgeois Liberalization.[80] In a speech to the National People's Congress on June 6, 1983, Premier Zhao Ziyang attributed the rise of counterrevolutionary activity and other criminality to the ideological and political apathy that had spread among Chinese bureaucrats.[81] The response was two-fold: the Ministry of Public Security (MPS) launched the Strike Hard Campaign and the MSS was established to counteract infiltration attempts by hostile forces.[82] MSS work summaries document that prior to 1989 the counterintelligence tasks of the ministry centered around detecting and neutralizing foreign and Taiwanese spies who engaged in subversion, sabotage, intelligence collection, the stealing of state secrets, and the deployment of propaganda for the purposes of psychological warfare (*xinli zhan* 心理战).[83] In short, the impetus for creating the MSS was the elevated external threat perception during the

---

[77] SMA B248_2_924 (1976); Li Peilin, Chen Guangjin, and Wang Chunguang, eds., *Zhongguo shehui xingshi fenxi yu yuce 2020* (Beijing: Shehui Kexue Wenxian Chubanshe, 2020), 262.

[78] On corruption, see *Neibu cankao* (no. 73/1981), esp. 10–14, and *Qingkuang huibian* (no. 549/1980). On retaliation, see *Qingkuang huibian* (no. 365/1980).

[79] Melanie Manion, *Retirement of Revolutionaries in China: Public Policies, Social Norms, Private Interests* (Princeton, NJ: Princeton University Press, 1993).

[80] Guojia Anquan Bu Bangongting, "Guojia anquan jiguan ji qi gongzuo" (1987) (document on file with the author).

[81] *Beijing Review*, 26:27 (July 4, 1983), xx–xxi, 6.

[82] Guojia Anquan Bu Bangongting, "Guojia anquan jiguan ji qi gongzuo" (1987).

[83] Guojia Anquan Bu Bangongting, "Guojia anquan jiguan ji qi gongzuo" (1987); Guojia Anquan Bu Bangongting, "1987 nian de guojia anquan gongzuo" (1989) (document on file with the author);

initial decade of reform. This parallels the cultural security concerns in Eastern Europe that led to the upgrading of pre-existing political police structures into the more specialized Sixth Directorate of State Security in Bulgaria (see Chapter 5) and the Fifth Directorate of the Soviet KGB (see Chapter 9).

Once the MSS began operations in July 1983, China joined the ranks of the handful of communist regimes having separate ministries to handle internal and state security.[84] As in the GDR, the creation of a new ministry did not mean that the MPS was sidelined from state security work.[85] Quite the opposite: throughout the 1980s, the MPS dedicated more staff to state security work than did the MSS. This institutional dualism persists to the current day: although the MSS has largely succeeded in eliminating the admittedly limited functions of the MPS in foreign intelligence work, there exists significant overlap between the counterintelligence mandate of the MPS and that of the MSS.

The MSS was established by drawing personnel from the MPS and from the Central Investigation Department (CID) of the Central Committee. Alongside the Second Department of the PLA General Staff, the CID had been the chief collector of foreign intelligence from the 1950s until the early 1980s.[86] There persists some uncertainty about the structure of the MSS,[87] though it is beyond doubt that the ministry handles both external intelligence and domestic counterintelligence. A recent study by a knowledgeable former Taiwanese intelligence operative lists eighteen functional divisions.[88] Support and human resources departments, party committees, and universities and think tanks also belong to

Guojia Anquan Bu Bangongting, "1988 nian de guojia anquan gongzuo" (1990) (document on file with the author).

[84] Such arrangements existed only in the GDR, the Soviet Union, and, after 1973, North Korea.

[85] In the Soviet Union, there was no overlap between the portfolio of the KGB and that of the Interior Ministry. The available data on North Korea do not allow for a reliable assessment of whether the MSS has established exclusive jurisdiction over the handling of state security threats.

[86] Michael Schoenhals, "Zhongguo gongchandang zhongyang diaocha bu jianshi," in Zhu Jiamu, ed., *Dangdai Zhongguo yu tade fazhan daolu: Di er jie dangdai Zhongguo shi guoji gaoji luntan lunwen ji* (Beijing: Dangdai Zhongguo Chubanshe, 2010), 252–72.

[87] In part, this reflects the re-organization and renumbering of various departments over time. As no official organization chart of the MSS has ever been released, it is challenging to reliably date these changes. See Nicholas Eftimiades, *Chinese Intelligence Operations* (Annapolis, MD: Naval Institute Press, 1994); Xuezhi Guo, *China's Security State: Philosophy, Evolution, and Politics* (New York: Cambridge University Press, 2012), 365; Mattis and Brazil, *Chinese Communist Espionage*, 55–56; Kan Zhongguo, "Inside the Chinese Intelligence Agencies," *BBC Monitoring International Reports*, February 8, 2006.

[88] These are: Confidential Bureau (机要局); International Intelligence Department (国际情报局); Political and Economic Intelligence Department (政经情报局); Taiwan, Hong Kong, and Macau Department (台港澳情报局); Intelligence Analysis Circulation Department (情报分析通报局); Work Guide Bureau (业务指导局); Counterespionage Intelligence Department (反间谍情报局); Counterespionage Reconnaissance Department (反间谍侦察局); Domestic Protection and Reconnaissance Department (对内保防侦察局); Foreign Protection and Reconnaissance Department (对外保防侦察局); Intelligence Information Center (情报资料中心局); Social Investigation Bureau (社会调查局); High Technology Bureau (技侦科技局); Technical Reconnaissance Department (Mail Inspection and Telecommunications Reconnaissance) (技术侦察

the MSS.[89] Altogether, it is estimated that over thirty departments existed within the ministry by the 2000s.[90]

The remarkably sophisticated internal structure of the MSS developed slowly. Its vertical expansion was also a lengthy process: it was not until 1998, for example, that the MSS had set up a branch in every province.[91] In the 1980s, the ministry focused on establishing a presence in the provincial-level municipalities and in some major coastal provinces. A Taiwanese source estimates that by 1989, offices had been created in fourteen cities and provinces, which are listed in Table 6.1. The source also presents the extremely rare opportunity to evaluate the size of the MSS full-time staff. Once we normalize the data by dividing them by the population of each provincial unit, we get a sense of the extreme variability in bureaucratic endowments across Chinese provinces: there was a nearly hundred-fold difference in the number of MSS officers allocated per million people in Beijing versus Shandong. Altogether, there were 14,570 MSS staff in these 14 provinces as of 1989.

One question that we need to address is whether the MSS officer saturation rate is too low. Several observations are in order. The first is that, as Table 6.1 reveals, Beijing compares favorably with the most conservative estimate of the size of State Security in 1989 in Bulgaria, excluding the various technical support divisions and the Praetorian Guard. Of course, a direct comparison shows that the MSS was very fragile at the end of the 1980s. The average number of MSS employees per million people in the fourteen provinces where the ministry had a presence as of 1989 was thirty-two times lower than the number of State Security officers per million people in Bulgaria in 1989. A comparison with the GDR reveals a 200-fold difference. However, we should be mindful that an accurate accounting of the staff dedicated to protecting state security cannot be limited only to the MSS. Multiple MPS departments were involved in this work either peripherally or fully: Social Order, Entry–Exit, Population Registration, and above all, the Political Protection Departments, which employed more staff than did the MSS. We can illustrate this point with an example from Guangxi, where the MSS had 332 employees in 1989 and the MPS Political Protection Department had 521.[92] As there is no reason to believe

---

局 [邮件检查与电信侦控]); Comprehensive Intelligence Analysis Department (综合情报分析局); Image Intelligence Department (影像情报局); Business Bureau (企业局); and Counterterrorism Bureau (反恐局). See Weng Yanqing, *Zhonggong qingbao zuzhi yu jiandie huodong* (Taipei: Xinrui Wenchuang, 2018), 109–10. Weng's discussion overlaps almost completely with Guo, *China's Security State*, 365.

[89] The University of International Relations and the China Institutes of Contemporary International Relations are the most prominent examples, respectively, of a university and a think tank.

[90] Guo, *China's Security State*, 364.

[91] Peter Mattis, "Assessing the Foreign Policy Influence of the Ministry of State Security," *China Brief* 11:1 (January 14, 2011), 5–8.

[92] Guangxi Zhuangzu Zizhiqu Gong'an Ju, *Guangxi gong'an tongji nianjian 1989* (Nanning: Guangxi Zhuangzu Zizhiqu Gong'an Ju Bangongshi, November 1991), 262; Weng, *Zhonggong qingbao zuzhi*, 111–12.

Table 6.1 Absolute Size and Relative Rate of Saturation with State Security Employees in China, Bulgaria, and the GDR in 1989

	Number of MSS Staff	MSS Staff per Million People
Beijing	4,334	403.2
Tianjin	1,681	197.3
Inner Mongolia	389	18.3
Liaoning	259	6.7
Jilin	392	16.3
Heilongjiang	355	10.1
Shanghai	2,111	165.4
Jiangsu	535	8.2
Zhejiang	633	15
Fujian	501	16.8
Shandong	348	4.3
Guangdong	2,245	36.2
Guangxi	332	8
Yunnan	518	14.2
TOTAL China (14 provinces)	14,570	**28.1**
Bulgaria (excluding all technical support units and the Praetorian Guard)	3,464	**384.9**
Bulgaria (all departments included)	8,012	890.2
German Democratic Republic	91,000	5,617.3

NB: Fourteen provinces with 46.7 percent of China's population.

Bulgaria State Security: 3,464 employees in departments for foreign intelligence, domestic counterintelligence, military counterintelligence, economic counterintelligence, counteracting ideological subversion, the antiterrorism battalion, and the state security division of the prosecutor's office. The list of 8,012 total employees includes the Praetorian Guard (which consisted of bodyguards, food caterers, and drivers), the operative-technical department, the surveillance department, the communications department, the archive, the information department, and the state security division of the police academy.

Sources: Author's dataset; Diniu Sharlanov, *Istoriia na komunizma v Bulgariia*, vol. 2 (Sofia: Ciela, 2009), 544; Weng, *Zhonggong qingbao zuzhi yu jiandie huodong*, 111–12 (addition errors reproduced as they appear in the source).

that Guangxi would be unique in terms of this ratio, we can conclude that throughout the 1980s, the MPS remained the main entity in charge of protecting state security.

Beyond personnel allocation statistics, we possess additional specific evidence of the ongoing involvement of the MPS in political protection after the creation of the MSS. The MPS continued to collect intelligence overseas,[93] but the essence of its contribution to state security was domestic counterintelligence. Data from various provinces attest to that. In Jiangsu, for instance, the focus of political-protection work in the 1980s included counteracting reactionary secret-society penetration (*fandong huidaomen fubi* 反动会道门复辟), active counterrevolutionaries (*xianxing fangeming anjian* 现行反革命案件), hostile forces (*didui shili* 敌对势力), and enemy conspiracies and sabotage (*didui fenzi yinmou pohuai huodong* 敌对分子阴谋破坏活动).[94] Secret societies were also a concern in Shandong, where the Qinghua Shengjiao (清华圣教) had more than 500 followers in 1988.[95] Similarly, data from Guangxi indicate that the MPS consistently investigated highly visible cases of counterrevolutionary activity that fell into several main categories, such as hostile propaganda and agitation (mostly the spreading of leaflets and the writing of antisocialist slogans in public places); distribution of anonymous letters; correspondence with hostile forces; organized anticommunist resistance; and secret societies.[96] In sum, there is no indication that the MPS relinquished its mandate to protect state security prior to the Tiananmen events in 1989.

The MPS executed its information-collection functions by expanding its visible social-order protection committees, small groups, and liaisons (see Figure 6.4).[97] The figure also includes other categories of visible informants, such as patrols, joint defense teams, and security guards.[98] In contrast to secret agents, the identity of social-order informants was publicly known and reinforced by armbands that identified them as intelligence collectors.

Aggregate data on an issue as sensitive as the number of informants in China are exceedingly rare. Detailed statistics on the geographical distribution of informants are even more difficult to obtain. Yet, the internal materials this study is based on do yield unusually detailed data on the main category of visible MPS informants, namely, members of the social-order protection committees and small groups (*zhi'an baowei weiyuanhui* 治安保卫委员会/ *zhi'an baowei xiaozu* 治安保卫小组), which operated under the aegis of work

[93] On overseas collection by the MPS prior to 1983, see *Gong'an jianshe*, no. 16 (1980), 5 and *Gong'an jianshe*, no. 3 (1980), 37–39. On collection after 1983, see Guo, *China's Security State*, 363.

[94] Jiangsu Sheng Difang Zhi Bianzuan Weiyuanhui, *Jiangsu sheng zhi: Gong'an zhi* (Beijing: Qunzhong Chubanshe, 2000), 96–97.

[95] *Jianguo yilai gong'an gongzuo*, 708.

[96] Guangxi Zhuangzu Zizhiqu Gong'an Ju, *Guangxi gong'an tongji nianjian 1988* (Nanning: Guangxi Zhuangzu Zizhiqu Gong'an Ju Bangongshi, July 1990).

[97] Individuals who signed social-order responsibility contracts are excluded from the dataset because they were ubiquitous in rural areas in the 1980s and 1990s and the MPS never counted them as informants.

[98] Contrary to the stylized fact, these individuals were not old grannies: retirees constituted less than one-tenth of the committee and small-group members in 1985–1991. However, older members were more numerous in the cities: internal sources indicate that in 1985–1991, up to 40 percent of the social-order informants in the urban areas were retirees.

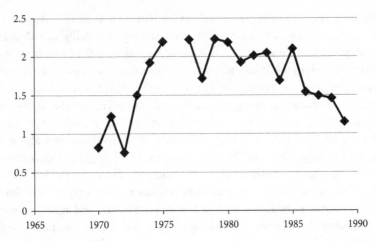

Figure 6.4 Visible police informants in China, 1970–1989 (as a percentage of the population).

Source: Author's dataset.

units, urban neighborhood committees, and rural village committees.[99] After their formal launch in 1951, social-order committees and the small groups underneath them engaged in preventing treason, spying, theft, arson, and other counterrevolutionary crimes.[100] According to regulations, the committees were expected to consist of three to eleven members and the small groups were to have three to five members.[101] Over time, there were significant fluctuations in their size. Internal materials allow us to calculate that in the 1980s–1990s committees had four to five members, whereas small groups consisted of two to three individuals.[102] These part-time intelligence collectors constituted about 70–80 percent of the visible informant corps in the 1980s and 1990s. Therefore, detailed data on their geographical distribution provide us with

[99] A sign of their importance is that these entities are mentioned in Article 111 of the 1982 Constitution. Article 111 specifies that social-order protection committees can be established under neighborhood and village committees, but it does not mention small groups or committees operating in work units. On urban neighborhood committees, see Benjamin L. Read, *Roots of the State: Neighborhood Organization and Social Networks in Beijing and Taipei* (Stanford, CA: Stanford University Press, 2012). On village committees, see Daniel C. Mattingly, *The Art of Political Control in China* (New York: Cambridge University Press, 2020).

[100] See Chapter 4 and Gong'an Bu, "Zhi'an baowei weiyuanhui zanxing zuzhi tiaoli" (August 8, 1952). Also see Zhang Houan and Bai Yihua, *Zhongguo nongcun jiceng jianzhi de lishi yanbian* (Chengdu: Sichuan Renmin Chubanshe, 1992), 202–7.

[101] Gong'an Bu, "Zhi'an baowei weiyuanhui zanxing zuzhi tiaoli" (August 8, 1952).

[102] Committees ranged from 4.43 to 4.95 members; small groups ranged from 2.2 to 2.96 members (data for 1985–1991).

unique insights into the spatial variation of one kind of information-gathering capacity in China.

Provincial-level statistics on the number of social-order protection committees and small groups in 1987 reveal extreme variation across China's then-existing twenty-nine provinces, ethnic autonomous regions, and provincial-level municipalities.[103] We can illustrate this variation by calculating the density of informants per square kilometer in each province: the variable has a minimum value of 0.012 in Tibet and a maximum value of 23.871 in Shanghai, with a mean of 4.219 and a standard deviation of 6.021 (see Figure 6.5). Another perspective on the spatial variation in the reach of the state across China is provided by calculating the share of the population that belonged to social-order protection committees and small groups: the informant saturation ranges from a low of 0.534 percent in Guangxi to a high of 3.06 percent in Beijing (see Figure 6.6), with a standard deviation of 0.599 and a mean of 1.196.

The 12,260,470 members of the social-order protection committees and small groups are equivalent to 1.14 percent of China's population in 1987. How can we interpret this figure? A comparative perspective may be helpful. As discussed in Chapter 2, a very liberal estimate of all visible and clandestine external intelligence and domestic counterintelligence agents and associates handled by the Ministry of State Security (Stasi) and the Ministry of the Interior (MdI) in East Germany did not exceed 1.9 percent of the population in 1987. The total number of overt and covert domestic counterintelligence informants of the two ministries in the GDR stood at 1.6 percent in 1987. Without a doubt, should it ever become possible to produce a complete inventory of all types of visible MPS intelligence collectors (1.49 percent in 1987, as shown in Figure 6.4), covert MPS agents, and clandestine MSS recruits, the tally would reveal that the counterintelligence penetration rate in China was significantly higher than that in the GDR, which is widely considered to have had an informant network with the highest saturation rate within the Eastern Bloc (see Chapter 2).

What explains the pattern of interprovincial variation? A key predictor of the number of social-order informants across Chinese provinces is the number of communist party members. The relationship is very powerful ($t = 8.76$; R-squared $= 0.7395$ in a bivariate regression) and robust to the omission of outliers (provincial-level municipalities) and to different specifications (in a bivariate regression where the dependent and independent variables are measured in percentages, the share of CCP members is still very highly significant, with

---

[103] Hainan and Chongqing did not attain provincial status until 1988 and 1997, respectively.

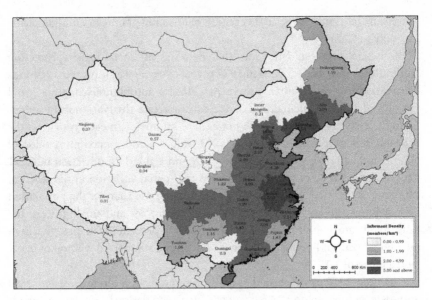

Figure 6.5 GIS map of the density of social-order informants per province in China, 1987 (members/km²).

Source: Author's dataset.

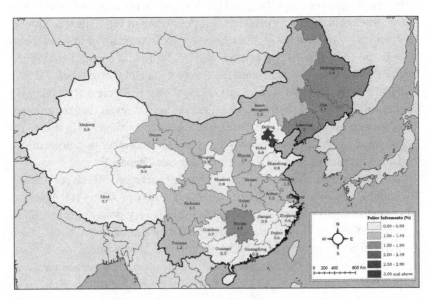

Figure 6.6 GIS map of the saturation of social-order informants per province in China, 1987 (as a percentage of the population).

Source: Author's dataset.

Table 6.2 Determinants of the Number of Visible Informants in Chinese Provinces, 1987

	M1 Bivariate	M2 Outliers Dropped	M3 Controls	M4 Outliers Dropped
Number of CCP members	0.2615*** (0.0298)	0.2628*** (0.0324)	0.2595*** (-0.0753)	0.2425*** (0.0829)
GDP (yuan)			2.55e-07 (2.80e-06)	9.81e-07 (3.16e-06)
Urbanization % (1985)			620.3259 (2,414.003)	331.1746 (4,058.922)
Territory (km^2)			0.0079 (0.0904)	0.0089 (0.0987)
Constant	17,364.23 (54,987.04)	11,824.68 (62,422.8)	-10,329.39 (118,590)	-3,904.754 (135,740.2)
N	29	26	29	26
R-squared	0.7395	0.7338	0.7409	0.7358

Source: Author's dataset.

Significance levels: * = 0.1; ** = 0.05; *** = 0.01.

NB: Outliers dropped in Model 2 and Model 4: Beijing, Tianjin, and Shanghai.

$t = 5.26$; the model has R-squared $= 0.5058$).[104] Further statistical tests presented in Table 6.2 show that the relationship between party members and social-order informants is robust to the inclusion of controls (GDP, urbanization, and provincial territory), none of which assume any level of conventional statistical significance in OLS specifications regardless of whether we omit the three provincial-level municipalities. The central finding of the analysis regarding the powerful relationship between party members and the number of social-order committee and small-group members is not surprising: those visible informants, who were publicly perceived as agents of the party-state, were indeed likely to be party members.

Internal materials reveal fewer details about the covert informants recruited by the MPS. Should detailed statistics on covert informants ever become available, we would expect to find that it would be less typical for these informants

---

[104] The percentage of CCP members is also the key predictor of informant density ($n = 29$; $t = 7.23$; R-squared $= 0.6593$), but that relationship is driven entirely by the three provincial-level municipalities, and it loses statistical significance when these three are excluded from the analysis ($n = 26$; $t = 1.03$; R-squared $= 0.032$).

to be party members. The logic is clear: to be effective, covert informants need to be able to infiltrate the groups of enemies that they are monitoring. As these enemies were unlikely to be party members, the covert informants would usually not belong to the party. Although the number of such clandestine police assets (eyes and ears, agents, secret forces, and friends) remains unknown, numerous police sources reference their existence and their recruitment from social milieus close to those of the enemies whom they had to secretly track: ex-convicts, for instance, were tasked with collecting intelligence on fellow former felons, who were placed on the targeted population roster.[105] The MPS roster survived the creation of the MSS and continued to function as an important mechanism for systematically monitoring known or suspected counterrevolutionaries. In sum, the MPS retained its role as a key collector of information on regime enemies after the establishment of the MSS.

Decision makers valued the intelligence that was collected by the MPS. There is direct evidence of the upward transmission of the information that was acquired through overt and covert techniques. In Liaoning, for instance, a special intelligence-collection small group was established in January 1986 to gather enemy, political, and social intelligence (*diqing, zhengqing, sheqing* 敌情, 政情, 社情) for distribution to the provincial PSB leadership as well as to the Political Protection Department, the Economic and Cultural Security Department, and the Technical Investigation Team; important information items were sent to the MPS in Beijing, with some forwarded to the central party leadership and obtaining *pishi*.[106] In short, institutional dualism in the monitoring of discontent by the MPS and the MSS persisted throughout the 1980s.

We can conclude with the general observation that creation of the MSS did enrich the information-gathering landscape in China by allocating specialized bureaucratic personnel to counteract external ideological threats and their domestic manifestations.

---

[105] *Jianguo yilai gong'an gongzuo; Gong'an jianshe*, no. 16 (1980), 5; *Gong'an jianshe*, no. 3 (1980), 37–39; Yu Botao, *Mimi zhencha wenti yanjiu* (Beijing: Zhongguo Jiancha Chubanshe, 2008). In Harbin, the PSB held a similar view that eyes and ears focusing on criminal activity should be recruited especially among younger criminals (*Heilongjiang gong'an*, no. 10 [1980], 13). Nationally, a 1984 regulation on recruiting social-order eyes and ears specified the three categories from which these assets should be drawn: former prison, labor camp, and reeducation-through-labor inmates; individuals who had violated the law or had committed minor crimes; and ordinary citizens (*jiben qunzhong* 基本群众). Except for ordinary citizens, the other categories involved individuals who would be included on the targeted population list. Thus, it is no surprise that the social-order agents were tasked with monitoring the targeted population (see Gong'an bu guanyu yinfa "Zhi'an ermu jianshe zanxing guiding" de tongzhi [October 20, 1984]).

[106] Liaoning Sheng Renmin Zhengfu Difangzhi Bangongshi, *Liaoning sheng zhi: Gong'an zhi, 1986–2005* (Shenyang: Liaoning Minzu Chubanshe, 2016), 45–46.

6.4 Selective Repression: Declining Indiscriminacy and Severity

Scholars have posited that more abundant information allows for a more precise targeting of repression.[107] In operationalizing this argument, the rate of repression is used as a proxy for targeting. The rate is a frequentist concept: it is either low or high. One potential problem arises when having to interpret a low rate of prosecution, which may reflect less crime rather than a targeted approach to prosecution. Thus, we need a different proxy for targeted repression. The concept that best captures targeting is selectivity. How might we measure selectivity? Here, we must take into account discriminacy and severity. Discriminacy can be ascertained by assessing the proportion of citizens who are prosecuted as a function of the number of individuals for whom the state security organs have evidence of their committing a crime. When assessing discriminacy, we should be aware that it can occur at any stage of the process, which starts with a decision to investigate a crime, collection of evidence, successful investigation, and subsequent transfer to the procuracy for indictment and arrest. Finally, the severity of punishment is the second criterion for assessing selectivity: it can range from execution without sentencing at one extreme to surveillance at the other. These criteria allow us to assess how selective the prosecution of political crimes has become over time.

Internal statistics on jail work reveal that after the Cultural Revolution there was a clear nationwide trend of a decline in the share of individuals imprisoned for counterrevolutionary crimes, both in absolute numbers and as a proportion of all prisoners (see Figure 6.7). However, as is well known, there were spikes in repression after the death of Mao. One occurred in the aftermath of Democracy Wall in 1979, when the MPS focused on illegal publications and organizations carrying out antiparty and antisocialist activities under the slogans of democracy, freedom, human rights, and reform.[108] Another was during the Strike Hard Campaign of 1983, which targeted both counterrevolutionaries and common criminals. Yet, these spikes in repression did not impact the grand total of individuals held for counterrevolutionary crimes, as the number of prisoners released was greater than the number of those who were newly incarcerated.

A significant signal about repressive intentions was issued in 1984, when the MPS sent a "Situation Report" (*Qingkuang fanying* 情况反映) to the Politburo

---

[107] Stathis N. Kalyvas, *The Logic of Violence in Civil War* (New York: Cambridge University Press, 2006); Martin K. Dimitrov and Joseph Sassoon, "State Security, Information, and Repression: A Comparison of Communist Bulgaria and Ba'thist Iraq," *Journal of Cold War Studies* 16:2 (Spring 2014), 4–31; Sheena Chestnut Greitens, *Dictators and Their Secret Police: Coercive Institutions and State Violence* (New York: Cambridge University Press, 2016).

[108] *Jianguo yilai gong'an gongzuo*, 471.

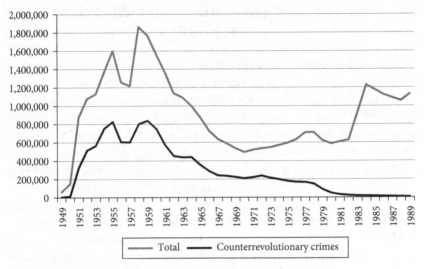

Figure 6.7 Prison population in China, 1949–1989.

Source: Author's dataset.

and the State Council that work with the Four Categories (*silei fenzi* 四类分子) had concluded and that from the founding of the PRC until 1984 altogether 20 million landlords, rich peasants, counterrevolutionaries, and bad elements (*di, fu, fan, huai* 地富反坏) had received reeducation-through-labor (*jiaoyu gaizao* 教育改造).[109] Thus, when the campaign-style targeting of counterrevolutionaries declined after 1984, the MPS deployed less violence in the handling of political dissent. The rate of political repression continued to decrease in subsequent years. Yet, the question of whether the indiscriminacy and the severity of repression also diminished stands unresolved, therefore making it difficult to adjudicate the issue of selectivity by using these aggregate data.

Direct evidence for the existence of selective repression prior to Tiananmen is provided by the unusually granular data on political-protection work from the Guangxi Zhuang Autonomous Region. Internal statistics demonstrate that the MPS continued to handle a range of counterrevolutionary crimes in the region throughout the 1980s. One category was counterrevolutionary propaganda and agitation (*fangeming xuanchuan shandong* 反革命宣传煽动), which encompassed the distribution of counterrevolutionary slogans (*fangeming biaoyu* 反革命标语), leaflets (*fangeming chuandan* 反革命传单), and letters (*fangeming xinjian* 反革命信件). Another was overseas counterrevolutionary

[109] *Jianguo yilai gong'an gongzuo*, 572–73.

Table 6.3 Investigation of Counterrevolutionary Crimes in Guangxi, 1988

	Cases Detected	Cases Registered for Investigation	Investigation Rate	Cases Solved	Resolution Rate (as % of cases investigated)
Slogans	41	9	21.9%	7	36.8%
Leaflets	6	2	33.3%	2	100%
Letters	19	5	26.3%	3	60%
Correspondence	131	8	6.1%	6	75%
Group	5	3	60%	3	100%
Secret society	4	1	25%	1	100%
Other	4	0	0%	NA	NA
TOTAL	210	28	13.3%	22	78.6%

Source: Guangxi gong'an tongji nianjian 1988, 19.

correspondence (*fangeming guagou* 反革命挂钩), in particular with KMT broadcast media and other spy organizations.[110] And the third was participation in counterrevolutionary groups or secret societies. The MPS kept statistics on the cases that had been detected (*fa'an* 发案), were subsequently registered for investigation (*li'an* 立案), and eventually got resolved (*po'an* 破案). The Guangxi data presented in Table 6.3 indicate that in 1988 only 13.3 percent of the instances of counterrevolutionary activity that had been detected were registered for investigation and that twenty-two cases (78.6 percent of those investigated) were eventually solved.[111] A mere 8 cases (3.8 percent of the 210 detected) were transferred

[110] For definitional issues, see the Supreme People's Court, Supreme People's Procuratorate and Ministry of Public Security "Notice on Questions of the Charge and Evidence in Cases of the Crime of Counterrevolutionary Correspondence" (最高人民法院，最高人民检察院，公安部 关于反革命挂钩案件的罪名罪证问题的通知), July 26, 1979, and *Jianguo yilai gong'an gongzuo*, 484. The notice stipulates that correspondence with the Soviet and Vietnamese media should be prosecuted in the same way as correspondence with Taiwanese media.

[111] *Guangxi gong'an tongji nianjian 1988*, 19. The low frequency of successful investigations when evidence of political crimes is present is unusual when put in the context of other communist regimes. In the Soviet Union, for example, the rate of successful investigation of cases of counterrevolutionary behavior was significantly higher than that in China: in 1983 (the latest year for which this type of data is available), authors were identified in 92.3 percent of the cases where counterrevolutionary propaganda and agitation were detected (calculated from a KGB report on anti-Soviet propaganda and agitation in 1983, Library of Congress, Volkogonov Papers, Box 28, February 9, 1984). In Guangxi, the authors were identified in twelve of the sixty-two cases (18.2 percent) of such activity detected in 1988. Thus, the rate of successfully concluded investigations of crimes against state security was much lower in China than it was in the Soviet Union.

to the procuratorate for criminal prosecution and indictment: 5 were cases of spying (*tewu jiandie* 特务间谍) and 3 of counterrevolutionary propaganda and agitation.[112] The majority of individuals were sentenced to surveillance or to imprisonment for less than five years.[113] Similar trends of increasing discriminacy and declining severity of punishment in the second half of the 1980s can be observed in other provinces as well,[114] thus supporting the conclusion that repression on the eve of Tiananmen was selective. However, these significant findings do not accord with the conventional wisdom about China.

This positive trend notwithstanding, a distinguishing characteristic of the Chinese model is that the overall rate of criminal prosecution for counterrevolutionary crimes was higher than that in Eastern Europe. A 1975 top-secret statistical memorandum prepared by KGB Chairman Andropov for General Secretary Brezhnev attests to the overwhelming dominance of prophylaxis over incarceration in the Soviet Union. The report indicates that in 1967–1974 there was a 1:96 ratio between those charged with committing especially serious state crimes (such as anti-Soviet propaganda and agitation) and those subjected to prophylactic measures.[115] This means that 1.05 percent of anti-state crimes in the Soviet Union ended with prosecution by the judicial authorities. By contrast, 3.8 percent of those involved in such crimes in Guangxi were charged.

What are the implications of these findings? One purpose of selective repression is to blackmail those who could have been imprisoned (but were not) to serve as informants. As the unusually rich data from Guangxi reveal, in 1988 as many as 40 percent of the social-order eyes and ears were recruited from among those who had engaged in illegal behavior or had committed minor infractions (and a further 13 percent were selected from among former prisoners and labor camp inmates).[116] They were tasked primarily with spying on individuals on the targeted population roster and in special professions (salons, bars, hotels). The higher selectivity of repression in the Soviet Union than in China suggests that the potential supply of individuals who could be recruited to serve as informants on the basis of compromising information was greater in the Soviet Union, thus allowing the KGB to be more discriminating in its recruitment practices.

---

[112] Guangxi Zhuangzu Zizhiqu Gaoji Renmin Fayuan, *Guangxi sifa tongji 1950–1994* (Nanning: Guangxi Zhuangzu Zizhiqu Gaoji Renmin Fayuan, December 1995), 22.

[113] *Guangxi sifa tongji*, 80.

[114] Beijing Shi Gaoji Renmin Fayuan, *Beijing shi sifa tongji ziliao huibian, 1949–1985* (Beijing Shi Gaoji Renmin Fayuan, September 1986), 8; Liaoning Sheng Gaoji Renmin Fayuan, *Liaoning sheng fayuan tongji ziliao huibian, 1949–1986* (Liaoning Sheng Gaoji Renmin Fayuan, July 1987), 16–17.

[115] "O nekotorykh itogakh predupreditel'no-profilakticheskoi raboty organov gosbezopasnosti," Volkogonov Papers, Box 28 (October 31, 1975), 1.

[116] *Guangxi gong'an tongji nianjian 1988*, 275.

A second conclusion that can be drawn is that a regime that is more selective in meting out repression is more secure that punishment has been appropriately targeted, which, in turn, depends on the volume and quality of the information available. Although China made extraordinary advances in improving its information-gathering capacity in the 1980s, it had not yet caught up with the Eastern European regimes in terms of their ability to produce fine-grained intelligence about regime enemies.

6.5 Voluntary Transmission

One of the main arguments of this book concerns the extraordinary value that voluntarily transmitted information has for evaluating citizen discontent. As petitioning was the most typical mechanism for voluntary transmission prior to 1989, this section will focus on documenting the overall volume of complaints and describing their content.

The available materials reveal that, over time, there were changes in the content of complaints that reflected the turbulent events in China's post-1949 political development. Political denunciations were frequent throughout the 1950s and during the radical phase of the Cultural Revolution, presenting a parallel to the Soviet Union under Stalin.[117] Throughout the 1970s and the early 1980s, tens of millions of petitions were received about rectifying the excesses of the Cultural Revolution.[118] However, during the entire 1949–1989 period, complaints also focused on problems with the fulfillment of the socialist social contract: job assignment difficulties, the provision of housing, poor living conditions, and the system for the rationing of staples.[119] In Shanghai, petitions about the social contract constituted almost half of the letters and visits handled by the district-level offices of the municipal government from 1973 to 1977.[120] Internal newspaper reporting indicates that citizens in Shanghai continued to focus on daily-life problems after the death of Mao.[121] For example, shortages of cotton batting (*xumian miantai* 絮棉棉胎) were a serious concern during the cold winter months of 1977.[122] Nationally, welfare complaints began to dominate after 1982, when rectification of the errors of the Cultural Revolution was officially declared

---

[117] On the Soviet case, see Sheila Fitzpatrick, *Tear Off the Masks! Identity and Imposture in Twentieth-Century Russia* (Princeton, NJ: Princeton University Press, 2005).

[118] For a sample of such complaints, see Shangfang Tongxun, *Chunfeng huayu ji* (Beijing: Qunzhong Chubanshe, 1981).

[119] Diao, *Renmin xinfang shilüe*.

[120] SMA B61_2_108 (1973–1977).

[121] See SMA A73_2_178_1 (1977) for *Jiefang ribao*'s January–March 1977 reports on citizen letters.

[122] SMA B248_2_1024 (December 8, 1977).

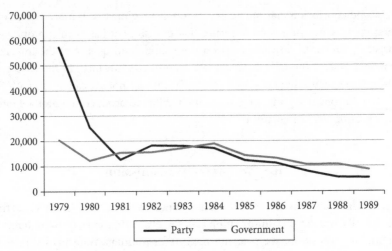

Figure 6.8 Citizen complaints in Gansu, 1978–1989.
Source: Gansu xinfang zhi 1949–1989, 49.

to be complete.[123] However, another trend was also evident in the 1980s: a drop in complaints occurring at the subnational level. Petitioning statistics from Tianjin reveal a decline from 77,913 letters and visits in 1979 to 23,570 in 1989.[124] Data on complaints to the party and government in Gansu, which are presented in Figure 6.8, document similar reductions in volume. Such rapid erosion in the frequency of citizen complaints suggests declining responsiveness.

The available data make it very difficult to systematically assess responsiveness to citizen complaints in China prior to 1989. Petitions were handled primarily by the Letters-and-Visits Offices (*xinfang ban* 信访办), which had been established at the national and subnational levels within the party, within various government agencies, and within enterprises. No source contains provincial- or national-level data on the proportion of petitions that had been resolved positively either in a single year or over time. However, the case of Bulgaria illustrates how trends in citizen complaints can reveal changes in responsiveness, namely, a drop in the number of petitions indicates a declining rate of positive resolution.[125] Data compiled from government documents and from *Renmin xinfang* (人民信访), an internal-reference journal that began publication for

---

[123] The share of rectification complaints dropped from 80 percent to 30 percent of all petitions between 1982 and 1986. See Isabelle Thireau and Hua Linshan, *Les Ruses de la démocratie: Protester en Chine* (Paris: Éditions du Seuil, 2010), 192.

[124] *Tianjin tongzhi: Xinfang zhi*, 188.

[125] Dimitrov, "What the Party Wanted to Know."

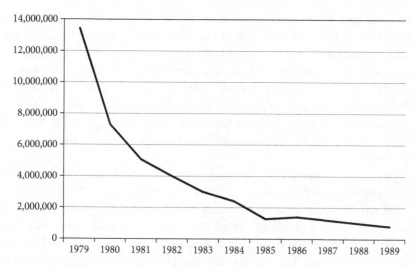

Figure 6.9 Citizen complaints in China, 1979–1989.
Source: Author's dataset.

letters-and-visits personnel in 1985, demonstrate that a sizable drop in the number of complaints occurred between 1984 and 1989 (see Figure 6.9). The Chinese regime reacted with alarm to this decline in the number of letters and visits. Numerous articles in *Renmin xinfang* stressed that government responsiveness to complaints is important for maintaining communist rule because petitions provide a channel for dialogue with the masses and for maintaining citizen loyalty.[126] These exhortations did not buck the trend, however. Letters and visits continued to decline, and citizens began to engage in practices such as repeat complaining and collective petitioning, both of which signaled their frustration with the system.[127]

In sharp contrast to Bulgaria, prior to 1989 letters and visits in China were overwhelmingly an urban phenomenon,[128] because the welfare commitments of the socialist social contract did not extend to rural residents.[129] There

---

[126] *Renmin xinfang*, no. 22 (1985), 2–3; *Renmin xinfang*, no. 7 (1986), 2–8, 19; *Renmin xinfang*, no. 4 (1987), 3–4.

[127] *Renmin xinfang*, no. 1 (1988), 15–17; *Renmin xinfang*, no. 2 (1989), 38–40.

[128] Bivariate OLS regressions based on 1986 data on provincial-level complaints gathered by the author indicate that the strongest predictor of the volume of complaints across Chinese provinces is population density ($t = 4.59$; R-squared $= 0.44$), which is a proxy for the level of urbanization.

[129] Andrew G. Walder, *Communist Neo-Traditionalism: Work and Authority in Chinese Industry* (Berkeley: University of California Press, 1986); Nara Dillon, *Radical Inequalities: China's Revolutionary Welfare State in Comparative Perspective* (Cambridge, MA: Harvard University Asia Center, 2015).

was widespread discontent among China's urbanites in the second half of the 1980s. On the one hand, they were distressed by newly announced policies that indicated that they would no longer be entitled to lifetime employment and generous benefits, known as the "iron rice bowl" (*tie fan wan* 铁饭碗).[130] In addition, urban workers were worried about the rising double-digit inflation.[131] As in Bulgaria, the regime had reneged on the socialist social contract, and city residents signaled their discontent by complaining less often. Voluntary transmission of information was in crisis in the lead-up to Tiananmen.

Most striking about the decline in complaints in China is that it did not have systemwide effects similar to those in Eastern Europe. The letters-and-visits system was never used extensively: in 1979, the peak year for petitioning during the entire 1949–1989 period, the central complaints offices in China received 769 letters and visits per million people, which was 5.8 times less than the central-level petitions in East Germany (4,464 per million people) and in Bulgaria (4,494 per million people).[132] China had developed a limited form of a welfare state that extended only to some urban residents, thus insulating the regime from the implications of potential nationwide urban and rural discontent like that which had occurred in Eastern Europe. The absence of a welfare dictatorship also changed the relationship between citizens and the state: except for some urbanites in 1989,[133] most citizens did not rely on the government for welfare support. This thus meant that the implications of the state's reneging on the social contract would be limited to some segments of the one-fifth of the population who lived in the urban areas. Support for the regime was high except in those cities with universities.[134] This stood in sharp contrast to the wider social implications of the malfunctioning welfare state in Eastern Europe.

[130] See the 1986 Law on Enterprise Bankruptcy. Also see Chapter 19 of the 1988 Law on Industrial Enterprises Owned by the Whole People (adopted April 13, 1988, and effective August 1, 1988), which stipulates that state-owned enterprises may be abolished through dissolution or bankruptcy.

[131] This was also demonstrated by the 1987–1989 national probability sample urban opinion polls conducted by Yang Guansan at the Economic System Reform Institute of China, which was established by Zhao Ziyang in 1987. According to Wenfang Tang, in early 1989 Yang wrote a secret report to Zhao about his findings, but the warning came too late to have an effect. See Wenfang Tang, "The 'Surprise' of Authoritarian Resilience in China," *American Affairs*, 2:1 (Spring 2018), 101–17.

[132] Calculations based on data in Diao, *Renmin xinfang shilüe*, 260; Mühlberg, *Bürger, Bitten und Behörden*, 177; and the Bulgarian Central State Archives (TsDA) f. 1B op. 55 a. e. 940 (1983), 28.

[133] Andrew G. Walder, "Workers, Managers, and the State: The Reform Era and the Political Crisis of 1989," *The China Quarterly*, no. 127 (1991), 467–92.

[134] Zhang Liang, comp., *The Tiananmen Papers* (New York: Public Affairs, 2001), 149.

The central argument of this section is two-fold. First, voluntary provision was not as widespread in China as it was in Eastern Europe, thus making it more difficult for the regime to obtain nuanced assessments of latent discontent and engage in anticipatory governance. This created challenges for fostering conditional loyalty. Second, loyalty among urbanites diminished greatly prior to 1989, yet given the limited social contract, the effect of this development was more manageable than it was in Eastern Europe.

6.6 Minority Management

Minority penetration presented a problem for the regime. In the wake of the 1959 Uprising, Tibet and Xinjiang were managed through a mix of strategies that involved both repression and co-optation. Repression was consistently more severe in Tibet than it was in Xinjiang. Consequently, co-optation (measured by the share of CCP membership) was less successful in Tibet, where erosion of party strength occurred in the mid-1980s. Incentives for voluntary provision were also insufficient, as demonstrated by the declining share of corruption denunciations in Tibet in the lead-up to the 1987 protests that resulted in the imposition of martial law. Although the capacity of the party-state to penetrate Tibet did improve after the 1959 Uprising, the regime remained unable to anticipate discontent. Legibility was higher in Xinjiang due to the less repressive overall environment. The strength of the party, the saturation rate of the informant network, and the integration of minorities among the police proved especially consequential for improving monitoring capacity in Xinjiang in the years before Tiananmen. As we detail in Chapter 8, the 1990s provided a test of whether the party-state was capable of anticipatory governance in both Tibet and Xinjiang and the 2000s cemented the idea of pursuing an ethnic assimilation solution very similar to the one adopted in Bulgaria in the 1980s.

6.6.1 The 1959 Uprising

The Tibetan Uprising began on March 10, 1959, as a direct consequence of rumors that the PLA would abduct the Dalai Lama when entering a Lhasa military compound to attend a dance performance. This news led to the mobilization of thousands of people who blocked off the road, thus preventing the Dalai Lama from leaving his palace to attend the performance. Protests escalated quickly during the next several days, with calls for Tibetan independence and women gathering outside the palace to protect the Dalai Lama (who eventually fled to India on March 17). None of the facts, except the number of victims, are contested.

It is also beyond dispute that the leaders "for the most part were caught off-guard by the event."[135] It is true that Mao was presented with various briefs about dissent among Tibetans, but mainly outside of Tibet.[136] It is also true that reports on spy organizations in Tibet had circulated in 1957 and 1958.[137] There had even been an alert about an uprising in Shannan (Lhoka) in southeastern Tibet in January 1959.[138] Lhasa, however, appeared to be stable. Based on the available information, the center could not anticipate the timing and scope of the Tibetan Uprising.

Once the protests erupted, the top leadership could not decide on a course of action. The Tibet Party Committee informed Beijing about the uprising as early as March 10. Mao was, of course, apprised of the developments immediately, but the fact that he was away in Wuhan slowed down the deliberative process. On March 11–14, Liu Shaoqi, along with Zhou Enlai and Deng Xiaoping, organized various meetings to discuss the situation. However, the Politburo did not convene until March 17 (the day that the Dalai Lama set off for India) and the decision to suppress the uprising and implement democratic reforms (*minzhu gaige* 民主改革) in Tibet was not announced until March 22. During this time, *Neibu cankao* did not cover the uprising at all. Its first report was published on March 24, a full two weeks after the start of the upheaval.[139]

The high tide of reporting on Tibet in *Neibu cankao* spanned the period from the end of March 1959 to January 1960. Three thematic foci can be discerned during those months. One was the international reaction to the events, not only in neighboring states like India and in hostile territory like the United States, Taiwan, and Japan[140] but also throughout the socialist Bloc (the USSR, Czechoslovakia, Hungary, Romania, and even Vietnam).[141] The general tenor of foreign coverage was negative, some assurances of support in the socialist camp notwithstanding. The second line of reporting concerned domestic reactions to the events in non-Tibetan areas. Various social strata in these parts of China were, according to *Neibu cankao*, nearly universally supportive of central policies toward the uprising.[142] Most interesting was the third thematic focus,

---

[135] Jian Chen, "The Tibetan Rebellion of 1959 and China's Changing Relations with India and the Soviet Union," *Journal of Cold War Studies* 8:3 (2006), 54–101, at 72.

[136] Xiaoyuan Liu, *The End of Revolution: The Chinese Communist Party in Tibet, 1949–1959* (New York: Columbia University Press, 2020), 252–63; Chen, "The Tibetan Rebellion of 1959," 69–70.

[137] *Neibu cankao*, no. 2426 (February 28, 1958), 8–12; *Neibu cankao*, no. 2600 (October 7, 1958), 3–10.

[138] Xizang Zizhiqu Gong'an Ting, *Xizang gong'an dashiji, 1950–1995* (Lasa: Xizang Zizhiqu Gong'an Ting, 1999), 75–76.

[139] *Neibu cankao*, no. 2734 (March 24, 1959), 12–13, 15–16.

[140] *Neibu cankao*, no. 2735 (March 25, 1959), 2–18; *Neibu cankao*, no. 2735 (March 25, 1959), 19–24; *Neibu cankao*, no. 2736 (March 26, 1959), 12–28.

[141] *Neibu cankao*, no. 2760 (April 26, 1959), 22–23; *Neibu cankao*, no. 2760 (April 26, 1959), 24; *Neibu cankao*, no. 2761 (April 28, 1959), 22; *Neibu cankao*, no. 2763 (May 1, 1959), 22–24; *Neibu cankao*, no. 2769 (May 12, 1959), 20.

[142] *Neibu cankao*, no. 2740 (March 31, 1959), 3–5; *Neibu cankao*, no. 2742 (April 2, 1959), 8–16.

which centered on reactions in Tibet itself and in areas with compact Tibetan populations. There was ongoing concern about overt discontent among Tibetans in Sichuan, Qinghai, and southern Gansu after the suppression of the Lhasa Uprising.[143] These were areas that had previously experienced a high level of activity by counterrevolutionary groups, bandits, and spies, often aided by the CIA or by other "hostile foreign forces." In Tibet itself, the situation proved to be complex. Although residents of Shigatse, loyal to the Panchen Lama, predictably expressed support for central policies,[144] students in Lhasa were worried about the Dalai Lama.[145] Reports of guerrilla activities and reactionary leaflets throughout Tibet continued to be filed until the end of 1959.[146] Then, in January 1960, coverage of Tibet in *Neibu cankao* dropped to levels even lower than before the uprising. For the entire five-year period between January 1960 and December 1964, a total of only fifteen reports that had any relation to Tibet (one about Tibetans, five about Lhasa, and nine about Tibet) were filed. The uprising had been dealt with.

6.6.2 Learning from the Tibetan Uprising

The uprising led to a postmortem that revealed just how poorly penetrated the region had been prior to 1959. Less than a year after the upheaval, the Ethnic Affairs Office produced a statistical compendium on the situation of minorities in China.[147] This compendium highlights that as of 1958, Tibet had a population of 1,273,969, of which 110,000 were religious workers and fewer than 5,000 were communist party members.[148] Whereas party members grew to 5,864 in 1959,[149] the share of minorities in the CCP was halved in the wake of the uprising: they had constituted 28.4 percent in 1958 (1,190 out of 4,186 party members), but then dropped to 15 percent in 1959 (875 out of 5,864 members);[150] farmers and herders were extremely underrepresented, amounting to 0.9 percent of party members in 1959.[151] This was the lowest level of CCP penetration among any

---

[143] *Neibu cankao*, no. 2754 (April 19, 1959), 2–4; *Neibu cankao*, no. 2829 (July 23, 1959), 15–16; *Neibu cankao*, no. 2829 (July 23, 1959), 16.

[144] *Neibu cankao*, no. 2756 (April 22, 1959), 12–14.

[145] *Neibu cankao*, no. 2741 (April 1, 1959), 11.

[146] *Neibu cankao*, no. 2950 (January 1, 1960), 14–15.

[147] Guojia Minwei Bangongting, *Quanguo shaoshu minzu qingkuang tongji ziliao 1949–1959* (Beijing: Guojia Minwei Bangongting, February 1960).

[148] *Quanguo shaoshu minzu qingkuang*, 9, 115, 119.

[149] Yuan Siming, ed., *Zhongguo gongchandang Xizang gongzuo 50 nian* (Beijing: Zhongguo Zangxue Yanjiu Zhongxin Dangdai Yanjiusuo, 2004), 387–88.

[150] *Zhonggong Xizang difang zuzhishi zhigao*, 250; Yuan, *Zhongguo gongchandang Xizang gongzuo*, 387–88.

[151] Yuan, *Zhongguo gongchandang Xizang gongzuo*, 387–88.

Table 6.4 Political Prisoners in Tibet and in China Overall, 1965–1989

	Individuals Imprisoned for Counter-revolutionary Crimes (national level)	As % of all Prisoners (national level)	Individuals Imprisoned for Counter-revolutionary Crimes (Tibet)	As % of all Prisoners (Tibet)	National:Tibet Ratio
1965	353,713	40.6	5,007	80	1:1.97
1976	169,496	28.76	2,314	80.01	1:1.78
1978	148,930	20.97	2,223	79.99	1:3.81
1984	15,768	1.28	47	4.87	1:3.8
1989	5,774	0.51	46	4.42	1:8.67

Source: Sifa Bu Jianyu Guanli Ju, *Dangdai Zhongguo jianyu tongji ziliao (1949–1989)* (Beijing: Sifa Bu Jianyu Guanli Ju, November 1998).

major minority group. Additionally, traditional propaganda tools were not widely used in Tibet: only 8,000 copies of *Quotations from Chairman Mao* had been published in Tibetan by September 1959, and the first movie theater in the region did not open until 1958.[152] In short, Tibet had proven impenetrable and thus illegible for the CCP.

Instead of facilitating trust that would lead to the voluntary provision of information by citizens, initially the leadership preferred to handle Tibet by imposing an extraordinarily high level of repression, as is made clear by the statistics on political prisoners presented in Table 6.4. Tibetan prisons incarcerated a significantly higher proportion of individuals for counterrevolutionary crimes than the national average. Beyond imprisoning Tibetans, in the wake of the uprising, the CCP also decided to destroy the monasteries and to greatly reduce the number of monks and nuns. Thus, by March 1961, only 553 of the 2,676 monasteries in Tibet remained.[153] Monks and nuns were reduced from 110,000 to 7,000 by 1961.[154] Suspicions of Buddhism increased in the following decades.[155]

Another strategy for managing Tibet was party building. By September 1965, the CCP had tripled in size by comparison with 1958: it had 14,830 members,[156]

[152] *Quanguo shaoshu minzu qingkuang*, 323, 375.
[153] *Zhonggong Xizang difang zuzhishi zhigao*, 73.
[154] *Zhonggong Xizang difang zuzhishi zhigao*, 4 (foreword) and 73.
[155] Lin Le, "China's Perception of External Threats and Its Current Tibet Policy," *The China Journal*, no. 76 (2016), 103–23.
[156] *Zhonggong Xizang difang zuzhishi zhigao*, 252.

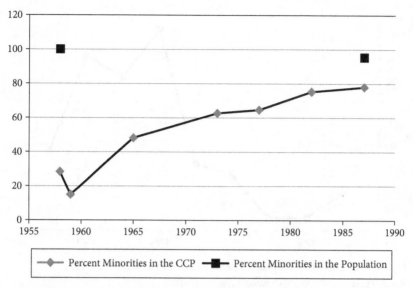

Figure 6.10 Share of minorities in the CCP in Tibet and in the general population in Tibet, 1958–1987.

Sources: Zhongguo gongchandang dangnei tongji ziliao huibian, 1921–2010, 11–16; Yuan, *Zhongguo gongchandang Xizang gongzuo 50 nian*, 387–88.

7,153 of whom belonged to ethnic minorities (48.23 percent).[157] The party also increased its presence in rural areas: one-third of its members in 1965 (4,349 individuals) were rural residents.[158] As we can see from Figure 6.10, the share of minorities recruited into the CCP continued to increase after 1965.

In addition, the party tried to promote voluntary information transfer by soliciting more complaints. As the available statistics on letters and visits to the Discipline Inspection Commission indicate, this initiative was increasingly successful for several years before all complaints work stopped in 1966 (see Figure 6.11).[159]

Information gathering can also be accomplished through informants. We do not know precisely how many police informants existed in the entire region of Tibet from the 1950s onward. But we do have some numerical indicators at

[157] Zhonggong Zhongyang Zuzhi Bu, *Zhongguo gongchandang dangnei tongji ziliao huibian, 1921–2010* (Beijing: Dangjian Duwu Chubanshe, 2011), 12.

[158] *Zhonggong Xizang difang zuzhishi zhigao*, 252. Given the small size of the party, however, only 0.36 percent of rural residents were CCP members in Tibet (as opposed to 1.73 percent nationally). See Zhonggong Zhongyang Zuzhi Bu, *Zhongguo gongchandang dangnei tongji ziliao huibian, 1921–2000* (Beijing: Zhonggong Zhongyang Zuzhi Bu Xinxi Guanli Zhongxin, 2002), 7. This source reports that the number of rural party members in Tibet in 1965 was 4,533.

[159] *Zhonggong Xizang difang zuzhishi zhigao*, 517–18.

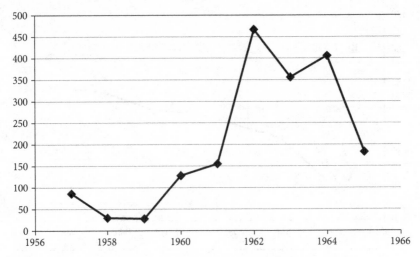

Figure 6.11 Discipline inspection denunciations in Tibet, 1957–1965.
Source: Zhonggong Xizang difang zuzhishi zhigao, 517–18.

the grassroots level. For example, a discussion in an internal police journal of the social-order protection committee of Samada village (population 1,700) in Kangma county reveals that in 1959 the committee had 13 members; membership expanded after the uprising and reached 19 in 1966.[160] The main function of the Samada social-order protection committee was to "collect, grasp, and report information on trends in enemy activities."[161] It is therefore beyond doubt that its members functioned as informants. The rate of roughly 1 informant per 130 residents in 1959 and 1 informant per 90 residents in 1966 in this Tibetan village is high by comparison with the size of the informant corps in Guangxi, for example, which had 1 informant per 233 residents in 1957,[162] but with the caveat that it is unconventional to compare a single village with an entire province.

Overall, the corps of full-time police officers and part-time informants allowed for a somewhat enhanced involuntary extraction of information after the 1959 Uprising. Though important, this could not be a substitute for voluntary transmission, which resumed in the form of denunciations after the Cultural Revolution but stayed very low in the 1980s (see Figure 6.12).[163] The lack of

[160] *Xizang gong'an*, no. 21 (1991/2), 2–4.

[161] *Xizang gong'an*, no. 21 (1991/2), 2.

[162] Calculated from data included in Guangxi Zhuangzu Zizhiqu Difang Zhi Bianzuan Weiyuanhui, *Guangxi tongzhi: Gong'an zhi* (Nanning: Guangxi Renmin Chubanshe, 2002), 551.

[163] In 1986, for example, only 106 letters and 4 visits were received by the discipline inspection authorities (see *Zhonggong Xizang difang zuzhishi zhigao*, 518).

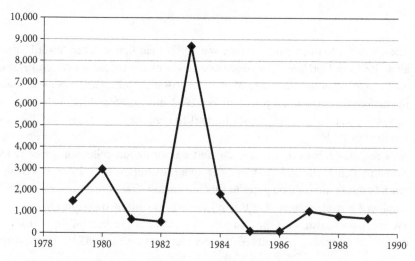

Figure 6.12 Discipline inspection denunciations in Tibet, 1979–1989.
Source: Zhonggong Xizang difang zuzhishi zhigao, 518.
NB: The peak in 1983 is related to the Strike Hard Campaign.

voluntary transmission reflects the incapacity of the CCP to build trust among the Tibetan population. The 1979 release of the 376 remaining 1959 Uprising prisoners and the removal of the designation of "rebels" (*panluan fenzi* 叛乱分子) from the more than 6,000 individuals who had undergone reeducation-through-labor after the uprising were steps in the right direction,[164] but the party remained unable to successfully penetrate the ethnic periphery. This is also highlighted by the fact that the share of CCP members as a proportion of the population in Tibet declined in 1982–1987 from 3.4 percent to 3.2 percent.[165] A general conclusion is that the ongoing use of brute force and the high levels of fear prevented the creation of institutions for the voluntary transmission of information that would have enabled the regime to monitor latent discontent and to anticipate its transformation into overt discontent. Involuntary extraction was also problematic. For those reasons, the 1987–1988 Lhasa riots, resulting in the imposition of martial law in March 1989, came as a surprise, just as the uprising back in 1959 had.[166]

[164] *Jianguo yilai gong'an gongzuo,* 423.
[165] *Zhongguo gongchandang dangnei tongji ziliao huibian, 1921–2010,* 15–16.
[166] *Jianguo yilai gong'an gongzuo,* 673, 685–86, 727–28.

6.6.3 Xinjiang

The approach to managing Xinjiang was softer than that adopted toward Tibet after the 1959 Uprising. One difference concerns the frequency of repression. As Table 6.5 indicates, the share of political prisoners in Xinjiang was lower than the national average for all years between 1952 and 1989 for which we have data, except 1976 and 1978. This stands in marked contrast to the trends in Tibet, as reported in Table 6.4.

A key reason for this trend is the better information-collection capacity in Xinjiang, which allowed for more selective prosecution of counterrevolutionaries. Several kinds of data point to this conclusion. One is that the Urumqi PSB employed a sizable share of ethnic minorities, as demonstrated in Figure 6.13. We also have statistics for the Urumqi city political protection police, which indicate that minorities constituted 22.6 percent of its staff in 1985.[167] It is difficult

Table 6.5 Political Prisoners in Xinjiang and in China Overall, 1952–1989

	Individuals Imprisoned for Counter-revolutionary Crimes (national level)	As % of All Prisoners (national level)	Individuals Imprisoned for Counter-revolutionary Crimes (Xinjiang)	As % of All Prisoners (Xinjiang)	National: Xinjiang Ratio
1951	326,497	37.4	ND	ND	
1952	512,252	47.47	1,996	43.16	1.1:1
1953	565,280	50.02	3,446	40.16	1.24:1
1956	604,532	48.05	3,741	40.91	1.17:1
1957	602,241	49.48	4,244	43.97	1.12:1
1958	800,027	42.96	4,818	27.24	1.58:1
1965	353,713	40.6	4,678	31.8	1.28:1
1976	169,496	28.76	5,046	31.32	0.9:1
1978	148,930	20.97	3,991	25.15	0.83:1
1984	15,768	1.28	247	1.04	1.23:1
1989	5,774	0.51	79	0.39	1.3:1

Source: Author's dataset.

[167] Wulumuqi Shi Gong'an Ju, *Wulumuqi gong'an zhi* (Urumqi: Xinjiang Renmin Chubanshe, 1998), 139.

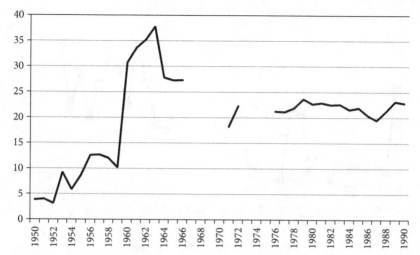

Figure 6.13 Percentage of minority police in the city of Urumqi, 1950–1990.
Source: Wulumuqi gong'an zhi, 135–37.

to interpret these numbers without a baseline. On the one hand, we can point out that both the overall share of minorities in the police and in the political-protection police declined over time. For political protection, the reduction was from 34.5 percent in 1953 to 22.6 percent in 1985; an even bigger drop occurred in the police overall, from a high of 37.8 percent in 1963 to a low of 19.5 percent in 1987.[168] At the same time, Urumqi was a predominantly Han city: in 1982, minorities made up 24.4 percent of its population.[169] It is clear from this statistic that the overall proportion of minorities in the PSB force, and, especially, in the political-protection division, was roughly on par with the share of non-Han residents in the city. This suggests that the extremely delicate issue of minority inclusion on the police force was handled thoughtfully during most of the pre-Tiananmen period.

Concerns about shortcomings in minority representation on the police force are further mitigated by the relatively stable size of the visible informant corps. In most years between 1951 and 1990, close to 1 percent of the population of Urumqi consisted of members of the social-order protection committees and the small groups. Although other cities had a higher penetration of the population (see Figure 6.14), Urumqi's record is, nevertheless, indicative of a stable capacity

[168] *Wulumuqi gong'an zhi*, 135–39.
[169] Ma Rong, "Population Distribution and Relations Among Ethnic Groups in the Kashgar Region, Xinjiang Uyghur Autonomous Region," in Robyn Iredale, Naran Bulik, and Fei Guo, eds., *China's Minorities on the Move: Selected Case Studies* (Armonk, NY: M.E. Sharpe, 2003), 105–22, at 112.

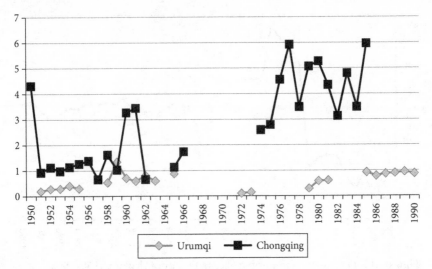

Figure 6.14 Membership in social-order protection committees and small groups as percentage of the population in Chongqing (1950–1985) and Urumqi (1951–1990).

Sources: Chongqing Shi Difang Zhi Bianzuan Weiyuanhui, *Chongqing shi zhi: Di 14 juan* (Chongqing: Xinan Shifan Daxue Chubanshe, 2005), 95–99; *Wulumuqi gong'an zhi*, 245.

to monitor the population. This applies both to the city and to the county of Urumqi. For example, a decision was made in 1964 in Urumqi County to register those suspected of political crimes and those endangering social order, to then open files on them, and to manage them according to type (*fenlei baoguan* 分类保管). This enabled a more granular approach to the targeted population roster. Very precise statistics on the targeted population list were kept during the decades after this decision was implemented.[170]

The substantial surveillance capacity in Urumqi explains the low incidence of political crime in the city. We possess data on political crimes for the period spanning 1949–1970. During this time, twenty-four political cases were detected each year.[171] By contrast, in the Xinjiang Production and Construction Corps (which had a population twice as large as that of Urumqi), 118 cases were detected per year during the period for which we have systematic data (1958–1965).[172] Political crime (organizing counterrevolutionary groups, distributing

---

[170] Wulumuqi Xian Gong'an Zhi Bianzuan Lingdao Xiaozu, *Wulumuqi xian gong'an zhi* (Urumqi: Xinjiang Renmin Chubanshe, 1997), 230–32.

[171] Calculated on the basis of data in *Wulumuqi gong'an zhi*, 165.

[172] Calculated from data in *Xinjiang shengchan jianshe bingtuan gong'an zhi* (Urumqi: Xinjiang Shengchan Jianshe Bingtuan Gong'an Zhi and Xinjiang Shengchan Jianshe Bingtuan Difang Zhi Bangongshi, 1999), 185. Police sources give no reason to believe that police capacity to detect political crimes in the Xinjiang Production and Construction Corps was superior to that in Urumqi.

Table 6.6 Political Cases in the City of Urumqi, 1979–1990

	Counterrevolutionary	Reactionary Leaflets	Anonymous Letters	Correspondence	Reactionary Rumors	Sabotage	Other	TOTAL
1979				1			1	2
1980				1			6	7
1981		7	2	7	2			18
1982		4	1	5	1			11
1983		1	1	4			4	10
1984	5	1	4				9	19
1985		4		7			1	12
1986		1	2	4			2	9
1987		1					6	7
1988		1	1	1				3
1989		32	8		22	1	5	68
1990	1	8	2				2	13

Source: Statistics on Political Crime in the People's Republic of China, Occasional Publications of the Dui Hua Foundation, No. 7 (April 2001), 20.

reactionary posters, writing anonymous letters, maintaining overseas correspondence, spreading reactionary rumors, and engaging in acts of sabotage and
treason) remained limited in Urumqi up until the Tiananmen Spring, as indicated by Table 6.6.

A final feature of the Xinjiang model is the more highly saturated party network than that which existed in Tibet. Although the slope of the increase in party
membership (as a percentage of the population) was steeper in Tibet than it was
in Xinjiang in the 1960s and 1970s, party size in Xinjiang remained consistently
higher relative to Tibet; also, the minority share in the CCP in Xinjiang came
closer to the minority share in the general population in Xinjiang than it did in
Tibet (see Figures 6.15 and 6.16). Most important, whereas Tibet experienced a
decline in party membership as a percentage of the population in the 1980s, no
similar erosion can be detected in Xinjiang. In short, co-optation in Xinjiang
was superior to that in Tibet. As a result, the level of overt discontent in Xinjiang
was considerably lower than that in Tibet up until 1989. The 1990s brought new
challenges, which will be discussed in Chapter 8.

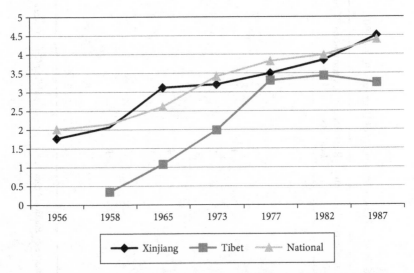

Figure 6.15 Increase in CCP membership, as a percentage of the population in
Tibet (1958–1987), Xinjiang (1956–1987), and nationwide (1958–1987).

Sources: Nationwide (1956–1987), Xinjiang (1956–1987), and Tibet (1965–1987): *Zhongguo
gongchandang dangnei tongji ziliao huibian, 1921–2010*, 11–16; Tibet 1958: *Zhonggong Xizang difang
zuzhishi zhigao*, 250.

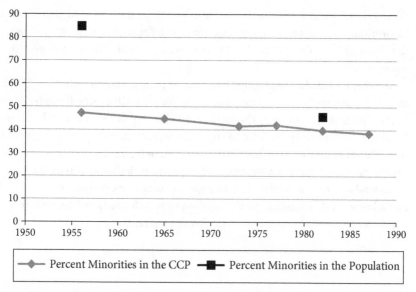

Figure 6.16 Minority share of the CCP in Xinjiang and in the general population in Xinjiang, 1958–1987.

Sources: Zhongguo gongchandang dangnei tongji ziliao huibian, 1921–2010, 11–16; Quanguo shaoshu minzu qingkuang tongji ziliao, 7.

To sum up, although penetration capacity varied to a certain extent, the legibility of territorially concentrated ethnoreligious minorities was an ongoing concern for the CCP. Different strategies were deployed toward the Uyghurs and the Tibetans. In Xinjiang, both surveillance capacity and minority co-optation were more successful, thus explaining the lower incidence of overt discontent relative to Tibet.

6.7   Conclusions

This chapter has analyzed the development of institutions for the involuntary collection and voluntary provision of information on popular discontent during the second, third, and fourth decades of the communist regime in China. Perhaps most surprising is that the existing institutions withstood the onslaught of the Great Leap Forward and the Cultural Revolution. It is not widely appreciated that although some had to suspend operation for years, many managed to survive and continued to collect information even during those disruptive episodes in China's political trajectory. Moreover, new institutions for the involuntary collection of information were created after the death of Mao. Cumulatively, this enabled a gradual transition to selective repression.

The chapter has also highlighted two lacunae in information collection. One is minority penetration, which was a blind spot for the CCP, especially with regard to the Tibetans. The other is the lackluster voluntary provision, which diminished the capacity of the regime to engage in anticipatory governance. Overall, information collection remained patchy and incomplete. The low levels of voluntary provision explain why although repression declined, it remained at a considerably higher level than that in Eastern Europe: the regime knew less and had a lower level of conditional loyalty than its counterparts in Eastern Europe, which necessitated a more frequent deployment of repression.

PART IV
SIMILAR CRISES, VARIED CONTEXTS, DIFFERENT REFORMS

Part IV discusses the divergent paths of the two countries after the crisis of 1989. The anticipatory information-gathering institutions in Bulgaria had issued warnings of the transformation of latent into overt discontent, but the incumbent was unable to assert control through either repression or redistribution. Elite insiders used their access to this information to stage a palace coup. Though he was aware of the preparations, the incumbent could not stop them. A process of democratization began that culminated in the opposition winning the elections at the end of 1991. Solving the dictator's dilemma in Bulgaria could not ensure the indefinite survival of either the incumbent or the regime. In China, the crisis of 1989 (which was largely unanticipated) could be handled through repression due to its more limited scope and the fact that soft-liners were a minority within the elite. Following suppression of the protests, ideological subversion became a top concern. It was counteracted by the promotion of indigenous cultural consumption and the introduction of a market social contract featuring welfare commitments that were universal in application but limited in scope. Low responsiveness to welfare concerns institutionalized disruptive protests rather than routine petitioning as the dominant mechanism for communicating grievances, thus further heightening regime insecurity. Technological advances facilitated a rapid police response by the end of the 2000s, thus allowing the regime to prevent the transformation of protests into upheavals. Having solved the mass constraint, regime insiders moved ahead with ethnic assimilation in the 2010s. By the arrival of COVID-19, China had developed the most sophisticated state capacity of any communist regime ever extant, yet information gathering rested overwhelmingly on involuntary extraction. Time will tell how long such a system based on routine disruptive contentious episodes can persist.

Several theoretically relevant conclusions that emerge from the two chapters should be highlighted. The Bulgarian case demonstrates that the dictator's dilemma can be solved, but this does not necessarily mean that the incumbent can avoid being deposed. A second finding is that information-gathering institutions can persist after the end of a dictatorship whose demise they have foretold—this occurred in Bulgaria and helped preclude an immediate win by the opposition in the first competitive elections in the democratizing postcommunist regime. The final theoretical insight from the Bulgarian case is that assimilation is not an optimal solution of the problem of ethnic minority impenetrability—grievances persist and, should they be visibly expressed, can destabilize the regime. All three findings have direct relevance for China's future.

The Chinese case similarly yields several theoretically relevant conclusions. One concerns the capacity of market communist regimes to survive with relatively low levels of voluntary provision of information through the complaints system and a high frequency of disruptive protests. This equilibrium would never have been possible in the centrally planned communist regimes but has persisted thus far in China. We should stress that complaints have declined, but not disappeared; they still play a role even in the age of social media. Second, the case of China demonstrates that technological advances do not obviate the need for human intelligence collectors—quite the opposite: China had a rate of counterintelligence informant penetration in the 2010s that was never matched by any communist regime in history. Finally, China shows that the advent of social media has not made internal reporting obsolete. On the contrary, leaders in the 2010s were even more dependent on internal media than before, as they had to use them to make sense of both online and offline dissent. Despite the extraordinary economic changes in China, the core of its classic communist information-gathering infrastructure persists.

7

Information-Gathering Institutions in Bulgaria, 1989–1991

One of the most consequential decisions in communist autocracies concerns the number of names on the list of recipients of classified information. Although the dictator may be able to restrict access to foreign and military intelligence or to reporting on coup-plotting attempts by the top elite, confidential information about levels of popular discontent has wider circulation, reaching from several dozen to as many as several hundred top-level recipients. This is a product of necessity: whereas findings about coup-plotting must remain top secret, intelligence about discontent cannot be passed along to only one recipient, as this would very rapidly overwhelm the capacity to make decisions. When the system operates with a sufficiently high level of responsiveness, a relatively wide circulation of classified intelligence is essential for anticipatory governance, which is contingent on addressing dissatisfaction during its latent stage. However, when responsiveness declines and popular discontent becomes unmanageable, information circulation enables those in the inner circle to plan a palace coup in light of the reporting about overt discontent. The tragic brilliance of the system is that the dictator is apprised of coup attempts but cannot stop them once a majority of his inner circle commits to join them.

This chapter analyzes how communist autocracies handle a crisis when sophisticated systems for the collection of information transmit detailed intelligence about a growing incapacity to manage overt discontent. The most consequential effect is that time horizons become extremely narrow: instead of strategic long-term thinking, elites are oriented toward short-term goals. In an attempt to hang on to power, the inner circle is willing to accept an increasingly more limited set of wins. Initially, the position of the dictator and the future of the system are fused. But the coup-plotters may decide that the incumbent should be replaced in order to preserve the single-party system. Subsequently, they may introduce competitive elections (thus relinquishing single-party rule), with the hope of decisive wins. Yet, if they only secure a modest win, the next step might be to agree to form a coalition government so as not to be forced to step down in response to popular protests. Ultimately, however, the party may be voted out of office, with elites agreeing to relinquish power and monetize their political capital by entering party-sponsored business ventures. Although this chapter focuses on

Dictatorship and Information. Martin K. Dimitrov, Oxford University Press. © Oxford University Press 2023.
DOI: 10.1093/oso/9780197672921.003.0007

Bulgaria in 1989–1991, parallel processes also began to unfold in 1989 in other Eastern European regimes.

This chapter makes several theoretical contributions. First, it demonstrates that solving the dictator's dilemma should not be equated with preserving the dictator's position. To prevent an ouster, the dictator must manage the popular threat (through the deployment of repression and redistribution) and eliminate coup attempts at their incipient stage, when they involve only one or two members of the inner circle. If popular discontent is rampant, the dictator may lose his or her grip over the inner circle and find him- or herself in the minority, thus facing an elevated risk of ouster. A byproduct of solving the dictator's dilemma is that information about discontent must circulate broadly among the elite, thus making it possible for the inner circle to engage in collective action against the incumbent when available intelligence indicates that a crisis point in the management of popular dissatisfaction has been reached. This finding highlights the need for existing theory to move beyond simple notions of the presence or absence of information and to examine both its content and the extent of its circulation.

Second, the chapter shows that reacting to available information in a situation of crisis is not always compatible with regime preservation. The actions of decision makers in Bulgaria in 1989–1991 displayed short-run rationality but did not help ensure resilience over the long term. Quite the opposite: with the benefit of hindsight, it is obvious that the net effect of the liberalization policies implemented in Bulgaria bears a striking resemblance to what scholars working on Taiwan and South Korea have described as "democratization from strength."[1] Unsurprisingly, initiating political liberalization sets the stage for the eventual surrender of power. However, the duration of this process varies: in Taiwan, it extended over thirteen years (1987–2000, with competitive elections taking place in 1996 and 2000); in Bulgaria, it lasted three years (1989–1991, with competitive elections in 1990 and 1991); and in the German Democratic Republic (GDR), it was completed within a single year. Although elites may hope for a prolonged transition (giving them sufficient time to develop an exit strategy), when democratization is initiated, it is impossible to foresee whether the process will unfold as speedily as it did in the GDR or as slowly as it did in Taiwan. In sum, moments of crisis make long-term planning exceedingly difficult. This does not mean that short-term decision making is uninformed or irrational.

Finally, although some of the institutions for collecting information were dissolved during the process of democratization in the GDR and the Soviet

---

[1] Dan Slater and Joseph Wong, "The Strength to Concede: Ruling Parties and Democratization in Developmental Asia," *Perspectives on Politics* 11:3 (September 2013), 717–33; Rachel Beatty Riedl, Dan Slater, Joseph Wong, and Daniel Ziblatt, "Authoritarian-Led Democratization," *Annual Review of Political Science* 23 (2020), 315–32.

Union, this did not occur in Bulgaria, where State Security, the party, and the media continued to supply intelligence to insiders, allowing them to engage in informed decision making as regime transformation was unfolding. Because these institutions are essential for regime preservation, it is worth considering whether the GDR would have lasted longer had the Stasi not been dissolved in December 1989 or whether the banning of the Communist Party of the Soviet Union (CPSU) after the August 1991 putsch accelerated the dissolution of the Soviet state. The relevant theoretical point here is that information-gathering institutions can outlast the single-party system that they are meant to serve and they can adapt to the needs of elites in a competitive authoritarian setting. This is another reminder that the relationship between information and regime resilience is complex and that the demise of communist autocracies may take place despite the persistence of information-gathering institutions that supply copious amounts of intelligence on issues that are of vital interest to the top decision makers.

A meta-theoretical point focuses on whether Bulgaria could have preserved its single-party welfare dictatorship had it carried out Chinese-style economic reforms. As this chapter shows, nearly every reform that was implemented in China prior to 1989 was also introduced in Bulgaria, in some cases decades earlier than in the People's Republic of China (PRC). However, these policies had limited effectiveness in the Bulgarian context due to different initial conditions, which fueled higher expectations of relative improvements in the standards of living in Bulgaria as opposed to those expectations in China. The other limitation of the reforms in Bulgaria was its more extensive central planning system, which made it difficult to restructure the state-owned enterprises (SOEs) without unleashing a widespread strike wave (this is indeed what happened when enterprise privatization occurred in the 1990s). The general point is that fundamental economic reforms were seen by the population as reneging on the socialist social contract. Thus, Chinese-style economic restructuring (which was indeed introduced) could not have saved the single-party system. The political liberalization unleashed in 1987–1989 depleted the repressive capacity of the regime, making it impossible to contemplate a nationwide crackdown in case of widespread organized protests resulting from economic dissatisfaction.

This chapter is organized as follows. Section 7.1 examines the Bulgarian crisis of 1989 that culminated with the formal end of single-party rule in January 1990. Section 7.2 analyzes whether Chinese-style economic reforms might have preserved single-party rule in Bulgaria. Section 7.3 details the series of decisions in 1990–1991 that resulted in the eventual electoral defeat of the party in October 1991. Section 7.4 focuses on the persistence of information-gathering institutions past 1989. Section 7.5 offers summary conclusions.

7.1 The End of Single-Party Rule in Bulgaria: January 1989–January 1990

When Bulgaria entered 1989 in the midst of limited political reforms that were unfolding against the background of economic stagnation, there were no indications that the single-party system would be eliminated within a year. The crucial factor that made the end of communist rule possible was the November 1989 palace coup. We should note that the successful execution of a coup is exceedingly rare: in fact, Zhivkov's ouster in 1989 is the only case of radical and prompt sidelining of a leader in Bulgaria's single-party regime trajectory.[2] The decision to begin coup preparations was taken in the summer of 1989 by several Politburo members. Their calculus was informed by secret reports they were receiving on domestic political unrest and economic grievances, as well as the evolving international situation. Importantly, Zhivkov was aware of the plot, but he could not stop it. This section provides further details on how the exit from communist rule unfolded and the role that information played in shaping the decision making of the coup-plotters, of the incumbent, and of the new leadership that assumed power in November 1989 and then moved to formally abolish the single-party system in January 1990.

7.1.1 Economic Stagnation and Popular Disaffection

Economic stagnation began in 1984 and became progressively worse as the regime moved toward 1989.[3] Several trends were detected by the information collectors and were transmitted through routine reports to Zhivkov and to other members of the elite. One was the rapid decline of citizen complaints (from 675,911 in 1984 to 334,408 in 1988),[4] which was correctly interpreted as an index of the eroding trust of citizens in the capacity of the regime to satisfy their requests for welfare.[5] The second was based on opinion polling, which indicated that as perestroika progressed in Bulgaria, *fewer* respondents agreed that it was proceeding well.[6] The drops in citizen self-assessments of personal

---

[2] The first general secretary (Georgi Dimitrov) died in office in 1949. The second (Valko Chervenkov) was demoted in 1954 to number two in the hierarchy, but he kept that powerful position until 1956. Zhivkov was the third general secretary, serving from 1954 until 1989.

[3] Martin K. Dimitrov, "Economic Shocks and Communist Regime Survival and Collapse," in Victor Shih, ed., *Economic Shocks and Authoritarian Stability: Duration, Financial Control, and Institutions* (Ann Arbor: University of Michigan Press, 2020), 41–71.

[4] Bulgarian Central State Archives (TsDA) f. 1B op. 55 a. e. 943 (1984), 8; TsDA f. 1B op. 55 a. e. 953 (1989), 3.

[5] Georgi Chukrin, *Zapiski ot totalitarnoto vreme: Kraiat* (Sofia: Iztok–Zapad, 2007), 85.

[6] TsDA f. 1B op. 55 a. e. 857 (February 2, 1989), 8. In November 1987, 55 percent of the respondents to a nationally representative poll of 2,444 adult Bulgarians thought that perestroika was progressing well; by October 1988, only 40 percent of respondents agreed with this statement.

well-being were precipitous: by October 1988, as many as 60 percent of the youth thought their standard of living was low, up from 25 percent in 1985.[7] The third trend was a foreign debt crisis: the reduction in Soviet oil shipments, which were valued at $2 billion per year in world prices, contributed to a rapid accumulation of $10 billion in foreign debt in 1985–1989 (equivalent to one full year of GDP).[8] According to a top-secret letter from the Central Bank that was circulated to Politburo members as coup-plotting commenced in July 1989, Bulgaria had no further export capacity and could no longer secure additional foreign loans or make payments on its existing obligations to the West.[9] A second letter from the Central Bank to the Politburo in October 1989 reiterated the gravity of the situation.[10] Thus, when regime soft-liners removed Zhivkov on November 10, 1989, they did so knowing that the country was facing bankruptcy. They were also aware that the economic liberalization measures paving the way for a transition from plan to market that had been promulgated in 1987–1989 were deeply unpopular with the citizenry, who feared that such measures would usher in unemployment and economic inequality.[11]

7.1.2 Public Protests as a Consequence of Political Liberalization

In 1987–1989, the regime promulgated a package of political liberalization measures. These included the introduction of semi-competitive grassroots elections (held in 1988),[12] media openness (which extended to the suspension of jamming of Western radio broadcasts in January 1989),[13] and the end of compulsory mass rallies (thus putting an end to "as if" compliance).[14] Although some of the policies were popular,[15] their net effect was to facilitate antiregime mobilization, especially because the liberalization measures sanctioned the creation of independent nongovernmental organizations (NGOs), which were, of course, thoroughly infiltrated with State Security informants.[16] The first NGO

---

[7] TsDA f. 1B op. 55 a. e. 857 (February 2, 1989), 50.

[8] TsDA f. 1B op. 100 a. e. 76 (1989), 8–9.

[9] TsDA f. 132P op. 15 a. e. 2 (July 18, 1989), 1–4.

[10] TsDA f. 132P op. 15 a. e. 10 (October 19, 1989), 3–4.

[11] TsDA f. 1B op. 55 a. e. 853 (December 1988), 24

[12] TsDA f. 1B op. 55 a. e. 691 (April 1988).

[13] TsDA f. 1B op. 64 a. e. 909 (March 23, 1989).

[14] *Rabotnichesko delo*, no. 212 (July 31, 1987), 1. On "as if" compliance, see Lisa Wedeen, *Ambiguities of Domination: Politics, Rhetoric, and Symbols in Contemporary Syria* (Chicago: University of Chicago Press, 1999).

[15] TsDA f. 1B op. 55 a. e. 651 (August 17, 1987); TsDA f. 1b op. 55 a. e. 623 (December 1987).

[16] See documents reproduced in Stefan Doinov, compiler, *Shesto upravlenie sreshtu neformalnite organizatsii v Bulgariia: Dokumentalen sbornik s materiali ot arkhivite na MVR i Tsentralniia durzhaven arkhiv* (Sofia: Fondatsiia Dr. Zheliu Zhelev, 1999).

was established in March 1988 to protect the Danubian city of Ruse from the spewing of toxic gases from a chemical plant located across the river in the Romanian city of Giurgiu. Subsequent NGOs included the Club for Support of Glasnost and Perestroika; the independent labor union *Podkrepa* (Support); and the *Ecoglasnost* movement, which organized demonstrations during the October 16 to November 3, 1989, Ecoforum held in Sofia under the auspices of the Conference on Security and Cooperation.

The most significant challenges to regime stability in Bulgaria emerged not from the Bulgarian ethnic majority but rather from the mobilization of the Turkish minority. In May 1989, antiregime demonstrations broke out in a number of villages, small towns, and mid-sized cities in areas with substantial minority populations. Estimates of the total number of participants vary, but they were certainly in the tens of thousands,[17] thus exceeding the size of the ecological protests that occurred in Ruse in 1987–1988 and in Sofia in October–November 1989. In contrast to the handling of the ecological movement, the Turkish unrest was brutally suppressed through the use of tear gas, pressurized water mixed with grit, blank bullets, and the manhandling of protesters by special riot control troops. At least several dozen Turks died during the suppression of the protests, in contradistinction to the ecological demonstrations, where there was not a single victim. Several high-profile minority leaders were extradited to the West.[18] Despite all these measures, the leadership felt that the situation was slipping out of control. Thus, Zhivkov declared on national TV on May 29, 1989, that the Turks were free to move to Turkey either temporarily or permanently.[19] Unable to solve the problem of minority discontent through the use of force, the top leadership decided to expel its Turkish citizens. This was a sign of weakness rather than strength.

Although one might expect that the dissidents among the Bulgarian majority would support the antiregime mobilization of the minority, most of the newly emerging Bulgarian NGOs did not embrace the Turkish cause. Due to disagreement among its core leadership on whether to engage with the Turkish grievances, the most important opposition group, the Club for Support of Glasnost and Perestroika, did not file a protest petition with the National Assembly until July 1989, a full two months after the suppression of the Turkish dissent. No further engagement with the Turkish cause occurred until after Zhivkov's ouster in November 1989. Although the leaders of some smaller provincial NGOs, such as the *Podkrepa* trade union and the Independent Organization for Defense of

---

[17] Veselin Angelov, ed., *Sekretno! Protestnite aktsii na turtsite v Bulgariia, januari–mai 1989: Dokumenti* (Sofia: Veselin Angelov, 2009), 8–56.

[18] Angelov, ed., *Sekretno! Protestnite aktsii na turtsite v Bulgariia*.

[19] Todor Zhivkov, "Edinstvoto na bulgarskiia narod e grizha i sudba na vseki grazhdanin na nasheto milo otechestvo," *Rabotnichezko delo*, no. 150 (May 30, 1989), 1.

Human Rights, openly sympathized with the Turkish movement, these NGOs did not have the moral clout of the capital-based Club for Support of Glasnost and Perestroika. The leaders of these provincial NGOs were imprisoned in the late spring and were not released until the early fall, when the Turkish protests had already subsided. Instead of forming a cross-ethnic alliance, the Turkish and Bulgarian NGOs advanced discrete agendas. This is similar to the April–June 1989 Tiananmen Square protests in China, when students and workers presented separate demands to the leadership instead of developing a unified platform.[20]

The decision to expel the Turks from Bulgaria at the end of May 1989 ushered in a full-blown crisis, as hundreds of thousands of people rushed to leave the country in the summer. Through its policies, the party had managed to deplete its stock of popular support by progressively alienating large segments of the population, including virtually the entire Turkish minority. The exodus ended in August, when Turkey unilaterally closed its borders. However, by that point more than one-third of the minority had already left the country and those remaining were making preparations to depart. The costs were economic (depleting the agricultural and manufacturing workforce) and political (extreme dissatisfaction with the system). This increased domestic pressure to explosive levels and strengthened the resolve of the coup-plotters to remove Zhivkov from power.

7.1.3 Alienating the Mid-Level Elites: Reducing the *Nomenklatura* and Eliminating Privileges

The most influential theories of authoritarianism emphasize the importance of elite loyalty for maintaining regime stability.[21] Although Zhivkov had skillfully nurtured unity until perestroika, a series of policies that he introduced in 1987–1989 alienated sizable portions of the elite. Most damaging was the August 1987 decision to implement administrative reforms. As a result of the restructuring, the number of provinces was cut from twenty-eight to eight, leading to a reduction in the size of the *nomenklatura* cadres by two-fifths.[22] Although these administrative reforms sought to reduce bloat in the party-state, they also alienated mid-level *apparatchiks*, who lost their sinecures as a result of the restructuring.

[20] Andrew G. Walder and Gong Xiaoxia, "Workers in the Tiananmen Protests," *Australian Journal of Chinese Affairs*, no. 29 (January 1993), 1–29.

[21] Jennifer Gandhi, *Political Institutions under Dictatorship* (New York: Cambridge University Press, 2008); Bruce Bueno de Mesquita and Alastair Young, "Political Survival and Endogenous Change," *Comparative Political Studies* 42:2 (January 2009), 167–97; Milan W. Svolik, *The Politics of Authoritarian Rule* (New York: Cambridge University Press, 2012).

[22] In 1977, there were 4,822 full-time *nomenklatura* positions in the party *apparat* at the central, provincial, district, and major enterprise levels in Bulgaria (party secretaries of basic party organizations are not included in this number). By 1989, there were only 2,925 (a reduction of 39.5 percent). See TsDA f. 1B op. 55 a. e. 222 (May 1989), 25.

Similar measures were introduced in other Eastern Bloc regimes, with identical effects.[23] By contrast, the norm for the retirement of revolutionaries in China and several successive reforms in the 1990s aimed at limiting the size of the *nomenklatura* did not destabilize the system.[24] These different outcomes reveal that limiting the size of the winning coalition by alienating members of the elite during difficult economic times is dangerous for regime stability—the booming economy in China created employment opportunities for laid-off cadres that were simply not present in Bulgaria or the Soviet Union in 1987–1989. But the experience of China also points to the importance of sequencing *nomenklatura* reforms by forcing the old guard to retire first and only then reducing the size of the mid-level *nomenklatura*, a strategy that neither Bulgaria nor the Soviet Union adopted.

The Bulgarian regime also introduced further reforms that led to a loss of loyalty among even larger segments of the elite. In 1987, the status of "active fighters against fascism and capitalism" was abolished.[25] This end of privileges affected not only the 88,000 active fighters (equivalent to 1 percent of the population), but their families as well. Other measures introduced in 1987 included an attempt to curtail the expense accounts and entertainment allowances of the top party and state leadership and to eliminate the designations "people's" (*naroden*) and "distinguished service" (*zasluzhil*), which were reserved for actors, painters, singers, and other artists.[26] Public discontent with the rise of a privileged elite was so widespread that a movie shot in 1986–1987 contained a comment that was labeled subversive: "All revolutions are directed against a privileged class."[27] These measures enjoyed public support,[28] but they were deeply unpopular with party cadres. The disaffected elites were then more likely to join the budding NGOs and turn against the regime.

---

[23] Jonathan Harris, *Subverting the System: Gorbachev's Reform of the Party's Apparat, 1986–1991* (Lanham, MD: Rowman & Littlefield, 2003). See also Philip Roeder, *Red Sunset: The Failure of Soviet Politics* (Princeton, NJ: Princeton University Press, 1993); Steven L. Solnick, "The Breakdown of Hierarchies in the Soviet Union and China: A Neoinstitutional Perspective," *World Politics* 48:2 (January 1996), 209–38; and Steven Solnick, *Stealing the State: Control and Collapse in Soviet Institutions* (Cambridge, MA: Harvard University Press, 1998).

[24] Melanie Manion, *Retirement of Revolutionaries in China: Public Policies, Social Norms, Private Interests* (Princeton, NJ: Princeton University Press, 1993); John P. Burns, "Strengthening Central CCP Control of Leadership Selection: The 1990 *Nomenklatura*," *The China Quarterly*, no. 138 (1994), 458–91; John P. Burns "'Downsizing' the Chinese State: Government Retrenchment in the 1990s," *The China Quarterly*, no. 175 (2003), 775–802.

[25] Martin K. Dimitrov, *Politicheskata logika na sotsialisticheskoto potreblenie* (Sofia: Ciela, 2018), 135–38.

[26] "Za neobkhodimostta ot dulboki promeni v atributite na vlastta v suotvetstvie s resheniiata na Iulskiia plenum (1987) na TsK na BKP," *Rabotnichesko delo*, no. 223 (August 11, 1987).

[27] This politically sensitive movie was not released in theaters until 1989. See *Margarit i Margarita*, director Nikolai Volev (Sofia: Studio Boiana, 1989).

[28] TsDA f. 1B op. 55 a. e. 651 (August 17, 1987); TsDA f. 1B op. 11 vr. a. e. 4 (August 23–30, 1987).

7.1.4 The External Factor

Liberalization in Bulgaria was influenced by diffusion dynamics from the Soviet Union and other Eastern European regimes.[29] China's status as an outsider vis-à-vis the Eastern Bloc explains why *negative* diffusion did not take place in the aftermath of the Tiananmen crackdown in June 1989: the massacre in faraway Beijing was simply irrelevant to protesters in Sofia, whereas successful regime transformation in neighboring countries such as Poland and Hungary was quite salient.[30] Could the Bulgarian dictatorship have survived had the Soviet Union continued to extend economic assistance and had it not encouraged the coup-plotters in 1989? Recently released Soviet documents demonstrate that the Soviet leadership was informed of the ongoing economic difficulties in 1988–1989 by its newly appointed ambassador to Sofia (Major General Viktor Sharapov, a Committee for State Security [KGB] operative, whose rapid career ascent had begun as an assistant to Andropov). The Soviet embassy received copies of confidential documents that were discussed by the Bulgarian Politburo,[31] dispatched regular updates on the parlous state of the economy to the Kremlin,[32] encouraged the coup-plotters,[33] and dissuaded Zhivkov from trying to hang on to power.[34] Although the regime probably would not have survived even if it had had Soviet support, the actions of the Soviet Union in 1984–1989 (and especially in 1988–1989) served as a catalyst for a speedier transition.

7.1.5 Information Flow in the Final Months before Regime Collapse

The archives produce a major discovery, namely, an important change occurred in the information transmitted to the top leadership in the early fall of 1989. Up until that point, Todor Zhivkov had been designated as "Recipient No. 1" of the most sensitive State Security reports. In September 1989, Zhivkov's name was stricken from a report that was meant to be sent to him as Recipient No. 1;

---

[29] Valerie Bunce, *Subversive Institutions: The Design and the Destruction of Socialism and the State* (New York: Cambridge University Press, 1999).

[30] Martin K. Dimitrov, "European Lessons for China: Tiananmen 1989 and Beyond," in Kyrill Kunakhovich and Piotr Kosicki, eds., *The Long 1989: Decades of Global Revolution* (New York: Central European University Press, 2019), 61–88.

[31] *Konets epokhi: SSSR i revoliutsii v stranakh Vostochnoi Evropy v 1989–1991 gg.: Dokumenty* (Moscow: Rosspen, 2015), 736–43, 746–51.

[32] *Konets epokhi*, 752–57.

[33] Kostadin Chakarov, *Ot vtoriia etazh kum nashestvieto na demokratite* (Sofia: Trud, 2001), 167, 171.

[34] Kostadin Chakarov, *Vtoriiat etazh* (Sofia: Plamuk, 1990), 106–7; Chakarov, *Ot vtoriia etazh*, 171–72.

instead, former Minister of the Interior (and current Politburo member) Dimitar Stoianov became Recipient No. 1. The information was sent to Zhivkov, but with a two-day delay.[35] By the summer of 1989, a majority of the Politburo was planning to oust Zhivkov.[36] Prompt intelligence on domestic developments was essential both for planning the coup and for defending against it. The plotters were aware of the rapidly increasing public discontent and the rise of NGOs,[37] because State Security provided this information to them immediately.

As with the ongoing coup preparations, Zhivkov was aware of the information-transmission delay and registered his displeasure in a letter he sent to the head of State Security.[38] Regardless, the pattern continued throughout the fall, when a subset of the Politburo was receiving briefs about domestic developments a day or two before the same information reached Zhivkov and the rest of the Politburo.[39] Even more interesting than this strategic delay of information on domestic developments is that intelligence on political instability in the Eastern Bloc was immediately transmitted to Zhivkov, who received reports of Honecker's impending ouster days before it happened.[40] Zhivkov was likewise extremely well briefed on developments in Poland and Czechoslovakia.[41] He continued to receive regular dispatches from the party along with internal media digests, which primarily covered the same issues as the delayed State Security reports.

How can we interpret this unanticipated discovery about the tardy transmission of State Security information on domestic instability and the prompt briefing on international developments? Some might see it as evidence of a lack of information. But the fact that the secret police reports were eventually transmitted and that the redundant party and internal media digests were continuously delivered does not support such an interpretation. Rather, it suggests that

[35] Archive of the Bulgarian Ministry of the Interior (AMVR) f. 1 op. 12 a. e. 943 (April–October 1989).

[36] Personal interviews with Dimutur Ivanov (June 24, 2008; July 1, 2008; July 7, 2008; October 1, 2008) (Sofia, Bulgaria); Chukrin, *Zapiski ot totalitarnoto vreme*; Chakarov, *Ot vtoriia etazh*. A majority of the eleven full Politburo members supported the coup: Petar Mladenov, Dobri Dzhurov, Georgi Atanasov, Yordan Yotov, Dimitar Stanishev, and Nacho Papazov; also in support was Politburo candidate member Andrei Lukanov (Maria Mateeva, *Subitiiata v Iztochna i Tsentralna Evropa: Khronologichen pregled, 1987–1997* [Sofia: Akademichno Izdatelstvo "Marin Drinov," 1998], 96).

[37] Specific reports made by the secret police to the top party leadership are reproduced in Doinov, comp., *Shesto upravlenie sreshtu neformalnite organizatsii*, and in Veselin Angelov, comp., *Lichno strogo sekretno: Durzhavna sigurnost sreshtu neformalnite organizatsii v Bulgariia 1987–1989* (Sofia: Simolini, 2012). See also Dimitar Ivanov, *Politicheskoto protivopostaviane v Bulgariia 1956–1989* (Sofia: Ares Press, 1994); Dimitar Ivanov, *Shesti otdel* (Sofia: Trud, 2004).

[38] Chakarov, *Ot vtoriia etazh*, 158.

[39] AMVR f. 1 op. 12 a. e. 943 (April–October 1989).

[40] AMVR f. 1 op. 12 a. e. 943 (October 12, 1989), 230–32.

[41] AMVR f. 1 op. 12 a. e. 943 (October 6, 1989), 174–75; AMVR f. 1 op. 12 a. e. 943 (October 16, 1989), 255–64; AMVR f. 1 op. 12 a. e. 943 (October 17, 1989), 281–86.

the delayed transfer provided yet another signal of the impending ouster. It is abundantly clear that Zhivkov remained well informed and that he anticipated his removal from power. Thus, the Bulgarian experience of regime transformation is not a case of a hapless despot who is caught unaware by the efforts of his associates to depose him.[42] In short, solving the dictator's dilemma did not allow Zhivkov (who had assumed power in 1954 and had achieved the longest tenure of any Eastern European post-Stalinist leader by 1989) to retain his position past November 1989.

7.1.6 The Coup and the Abolition of Single-Party Rule

The coup-plotters operated with Soviet reassurance, which was expressed by Gorbachev, by the Soviet ambassador, and by the KGB representative in Sofia. The U.S. ambassador also extended his support.[43] What aided the soft-liners was the emergence of new protests in the capital on October 26 and November 3. The reformists were therefore emboldened by these developments and went ahead with the planned ouster of Zhivkov, who failed to dissuade them or to obtain Soviet or U.S. support. On November 9, a Politburo meeting decided that it would accept Zhivkov's resignation as general secretary of the Bulgarian Communist Party on November 10, during a regularly scheduled plenum of the Central Committee. On November 10, a new leader of the Bulgarian Communist Party was appointed: reformist Petar Mladenov, who had served as minister of foreign affairs since 1971.

One puzzling aspect of the transition is why Mladenov put an end to single-party rule within two months after his accession to the top position in the party-state hierarchy. Massive rallies by the ethnic majority took place in November and early December, when the opposition movement was formally established under the umbrella of the Union of Democratic Forces. On December 14, a large-scale demonstration in front of the National Assembly demanded abolition of Article 1 of the Constitution, which designated the communist party as the leading party in Bulgaria (thus, abolition of Article 1 meant the legalization of opposition parties). The labor union *Podkrepa* organized a national strike at the end of December 1989. The Turkish minority, who were victims of the Regenerative Process, demanded that their Turkish-Arabic names be restored. Roundtable negotiations between the opposition and the communist party began in early January 1990. In the face of this rapid escalation of tensions, the

---

[42] All of Zhivkov's aides note his steady interest in classified reporting. See especially Chakarov, *Vtoriiat etazh*; Chakarov, *Ot vtoriia etazh*; and Niko Iakhiel, *Todor Zhivkov i lichnata vlast* (Sofia: M8M, 1997), 415.

[43] Alekseniia Dimitrova, *Sekretnite dokladi na Sol Polansky za 10 noemvri* (Sofia: Trud, 2019).

communist-controlled legislature voted to abolish Article 1 of the Constitution on January 15, 1990. In the end, the communist party agreed to the demands of the opposition to schedule competitive elections for June 1990—but the plan of the party was to win those elections, not to step down.

Importantly, information provision continued after Zhivkov's ouster. The archival documents leave no doubt that the party and State Security kept the top decision makers apprised of all political developments. Prior to the December 14 rally, the leadership was informed about preparations for strikes and protests; about imminent demands to abolish Article 1 and to restore the names of the Turks; and about the transformation of informal political movements into proto-political parties.[44] Thus, the decision to end single-party rule was made with access to abundant information.

7.1.7 Summing Up

The ouster of Zhivkov resulted from changes in the domestic situation (the actions of human rights NGOs and independent trade unions; the expulsion of the Turkish minority following failure to suppress its discontent; and the deepening economic deterioration); from new international developments (Western radio broadcasts were no longer jammed, thus enabling the horizontal spread of information about organized challenges to the system; Eastern European regimes were undergoing political transformations that moved them farther away from single-party rule; and the Soviet Union did not intervene to stop these liberalizing processes); from alienating the *nomenklatura*; and, most consequentially, from the decision of members of the inner circle to defect and to begin to plot a coup. Once Zhivkov was removed, the situation became more volatile, with the opposition movement coalescing and mass protests emerging. Ending single-party rule was a tactical maneuver by the softliners that allowed for a temporary cooling down of social tensions, as preparations for holding competitive elections were being made.

7.2 Counterfactuals: Could Economic Reforms Have Saved the System?

A question that needs to be addressed is whether Bulgaria could have delayed democratization by pursuing economic liberalization. Although this is not widely appreciated, Bulgaria had implemented various reforms prior to 1989 that

---

[44] AMVR f. 1 op. 12 a. e. 946 (November 27–December 8, 1989).

matched or even exceeded those in China. The fact that they did not have the same effect in Bulgaria reflects differences in timing, levels of development, and the share of economic activity that was regulated by the plan. Another obstacle was the fact that liberalization ultimately necessitated dismantling the socialist social contract of welfare benefits and price stability; such measures were met with strong hostility by the populace. Thus, rather than shoring up the system, economic reforms accelerated the unraveling of the welfare dictatorship.

7.2.1 Personal Plots

Although land was collectivized during the initial decade of communist rule in Bulgaria, by the early 1960s rural residents had access to auxiliary plots that they could use to produce food for personal consumption or for sale to the state (at official procurement prices) or to other citizens (at farmers' markets).[45] Over time, access to these plots was granted to urban residents. Use for animal husbandry was also permitted. Although individuals could not buy or sell the plots, the literature in English and Bulgarian describes them as private or personal, because they were treated as such by the families who worked them, with the expectation that they would keep them in perpetuity.[46] By 1985, two-thirds of Bulgarians were allocated 2.01 million plots with a mean size of 0.319 hectares.[47] In China, the average household-farming plot had a size of 0.446 hectares in 1986.[48] However, taking into account that the Bulgarian households with access to land had a mean size of three, and rural households in China had a size of five, the amount of land per household member in Bulgaria was larger than that in China (0.106 hectares vs. 0.0881 hectares). Productivity was remarkably high: though they comprised less than one-fifth of the arable land, by 1988 these plots generated one-half of the vegetables and fruit; 40 percent of meat production; and a quarter of the milk produced in the country.[49] We should underscore that in contrast to China, these plots persisted alongside agricultural collectives. Citizens proved capable of managing them after hours and on weekends. The existence of these plots is a key reason why the 1987 initiative to begin the process of decollectivization was so poorly received by rural residents: they wanted both

---

[45] Iliiana Marcheva, *Politikata za stopanska modernizatsiia v Bulgariia po vreme na Studenata voina* (Sofia: Letera, 2016), 247–50.

[46] Ivan Elenkov, *Orbiti na sotsialisticheskoto vsekidnevie* (Sofia: Ciela, 2018); Marcheva, *Politikata za stopanska modernizatsiia*; Glenn E. Curtis, ed., *Bulgaria: A Country Study* (Washington, DC: GPO for the Library of Congress, 1992).

[47] Elenkov, *Orbiti na sotsialisticheskoto vsekidnevie*.

[48] Fu Chen and John Davis, "Land Reform in Rural China Since the mid-1980s," http://www.fao.org/3/x1372t/x1372t10.htm (accessed April 19, 2022).

[49] Curtis, ed., *Bulgaria: A Country Study*.

job security in the collective farms and supplementary income from their personal plots.[50]

7.2.2 Private Businesses

As with the personal plots, the liberalization of restrictions surrounding private business can be traced back to the 1960s, when retirees and some groups of employees were permitted to provide a limited set of repair, transportation, construction, and tailoring services.[51] The scope of legally sanctioned activities was expanded in the late 1960s, with the very important addition of medical services.[52] Some of the permissible operations were unusual: in 1967, the country's best known fortune teller, Baba Vanga, was allowed to charge fees for clairvoyant services; most other psychics operated illegally.[53] Although policies fluctuated throughout the 1970s, by the early 1980s small cafés, bars, and restaurants could be leased and, under certain conditions, owned by individuals or families, especially if they operated on a semi-permanent seasonal basis at the seaside or mountain resorts.[54] Private cooperatives were subsequently allowed, and in January 1989, citizens were permitted to establish firms and to hire employees on a permanent or temporary basis. Thus, nearly a full year before the beginning of democratization, private business had been legalized.

7.2.3 Industrial Groups

One of the most remarkable experiments during communist rule in Bulgaria was the creation of the Texim Industrial Group, which existed under various

---

[50] Iliiana Marcheva, "Ideite za reshavane na agrarniia vupros v Bulgariia v kraia na 80-te i nachaloto na 90-te godini na XX vek," in Evgeniia Kalinova, Mikhail Gruev, Liudmila Zidarova, eds., *Prelomni vremena: Iubileen sbornik v chest na 65-godishninata na professor Liubomir Ognianov* (Sofia: Universitetsko Izdatelstvo "Sv. Kliment Okhridski," 2006), 855–80, at 858–63.

[51] Marcheva, *Politikata za stopanska modernizatsiia,* 250–54.

[52] Vladimir Migev, "Chastniiat sektor v bulgarskata ikonomika prez 60-te godini na XX vek," in Stela Dermendzhieva, Veliko Lechev, and Petko St. Petkov, eds., *Sbornik v chest na dots. d-r Mincho Minchev: Izsledvaniia po sluchai 60 godini ot rozhdenieto mu* (Veliko Turnovo: Universitetsko Izdatelstvo "Sv. Sv. Kiril i Metodii," 2006), 130–45, at 140–41. Doctors had to be employed full-time in a state hospital and could only engage in private work for a limited number of hours. Prohibitions existed for treating tuberculosis and venereal diseases as well as for performing abortions in private offices.

[53] Petar Stoianov, *Shesto upravlenie: Moiata istina,* vol. 2 (Sofia: Daniela Ubenova, 2009), 233.

[54] Iliiana Marcheva, "Politikata po agrarniia vupros v Bulgariia v konteksta na 'perestroikata' na sotsializma v kraia na 80-te godini," in Dermendzhieva, Lechev, and Petkov, eds., *Sbornik v chest na dots. d-r Mincho Minchev,* 204–30, at 209.

names in the 1960s.[55] At the height of its power, Texim had 45,000 employees (equivalent to 1 percent of the working-age population), thus making it the largest firm in the country.[56] Even more remarkable than its size is that the company was highly profitable, generating hundreds of millions of dollars for the strained state budget. What made this success possible was the patronage of the Politburo and State Security (the company head, Georgi Naidenov, was a highly placed intelligence officer). The business activities of Texim were broad: weapons and drug smuggling (mostly in the Middle East and North Africa); evading CoCom export controls (by setting up phantom firms in the West); re-exporting Soviet raw materials purchased at Council for Mutual Economic Assistance (COMECON) rates to third countries that paid world prices for them; truck freight, sea, and air transportation; and the domestic manufacturing of sought-after goods, such as Coca-Cola, which generated extremely high profit margins. Texim also operated a handful of luxury stores and other businesses ranging from dry cleaners to highly profitable greenhouses for winter production of vegetables. Finally, Texim had its own bank, even though banking was strictly regulated by the state.[57]

Against this background, the decision to dissolve the industrial group in 1969 and to imprison its president may appear baffling. Historians have yet to agree on the key explanation for this outcome, though it appears that Texim was disbanded because it was too successful. Its president, Georgi Naidenov, was accused of running the industrial group like a capitalist firm, with the blind pursuit of profit.[58] In the wake of the Prague Spring, deviations from state control of industry were not permissible.[59] Mr. Naidenov's other transgression was that he engaged in currency speculation against the ruble, thus attracting the wrath of the Soviet minister of foreign trade.[60] Ultimately, the external factor appears to have been the essential catalyst for punishing the successful entrepreneur. The case of Texim demonstrates that economic experiments could be wildly successful, but it also shows that the Soviet Union would not tolerate them because they deviated from the principles of central planning and intra-bloc trade.

[55] Petia Slavova, *Ogranichenata diktatura v Bulgariia prez 60-te godini na 20-ti vek. Izsledvane na izkliuchenieto: Sluchaiat Texim* (Sofia: Ciela, 2017).

[56] Liliia Stoeva, comp., *'Aferata' Texim v svidetelstva i dokumenti* (Sofia: Teximreklama, 1994).

[57] Marcheva, *Politikata za stopanska modernizatsiia*, 254–65.

[58] Angel Solakov, *Predsedateliat na KDS razkazva* (Sofia: Teximreklama, 1993), 31–44.

[59] Marcheva, *Politikata za stopanska modernizatsiia*, 265–77.

[60] Stoeva, *'Aferata' Texim*, 247.

7.2.4 Foreign Direct Investment and Special Economic Zones

Joint ventures with foreign companies were legalized in 1980.[61] They existed primarily in the hospitability sector (e.g., the New Otani and Sheraton hotels in the capital) and in retail trade, with very few in manufacturing. Efforts were made to attract more foreign capital from Japan, Austria, and especially the Federal Republic of Germany. Discussions about setting up a duty-free zone in the Danube ports of Ruse or Vidin took place throughout the mid-1980s, though eventually the second-biggest city in the country (Plovdiv) was declared a special economic zone in 1989.[62] Perhaps the most important decision in terms of attracting foreign capital was made in January 1989, when the rules for foreign direct investment (FDI) were greatly simplified. The one persistent obstacle, however, was Soviet opposition to cooperation with Western firms.[63] China had no similar constraints when pursuing Western FDI,[64] when experimenting with state-sponsored industrial groups,[65] or when it made its decision to grow out of the plan.[66] Bulgaria, like the other Eastern Bloc countries, was economically shackled by its trade alliance with the Soviet Union.

7.2.5 Summing Up: The Incompatibility of Market Reforms and the Socialist Social Contract

This examination of economic reforms in Bulgaria yields several theoretically relevant conclusions. One is that by 1989 Bulgaria and China had progressed to a similar stage in their reforms. Yet, they did so at a different speed. By the late 1980s, private family farming had reached its limits in Bulgaria. Other reforms, like private business and foreign-invested enterprises, might have proceeded much further, but Soviet opposition did not allow for that to happen. The most challenging task was to reform the inefficient state-owned enterprises—this was deeply unpopular in China (it was delayed by nearly a decade due to the Tiananmen demonstrations) and in Bulgaria, where the more extensive use of central planning and the greater share of industrial production in the country's

---

[61] Marcheva, *Politikata za stopanska modernizatsiia*, 433.

[62] TsDA f. 1B op. 101 a. e. 2284 (January 9, 1989).

[63] Marcheva, *Politikata za stopanska modernizatsiia*, 517–28.

[64] Julian Gewirtz, *Unlikely Partners: Chinese Reformers, Western Economists, and the Making of Global China* (Cambridge, MA: Harvard University Press, 2017).

[65] Lisa A. Keister, *Chinese Business Groups: The Structure and Impact of Interfirm Relations during Economic Development* (New York: Oxford University Press, 2000); James Mulvenon, *Soldiers of Fortune: The Rise and Fall of the Chinese Military–Business Complex, 1978–1998* (Armonk, NY: M.E. Sharpe, 2001).

[66] Barry Naughton, *Growing Out of the Plan: Chinese Economic Reform, 1978–1983* (New York: Cambridge University Press, 1995).

GDP made the task correspondingly more difficult.[67] Urban industrial restructuring was a painful process. Had it been possible to attempt to carry it out prior to 1989, it is likely that it would have accelerated democratization by unleashing popular discontent, rather than helping the regime to stabilize its rule. In sum, the fact that the communist autocracies that successfully marketized without democratizing had poor agrarian economies at the beginning of the reform process (China, Vietnam, and Laos) attests to the impossibility of rapidly dismantling advanced centrally planned industrial economies without provoking massive popular unrest.

A further complication in the Bulgarian case is that radical economic reforms required abolishing the socialist social contract, which guaranteed jobs, welfare benefits, and price stability. The economic reforms that were unveiled in 1987–1989 were fundamental: the role of planning in industry and agriculture would be drastically reduced, the creation of special economic zones would henceforth be authorized, the monobank would be replaced with a system of seven commercial banks, and private firms would be legalized.[68] Although there was no wholesale privatization or price liberalization, these changes nevertheless explicitly laid the groundwork for a shift from the plan to a market economy. Yet, instead of shoring up confidence in the system, the publicized blueprints for economic transformation created uncertainty: citizens neither understood nor believed in the initiatives that sought to establish private economic activity.[69] Furthermore, as the reform announcements did not specify how the losers from the reforms would be protected, both rural and urban residents suffered serious anxieties about the potential for unemployment once the market was introduced.[70] Rural reforms that aimed to increase the profitability of agricultural cooperatives (and provided for the possibility of bankruptcy of unprofitable entities) were similarly met with hostility from farmworkers.[71] Such measures were highly unpopular.

The economic difficulties meant that the leadership could not fulfill its obligations under the socialist social contract. Citizens responded by withdrawing their conditional loyalty: they complained less often (despite the worsening economic situation), and they used the political liberalization measures introduced in 1987–1989 to visibly express their dissatisfaction with the system. The much-needed market transition would only be implemented after the end of

---

[67] On the limited extent of central planning in China, see Yasheng Huang, "Information, Bureaucracy, and Economic Reforms in China and the Soviet Union," *World Politics* 47:1 (October 1994), 102–34.

[68] Gospodinka Nikova, "Zhivkovata ikonomicheska reforma, perestroikata i startut na skritata privatizatsiia v Bulgariia," *Istoricheski pregled*, no. 5–6 (2003), 92–125.

[69] Martin Ivanov, *Reformatorstvo bez reformi* (Sofia: Ciela, 2008).

[70] Opinion polling revealed that, as of October 1988, only 15 percent of the population thought that unemployment was an acceptable part of life under socialism. See TsDA f. 1b op. 55 a. e. 853 (December 1988), 24.

[71] Marcheva, "Ideite za reshavane na agrarniia vupros," 858–63.

single-party rule. Although social contracts can exist under a market economy (as in contemporary China and post–Soviet Russia),[72] they feature many fewer government commitments to supply benefits than under a typical welfare dictatorship, as exemplified by the GDR or Bulgaria.[73] Importantly, there was no welfare dictatorship in China in 1989, thus allowing decision makers to engage in reform with fewer constraints than their counterparts in Eastern Europe. One example, provided by Cuba, which created a welfare dictatorship identical to those that arose in Eastern Europe, indicates that these economically inefficient but politically expedient models may persist for a very long time: as of 2022, the Cuban party-state still guarantees employment (though self-employment has been legal in one form or another since the 1990s), universal healthcare and education, and limited food rations; the effects of the currency reform introduced in 2021 (along with measures that expand the scope for private business) remain to be seen. The extent of entitlements has declined since 1989, but the state provision of benefits has not disappeared because, as in Bulgaria, welfare is essential to maintain the single-party system.

7.3 Moving from Competitive Authoritarianism to Democracy, January 1990–October 1991

In the summer of 1989, the reformist faction within the top party leadership began taking calculated risks. Yet, with each subsequent move, the range of desirable outcomes became narrower. Zhivkov's ouster in November 1989 only gave the party another two months of complete monopoly over the political system. In the twenty-two months between the beginning of January 1990 and the end of October 1991, Bulgaria underwent an extraordinary evolution from a competitive authoritarian regime to a multiparty democracy. This section engages with the theoretically relevant question of why the communist party agreed to step down after losing the elections in 1991.

The most consequential initial decision was to begin roundtable negotiations between the communist party and the opposition, which lasted from January 3 until mid-May 1990 and reached a consensus on several issues: abolition of Article 1 of the Constitution; dissolution of the Sixth Directorate of State Security (the political police); removal of party organizations from the army, the police, the judicial system, the diplomatic corps, all educational establishments, agricultural cooperatives, firms, and government entities; and the organization of

---

[72] Linda Cook and Martin K. Dimitrov, "The Social Contract Revisited: Evidence from Communist and State Capitalist Economies," *Europe–Asia Studies* 69:1 (2017), 8–26.

[73] Dimitrov, *Politicheskata logika na sotsialisticheskoto potreblenie*; Dimitrov, "Economic Shocks and Communist Regime Survival and Collapse."

elections for a Grand National Assembly tasked with drafting a new constitution. The party agreed to hold elections in June 1990 with the expectation that it would win them. This is indeed what happened: the ex-communist (renamed socialist) party managed to secure 52.75 percent of the seats in the legislature.[74] Despite obvious manipulation,[75] the opposition accepted the electoral outcome.

What the top-level party strategists could not anticipate is that they would be haunted by a statement by General Secretary Petar Mladenov during the December 14, 1989, protests. As no decision was being announced regarding their demands to abolish Article 1, the crowds of protesters grew larger and angrier on the evening of December 14. Unable to calm them down, Mladenov mentioned to the minister of defense standing next to him that "[i]t would be best if the tanks were to come." This statement did not accord with the reformist image that the newly elected General Secretary Mladenov wanted to project. The statement was initially hidden from the public but it was eventually revealed between the first and the second round of the June 1990 elections. Shortly thereafter, a tent encampment appeared in the center of the capital, protesting the electoral outcome and demanding that Petar Mladenov resign from his position as president (he had assumed the post in April 1990, following abolition of the State Council). Mladenov stepped down on July 6, 1990. Although Mladenov's resignation was an unwelcome loss, the party retained its majority in parliament and its complete control over the cabinet.

The summer and fall of 1990 brought new challenges to the party's hold on power. Zheliu Zhelev, leader of the opposition, assumed the ceremonial post of president on August 1. At that point, the country was being rocked by anticommunist protests, hunger strikes, work stoppages, and acts of civil disobedience. On August 26, a fire erupted in the party headquarters building. A new cabinet was introduced in September 1990, but, like the previous one, it was fully controlled by the ex-communists. Antigovernment protests continued throughout the fall, thus necessitating the formation of yet another cabinet.

The obvious choice for prime minister was Petar Beron, a noted zoologist and Ecoglasnost activist prior to November 1989, who had been elected leader of the opposition when Zheliu Zhelev assumed the presidency in August 1990. Had Beron become premier, the anticommunist parties would have gained complete

[74] Technically, the elections occurred in two rounds (on June 10 and June 17), but only 18 of the 400 seats in the Grand National Assembly were contested during the second round.

[75] Apart from overt manipulation, rumors were disseminated by State Security to discourage voting for the opposition. For example, agents among the Turkish minority spread rumors aimed at preventing the Turks from voting for the Union of Democratic Forces (the main opposition party) (AMVR f. 1 op. 12 a. e. 1000 [April 11, 1990], 144). In addition, rumors were being circulated about violence by opposition activists against ex-communist party members, aiming to ensure higher electoral turnout among supporters of the former communist party (AMVR f. 1 op. 12 a. e. 1002 [May 24–June 10, 1990]).

control over the executive. The communist leadership was determined to prevent such an outcome. In late November 1990, it became known that Beron had served as an informant and was passing on intelligence about Ecoglasnost and the formation of the opposition movement to State Security.[76] This explosive news (which was leaked to the newspaper *Duma*, official organ of the former communist party) discredited Beron and made it impossible for him to be appointed prime minister. Instead, a coalition government was formed on December 22, 1990, in which three ministerial seats (out of eighteen) were allocated to the opposition. By sidelining Beron, the ex-communist party managed to maintain control over the executive for another ten months. The Union of Democratic Forces won a plurality of the vote in the October 1991 parliamentary elections. With the support of the Turkish party, the Movement for Rights and Freedoms, the opposition was able to form a cabinet. This put an end to control over the legislature and the executive by the ex-communist party.

One question that arises is why the former communist party agreed to accept the results of the 1991 elections and to step down from power. The answer is that its elite had an attractive exit option, namely, it could trade political power for economic prowess by entering party-affiliated business ventures.[77] The availability of this lucrative option allowed the transition process to conclude with the opposition assuming political control of the country.

7.4 Continuity in Information Provision after 1989

The end of the single-party system did not lead to a demise of the information-gathering institutions that had been created to sustain it. On the contrary, these entities continued to generate classified reporting that guided the decision-making process of the communist elites, who had to accept ever-diminishing wins until they lost power completely.

7.4.1 Continuity: The Information-Sociological Center

The Information-Sociological Center of the Central Committee of the Bulgarian Communist Party continued to collect and transmit reports on the popular mood after Zhivkov's ouster and the coalescing of the opposition movement at the end of 1989. As before, voluntarily transmitted information remained its focus. Whereas the systematic analysis of citizen letters had been the most

---

[76] *Duma*, November 22, 1990.
[77] Martin K. Dimitrov, "Kémekből oligarchák," *Arc és Álarc* (Fall–Winter 2017), 9–34.

valuable vector for obtaining such intelligence prior to the changes, the rapid evolution of the events in November–December 1989 elevated the importance of other mechanisms that could accelerate assessments of the popular mood. In parallel with the GDR after Honecker's resignation (see Chapter 9), the party turned to the systematic analysis of phone calls, which allowed for faster assessments of public opinion than the time-consuming study of letters.[78] As polling became more reliable due to the decline in preference falsification, the Information-Sociological Center also developed questionnaires that measured the impact of specific triggers of socioeconomic dissatisfaction (shortages, price inflation, job insecurity) and tried to assess levels of support for the party among the general population.[79]

Both before and after the watershed of November 1989, information was collected with the goal of supporting party rule. In the context of the transition to a multiparty system and the scheduling of competitive elections for June 1990, the main goal of the Information-Sociological Center was to help the communists secure an electoral victory by supplying the leadership with timely intelligence that would allow it to anticipate evolving trends in popular dissatisfaction and to counteract their transformation into increased support for the opposition.[80] As the party renamed itself "socialist" in February 1990 and established an election preparation headquarters in March 1990, the Information-Sociological Center set up an Information, Analysis and Planning Group within the Election Preparation Center.[81] Moreover, two new working groups were created under the umbrella of the Information-Sociological Center: a Coordination Group and a "Hello, Bulgarian Socialist Party!" Group.[82] Survival of the information-gathering apparatus meant that in addition to an organizational advantage (cells that penetrated down to the grassroots and could mobilize voters), the party enjoyed a decisive informational advantage over the opposition, which had no capacity to generate intelligence for intra-party use prior to the elections of June 1990.

Although the party won the elections, there was significant doubt among supporters of the opposition whether the polling had been free and fair. Voter intimidation took place both in the lead-up to the elections and on voting day; more importantly, a strong suspicion of manipulation of the ballot count became entrenched in the summer of 1990. Opposition supporters erected a tent encampment, named "the City of Truth," in the center of Sofia and workers and

---

[78] Bulgarian State Security Dossier Commission (AKRDOPBGDSRSBNA-M) f. 1 op. 11 a. e. 921 (April 1990), 54–59.

[79] AKRDOPBGDSRSBNA-M f. 1 op. 11 a. e. 921 (April 1990), 80–97.

[80] AKRDOPBGDSRSBNA-M f. 1 op. 11 a. e. 921 (February 27, 1990), 1–8, at 8.

[81] AKRDOPBGDSRSBNA-M f. 1 op. 11 a. e. 921 (March 13, 1990), 12–17.

[82] AKRDOPBGDSRSBNA-M f. 1 op. 11 a. e. 921 (April 1990), 54–59; AKRDOPBGDSRSBNA-M f. 1 op. 11 a. e. 921 (May 2, 1990), 66–73.

students demanded accountability from the socialist party. Under such heightened tensions, flames engulfed the imposing Central Committee building in August 1990. Officially attributed to vandals, the fire mysteriously struck only one part of party headquarters: the operational archive, which housed materials of the Information-Sociological Center, of the Election Preparation Center, and of the Finance Department; these were precisely the documents that could demonstrate whether the election had been stolen. Due to the archival losses during the fire, it was widely believed that the Information-Sociological Center ceased to exist in November 1989. However, given the difficulties of completely destroying archival records (see Chapter 2), copies of the bulletins and reports produced by the Information-Sociological Center survived as they were being sent to and duly preserved by the other pre-1989 information-gatherer that outlasted single-party rule, namely, State Security.[83]

7.4.2 Continuity: State Security

In the immediate aftermath of the November 1989 events, public pressure to dissolve the secret police was building very rapidly. Within two weeks of Zhivkov's ouster, his successor informed the leadership of State Security that the Sixth Directorate would have to be disbanded.[84] In January 1990, roundtable negotiations between the communist party and the opposition reached an agreement to discontinue the use of technical surveillance methods, such as phone tapping, audio and video monitoring, and control of correspondence.[85] Given strong public sentiments against State Security, its capacity to persist through July 1991 is both empirically surprising and theoretically illuminating.[86]

The durability of State Security reveals the protean adaptive powers of institutions. It also highlights how survival necessitated cunning and subterfuge. Thus, although the fearsome Sixth Directorate (political police) was officially dissolved in January 1990, very few of its employees were fired from the Ministry of the Interior; most were transferred either to the newly created Organized Crime Directorate or to the freshly minted National Service for the Protection of the Constitution, which was also staffed by former employees of the second (counterintelligence) and fourth (antisabotage) directorates of State

---

[83] Because the surviving copies of these party documents produced after November 1989 are located in the State Security archive, they are referenced as AKRDOPBGDSRSBNA-M.

[84] AKRDOPBGDSRSBNA-M f. 1 op. 12 a. e. 936 (November 25, 1989).

[85] AKRDOPBGDSRSBNA-M f. 58 op. 1a a. e. 519 (February 9, 1990), 26.

[86] The 1974 decree governing the operation of State Security was formally repealed in July 1991.

Security.[87] These personnel transfers were not officially announced and thus they did not result in a public outcry. With regard to operational methods, technical surveillance persisted (albeit at a lower frequency than before 1989).[88] More importantly, because it was never discussed and it was declared off-limits during the roundtable negotiations, the deployment of agents not only continued but even increased,[89] in order to compensate for the decline in technical surveillance. As some assets were reluctant to provide intelligence,[90] adaptive responses had to be developed: the Ministry of the Interior increased the use of material incentives for agent work and redirected some criminal informants to State Security targets.[91] Overall, however, the general intelligence-generation infrastructure was preserved despite extraordinarily strong anti–State Security public sentiment.

Having survived the initial transformation of single-party rule, State Security faced several main tasks. The paramount goal was to secure a victory for the communist party in the 1990 elections.[92] This target was clearly articulated during numerous meetings of the Ministry of the Interior leadership, and it was transmitted down to the regional police directorates. Information was essential for accomplishing this goal. The collection mechanisms remained identical to those that were deployed prior to 1989: the opposition was thoroughly infiltrated with agents and, though officially off-limits, technical surveillance was used as needed.[93] Blackmail was deployed as well: when the opposition wanted to release the December 14 "tank" tape in the lead-up to the June 1990 elections, it was threatened that the list of State Security informants in its ranks would be leaked,[94] thus greatly reducing its share of the vote.[95] It is not accidental that Liuben Gotsev (a high-ranking State Security operative whose official cover was first vice-minister of foreign affairs) was put in charge of the Election Preparation Center of the Bulgarian Socialist Party; this appointment ensured that the information-gathering activities of the party and the repressive organs would be

---

[87] AKRDOPBGDSRSBNA-M f. 1 op. 12 a. e. 987 (April 24, 1990), 33–45; Khristo Khristov, *Ubiite "Skitnik": Bulgarskata i britanskata durzhavna politika po sluchaia Georgi Markov* (Sofia: Ciela, 2006), 487.

[88] AKRDOPBGDSRSBNA-M f. 1 op. 12 a. e. 996 (April 20, 1990), 1–42, at 12.

[89] AMVR f. 1 op. 12 a. e. 999 (February 20, 1990), 74; AKRDOPBGDSRSBNA-M f. 1 op. 12 a. e. 996 (April 20, 1990), 1–42, at 19.

[90] AMVR f 1 op. 12 a. e. 967 (January 10, 1990), cited in Khristov, *Ubiite "Skitnik,"* 502–3; on agents among the Turkish minority, see AMVR f. 1 op. 12 a. e. 999 (February 9, 1990), 57.

[91] AKRDOPBGDSRSBNA-M f. 1 op. 12 a. e. 981 (June 26, 1990), 1–28, at 6–7, 11–12, 27.

[92] AMVR f. 1 op 12 a. e. 967 (January 10, 1990), as cited in Khristov, *Ubiite "Skitnik,"* 482–85.

[93] AMVR f. 1 op. 12 a. e. 946 (November 27–December 8, 1989); AKRDOPBGDSRSBNA-M f. 1 op. 12 a. e. 996 (April 20, 1990), 1–42.

[94] For a similar argument applied to a different context, see Monika Nalepa, *Skeletons in the Closet: Transitional Justice in Post-Communist Europe* (New York: Cambridge University Press, 2010).

[95] See the Bulgarian International Television interview with former Union of Democratic Forces leader Petko Simeonov, September 9, 2017, https://www.youtube.com/watch?v=K-GyOf__Ij0 (accessed August 15, 2018).

coordinated.[96] It is worth emphasizing that the monitoring of the opposition and of social discontent continued past the June 1990 elections.[97] State Security did what it knew how to do: it collected information, even when the groups involved (e.g., students and other members of the intelligentsia) were no longer supposed to be monitored.

Apart from maintaining continuous surveillance, State Security deployed several kinds of insurance policies. One was to destroy the personal and operational files of former State Security agents. This process was chaotic and highly variable regionally due to the extraordinary amount of discretionary decision making stipulated by the initial and the revised internal guidelines; it resulted in eliminating 40.3 percent of the State Security agent files that had been archived as of January 1990.[98] The aim was to limit wide societal circulation of potentially explosive evidence of the unsavory intelligence-gathering methods used by State Security at a time when public hostility to the political police was very high.

The second insurance policy involved monetizing knowledge. This could be accomplished through several different vectors. One was the selling of information to the opposition.[99] It is not clear how often this occurred, but concerns that some State Security employees were not loyal to the party were repeatedly expressed by the leadership of the Ministry of the Interior in the lead-up to the June 1990 elections.[100] The motivations of those who passed intelligence on to the opposition are not documented, though political uncertainty and the possibility that the opposition might win the elections must have incentivized some State Security operatives to demonstrate their anticommunist bona fides.

The secret police also capitalized on a byproduct of the process of agent file destruction, namely, as documents were being examined to determine whether they should be preserved, information that some prominent individuals had been or still were informants began to circulate among State Security employees. This knowledge could then be used to blackmail the agents, who did not want their identity to be revealed, especially if they were publicly known opposition members. The names of such individuals could be leaked or sold to the press; such leaks prompted the newly elected Grand National Assembly to form a special commission in the summer of 1990 to investigate how many of its deputies had been or were still State Security agents. The secret police carefully monitored reactions to the publicizing of the identities of its collaborators.[101] The next salvo occurred in April 1991, when the names of 33 deputies in the Grand

96 AKRDOPBGDSRSBNA-M f. 1 op. 11 a. e. 921 (April 17, 1990), 53.
97 AMVR f. 1 op. 12 a. e. 1004 (July 21, 1990), 151.
98 Khristov, *Ubiite "Skitnik,"* 513–14.
99 AKRDOPBGDSRSBNA-M f. 1 op. 12 a. e. 981 (June 26, 1990), 1–28, at 13.
100 AKRDOPBGDSRSBNA-M f. 1 op. 12 a. e. 981 (June 26, 1990).
101 AMVR f. 1 op. 12 a. e. 1003 (December 20, 1990), 22–24.

National Assembly (out of 400) who had collaborated with the political police were published.[102] These piecemeal leaks demonstrated how valuable such information might be about other informants, whose identity had not yet been publicly revealed.

A final vector for monetizing knowledge was the setting up of businesses.[103] One prominent case, which illustrates how access to files could facilitate financial success, is that of Dimitar Ivanov, who was head of the Sixth Department of the Sixth Directorate (political police) of State Security. The Sixth Department enjoyed the unusual prerogative to maintain a specialized set of agent files that was entirely separate from the general State Security informant registry.[104] The reason was that this department handled the extremely sensitive issue of organized crime and corruption at the highest echelons of the party-state. Further evidence of the special status of the Sixth Department is that it bypassed the standard reporting chain and dispatched regular intelligence briefs directly to Todor Zhivkov. After the 1989 changes, the agent files and the confidential reports sent to Zhivkov disappeared. It is not clear where these documents might currently be located, though existing scholarship assumes that they were never destroyed.[105] Most revealing about the post-1989 trajectories of State Security employees is that Dimitar Ivanov successfully remade himself from a head of the Sixth Department (and a person responsible for safeguarding the secrets contained in its archive) into a thriving businessman, as reflected by his position as vice-president of the largest private conglomerate during the 1990s.[106] Although an in-depth discussion of the multiple trajectories through which State Security employees and agents transformed their knowledge and network membership into business success after 1989 is beyond the scope of this study, it is relevant that 90 percent of Bulgaria's oligarchs in the 2000s had a demonstrable prior connection to the communist-era State Security.[107]

In sum, the archival documents leave no doubt that State Security kept the leadership apprised of all political developments after November 1989, key among which was the formation of opposition parties.[108] One discovery is that rather than welcoming elections as an opportunity to assess their level of popularity (as the literature argues), regime insiders feared that competitive elections might reveal that the majority of the population was opposed to the party,[109]

[102] *Faks*, April 17, 1991.

[103] AKRDOPBGDSRSBNA-M f. 1 op. 12 a. e. 981 (June 26, 1990), 1–28, at 26.

[104] Momchil Metodiev and Mariia Dermendzhieva, *Durzhavna sigurnost—Predimstvo po nasledstvo: Profesionalni biografii na vodeshti ofitseri* (Sofia: Ciela, 2015), 796.

[105] Khristov, *Ubiite "Skitnik,"* 570; Metodiev and Dermendzhieva, *Durzhavna sigurnost*, 794.

[106] Personal interviews with Dimitar Ivanov (June 24, 2008; July 1, 2008; July 7, 2008; October 1, 2008) (Sofia, Bulgaria).

[107] Dimitrov, "Kémekből oligarchák."

[108] AMVR f. 1 op. 12 a. e. 946 (November 27–December 8, 1989); AMVR f. 1 op. 12 a. e. 998 (January 4, 1990), 34.

[109] AMVR f. 1 op. 11a a. e. 933 (April 23, 1990).

thus making it imperative to secure a victory through any means. Perhaps the most important discovery that emerges from the archives is that in late July 1990 the leadership was apprised of rapidly increasing support for a petition to create a parliamentary commission to examine the party and state archives;[110] this document presents in a new light the fire in August 1990 that destroyed evidence about financial and electoral irregularities that was presumably located at the party headquarters. Information transfer continued in the fall of 1990, when the ex-communist government was briefed on the economic chaos that was spreading throughout the country, which had defaulted on its foreign loan payments but was still trying to maintain subsidized prices.[111] In short, intelligence collection continued apace. State Security aimed to use its informational advantage to remain relevant during the transition period.[112]

7.4.3 Continuity: Secret Bulletins after 1991

Secret bulletins persisted in Bulgaria into the 2010s.[113] One example is provided by the Presidential Administration, which had a special group focusing on strategic policy, analysis, and forecasting. Staffed by four full-time analysts, the group generated daily, weekly, and monthly bulletins for the president and another twenty high-level recipients within the Presidential Administration. The bulletins were prepared on the basis of classified intelligence (extracted from the digests supplied by the External Intelligence Directorate, the Domestic Counterintelligence Service, the Military Intelligence Directorate, the Foreign Ministry, the Finance Ministry, and the Central Bank); publicly accessible newswires; and information personally collected by employees of the group. The bulletins varied in length: two pages for the daily; three to ten pages for the weekly; and no more than twenty pages for the monthly, which was usually an analytical brief on an issue of current interest (e.g., youth unemployment). The daily bulletin was typically organized in the form of a table, listing specific noteworthy events, the source reporting on these events, and an internal assessment of their importance. The weekly bulletin contained up to fifteen paragraph-length analytic descriptions of important long-term developments (such as the civil war in Syria), similarly acknowledging the source of the intelligence (which was often attributed to specific experts) and assessing its value. The ranked

[110] AMVR f. 1 op. 12 a. e. 1004 (July 21, 1990), 151.

[111] AMVR f. 1 op. 12 a. e. 1006 (October 25, 1990), 170–76; AMVR f. 1 op. 12 a. e. 1006 (December 21, 1990), 99.

[112] As documents from the Bulgarian Telegraph Agency are not available past November 10, 1989, we cannot use internal materials to discuss how it reacted to the transition.

[113] Paragraph based on an interview with a Presidential Administration official, July 25, 2013 (Sofia).

priority order for topical inclusion in the internal bulletins was domestic political developments, followed by coverage of Bulgaria in the foreign media, and
ending with key international developments. Although concrete feedback and
specific follow-up by the recipients of the bulletin were rare, most addressees
read these briefs closely.

Survival of the secret bulletins well into the 2010s leads to some general
remarks. One is that even in a democratic setting, leaders need specialized assistance to navigate the available information. The other is that these bulletins
are based on intelligence-gathering mechanisms that are remarkably similar to
those used under communism, with two crucial differences: there is no party
information, nor is there any internal journalistic reporting. This helps highlight
the communist institutional difference in intelligence collection.

7.5 Conclusions

This chapter has analyzed the process of democratization in Bulgaria in 1989–
1991. As argued in this book, regime stability in the later decades of communist rule rested on three pillars: selective repression and extensive redistribution
(which jointly constituted a welfare dictatorship); and ideological vigilance that
involved warding off external influences by promoting indigenous cultural consumption and national pride. Chapter 5 demonstrated that by 1988 the power
holders were incapable of maintaining ideological vigilance. Soon thereafter,
the welfare dictatorship came under extreme stress as well. The political liberalization initiated in 1987–1988 meant that repressive capacity was greatly
constrained; this was true even in terms of handling minority unrest, as when
the regime decided to expel the Turks in a public admission of its incapacity
to solve the problem. To make matters worse, the foreign debt crisis severely
constrained the ability of the regime to satisfy popular consumption needs.
The economic reforms announced in July 1987–January 1989 clearly indicated
movement in the direction of an eventual dismantling of the socialist social
contract, which guaranteed full employment, subsidized services, and price stability. In short, all three pillars of regime stability were severely weakened by the
summer of 1989.

The problem for the incumbent was that classified information about politically and economically motivated discontent circulated widely within the top
echelons of the party leadership, thus allowing members of the Politburo to begin
planning a palace coup. Successful execution of the coup was not the result of a
lack of intelligence: on the contrary, the leader was apprised of the preparations,
but he was unable to stop them, as a majority of the Politburo was united against
him. The case of Bulgaria has general relevance for theories of information in

autocracies, as it demonstrates that solving the dictator's dilemma cannot ensure indefinite tenure for the dictator. The wide circulation of sociopolitical intelligence allows members of the elite to coordinate and to sacrifice a vulnerable dictator in hopes of preserving the system.

This chapter presents evidence that is relevant for existing theories of democratization from strength. The measures implemented in Bulgaria in 1987–1988 and especially in 1989–1991 bear a striking resemblance to the democratization initiatives in Taiwan. Yet, the Guomindang (KMT) enjoyed thirteen years in office after initiating democratization in 1987, whereas the Bulgarian Communist Party was forced to step down after two years of liberalization in October 1991. The challenge in the case of Bulgaria was that the political transformation had to be accompanied by painful economic reforms, which shortened the lifespan of the transitional communist regime and forced it to carry out two rounds of competitive elections within a very short timeframe (1990 and 1991 vs. 1996 and 2000 in Taiwan). The win-set for the top decision makers was becoming progressively smaller. However, this does not mean that their actions did not display short-term rationality.

A final theoretically relevant argument that emerges from this chapter concerns the capacity of information-gathering institutions to outlast the regime that they were created to serve. These institutions continued to supply the ex-communist party with intelligence as it was trying to secure its hold on power after November 1989. Had these institutions been dissolved (as occurred in the Soviet Union and East Germany), the capacity of the party to persist for as long as it did once democratization was initiated would have been uncertain. The survival of information-gathering institutions past 1989 demonstrates their centrality to autocratic rule. At the same time, it also highlights the limits of intelligence, namely, under conditions of crisis, even well-informed autocrats may be forced to resign.

8

Information-Gathering Institutions in China, 1989–2019

This chapter analyzes the development and evolution of information-gathering institutions during the three decades that separate the Tiananmen Massacre from the arrival of COVID-19.[1] The entire 1989–2019 period was marked by a singular focus on collecting the information that was necessary to maintain social and political stability. Threat perceptions were elevated due to heightened levels of domestic discontent that, in the view of the party, stemmed at least in part from the actions of hostile foreign forces. For this reason, the paramount task was to neutralize the known vectors of external influence (by promoting cultural security) and to systematically identify the domestic enemies who posed a threat to social stability. The mechanisms used to collect information were continuously upgraded and became increasingly more technologically sophisticated. Yet, artificial intelligence (AI) and smart policing did not displace traditional human intelligence. Informants persisted and even increased in number in the 2010s. In the months prior to the arrival of COVID-19, China had both the most technologically sophisticated counterintelligence infrastructure and the highest penetration, with visible and covert informants, of any communist regime ever extant. No effort was spared to ensure stability, which directly contributed to resilience, according to internal regime understandings.

These achievements in involuntary information collection notwithstanding, the chapter also details two consequential failures that characterize the entire post-1949 period but whose impact became especially palpable in the decades after 1989. The first concerns the voluntary transfer of information. The Eastern European examples demonstrate that credible commitments by the party-state to provide welfare and to engage in selective repression are required to incentivize citizens to supply information about their welfare needs through the complaints system. When this process is regularized and responsiveness is sufficiently high, petitioning constitutes a source of stability by binding citizens and the regime to a bargain wherein the regime satisfies the welfare needs of the population and citizens reward it by remaining quiescent. No such equilibrium ever arose nationwide in China, despite efforts to encourage citizen complaints in the

---

[1] The effects of the pandemic on information gathering are discussed in Chapter 10.

Dictatorship and Information. Martin K. Dimitrov, Oxford University Press. © Oxford University Press 2023.
DOI: 10.1093/oso/9780197672921.003.0008

1990s. The low responsiveness to letters and visits meant that the mechanism which served as the foundation of anticipatory governance in Eastern Europe (by enabling reacting to latent discontent prior to its transformation into public displays of dissatisfaction) was increasingly perceived as a source of instability in China, as growing numbers of aggrieved citizens, whose individual petitions were unsuccessful, swiftly proceeded to express their frustrations through collective action. Although protests are also a means for information transfer, they pose a direct threat to social stability (because they allow information to circulate horizontally rather than only vertically, as with written complaints) and therefore are not welcomed by the party. As rates of complaining continued to decline and protests were swiftly repressed in the 2010s, the chances of using a welfare compact as the wellspring of regime stability continued to erode further. China did not, and likely will not, develop anticipatory governance centered on the successful management of latent discontent assessed through voluntarily transmitted information.

The second failure concerns the penetration of compactly settled ethnoreligious minorities. The challenge of handling Tibetans preceded 1989 and has persisted in the decades since then. What has emerged forcefully since the 1990s is that Uyghurs, who had been successfully managed in previous decades, also harbored high levels of discontent. Both groups remained illegible to the regime, thus leading to the adoption of heavy-handed tactics like grid policing, which was first used in Tibet and then applied in Xinjiang. The Uyghurs were also subjected to mass detention in reeducation centers, with very crude algorithms determining who might be a potential threat and therefore should be sent to a camp. Although some may see such displays of brute force as evidence of regime strength, this book conceptualizes them as indicia of an incapacity to deploy targeted repression and of a failure to incentivize citizens to voluntarily provide the necessary information to produce fine-grained anticipatory assessments of latent discontent that can then be used to prevent the rise of overt dissatisfaction. The deployment of force has further eroded support for the party among members of these minorities, thus creating significant uncertainties about the future.

China's persistence for more than three decades since the Tiananmen Massacre demonstrates that communist regimes were not doomed to fail after 1989. Survival is possible, though it has involved several tradeoffs. One is that persistence was achieved by sacrificing political liberalization, which seemed to be plausible before Tiananmen but not afterward. Another is that although repression meted at the Han majority became selective over time, it barely reached the low levels of frequency and severity that were practiced in Eastern Europe in the later decades of communist rule. The final tradeoff is that compactly settled ethnoreligious minorities were subjected to totalistic repression as a result of their ongoing illegibility for the party-state. Overall, the Chinese model prioritized involuntary collection over voluntary provision of information, handling political dissent and independent associational life with an iron grip, and responding to welfare grievances once they were expressed as overt collective discontent rather than when they were still latent instances of individual dissatisfaction. Technology has helped keep the system together, with the effect of facilitating repression. However, the long-term viability of this model is uncertain, as attested by opinion polling that indicates the eroding legitimacy of the party in the 2010s and the growing willingness of citizens to join protests and strikes.

The chapter is organized as follows. Section 8.1 discusses the impact that Tiananmen and the end of communist rule in Eastern Europe had on information-gathering priorities, paying specific attention to how elevated foreign and domestic threat perceptions transformed stability maintenance into a top state security concern. The chapter then examines traditional and new techniques for the involuntary collection of information used after 1989 by the police (Section 8.2). Section 8.3 analyzes problems in voluntary information transfer through complaints as well as the role of protests and online comments. Section 8.4 discusses the coordinating role of the party in public-opinion monitoring. Section 8.5 focuses on information collection among minorities, especially Tibetans and Uyghurs. Section 8.6 offers concluding reflections about information gathering in post-1989 China.

Before we proceed further, we should make a general statement about the systems for information transfer during the period examined in this chapter. The existing literature has documented a wide range of sources that were available to the top Chinese decision makers as they evaluated visible acts of dissatisfaction with the regime during the 1989 Tiananmen protests: these included Ministry of Public Security (MPS) and Ministry of State Security (MSS) reporting, People's Liberation Army (PLA) overviews, party reporting, internal journalistic digests, and briefs from various ministries and commissions.[2] Internal reporting assumes particular importance in times of crisis. For example, during the two-and-a-half months between April 15 and the end of June 1989, Xinhua generated 1,427 internal reports (double the usual amount); on some days, as many as 50 internal reports were dispatched. Xinhua also sent important news directly by fax to the General Office of the Central Committee and to the Office of the

[2] Zhang Liang, comp., *The Tiananmen Papers* (New York: Public Affairs, 2001). Ezra Vogel also provides evidence of the rich variety of documents that were absorbed on a daily basis by Deng Xiaoping (see Ezra F. Vogel, *Deng Xiaoping and the Transformation of China* [Cambridge, MA: Belknap Press of Harvard University Press, 2011], 378). The grassroots inspection tours that central leaders undertook to learn firsthand about the lives of ordinary citizens were another source of information (see Wen Jiabao, "Zai hui Xingyi yi Yaobang," *Renmin ribao*, April 15, 2010, 2).

State Council during the 1989 Tiananmen protests.[3] During such times, internal reports greatly outnumber those issued for public dissemination.[4]

Despite technological evolution, there was no radical change in bureaucratic reporting genres after 1989. All previous channels continued to operate, though they became increasingly specialized, allowing leaders to benefit from an ever-expanding range of documents to shed light on trends in discontent. Party reporting focused primarily on information voluntarily provided through complaints and discipline inspection denunciations.[5] Social investigations were also carried out on behalf of the party, with results published in internal bulletins.[6] The MPS took charge of reporting on dissent. Both Xinhua and the police monitored harmful Internet content. In addition, classified news bulletins were produced.[7] These channels for information collection were replicated further down in the system, with even grassroots officials enjoying access to some internal-reporting streams at appropriate levels of classification for their rank.[8] Since 1989 leaders at all tiers of the political system have received abundant information about levels of discontent, though this "democratization" of intelligence has, counterintuitively, only served to increase their insecurity about effectively managing popular dissatisfaction.

8.1 The Impact of 1989 on Information Gathering: Cultural Security and Stability Maintenance

The year 1989 was a momentous time for China, mostly because of the domestic protests that engulfed the capital as well as some 340 other cities.[9] In addition to these events in China, the year also set in motion the unraveling of communist rule throughout Eastern Europe. The conclusions that the party drew from these developments shaped its understandings of threats to state security during the following three decades. The first lesson was that hostile foreign forces were bent on subverting China's political stability by supporting regime enemies inside the

---

[3] *Xinhua she dashiji (1931–2001)*, vol. 3 (Beijing: Xinhua She, 2002), 77.

[4] This continued past 1989: for example, during the EP-3 spy-plane incident in April 2001, Xinhua produced 414 internal reports versus 219 public reports. See *Xinhua she dashiji (1931–2001)*, vol. 3, 169.

[5] The central information transmission node within the party is the General Office. See Wen-hsuan Tsai and Xingmiu Liao, "The Authority, Functions, and Intrigue of the General Office of the Chinese Communist Party," *The China Journal*, no. 80 (July 2018), 46–67.

[6] See, for example, *Guangdong shengqing neican*, no. 103 (May 28, 2011), http://www.gdsqfb.org.cn/text/974.html (accessed June 30, 2021).

[7] Key Xinhua news bulletins have persisted, including the highly classified *Guonei dongtai qingyang*. See *Jianguo yilai gong'an gongzuo dashi yaolan (1949–2000)* (Beijing: Qunzhong Chubanshe, 2003), 1290.

[8] For example, the classified *Renmin ribao* news bulletin entitled *Neibu canyue*.

[9] Zhang, comp., *The Tiananmen Papers*, viii.

country. As in Eastern Europe in the 1960s, the response strategy was to ward off external ideological influences by safeguarding cultural security. The second lesson, which crystallized gradually, involved conceptualizing any type of protest, be it political or socioeconomic, as a threat to stability maintenance and thus to state security. The targeted population roster, which was used to monitor individuals who harbored both political and socioeconomic grievances, functioned as the fulcrum of the information infrastructure that undergirded the protection of state security.

8.1.1   Hostile Foreign Forces as a Threat to Political Security

The creation of the Ministry of State Security in 1983 was guided by a doctrine that identified external forces as the main threat to state security; this paralleled the thinking in Eastern Europe in the 1960s and 1970s (see Chapters 5 and 9). Although it had emerged prior to 1989, this understanding was firmly consolidated as a result of the domestic and international events of 1989–1991. After 1989, leadership perceptions of threats to state security began to increase. According to Chinese scholars, this is publicly manifested by the higher frequency of the use of the words "security" (*anquan* 安全) and "state security" (*guojia anquan* 国家安全) in official reports (*dahui baogao* 大会报告) delivered to the party congress. Thus, at the Fourteenth Party Congress in 1992, "security" was used four times and "state security" once; by contrast, at the Seventeenth Congress in 2007, "security" was used twenty-three times and "state security" six times.[10]

In the internal understandings of the Ministry of State Security during the initial post-Tiananmen period, the main threat to state security originated from "peaceful evolution" (*heping yanbian* 和平演变),[11] a strategy to subvert socialism from within through economic, cultural, and political means, such as trade, promotion of Western lifestyles, and pressure on the communist world to protect human rights.[12] Thus, after the end of the Cold War, in the worldview of Chinese policy makers the West replaced Taiwan and the Soviet Union as the main source of threat. Internal government documents identify "hostile overseas forces" (*jingwai didui shili* 境外敌对势力) as responsible for promoting the strategy of peaceful evolution.[13] The focus on hostile foreign forces has remained

[10] Guoji Guanxi Xueyuan Guoji Zhanlüe yu Anquan Yanjiu Zhongxin, *2009 nian Zhongguo guojia anquan gailan* (Beijing: Shishi Chubanshe, 2010), 32.
[11] Guojia Anquan Bu Bangongting, "1990 nian de guojia anquan gongzuo" (1991) (document on file with the author).
[12] *Neibu canyue*, no. 40 (1991).
[13] Guojia Anquan Bu Bangongting, "1989 nian de guojia anquan gongzuo" (1990) (document on file with the author); Guojia Anquan Bu Bangongting, "1990 nian de guojia anquan gongzuo" (1991).

a constant in thinking about state security, even if peaceful evolution is used less today. Perhaps the best illustration of the external threat to state security is found in a treatise on stationing of troops and state security in Xinjiang, which presents social stability in the region as the innermost of four concentric circles; the outermost circle is external hostile forces (*guowai didui shili* 国外敌对势力), followed by separatist forces (*fenlie shili* 分裂势力) and extreme nationalism (*jiduan minzu zhuyi* 极端民族主义).[14] Overseas forces have also been identified as the motor driving the three evil forces (*sangu shili* 三股势力) of terrorism, separatism, and religious extremism in Xinjiang.[15]

The notion of external forces posing a threat to social stability extends beyond the specific issue of Xinjiang. In 2010, for example, an internal petitioning journal argued that hostile overseas forces use the pretext of rights defense (*weiquan* 维权) to promote anti-Chinese ideas like Tibetan independence, Eastern Turkestan, the democracy movement, and Falun Gong.[16] This type of attribution bears striking resemblance to the doctrinal orientation of Eastern European state security services from the late 1960s onward, whereby external (primarily Western) forces engaging in ideological subversion were identified as the main threat to state security. There is also a similarity in the response to this Western threat in the context of China and Eastern Europe, namely, fostering national pride through grandiose spectacles (the Olympics in China and historical celebrations in Eastern Europe) and patriotic education, which had the effect of exacerbating ethnic minority political alienation. Another similarity is the shared concern with cultural security (*wenhua anquan* 文化安全),[17] which requires limiting the impact of Western culture by either blocking or regulating access and, equally important, by developing indigenous cultural products to replace foreign imports, or at least to distract citizens from the desire to consume them.[18]

The doctrine of cultural security predates 1989.[19] Yet, it was only after Tiananmen that guarding against harmful foreign influences became a central component of the strategy of stability maintenance. Concerns about cultural security in the 1990s reflected unease about the promotion of universal values after

[14] Zhang Anfu, *Qingdai yilai Xinjiang tunken yu guojia anquan* (Beijing: Zhongguo Nongye Chubanshe, 2011), 203.

[15] "Jianjue daji 'sangu shili,'" *Renmin ribao*, July 1, 2013.

[16] *Renmin xinfang*, 2/2010 (313), 6. On Tibet, see Lin Le, "China's Perceptions of External Threats and Its Current Tibet Policy," *The China Journal*, no. 76 (2016), 103–23. On Falun Gong, see James W. Tong, *Revenge of the Forbidden City: The Suppression of the Falungong in China, 1999–2005* (New York: Oxford University Press, 2009).

[17] Zhang Xiaoping, *Dangqian Zhongguo wenhua anquan wenti yanjiu* (Beijing: Shehui Kexue Wenxian Chubanshe, 2012).

[18] Han Yuan, *Zhongguo wenhua anquan pinglun* (Beijing: Shehui Kexue Wenxian Chubanshe, 2016).

[19] On cultural protection work in the 1950s, see Chapter 6.

the dissolution of the USSR. China's entry into the World Trade Organization (WTO) in 2001 exacerbated pre-existing fears about the impact of external forces on domestic stability. In 2014, Xi Jinping included cultural security in his definition of comprehensive state security (*zongti guojia anquan guan* 总体国家安全观).[20] In Article 23 of the 2015 National Security Law, preventing and resisting the impact of harmful culture were explicitly discussed. Since then, the concept has been firmly integrated into Chinese notions of comprehensive state (national) security. Analysts are united in their assessment that the primary danger is ideological, but they differ in terms of how explicitly they discuss the specific vectors through which this external ideological influence may impact China. A partial list includes the spread of literary and artistic works; the diffusion of traditional media (newsprint, radio, and TV broadcasts); religious proselytizing, cult propaganda, and NGO activities; international scholarly exchange; and the circulation of harmful content through the Internet and social media.[21] An overarching concern is to counteract linguistic hegemony (*yuyan baquan* 语言霸权), which reflects the global cultural dominance of English.[22] Overall, cultural security is a broad concept covering a wide swath of activities that present a potential threat to the Chinese polity by spreading harmful foreign ideas.

8.1.2 Defending Cultural Security

We can derive different perspectives on the two main strategies for protecting cultural security by reading scholarly analyses and by examining internal government documents. Scholarly analyses contain mainly prescriptive recommendations, which are nevertheless informative of the desiderata associated with safeguarding cultural security. First is ideological construction, which includes both reinvigorating Marxism-Leninism and promoting traditional Confucian culture.[23] Other strategies involve sponsoring indigenous artistic production of literary and creative works. Related to this is an emphasis on increasing Chinese-language content on the Internet and elevating the status of Mandarin, including by sponsoring Confucius institutes. Finally, scholars highlight the importance of patriotic education and of steady vigilance against the ideological impact of international scholarly exchange. The ultimate goal of their recommendations is to foster cultural awareness and ethnic culture.[24]

---

[20] http://www.xinhuanet.com//politics/2014-04/15/c_1110253910.htm (accessed April 19, 2022).

[21] Han, *Zhongguo wenhua anquan pinglun.*

[22] Yang Shisheng and Zhang Yuxian, "Quanqiuhua xiade wenhua baquan yu wenhua anquan," *Qianyan*, no. 24 (2010), 160–62.

[23] Zhang, *Dangqian Zhongguo wenhua anquan.*

[24] Zhao Yingchen, "Quanqiuhua beijing xiade Zhongguo wenhua anquan," *Lanzhou xuekan*, no. 6 (2004), 36–38.

Fundamentally, these measures aim to counteract Western cultural hegemony (*xifang wenhua baquan* 西方文化霸权) by raising the profile of indigenous cultural production and building cultural soft power. These strategies are quite similar to those adopted by the Eastern European regimes in the 1960s and 1970s when promoting indigenous cultural consumption was understood as one part of a two-pronged response to ideological infiltration (see especially Chapter 5).

Internal sources give us insight into the second prong, which as in Eastern Europe, was a defensive response to cultural infiltration (*wenhua shentou* 文化渗透). These materials indicate that, like the rest of the state security portfolio, the cultural protection mandate is shared between the MSS and the MPS. The available MSS materials are short on specifics in terms of the concrete actions taken by the ministry to protect cultural security. By contrast, the MPS documents yield several important insights about the defensive police response to cultural infiltration. The first concerns placement of the cultural protection departments within the MPS organizational chart. The documents clearly demonstrate that these divisions formed a part of the state security protection system (*guojia anquan baowei xitong* 国家安全保卫系统) as early as 2000.[25] Second, like other units in charge of safeguarding state security, the cultural protection police rely on informants who provide them with intelligence that is used to investigate and neutralize specific threats. Third and most important, the scope of cultural protection work is vast, including everything from identifying politically subversive publications and monitoring religious and cult activities to maintaining control over political stability in universities and research institutes. The Internet is also surveilled for harmful content. In sum, the amorphous cultural security protection mandate of the MPS is so expansive that it has already enveloped nearly the entire MPS state security protection portfolio. This is consistent with dominant understandings that ideological infiltration is the root cause of domestic state security problems that run the gamut from human rights to minority unrest. The unusual breadth of cultural security can thus be a useful lens into Chinese understandings of how external forces impact domestic political processes.

There was continuity with the pre-1989 period in terms of specific cultural security threats. In August 1989, the MPS issued a notice on resisting foreign reactionary propaganda and political infiltration activities by cooperating with Customs and the post office to inspect and seize hostile propaganda materials.[26] Two manifestations of the threat were identified. One was strikes: by 1992, the

---

[25] In Beijing, for example, the PSB state security system (*guojia anquan baowei xitong*) consisted of four departments: the Domestic Security Protection Team (*guonei anquan baowei zongdui*); the Cultural Protection Department (*wenhua baowei chu*); the Mobile Technology Department (*xingdong jishu chu*); and the Entry–Exit Inspection (*churujing guanli chu*). See Beijing Shi Gong'an Ju, *Beijing gong'an nianjian 2001* (Beijing: Zhongguo Renmin Gong'an Daxue Chubanshe, 2001).

[26] *Jianguo yilai gong'an gongzuo*, 756.

police stressed the need to protect political stability and social order by neutralizing strikes and reactionary propaganda driven by hostile foreign forces within firms.[27] The other was black societies (gangs).[28] A 1990 MPS notice clearly states that gangs from Taiwan, Hong Kong, and Macao had infiltrated China, both engaging in economic crimes like smuggling and, by linking up with domestic and foreign enemies, in antiparty, antisocialist, and anti–central government political activities.[29] A related threat was overseas secret-society infiltration.[30] The concern was so serious that in 1992 the political protection departments gathered to attend a national conference on secret-society infiltration.[31] Religious safety pre-occupied the attention of the MPS for the remainder of the 1990s, when the popularity of Falun Gong also increased exponentially.[32] Coastal provinces like Shandong, Liaoning, and Fujian were especially vulnerable.[33] In Fujian, the threats included Taiwanese influence, secret societies, Falun Gong, and foreign-inspired labor NGOs.[34] Sustained efforts to ensure cultural security by counteracting hostile foreign forces persisted in the 2000s and 2010s.

The focus on external forces as the main state security threat also impacts how China views foreigners. A treatise from 1990 outlines the seven main ways in which foreign countries conduct spy activities: under diplomatic cover; using the guise of technical cooperation and trade; by deploying overseas Chinese who are visiting relatives or traveling in China; by passing off their intelligence gathering as journalistic work; by exploiting the venality or vulnerability of officials who pass along classified materials in exchange for bribes or as a result of honeypot entrapment (*seqing gouyin* 色情勾引); by recruiting Chinese citizens while they are abroad for study, work, or leisure; and by cultivating the children of high-ranking cadres.[35] The emphasis is on intelligence collection executed by foreign citizens. This is consistent with provincial statistics, which indicate that nearly one-quarter of the foreigners imprisoned in Shanghai between 1949 and

[27] *Jianguo yilai gong'an gongzuo*, 905–6.

[28] *Jianguo yilai gong'an gongzuo*, 811.

[29] *Gong'an jianshe*, no. 10/860 (1990), 12–15.

[30] *Jianguo yilai gong'an gongzuo*, 886.

[31] *Jianguo yilai gong'an gongzuo*, 917.

[32] *Jianguo yilai gong'an gongzuo*, 1026–27, 1053–54, 1247–49, 1375–76. An interesting question is why the MPS subjects small-scale Protestant house churches to infiltration and surveillance but not to outright crackdowns (Marie-Eve Reny, *Authoritarian Containment: Public Security Bureaus and Protestant Churches in Urban China* [New York: Oxford University Press, 2018]). The followers of those churches are typically not perceived as subversive, in contrast to Falun Gong practitioners, Muslims, and Tibetan Buddhists.

[33] Shandong Sheng Gong'an Ting, *Shandong gong'an nianjian 2010* (Beijing: Zhongguo Guoji Wenhua Chubanshe, 2010), 96; Liaoning Sheng Renmin Zhengfu Difangzhi Bangongshi, *Liaoning sheng zhi: Gong'an zhi 1986–2005* (Shenyang: Liaoning Minzu Chubanshe, 2016), 47–49.

[34] Fujian Sheng Difang Zhi Bianzuan Weiyuan Hui, *Fujian sheng zhi: Gong'an zhi 1990–2005* (Beijing: Shehui Kexue Wenxian Chubanshe, 2011), 15–17.

[35] Yu Zhonggui, *Fangjian baomi yu guojia anquan* (Beijing: Guofang Daxue Chubanshe, 1990), 127–42.

2000 were held on charges of counterrevolutionary crimes.[36] An awareness of the bureaucratic understandings of the threat posed by foreigners may help explain why, for example, an underdeveloped province like Guangxi would allocate 154 police to focus on management of the 329,692 foreigners who entered the region in 1989, equaling 1 entry–exit police officer per 2,140 tourists (in the same year, 542 *hukou* police managed the 8.67 million households in Guangxi, equaling 1 police officer per 16,000 households).[37] These views of the threats to state security posed by foreigners persisted well into the 2010s, as demonstrated by cartoons found in displays on Chinese streets that aimed to sensitize citizens to foreign spies posing as tourists or students (or, alternatively, pretending to be in love with Chinese women in order to extract state secrets). Ensuring cultural security by counteracting hostile foreign forces has become ingrained in Chinese thinking about protecting state security.

8.1.3 The Imperative of Stability Maintenance in China

Although hostile foreign forces threaten cultural security, their impact is slow and mediated, thus allowing for a response to be calibrated and deployed in a measured way. Tiananmen forcefully brought the realization that collective action can suddenly pose a nationwide threat to political stability. Since then, the leadership has drawn a direct link between maintaining stability and protecting state security.

For any student of current-day China, the notion that protests are a threat to social stability is a stylized fact. Yet, this understanding did not exist under Mao or during the initial reform period. It only emerged in the aftermath of the 1987 Lhasa riots. In 1988, both the MPS and the People's Armed Police (PAP) were conducting retrospective evaluations of their suppression of the unrest. The MPS described its actions in Tibet as "protecting state security and social order and stability" (*baowei guojia anquan he shehui zhi'an wending* 保卫国家安全和社会治安稳定),[38] whereas the PAP referred to handling "a sudden incident impacting social order" (*zhi'an tufa shijian* 治安突发事件).[39] Furthermore, the PAP claimed that it had "protected social order" (*weihu le shehui zhi'an* 维护了社会治安) by suppressing the protests.[40] These examples illustrate that the

[36] The exact number is 22.5 percent (98 out of 435 foreigners). See *Zhonghua renmin gongheguo jianyu shi, 1949–2000* (Beijing: Zhongguo Jianyu Xuehui, 2004), 472.

[37] Calculated from data in *Guangxi gong'an tongji nianjian 1989* (Nanning: Guangxi Zhuangzu Zizhiqu Gong'an Ju Bangongshi, November 1991).

[38] *Jianguo yilai gong'an gongzuo*, 686.

[39] Wujing Zongbu Zhengzhi Bu, "1988 nian de wujing budui gongzuo" (1990) (document on file with the author).

[40] "1988 nian de wujing budui gongzuo."

vocabulary that would come to inflect general thinking about protests in 1989–2019 was already in use by the security services prior to Tiananmen—but only to describe political contention on China's periphery that was inspired by hostile foreign forces.

The year of 1989, which featured student and worker protests, brought to the fore that both political and socioeconomic contention posed an immediate threat to state security. Protests in the capital and other major cities were described as social chaos (*shehui dongluan* 社会动乱).[41] To this, the MSS juxtaposed its mission to guard against hostile foreign forces and to protect state security and stability (*baowei guojia anquan he wending* 保卫国家安全和稳定).[42] In turn, internal MPS materials talked about political stability (*zhengzhi wending* 政治稳定), social order (*shehui zhi'an* 社会治安), social stability (*shehui wending* 社会稳定), and political and social stability (*shehui zhengzhi wending* 社会政治稳定).[43] The police equated protecting state security with stability maintenance—and stability maintenance required preventing large-scale collective action. This was a new idea because in the 1980s only political protests were understood to be state security threats, whereas socioeconomic protests represented a lesser threat to maintaining social order (*zhi'an* 治安).

The 1990s were a decade of mismatch between doctrinal thinking about contention and the actual behavior of the police on the ground. Throughout the decade, the top priority of the regime was to detect and neutralize overt political discontent. Although both political protests and socioeconomic contention compromised stability, there was a clear rank-ordering of threats. This meant that the reaction to political dissent was harsher than that to socioeconomic contention, with repression being the most likely response to political protest and concessions being a possible outcome for socioeconomic grievances. This more lenient approach to socioeconomic protests explains why they grew so rapidly in the 1990s, when Falun Gong occupied most of the attention of the police. However, the Color Revolutions and the Arab Spring served as a powerful reminder to the security apparatus that socioeconomic grievances can be rapidly transformed into regime-destabilizing political contention. For this reason, by the early 2010s, theory and practice were aligned, and any type of collective action was seen as a threat to state security. In 2014, protecting societal security (*shehui anquan* 社会安全) was officially included in the concept of comprehensive state security.

By conceptualizing any kind of contention as a state security threat, China reached an understanding of protest that was similar to the one that existed in

---

[41] Gong'an Bu Bangongting, "1989 nian de gong'an gongzuo" (1990).
[42] Guojia Anquan Bu Bangongting, "1989 nian de guojia anquan gongzuo" (1990).
[43] *Jianguo yilai gong'an gongzuo*, 733–48, 756, 810–11, 842–43.

pre-1989 Eastern Europe, where the leadership was made nervous by large-scale collective action regardless of whether it stemmed from economic or political grievances. This thinking produced clear benefits for the top leadership: one extraordinary feature of the Eastern European model is that most communist regimes enjoyed decades of rule without major upheavals. The most systematic available data on this issue are for the Soviet Union. We have two different estimates of civil unrest during the pre-1989 period. One is from 1988, when the Committee for State Security (KGB), at Gorbachev's request, generated a list of 24 cases of protests with more than 300 participants that had taken place between 1957 and 1986.[44] The other is a National Intelligence Council count of 281 demonstrations, strikes, riots, and acts of political violence that took place between 1970 and 1982, ranging in size from a single participant to over 10,000 protesters.[45] Despite such different estimates, both sources point to the fact that protest in the Soviet Union was a rare event. Although pejoratively referred to as the period of stagnation (*zastoi*), those years, from a contemporary Chinese perspective, appear to be a time of social stability. All communist regimes come to value stability maintenance once they experience nationwide regime-destabilizing protests (or observe them in other countries and draw the requisite lessons). This occurred in Eastern Europe when the leadership dissected regime-destabilizing experiences, such as the 1953 nationwide worker unrest in the German Democratic Republic (GDR), the 1956 uprisings in Poland and Hungary, and the Prague Spring in 1968. In China, the inflection point was the postmortem of Tiananmen and the dissolution of the communist regimes in Eastern Europe.

8.1.4 The Stability Maintenance Mandate of the MPS since 1989

Who is responsible for maintaining stability in China? In the period after 1989, the Ministry of State Security (MSS) and the Ministry of Public Security (MPS) have shared the state security portfolio. They have joint responsibility for monitoring foreign citizens, companies, NGOs, and Chinese citizens who have contacts with foreigners. Both ministries also engage in political protection (*zhengbao* 政保) that extends to preventing enemy forces and individuals from carrying out acts of hostility or sabotage of socialist property; ethnic separatism; sabotage under the guise of religion; incitement of sabotage by illegal

---

[44] "O massovyh besporiadok s 1957 goda," *Vestnik*, no. 6/1995, 146–54; V. A. Kozlov, *Massovye besporiadki v SSSR pri Khrushcheve i Brezhneve (1953–nachalo 1980-kh gg.)* (Novosibirsk: Sibirskii Khronograf, 1999).

[45] *Dimensions of Civil Unrest in the Soviet Union* (Washington, DC: National Intelligence Council, April 1983).

organizations and publications; and other counterrevolutionary and reactionary activities.[46] However, they also have areas of near-exclusive jurisdiction. Overseas, Hong Kong, Macau, and Taiwan intelligence is carried out almost fully by the MSS. In turn, day-to-day stability maintenance is handled by the MPS and the PAP, with little MSS involvement.

Stability maintenance has constituted a core task for the MPS since 1989, when protests of all kinds came to be understood by the police as threats to social and political stability (*weihai shehui zhengzhi wending* 危害社会政治稳定).[47] It is important to stress that the MPS was not interested in the *type* of protest but rather in the *tactics* of the protesters. It sought to safeguard against threats to stability by curbing sudden incidents, including demonstrations, factory and school strikes, petitions, illegal activities, and other disturbances—regardless of whether they arose on political or economic grounds.[48] This understanding continued in the 1990s, when, following a conference on political protection work, maintaining social stability was included among the state security responsibilities of the MPS. This wide remit yielded an extraordinarily broad portfolio.

In 1998, the MPS issued a regulation on handling sudden incidents, which reiterated that the police response was to be guided by protest tactics threatening stability, regardless of the grievances involved.[49] A notice on state security work by the MPS was issued in 1999, clarifying that domestic security protection (*guonei anquan baowei* 国内安全保卫, or *guobao* 国保) mainly involved ensuring stability maintenance.[50] In December 1999, a state security protection circular enumerated the tasks of grassroots police stations, which included: collection of internal enemy intelligence and evaluation of the factors impacting political stability in the areas under their jurisdiction; controlling management of the targeted population, complex locations and key places (*fuza changsuo he zhongdian diwei* 复杂场所和重点地位); carrying out basic investigations to protect domestic security; and successfully implementing propaganda education.[51]

This doctrinal evolution notwithstanding, the need to eliminate Falun Gong temporarily slanted the state security enforcement portfolio toward handling cults and illegal religious activities.[52] As the Falun Gong threat appeared more manageable in the 2000s, emphasis shifted to skip-level petitioning (越级上方

[46] *Jianguo yilai gong'an gongzuo*, 932.

[47] *Xinjiang shengchan jianshe bingtuan gong'an zhi* (Urumqi: Xinjiang Shengchan Jianshe Bingtuan Gong'an Zhi and Xinjiang Shengchan Jianshe Bingtuan Difang Zhi Bangongshi, 1999), 188–89.

[48] *Xinjiang shengchan jianshe bingtuan gong'an zhi*, 188–89.

[49] Gong'an Bu Bangongting Yanjiushi, *Quntixing shijian yanjiu* (Beijing: Gong'an Bu Bangongting Yanjiushi, June 2000), 557–62.

[50] *Jianguo yilai gong'an gongzuo*, 1287–88.

[51] *Jianguo yilai gong'an gongzuo*, 1294.

[52] Changchun Shi Gong'an Ju, *Changchun gong'an nianjian 2001–2003* (Changchun: Changchun Shi Gong'an Ju, 2004), 128–29; *Fujian sheng zhi: Gong'an zhi 1990–2005*, 15–17; Hubei Sheng Gong'an Ting, *Hubei gong'an zhi 1949–2009* (Wuhan: Hubei Sheng Gong'an Ting, 2010), 337–39.

yueji shangfang), and, eventually, to protests. Maintaining social stability was a consistent veto target (*yipiao foujue* 一票否决) in cadre evaluations throughout the 2000s,[53] thus explaining the extraordinary nervousness with which local leaders reacted to potentially destabilizing acts of contention. The 2007 Collective Incidents Law added new emphasis to the role of the police in handling these problems. The 2008 Olympics required further expansion of security budgets, which persisted into the 2010s. Advances in technology allowed the police to adapt to protests in the digital age. Extensive monitoring of all telecommunications means that the most sensitive protests in the 2010s could be nipped in the bud. For those that did occur, grid urban policing, which relies on a high density of surveillance cameras and big data algorithms, enabled a rapid reaction.[54] Surveillance extended to rural areas as well through the Sharp Eyes (*xueliang* 雪亮) Project. Future advances in AI will enable an ever speedier and more precise response to protests and will make negotiation and compromise even less likely.

8.1.5 Selective Enforcement of State Security Laws after Tiananmen

Previously unavailable internal statistics from Guangxi shed light on the severity of prosecutions for counterrevolutionary crimes. Although Guangxi had the highest proportion of counterrevolutionary prisoners of any Chinese province in 1951 (84,334 individuals or 93.73 percent of all those imprisoned), by 1989 its counterrevolutionary inmates numbered as few as 150 (0.28 percent of the prison population).[55] But what can we expect about the severity of prosecution based on these statistics? Internal sources reveal that enforcement was highly selective.[56] Table 8.1, for example, indicates that in 1989 as few as 5 percent of the counterrevolutionary crimes discovered by the Guangxi PSB culminated in arrest (twenty individuals) or reeducation-through-labor (one individual). By 1991, the proportion of cases that concluded with arrest or reeducation had declined to 1.8 percent, which is equivalent to the number of cases that resulted in arrest in Bulgaria in the early 1970s (see Chapter 5 and Table 8.2). This offers

---

[53] Hou Linke and Liu Mingxing, "Zhongguo jiceng zhengfu de ganbu kaohe yu gongzuo zhineng: Yunzhuan zhidu yu gaige kunjing" (2014), http://www.escience.cn/system/download/68096 (accessed November 10, 2019). Failure to meet veto targets can negate successful performance in other areas and thus block career advancement.

[54] *Gong'an yanjiu*, no. 6 (2017), 34–39; *Gong'an yanjiu*, no. 6 (2017), 40–46; *Gong'an yanjiu*, no. 6 (2017), 65–70. Importantly, grid policing also uses human intelligence collectors: see Huirong Chen and Sheena Chestnut Greitens, "Information Capacity and Social Order: The Local Politics of Information Integration in China," *Governance* (2021), DOI: 10.1111/gove.12592.

[55] Sifa Bu Jianyu Guanli Ju, *Dangdai Zhongguo jianyu tongji ziliao (1949–1989)* (Beijing: Sifa Bu Jianyu Guanli Ju, November 1998), 68, 76.

[56] Also see Chapter 6 on 1988 Guangxi statistics.

Table 8.1 Counterrevolutionary Crimes in Guangxi, 1989

	Cases Discovered by the PSB	Cases Investigated by the PSB	Cases Clarified by the PSB	PSB/MSS Cases Accepted by the Procuratorate	Cases Solved	Individuals Arrested	Reeducation-through-Labor
Slogans	230	157	83	73	55		
Leaflets	36	16	7	20	14		
Domestic letters	36	14	5	22	11		
Foreign correspondence	148	135	114	13	10		
Group	13	10	10	3	3		
Secret societies	5	2	2	3	3		
Explosions	1	1	1	1	1		
Murder	1	1	1				
Other	90	37	34	44	37		
TOTAL	560	373	257	179	134	20	1

Source: Guangxi gong'an tongji nianjian 1989.

Table 8.2 Counterrevolutionary Crimes in Guangxi, 1991

	Cases Discovered by the PSB	Cases Investigated by the PSB	Cases Clarified by the PSB	PSB/MSS Cases Accepted by the Procuratorate	Cases Solved	Individuals Arrested	Reeducation-through-Labor
Slogans	111	76	52	14	11		
Leaflets				3	1		
Domestic letters	11	9	8	7	6		
Foreign correspondence	85	72	69	3	2		
Group	5	5	3				
Secret societies	4	1	1	6	6		
Explosions							
Murder							
Other	114	27	24	3	3		
TOTAL	330	190	157	36	29	6	0

Source: Guangxi gong'an tongji nianjian 1991 (Nanning: Guangxi Zhuangzu Zizhiqu Gong'an Ju Bangongshi, May 1993).

powerful evidence that China was already practicing selective enforcement of state security laws and regulations on the eve of Tiananmen and that prosecution became even more selective after Tiananmen.

Given that the Political Protection Department (*zhengbao ju* 政保局) of the Guangxi PSB had nearly as many police as the crucial Household Registration Department (*huji ju* 户籍局) (521 vs. 542 officers),[57] we face another question—namely, considering that the PSB had no shortage of personnel to investigate counterrevolutionary crimes, why did so few of those who committed them end up in prison? The chapters on Eastern Europe generate two hypotheses about the utility of non-imprisonment: the first is that those who are not arrested may be recruited through blackmail to serve as informants, and the second is that non-imprisonment does not mean immunity from surveillance, as demonstrated by the logic of the targeted population roster.

8.1.6 Monitoring Domestic Enemies through the Targeted Population Roster

Police materials published after the 1989 Tiananmen protests use interchangeably the concepts of domestic security protection and stability maintenance (*weihu wending* 维护稳定).[58] Accurate threat information was needed to ensure stability. Collection of this intelligence was guided by the categories on the targeted population list. These evolved between the 1990s and the 2010s. Prior to the abolition of counterrevolutionary crimes, individuals suspected of engaging in the following types of behaviors were tracked for inclusion on the roster: conspiracies to hijack planes (*jiechi feiji* 劫持飞机) and subvert trains (*dianfu lieche* 颠覆列车); spy or agent activity; and writing slogans, leaflets, anonymous letters, or organizing counterrevolutionary activities under the guise of religion.[59] The targeted population roster changed when the category of crimes of endangering state security replaced counterrevolutionary crimes in 1997. By 2010, the following subcategories had emerged on the list: state security protection (*guobao* 国保); anticult (*fan xiejiao* 反邪教); social order (*zhi'an* 治安); criminal suspects (*xingxian* 刑嫌); and Internet users (*wangshang* 网上).[60] Inclusion on the list

---

[57] *Guangxi gong'an tongji nianjian 1989.*

[58] Ji'nan Gong'an Nianjian Bianzuan Weiyuanhui, *Ji'nan gong'an nianjian 2010* (Ji'nan: Ji'nan Gong'an Nianjian Bianzuan Weiyuanhui, 2010), 130–32.

[59] *Xinjiang shengchan jianshe bingtuan gong'an zhi*, 214–15.

[60] Shandong Sheng Gong'an Ting, *Shandong gong'an nianjian 2011* (Beijing: Zhongguo Guoji Wenhua Chubanshe, 2011), 104; Lincang Shi Gong'an Zhi Bianxuan Weiyuanhui Bangongshi, *Lincang gong'an nianjian 2010* (Lincang: Lincang Shi Gong'an Zhi Bianxuan Weiyuanhui Bangongshi, 2010), 63.

was based on intelligence collected by eyes and ears and other informants.[61] Those on the list were controlled during sensitive periods and were monitored for behaviors like participation in special group gatherings (*teshu qunti juhui huodong* 特殊群体聚会活动) or collective petitioning.[62] It bears pointing out that individuals on the list could also be recruited to serve as informants tasked with providing intelligence about others on the roster.[63]

Although precise data on the share of individuals whose names were on the targeted population roster for political reasons are difficult to obtain, it is clear that in post-Mao China the roster was gradually transformed from a mechanism primarily for managing counterrevolutionaries into a tool for dealing with non-political criminality. Nevertheless, political transgressions did lead to placement on the list. This process was characterized by extraordinary temporal and geographic variation. For example, in the Xinjiang Production and Construction Corps, individuals suspected of engaging in counterrevolutionary crimes constituted no more than 1.5 percent of the roster in 1989–1997.[64] In the rest of Xinjiang, by contrast, those suspected of endangering state security accounted for 23.9 percent of the roster in 2000.[65] Finally, state security suspects, anticult suspects, criminal suspects, and Internet users constituted 98.8 percent of the roster in Shandong in 2010.[66] Those who engage in political transgressions are still managed via the list, thus elevating the importance the MPS attaches to obtaining accurate information through its surveillance network.

To sum up, alongside the MSS, the MPS has been a key entity in charge of developing rosters of domestic regime enemies since 1989. Broad conceptualizations of stability maintenance and cultural security have guided the designation of specific categories of individuals as threats to domestic security. Identifying these enemies has been accomplished through a series of techniques for the involuntary collection of information by the police, which are discussed in the next section.

---

[61] Gong'an Bu San Ju, ed., *Zhonghua renmin gongheguo hukou guanli ziliao huibian 1950–2014* (Beijing: Zhongguo Renmin Gong'an Daxue Chubanshe, 2015), 1643–51, at 1645; *Shandong gong'an nianjian 2011*, 104; *Lincang gong'an nianjian 2010*, 63.

[62] *Ji'nan gong'an nianjian 2010*, 131. See also Rory Truex, "Focal Points, Dissident Calendars, and Preemptive Repression," *Journal of Conflict Resolution* 63:4 (2019), 1032–52; Jennifer Pan, *Welfare for Autocrats: How Social Assistance in China Cares for Its Rulers* (New York: Oxford University Press, 2020); H. Christoph Steinhardt, "Defending Stability Under Threat: Sensitive Periods and the Repression of Urban Protest in China," *Journal of Contemporary China* 30:130 (2021), 526–49.

[63] In 1996, the head of the MPS *hukou* department revealed that the targeted population facilitated the identification of 251,000 individuals who had to be punished, provided 389,000 investigative clues, and helped solve 274,000 cases. *Zhonghua renmin gongheguo hukou*, 1645.

[64] Calculated from *Xinjiang shengchan jianshe bingtuan gong'an zhi*, 214–15.

[65] Calculated from Xinjiang Weiwuer Zizhiqu Difang Zhi Bianzuan Weiyuanhui, *Xinjiang tongzhi: Gong'an zhi* (Urumqi: Xinjiang Renmin Chubanshe, 2004), 514.

[66] Calculated from *Shandong gong'an nianjian 2011*, 104.

8.2   Police Techniques for Identifying, Registering, and Managing Enemies

The involuntary collection of information after 1989 presents numerous continuities with the pre-1989 period in terms of the techniques used to identify threats to state security, most notably the ongoing reliance on full-time staff and part-time visible and secret informants. There were important innovations as well, in particular the 110 hotline, grid policing, and Internet monitoring. A relevant caveat is that after 1989 the party was no longer involved in direct assessments of the enemy threat. The party did, however, continue to compile and analyze voluntarily provided information and, since the 2010s, to collect intelligence involuntarily through systematic Internet monitoring.

8.2.1   Innovations: From the 110 Hotline to Grid Policing

Information transmission is facilitated by techniques like a uniform telephone number that enables citizens to alert the police about any suspicious behavior they witness. After the successful introduction of the 110 hotline in Guangzhou in January 1986, a notice on expanding the 110 network to large- and medium-sized cities was issued by the MPS in April 1987.[67] The purpose of the hotline was to ensure a timely and resolute response to criminal activity as well as the effective handling of sudden incidents, the maintenance of social order, and the prevention of disasters.[68] In 1986, Guangzhou received 2,235 calls that focused primarily on criminal matters, violations of social order, and traffic incidents; in addition, some citizens provided information about individuals who were wanted by the police. Efforts were made to ensure that personnel would reach the scene within five minutes of receiving a call.[69] The network expanded rapidly and covered all 217 prefectural-level cities by 1997.[70] The value that the MPS attaches to this technology is revealed by the fact that information about the 110 hotline is printed in the section of the police yearbooks dedicated to intelligence-collection activities (qingbao gongzuo 情报工作).[71]

Internal police materials provide direct evidence of the utility of hotline tip-offs, which were used to draft a range of intelligence bulletins. Some were directly

[67]   Zhongguo renmin gong'an shigao (Beijing: Jingguan Jiaoyu Chubanshe, 1997), 398.

[68]   Jianguo yilai gong'an gongzuo, 663.

[69]   Jianguo yilai gong'an gongzuo, 1086.

[70]   Jianguo yilai gong'an gongzuo, 1087, 1135–36. The 1990s was also the decade when the internal telecommunications system of the MPS (which included computers) was created and expanded (see Zhongguo renmin gong'an shigao [1997], 411).

[71]   See, for example, Shanghai Gong'an Nianjian Bianji Bu, Shanghai gong'an nianjian 2010 (Shanghai: Tongji Daxue Chubanshe, 2010), 95–97.

based on the information extracted from the hotline. For example, in 2010 the Shanghai PSB generated 266 issues of a daily 110 police intelligence bulletin (*meiri 110 jingqing tongbao* 每日110警情通报).[72] In the same year, the Shanghai police produced two other briefs that relied on hotline information, in addition to other sources. The first was a digest of important intelligence (*yaoqing zhaibao* 要情摘报), which was issued 2,096 times in 2010.[73] The second, appearing 316 times in 2010, focused on current important public-security intelligence (*jinri gong'an yaoqing* 今日公安要情).[74] The value of such intelligence is that it is based on information transmitted voluntarily by citizens and it does not require massive investments for the recruiting and training of informants. Although most of it is noise (in 2010, it helped the Shanghai police crack 259 criminal cases,[75] or 0.6 percent of the total cases solved),[76] the number of police bulletins based on it suggests that its value lies elsewhere—namely, alongside other sources of information, it was used to measure the pulse of public opinion.

The 110 hotline has proven capable of adapting to the evolution of technology. In the 1990s, citizen 110 tip-offs were made exclusively by phone. The dominance of telephone lines persisted into the 2000s. Even though the police made use of the Internet and instituted a 110 police chief's mailbox (*juzhang xinxiang* 局长信箱), such technological advances did not obliterate the phone. There is no more powerful example of the importance of legacy technologies in police work than the case of Shanghai. Although it is invariably one of the two cities with the highest Internet penetration rate in China, its residents overwhelmingly chose to reach the police by phone. In 2010, the Shanghai police 110 service center was contacted 12.11 million times by phone; by contrast, only 17,112 tip-offs were received by mail and 830 were sent by email to the police chief's mailbox.[77] By 2012, mail tip-offs had declined to 16,738.[78] As of 2021, citizens could alert the police (*baojing* 报警) by writing a letter on 110 letterhead and depositing it into a 110 mailbox; by sending an email; through WeChat; or by making a phone call.[79] As in the past, monetary rewards are still disbursed to those who provide especially valuable information. Today, the 110 complaints hotline remains an important part of smart policing. Handled by a command center (*zhihui zhongxin* 指挥中心), smart policing uses artificial intelligence algorithms to aggregate information received through social media, phone calls,

---

[72] Shanghai Gong'an Nianjian Bianji Bu, *Shanghai gong'an nianjian 2011* (Shanghai: Tongji Daxue Chubanshe, 2011), 122.

[73] *Shanghai gong'an nianjian 2011*, 122.

[74] *Shanghai gong'an nianjian 2011*, 122.

[75] *Shanghai gong'an nianjian 2011*, 117.

[76] A total of 44,731 cases were solved in 2010 (*Shanghai gong'an nianjian 2011*, 149).

[77] *Shanghai gong'an nianjian 2011*, 117–18, 122.

[78] Shanghai Gong'an Nianjian Bianji Bu, *Shanghai gong'an nianjian 2013* (Shanghai: Tongji Daxue Chubanshe, 2013), 86.

[79] https://gaj.sh.gov.cn/shga/mail110 (accessed June 30, 2021).

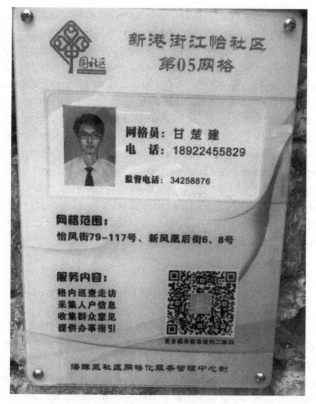

Figure 8.1 Grid policing contact information in Guangzhou.
Source: Photo taken by the author in Guangzhou, June 2016.

and surveillance cameras.[80] Thus, legacy technologies like phone hotlines have survived and have been integrated as essential components of advanced urban grid policing surveillance platforms in the age of big data and AI (see Figure 8.1 for the integration of legacy and recent technologies in grid policing).

8.2.2 Innovation: Police Internet Monitoring

Since the 1990s, the police have been monitoring the Internet, in addition to other telecommunications channels. Internet policing initially involved the closing down of illegal Internet cafés, but it quickly transitioned to the deletion

---

[80] *Gong'an yanjiu*, no. 6 (2017), 34–39; *Gong'an yanjiu*, no. 6 (2017), 40–46; *Gong'an yanjiu*, no. 6 (2017), 65–70.

of harmful content by the MPS Internet Security Protection Department and its affiliates located in Internet service providers (ISPs) and social media companies.[81] In the 2010s, the Internet police units focused on detecting illegal information (arms and explosives; prostitution and pornography; fraud; etc.) and detaining the individuals who facilitated its circulation.[82] Internet giants coached the police on how to identify and deal with illegal information: in Beijing alone, 400 police received such training by Sina and Baidu in 2013.[83] In that year, the Beijing PSB identified 5.85 million dangerous items and cleaned up 457,000 illegal items from the Internet.[84] In other provinces, considerably less was done: in Shandong, for example, the Internet police (*gonggong xinxi wangluo anquan jiancha zongdui* 公共信息网络安全监察总队) compiled statistics on 211,000 false information items.[85] The importance of Web monitoring is revealed by the fact that classified intelligence bulletins provided higher-level leaders with information on Internet safety.[86]

8.2.3 Continuity: Secret Investigation Work

One of the areas where significant continuities exist from the pre-1989 period is the use of secret investigative work (*mimi zhencha* 秘密侦查) for collecting information.[87] These activities are conducted either with or without deception. Agent work involves deception, whereas technical surveillance does not.

Nondeception methods of secret investigation center around technical surveillance, which is usually executed by full-time staff.[88] In China, these practices include covert eavesdropping (*mimi jianting* 秘密监听); secret photography, audio, and video recording (*milu mipai* 秘录秘拍); covert identification (*mimi bianren* 秘密辨认); secret searching for and collection of evidence (*misou miqu* 秘搜秘取); tailing (*genzong dingshao* 跟踪盯梢), surveillance (*shouhou jianshi* 守候监视), and outside reconnaissance (*waixian zhencha* 外线侦察); and, finally, examination of correspondence (*youjian jiancha* 邮件检查). In the days of analog technology, communications surveillance was limited to opening people's mail and to phone tapping (*dianhua zhenting* 电话侦听). With technological

---

[81] *Jianguo yilai gong'an gongzuo*, 1355.
[82] *Ji'nan gong'an nianjian 2010*, 142–45.
[83] Beijing Shi Gong'an Ju, *Beijing gong'an nianjian 2014* (Beijing: Beijing Shi Gong'an Ju, 2014), 155.
[84] *Beijing gong'an nianjian 2014*, 155.
[85] *Shandong gong'an nianjian 2011*, 125.
[86] Zhejiang Gong'an Shizhi Bianzuan Weiyuanhui, *Zhejiang gong'an nianjian 2015* (Hangzhou: Zhejiang Guji Chubanshe, 2015), 63; *Shandong gong'an nianjian 2011*, 125.
[87] Unless otherwise noted, the discussion of secret investigative work is based on Yu Botao, *Mimi zhencha wenti yanjiu* (Beijing: Zhongguo Jiancha Chubanshe, 2008).
[88] See 1985 temporary MPS regulation on technical surveillance measures (技术侦查手段的使用原则).

changes, electronic interception and monitoring (*dianzi zhenting dianzi jiankong* 电子侦听电子监控) have been added to the list of techniques used in secret investigations. In addition to these surveillance methods, the Chinese security apparatus carries out covert arrests (*mimi daibu* 秘密逮捕). We do not know the frequency with which these techniques are deployed. The persistence of so many analog methods, however, indicates that the digital age has expanded the scope of secret investigation work but has not rendered traditional mechanisms for human and technical surveillance obsolete.

The nomenclature of agents in contemporary China is quite broad. They are interchangeably referred to as *teqing* (特情), *ermu* (耳目), *xianren* (线人), hidden forces (*yinbi liliang* 隐蔽力量), or secret forces (*mimi liliang* 秘密力量).[89] One distinction is between criminal and political agents, who are sometimes called secret political protection forces (*zhengbao mimi liliang* 政保秘密力量).[90] Another is based on the deception tradecraft these agents deploy: entrapment (*youhuo* 诱惑), which can be pecuniary or sexual; penetration (*wodi* 卧底) of illegal or criminal organizations; controlled delivery of contraband goods (*kongzhi xia jiaofu* 控制下交付), aimed at developing relations with criminals and generating evidence that can lead to their arrest; prison work (*yunei teqing* 狱内特情),[91] which involves planting agents to extract further incriminating evidence from arrested or sentenced cellmates; and antidrug operations (*jidu teqing* 缉毒特情).[92] In contrast to citizens engaged in social-order protection (who gather information publicly or semi-publicly), all agents operate undercover with the aim of collecting evidence (*mimi huoqu moxie wuzheng* 秘密获取某些物证). Despite its breadth, the range of agents and the scope of agent work in contemporary China are consistent with the experience of the Eastern European communist regimes.

Although both the MPS and the MSS recruit secret informants, their number and compensation remain extremely carefully guarded secrets. Fortunately, internal police materials shed some light on these matters. Such documents reveal that in 1990 there were 3,243 social-order eyes and ears (*zhi'an ermu* 治安耳目) in Dalian for managing the targeted population of 25,311; *ermu* focused in particular on special professions.[93] The Dalian statistics allow us to calculate the penetration of eyes and ears (1,629.6 per million people),[94] in addition to

---

[89] Based on general regulations from 1981, 1984, and 2000. Also see *Xinjiang shengchan jianshe bingtuan gong'an zhi*, 188–89.

[90] *Xinjiang shengchan jianshe bingtuan gong'an zhi*, 186.

[91] See 1986 regulations on prison agents.

[92] See 2001 regulations on antidrug agents.

[93] Dalian Shi Shizhi Bangongshi, *Dalian shi zhi: Gong'an zhi* (Beijing: Fangzhi Chubanshe, 2004), 254. Special professions (*tezhong hangye* 特种行业) included hotel and entertainment venue employees; those who sold old and antique goods; the seal-and-carving craftspeople; and those who performed repairs, including of cameras and radios. See Yu Ying, *Gong'an xingzheng zhishi wenda* (Harbin: Heilongjiang Renmin Chubanshe, 1986), 62–65.

[94] The city had a population 1.99 million in 1990.

the saturation rate of the eyes-and-ears network among the targeted population (a ratio of one informant per eight individuals on the roster). Dalian was not unique: police sources indicate that Fujian deployed *ermu* in an identical way.[95] Internal police materials also shed light on the use of spies (*teqing*), who are better trained and more highly valued than eyes and ears: for example, such sources make clear that in Changchun there were under 1,000 spies in 2003 (for a population of over 3 million people), one-tenth of whom were top spies (*jianzi teqing* 尖子特情).[96] Very importantly, the sources also allow us to glean the amount of subsidies for agent work. In Changchun, for instance, the subsidy fund for spies (*teqing gongzuo zhuanxiang jingfei* 特情工作专项经费) was equivalent to RMB 500,000 in 2003;[97] this suggests that on an annual basis the subsidy for an average agent was about RMB 500 (US$60). This was not a paltry sum, but neither was it significant. It was equivalent to about one week's wages in Changchun at the time. Research on the GDR estimates that Stasi informants received a subsidy commensurate with the price of an annual TV subscription, which was also equivalent to a week's wages.[98] It is clear that secret investigation work in China exhibits numerous parallels to that in Eastern Europe.

8.2.4 Continuity: Visible Informants

The groups of informants who enabled social-order protection work underwent significant stresses and strains after 1989, but they have survived and thrived to the current day. Prior to the reform period, these social-order protection committees and small groups functioned primarily at the level of urban neighborhoods and rural communities, but some were also based within factories, mines, schools, firms, and government units. In the 1980s, there was a proliferation of additional entities conducting surveillance under the direction of the police: joint defense teams, patrols, armed guards (*wuzhuang shouwei* 武装守卫),[99] and security companies all engaged in information gathering. In Chengdu, for example, the landscape of visible informants in 1989 included the following social-order protection organizations (*zhi'an fangfan zuzhi* 治安防范组织): social-order protection committees; social-order protection small groups; protection teams and companies (*bao'an dui/gongsi* 保安队, 公司); social-order joint protection teams (*zhi'an lianfangdui* 治安联防队); social-order protection

---

[95] *Fujian sheng zhi: Gong'an zhi 1990–2005*, 69.

[96] *Changchun gong'an nianjian 2001–2003*, 130.

[97] *Changchun gong'an nianjian 2001–2003*, 129.

[98] Barbara Maria Piotrowska, "The Price of Collaboration: How Authoritarian States Retain Control," *Comparative Political Studies* 53:12 (2020), 2091–117.

[99] Gansu Sheng Difang Shi Zhi Bianzuan Weiyuanhui, *Gansu sheng zhi: Gong'an zhi* (Lanzhou: Gansu Wenhua Chubanshe, 1995), 226–28.

offices or teams (*zhi'an shi/dui* 治安室, 队); social-order protection posts (*zhi'an gangting* 治安岗亭); factory and school protection teams (*huchang, huxiao dui* 护厂, 护校队); night duty points (*yejian zhiqin dian* 夜间执勤点); and neighborhood watch small groups (*linli shoulou xiaozu* 邻里守楼小组).[100] Efforts were made throughout the 1980s to improve quality by reducing the share of retirees and by conducting yearly evaluations that categorized each protection committee based on whether it was good, satisfactory, or unsatisfactory.[101] For example, the number of associations that were evaluated as "ineffective" (*buqi zuyong de* 不起作用的) by the Guangxi PSB declined from 9.9 percent in 1989 to 6.1 percent in 1991.[102] Because the value of information increased after Tiananmen, the regime aggressively sought to obtain intelligence.

The 1990s put the system to a test. One complication was that the rise of security companies and the overall marketization of society raised the importance of compensating social-order protection committee members for their efforts. In the 1950s and 1960s, no stipend was provided for social-order protection work (*jihu meiyou shenme butie, quankao zhengzhi juewu* 几乎没有什么补贴,全靠政治觉悟); in the 1980s, with the introduction of various responsibility systems and the collection of a range of levies, local governments began to set aside funds to compensate members of the social-order protection committees with subsidies for living expenses (*shenghuo butie* 生活补贴) or for lost work (*wugong butie* 误工补贴), but no economic compensation was offered to the members of social-order protection committees in enterprises (*qishiye danwei de zhibao renyuan you zhengzhi rongyu daiyu, meiyou jingji baochou* 企事业单位的治保人员有政治荣誉待遇, 没有经济报酬).[103] Although most informants worked as uncompensated volunteers (*yiwu, meiyou baochou* 义务, 没有报酬), in some places they were compensated (*geiyu shidang de butie* 给予适当的补贴) from the public protection fee (*zhi'an fei* 治安费).[104] In the 1990s, some social-order protection committees were forced to disband due to financial pressures, especially in the countryside. Others were dissolved because they exceeded their legal mandate.[105] Although the police responded to this exigency by forcing

[100] Chengdu Shi Difang Zhi Bianzuan Weiyuanhui, *Chengdu shi zhi: Gong'an zhi* (Chengdu: Sichuan Renmin Chubanshe, 1999), 250.

[101] Beijing Shi Difang Zhi Bianzuan Weiyuanhui, *Beijing zhi: Zhengfa juan: Gong'an zhi* (Beijing: Beijing Chubanshe, 2003), 344; Jiangsu Sheng Difang Zhi Bianzuan Weiyuanhui, *Jiangsu sheng zhi: Gong'an zhi* (Beijing: Qunzhong Chubanshe, 2000), 274; Jiangxi Sheng Gong'an Zhi Bianzuan Weiyuanhui, *Jiangxi sheng gong'an zhi* (Beijing: Fangzhi Chubanshe, 1996), 61.

[102] *Guangxi gong'an tongji nianjian 1989*; *Guangxi gong'an tongji nianjian 1991*.

[103] Shandong Sheng Difang Shizhi Bianzuan Weiyuanhui, *Shandong sheng zhi: Gong'an zhi* (Ji'nan: Shandong Renmin Chubanshe, 1995), 319.

[104] Ningxia Gong'an Zhi Bianzuan Weiyuanhui, *Ningxia gong'an zhi* (Yinchuan: Ningxia Renmin Chubanshe, 2000), 299.

[105] Sichuan Sheng Difang Zhi Bianzuan Weiyuanhui, *Sichuan sheng zhi: Gong'an zhi 1986–2005* (Beijing: Fangzhi Chubanshe, 2014), 101; *Beijing zhi: Zhengfa juan*, 349.

communities to enter into social-order performance contracts,[106] the general trend in the late 1990s was toward limiting the size of the informant corps.

This was rapidly reversed. Having undergone a retrenchment during the deepening of the market transition of the 1990s, the social-order protection committees experienced substantial growth in the mid-2000s and 2010s. In Shandong, for example, between 1992 and 2000, the joint defense teams were reduced from 409,000 to 193,000 members, due to the elimination of the public security joint defense fee (*nongcun zhi'an lianfang fei* 农村治安联防费).[107] As the joint defense team members were reclassified as assistant police (*xiejing* 协警) in the 1990s and 2000s, new categories were created. For instance, by 2010 the group defense patrol teams (*qunfang qunzhi xunluo liliang* 群防群治巡逻力量) had 423,000 members.[108] In Shanghai, along with the familiar social-order protection committees, the following types of new visible informants existed in 2012: social-order auxiliary forces (*zhi'an fuzhu liliang* 治安辅助力量); social protection teams (*shebao dui* 社保队); and mass protection and mass order teams (*qunfang qunzhi duiwu* 群防群治队伍).[109] Likewise, Chaoyang masses (*Chaoyang qunzhong* 朝阳群众) were added to the familiar categories of social-order protection committees and small groups, residential surveillance teams, liaisons, and patrols in Beijing. When we factor in the ubiquitous security companies, whose operation is controlled by the police, we can conclude that the visible informant saturation rate in contemporary China is high.

Precisely how high is an important empirical question. No official statistics have been released, but they can be compiled from subnational police almanacs, gazetteers, and yearbooks. One complication is that some provinces list information about joint defense teams, patrols, and neighborhood watches—but many do not, even though these surveillance mechanisms exist in those provinces as well. Figure 8.2 reports on the data that can be extracted from police sources, without imputing numbers for categories of visible informants that are not listed in the sources. These caveats mean that Figure 8.2 is an underestimate of the share of visible MPS informants in China. Nevertheless, the trend is clear: the number of informants declined in the mid-1990s, but thereafter it increased. On average, social-order MPS informants between 1989 and the 2010s constituted 1 percent–2 percent of the population. This saturation rate is astonishingly high—all the more so when we take into consideration that it is an undercount.

---

[106] Guangdong Sheng Difang Shizhi Bianzuan Weiyuanhui, *Guangdong sheng zhi: Difang zhi* (Guangzhou: Guangdong Renmin Chubanshe, 2001), 196; *Xinjiang shengchan jianshe bingtuan gong'an zhi*, 205–6, 255–68.

[107] Shandong Sheng Difang Shizhi Bianzuan Weiyuanhui, *Shandong sheng zhi: Gong'an zhi 1986–2005* (Ji'nan: Shandong Renmin Chubanshe, 2013), 153.

[108] *Shandong gong'an nianjian 2011*, 106.

[109] *Shanghai gong'an nianjian 2013*, 126, 141.

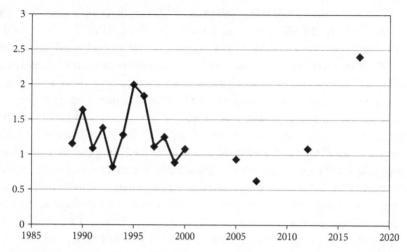

Figure 8.2 Visible police informants in China, 1989–2017 (as a percentage of the population).
Source: Author's dataset.

Even more revealing is the answer to a question that was newly added to the China Social Survey in 2017. Respondents were asked whether they had participated as volunteers in a social-order protection group (*zhi'an fangfan* 治安防范) during the previous year. Surprisingly, 3.5 percent replied in the affirmative.[110] When we take into account that only those over 18 years of age could participate in the survey, this means that as of 2017, fully 2.4 percent of the population of China had been active as social-order police informants during the previous twelve months. As a result, China is a leader among communist countries in terms of the rate of its penetration of society with human intelligence collectors. This staggering finding is an undercount, as respondents were only asked about their participation as visible informants. A complete tally of the penetration rate of informants would take into account the number of secret collectors who work as MPS eyes and ears or as MSS agents.[111] These caveats notwithstanding, the self-reported participation in visible police informant networks constitutes concrete proof that social surveillance by police volunteers has not only survived but also has increased in the age of social media and AI-enabled smart policing.

[110] Li Peilin, Chen Guangjin, and Zhang Yi, eds., *Zhongguo shehui xingshi fenxi yu yuce 2019* (Beijing: Shehui Kexue Wenxian Chubanshe, 2019), 149.
[111] The only available estimate is based on an interview with a county-level MPS official who surmised that 3 percent of the population in his county served as informants. See Peter L. Mattis, "China's Adaptive Approach to the Information Counter-Revolution," *China Brief* 11:10 (June 3, 2011), 5–8, at 6.

What is the function of visible informants? One argument might be that they provide clues to the police that prove useful in solving cases. This is certainly true, but the frequency with which it happens is low. Consider Beijing, where in 1995 there were 735,471 members of the social-order protection committees and small groups (6.2 percent of the capital's population). Those individuals were only one part of the visible informant network: others included joint defense teams, security companies, volunteer factory patrols, and neighborhood watch members (*kanlou huyuan liliang* 看楼护院力量). All of these individuals supplied a grand total of 33,564 suspicious clues to the Beijing police and assisted in solving 2,481 cases in that year.[112] These paltry numbers suggest that the real utility of visible informants might not reside in supplying actionable intelligence on petty criminals but rather in providing information on brewing social instability.[113] This information is then used to determine placement on the targeted population roster, which has a category reserved for state security violations.[114] Thus, from the point of view of the MPS, the utility of developing an informant corps resides in continuously updating the targeted population roster with current intelligence.

8.2.5 Continuity: Full-Time Police Staff

The personnel allocation of the MSS is unknown, except for the 1989 data on fourteen provinces reported in Chapter 6. The personnel allocation of the MPS is known, though it should be interpreted with an understanding that it is an undercount, as the PAP troops that assist in maintaining stability and individuals who are employed full-time by the police in *bianwai* (编外) positions are not systematically counted.[115] With these caveats, we can make the following observations. Prior to 1989, the official public security personnel allocation grew from 190,000 in 1951 to 408,000 in 1958 and 650,000 in 1985.[116] But it is the post-Tiananmen expansion that is most impressive. Greitens, relying on research by Scoggins and O'Brien, cites a figure of 1.38 police per 1,000 residents in 2009.[117] Internal personnel compendia supply significantly higher numbers: in

---

[112] *Beijing zhi: Zhenggfa juan*, 345.

[113] *Sichuan sheng zhi: Gong'an zhi 1986–2005*, 100.

[114] *Shandong gong'an nianjian 2011*, 104; *Lincang gong'an nianjian 2010*, 63.

[115] Although the number of uniformed PAP assisting the MPS in 2010 is not known, detailed personnel statistics for 1986–1991 on file with the author allow us to calculate that in 1986–1991 the mean ratio of MPS police to PAP police was 1.2:1.

[116] *Jianguo yilai gong'an gongzuo*, 33, 157, 564.

[117] Sheena Chestnut Greitens, "Rethinking China's Coercive Capacity: An Examination of PRC Domestic Security Spending, 1992–2012," *The China Quarterly*, no. 232 (December 2017), 1002–25, at 1013. Identical statistics are also contained in Lena Y. Zhong, "Community Policing in China: Old Wine in New Bottles," *Police Practice and Research* 10:2 (April 2009), 157–69, at 157.

2010, there were 2 political-legal officers and 4 civilian political-legal staff per 1,000 residents.[118] The 1,957,529 police (*jingcha* 警察) constituted 74.4 percent of the political-legal officers.[119] Importantly, the political-legal system included the MSS; although its personnel allocation is highly confidential, classified police materials reveal that in 2010 there were 311,349 intelligence and investigation personnel (*zhengfa qingbao he zhencha rencai ziyuan* 政法情报和侦察人才资源) and 87,112 emergency personnel (*zhengfa yingji rencai ziyuan* 政法应急人才资源) for use in protecting social stability.[120] Both categories of personnel serve the MPS and the MSS, thus providing some glimpses into the secretive world of MSS personnel statistics.

The internal organization of the MPS is more revealing of its approach toward safeguarding state security than the raw personnel numbers. Until the 1980s, the MPS office centrally responsible for handling dissent was the Political Protection Department (*zhengbao chu* 政保处). In the 1980s, there was a constant focus on strengthening the investigation of international conspiracies organized by the Soviet Union, of Taiwanese spies, and of counterrevolutionary cases.[121] In the 1990s, the political protection departments were renamed domestic security protection departments. The threat of Falun Gong, which had appeared in some provinces as early as 1992,[122] was managed by the 610 offices,[123] which were rebranded as the Provincial PSB Offices on Preventing and Handling Cult Crimes (*sheng gong'an ting fangfan he chuli xiejiao fanzui gongzuo chu* 省公安厅防范和处理邪教犯罪工作处) in the 2000s.[124] A final innovation of the 2000s was the creation of units focusing on mass incidents.[125] Thus, a fuller accounting of the departments responsible for managing dissent would include the Domestic Security Protection Department (*Guobao* Department), the 610 Office (Anticult Department), the Mass Incidents Department, the Social Order Department, the Household Registration (*huji* 户籍) Department, and the Entry–Exit Department.

---

[118] Zhonggong Zhongyang Zuzhi Bu, *Quanguo rencai ziyuan tongji ziliao huibian 2010* (Beijing: Zhonggong Zhongyang Zuzhi Bu, 2012), 278–84. The 2,720,156 political-legal personnel (or 1:500 residents) were assisted by 5,310,747 staff from outside the formal political-legal system (依托, 购买, 雇用体制外的人才).

[119] For a different breakdown listing the MPS as having at least 1.58 million officers, see *Quanguo rencai ziyuan tongji*, 278–84.

[120] *Quanguo rencai ziyuan tongji*, 278–84.

[121] Hubei Sheng Gong'an Ting, *Hubei gong'an zhi 1949–2009* (Wuhan: Hubei Sheng Gong'an Ting, 2010), 337–39.

[122] *Hubei gong'an zhi 1949–2009*, 337.

[123] In some regions of certain provinces, the 610 Office is included in the State Security Office [国保支队 [含"610"办]). See Hunan Sheng Difangzhi Bianzuan Weiyuanhui, *Hunan sheng zhi: Gong'an zhi* (Zhuhai: Zhuhai Chubanshe, 2009), 716–17.

[124] *Ji'nan gong'an nianjian 2010*, 137–41; *Hubei gong'an zhi 1949–2009*, 337–39.

[125] In Changchun, this department was created in 2006 with ten personnel. There were 1,159 mass incidents with 77,164 participants in Changchun in that year. Changchun Shi Gong'an Ju, *Changchun gong'an nianjian 2004–2006* (Changchun: Changchun Gong'an Ju, 2008), 103–4.

As the MPS division most directly responsible for protecting state security, the *Guobao* Department deserves further attention. In general, it is exceedingly difficult to obtain specific empirical information on this department, but details are available for Hunan, Zhejiang, and the city of Changchun in Jilin province. The Hunan data clarify the internal organization of the Domestic Security Protection Department (*Guobao* Department) in the 2000s: it consisted of a comprehensive intelligence research office (*zonghe qingbao yanjiu shi* 综合情报研究室), a religious and democratic work detachment, which also carried the nameplate of a mobile investigation detachment (*zongjiao minzhu gongzuo zhidui, jiagua jidong zhencha zhidui paizi* 宗教民主工作支队，加挂机动侦察支队牌子), an economic and cultural security protection detachment (*jingji wenhua baowei gongzuoren zhidui* 经济文化保卫工作人支队), and an overseas research detachment (*jingwai yanjiu zhidui* 境外调研支队).[126] Closely affiliated with the *Guobao* Department, which was also known as the First Department (一处), were the 610 Office or 26th Department ("610" 办公室 [二十六处]) and the Counterterrorism or 27th Department (反恐怖处 [二十七处]).[127] The Zhejiang data provide information on the size of the intelligence division of the Domestic Security Protection Department: in 2013, a total of 683 police (*qingbao zhuanye minjing* 情报专业民警) and 622 civilian workers (*wenzhi renyuan* 文职人员) were employed in the provincial intelligence center (*qingbao zhongxin* 情报中心).[128] Finally, rich data from Changchun shed light on the tasks of the *Guobao* Department and on its personnel allocation. The mission of the State Security Department was to protect social political stability (*weihu shehui zhengzhi wending* 维护社会政治稳定).[129] Its specific tasks included antisubversion and anti-infiltration (*fan dianfu fan shentou* 反颠覆反渗透), which were carried out by confiscating religious materials (bibles and Falun Gong propaganda); by seizing illegal political publications on the lives of leaders and on elite Zhongnanhai machinations; by identifying places of illegal religious activities; and by detaining, fining, and educating the leaders and some of the followers of those religious organizations.[130] At the time, the *Guobao* Department relied on 125 employees to execute these tasks.[131] In sum, internal police sources highlight the ongoing central role of the MPS in counteracting numerous domestic threats to state security during the post-1989 period.

---

[126] *Hunan sheng zhi: Gong'an zhi*, 717–19.
[127] *Hunan sheng zhi: Gong'an zhi*, 717–19.
[128] Zhejiang Gong'an Shizhi Bianzuan Weiyuanhui, *Zhejiang gong'an nianjian 2014* (Hangzhou: Zhejiang Guji Chubanshe, 2015), 126.
[129] *Changchun gong'an nianjian 2001–2003*, 120.
[130] *Changchun gong'an nianjian 2001–2003*, 124–25.
[131] *Changchun gong'an nianjian 2001–2003*, 121.

8.2.6 Continuity: Police Reporting and the Transfer of Information

Another area of continuity with the pre-1989 period is the transfer of intelligence to the higher levels. Internal statistics allow us to document that such transfer is always selective. For example, the Liaoning PSB gathered enemy, political, and social intelligence (*diqing, zhengqing, sheqing* 敌情, 政情, 社情).[132] In 1986–2000, the Liaoning political protection units collected over 400,000 items of these three types of intelligence and transmitted to the provincial party and government and to the MPS 3,253 important information items, some of which were used by the central leadership or resulted in instructions (*pishi* 批示).[133] In 2001–2005, Liaoning was in a leading national position in terms of the collection and upward transmission of domestic security protection intelligence; in 2005, over 70,000 intelligence items were collected, of which 3,500 were deemed important and 360 were transmitted upward.[134] Even rarer than transmission is a leadership *pishi*: in 2010 in Ji'nan, 4,540 pieces of intelligence were reported upward, with 72 resulting in instructions (*pishi*).[135] Rather than being indiscriminate, transfer is carefully considered so that top leaders are not buried in an avalanche of information.

8.2.7 Summing Up

The MPS has developed new techniques for the involuntary collection of information, including adapting old methods to the post-1989 realities. A large amount of intelligence is gathered, which overwhelmingly is used for counteracting dissent and maintaining stability at the local level. But as in other communist regimes, such information in China is rarely deemed sufficiently important to be transferred to the higher-level authorities. The logic of selective transmission goes against the conventional wisdom of willful suppression of upward information flows in the bureaucracy.

8.3 Petitions, Protests, and Online Comments: From Private Requests for Services to the Public Broadcasting of Grievances

The main mechanism for the voluntary transmission of information in communist regimes has traditionally been citizen complaints. Protests are also

---

[132] *Liaoning sheng zhi: Gong'an zhi, 1986–2005*, 45.
[133] *Liaoning sheng zhi: Gong'an zhi, 1986–2005*, 46.
[134] *Liaoning sheng zhi: Gong'an zhi, 1986–2005*, 46.
[135] Over 1,000 of the 4,540 pieces were signals (*yujing xinxi* 预警信息). See *Ji'nan gong'an nianjian 2010*, 132.

informative (and voluntary), but this information is disseminated both vertically and horizontally, in contrast to complaints, which are private requests for services that are transmitted only vertically. Since the 1990s, the Internet has provided an additional avenue for citizens to voluntarily communicate their views—posting on websites and social media with their real names. Like protests, Internet posts allow for the public airing of grievances, thus calling for a response different from the one issued to complaints.

Before we proceed with the analysis, it is worth highlighting the key differences between Eastern Europe and China. Complaints were the principal channel for voluntary information transmission in Eastern Europe.[136] A stark divergence is that because the complaints system functioned well, protests were infrequent. In contrast to China, complaints were typically individual (rather than collective), and they were delivered in writing (instead of in person). Complaining was a routine private act of communicating with the government, which was made possible by a low-repression high-redistribution equilibrium. Citizens issued requests about welfare benefits that were consistent with the socialist social contract; until economic conditions deteriorated in the mid-1980s, the party-state was able to satisfy these demands. Because it enabled anticipatory governance, voluntary information transmission through letters was welcome in Eastern Europe.

Voluntary transfer had a different trajectory in China. Although the central government promoted written petitions after 1989 (and levels of repression declined, as illustrated by the granular Guangxi data reviewed in Section 8.1), local governments often lacked the capacity to address the grievances outlined in them. Low responsiveness, in turn, led to a decline in petitioning and a rise in protests, thus threatening social stability. A second effect of the weakness of the traditional letters-and-visits system was that more citizens turned to online complaint forums. This only heightened regime insecurity, given the potential of online comments to catalyze offline contention. The net result was that the type of voluntary provision that was desired (through letters and individual visits) declined, whereas transfer through online posts and offline protests continued to grow. Although the government preferred private vertical communication, it was confronted with threatening public expression of discontent that could spread horizontally and catalyze further dissatisfaction. For this reason, by the 2010s the modal forms of voluntary information transfer were discouraged, rather than being promoted by the regime.

---

[136] The Internet did not emerge in Eastern Europe until after 1989, and competitive elections did not exist, except at the beginning and end of regime tenure.

8.3.1 Complaints 1989–2004

Between June and September 1989, Shanghai mayor Zhu Rongji, General Secretary Jiang Zemin, Politburo Standing Committee member Qiao Shi, and Premier Li Peng each made separate statements about the importance of providing prompt and detailed responses to citizen complaints.[137] In August 1989, the top leadership convened a meeting in Beijing of ten directors of provincial-level letters-and-visits bureaus,[138] and in September 1989 the Central Bureau of Letters and Visits sent out a notice to all provincial-level party and government offices regarding strengthening complaints work.[139] The system of citizen petitions had never before received as much sustained attention from the top leadership as it did at this time. This is not surprising, considering that the top echelon of the party-state wanted to regain the trust of the masses through increased responsiveness to complaints. Central-level leaders also thought that greater responsiveness would maintain stability by preventing the escalation of individual grievances into group petitions or visits to Beijing.

In the early 1990s, the center undertook a vertical expansion of the complaints network to the township level and eventually to the villages.[140] This led to an increase in the number of letters and visits, thus re-integrating citizens into the system (see Figure 8.3). My provincial complaints dataset indicates that in marked contrast to the pre-Tiananmen period when urban petitions dominated, complaints in the 1990s came primarily from rural residents, who were expressing dissatisfaction with excessive taxation, high compulsory procurement quotas, cadre malfeasance, and corrupt implementation of village elections. However, in addition to this increase in the volume of petitions, there was also a rising number of individuals who escalated their complaining by visiting Beijing to remonstrate in person and by organizing mass protests.[141] By the early 2000s, most petitions came from unemployed urban workers, who were expressing their dissatisfaction with enterprise restructuring and were demanding social welfare payments and poverty relief. The number of complaints increased very rapidly, and by 2004 it stood at 13.7 million, more than double the 5.5 million petitions received in 1997 (see Figure 8.3). But it was the increasing frequency of mass incidents that the regime found most worrisome: between 1997 and 2004,

---

[137] *Renmin xinfang*, no. 10 (1989), 2; *Renmin xinfang*, no. 11 (1989), 2–4.
[138] *Renmin xinfang*, no. 10 (1989), 3–8.
[139] *Renmin xinfang*, no. 2 (1990), 2–3.
[140] On this process in Zouping County (Shandong province), see *Zouping nianjian 1986–1995* (Ji'nan: Jilu Shushe, 1997), 83–84.
[141] *Renmin xinfang*, no. 12 (1998), 11–13.

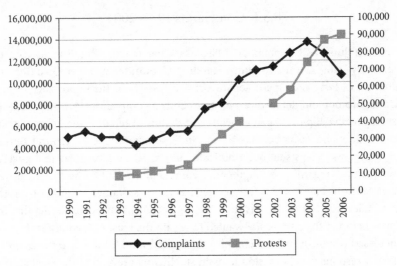

Figure 8.3 Number of citizen complaints and protests in China, 1990–2006.
Source: Author's dataset.

they quintupled—from 15,000 to 74,000.[142] Maintaining social stability, a primary concern after Tiananmen, suddenly acquired a new urgency.

8.3.2 Decline in Complaints Received by the Letters-and-Visits Bureaus since 2005

Petitions handled by the *xinfang* offices declined after 2004 (see Figure 8.4). The frequency of complaining is low not only in absolute but also in relative terms: at 3.5 per 1,000 people, the rate of complaining in 2017 was an order of magnitude smaller than the lowest volume of complaints in Bulgaria, which stood at 36.67 per 1,000 at its nadir in 1987.[143] A further sign of erosion of trust in the system is that, in contrast to the Eastern Bloc where 90 percent of the petitions were individual and in writing, most *xinfang* in China involved escalation tactics like

---

[142] Andrew Wedeman, "Enemies of the State: Mass Incidents and Subversion in China," paper presented at the Annual Meeting of the American Political Science Association, Toronto, September 2009.

[143] Survey research finds higher rates of complaining, because citizens are asked whether they have contacted the authorities through letters and visits or in other ways. For this imprecise estimate on the rate of complaining, see Diana Fu and Greg Distelhorst, "Grassroots Participation and Repression under Hu Jintao and Xi Jinping," *The China Journal*, no. 79 (2018), 100–22, at 114 (referring to the 2010 wave of the General Social Survey).

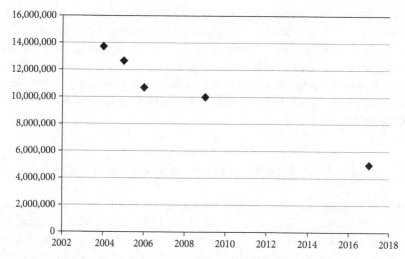

Figure 8.4 Complaints lodged at letters-and-visits offices, 2004–2017.
Source: Author's dataset.

in-person visits or collective petitioning.[144] What is especially worrisome about the decline registered in Figure 8.4 is that it has occurred in conjunction with a rise in the number of petitions that were lodged at the central level in Beijing and a dramatic increase in the frequency of mass incidents, mostly at the subnational level. Both petitioning in Beijing and participating in mass incidents indicate that citizens do not believe that their grievances can be resolved through the formal complaints channels available at the local level.

One of the key obstacles preventing citizens from trusting the petitioning system is the behavior of local officials. The 2014 reforms of the letters-and-visits system eliminated the number of petitions that escalate from localities to the higher levels as one of the criteria for evaluating the performance of local officials, aiming to reduce the incentives of local cadres to suppress petitions.[145] A related reform has been the phasing out of *paiming tongbao zhidu* (排名通报

[144] All provinces for which we have disaggregated data indicate similar trends. For example, in Guangxi, a total of 188,200 individuals complained in 2006 by post or in person, broken down as follows: 31,819 letters, 6,034 of which were collective letters signed by 41,649 people; 23,866 individual visits; and 5,458 collective visits by 96,900 people. In the 2010s, in-person visits still accounted for about half of the complaints handled by the petitioning offices, despite efforts to promote the electronic submission of letters. In Anhui, for example, 45.5 percent of petitions were made in person in 2016. See Anhui Nianjian Bianzuan Weiyuanhui, *Anhui nianjian 2017* (Hefei: Anhui Nianjian Chubanshe, 2017), 105.

[145] Zhonggong Zhongyang Bangongting and Guowuyuan Bangongting, *Guanyu chuangxin qunzhong gongzuo fangfa jiejue xinfang tuchu wenti de yijian* (February 25, 2014).

制度), the practice of ranking localities on the basis of the number of complaints that escalate to higher levels.[146] Local cadres benefited from the change, as they would no longer receive a lower performance review should petitions that could not be resolved locally escalate. However, as these policies did not succeed in incentivizing citizens to stop protesting and to utilize the letters-and-visits system, there was a new urgency to handle protests in a manner that would maintain social stability.

8.3.3 The New Normal: Protest Response After 2012

Protests in autocracies are rare events that have the potential to unleash cascades of destabilization.[147] For this reason, they are typically met with a resolute response. China appears exceptional in terms of this empirical pattern, as it has withstood well over 1 million acts of contention since 1989 without unraveling. The literature argues that socioeconomic protests (rightful resistance) and nationalist protests are likely to be tolerated,[148] in contrast to the rare instances of political dissent, which are harshly repressed in light of their capacity to threaten stability.[149] In general, scholars maintain that since 1989 protests have been more likely to be tolerated in China than to be repressed.[150] Large-scale, disruptive (forceful), and public events, especially when they took place in urban areas, were more likely to succeed.[151] In explaining accommodation, scholars highlight the benefits that accrue from demonstrating responsiveness to protests. The

---

[146] "Xinfang paiming tongbao zhidu yi bei quxiao," *Caijing*, November 11, 2013.

[147] Timur Kuran, "Now Out of Never: The Element of Surprise in the East European Revolution of 1989," *World Politics* 44:1 (1991), 7–48; Susanne Lohmann, "The Dynamics of Informational Cascades: The Monday Demonstrations in Leipzig, East Germany, 1989–91," *World Politics* 47:1 (1994), 42–101.

[148] Kevin J. O'Brien and Lianjiang Li, *Rightful Resistance in Rural China* (New York: Cambridge University Press, 2006); Jessica C. Weiss, *Powerful Patriots: Nationalist Protest in China's Foreign Relations* (New York: Oxford University Press, 2014).

[149] Elizabeth J. Perry, *Challenging the Mandate of Heaven: Social Protest and State Power in China* (Armonk, NY: M.E. Sharpe, 2002), esp. ix–xxxii.

[150] Yanqi Tong and Xiaohua Lei, *Social Protest in Contemporary China, 2003–2010: Transitional Pains and Regime Legitimacy* (New York: Routledge, 2014); Yao Li, *Playing by the Informal Rules: Why the Chinese Regime Remains Stable Despite Rising Protests* (New York: Cambridge University Press, 2019). For more nuanced treatments that still find very high (even if not dominant) levels of toleration, see Yongshun Cai, *Collective Resistance in China: Why Popular Protests Succeed or Fail* (Stanford, CA: Stanford University Press, 2010); Xi Chen, *Social Protest and Contentious Authoritarianism in China* (New York: Cambridge University Press, 2012); Christopher Heurlin, *Responsive Authoritarianism in China: Land, Protests, and Policymaking* (New York: Cambridge University Press, 2016); Manfred Elfstrom, "Two Steps Forward, One Step Back: Chinese Reactions to Labor Unrest," *The China Quarterly*, no. 240 (2019), 855–79; and Manfred Elfstrom, *Workers and Change in China: Resistance, Repression, Responsiveness* (New York: Cambridge University Press, 2021).

[151] Cai, *Collective Resistance in China*; Chen, *Social Protest and Contentious Authoritarianism in China*.

basic contention is that the regime increases its level of support by appearing accountable to popular demands.[152] A related claim is that the center welcomes protests, as they help alleviate information problems of higher-level leaders regarding local-level malfeasance.[153] Finally, scholars argue that protests are not only compatible with but are even necessary for ensuring stability.[154] In sum, the typical protest is not repressed, as it is not a source of concern for the leadership. China thus emerges as a sui generis autocracy that is tolerant of protests.

The bulk of the research on the toleration of protests is based on data that do not extend past the end of Hu Jintao's second term.[155] Thus, we need to ask a different question, namely, have regime attitudes toward protest activity changed under Xi Jinping? To address this issue, I rely on an analysis of over 65,000 cases of protest that span the period from November 2013 to June 2016.[156] The central finding is that the dominant outcome in cases of protest is overwhelmingly repression. Contrary to conventional wisdom, negotiation and compromise constitute a highly exceptional result from contentious activity.[157] A related finding is that public security spending is sensitive to protests: in 2014, the relationship between protests and expenditures on public security was very strong ($t = 9.13$ and R-squared of 0.74 in a bivariate regression). What explains this? We need to take into account that several trends, all of which precede Xi's assumption of power, converged by 2012–2013, leading to a harsher response to protests by the security apparatus.

The first development was that the rise of protests continued unabated. The actual number became a closely guarded secret in 2005, when it reached

---

[152] Ching Kwan Lee and Yonghong Zhang, "The Power of Instability: Unraveling the Microfoundations of Bargained Authoritarianism in China," *American Journal of Sociology* 118:6 (May 2013), 1475–1508; Heurlin, *Responsive Authoritarianism in China*.

[153] Peter L. Lorentzen, "Regularizing Rioting: Permitting Public Protest in an Authoritarian Regime," *Quarterly Journal of Political Science* 8:2 (2013), 127–58.

[154] Chen, *Social Protest and Contentious Authoritarianism in China*.

[155] This is true even of very recent studies such as Elfstrom, "Two Steps Forward, One Step Back" (who relies on data from 2003 to 2012) and Li, *Playing by the Informal Rules* (who uses data for 2001–2012). Christian Goebel, "Social Unrest in China: A Bird's Eye View," in Teresa Wright, ed., *Handbook of Protest and Resistance in China* (Cheltenham, UK: Edward Elgar, 2019), 27–45 and Han Zhang and Jennifer Pan, "CASM: A Deep Learning Approach for Identifying Text and Image Data from Social Media," *Sociological Methodology* 49:1 (2019), 1–57 use the Wickedonna dataset but address questions that are very different from those examined in this study. Zhang and Pan, "CASM" use the data to develop machine-learning algorithms that can identify protests. Goebel, "Social Unrest in China" uses machine learning to develop a topic model for classifying the protests by type of grievance. Neither Goebel, "Social Unrest in China," nor Zhang and Pan, "CASM," focus on the central puzzle analyzed in this study, namely, how do protest tactics condition government response.

[156] Martin K. Dimitrov and Zhu Zhang, "The Political Economy of Stability Maintenance under Xi Jinping," in Lowell Dittmer, ed., *China's Political Economy in the Xi Jinping Epoch: Domestic and Global Dimensions* (Singapore: World Scientific, 2021), 127–62. The Dimitrov and Zhang dataset is built from the textual reports of protests compiled by Li Yuyu and Li Tingyu on their Wickedonna blog.

[157] This occurs in less than 1 percent of the 2,604 well-publicized high-profile cases in the Dimitrov and Zhang dataset ("The Political Economy of Stability Maintenance") that were most likely to be large-scale and disruptive.

87,000. Since then, occasional estimates about individual years have emerged, documenting an ongoing increase,[158] with some accounts putting the volume of protests at 180,000 in 2010.[159] Scholars with access to internal statistics cite lower figures but nevertheless note an alarming rise by the end of Hu's second term, with protests reaching 165,000 in 2013.[160] In addition to their sheer number, contentious episodes presented a challenge because they were difficult to resolve, as grievances increasingly stemmed from transactions between two private parties (e.g., a nonstate-owned firm and its employees), thus making it difficult for the government to intervene and adjudicate the dispute. Even more consequential was that tolerating land grabs and the illegal demolition of housing to make way for lucrative development projects had become widespread as a result of the failure of the central government to adequately fund local governments. These realities imposed constraints on the capacity of higher-level political actors to solve systemic problems through one-off financial largesse ("buying stability").[161]

The second development was the declining popularity of the party-state (see also the opinion research reviewed in Section 8.4), which was demonstrated by information collected through different channels and communicated in internal (*neibu*) sources. Internal reports indicate that petitioning shows trust, whereas protests do not; petitions are to be encouraged, whereas protests are not.[162] Thus, one alarming indicator for insiders was the declining volume of petitions, which was connected to the growth in the number of protests (they are substitutes, not complements).[163] This link was initially established in the 2000s in internal police materials that aimed to identify the triggers of contentious activity and found that 62.2 percent of mass incidents in 2000–2004 stemmed from unsuccessful petitions.[164] The Dimitrov and Zhang protest dataset also indicates a powerful relationship between petitions and protests: in 2014, the effects of corruption complaints were very strong ($t = 4.34$ and R-squared of 0.37 in a bivariate regression).[165] The weakness of the complaints system and the extraordinary efforts

[158] Wedeman, "Enemies of the State."

[159] Sun Liping, "Shehui shixu shi dangxia de yanjun tiaozhan," *Jingji guancha bao*, February 25, 2011.

[160] Zhang Mingjun and Chen Ming, "2013 niandu Zhongguo shehui dianxing quntixing shijian fenxi baogao," *Zhongguo shehui gonggong anquan yanjiu baogao*, no. 5 (2014), 3–12.

[161] Hiroki Takeuchi, *Tax Reform in Rural China: Revenue, Resistance, and Authoritarian Rule* (New York: Cambridge University Press, 2014).

[162] Tian Xianhong, "Yishi xingtai zhuanxing yu xinfang zhuli de lunli kunjing," *Zhanlüe yu guanli: Neibu ban*, nos. 5–6 (2012), 39–54.

[163] Martin K. Dimitrov, "Internal Government Assessments of the Quality of Governance in China," *Studies in Comparative International Development* 50:1 (March 2015), 50–72.

[164] Lin Weiye and Liu Hanmin, *Gong'an jiguan yingdui quntixing shijian shiwu yu celüe* (Beijing: Zhongguo Renmin Gong'an Daxue Chubanshe, 2008), 3. See also *Quntixing shijian yanjiu*.

[165] Dimitrov and Zhang, "The Political Economy of Stability Maintenance."

by the authorities to maintain stability by preventing citizens from petitioning Beijing meant that by the 2010s the most aggrieved individuals bypassed the letters-and-visits system altogether and turned directly to protests.

The final factor explaining the harsher response to protests was the increasing availability of smartphones, which meant that the overwhelming majority of Internet users in China can access the Web through mobile devices, allowing them to exchange information in real time and making it easier for online contention to spill offline.[166] Concerns mounted about the rapidity with which contentious episodes could be organized with the help of mobile phones.[167] This was based both on domestic experiences and on international examples, such as the Arab Spring, the anti-Putin protests in 2012, and Euromaidan—all of which were facilitated by smartphones.[168] Given the level of grievances and the lack of popularity of the party, protests often became violent, thus raising the probability of destabilization.[169] Internal analysis of violent episodes of contention indicated that participants included evil elements, ex-convicts, drug addicts, and the like.[170]

The theory on protest response under Xi is consistent with recent findings about a general repressive turn during the 2010s,[171] about the dire straits of workers who experience "informed disenchantment" with the legal system (and who are thus more likely to engage in violent protests),[172] and about the high risk of engaging in visible acts of contention,[173] especially when directed against the central government.[174] The goal here is to present a theory of the main factors that explain the repressive response to contention under Xi Jinping, which stands in contrast to the more tolerant approach to protest prior to 2012 that has been amply documented in the literature on contention. Unfortunately, the data

---

[166] Xie Yungeng, ed., *Zhongguo shehui yuqing yu weiji guanli baogao 2013* (Beijing: Shehui Kexue Wenxian Chubanshe, 2013).

[167] Cui Yadong, *Quntixing shijian yingji guanli yu shehui zhili: Weng'an zhiluan dao Weng'an zhizhi* (Beijing: Zhonggong Zhongyang Dangxiao Chubanshe, 2013), 48.

[168] Zhang Xianlong, "Hulianwang huanjing xia de yishi xingtai anquan jianshe," *Neibu canyue*, no. 28 (2013), 3–13; Lu Baichun and Zhu Junwei, "E yingdui xinxing meiti fumian yingxiang de zuofa ji wenti," *Neibu canyue*, no. 25 (2013), 43–48.

[169] Yan Daocheng, *Quntixing shijian zhong de wangluo yuqing yanjiu* (Beijing: Xinhua Chubanshe, 2013)

[170] Wang Cijiang, *Chongtu yu zhili: Zhongguo quntixing shijian kaocha fenxi* (Beijing: Renmin Chubanshe, 2013), 56; Cui, *Quntixing shijian yingji guanli*, 50–51.

[171] Yuhua Wang and Carl Minzner, "The Rise of the Chinese Security State," *The China Quarterly*, no. 222 (June 2015), 339–59; Suzanne E. Scoggins, *Policing China: Street-Level Cops in the Shadow of Protest* (Ithaca, NY: Cornell University Press, 2021); Lynette Ong, *Outsourcing Repression: Everyday State Power in Contemporary China* (New York: Oxford University Press, 2022).

[172] Mary Gallagher, *Authoritarian Legality in China: Law, Workers, and the State* (New York: Cambridge University Press, 2017).

[173] Diana Fu, *Mobilizing Without the Masses: Control and Contention in China* (New York: Cambridge University Press, 2017).

[174] Chih-Jou Jay Chen and Yong-shun Cai, "Upward Targeting and Social Protest in China," *Journal of Contemporary China* 30:130 (2021), 511–25.

indicate that compromise and negotiation are now highly atypical responses, regardless of whether citizens have political or socioeconomic grievances. Under Xi Jinping, all protests are considered a threat to state security. What remained primarily a doctrinal matter in police almanacs in the 1990s has become a reality in the 2010s. This is the new normal.

8.3.4 Online Complaints

In addition to petitions and protests, online complaints serve as a third main channel for transmission of information in contemporary China. But there is conceptual confusion about the operationalization of online complaints in the context of China. Three distinct types of activities are relevant here: letters transmitted electronically, whose content is not made publicly available; public posts using real names; and negative comments on webpages and social media written under a pseudonym. Although all three kinds of online activity transmit information about popular grievances, their authors have different intent, include different content in them, and direct them to different audiences. Moreover, regime insiders regard these three types of online behavior differently.

Sending a letter electronically (*wangshang xinfang* 网上信访) involves filling out a form that contains relevant identification information and supplying a detailed explanation of the concern; the online portal or app also allows citizens to attach files documenting their grievance. Instead of using the postal service, petitioners can transmit their letters electronically. The system is user-friendly, thus explaining why online complaining rapidly gained in popularity after its introduction in the 2000s. By 2017, most provinces in China reported that over one-half of the letters received by their complaints offices were sent electronically. It should be noted, however, that letters transmitted electronically are no different from those sent by regular mail: their content is not publicized, so they represent a private act of communication between citizens and the government—individuals voluntarily transmit to the government information that is meant for internal use. We should also emphasize that the volume of complaints sent to the letters-and-visits offices continued to decline throughout the 2010s despite the growing popularity of the electronic submission of letters and the fact that the government welcomes this form of citizen participation.

The low effectiveness of the traditional letters-and-visits system and the high Internet penetration rate explain the growing popularity of the second option: online complaints (*wangluo jubao* 网络举报), to which I refer as "public posts" to avoid confusion. Introduced in the late 2000s as part of the Open Government Information Initiative, public posts appear on numerous platforms.

One forum for such content is the "mayor's mailbox,"[175] which has attracted significant scholarly attention.[176] Mayors' mailboxes primarily highlight concerns about socioeconomic matters like the provision of public goods and social services; a small number of posts focus on economic disputes over property rights; and very few (4 percent) report instances of corruption.[177] A key finding in the literature is that only some of these citizen communications are made public and that priority is given to content that reflects positively on the local government.[178] This is consistent with evidence from Jiangxi, for instance, where the "ask the government" portal explicitly states that citizens may only complain about a limited set of issues and that publication is at the discretion of portal administrators.[179] In the ten years between March 2011 and February 2020, the portal posted 77,736 letters.[180] Although we do not know what percentage of online complaints were selected for publication, it is relevant to keep in mind that in a single year (2014) the Jiangxi letters-and-visits offices received 323,300 complaints.[181] Selective publication notwithstanding, scholars argue that levels of responsiveness are reasonably high (perhaps reaching 43 percent).[182] The lengths to which grassroots propaganda officials go in order to investigate public posts are documented by the Zhanggong and Jiujiang Propaganda Department datasets (see Section 8.4). The reason for such attention is clear: publicized but unaddressed social grievances may facilitate the transformation of online dissent into offline contention.

The third type of online expression of grievances is negative commentary, which is described by propaganda officials as negative sentiment (*fumian yuqing* 負面輿情).[183] Although public posts and negative comments have similarities

---

[175] This forum has different designations across China, but the modal category (in 65 percent of the cases) is "mayor's mailbox." See Greg Distelhorst and Yue Hou, "Constituency Service under Non-Democratic Rule: Evidence from China," *The Journal of Politics* 79:3 (2017), 1024–40, at 1026 (n. 4).

[176] Jidong Chen, Jennifer Pan, and Yiqing Xu, "Sources of Authoritarian Responsiveness: A Field Experiment in China," *American Journal of Political Science* 60:2 (2016), 383–400; Distelhorst and Hou, "Constituency Service under Non-Democratic Rule"; Greg Distelhorst and Diana Fu, "Performing Authoritarian Citizenship: Public Transcripts in China," *Perspectives on Politics* 17:1 (2019), 106–21.

[177] Distelhorst and Hou, "Constituency Service under Non-Democratic Rule," at 1035–37.

[178] Chen, Pan, and Xu, "Sources of Authoritarian Responsiveness." On the image that is promoted through government webpages, see Jennifer Pan, "How Chinese Officials Use the Internet to Construct Their Public Image," *Political Science Research and Methods* 7:2 (2019), 197–213.

[179] https://wenz.jxnews.com.cn/ms/index.php/Home/Index/yqzd/p/1 (accessed June 30, 2021).

[180] https://wenz.jxnews.com.cn/ms/index.php/Home/Index/yqzd/p/1 (accessed June 30, 2021).

[181] Jiangxi Sheng Difang Bianzuan Weiyuanhui, *Jiangxi nianjian 2015* (Beijing: Zhongguo Shidai Jingji Chubanshe, 2015), 71.

[182] Distelhorst and Hou, "Constituency Service under Non-Democratic Rule," at 1029. See also Chen, Pan, and Xu, "Sources of Authoritarian Responsiveness" and Zheng Su and Tianguang Meng, "Selective Responsiveness: Online Public Demands and Government Responsiveness in Authoritarian China," *Social Science Research* 59 (2016), 52–67.

[183] See Zhanggong and Jiujiang datasets.

(both are seen by the party as threats due to their potential to disrupt social stability), there are some consequential differences. One is that public posts are made with real names (*shiming jubao* 实名举报), while negative comments are typically pseudonymous. An additional distinction is that negative comments tend to be less specific than public posts, and they make general allegations about corruption or incompetence without supplying much detail.[184] Finally, and most important, public posts differ from negative comments in terms of whether or not they can be described as voluntarily transmitted information. There is no doubt that when citizens (no matter whether they are Big Vs or ordinary netizens) post online with their real names, they want this information to be transmitted to the authorities. At the other extreme, it is also uncontroversial that when the government reads personal messages on WeChat, it is collecting information involuntarily. Negative comments lie somewhere in between: they are more akin to a public conversation between strangers—it can be overheard and subsequently analyzed by the authorities, but this is not its express intended purpose. The Zhanggong and Jiujuang propaganda datasets richly document the efforts that were made to identify negative public sentiment and to counteract it through strategies that ranged from infusing popular commentary to actually addressing the problem (though, inevitably, there were also cases when nothing was done, with the expectation that negative comments would not impact online opinion as they would not lead to a public reaction in the form of a response or a re-tweet).

8.3.5 Summing Up

When it comes to the voluntary transmission of information, autocracies prefer private individual communications, which enable the continuous assessment of latent discontent and the deployment of anticipatory governance. To use a popular metaphor in political science,[185] individual written complaints are like police patrols: they allow for grievances to be systematically identified and resolved, reinforcing a relationship of reciprocal obligation between citizens and the regime that involves a tacit understanding that the citizens will remain quiescent provided that the government satisfies

---

[184] Propaganda officials also classify as negative comments reports about incidents, accidents, and natural disasters. Such content has the potential to negatively impact public opinion.

[185] Mathew McCubbins and Thomas Schwartz, "Congressional Oversight Overlooked: Police Patrols versus Fire Alarms," *American Journal of Political Science* 28:1 (1984), 165–79.

their welfare needs. This system thrived in Eastern Europe, but it never developed in China. Although private written complaints by individual citizens exist, their frequency has always been low and has undergone further declines in the past two decades, despite the option of sending electronic petitions. The low effectiveness of private petitioning explains the popularity of publicly observable mechanisms for articulating grievances: collective in-person petitions; protests; public posts; and online negative comments. These channels transmit information as well, but in doing so, they put extraordinary pressure on the government to act quickly to resolve pressing grievances that have been publicized. Thus, their function is akin to fire alarms. The modal response to this ongoing massive expression of visible discontent has shifted from accommodation to repression. Information transmission through protests and online negative comments is discouraged. In sum, the imperative of stability maintenance has overridden the party's understanding that citizens should be incentivized to transmit information voluntarily via all avenues that are available to them.

8.4 The Role of the Party in Coordinating Public-Opinion Monitoring

As both a producer and the ultimate consumer of information, the Chinese Communist Party (CCP) determines what intelligence is collected by other agencies and by its own departments. We can illustrate this process by analyzing how the CCP has approached the monitoring of public opinion since 1989. Outside the party, three main avenues have been used to accomplish this task: opinion polling; internal media reporting; and police and secret police assessments of threats to stability presented by the enemy contingent and by trends in the public mood. All three channels traditionally involved involuntary collection, though opinion polling gradually shifted toward voluntary provision. Within the party, information on public opinion has been compiled using both voluntarily provided information (in the form of citizen complaints, protests, and public posts), as well as involuntary extraction based on analyses of other online and offline expressions of discontent. As previous sections have already discussed involuntary collection by the security services and voluntary provision, this section will focus on opinion polling, internal media reporting, and involuntary collection by the party. We will also engage with the question of information aggregation and transfer.

8.4.1 Opinion Polling: From Involuntary to Voluntary

Opinion research has found very high levels of support for the central government in China,[186] leading to a scholarly debate on whether respondents engage in preference falsification when answering sensitive survey questions.[187] Although resolving this debate is impossible, evidence from Eastern Europe is useful for putting it into perspective: opinion research there was marred with problems into the 1980s, but started to improve radically in its informational value during perestroika, when the quality of the questions asked was elevated and the level of fear about repercussions decreased.[188] China in the 2010s is comparable to the Soviet Union during the height of perestroika, when opinion polling became a meaningful instrument for assessing public attitudes. Whereas there were journalistic reports of compulsory participation in surveys into the late 2000s,[189] such practices were becoming less common in the 2010s, thus raising the possibility that opinion polling is transitioning from being a channel for involuntary extraction into an avenue for voluntary provision.

Opinion polling in the 2010s has produced some contradictory findings. On the one hand, we have surveys that raise profound doubts about the validity of their results. For example, a national probability proportional to size (PPS) sampling survey of life satisfaction conducted in 2011 by the Chinese Academy of Social Sciences revealed that the happiest citizens live in Tibet, Shandong, and Xinjiang.[190] Yet, other results are much less flattering for the CCP. In particular, Internet public opinion has been increasingly critical of the party-state,[191] with the police consistently topping the list of government agencies that are criticized

---

[186] Lianjiang Li, "Political Trust in Rural China," *Modern China* 30:2 (2004), 228–58; Bruce Dickson, *The Dictator's Dilemma: The Chinese Communist Party's Strategy for Survival* (New York: Oxford University Press, 2016), 214–61; Wenfang Tang, *Populist Authoritarianism: Chinese Political Culture and Regime Sustainability* (New York: Oxford University Press, 2016).

[187] Darrel Robinson and Marcus Tannenberg, "Self-Censorship of Regime Support in Authoritarian States: Evidence from List Experiments in China," *Research and Politics* 6:3 (2019), 1–9; Ashley Esaray, Daniela Stockmann, and Jie Zhang, "Support for Propaganda: Chinese Perceptions of Public Service Advertising," *Journal of Contemporary China* 26:103 (2017), 101–17; Xuchuan Lei and Jie Lu, "Revisiting Political Wariness in China's Public Opinion Surveys: Experimental Evidence on Responses to Politically Sensitive Questions," *Journal of Contemporary China* 26:104 (2017), 213–32; Junyan Jiang and Dali L. Yang, "Lying or Believing? Measuring Preference Falsification from a Political Purge in China," *Comparative Political Studies* 49:5 (2016), 600–34.

[188] Martin K. Dimitrov, "Tracking Public Opinion Under Authoritarianism: The Case of the Soviet Union under Brezhnev," *Russian History* 41:3 (2014), 329–53.

[189] "China Town Given Survey Answers," BBC News, December 31, 2008, http://news.bbc.co.uk/2/hi/asia-pacific/7806204.stm (accessed April 19, 2022).

[190] Wang Junxiu and Quan Jing, "2011–2012 nian Zhongguo jumin shenghuo manyi du diaocha baogao," in Wang Junxiu and Yang Yiyin, eds., *Zhongguo shehui xintai yanjiu baogao, 2012–2013* (Beijing: Shehui Kexue Wenxian Chubanshe, 2013), 52–70.

[191] Peng Xiao, "Wangluo kongjian yu woguo guojia anquan," *Neibu canyue*, no. 25 (2013), 10–22; "Woguo wangluo yulun tufa shijian de jiben taishi ji duice jianyi," *Lingdao canyue*, no. 27 (2014), 8–12.

in various online forums.[192] Most consequential is that in 2013 an internal pub-lication sounded an alarm about the results of the China Social Survey, which documented the deep erosion of trust in the party-state, the police, and the courts.[193] The 2015 China Social Survey revealed that only 55.8 percent of citizens trust party and government officials somewhat or very much, with the rest of the respondents expressing moderate or high distrust or refusing to answer.[194] In the same survey, 49.9 percent agreed with the statement that voting in village and neighborhood elections does not have an impact on the final electoral outcome (i.e., they expressed concerns about ballot box manipulation).[195] In the 2017 wave of the survey, 56.1 percent of respondents supported this statement.[196] In the 2019 China Social Survey, 49.42 percent concurred that participating in political activities has no impact on the government.[197] Thus, as is acknowledged both in internal and publicly available materials, the informational value of survey research has increased in the 2010s. Consistent with the insights produced by analyzing citizen complaints and protests, Chinese opinion research reveals that popular dissatisfaction has increased substantially.

8.4.2 Internal Media at the Central Level

Additional avenues for information collection exist in contemporary China. Internal journalism has survived and thrived, but it has also expanded its purview to integrate analysis of Internet public opinion. In addition, numerous commercial companies provide public-opinion monitoring services.

The difference between the public and the internal media persists to the current day. Chinese journalists are encouraged to write information (*xinxi* 信息) for internal periodicals and news (*xinwen* 新闻) for public outlets. A leaked

[192] Li Peilin, Chen Guangjin, and Zhang Yi, eds., *Zhongguo shehui xingshi fenxi yu yuce 2015* (Beijing: Shehui Kexue Wenxian Chubanshe, 2014), 232; Li Peilin, Chen Guangjin, and Zhang Yi, eds., *Zhongguo shehui xingshi fenxi yu yuce 2016* (Beijing: Shehui Kexue Wenxian Chubanshe, 2015), 224; Li Peilin, Chen Guangjin, and Wang Chunguang, eds., *Zhongguo shehui xingshi fenxi yu yuce 2020* (Beijing: Shehui Kexue Wenxian Chubanshe, 2020), 264. At the same time, the 2019 China Social Survey revealed that respondents considered the government's performance in social-order protection the best among thirteen policy areas, with 85.33 percent evaluating it as good (Li, Chen, and Wang, eds., *Zhongguo shehui xingshi fenxi yu yuce 2020*, 134).

[193] Zou Zichun, "Minzhong dui dangzheng renyuan de 'bu xinren' wenti ji duice jianyi," *Lingdao canyue*, no. 29 (2014), 23–26.

[194] Li, Chen, and Zhang, eds., *Zhongguo shehui xingshi fenxi yu yuce 2015*, 123. Wording is especially important: when asked about trusting the government (not government officials) in the 2019 China Social Survey, 93.2 percent of respondents report trusting the central government; 70.38 percent the district and county government; and 61.85 percent the grassroots government. See Li, Chen, and Wang, eds., *Zhongguo shehui xingshi fenxi yu yuce 2020*, 128.

[195] Li, Chen, and Zhang, eds., *Zhongguo shehui xingshi fenxi yu yuce 2015*, 132.

[196] Li, Chen, and Zhang, eds., *Zhongguo shehui xingshi fenxi yu yuce 2019*, 157.

[197] Li, Chen, and Wang, eds., *Zhongguo shehui xingshi fenxi yu yuce 2020*, 138.

directive from 2011 on writing reports for the party and government sheds light on the different expectations involved in generating internal information and in producing public news stories.[198] Information reports are supposed to help leaders reach decisions and should be presented in an objective and clear writing style. By contrast, apart from entertaining the masses, news serves to propagandize, to educate citizens, and to guide public opinion and should thus be presented in ornate language that uses metaphors and analogies. This document also specifies the kinds of information (on disasters, epidemics, and sudden incidents), whose casual release to the public may impact social stability; such information should appear in the public media only with prior approval from the senior leader at the relevant level.[199] Internal media therefore continue to serve as a repository for negative information; the role of the public media, as has been stressed by Xi Jinping, is quite different from that of the classified media, namely, to correctly guide public opinion (zhengque yulun daoxiang 正确舆论 导向) by emphasizing positive publicity (zhengmian xuanchuan weizhu 正面宣 传为主).[200]

Rather than being fossils of a bygone chapter of communist governance, internal media have remained indispensable in the era of the Internet and social media, when the importance of the rapid collection and transmission of information on brewing popular discontent to regime insiders has increased exponentially. Chinese leaders receive a broad array of classified reports on public sentiments, including regular briefings on Internet public opinion.[201] This transfer of information notwithstanding, a stylized fact about communist regimes is that leaders ignore the reports sent to them.[202] One feature of the Chinese internal reporting system allows us to test this assumption: leaders have the option to ignore the information; to read it; or to read it and issue instructions (pishi). Reports that result in instructions are prized by bureaucracies, which means that they are likely to be referred to in official organizational histories,

---

[198] "Dangzheng xinxi xie gongzuo de jidian tihui," http://www.zk168.com/fanwen/fanwenxinde_274744 (accessed April 5, 2019).

[199] "Dangzheng xinxi xie gongzuo de jidian tihui."

[200] David Bandurski, "Under Xi, the Media Has Turned from a 'Mouthpiece of the Masses' to the Party's Parrot," Hong Kong Free Press, June 21, 2016, https://www.hongkongfp.com/2016/06/21/under-xi-the-media-has-turned-from-a-mouthpiece-of-masses-to-the-partys-parrot/ (accessed April 19, 2022).

[201] For the types of Internet-monitoring reports that Xinhua News Agency has been preparing since the late 1990s, see Xinhua News Agency, Xinhua she nianjian 1997–2016 (Beijing: Xinhua She, 1997–2016). See also Wen-hsuan Tsai, "How 'Networked Authoritarianism' Was Operationalized in China: Methods and Procedures of Public Opinion Control," Journal of Contemporary China 25:101 (2016), 731–44.

[202] Frank Dikötter, Mao's Great Famine: The History of China's Most Devastating Catastrophe, 1958–1962. (New York: Walker & Co., 2010).

thus generating empirical evidence that scholars can use to study leadership engagement with bureaucratic reporting.[203]

We have evidence of steadily increasing leadership engagement with Xinhua materials. Prior to the reform era, such instructions were extremely rare: Mao wrote comments occasionally in the 1950s and even an avid reader like Zhou Enlai issued no more than forty-two comments or instructions (*pishi huo zhishi* 批示或指示) on *Cankao xiaoxi* and *Cankao ziliao* reports in 1972 (a peak year in terms of his engagement with internal reference bulletins).[204] Contrast this with the situation in the 1980s, when between January 1980 and June 1984 top leaders (at and above the rank of vice-premier) issued instructions on 742 Xinhua internal reports, which is equivalent to all instructions generated in the previous thirty-year period.[205] The rate of issuance of instructions intensified in the following decades. Thus, in 2005 central leading cadres (*zhongyang lingdao* 中央领导) produced instructions on 1,460 internal reference reports prepared by Xinhua News Agency; by 2011, the number of reports receiving instructions by the top leadership had risen more than three-fold to 4,557.[206] This rapid increase attests both to the value that leaders attach to internal reporting and to the frequency with which these reports inform policy decisions: according to the internal rules of the Chinese bureaucracy, a report that has received a *pishi* automatically acquires the status of a policy document.[207] In sum, internal journalistic reporting remains indispensable to top leaders in the age of social media.

8.4.3 The Role of Internal Media in Grassroots Governance

A second trend that can be best described as "the democratization of intelligence" has occurred during the last decade in China. Whereas previously internal journalistic reporting was a closely guarded privilege of high-level cadres, commercial pressures have recently made intelligence available to grassroots leaders as well. As scholars have argued, outfits like Nanfang Media Group provide intelligence for sale to any government entity or company that wants to buy it.[208]

---

[203] On MPS materials that resulted in a *pishi* from Hu Yaobang or Hu Jintao, see *Jianguo yilai gong'an gongzuo*, 517, 545, 1290.

[204] *Xinhua she dashiji (1931–2001)*, vol. 2, 107.

[205] *Xinhua she dashiji*, vol. 3, 41. Hu Yaobang personally issued 496 instructions during the four-and-a-half-year period.

[206] Calculated from Xinhua News Agency, *Xinhua she nianjian 2006* (Beijing: Xinhua She, 2007), 198, and Xinhua News Agency, *Xinhua she nianjian 2011* (Beijing: Xinhua She, 2012), 259.

[207] Wen-Hsuan Tsai, "A Unique Pattern of Policymaking in China's Authoritarian System: The CCP's *Neican/Pishi* Model," *Asian Survey* 55:6 (November/December 2015), 1093–115.

[208] Tao Wu and Bixiao He, "Intelligence for Sale: The 'Party-Public Sentiment, Inc.' and Stability Maintenance in China," *Problems of Post-Communism* 67:2 (2020), 129–40.

We can illustrate the democratization of intelligence by observing the access to internal reporting enjoyed by the Jiujiang Prefecture Propaganda Department.[209] Leaked internal data indicate that officials in this relatively low-level government office have had access to a wide array of central-level reports. For example, the weekly *Yuqing guancha (dangzheng ban)* (舆情观察 [党政版]) contains reports on the official *weibo* (微博); social media posts by famous personalities; top news items; most frequent keyword searches; most viewed photos, cartoons, and videos; as well as analytical reports on Internet public opinion.[210] In addition, the Jiujiang officials received central-level reports from nongovernment commercial news providers like Ant Vision (蚁坊社会热点舆情分析) and Cionic (中智东方情报简讯), both of which monitored social media in order to issue warning signals about the rise of major national-level public-opinion incidents; these companies, which worked with the MPS, essentially relied on a scaled-down version of the Golden Shield Project (*jindun gongcheng* 金盾工程) database to determine the identity and social networks of individuals who posted online content.

Another type of reporting that has become available to grassroots cadres is custom-based daily and weekly assessments of public opinion that can be produced for any specific locality. Xinhua News Agency reveals that these reports are generated through the Xinhua public-opinion management system (*yuqing guanli xitong* 舆情管理系统), consisting of over 700 popular print media from mainland China, Taiwan, Hong Kong, and Macau, as well as over 300 major websites and over 300 discussion forums. For example, public opinion about Jiujiang prefecture in one week of October 2014 consisted of 159 items from the traditional print media; 908 items from the online media; and 509 items from discussion forums.[211] Once identified, these items can be scored in terms of their tone (positive, neutral, negative), with negative public opinion highlighted for additional attention.

In general, over the last decade there has been a proliferation of internal reporting aimed at lower-level cadres. Different entities generating these reports vary in terms of the source material they use. Commercial media monitoring firms, for example, mostly count the frequency with which various keywords are used; by contrast, traditional purveyors of internal journalistic intelligence

---

[209] Data from Jiujiang Prefecture serve as the basis of Jennifer Pan and Kaiping Chen, "Concealing Corruption: How Chinese Leaders Distort the Upward Reporting of Online Grievances," *American Political Science Review* 112:3 (2018), 602–20 and Yongshun Cai and Titi Zhou, "Online Political Participation in China: Local Government and Differentiated Response," *The China Quarterly*, no. 238 (June 2019), 331–52. Although I believe that the Jiujiang dataset that I am using is nearly identical to the one referenced by Pan and Chen, "Concealing Corruption" and Cai and Zhou "Online Political Participation in China," I obtained this dataset independently and the questions I ask based on it are different from those explored by either Pan and Chen or Cai and Zhou.

[210] See *Yuqing guancha (dangzheng ban)*, no. 16 (October 17, 2014).

[211] *Jiujiang shi yuqing jiance zhoubao*, no. 40 (October 6–10, 2014).

like Xinhua or Nanfang Media Group monitor both online and print media and even engage in some good old-fashioned legwork when assessing the newsworthiness of public opinion; this is why the old purveyors of internal reporting have retained their customer appeal in the digital age. The end result of the abundance of internal reporting is more nimble governance, not only at the central level but also at the grassroots. These reports allow leaders to react to online and offline public-opinion crises quickly to achieve their paramount goal of stability maintenance.

8.4.4 Party Department Reporting

In addition to external sources of information, the party has its own internal information-collection mechanisms. All party departments produce regular reports, which circulate both horizontally (to the party secretary) and vertically to superior party units. The departments most closely associated with assessing public opinion are those in charge of complaints (letters-and-visits offices and discipline inspection) and those that handle propaganda. Complaints work has been discussed at length throughout this book, but the reporting flow of propaganda departments in China has not been examined in previous chapters. Two leaked datasets from Jiangxi province allow us to gain direct insight into the reporting patterns of district-level (Zhanggong) and prefecture-level (Jiujiang) Internet propaganda offices (*wangxuan ban* 网宣办) in 2013–2014.[212] The datasets provide rich detail on the subordinate bureaus that sent information to Zhanggong and Jiujiang that was necessary to produce assessments of online public opinion, which were, in turn, transmitted to superior propaganda departments (Ganzhou prefecture for Zhanggong and Jiangxi province for Jiujiang) and to party secretaries at the same level. The datasets show that both commercial opinion monitoring and subordinate party departmental reporting triggered considerable efforts by propaganda officials to promptly identify the root cause of negative online public opinion and to then expeditiously decide how to respond (the options involved allowing the issue to subside by doing nothing; instructing government commentators to infuse positive content; or taking specific actions to address the articulated online grievances). The relatively low rank of these propaganda departments within the party hierarchy and

---

[212] Gary King, Jennifer Pan, and Margaret E. Roberts, "How the Chinese Government Fabricates Social Media Posts for Strategic Distraction, Not Engaged Argument," *American Political Science Review* 111:3 (2017), 484–501 use the Zhanggong and Jiujiang datasets to study the 50-cent party. Pan and Chen, "Concealing Corruption" use the Jiujiang dataset to assess the concealment of corruption in upward reporting.

the fact that negative comments appeared overwhelmingly on national platforms significantly restricted the capacity to censor content.

8.4.5 Upward Reporting: Selective Transfer or Willful Suppression?

As this book argues, information transfer is always hierarchical and selective: higher levels only need to know about certain matters that are relevant to them. Selective transfer is different from the willful suppression of information. However, selective transfer and the hiding of information are observationally equivalent. Distinguishing between the two is impossible, as it requires both a complete registry of the information that is available to lower-level authorities and strong assumptions that are difficult to justify theoretically about what information should be transferred upward.

In an article based on the Jiujiang dataset, Pan and Chen code 822 textual reports of negative online sentiments that were received by Jiujiang propaganda officials through daily and weekly Xinhua bulletins on online public opinion in January–November 2014.[213] The authors also identify 590 textual reports of negative sentiments (which they call complaints) in the biweekly online public-opinion briefs that were prepared by the Jiujiang officials and transmitted to the Jiangxi Provincial Propaganda Department. A subset of the textual reports concerns corruption (wrongdoing): 245 in the Xinhua bulletins and 156 in the biweekly briefs. Pan and Chen find that the frequency of upward reporting of wrongdoing in the prefecture and in six patronage counties is lower in the biweekly briefs than it is in the Xinhua bulletins (see Table 8.3). They use this information to conclude that the Jiujiang officials suppressed reporting on corruption in the biweekly updates on public opinion that were sent to provincial officials.

How might we be able to ascertain whether we are dealing with selective reporting? Analysis of the twenty-one original biweekly briefs (*wangluo yuqing zhuanbao* 网络舆情专报) submitted to the Jiangxi Provincial Propaganda Department indicates that the higher-ups were apprised of 1,720 instances of negative sentiment in January–November 2014. This is 191.5 percent higher than the 590 negative reports identified by Pan and Chen in the same biweekly briefs. It is also twice higher than the 822 reports in the briefs that Xinhua sent

---

[213] Pan and Chen, "Concealing Corruption." The article describes the Xinhua reports as produced by the Jiujiang Propaganda Department (which is not correct, as these were Xinhua bulletins) and as not sent upward (which is technically correct, though uninformative, as the reason why the Xinhua reports were not sent to the Jiangxi Provincial Propaganda Department is that they were generated for a lower-level recipient, namely, the prefectural-level Jiujiang propaganda officials, who would then use them to prepare the reports that were meant for the provincial-level officials).

Table 8.3 Reports of Negative Online Sentiments in Jiujiang, 2014

	Wrongdoing in Xinhua Reports (Pan and Chen 2018)	Wrongdoing Reported to the Province (Pan and Chen 2018)	Wrongdoing Reported to the Province (Dimitrov)	All Negative Sentiment Reported to the Province (Dimitrov)
Prefecture	61 (24.9%)	17 (10.9%)	23 (26.1%)	639 (37.1%)
Patronage counties	116 (47.3%)	71 (45.5%)	42 (47.7%)	731 (42.5%)
Nonpatronage counties	68 (27.7%)	68 (43.6%)	22 (25%)	350 (20.3%)
TOTAL	245 (100%)	156 (100%)	88 (100%)	1,720 (100%)

Sources: Pan and Chen, "Concealing Corruption"; calculations by the author, based on the original reports in the Jiujiang dataset. The names of the six patronage counties, which are identified as W, L, H, Y, D, and X in Pan and Chen, "Concealing Corruption," were determined by analyzing the original dataset and documents on the administrative organization of Jiujiang prefecture. These counties are Wuning, Lushan, Hukou, Yongxiu, Duchang, and Xiushui.

NB: There were eighty-eight textual reports of corruption (*jubao*); as one of them was pan-regional/province-wide, the percentage calculations for the eighty-seven prefecture, patronage counties, and nonpatronage counties reports add up to 98.8 percent rather than 100 percent.

to the Jiujiang officials. This result showcases that the Xinhua reports analyzed by Pan and Chen are not the only source by which the Jiujiang Propaganda Department obtained information about negative public opinion. It is impossible to know whether the 1,720 instances of negative online sentiment were reported selectively, though this seems unlikely given the total number of reports and their distribution across the prefecture and its associated county as well as the patronage and nonpatronage counties (see Table 8.3). Analysis of the original briefs indicates that the total volume of negative sentiment in every two-week period is reported in histograms (thus allowing us to calculate the 1,720 figure for January–November 2014) and some noteworthy cases are then selected for specific mention. It is not clear how Pan and Chen code wrongdoing (corruption), but there are eighty-eight illustrative mentions of corruption reporting (*jubao*) in the biweekly briefs; only fifty-two of those are coded as wrongdoing by Pan and Chen. Analysis of these eighty-eight reports does not indicate that either the prefecture or the patronage counties are shielded from reporting of wrongdoing: in fact, they jointly constitute three-quarters of the corruption cases reported to the Jiangxi Provincial Propaganda Department (see Table 8.3).[214]

---

[214] Surprisingly, there was no follow-up from the Provincial Propaganda Department: sixteen of the seventeen messages sent to the Jiujiang officials by the Jiangxi Propaganda Department were automatic responses. The only message with an actual text was sent on May 12, 2014, to all prefectures

These striking results, which contradict stylized understandings in the literature on China, point to an element of the upward reporting that is not given due consideration by Pan and Chen: in addition to provincial officials, the biweekly reports were sent to seventy recipients that included the Jiujiang party secretary, city mayor, the heads of the prefectural legislatures, the prefectural standing committee, all Jiujiang county and district propaganda departments, and other relevant offices.[215] In fact, the reports were much more closely read by local officials, as reflected by the fact that the Jiangxi Propaganda Department did not send a single instruction (*pishi*) in response to the seventy-one bulletins on online public opinion that it received from Jiujiang in 2013, whereas the prefectural leadership issued more than fifty instructions.[216] Misleading both higher-ups and officials at the local level about the incidence of negative public opinion would have disastrous consequences for social stability—this might be why we see that the prefecture and patronage counties account for the bulk of reported negative online sentiment (1,370 out of 1,720 cases) and of illustrative mentions of wrongdoing (65 out of 88 cases). Although some selection is inevitably at work when cases are chosen for illustrative mention (listing all 1,720 cases of negative opinion in detail would make the reports excessively long), in contrast to what Pan and Chen argue, there is no evidence of willful suppression of information to benefit the prefecture or patronage counties. Quite the opposite, the histograms of negative public opinion included in the twenty-one biweekly briefs focus attention on the prefecture and patronage counties. This extended example illustrates the value of research informed by archival ethnography, which stresses the importance of analyzing documents in their totality rather than extracting and coding only a portion of the data contained in them.

8.4.6 Summing Up

The CCP relies on a vast array of information that is transmitted to it by external collectors and is compiled internally by party departments. This allows for visible expressions of discontent to be identified and neutralized before they get transformed into even more serious threats to social stability. The party has played a leading role of directing and coordinating the assessment and response to public opinion in post-1989 China.

in Jiangxi province with very brief technical guidelines on the length, frequency, and formatting of the biweekly online public-opinion briefs.

[215] See distribution list in *Wangluo yuqing zhuanbao*, no. 73 (May 14, 2014), 6.

[216] See relevant details in *2012 nian Jiujiang shiwei xuanchuan bu ziping baogao* (March 11, 2013), 6.

8.5 Minorities

This book has argued that imperfect visibility presents a barrier for minority penetration. The 1990s demonstrated the regime's incapacity to make legible the two restive minorities of Tibetans and Uyghurs. As protests in Tibet preceded the Tiananmen events, the leadership turned to the Tibetan problem immediately after June 1989. Concerns that the Dalai Lama might use "peaceful evolution" as a strategy for achieving Tibetan independence made securing compliance in Tibet through continuous repression an attractive option for the top decision makers.[217] In the early 1990s, as various former Soviet republics inhabited by Uyghur kin groups became independent states, there were more frequent indications of growing discontent in Xinjiang as well. This led to concerns among the leadership that the Uyghurs might pursue separatism. Even before 9/11, this minority was understood as a vector for the spread of Islamic fundamentalism and terrorism. The regime's response to this threat featured even stricter measures than those applied in Tibet.

Importantly, there is no evidence of successful co-optation of members of the minority in either of the two regions during the 1990s. There was also a low level of voluntary provision of information through citizen complaints. Cumulatively, the barriers to involuntary extraction and voluntary provision meant that the Tibetans and the Uyghurs remained illegible for the regime. This closely parallels the situation with the Turks in Bulgaria prior to the start of the Regenerative Process, which is discussed in Chapter 5. The Chinese government's response to the Tibetan and, especially, Uyghur unrest since 2008 bears striking resemblance to the policies that the Bulgarian regime unleashed against the Turks in the 1980s.

8.5.1 The Tibetan Problem

Unrest in Tibet began in the fall of 1987, when riots emerged in Lhasa and various other localities inhabited by Tibetans; according to the official Chinese understanding, these events were inspired by external forces, mainly the Dalai Lama and his supporters among the American and European political elite.[218] An internal police source reports as many as twenty separate major riots (*saoluan shijian* 骚乱事件) between 1987 and 1991 in Tibet.[219] A quote from Jiang Zemin,

---

[217] Renzhen Luose, Xie Gangzheng, and Chen Zhichun, *Suowei 'Xizang wenti' de lishi yu xianzhuang* (Chengdu: Sichuan Zangxue Yanjiusuo, 2001).

[218] Qin Weidong, *Xizang wenti beiwanglu* (Lanzhou: Lanzhou Junqu Zhengzhibu Lianluobu, 1990), esp. 1–59.

[219] *Xizang gong'an*, no. 25 (1991/6), 12.

which is reproduced in an internal compendium, summarizes how the top leadership understood the issue of Tibet in the 1990s: "The Dalai problem is not a religious problem. The Dalai clique is an organized and well-directed separatist clique. The Dalai Lama is decidedly not merely a religious figure, rather he is a political exile who engages in separatist activities."[220] The response, which was driven by panic, further alienated the Tibetans.

One measure that was implemented in the wake of the 1987–1989 protests was a rectification of the informant corps. An internal police journal reveals that the social-order protection committee in Samada village underwent an "adjustment" (*tiaozheng* 调整) in 1990, which led to a reduction in its size.[221] Although the social-order protection committee had had as many as nineteen members during the Cultural Revolution, in 1990 its staff numbered a mere five individuals. However, in contrast to 1959, when only six of its thirteen members belonged to the party, in 1990 all five were party members.[222] These statistics demonstrate that because of its distrust of nonparty members, the PSB actively limited its information-gathering capacity by reducing the size of its informant corps. Moreover, to the extent that a position as an informant carried perks, it functioned as a strategy of co-optation; therefore, reducing the informant corps diminished the capacity of the regime to co-opt Tibetans.

The rest of the package of measures implemented toward members of the minority created a further sense of resentment among Tibetans. For example, separatism in Shigatse was dealt with by carrying out extensive patriotic education activities aimed at impressing upon Tibetans the importance of protecting national unity and maintaining ethnic harmony.[223] Both cadres and ordinary folk were required to make a commitment not to believe in or to spread rumors and to promptly report separatist rumors and activities to the authorities.[224] In addition, as "separatist foreign forces infiltrate temples" (*jingwai fenlie shili ba simiao zuowei shentou de zhongdian* 境外分裂势力把寺庙作为渗透的重点), the temples had to be rectified.[225] In practice, this meant reducing the number of monks and nuns,[226] closing down some temples, and subjecting all others to strict surveillance. In short, the 1990s sent a clear signal to the Tibetan minority that the regime would continue to respond with repression to any attempts to promote Tibetan independence and traditional Tibetan cultural values. Tibetans

---

[220] Renzhen Luose et al., *Suowei 'Xizang wenti,'* p. 1 of unpaginated introduction.

[221] *Xizang gong'an*, no. 21 (1991/2), 2–4.

[222] *Xizang gong'an*, no. 21 (1991/2), 2–4.

[223] *Xizang gong'an*, no. 22 (1991/3), 16–19.

[224] *Xizang gong'an*, no. 22 (1991/3), 17.

[225] *Xizang gong'an*, no. 22 (1991/3), 17.

[226] In 1998, there were 46,380 monks and nuns (Yuan Siming, ed., *Zhongguo gongchandang Xizang gongzuo 50 nian* [Beijing: Zhongguo Zangxue Yanjiu Zhongxin Dangdai Yanjiusuo, 2004], 381). In 1958, Tibet had 110,000 religious workers (*Quanguo shaoshu minzu qingkuang tongji ziliao 1949–1959* [Guojia Minwei Bangongting, February 1960]).

were not trusted to carry out this repression: as revealed by statistics on party building, non-Han never constituted more than 5 percent of party members in the Tibetan People's Armed Police during 1999–2005.[227] Finally, the rapid increase in investment in the Tibetan Autonomous Region was understood by minority members as yet another lever through which the center would exercise control over the region by making it dependent on ongoing substantial fiscal transfers.[228]

8.5.2 Unrest in Xinjiang

Starting with the Baren incident in April 1990, Xinjiang experienced more than 100 separatist riots, explosions, and acts of sabotage prior to the March 19, 1996, Politburo Standing Committee meeting that outlined a series of measures aimed at protecting stability in the autonomous region.[229] Apart from emphasizing ideological vigilance and the strengthening of party presence at the grassroots level, the meeting stressed the importance of guiding minority religion and education, with the eradication of underground Quranic study centers and military training establishments designated as a priority.[230] Repressive measures were also highlighted, including the strengthening of antiseparatist public and state security organs; expansion of the Xinjiang Production and Construction Corps (XPCC) and the PLA; and stopping the activities of external forces promoting separatism. The Politburo Standing Committee meeting also emphasized the importance of faster economic development and improving the livelihood of the people for maintaining stability in the autonomous region.[231]

Echoing earlier statements about the intersection of politics and religion in Tibet, CCP Document No. 7 from 1996 states that "we must clearly see that the main threats to stability in Xinjiang are ethnic separatism and illegal religious activity."[232] Part of the package of countermeasures included specific actions in the sphere of ideology and propaganda, such as emphasizing political education

---

[227] *Zhongguo renmin wuzhuang jingcha budui Xizang zongdui zuzhi shi (1999–2006)* (Lasa: Zhongguo Renmin Wuzhuang Jingcha Budui Xizang Zizhiqu Zongdui Shizhi Bianshen Weiyuanhui, 2006), 73.

[228] Andrew M. Fischer, "Subsidizing Tibet: An Interprovincial Comparison of Western China Up to the End of the Hu–Wen Administration," *The China Quarterly*, no. 221 (March 2015), 73–99.

[229] Data on incidents from Justin V. Hastings, "Charting the Course of Uyghur Unrest," *The China Quarterly*, no. 208 (December 2011), 893–912. A summary of the main decisions of the Politburo Standing Committee meeting can be found in *Xinjiang wending gongzuo wenjian xuanbian* (Urumqi: Zhonggong Xinjiang Weiwuer Zizhiqu Weiyuanhui Bangongting, 1999), 3–9.

[230] *Xinjiang wending gongzuo,* 3–9.

[231] *Xinjiang wending gongzuo.*

[232] Cited in *Gaodu zhongshi woqu yishi xingtai lingyu de fan fenlie douzheng* (Urumqi: Zhonggong Xinjiang Weiwuer Zizhiqu Dangwei Xuanchuanbu, 2000), 2.

(especially of peasants, nomads, and minors); controlling religious institutions; rectifying cultural markets by destroying reactionary propaganda and the illegal religious publications found in them; and energetically engaging in external propaganda aimed at effectively debunking Western separatist efforts advanced under the guise of support for the freedom of religious expression or the protection of human rights.[233]

The end of the 1990s and the early 2000s were a period of major doctrinal evolution regarding the Uyghur threat, which involved conceptualizing Xinjiang not only as a separatist region but also, in contrast to Tibet, as a hotbed of terrorism fueled by Islamic fundamentalism. An early 2004 general assessment of the international factors affecting political security in Chinese border areas included globalization and the worldwide waves of nationalism and terrorism.[234] A more nuanced evaluation of the sources of terrorism specifically in Xinjiang appeared at the end of 2004.[235] It similarly focused on international factors (the forces of Islamic extremism) but also highlighted domestic cultural security lapses, such as neglecting the importance of political education, insufficient control over cultural markets and mosques (used for preaching religious extremism), and the slow pace of economic and social development in the region.[236] Remarkably, these doctrinal adjustments, which were consistent with a global change in attitude toward Muslims after 9/11, occurred against the background of declining overt Uyghur discontent in China. Their effect was to increase alienation among members of the minority, thus making it even more illegible and impenetrable for the center. The low frequency of overt discontent among the Uyghurs after 1998 did not mean that they were satisfied, as would be demonstrated through another riot wave that began in 2007 and justified the imposition of draconian control in the region in the 2010s.

8.5.3 Involuntary Extraction in Xinjiang

The MPS was the chief entity tasked with the involuntary collection of information in Xinjiang. Numerous concerns occupied the police since conducting a Xinjiang investigation in August 1989.[237] A counterrevolutionary organization, the East Turkestan Islamic Party, was neutralized in 1992 and a planned

---

[233] *Gaodu zhongshi woqu yishi xingtai*, 1–12.

[234] *Zhongguo xibu minzu diqu kongbu fanzui wenti yanjiu* (Beijing: Gong'an Bu, January 2004), 1–4.

[235] *Guoji yisilan jiduan shili dui Xinjiang de yingxiang* (Beijing: Guowuyuan Fazhan Yanjiu Zhongxin, December 2004).

[236] *Guoji yisilan jiduan shili*, 305–19.

[237] *Jianguo yilai gong'an gongzuo*, 756.

explosion at the opening of Fourteenth Party Congress was thwarted.[238] In 1993, the police dealt with the aftermath of a Kashgar explosion that was supported by the East Turkestan Islamic Party and by the East Turkestan Islamic Reform Party commandos (*Dongtu'erqisitan yisilan gaige dang tuji dui* 东土耳其斯坦伊斯兰改革党突击队).[239] By 1997, the MPS had reached the conclusion that violence and unrest in Xinjiang were driven by ethnic separatism and religious extremism.[240]

After Tiananmen, visibility in the Xinjiang Production and Construction Corps diverged from that in the rest of Xinjiang. In the XPCC, the focus of the police after 1989 shifted to safeguarding (*yufang* 预防) against instability and sudden incidents through the collection of enemy and social intelligence as well as information on the reactions of different segments of society to important domestic and international events. In order for information to be anticipatory (*chaoqian baojing* 超前报警 "sound an advance alarm"), a decision was made in 1990 that multiple channels had to be used, including the development of "hidden forces" (*yinbi liliang* 隐蔽力量) of intelligence collectors. The emphasis was on prevention (*yifang weizhu* 以防为主) of infiltration (*fang shentou* 防渗透), sabotage (*fang pohuai* 防破坏), and sudden incidents (*fang tufa shijian* 防突发事件). An intelligence-collection network was to be set up at all administrative levels of the production and construction corps. As Table 8.4 reveals, intelligence was classified into enemy, political, social, border area, and other and it was used to detect, prevent, and curb demonstrations, factory and school strikes, petitions, illegal religious activities, and other disturbances. Information collection was driven by the understanding of the MPS that hidden informants (also called *zhengbao mimi liliang* 政保秘密力量) were essential for maintaining political stability (*weihu zhengzhi wending* 维护政治稳定).[241] These tasks were accomplished by deploying secret forces (*mimi liliang* 秘密力量) to collect intelligence (*qingbao xinxi* 情报信息) about key units and suspicious individuals on the targeted population roster. The results of that work are presented in Table 8.4.

A major difference between the XPCC and the rest of Xinjiang has to do with the informant network saturation rate. In the XPCC, 357,401 individuals signed a social-order protection responsibility contract in 1997.[242] This means that in

---

[238] *Jianguo yilai gong'an gongzuo*, 917.

[239] *Jianguo yilai gong'an gongzuo*, 944.

[240] *Jianguo yilai gong'an gongzuo*, 1109–11.

[241] *Xinjiang shengchan jianshe bingtuan gong'an zhi*, 186.

[242] *Xinjiang shengchan jianshe bingtuan gong'an zhi*, 205–6, 255–68. The social-order protection responsibility system (*zhi'an zeren chengbao zerenzhi* 治安责任承包责任制) was introduced in the production and construction corps in 1984. It appears that every rural household signed such a contract, as 356,964 of the 357,401 individuals were in villages; there were 726,101 households in the XPCC in 1997 (*Xinjiang shengchan jianshe bingtuan gong'an zhi*, 207), with rural residence holders

Table 8.4 Types of Intelligence Collected by the Xinjiang Production and Construction Corps and Their Use to Identify, Prevent, and Curb Political Threats, 1993–1997

	1993	1994	1995	1996	1997
Enemy intelligence	90	2	8	3	13
Political intelligence	866	20	45	33	80
Social intelligence	125	408	505	268	335
Border area intelligence	31	58	76	35	17
Other intelligence	39	15		55	23
TOTAL intelligence collected	1,117	503	1,602	1,267	1,355
Used to detect, prevent, and curb: a) demonstrations, worker strikes, and petitions	4	24	110		5
b) student strikes	18	2			32
c) illegal religious accidents	85	16	26	19	11
d) other disturbances		38	94	28	36

Source: *Xinjiang shengchan jianshe bingtuan gong'an zhi*, 189.
NB: Addition errors reproduced here as they appear in the source.

the XPCC, 15.9 percent of the population in 1997 were members of social-order protection committees or had signed a social-order responsibility contract. By contrast, penetration was less successful in other parts of Xinjiang: in Urumqi, only 1 percent of the population were members of social-order protection committees in 2000.[243] With a much larger informant network, the XPCC had a smaller list of counterrevolutionaries: in 1997, only 66 of the 4,914 individuals on the targeted population roster (1.3 percent) were suspected of political crimes or organizing counterrevolutionary activities under the guise of religion.[244] In Xinjiang overall, the targeted population in 2000 amounted to 31,408 (23.9 percent of whom were suspected of endangering state security).[245] The police had to deal with mass gatherings and riots (*chuzhi gelei juzhong naoshi, saoluan shijian* 处置各类聚众闹事, 骚乱事件), which included illegal assemblies and demonstrations (*feifa juzhong, youxing shijian* 非法聚众, 游行事件) and serious

accounting for 1,283,523 of the 2,383,983 residents of the XPCC (urban resident holders made up the remaining 1,100,460); assuming slightly larger rural households, the rural/urban household split was probably 50/50, thus making it plausible that there were around 360,000 rural households and that each and every one signed a social-order protection performance contract.

[243] *Xinjiang tongzhi: Gong'an zhi*, 374.
[244] *Xinjiang shengchan jianshe bingtuan gong'an zhi*, 211–15.
[245] *Xinjiang tongzhi: Gong'an zhi*, 514.

political riots (*yanzhong zhengzhi saoluan shijian* 严重政治骚乱事件).[246] This was a formidable task that could not be executed without a major increase in personnel allocation and recruitment of minority informants.[247]

8.5.4 Voluntary Provision of Information

As neither Tibet nor Xinjiang provides disaggregated statistics on complaints by ethnic status, we cannot make any definitive statements about the number of petitions lodged by ethnic minorities in these two regions. Data for citizen complaints during the 1990s indicate that Tibet almost invariably had the lowest level of petitions on a per capita basis of any province in China, and Xinjiang was either in the bottom half or in the bottom third. This suggests that should letters-and-visits data for Tibetans and Uyghurs ever become available, they would indicate a low frequency of voluntary transmission of information through citizen complaints. Such a finding would be consistent with one of the main arguments of this book, namely, that petitioning through the officially approved channels represents trust in the system. This trust cannot develop in an increasingly repressive environment such as that emerging in Xinjiang and Tibet in the 1990s and becoming firmly entrenched since 2008. Figures 8.5 and 8.6, which present statistics on corruption denunciations, offer further indications of the decline in trust.

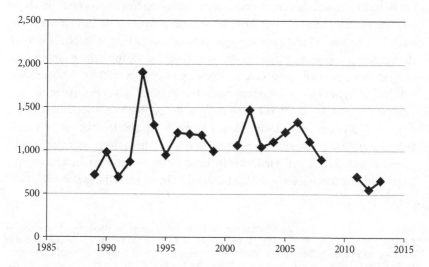

Figure 8.5 Discipline inspection denunciations in Tibet, 1989–2013.

Sources: Zhonggong Xizang difang zuzhishi zhigao 1950–1999 (Lasa: Zhonggong Xizang Zuzhibu, 2000), 518–19; *Xizang nianjian* (Lasa: Xizang Renmin Chubanshe, various years).

[246] *Xinjiang tongzhi: Gong'an zhi*, 380–85.
[247] Adrian Zenz and James Leibold, "Securitizing Xinjiang: Police Recruitment, Informal Policing, and Ethnic Minority Co-Optation," *The China Quarterly*, no. 242 (June 2020), 324–48.

Figure 8.6 Discipline inspection denunciations in Xinjiang, 1999–2012.
Source: Xinjiang nianjian (Urumqi: Xinjiang Nianjian She, various years).

8.5.5   Minority Management since 2008: The Failure of Co-optation

Prominent scholars argue that although communist regimes initially rule through mobilization, they eventually transition to governance through inclusion.[248] A threat to resilience is presented by the emergence of groups that are not subject to inclusion and that can successfully organize against the regime. This book maintains that the incapacity of the Chinese regime to penetrate the two compactly settled minorities of Tibetans and Uyghurs has presented the main obstacle to inclusion and co-optation. Although efforts to co-opt more minority members into the party increased after the Tibetan Uprising of 1959, as of 2006 Tibetans and, especially, Uyghurs were underrepresented in the CCP when compared to their share of the population.[249] The incapacity of the regime to co-opt Tibetans and Uyghurs is also illustrated by the theoretically anticipated low volume of voluntarily transmitted information from these minorities through citizen complaints.

The main indicator of the failure of inclusion is the rise of overt discontent. This began with Tibetan unrest in the lead-up to the Olympics in the spring of 2008.[250]

---

[248] Kenneth Jowitt, *New World Disorder: The Leninist Extinction* (Berkeley: University of California Press, 1992), 77. See also Barbara Geddes, "Stages of Development in Authoritarian Regimes," in Vladimir Tismaneanu, Marc Morjé Howard, and Rudra Sil, eds., *World Order After Leninism* (Seattle: University of Washington Press, 2006), 149–70.

[249] For statistics on the number of Uyghurs and Tibetans in the party, see Zhonggong Zhongyang Zuzhi Bu, *Zhongguo gongchandang dangnei tongji ziliao huibian, 1921–2010* (Beijing: Dangjian Duwu Chubanshe, 2011), 194.

[250] Much like the spectacle of the 1300th anniversary of the Bulgarian state (see Chapter 5), the 2008 Olympics were seen by aggrieved minorities as a celebration for the ethnic majority.

In addition, Xinjiang was rocked by violent clashes between Han Chinese and Uyghurs for nearly a decade after 2008. This contradicts a survey finding from 2011 reported in Section 8.4, which indicates that the Tibetans and the Uyghurs are among the most satisfied Chinese citizens.[251]

This book argues that communist regimes turn to the problem of ethnic minorities when both elite and mass constraints are low. In China, the successful hosting of the 2008 Olympics demonstrated to the regime that it was capable of managing mass discontent. Despite a rapid increase in protests and considerable anxiety about potential disruptions to social order, 2008 did not bring about unanticipated nationwide eruptions of discontent. China's successful weathering of the global financial crisis and of the Arab Spring gave further confidence to regime insiders that, as far as the ethnic majority was concerned, the popular threat was at a manageable level. With regard to the elite threat, the sidelining of Bo Xilai in 2012 and the subsequent investigations of the rest of the "new Gang of Four" (Xu Caihou, Zhou Yongkang, and Ling Jihua) demonstrated Xi Jinping's capacity to manage elite rivals. Other key targets identified in 2012–2014 were eliminated through sentencing by 2016.[252] Thus, by August 2016, when Chen Quanguo was appointed party secretary of Xinjiang, the elite threat had been neutralized as well. This means that the regime was ready to address minority discontent in a more systematic fashion.

The regime first turned to discontent in Tibet, where the 2008 riots had resulted in massive investment in the security apparatus. Under Chen Quanguo's watch as party secretary in 2011–2016, the so-called grid-management system (*wanggehua guanli* 网格化管理) was implemented throughout the autonomous region.[253] This system employs sophisticated monitoring technology that enables the police and paramilitary forces to respond to social unrest extremely efficiently. The result has been a lack of overt expressions of discontent. This statement might not square with statistics indicating that the number of self-immolations since 2009 reached 157 by 2019 (and 159 by 2022).[254] However, nearly all self-immolations have taken place outside of the Tibet Autonomous Region.

In contrast to Tibet, overt discontent continued in Xinjiang. In the wake of Uyghur unrest in June 2013, the Xinjiang Police Department issued a public notice offering rewards of 50,000–100,000 yuan (about $8,300–$16,600), along with guarantees of anonymity and protection, to informants from any ethnic

---

[251] Wang and Quan, "2011–2012 nian Zhongguo jumin shenghuo manyi du."

[252] In general, see Yuen Yuen Ang, *China's Gilded Age: The Paradox of Economic Boom and Vast Corruption* (New York: Cambridge University Press, 2020).

[253] James Leibold, "Surveillance in China's Xinjiang Region: Ethnic Sorting, Coercion, and Inducement," *Journal of Contemporary China* 29:121 (2020), 46–60.

[254] International Campaign for Tibet, "Self-Immolations by Tibetans," https://www.savetibet.org/resources/fact-sheets/self-immolations-by-tibetans/ (accessed April 19, 2022).

group (*ge minzu qunzhong* 各民族群众) who provide tips that could be used to solve cases of violent terrorism.[255] The persistence of ethnic unrest in Xinjiang well past 2013 testifies to the failure of this policy. The response of the central government has been to step up repression. One indicator of this approach has been increased prosecution of political crimes: with slightly more than 1 percent of the population of China, the Xinjiang Uyghur Autonomous Region accounts for roughly half of the individuals prosecuted for crimes of endangering state security (*weihai guojia anquan zui* 危害国家安全罪) in the 2000s and 2010s.[256] This approach is counterproductive in the long term as it does not increase the loyalty of minority members and it exacerbates the pre-existing ethnic tensions.

Ethnic policy in Xinjiang experienced a major overhaul after Xi Jinping's 2014 speech and Chen Quanguo's appointment as party secretary in August 2016.[257] Chen brought to Xinjiang techniques like the grid management system that he had perfected in Tibet. However, the intensity of his policies reached an extreme level that went beyond the experience of Tibet. Capitalizing on internal understandings of Islam as a religion that can lead to instability, a battery of policies was implemented following promulgation on March 29, 2017, of the Xinjiang Uyghur Autonomous Region De-Extremification Regulations.[258] Under these regulations, practices such as veiling, "abnormal beards used to promote religious fanaticism" (*yi feizhengchang xuxu xuanran zongjiao kuangre* 以非正常蓄须渲染宗教狂热), refusal to watch state TV and radio, refusal to send one's children to national education classes, and giving overly Islamic names to babies (Islam, Quran, Mecca, Jihad, Medina, Imam, Hajj, Saddam) were forbidden.[259] Mosque attendees were subjected to strict surveillance and citizens who fasted during Ramadan were punished.[260] A list of seventy-five signs of extremism, including praying with legs wide apart and abstaining from drinking alcohol, were prepared to assist officials in detecting extremists.[261] These are all examples of restrictions on religious expression, which generally parallel the Regenerative Process that unfolded in Bulgaria in 1984–1989.

A unique feature of the Xinjiang experience, however, involves the use of advanced AI technology to subject the population of the entire ethnic autonomous

---

[255] *Jiefang ribao*, July 3, 2013, 3.

[256] Hastings, "Charting the Course of Uyghur Unrest"; *Zhongguo tongji nianjian* (Beijing: Zhongguo Tongji Chubanshe, various years).

[257] *Xinjiang Papers* (https://uyghurtribunal.com/statements/, accessed April 19, 2022); Sean R. Roberts, *The War on the Uyghurs: China's Campaign Against Xinjiang's Muslims* (Princeton, NJ: Princeton University Press, 2020).

[258] "Xinjiang weiwuerzu zizhiqu qu jiduanhua tiaoli," March 29, 2017.

[259] "Xinjiang weiwuerzu zizhiqu qu jiduanhua tiaoli."

[260] http://www.rfa.org/english/news/china/muslims-ramadan-06142017134547.html/, June 14, 2017 (accessed April 19, 2022).

[261] "Shibie zongjiao jiduan huodong (75 zhong juti biaoxian) jichu zhishi," June 19, 2017.

region to totalistic surveillance.[262] This goes beyond the use of face-recognition technology, the inscription of QR codes into every kitchen knife sold in Xinjiang (containing information on the customer's ID number, photo, ethnicity, and address), the routine checking of personal electronics for subversive content, and the requirement that all vehicles be equipped with location trackers. An effort is now under way to complete a biometric database that contains iris scans, DNA samples, fingerprints, and blood samples of the entire population.[263] Technological advances and cheap data have given the Chinese state access to surveillance tools that make the Stasi's efforts to obtain a "scent preserve" (*Geruchskonserve*) of every criminal suspect and political dissident in the GDR seem decidedly premodern.[264]

And yet there is one indicator that triumphalist thinking about the surveillance capacity of the Chinese state should be tempered. This book argues that more abundant information enables more selective and precisely targeted repression. News emerged from Xinjiang about a 731 percent increase in criminal arrest rates for Uyghurs in 2016–2017 and about the sending of a million Uyghurs (10 percent of the Uyghur population) to reeducation camps.[265] The comparable statistics for Bulgaria are that up to 0.3 percent of the Turkish population was held in the reopened labor camps during 1984–1989 and that arrests of Turks tripled during the Regenerative Process. What the Chinese statistics suggest is that the state is not omniscient or omnipotent. Indeed, they reveal a state in panic because it has failed to penetrate an ethnoreligious minority and has definitively abandoned the goal of promoting voluntary information transfer through citizen complaints. Overall, the use of indiscriminate repression demonstrates that the Chinese state lacks the fine-grained information that is necessary for anticipatory governance in Xinjiang. To the extent that the Bulgarian ethnic assimilation policies toward the Turks present a useful parallel, the Chinese state may be able to eliminate expressions of overt discontent through the implementation of repressive measures. However, the absence of overt discontent does not mean citizen satisfaction. Most importantly, failure to accurately assess and counteract latent discontent may have serious negative consequences for regime stability.

---

[262] Darren Byler, *Terror Capitalism: Uyghur Dispossession and Masculinity in a Chinese City* (Durham, NC: Duke University Press, 2022).

[263] https://www.hrw.org/news/2017/12/13/china-minority-region-collects-dna-millions (accessed April 19, 2022).

[264] Cristina Vatulescu, *Police Esthetics: Literature, Film, and the Secret Police in Soviet Times* (Stanford, CA: Stanford University Press, 2010), 13.

[265] http://www.duihuaresearch.org/search/label/ESS (accessed July 19, 2017); https://uyghurtribu nal.com/statements/ (accessed April 19, 2022).

8.6 Conclusion

This chapter has analyzed the evolution of information-gathering institutions in China during the three decades that separate the Tiananmen Spring from 2019. The challenges of soliciting voluntary provision through letters and of simultaneously penetrating and co-opting minorities persisted, and it became evident that the party-state was incapable of resolving them. The response has been to strengthen involuntary extraction through increasingly sophisticated methods of human and technological surveillance. The imperative since Tiananmen has been to maintain stability. Instead of anticipatory governance oriented toward identifying latent discontent and preventing it from being transformed into visible acts of opposition to the regime by satisfying the welfare demands of the population, China has practiced ex-post governance focused on detecting and neutralizing visible acts of dissent. Single-party rule has survived in China, but it has been placed under considerable stress. Its capacity to persist with declining levels of voluntary provision and an erosion of public trust will be discussed in the concluding chapter of this study.

PART V

GENERALIZABILITY
OF THE THEORY

Part V concludes the study by engaging with the question of the generalizability of the argument, which is approached by discussing scope conditions (Chapter 9) and the relationship between information and regime resilience (Chapter 10).

All regimes need information, which is essential for establishing a panoptical vision over society. A feature limited to autocracies is that they also experience the dictator's dilemma, where those in power are uncertain about the support they have among members of the elite and the masses. Solving the dilemma requires the collection of information on levels of opposition to the regime. As monitoring elites is considerably simpler than assessing the mood of the masses, most attention internally within autocracies is devoted to tracking popular discontent. Single-party communist autocracies exhibit specificities in terms of the range of mechanisms deployed to compile actionable intelligence. The case studies in Chapter 9 are used to generate further evidence about these specificities and to test whether the institutional solutions to the information problem presented in the book thus far apply to noncommunist regimes as well.

Empirically, these case studies (which extend to the full range of autocracies: single-party communist; Leninist non-communist; single-party non-Leninist; multiparty; and regimes without parties) demonstrate the gradation of institutional endowments across nondemocracies: those without any parties possess the lowest number of information-gathering agencies, whereas single-party communist regimes develop the full complement of institutions discussed in this book; the remaining regime types fall in the middle in terms of the extent of their information-collection mechanisms. The case studies also demonstrate that identical institutions can have different functions across various types of regimes: for example, the absence of a social contract in Taiwan led to a low level of voluntary transmission of information through complaints, even though numerous avenues existed for lodging such complaints. A final empirical finding is that regardless of regime origins and initial information-gathering arrangements, all communist autocracies eventually develop the same complement of institutions for assessing popular discontent, thus attesting to the communist difference in information collection.

The case studies in Chapter 9 provide further process-tracing evidence that strengthens some of the major theoretical arguments of the book about features of information gathering. One is the tradeoff between information quality and repression: namely, the frequency, indiscriminacy, and severity of repression all decline as the quality of information improves. The second theoretically relevant finding concerns the capacity of redundancy to compensate for the biases of different sources of information (e.g., rosy party reporting vs. entirely negative State Security briefs in the early years of the Soviet Union), to help regime insiders cross-check the available intelligence, and to increase their confidence in the decisions they make. A final theoretical insight is that at the end of communist rule incumbents had abundant information (they had solved the dictator's dilemma) but were unable to act on it and to avoid being deposed. Although all of these findings emerge in prior chapters and are developed throughout the book, Chapter 9 helps consolidate our certainty that these are generalizable phenomena in communist regimes, rather than sui generis features of the Bulgarian or the Chinese case.

Chapter 10 turns to concluding reflections. This book is fundamentally interested in the relationship between information and regime resilience, which involves regime capacity to survive a shock and implement adaptive institutional changes as a result of learning. Surviving a shock requires the deployment of brute repression; this type of response does not necessitate detailed information. However, resilience cannot rest on a high level of repression. The book indicates that two models are possible. One is a classic communist welfare state and the other is a market welfare state. Neither model can ensure indefinite survival, even if the market model reduces some of the pressure on the party-state to engage in redistributive spending. In both models, the capacity to respond to information may diminish over time. When this occurs, overt opposition to the system increases and the likelihood of regime breakdown is greater. This argument has specific implications for the future of China. The suppression of offline and online contention does not bode well for the regime, as it indicates that the party-state is unwilling to respond to popular input. The policies in Tibet and Xinjiang are sending an even stronger signal about this deficiency. A communist regime that ignores popular opinion is destined to face surprise eruptions of discontent, which can present a threat to systemic stability.

9

Scope Conditions

Authoritarian Information-Gathering Institutions

Thus far, the argument of this book about the use of involuntarily extracted and voluntarily provided information to guide decisions about repression and concessions in autocracies has been tested through evidence generated primarily by the single-party communist regimes of Bulgaria and China. This chapter engages with a group of nondemocratic regimes to which this argument might extend.

When thinking about scope conditions, two related concerns arise. First is the very existence of information-gathering institutions. An empirical question that must be addressed is whether these institutions can be found only in some types of autocracies or whether, by contrast, they are universal. The chapter presents evidence that although some of these institutions, such as the state security system, do indeed exist in most regimes, the full complement is found only in communist dictatorships. Remarkably, even though the sequencing pattern in which these institutions emerge displays some variation across communist autocracies, in the end all regimes that belong to this class develop the set of mechanisms for voluntary provision and involuntary collection that are detailed in the chapters on Bulgaria and China. This helps us highlight the communist specificity of intelligence-gathering institutions in dictatorships.

The second issue concerns the functions of these institutions. We need to be mindful that institutions may assume roles that are different from those intended by their creators. Obsolescence also occurs, as illustrated by some of the cases discussed in this chapter. A further complication arises from the fact than an identical institution may serve different purposes across a range of regimes. To uncover the functions of institutions, we need detailed empirical evidence on the complete set of information-gathering mechanisms in different countries. At a theoretical level, this type of material enables us to identify the tradeoffs that exist when some institutions are present, but others are not. Methodologically, the evidence presented in this chapter and throughout the book, allows us to highlight the value of archival ethnography for opening the black box of authoritarian politics and identifying deep processes rather than surface dynamics.

The chapter is organized as follows. Through a series of short case studies based on primary sources, it reviews the information-gathering infrastructure

Dictatorship and Information. Martin K. Dimitrov, Oxford University Press. © Oxford University Press 2023.
DOI: 10.1093/oso/9780197672921.003.0009

of different types of autocracies: communist single-party (the Soviet Union, the German Democratic Republic [GDR], and Cuba); Leninist noncommunist single-party (Taiwan 1949–1987); non-Leninist single-party (Iraq 1968–2003); multiparty (Russia, 2000–present); and nonparty (Chile 1973–1989 and Argentina 1976–1983). These investigations reveal that the full complement of intelligence-gathering institutions that are needed for a low-repression high-redistribution governance model is most likely to emerge in a communist single-party regime that has a centrally planned economy. Leninist noncommunist regimes share many similarities with communist regimes, but they do not reach a low-repression high-redistribution equilibrium, because the lack of a social contract and elevated levels of repression-induced fear limit citizen willingness to voluntarily transmit information. Non-Leninist single party regimes have smaller parties, thus reducing their information-gathering capacity to the monitoring of overt discontent. In multiparty systems, the party in power typically plays no significant intelligence-gathering role; however, if these autocracies are successors of single-party communist regimes, institutional legacies may help maintain pervasive involuntary collection and substantial voluntary transmission; although this cannot translate into the same level of redistribution as that which exists under central planning, these regimes can nevertheless develop a moderate-repression moderate-redistribution equilibrium not dissimilar from the one currently in place in China. Finally, in countries without political parties, information gathering is extremely limited and extends only to intelligence and counterintelligence that can be used to inform decisions about the deployment of repression against regime opponents; there is no systematic collation of intelligence to guide redistributive choices.

These case studies help outline the scope conditions for the argument. Only single-party communist regimes with a centrally planned economy are likely to develop complex information states where the party, State Security, and internal media supply involuntarily collected and voluntarily provided information that can be used to guide decisions about repression and concessions. In market economies, moderate redistribution and moderate repression may exist in communist (China), Leninist noncommunist (Taiwan), or multiparty postcommunist regimes (Russia); however, because redistribution is moderate, these autocracies are likely to have lower levels of stability (i.e., more protests) than centrally planned communist information states. In noncommunist regimes with small parties, intelligence gathering is crude and geared more toward repression; in dictatorships without parties, information is used only for repression. Overall, these case studies highlight the essential role that the party plays in generating intelligence and in coordinating information-gathering activities.

9.1 Origins of the Soviet Information State

Analyzing the creation of an information state in the Soviet Union highlights the complex interactions between the pre-existing and the newly established bureaucracies tasked with tracking popular discontent. During the initial decade of postrevolutionary governance, the Soviet leadership created institutions such as the All-Russian Extraordinary Commission (Cheka) and the Red Army that were nominally new but in practice had appropriated most of the intelligence-collection techniques of the Tsarist secret police and army. Some existing entities, such as the telegraph agency, were given a new mandate to monitor domestic discontent. Finally, there were organizations like the communist party that had never engaged in the systematic tracking of popular discontent, let alone in the coordination and supervision of such information-collection activities by other bureaucratic actors. The initial decade of communist rule was a period of rapid institution building, adjustment, and re-appropriation. This was also a time when intense rivalries emerged among the various bureaucracies in charge of tracking dissent, resulting in the exclusion of the telegraph agency and of the Red Army from producing assessments of popular discontent. By the end of the 1920s, the basic armature of the information state was in place: involuntary collection was executed by the Cheka and the party, whereas the print media were assigned the new task of preparing analytical summaries of the grievances that citizens had voluntarily revealed by writing complaint letters. This blueprint of the information state would be reproduced by all communist regimes at some point in the trajectory of their institutional development.

9.1.1 Russia: State Security Precursors

There should be no doubt that the Russian Empire developed sophisticated techniques for identifying enemies of the state. The Third Department of the Emperor's Office, established in the wake of the unanticipated December Uprising of 1825, was tasked with detecting and counteracting political dissent.[1] Building on the expertise of its predecessors, such as the Secret Office of the Ministry of the Interior, the Third Department monitored antimonarchical and antistate activities; sects and schisms; money falsification; political prisoners; and the activities of foreigners.[2] The Third Department was also in

---

[1] V. M. Sidorova, "Vysshuiu politsiiu v Rossii ozhidali so strakhom: Zhandarmy o sebe samikh," in V. K. Bylinin, ed., *Trudy Obshchestva izucheniia istorii otechestvennykh spetssluzhb*, vol. 1 (Moscow: Kuchkovo Pole, 2006), 14–24, at 14.

[2] Sidorova, "Vysshuiu politsiiu," 14–15.

charge of compiling statistics on all major incidents throughout the country. It reported regularly to the emperor and produced overviews of public opinion (*obzory obshchestvennogo mneniia*), which were subsequently reclassified as moral-political overviews (*nravstvenno-politicheskie obozreniia*).[3] The Third Department relied on its thirty-five full-time staff, a corps of gendarmes that had about 5,500 men,[4] and an unspecified number of informants.[5] The intelligence collected was entered into individual and group files; in 1850, there existed more than 10,000 operational and 29,589 archived files.[6] In the second half of the nineteenth century, the functions of the secret police were gradually assumed by the Ministry of the Interior, which formally established the Department for the Protection of Public Order and Safety (*okhranka*) in 1881. The *okhranka* relied on full-time staff, surveillance agents (*fileurs*), and informants (*osvedomiteli*). Like the Third Department, it used perlustration of correspondence (a function taken over by the army during World War I) and it kept files on those who were politically unreliable—in 1917, the Moscow *okhranka* had card files on one-sixth of the city's inhabitants.[7] After the October Revolution, State Security (the VChK) adapted the existing methods to the political needs of the new government and redefined the categories of individuals who should be counted as enemies; however, it is important to stress that there was not a radical change in State Security information-collection methods during the initial years of Soviet rule.

9.1.2 Information Gathering during the Initial Postrevolutionary Period

In the aftermath of the October Revolution, four parallel systems for intelligence collection apprised the leadership of the popular mood: the Bolshevik party,[8] the army, the media, and State Security. Revealing the value it placed on such intelligence, only three days after October 25, 1917, the Bolshevik leadership sent a questionnaire to regional party committees about popular attitudes toward the

---

[3] For a sample report, see State Archive of the Russian Federation (GARF) f. 109 op. 223 d. 6 l. 161–74 (1841), reproduced in Sidorova, "Vysshuiu politsiiu," 15–18.

[4] Data for 1850 from GARF f. 109 op. 231 d. 1A l. 339–64a (December 4, 1850), reproduced in Sidorova, "Vysshuiu politsiiu," 18–21 (data at 20).

[5] Altogether, there were 10,000–40,000 secret police agents in prerevolutionary Russia (Vladlen S. Izmozik, *Glaza i ushi rezhima: Gosudarstvennyi politicheskii kontrol' za naseleniem Sovetskoi Rossii v 1918–1928 godakh* [St. Petersburg: St. Petersburg University of Finance and Economics Press, 1995], 19).

[6] GARF f. 109 op. 231 d. 1A l. 339–364a (December 4, 1850), reproduced in Sidorova, "Vysshuiu politsiiu," 18–21 (data at 20).

[7] Izmozik reports that the *okhranka* had cards on 300,000 individuals (Izmozik, *Glaza i ushi rezhima*, 18). Moscow's population at the time was 1.8 million.

[8] The Russian Social Democratic Labor Party (Bolsheviks) was transformed into the Russian Communist Party (Bolsheviks) in 1918.

revolution.[9] In June 1918, the party Central Committee created an Information Department to track the state of grassroots party organizations and the mood of the people.[10] Alongside the party, the Red Army political directorate also issued regular bulletins that assessed popular discontent.[11] The perlustration of correspondence was such an important channel for the collection of information that the army tasked as many as 10,000 people with reading letters and telegrams in 1919.[12] The third entity that collected intelligence was the Russian Telegraph Agency (*Rossiiskoe telegrafnoe agentstvo*, or ROSTA), which began issuing weekly bulletins on the popular mood in 1918. In the following year, ROSTA established a Department of Special Information that served the needs of the government,[13] the legislature,[14] and the party;[15] the department enjoyed extraordinary discretion in producing bulletins and it had access not only to ROSTA's internal journalistic network but also to intelligence collected by the party, by various government agencies, and most crucially, by State Security.[16] However, the broad access to information and the coordinating function enjoyed by the newswire agency aroused discontent. The army called into question the political bona fides of journalists and their capacity to safeguard the various state, military, and political secrets they encountered. The recommendation was to transfer ROSTA's functions of monitoring dissent to the party.[17] This means that, similar to Bulgaria but in contrast to China, the telegraph agency could not be trusted to handle secret information on domestic matters during the initial decades of communist rule.[18]

---

[9] Izmozik, *Glaza i ushi rezhima*, 26.

[10] Izmozik, *Glaza i ushi rezhima*, 27–28.

[11] Izmozik, *Glaza i ushi rezhima*, 36–40.

[12] Izmozik, *Glaza i ushi rezhima*, 50. Control of correspondence was not a Russian or Soviet trademark. Under the Third Republic, the *Service du contrôle technique* was established in France; in December 1943, it inspected 2.44 million letters, in addition to reading 1.77 million telegrams and intercepting 20,811 phone calls. See Peter Holquist, "'Information Is the Alpha and Omega of Our Work': Bolshevik Surveillance in Its Pan-European Context," *The Journal of Modern History* 69:3 (September 1997), 415–50, at 445.

[13] The Council of People's Commissars (*Sovet narodnykh komissarov*, or Sovnarkom) was the predecessor of the Council of Ministers, which was established in 1946.

[14] The All-Russian Central Executive Committee (*Vserossiiskii tsentral'nyi ispolnitel'nyi komitet*) was the highest legislative body in between sessions of the All-Russian Congress of Soviets. The system existed until the creation of the Supreme Soviet in 1938.

[15] A. V. Golubev, *Esli mir obrushitsia na nashu respubliku: Sovetskoe obshchestvo i vneshnaia ugroza v 1922–1941 godakh* (Moscow: Direct Media, 2020), 25.

[16] Izmozik, *Glaza i ushi rezhima*, 32.

[17] Izmozik, *Glaza i ushi rezhima*, 33.

[18] Xinhua was created by the CCP, whereas ROSTA emerged as a private newswire. In Bulgaria, the telegraph agency was controlled by the Ministry of Foreign Affairs, which was not headed by a communist during the initial years after the 1944 coup.

The growing stature of the fourth intelligence gatherer, the VChK (Cheka),[19] quickly put an end to the monitoring of domestic discontent by ROSTA and the army. Created one month after the revolution, the purpose of the Cheka was to collect information for state organs (*gosinformatsiia*) that revealed the moods of all social groups and the factors influencing changes in those moods.[20] Remarkably, by the end of 1918, State Security commissions existed in 40 *guberniia* and 365 *uezd*.[21] The Cheka staff also grew rapidly, from 219 in March 1918 to 60,000 by 1921.[22] As it became more powerful, the VChK assumed a greater role in information collection. It started issuing regular weekly overviews from January 1, 1920; these replaced the confidential ROSTA bulletins on the popular mood.[23] As the civil war became less intense and moved to the borderlands, the Cheka asserted itself by taking control over perlustration from the Red Army in August 1920.[24] When the civil war came to a close in 1922–1923, the military stopped functioning as an independent generator of information on the popular mood. By 1923, State Security was able to successfully monitor the loyalty of soldiers through its network of political commissars in the armed forces.

Thus, in the early 1920s, the foundations of a system for intelligence collection were firmly established: domestic discontent was assessed through information involuntarily extracted primarily by State Security and secondarily by the party, with ROSTA (which became the Telegraph Agency of the Soviet Union, or TASS in 1925) having a mandate to issue confidential reports on international affairs. The perlustration of correspondence remained important for

---

[19] The All-Russian Extraordinary Commission (*Vserossiiskaia chrezvychainaia komissiia*, or VChK or simply Cheka) existed from December 1917 until February 1922. Its successor was the State Political Directorate (*Gosudarstvennoe politicheskoe upravlenie*, or GPU). In December 1923, the GPU was transformed into the Joint State Political Directorate (*Ob'edinënnoe gosudarstvennoe politicheskoe upravlenie*, or OGPU). In 1934, the OGPU was superseded by the People's Commissariat for Internal Affairs (*Narodnyi komissariat vnutrennikh del*, or NKVD). Three other agencies handled state security prior to the creation of the KGB in 1954: the People's Commissariat for State Security (*Narodnyi komissariat gosudarstvennoi bezopasnosti*, or NKGB); the Ministry of State Security (*Ministerstvo gosudarstvennoi bezopasnosti*, or MGB); and the Ministry of the Interior (*Ministerstvo vnutrennikh del*, or MVD). The Committee for State Security (*Komitet gosudarstvennoi bezopasnosti*, or KGB) existed from 1954 to 1991. For further details, see A. I. Kokurin and N. V. Petrov, comps., *Lubianka: Organy VChK-OGPU-NKVD-NKGB-MGB-MVD-KGB, 1917–1991* (Moscow: Mezhdunarodnyi Fond "Demokratiia," 2003).

[20] This was formalized several years later in VChK Order 85/23, February 1922 (referenced in Izmozik, *Glaza i ushi rezhima*, 3).

[21] Viktor M. Chebrikov, ed., *Istoriia sovetskikh organov gosudarstvennoi bezopasnosti: Uchebnik* (Moscow: KGB Academy, 1977), 58.

[22] Izmozik, *Glaza i ushi rezhima*, 75. By 1931, the OGPU had 25,886 staff persons; 45,612 border troops (with 20,529 horses); and 19,950 internal troops (with 7,556 horses) (see O. B. Mozokhin, ed., *Politbiuro i organy gosudarstvennoi bezopasnosti: Sbornik dokumentov* [Moscow: Kuchkovo Pole, 2017], 269–70).

[23] Izmozik, *Glaza i ushi rezhima*, 67.

[24] Izmozik, *Glaza i ushi rezhima*, 74.

tracking discontent within the army and among dissidents, but not for assessing the mood of broader segments of society. It its stead, analysis of letters voluntarily submitted by citizens to the media and to the party emerged as a valuable window onto the popular mood. Lenin made numerous statements about the utility of allowing citizens to complain and of tracking the volume of petitions.[25] He also stressed the importance of responding to citizen letters.[26] According to Lenin, complaints had two functions. First, they provided the government with information about popular discontent and made it possible for problems of governance like bureaucratism (*biurokratizm*) and red tape (*volokita*) to be identified and dealt with. Second, they enabled the "involvement of the wide masses in the work of the soviets."[27] After the death of Lenin, reports on letters sent to newspapers continued to be regularly prepared for the leadership.[28] This system for aggregating voluntarily transmitted information persisted without major changes until the end of the Soviet Union.

9.1.3   Party Information in the 1920s and 1930s: The Closed Letters System

In 1922, the Central Committee Organization Bureau began requiring regional party leaders to produce regular confidential materials that were variously called political letters (*politicheskie pis'ma*), personal letters (*lichnye pis'ma*) or, most commonly, closed letters (*zakrytye pis'ma*).[29] These monthly reports of two pages were to cover the economic situation, the mood of the people, recent enemy activity, the work of the soviets, and the life of the party organization.[30] Once received by the Organization Bureau, the closed letters were used to prepare a monthly report on the regional situations that would then be presented to the Central Committee Secretariat, which determined to whom this important document would circulate.[31] As scholars have noted, a major shortcoming

[25] In an often-cited 1922 letter to the editor of the newspaper *Bednota* (The Rural Poor), Lenin asked for a biweekly report on the number of peasant complaints to the newspaper, their mood, and the burning questions of the day (*zloby dnia*) they raised. See Vladimir I. Lenin, *Polnoe sobranie sochinenii*, vol. 54 (Fifth Edition) (Moscow: Izdatel'stvo Politicheskoi Literatury, 1970), 143–44.

[26] Vladimir I. Lenin, *Polnoe sobranie sochinenii*, vol. 50 (5th ed.) (Moscow: Izdatel'stvo Politicheskoi Literatury, 1969), 227, 323

[27] Vladimir I. Lenin, *Polnoe sobranie sochinenii*, vol. 38 (5th ed.) (Moscow: Izdatel'stvo Politicheskoi Literatury, 1969), 169.

[28] Izmozik, *Glaza i ushi rezhima*, 88.

[29] G. A. Kurenkov, *Ot konspiratsii k sekretnosti: Zashchita partiino-gosudarstvennoi tainy v RKP (b)–VKP (b) 1918–1941 gg.* (Moscow: AIRO-XXI, 2015), 53–54.

[30] Izmozik, *Glaza i ushi rezhima*, 89.

[31] Kurenkov, *Ot konspiratsii k sekretnosti*, 59–60.

of party digests (*svodki*) during the initial years of communist governance was that that they focused on successes in party building, aiming to present the situation in a positive light, and they were not sufficiently critical.[32] Army reports on the popular mood had suffered from the same deficiency, which was a key reason why they fell into disuse after 1920 and were eliminated altogether several years later.[33] As ROSTA was not allowed to monitor domestic dissent after 1920, reporting by State Security promptly displaced party digests and became the most important channel for assessing discontent during the early years of communist rule.

9.1.4 State Security Information in the 1920s and 1930s: Social-Political Overviews

In sharp contrast to the stylized fact that critical information is suppressed in autocracies, the top Soviet leadership received a steady stream of negative news on the popular mood in the form of State Security briefs. These reports reflected the major challenges that the regime faced in the first years of its existence. Initially, the internal organization of the bulletins was variable. For example, the March 1922 overview of the political and economic situation covered the following matters: the mood of workers, peasants, and Red Army servicemen; patterns in the spread of banditry;[34] the activities of organized counterrevolutionaries (anarchists, Mensheviks, left and right socialist revolutionaries [SR, or *essers*], monarchists, and cadets); and the attitudes of the clergy.[35] Several months later, the requirements for the content of these reports were standardized— beginning in May 1922, they had to cover the political mood (defined internally as popular attitudes toward the regime); strikes and the reasons for them (the economic situation, political influence, poor management); peasant uprisings; food distribution problems; banditry; sabotage; and other counterrevolutionary activity.[36] Needless to say, the Cheka aimed to develop a panoptical capacity throughout the country.

---

[32] Izmozik, *Glaza i ushi rezhima*, 100–2; Lesley A. Rimmel, "Svodki and Popular Opinion in Stalinist Leningrad," *Cahiers du Monde Russe* 40: 1–2 (January–June 1999), 217–34, at 218.

[33] Izmozik, *Glaza i ushi rezhima*, 100–2.

[34] By 1922, the Cheka and the Red Army had eliminated 89 large bands with 56,000 members (Chebrikov, ed., *Istoriia sovetskikh organov gosudarstvennoi bezopasnosti*, 174).

[35] Central Archive of the Federal Security Service (TsA FSB) f. 1 op. 6 d. 116 l. 176–83 (March 1922), reproduced in *"Sovershenno sekretno": Lubianka—Stalinu o polozhenii v strane (1922–1934 gg.)*, vol. 1 (Moscow: Institute of Russian History of the Russian Academy of Sciences, 2000), 89–95.

[36] L. P. Kolodnikova, *Sovetskoe obshchestvo 20-kh godov XX veka: Po dokumentam VChK-OGPU* (Moscow: Nauka, 2009), 69–72. Additional drivers of discontent included electoral constraints, as well as the lack of independent labor unions and a peasant party.

These briefs were produced by the Information Department of the state security agency with varying periodicity (daily; weekly; biweekly; monthly). In addition to regular reports, specialized intelligence bulletins were prepared on issues ranging from the prevalence of drunkenness and moonshine production (the so-called *p'iansvodka*, or drunkenness bulletin) to the spread of cannibalism and the incidence of various economic problems.[37] The reports did not paint a rosy picture: they detailed the urban strike wave of the 1920s; rural discontent during the forced collectivization (in 1930 alone, there were at least 2.7 million participants in peasant protests and armed uprisings);[38] and the broad appeal of counterrevolutionary organizations.[39] One distinctive feature of State Security reporting was its near complete lack of positive information.[40] This stood in marked contrast to the internal party bulletins at the time.

State Security briefs managed to be both comprehensive and specific. Evidence of their comprehensiveness is provided by the fact that in 1931 the Joint State Political Directorate (OGPU) reporting covered 3,300 administrative units located throughout the Soviet Union.[41] This geographic reach stands in contradistinction to the extreme paucity of comprehensive overviews of sociopolitical problems in Chinese intelligence bulletins: *Neibu cankao* contained reports on only one such issue (namely, reactions to the death of Stalin) in the sixteen years for which we have continuous access (see Chapters 4 and 6). It is important to stress that in the Soviet Union comprehensiveness did not come at the expense of specificity. These twin goals were easier to achieve when briefs focused on a problem in a limited number of regions (e.g., on armed rebellions by ethnic minorities in the Caucasus, Central Asia, or other border areas).[42] But even geographically broad reports often brought problems to life by providing concrete empirical details: for example, overviews of supply problems in 1929 listed various shortages (of salt, matches, salami, and canned fish)—but it was the low quality of bread that most aggravated consumers. Specifically, the meager rations often included bread that was either moldy or had impurities, such as sawdust, straw, sand, oatmeal husks, rotten fish, and expired fruit.[43] Sometimes, a catchy phrase could also add specificity, as demonstrated by the conclusion of a report

[37] On *p'iansvodka*, see Kolodnikova, *Sovetskoe obshchestvo 20-kh godov XX veka*, 88; on cannibalism, see document no. 320 (TsA FSB f. 2 op. 11 d. 1035 l. 5–6 [August 1, 1933]), reproduced in *Sovershenno sekretno* (vol. 10, pt. 2), 495.
[38] For a higher estimate, see Mozokhin, ed., *Politbiuro i organy gosudarstvennoi bezopasnosti*, 36.
[39] See document no. 327 (TsA FSB f. 2 op. 11 d. 1496 l. 2–21 [December 1933]), reproduced in *Sovershenno sekretno* (vol. 10, pt. 2), 521–37, and document no. 329 (TsA FSB f. 2 op. 11 d. 1031 l. 1–54 [December 25, 1933]), reproduced in *Sovershenno sekretno* (vol. 10, pt. 2), 539–63.
[40] *Sovershenno sekretno* (vol. 4), 16.
[41] *Sovershenno sekretno* (vol. 9), 21.
[42] *Sovershenno sekretno* (vol. 9), 59.
[43] *Sovershenno sekretno* (vol. 7), 14.

in 1930, which states that "the people's mood is beastly" (*nastroenie naroda zverinoe*).[44]

9.1.5 Maintaining Secrecy in the Circulation of Sensitive Information

In the Soviet Union, objective (*dostovernoe*) reporting on popular discontent was considered valuable political information that was so sensitive that it could not circulate widely beyond the highest echelons of the party-state.[45] Having received word of the content of such sociopolitical overviews, lower-level leading cadres expressed dissatisfaction with the tailored OGPU reports they read and demanded access to the broad overview materials prepared for the Central Committee.[46] However, the OGPU held firm and limited circulation of these prized documents to the Politburo and the Central Committee. In 1923, they were printed in thirty-four to thirty-six copies and distributed to a very narrow list of recipients in Moscow.[47] By 1929, sociopolitical briefs were sent to a larger group of 120 leading cadres throughout the Soviet Union, yet none of these individuals had status below that of a Central Committee member.[48] State Security closely guarded its secrets until the very end of communist rule: for example, in the 1960s–1980s the annual reports of the Committee for State Security (KGB) were typically issued in a single copy addressed to the general secretary, who would then circulate these documents to the other Politburo members and ask them to indicate that they have reviewed them by signing in the margin on the top page.[49] Less sensitive intelligence briefs had a wider circle of recipients, though copies could only be dispatched to individuals on a precleared distribution list.

The party devoted significant attention to maintaining secrecy and controlling the flow of information, as evidenced by the fact that in 1919–1941 the Politburo, the Organization Bureau (*Orgbiuro*), and the Central Committee Secretariat discussed 564 different agenda items concerning the protection of information.[50] Within the Secretariat, the Special Department (later renamed the General Department) was in charge of information transfer to the leadership.

---

[44] *Sovershenno sekretno* (vol. 8), 47.

[45] *Sovershenno sekretno* (vol. 6), 15.

[46] Mozokhin, ed., *Politbiuro i organy gosudarstvennoi bezopasnosti*, 240.

[47] For a distribution list, see *Sovershenno sekretno* (vol.1), 49–50.

[48] *Sovershenno sekretno* (vol. 7), 12.

[49] Based on the analysis of KGB annual reports for 1962, 1967, 1975, 1976, 1977, 1978, 1980, 1981, 1982, 1985, 1986, 1988, and 1989 (contained in Center for Preservation of Contemporary Documentation [TsKhSD] f. 89 and in Library of Congress, Volkogonov Papers, Box 28).

[50] Kurenkov, *Ot konspiratsii k sekretnosti*, 102.

The information flow controlled by this department included inner-party, government, and KGB reports; overviews of citizen letters; and decryptions of encoded telegrams.[51] Top leaders also had access to encrypted high-frequency telephone connections. In 1939, the system had 290 users.[52] It persisted and expanded after the war, with a high-frequency phone serving as a status symbol of a high-level *apparatchik*.[53] Another marker of secrecy was that the most important documents (secret Politburo agenda items and decisions made on such items, as well as certain party and KGB reports) were kept in the so-called special files (*osobye papki*), which had very limited circulation. In short, the party went to great lengths to prevent the dissemination of the most sensitive intelligence beyond a select circle of 100 or so recipients. With only a few exceptions, it was not possible to restrict reports solely to the top leader. The Soviet Union was a modern bureaucratic state, which required that those in charge of making governance decisions have access to the relevant information.

In sum, within a decade of the establishment of the Soviet Union, the process of rapid building and re-appropriation of institutions resulted in sidelining the telegraph agency and the army from monitoring internal dissent and in tasking State Security, the party, and the print media with the collection, analysis, and transmission of information on popular discontent that had been involuntarily extracted or voluntarily provided by the citizenry.

9.2 Information Gathering in the Soviet Union after World War II

Although there was no radical break in the systems for the collection of information, several important innovations occurred after World War II. The internal bulletins of the telegraph agency became a key source of foreign news. Party reporting incorporated regular analysis of voluntarily provided information (in the form of citizen letters) and drew on new forms of involuntary collection such as opinion polling. Various media outlets also generated briefs on citizen letters.

---

[51] V. I. Boldin, *Krushenie pedestala: Shtrikhi k portretu M. S. Gorbacheva* (Moscow: Respublika, 1995), 251–56. The number of these encoded telegrams was substantial: they amounted to 147,600 in 1973 and 129,000 in 1974 (Volkogonov Papers, Box 28 [December 31, 1974], Chernenko report to the Politburo, 15). On the use of encryption more generally, see Tat'iana Soboleva, *Istoriia shifroval'nogo dela v Rossii* (Moscow: Olma Press, 2002).

[52] V. V. Pavlov, "Iz istorii sozdaniia i razvitiia sistemy pravitel'stvennoi elektrosviazi sovetskogo gosudarstva (1930–1941 gg.)," in Bylinin, ed., *Trudy Obshchestva isuzheniia istorii*, vol. 1, 75–88, at 79.

[53] This is a universal status symbol across communist regimes. On the "red machine" in China, see Richard McGregor, *The Party: The Secret World of China's Communist Rulers* (New York: HarperCollins, 2010), esp. 1–33.

Most important, State Security greatly reduced its agent network and the number of citizens who were subjected to surveillance. These steps served as preludes to deploying a new strategy for dealing with dissent that relied on the selective repression of only a fraction of those who had violated state security laws. Despite these sophisticated advances in policing, monitoring minorities constituted an important scotoma in intelligence work. This section reviews these changes and concludes with some general reflections about the Soviet case with respect to our theory of information.

9.2.1 Citizen Letters and Opinion Polling as Sources of Information

Even though the analysis of citizen letters sent to the media and to the party began in the 1920s,[54] awareness of their utility for monitoring popular discontent was enhanced after World War II. Because citizens wrote to a wide range of recipients, numerous overviews of the content of these letters were produced by the print media,[55] by the electronic media,[56] by the legislature,[57] by government agencies,[58] and, of course, by the party.[59] In contrast to Bulgaria, there existed no one entity that collated these individual reports and generated a single document presenting the composite number of complaints and analyzing trends in the voluntary provision of information over time. In other ways, however, the Soviet Union was similar to countries in Eastern Europe. Namely, attention to citizen letters persisted all the way through the end of communist rule;[60] however, as the capacity to satisfy the redistributive demands of the population declined in the second half of the 1980s, there was a corresponding drop in the number

---

[54] Aleksandr IA. Livshin and Igor' B. Orlov, eds., *Pis'ma vo vlast' 1917–1927: Zaiavleniia, zhaloby, donosy, pis'ma v gosudarstvennye struktury i bol'shevistkim vozhdiam* (Moscow: ROSSPEN, 1998); Aleksandr IA. Livshin, Igor' B. Orlov, and Oleg B. Khlevniuk, eds., *Pis'ma vo vlast' 1928–1939: Zaiavleniia, zhaloby, donosy, pis'ma v gosudarstvennye struktury i sovetskim vozhdiam* (Moscow: ROSSPEN, 2002).

[55] Martin K. Dimitrov, "Tracking Public Opinion Under Authoritarianism: The Case of the Soviet Union under Brezhnev," *Russian History* 41:3 (2014), 329–53, esp. 342–51.

[56] See, for example, the overviews of letters to the television in 1972 (GARF f. R6903 per. 36 d. 2 [1973]), January 1973 (GARF f. R6903 per. 36 d. 15 [1973]), 1978 (GARF f. R6903 per. 36 d. 79 [1979]), 1981 (GARF f. R6903 per. 36 d. 117 [1982]), and 1984 (GARF f. R6903 per. 36 d. 156 [1985]).

[57] GARF f. R7523 per. 92 d. 39 (1946); GARF f. R7523 per. 136 d. 962 (1981).

[58] V. Mal'kov, *V uchrezhdenie postupila zhaloba* (Moscow: Moskovskii rabochii, 1972) and Viktor I. Remnev, *Pravo zhaloby v SSSR* (Moscow: Znanie, 1982).

[59] During a December 31, 1974, Politburo meeting, Chernenko reported that the Central Committee had received 350,000 letters in 1974, see Volkogonov Papers, Box 28 (1975), 11–13. Also see "O rabote s pis'mami trudiashchikhsia, postupivshimi v period podgotovki k XXV s''ezdu KPSS," TsKhSD f. 89 per. 26 d. 6 l. 1–9 (March 31, 1976).

[60] Gorbachev Fund, Document 26018 (September 30, 1987); GARF f. R9654 per. 10 d. 470 (1990).

of complaints sent to the party and state (though not to the media).[61] These trends parallel declines in complaints prior to 1989 in China, the GDR, and Bulgaria.[62]

Opinion research was introduced in the 1960s, when the Politburo authorized polling, and the KGB,[63] newspapers,[64] and numerous ministries and committees started fielding questionnaires.[65] The survey administration was deficient in various ways (usually employing convenience sampling or poorly implemented stratified quota sampling) and participation was typically coerced, thus producing research findings of questionable validity.[66] In the second half of the 1980s, questionnaire design and sampling methods improved, participation became voluntary, and levels of fear that anonymity was not protected declined; consequently, the reliability and validity of surveys were elevated. In the final years of Soviet rule, citizens felt less inhibited in expressing direct criticism of the regime.[67]

9.2.2 TASS Information Collection: Classified Bulletins

As the central news agency of the Soviet Union, TASS had three functions: it dictated the tone of all copy printed domestically; it took charge of the international dissemination of official announcements about developments within

---

[61] Russian Center for the Preservation and Study of Documents of Most Recent History (RTsKhIDNI) f. 646 per. 1 d. 3 (1990), 11. On media letters, see Christopher Cerf and Marina Albee, eds., *Small Fires: Letters from the Soviet People to* Ogonyok *Magazine, 1987–1990* (New York: Summit Books, 1990); Ron McKay, ed., *Letters to Gorbachev: Life in Russia through the Postbag of* Argumenty i Fakty (London: Michael Joseph and New York: Viking Penguin, 1991); Jim Riordan and Sue Bridger, *Dear Comrade Editor: Readers' Letters to the Soviet Press under Perestroika* (Bloomington: University of Indiana Press, 1992).

[62] On China, see Martin K. Dimitrov, ed., *Why Communism Did Not Collapse: Understanding Authoritarian Regime Resilience in Asia and Europe* (New York: Cambridge University Press, 2013), esp. 289–93; on the GDR, see Martin K. Dimitrov "Anticipating Crises by Collecting Information on Levels of Popular Discontent," in Christoph Stefes and Johannes Gerschewski, eds., *Crises in Autocracies* (Boulder, CO: Lynne Rienner, 2017), 21–41, esp. 28–30; on Bulgaria, see Martin K. Dimitrov, "What the Party Wanted to Know: Citizen Complaints as a 'Barometer of Public Opinion' in Communist Bulgaria," *East European Politics and Societies and Cultures* 28:2 (May 2014), 271–95.

[63] Vladimir Shlapentokh, *The Politics of Sociology in the Soviet Union* (Boulder, CO: Westview Press, 1987), 126–27.

[64] B. A. Grushin, "Institut obshchestvennogo mneniia—otdel *Komsomol'skoi pravdy*," in A. I. Volkov, M. G. Pugacheva, and S. F. Iarmoliuk, eds., *Pressa v obshchestve: Otsenki zhurnalistov i sotsiologov. Dokumenty* (Moscow: Institut Sotsiologii RAN, 2000), 46–64.

[65] On the Politburo decision, see TsKhSD f. 4 op. 20 d. 356 l. 17–18, "Postanovlenie Politbiuro TsK KPSS 'Ob organizatsii Instituta konkretnykh sotsial'nykh issledovanii Akademii nauk SSSR'" (May 22, 1968).

[66] Dimitrov, "Tracking Public Opinion Under Authoritarianism," esp. 338–41.

[67] Dimitrov, "Tracking Public Opinion Under Authoritarianism"; All-Union Center for the Study of Public Opinion (VTsIOM), *Obshchestvennoe mnenie v tsifrakh*, no. 8 (Moscow: VTsIOM, April 1990).

the Soviet Union; and it issued confidential briefs with restricted circulation. However, in contrast to Xinhua, its classified bulletins only contained international news. As in China, publications with higher levels of secrecy had smaller circles of recipients. Most restricted were the bulletins of the Classified Publications Department (*otdel zakrytoi pechati*), which detailed international criticism of the Soviet Union and of its leaders and thus could circulate only to the top leadership.[68] A step below were the weekly briefs entitled "Information Letters of TASS Correspondents" (*Informatsionnye pis'ma korrespondentov TASS*), which were published in fewer than 200 copies that were then dispatched to the top echelon of the party-state right below the Politburo.[69] These reports were meant to focus on matters deemed too sensitive for discussion in the official media. Analysis of the bulletins issued in the first quarter of 1984, for example, reveals that they indeed covered sensitive issues like support for Solidarity among the youth, journalists, and the clergy in Poland; the economic difficulties experienced by Bulgaria, Romania, Cuba, and Poland; antisocialist incidents in Czechoslovakia; the peace movement in the GDR; and the economic, political, and military developments in China (at the time, the Sino–Soviet split was still extant).[70] At the lowest level of classification were various internal newspapers, which combined materials that were fit for print with "supplementary" information (*dopolnitel'naia informatsiia*), which was not suitable for dissemination in the official press.[71] There also existed an internal circulation bulletin on international affairs that was meant for propaganda workers; it had a large print-run (38,500 copies in 1980).[72] Such strictly regimented circulation of information ensured that reporting and analysis of the most sensitive international news would be restricted to a small circle of recipients; TASS newswire items could then be cross-checked against Ministry of Foreign Affairs and KGB intelligence reports.[73] There is no evidence that, unlike ROSTA during the initial years of Soviet rule, TASS published classified bulletins on domestic news for the leadership. Internal journalistic reporting on the popular mood by the print and electronic media filled this niche.[74]

---

[68] Valeriia Viacheslavovna Bitiutskaia, "Sovetskoe informatsionnoe agentstvo: Evoliutsiia soderzhaniia i tekhnologii deiatel'nosti (po materialam TASS)" (Ph.D. Dissertation, St. Petersburg State University, 2019), 106–7. These regularly issued top-secret bulletins had a white cover ("white TASS"); occasional bulletins of supplementary information with a red cover were known as "red TASS." See Andrei V. Ostal'skii, *Sud'ba nerezidenta: Noveishaia istoriia v zerkale biografii* (St. Petersburg: Pal'mira, 2018), 189–90.

[69] The bulletins issued during the first quarter of 1984 had print-runs between 182 and 186 copies (see GARF f. R4459 op. 45 d. 25 [1984]).

[70] GARF f. R4459 op. 45 d. 25 (1984), bulletins nos. 1–13 (January 6–March 30, 1984).

[71] Bitiutskaia, "Sovetskoe informatsionnoe agentstvo," 107.

[72] TsKhSD f. 89 per. 31 d. 35 (March 12, 1980) and TsKhSD f. 89 per. 46 d. 49 (March 12, 1980).

[73] Bitiutskaia, "Sovetskoe informatsionnoe agentstvo," 109.

[74] Dimitrov, "Tracking Public Opinion under Authoritarianism," esp. 343–46.

9.2.3 State Security Information Gathering: Agents and Full-Time Staff

Rather than the party or the media, State Security was the key collector of information on dissent throughout the lifespan of the Soviet Union. From its very beginnings, it made extensive use of agents. As of 1921, there existed three categories of assets. The first was informants, who were recruited on patriotic grounds from social groups close to the communists. The second group was agents focusing on anti-Soviet activity, who were selected for collaboration with the Cheka in prisons or counterrevolutionary groups. Their success was based on the fact that those under surveillance trusted them. This trust did not extend to the Cheka itself, which watched the agents for potential acts of provocation and treason. The final group was full-time staff members, who were used as penetration agents for the most sensitive tasks, such as uncovering subversive plans of anti-Soviet parties, organizations, and groups.[75] At the same time, residents were introduced to manage informants, whose numbers grew very rapidly, especially in rural areas.[76] By 1924, the ranks of the agent network had increased to 8,000–10,000.[77] As in other countries, blackmail was used to recruit at least some of the agents. However, as early as 1930, this practice gave rise to complaints from individuals who were forced to cooperate with State Security.[78] For this reason, material inducements gradually assumed greater importance to reward agents; this contradicts stylized facts about the blackmailing of secret collaborators.[79] Other methods, which parallel the experience of both China and Bulgaria, include the identification of assets among former camp inmates. For example, 60 percent of the agents recruited in 1956–1957 in the Ukrainian Soviet Socialist Republic to fight against Ukrainian nationalism were former camp inmates.[80]

Full-time State Security staff increased correspondingly, more than tripling from about 30,000 in the 1920s to nearly 100,000 on the eve of World War II.[81]

---

[75] Chebrikov, ed., *Istoriia sovetskikh organov gosudarstvennoi bezopasnosti*, 141–42.

[76] Chebrikov, ed., *Istoriia sovetskikh organov gosudarstvennoi bezopasnosti*, 141–42; on residents in external intelligence, see Chebrikov, ed., *Istoriia sovetskikh organov gosudarstvennoi bezopasnosti*, 307.

[77] Izmozik, *Glaza i ushi rezhima*, 117; Nicolas Werth, "L'OGPU en 1924: Radiographie d'une institution à son niveau d'étiage," *Cahiers du Monde Russe* 42:2–4 (June–December 2001), 397–421, at 399.

[78] Chebrikov, ed., *Istoriia sovetskikh organov gosudarstvennoi bezopasnosti*, 237.

[79] Mozokhin, ed., *Politbiuro i organy gosudarstvennoi bezopasnosti*, 174; Izmozik, *Glaza i ushi rezhima*, 132.

[80] Chebrikov, ed., *Istoriia sovetskikh organov gosudarstvennoi bezopasnosti*, 523.

[81] Chebrikov, ed., *Istoriia sovetskikh organov gosudarstvennoi bezopasnosti*, 136; Mozokhin, ed., *Politbiuro i organy gosudarstvennoi bezopasnosti*, 269–70 and 594–96; Nikita Petrov, Françoise Corde-Baudrillard, and Catherine Klein-Gousseff, "Les transformations du personnel des organes de sécurité soviétiques, 1922–1953," *Cahiers du Monde Russe* 42:2–4 (2001), 375–96, at 376.

Following further expansion during the war, the number of staff exceeded half a million during the final years of Stalin's rule.[82]

9.2.4 Reducing the Agent Network and the Extent of Operational Surveillance

One of the most consequential decisions after World War II was made in 1951 and it involved reducing the scope of the operational-reporting system for anti-Soviet and enemy activity, which was equivalent to the targeted population roster in China or the enemy contingent list in Bulgaria. The number of individuals subjected to preliminary checks was limited and 1,647,175 files were archived, as they were based on dated compromising material and contained no evidence of recent antistate activities; those who were excluded from the operational-reporting system comprised individuals suspected of being fascist collaborators as well as kulaks, former oppositionists, and ex-clergy. Thereafter, the focus was on foreign espionage activities in the USSR as well as on anti-Soviet and enemy activity. These measures resulted in a six-fold overall contraction of operational reporting from 2,328,632 to 400,000 individuals.[83]

The timing of this decision cannot be linked to standard understandings of what drives declines in repression, such as de-Stalinization (the death of Stalin had not yet occurred); domestic mass constraints (there had been no widespread discontent that, after being resolutely suppressed, might have required a softer long-term governance strategy); or external pressure to reduce the levels of repression (this would only occur in later decades).[84] Instead, there existed a high level of self-assurance within the secret police that it could handle dissent through a more targeted approach that required fewer human resources. Although no Soviet document has become available that explicitly articulates an awareness of the tradeoff between pervasive repression and the quality of information in the late 1940s, the fact that such materials have appeared in Bulgaria points to their likely existence in the KGB archives for the early 1950s as well.[85] We cannot interpret the 1951 decision in any other way except as an indicator that the secret police were moving toward a selective repression equilibrium that would be made possible by higher-quality information.

---

[82] In 1952, the MGB had a staff of 543,347 (of which 259,061 were militia) (Petrov et al., "Les transformations du personnel," 396).

[83] Mozokhin, ed., *Politbiuro i organy gosudarstvennoi bezopasnosti*, 622–23.

[84] Daniel C. Thomas, *The Helsinki Effect: International Norms, Human Rights, and the Demise of Communism* (Princeton, NJ: Princeton University Press, 2001).

[85] Bulgarian Central State Archives (TsDA) f. 1B op. 64 a. e. 185 (November 21, 1953), 1–10.

The size of the informant network was also reduced in 1951, with the number of agents declining by 30 percent (from 1,503,404 to 1,051,834).[86] There were further waves of staff and agent contractions in 1952–1955.[87] By the 1960s, the KGB had a significantly leaner network of agents (164,774 in 1962 and 166,346 in 1967),[88] which amounted to less than 0.1 percent of the Soviet population.[89] Even if we were to add trusted persons (*doverennye litsa*), who were sometimes counted as agents by the KGB, the agent network would constitute no more than 0.2 percent of the population in the 1960s,[90] thus being substantially smaller than that in the GDR, let alone China. KGB documents from the 1980s indicate that the understanding that the network of agents had to be numerically small but of a high quality persisted until the last decades of Soviet rule.[91]

These steps paved the way for the adoption of prophylaxis in the mid-1950s,[92] which rested on the assumption that all crime can be detected and most individuals who engage in violating state security laws are not driven by hostile or nationalist intentions.

9.2.5 Institutional Innovation in the Handling of Dissent: Prophylaxis and Selective Repression

The annual reports of the KGB and its more specialized yearly briefs on the circulation of anti-Soviet materials provide us with a rare glimpse into the levels of dissent in Soviet society in the 1960s–1980s. They present a surprising picture: after 1967, there was a gradual *increase* in anti-Soviet activity accompanied by a steady *decrease* in harsh punishments for such activity. For example, the number of anonymous anti-Soviet materials (leaflets, letters, and graffiti) discovered by

[86] Mozokhin, ed., *Politbiuro i organy gosudarstvennoi bezopasnosti*, 627.

[87] Chebrikov, ed., *Istoriia sovetskikh organov gosudarstvennoi bezopasnosti*, 506; Mozokhin, ed., *Politbiuro i organy gosudarstvennoi bezopasnosti*, 709. These reductions have also been noted by scholars working on the Lithuanian case, where KGB informants declined from 28,000 to 9,000 in 1952. See Amir Weiner and Aigi Rahi-Tamm, "Getting to Know You: The Soviet Surveillance System, 1939–1953," *Kritika: Explorations in Russian and Eurasian History* 13:1 (Winter 2012), 5–45, at 33–34.

[88] 1962 KGB Annual Report, Volkogonov Papers, Box 28 (February 1963), 7; 1967 KGB Annual Report, TsKhSD f. 89 per. 51 d. 3 (May 6, 1968), 7 (the 1967 report reveals that 24,952 individuals constituted 15 percent of the agents).

[89] The Soviet Union had a population of 234.8 million in 1967.

[90] Systematic data on trusted persons are not available, but Lithuanian KGB statistics indicate that the ratio of agents to trusted persons was 1:1.14 in 1967 and 1:1.49 in 1971 (see Lithuanian KGB Archive [Lietuvos] f. K1 per. 1 d. 793 [1972], 53–55). If we assume that this ratio was consistent throughout the Soviet Union, we can produce estimates of a total number of 355,000 agents and trusted persons in 1967 (0.15 percent of the population) and 416,000 in 1971 (0.17 percent of the population).

[91] TsKhSD f. 89 per. 18 d. 84 (June 2, 1983).

[92] Chebrikov, ed., *Istoriia sovetskikh organov gosudarstvennoi bezopasnosti*, 503.

Table 9.1 Individuals Charged with Crimes against the State by the Soviet KGB versus Individuals Subjected to Prophylaxis, 1959–1974

	1959–1962	1963–1966	1967–1970	1971–1974
Prophylaxis			58,298	63,108
Charged with antistate crimes	5,413	3,251	2,456	2,423
a) treason and espionage	1,038	465	433	359
b) anti-Soviet propaganda and agitation	1,601	502	381	348
c) smuggling and currency violations	634	577	565	875
d) illegal border crossings	926	613	704	553
e) other antistate crimes	1,025	1,042	347	276

Source: "O nekotorykh itogakh predupreditel'no-profilakticheskoi raboty organov gosbezopasnosti," Volkogonov Papers, Box 28 (October 31, 1975), 2.

NB: Subcategories a)–e) are a partial list and do not include all types of antistate crimes.

the KGB doubled between 1967 and 1981, from 11,856 to 23,106.[93] However, whereas 10 percent of the identified authors of such anti-Soviet materials were charged with committing crimes against the state in 1967, this proportion had declined to 3 percent by 1981.[94] There was a similar reduction in the rates of prosecution for other state crimes, such as illegal border crossings. Also, fewer persons were being indicted for the most serious transgressions against the state, such as treason, espionage, and revealing state secrets (see Table 9.1). Quite surprisingly, KGB statistics show that 54 percent of the individuals charged with crimes against the state in 1975–1977 were targeted for illegal economic activity (smuggling and currency violations) rather than for political dissent, as demonstrated in Table 9.2.[95]

As the KGB gradually turned away from harshly repressive measures like mass incarcerations, a softer type of repression emerged as the dominant response to political dissent.[96] This was prophylaxis (*profilaktika*), which involved

[93] See 1967 KGB Annual Report, Volkogonov Papers, Box 28 (May 6, 1968), 7 and 1981 KGB Report on the Search for Authors of Anonymous Anti-Soviet Materials, Volkogonov Papers, Box 28 (April 18, 1982), 1. The documents suggest that the increase reflects a higher volume of anti-Soviet activity, not stepped-up enforcement.

[94] 1967 KGB Annual Report, Volkogonov Papers, Box 28 (May 6, 1968), 8 and 1981 KGB Annual Report, Volkogonov Papers, Box 28 (April 18, 1982), 3.

[95] Calculated from 1975 KGB Annual Report (March 30, 1976), 1976 KGB Annual Report (February 28, 1977), and 1977 KGB Annual Report (March 27, 1978), Volkogonov Papers, Box 28.

[96] Moshe Lewin, *The Soviet Century* (London: Verso, 2005), 191–201.

Table 9.2 Individuals Charged with Crimes against the State in the Soviet Union, 1959–1988

	1. Total Number Charged	2. Total Number Charged with Serious Crimes	2a. Charged with Anti-Soviet Crimes	3. Total Number Charged with Less Serious Crimes	3a. Charged with Crimes of Smuggling and Currency Violations	4. Charged with Other Crimes	5. Prophylaxis (not charged)
1959–1962	5,413		1,601		634		
1963–1966	3,251		502		577		
1967–1970	2,456		381		565		58,298
1971–1974	2,423		348		875		63,108
1975	485		76		247		
1976	617		69		347		
1977	507		48		281		
1978		65	55		200		15,590
1979			56				
1980	433	91	80	283	178	57	
1981	557	79	36	341			18,408
1982	776	72	39	491		213	19,896
1983			101				
1984			81				
1985			97	417		61	15,274
1986			90	343		57	10,275
1987				243			
1988			34	183			

Sources: Volkogonov Papers Box 28; TsKhSD f.89 per. 51 d. 4 (1980); TsKhSD f. 89 per. 51 d. 7 (1986); TsKhSD f.89 per. 51 d. 9 (1987); TsKhSD f. 89 per. 51 d. 10 (1987); TsKhSD f. 89 per. 51 d. 12 (1988); TsKhSD f. 89 per. 51 d. 13 (1986); TsKhSD f. 89 per. 51 d. 15 (1989).

summoning individuals for a "chat" (*beseda*) with KGB personnel and representatives of social organizations. Another prophylactic measure was public criticism by a comrades' court. Confinement to psychiatric hospitals was also used,
but it was implemented in 10–20 percent of the cases, and this was not the dominant form of prophylaxis.[97] A 1975 top-secret statistical memorandum prepared
by KGB head Andropov for General Secretary Brezhnev attests to the overwhelming dominance of prophylaxis over incarceration. The report indicates
that in 1967–1974 there was a 1:96 ratio between those charged with committing
especially serious state crimes (such as anti-Soviet propaganda and agitation)
and those subjected to prophylactic measures.[98] Prophylaxis was effective, as
only 0.12 percent of the individuals who were subjected to it in 1967–1974 were
subsequently charged with recidivism.[99]

The emphasis on prophylaxis reflected a new sense in the KGB that it could
account for the reasons why individuals committed antistate crimes and
it could use penal measures only against those who were driven by hostile
beliefs (*vrazhdebnye ubezhdeniia*) or nationalist attitudes (*natsionalisticheskie
nastroeniia*). According to the KGB's own classification, antistate crimes might
also arise due to susceptibility to ideological subversion (listening to foreign
broadcasts); political immaturity; psychiatric illness; hooliganism; shortages of
goods and personal financial difficulties; as well as suffering insults or being the
victim of illegal acts of officials. However, when individuals committed crimes
due to nonhostile reasons, they were only subject to prophylaxis.[100] This was even
true for terrorist activities, which, in the KGB's evaluation, were only occasionally the result of hostile beliefs and nationalist attitudes. For example, the KGB
investigated 116 individuals who issued terrorist threats in 1977, but it determined that only five of them were driven by hostile anti-Soviet intent and therefore should receive criminal punishment.[101] The use of prophylaxis constitutes
specific empirical proof of the adoption of highly selective repression in the later
decades of Soviet rule.

The transition to selective repression was a slow process that did not gain mo-
mentum until the 1960s (see Table 9.2). During the initial years of Soviet rule,
governance was brutal. For example, from December 1917 to January 1919,
the VChK arrested 11,932 individuals (half for bureaucratic corruption and

---

[97] KGB reports for 1967, 1975, 1976, 1977, 1978 (April 2, 1979), 1980 (March 31, 1981), 1981
(April 18, 1982), and 1982 (March 15, 1983), Volkogonov Papers, Box 28.

[98] "O nekotorykh itogakh preduprediteľno-profilakticheskoi raboty organov gosbezopasnosti,"
Volkogonov Papers, Box 28 (October 31, 1975), 1.

[99] "O nekotorykh itogakh," 2.

[100] See, for example, the 1975 Report on the Search for Authors of Anonymous Anti-Soviet
Materials, Volkogonov Papers, Box 28 (March 13, 1976), 4.

[101] "O rezuľtatakh raboty organov KGB po bor'be s terroristicheskimi proiavleniiami,"
Volkogonov Papers, Box 28 (March 27, 1978), 1.

speculation).[102] At the end of 1924, the OGPU Secret Department kept files on 99,680 individuals but it arrested only 4,097.[103] Arrests for counterrevolutionary agitation (since 1941 anti-Soviet agitation) peaked in the 1930s, but they gradually decreased after World War II.[104] In 1954–1958, some 9,406 individuals were sentenced for disseminating anti-Soviet propaganda. In later years, these numbers declined precipitously and a mere 2,781 were arrested during the 1959–1991 period for such crimes.[105] There were 1,353 individuals who were sentenced in 1967–1982 for spreading harmful statements that endangered state and social order.[106] Softer treatment of deluded citizens (*gumannoe otnoshenie k zabluzhdavshimsia grazhdanam*) was combined with resolute obstruction (*peresechenie*) of criminal activity.[107] Prophylaxis, agent-operational surveillance to uncover whether those who engaged in crimes against the state had hostile intentions, and selective repression emerged as the dominant mechanisms for dealing with dissent in the post-World War II period.

What made selective repression possible was the rise of specialization, which was exemplified by the establishment of a discrete department in charge of handling anti-Soviet activities. Created in 1967 with 201 employees, by 1982 the Fifth Department of the KGB had expanded to 424 central-level staff.[108] According to its long-time head Filipp Bobkov, it had 2,500 central- and local-level employees throughout the Soviet Union (about 10 people per oblast).[109] The agent network of the Fifth Departments was considered optimal, with about 200 agents per oblast.[110] This allows us to estimate about 40,000 agents at the subnational level and 10,000 at the central level for the political police (about 50,000 nationwide for the network of local-level Fifth Departments and the central-level Fifth

---

[102] Mozokhin, ed., *Politbiuro i organy gosudarstvennoi bezopasnosti*, 85.

[103] Izmozik, *Glaza i ushi rezhima*, 120.

[104] Sarah Davies, *Popular Opinion in Stalinist Russia: Terror, Propaganda and Dissent, 1934–1941* (New York: Cambridge University Press, 1997), 16; Vladimir N. Khaustov, "Razvitie sovetskikh organov gosudarstvennoi bezopasnosti, 1917–1953 gg," *Cahiers du Monde Russe* 41:2–4 (June–December 2001), 357–73, at 372.

[105] O. M. Khlobustov, "Fenomen Andropova," in Bylinin, ed., *Trudy Obshchestva isuzheniia istorii*, vol. 1, 192–202, at 198–99. In 1959–1991, the total number of individuals sentenced for state crimes was 14,689. Of those, 5,483 were jailed for especially dangerous crimes, including anti-Soviet propaganda and agitation (the breakdown of those arrests by years is as follows: 1959–1961: 1,442; 1963–1967: 600; 1967–1982: 552).

[106] Khlobustov, "Fenomen Andropova," 199.

[107] TsKhSD f. 89 p. 51 d. 9 (January 26, 1987), 7.

[108] Kokurin and Petrov, comps., *Lubianka*, 166–68.

[109] Khlobustov, "Fenomen Andropova," 197. Taking into account central-level staff, Bobkov's statement assumes that there were roughly 200 oblasts, which is about 50 more than the number that actually existed. Some union republics, like those in the Baltic region, did not have oblasts, although the KGB certainly had a strong presence in these border regions: for example, we know that the Fifth Department of the Lithuanian KGB had fifty-six staff in 1971 (Lietuvos f. K1 op. 1 a. e. 793 [1972], 57).

[110] Khlobustov, "Fenomen Andropova," 197.

Directorate).[111] The Fifth Directorate was in charge of counteracting ideological subversion. Specifically, this meant focusing on intellectuals, students, youth, religious groups, and on individuals and organized groups that engaged in anti-Soviet propaganda and agitation. Creation of the directorate underscores how seriously KGB Chairman Yuri Andropov took the threat of Western ideological infiltration. It also reveals the extraordinary self-confidence of the KGB whereby it could handle political dissent in the Soviet Union with 2,500 staff and 50,000 agents.

9.2.6 The Challenge of Managing Ethnic Minorities

Throughout its existence, the Soviet Union could not solve the problem of minority discontent. State Security reports from the 1920s indicate that individual and group resistance took place primarily in the non-Russian republics and in minority areas of the Russian Soviet Federative Socialist Republic. KGB reports from the 1960s–1980s paint a similar picture of remarkable continuity in terms of the location of minority unrest and the ethnic identity of the main internal enemies of the regime.[112]

The optimal solution to the problem was to ensure higher levels of penetration by recruiting more full-time staff and informants from among minority groups. However, the Soviet Union was not successful on either count. Longitudinal data on the national origin of State Security employees indicate that Slavs were overrepresented and that this disproportion increased over time. Thus, whereas Slavs constituted 80 percent of full-time staff in the 1920s–1930s,[113] by 1950 they made up 90 percent of the Ministry of State Security (MGB) personnel.[114] The agent network was similarly characterized by an insufficient saturation with minorities. Parallel to Bulgaria and China, the KGB experienced difficulties recruiting

---

[111] We have the exact number of the agents in the Lithuanian Soviet Socialist Republic, where the Fifth Department had a total of 389 informants in 1971 (Lietuvos f. K1 op. 1 a. e. 793 [1972], 53). We also possess statistics on the total size of the KGB network in Lithuania in 1967 (3,800 agents), 1971 (4,182 agents); and 1978 (4,967 agents) (Lietuvos f. K1 op. 1 a. e. 793 [1972], 53; Lietuvos f. K1 op. 10 a. e. 372 [January 30, 1979], 182).

[112] 1962 KGB Semi-Annual Report, TsKhSD f. 89 per. 51 d. 1 (July 25, 1962), 1; 1967 KGB Annual Report, TsKhSD f. 89 per. 51 d. 3 (May 6, 1968), 6; 1975 KGB Annual Report, Volkogonov Papers, Box 28 (March 30, 1976), 9; 1985 KGB Annual Report, TsKhSD f. 89 per. 51 d. 7 (February 19, 1986), 6; 1986 KGB Report on Anti-Soviet Activity, TsKhSD f. 89 per. 51 d. 10 (February 26, 1987), 1. See also Chebrikov, ed., Istoriia sovetskikh organov gosudarstvennoi bezopasnosti, 545.

[113] 78.9 percent of OGPU staff in 1928 (Chebrikov, ed., Istoriia sovetskikh organov gosudarstvennoi bezopasnosti, 200) and 80 percent of the NKVD in 1937 (Petrov et al., "Les transformations du personnel," 395).

[114] Petrov et al., "Les transformations du personnel," 395. An additional relevant datum is that in 1947 Lithuanians were a minority among KGB staff in Lithuania (see Arvydas Anušauskas and Christine Colpart, "La composition et les méthodes secrètes des organes de sécurité soviétiques en Lituanie, 1940–1953," Cahiers du Monde Russe 42:2–4 [April–December 2001], 321–55, at 327–28).

Muslim clerics to its agent corps.[115] The incapacity to pre-empt the overt expression of discontent through sufficient penetration meant that minorities in the Soviet Union were more likely than Russians to be punished for engaging in anti-state crimes. On this dimension as well, there is a parallel between the Soviet experience and that of a range of communist regimes with sizable minority populations: the examples of disproportionately high imprisonment for anti-state crimes of Croats in the 1970s and Kosovars in the 1980s in Yugoslavia,[116] of Tibetans and Uyghurs in China, and of Turks in Bulgaria suffice to demonstrate this point.

9.2.7 General Theoretical Conclusions from the Soviet Case

We can draw several general conclusions from the preceding two sections. The first is that although the party was a key supplier of information in the Soviet Union, the telegraph agency rather than State Security was initially tasked with coordinating functions in the area of information collection. This decision had path-dependent effects that could be undone only gradually. In the Soviet case, both the telegraph agency and the army were eventually sidelined from monitoring discontent, thus producing a blueprint for communist information collection involving the triumvirate of State Security, the communist party, and internal media. Despite some additions and modifications, this structure persisted until the end of Soviet rule. Perhaps most importantly, the Soviet institution-building blueprint was replicated, in full or in adapted form, in all communist regimes.

Another generalizable lesson from the Soviet Union has to do with the tradeoffs between improved information quality and the intensity of repression. The Soviet Union found itself on the standard pathway of declining repression, which occurs at various points in time in different regimes. What is common across the communist universe is that the frequency, indiscriminacy, and severity of repression all decrease when the quality of information improves. With the exception of minority penetration, which remained a blind spot for the regime, the bureaucracies that monitored popular discontent greatly improved their understanding of the sources of dissatisfaction and developed sophisticated strategies for counteracting them. Gradually, highly selective repression was combined with strategic redistribution that aimed to satisfy the material and

---

[115] Chebrikov, ed., *Istoriia sovetskikh organov gosudarstvennoi bezopasnosti*, 508.

[116] In 1988, for example, 60 percent of those sentenced for antistate crimes in Yugoslavia were from the autonomous region of Kosovo, even though Kosovars made up less than 10 percent of the population of Yugoslavia at the time (Savezni zavod za statistiku, *Statistički godišnjak Jugoslavije 1989* [Belgrade: Zavod, 1989], 624).

cultural consumption needs of the population.[117] This formed the pillar of regime stability in the later years of the USSR.

The third and perhaps most consequential generalizable conclusion concerns the tradeoffs between different information channels. In the 1920s–1930s, party information focused both on party building and on the popular mood (dissent), whereas State Security only tracked discontent. Party information tended to be positive. By contrast, a characteristic of the OGPU reports is their near complete lack of positive information; this was by design, as their task was to track dissent. Given that State Security was interested in expanding its budget, it tended to exaggerate the threat, rather than to minimize it, in alarming briefs on "the general political situation" (a term used by the OGPU interchangeably with "the mood of the masses" and "the popular mood"). Therefore, we need not worry about underreporting in the case of internal State Security documents. Another potential concern is with the suppression of information. We cannot assume that all intelligence should be transmitted upward. If that were to happen, it inevitably would lead to decision maker overload. By default, information becomes more selective as it travels up the pyramid of power. Selective transmission of intelligence, however, is different from suppression of negative information. We can say that State Security reporting included a high volume of negative news in its bulletins for the leadership and that although from 1922 until his death in January 1924, Lenin was excluded from receiving such reports,[118] there is no evidence of the systematic suppression of access to information for other top leaders during the Soviet period.

One meta-theoretical point that emerges from the Soviet case concerns the utility of having multiple sources for tracking dissent that often generate redundant information. Researchers who have directed the project of publishing selected materials from the Cheka archives for the 1922–1934 period have concluded that those multiple sources were indeed redundant, but the duplication of intelligence allowed leaders to get closer to an objective assessment of dissent by cross-checking the information received through different channels.[119] Fostering redundancy reflects the view that the validity (*dostovernost'*) of information is a function of its variegated sourcing. Such understandings persisted until the very end of Soviet rule. Yegor Ligachev, for example, opined that having access to intelligence from multiple sources allowed leaders to compare and contrast the information they received.[120] Thus, in the Soviet Union redundancy was a desired outcome of the information-collection efforts of the bureaucracies tasked with monitoring popular discontent.

[117] On cultural consumption requests sent to *Literaturnaia gazeta*, see Dimitrov, "Tracking Public Opinion Under Authoritarianism," esp. 348–49.

[118] Kolodnikova, *Sovetskoe obshchestvo 20-kh godov XX veka*, 111.

[119] *Sovershenno sekretno* (vol. 9), 23.

[120] Leonid Mlechin, *KGB: Predsedateli organov gosbezopasnosti: Rassekrechenye sud'by*, 3rd ed. (Moscow: Tsentrpoligraf, 2002), 667. Ligachev held various leadership posts, the highest of which was second secretary of the Communist Party of the Soviet Union (CPSU) in 1985–1990.

9.3 The German Democratic Republic, 1949–1989

Although it is often considered to be the paradigmatic case of communist information gathering, the GDR is unusual in several respects. In contrast to other communist countries, the GDR was created after a four-year period of direct Soviet
administration of the eastern states of Germany. This means that many of the initial
governance challenges that confront communist autocracies were dealt with prior
to the establishment of the regime. These features made governance in the GDR
simpler than that in other communist dictatorships, and they allowed for a very
rapid adoption of mass surveillance.

Another atypical feature of the GDR is that the leadership had access to two
sources of information that were not available to the same extent to the rulers of
other communist regimes: a heavy Soviet security presence that also involved information gathering and the West German media, whose coverage of the GDR was
closely followed by the leadership.

Finally, though not unique, the creation of separate ministries of the interior and
of state security is unusual for a small country. The inter-bureaucratic rivalry that
emerged led to a multiplication of the channels for the collection of information but
also resulted in inflated personnel and informant rosters.

With these caveats, we can proceed to a discussion of several features of the
East German case (origins, transition to mass surveillance, information-gathering
avenues, patterns of transmission of intelligence, and information at the end of
the regime) that yield additional process-tracing evidence to help us highlight the
tradeoffs between different intelligence-gathering institutions and to elucidate the
scope conditions for the argument presented in this book.

9.3.1 Regime Establishment and Mass Surveillance

The GDR was established only six days after the People's Republic of China
(PRC) on October 7, 1949. The leadership of the newly created state was given
a tabula rasa without a parallel in the communist world. Several features should
be highlighted. First, the Nazi Party, which was the most formidable opponent
of communist ideology, had been dissolved in 1945 and its activists had been
executed or sent to prisons and labor camps by the Soviet military administration.[121] Four non-Marxist parties were allowed to operate legally (the Christian-
Democratic Union; the Democratic Farmers' Party; the Liberal-Democratic
Party; and the National Democratic Party), but only within the umbrella of the
National Front; thus, like Bulgaria and China, de facto the GDR had a single

---

[121] Ilko-Sascha Kowalczuk and Stefan Wolle, *Roter Stern über Deutschland: Sowjetische Truppen in der DDR*, 2nd rev. ed. (Berlin: Ch. Links, 2010), esp. 80–82.

party.[122] Second, the country was monoethnic, which meant that the regime never had to confront the challenge of penetrating ethnic minorities. Finally, there were no underground groups of armed individuals ("bandits"), thus eliminating the potential regime threat that existed during the initial decades of communist rule in the USSR (*lesnye bratia*), Bulgaria (*goriani*), Cuba (*bandidos*), and of course, China (*tufei* 土匪).

This unusually auspicious set of circumstances means that the State Security apparatus initially had a limited portfolio: counteracting economic sabotage; monitoring the National Front parties; and penetrating churches, sects, and social organizations with links to the West.[123] Importantly, the Stasi lacked an awareness of the necessity to deploy nationwide surveillance prior to the unanticipated 1953 Worker Uprising.[124] Given the high quality of its personnel, however, it quickly developed such a capacity in the wake of the Uprising, as revealed by a close analysis of its stream of classified reporting throughout 1953.[125]

We should note that in stark contrast to other communist regimes, the GDR did not experience an organized underground movement until the second half of the 1980s. What the Stasi considered to be "organized enemy activity" (*organisierte Feindtätigkeit*) in the months after the June 1953 Worker Uprising involved spreading leaflets or striking the odd grassroots party *apparatchik* or police officer with a club,[126] not terrorism or armed resistance. This effectively put the GDR in an exceptionally privileged position with regard to organized opposition to communist rule for most of the period between June 1953 and the demise of single-party rule in 1989–1990.

9.3.2 Mass Surveillance through the Ministries of State Security and the Interior

Like the PRC and the Soviet Union, the GDR had separate ministries of the interior (*Ministerium des Innern*, or MdI) and of state security (*Ministerium für Staatsicherheit*, or MfS, also known as the Stasi).[127] Yet while the Ministry of the

---

[122] Akademie für Staats- und Rechtswissenschaft der DDR Potsdam-Babeslberg, *Handbuch gesellschaftlicher Organisationen in der DDR: Massenorganisationen, Verbände, Vereinigungen, Gesellschaften, Genossenschaften, Komitees, Ligen* (Berlin: Staatsverlag der Deutschen Demokratischen Republik, 1985), 126–31.

[123] Gary Bruce, "The Prelude to Nationwide Surveillance in East Germany: Stasi Operations and Threat Perceptions, 1945–1953," *Journal of Cold War Studies* 5:2 (Spring 2003), 3–31.

[124] Bruce, "The Prelude to Nationwide Surveillance."

[125] For the original reports, see Roger Engelmann, ed., *Die DDR im Blick der Stasi: Die geheimen Berichte an die SED-Führung 1953* (Göttingen: Vandenhoeck and Ruprecht, 2013).

[126] Stasi Records Archive (BStU MfS) AS 39/58 Bd. 2 Bl. 97–107 (October 21, 1953).

[127] As of 1973, North Korea also had separate ministries, but we lack fine-grained information on their operation.

Interior played no role in handling political dissent in the Soviet Union after the KGB began operations,[128] East Germany closely resembles the case of China in terms of sequencing (in both countries, the Ministry of State Security was established after the Ministry of the Interior) and functions (the Ministry of the Interior did not lose its state security portfolio after creation of the Ministry of State Security). However, while there was a thirty-four-year lag between the establishment of the two ministries in China, the East German Ministry of State Security (the Stasi) began operations only four months after creation of the GDR. From 1950 until the end of the regime, the two ministries functioned in close coordination.[129] It should be noted that cooperation did not mean unconditional trust. The Ministry of the Interior was the most heavily penetrated government agency in the GDR, with 10–20 percent of its employees serving as part-time Stasi informants (*inoffizielle Mitarbeiter*, or IM);[130] in addition, several hundred full-time Stasi staff worked under the cover of policemen (these individuals were known as *Offiziere im besonderen Einsatz*, or OibE).[131] This close supervision reflects the informal understanding that the Stasi outranked the people's police and could exercise all of its powers, if needed.

As in China, significant overlap between the functions of the two ministries existed with regard to counteracting security threats. This is clearest when we examine the portfolio of Department K1 of the People's Police (*Abteilung K1 der Deutschen Volkspolizei*), which is equivalent to the State Security (*guobao* 国保) Department of the Ministry of Public Security (MPS) in China. In addition to handling antistate crimes, the tasks of the department included counteracting criminal violations of state and public order (*Bekämpfung von Verbrechen gegen die DDR sowie Straftaten gegen die staatiche und öffentliche Ordnung*), in particular political provocations such as spreading leaflets, writing slogans, and destroying flags and other state symbols.[132] Within the Stasi, Department XX had functions paralleling those of Department K1 of the Ministry of the Interior. Overlap also existed in terms of control over entry into and exit from the country, which was carried out by the Ministry of the Interior and by the Passport Control Department of the Stasi. In addition, the Ministry of the Interior was responsible for youth with negative attitudes, assessed the motivations of those who requested

---

[128] The KGB was created in 1954. During periods of elevated coup threats, especially in 1934–1943 and 1953–1954, the internal and state security portfolios were fused into a single bureaucracy.

[129] See Article 20.2 of the Law on the Tasks and Powers of the German People's Police (1968).

[130] Georg Herbstritt, ed., *Die Lageberichte der Deutschen Volkspolizei im Herbst 89: Eine Chronik der Wende im Bezirk Neubrandenburg*, 2nd rev. ed. (Schwerin: Die Landesbeauftragte für die Unterlagen des Staatssicherheitsdienstes der ehemaligen Deutschen Demokratischen Republik, 2009), 264–65.

[131] Steffen Alisch, "Das Ministerium für Staatssicherheit: Schild und Schwert der Partei," in Joachim Kallinich and Sylvia de Pascuale, eds., *Ein offenes Geheimnis: Post- und Telefonkontrolle in der DDR* (Heidelberg: Braus, 2002), 33–41, at 36.

[132] Herbstritt, ed., *Die Lageberichte der Deutschen Volkspolizei*, 32–34.

to emigrate from the GDR, and kept watch on Westerners visiting the country.[133] These examples leave no doubt that safeguarding state security was jointly executed by the two ministries. In this regard, the GDR and China are similar.

Mass surveillance was deployed by the two ministries, which relied on full-time staff, on technical means, and on part-time covert and overt informants (who jointly did not exceed 2 percent of the population in 1989, as demonstrated in the Appendix to Chapter 2). Major changes in the size of the full-time employee corps took place throughout the lifespan of the GDR. The Stasi started out as a small bureaucracy: it had 4,500 staff in 1951, compared with 67,000 police working for the Ministry of the Interior.[134] However, continuous expansion of Stasi personnel over the ensuing decades meant that by 1989 there were more State Security staff than policemen (91,015 vs. 88,000).[135] Although the methods through which the Stasi and the police collected intelligence shared commonalities, the emphasis of the Stasi was on secret information gathering, whereas the police operated in a more visible manner. Another difference is that the Stasi employed technical surveillance with a greater frequency than the police, which relied overwhelmingly on human collection through its network of informants and full-time staff. Jointly, the Stasi and the Ministry of the Interior ensured systematic penetration of the entire country.

9.3.3 State Security Reports and Their Transmission to the Leadership

A central question in studies of authoritarianism concerns information transfer. We have access to an extraordinary collection of Stasi reports on domestic politics for thirteen years between 1953 and 1989.[136] This corpus reveals that State Security focused primarily on external intelligence: reports on domestic politics constituted only 27.8 percent of the briefs generated by the Stasi in 1961–1989.[137] Produced by the Central Evaluation and Information Group (*Zentrale Auswertungs- und Informationsgruppe*, or ZAIG),[138] these reports allow us

---

[133] Herbstritt, ed., *Die Lageberichte der Deutschen Volkspolizei*, 268.

[134] Herbstritt, ed., *Die Lageberichte der Deutschen Volkspolizei*, 264.

[135] Herbstritt, ed., *Die Lageberichte der Deutschen Volkspolizei*, 264.

[136] These reports appear in the series *Die DDR im Blick der Stasi: Die geheimen Berichte an die SED-Führung* and cover the years of 1953, 1956, 1961, 1963, 1964, 1965, 1968, 1976, 1977, 1981, 1983, 1988, and 1989.

[137] Jens Gieseke, "Annäherungen und Fragen an die 'Meldungen aus der Republik,'" in Jens Gieseke, ed., *Staatsicherheit und Gesellschaft: Studien zum Herrschaftsalltag in der DDR* (Göttingen: Vandenhoeck and Ruprecht, 2007), 79–98, at 86.

[138] The ZAIG network had 1,227 employees in 1989. See Mark Schiefer and Martin Stief, eds., *Die DDR im Blick der Stasi 1989* (Göttingen: Vandenhoeck and Ruprecht, 2019), 49.

Table 9.3 Stasi Domestic Counterintelligence Reports Sent to Non-Stasi Recipients in the GDR (selected years)

	Total	KGB	Party General Secretary	Secretary for Security	Interior Minister	Church Working Group	Trade and Supply Secretary	Hard Currency Division	Berlin Party Secretary
1956	537	317	238	190			9		175
1961	260	45	68	86			6		7
1963	233	20	78	154	2		5		34
1964	380	39	154	244	2	3	4		52
1965	305	20	72	190	10				47
1968	276	26	30	129	5	48	2		73
1976	292	26	88	42	14	38		52	9
1977	296	29	102	34	18	33		52	23
1981	253	15	48	41	15	30	3	51	22
1983	408	17	60	37	12	41		50	23
1988	279	13	84	122	28	74	85	52	42
1989	262	9	46	92	38	57	70	48	47

Source: Calculations by the author, based on Die DDR im Blick der Stasi.
NB: Some reports had a single addressee, but most were dispatched to multiple recipients. Top overall recipient in bold. The 1953 reports do not contain information to code the recipients.

to study the content of the domestic intelligence that was transmitted to the leadership—and, most importantly, to systematically determine who were the recipients of this information (see Table 9.3).

The table raises many questions, one of which is crucial: Did the Stasi withhold information from Erich Honecker, who was the general secretary of the party from 1971 to 1989? The short answer is negative. Close inspection of the data in Table 9.3 reveals that the general secretary was the top recipient of Stasi reports in only three of the twelve years for which we have detailed data—and in each of those years (1976, 1977, and 1983) this position was held by Honecker. The list of top recipients is instructive: in seven of the twelve years, the top addressee was the Central Committee Secretary for Security (a powerful post that Honecker held in 1958–1971); in the remaining two years, the top place was taken by the KGB (in 1956) and by Dr. Herta König, who received more reports than Honecker in 1981. Does this mean that Dr. König was the best-informed person in the GDR? That conclusion would be unwarranted, as the reports she received were weekly updates on the hard currency receipts from Western visitors to the GDR. This was confidential information that Dr. König needed given her position as head of the Hard Currency Department in the Ministry of Finance; others had no necessity for such intelligence. This demonstrates that the Stasi reporting was not universal: different reports were tailored to the needs of specific addressees. For this reason, we cannot expect that *any* one recipient would have received all the reports.

A further complication is that any statistics indicating a drop in the number of Stasi reporting reaching the general secretary have to take into account that not all information was transferred to him through the official reporting streams. It is known that Honecker had a regular tête-à-tête with the minister for state security after standing Politburo meetings. While we cannot ascertain what information Minister Mielke passed along during those one-on-one talks, it is likely that it was highly sensitive.[139] These private meetings with the minister help clarify another peculiarity of Stasi reporting: starting in 1972 a series of reports on popular reactions were produced but these so-called O-reports (*O-Berichte*) were almost exclusively for internal use by the Stasi, and they were only occasionally sent to Honecker. However, as scholars have noted, more often than not, the content of the O-reports was eventually included in the information that was sent out to non-Stasi recipients.[140] To this we should add that the weekly meetings between Honecker and Mielke provided another potential channel through which the content of the O-reports could have reached the general secretary. Overall, there is no unambiguous evidence that the Stasi deliberately withheld information from him.

We do have evidence that, although he read them avidly before becoming general secretary, Honecker started to value the Stasi reports less over the course of the 1970s and 1980s.[141] What might explain this? Like all dictators,[142] Honecker aimed to foster multiple channels for the supply of information. The corollary is that some channels attracted less attention over time. In the area of reporting on incidents of a political nature, the Stasi's main competitor was the Ministry of the Interior, which supplied daily information bulletins (*Tagesinformationen*) that persisted until the end of the regime.[143]

---

[139] Henrik Bispinck, ed., *Die DDR im Blick der Stasi: Die geheimen Berichte an die SED-Führung 1977* (Göttingen: Vandenhoeck and Ruprecht, 2012), 47.

[140] Siegfried Suckut, ed., *Die DDR im Blick der Stasi 1976* (Göttingen: Vandenhoeck and Ruprecht, 2009), 17.

[141] Reinhold Andert and Wolfgang Herzberg, *Der Sturz: Erich Honecker im Kreuzverhör* (Berlin: Aufbau-Verlag, 1990), 312.

[142] Ryszard Kapuscinski, *The Emperor* (New York: Vintage, 1989), 7–11.

[143] Foundation Archives of the Parties and Mass Organizations of the GDR in the Federal Archives (SAPMO) DY 30/906 (1981–1989); SAPMO DY 30/IV 2/2.039/333 "Gewährleistung der öffentlichen Ordnung und Sicherheit" (October 22, 1989); and Herbstritt, ed., *Die Lageberichte der Deutschen Volkspolizei*.

9.3.4 Information Channels and Their Relative Ranking

All German leaders from President Wilhelm Pieck to General Secretary Honecker valued voluntarily transmitted information. Citizens were encouraged to send complaints (*Eingaben*) to the party, government, the legislature, and the media. They could also visit party and government functionaries in person. This was highlighted even in first-grade primers.[144] Citizen communications were so highly valued that districts competed to report more complaints.[145] Scholars have also noted the tendency of party and state organs to classify all citizen communications in the 1980s as complaints in order to demonstrate government effectiveness, closeness to the masses, and trust.[146] There is archival evidence that the top leadership was regularly apprised of the volume and tenor of citizen complaints received by the party, the government, and the press.[147]

When it comes to involuntary collection of information, an abundance of channels existed: Stasi and police reporting;[148] party information; and opinion polling, which featured lack of trust on the part of survey subjects that their answers would remain anonymous. Like other communist regimes, the GDR also established a Youth Research Institute (*Zentralinstitut für Jugendforschung*, or ZIJ) and a Central Committee Opinion Research Institute (*Institut für Meinungsforschung beim Zentralkomitee der SED*, or IfM). Occasionally, the Soviet Union also supplied information that the GDR leadership might have otherwise ignored.[149]

Each leader ranked these information sources differently. Honecker valued personal observations, direct reporting from grassroots party branches, and Worker–Peasant Inspection reports more highly than the Stasi bulletins.[150] His predecessor, Walter Ulbricht, was interested in opinion polling,[151] as evidenced by the establishment of the Central Committee Opinion Research Institute in 1964. This should not be surprising: it reflects personal style and a difference

---

[144] "Unseren Präsidenten besuchen in Berlin viele Menschen, Männer und Frauen aus Stadt und Land. Sie sprechen ihre Wünsche aus. Er hört alle an, er spricht mit allen. Er hilft ihnen, wo er helfen kann. Deshalb liebt unser Volk unseren Präsidenten Wilhelm Pieck." See Johannes Feuer, Robert Alt, and Hans Baltzer, *Lesen und Lernen*, 6th rev. ed. (Berlin: Volk und Wissen Volkseigener Verlag, 1954), 129.

[145] Paul Betts, *Within Walls: Private Life in the German Democratic Republic* (New York: Oxford University Press, 2010), 175.

[146] Jonathan R. Zatlin, "Eingaben und Ausgaben: Das Petitionsrecht und der Untergang der DDR," *Zeitschrift für Geschichtswissenschaft* 45:10 (1997), 902–17, n. 49, at 912–13.

[147] SAPMO DY 30/IV 2/1/529 (1976); SAPMO DY30/913 (1981); Ellen Bos, *Leserbriefe in Tageszeitungen der DDR: Zur "Massenverbundenheit" der Presse 1949–1989* (Opladen: Westdeutscher Verlag, 1993).

[148] *Die DDR im Blick der Stasi*; Herbstritt, *Die Lageberichte der Deutschen Volkspolizei*.

[149] On summoning the GDR leadership to Moscow prior to the 1953 Uprising to alert them about discontent, see Bruce, "The Prelude to Nationwide Surveillance," 25.

[150] Andert and Herzberg, *Der Sturz*, 313.

[151] Andert and Herzberg, *Der Sturz*, 311.

in emphasis that is perhaps reminiscent of how different U.S. leaders treat the *President's Daily Brief* (PDB).[152]

An extraordinary feature of the GDR information environment is that in addition to the state-collected intelligence, the leadership received a high volume of reporting on popular dissatisfaction from the Western media: West German TV could not be blocked and print media, which were inaccessible to ordinary citizens, were delivered to the top leaders. Easy access to alternative sources of information explains why the Central Committee Opinion Research Institute was closed down in 1979.[153] Admittedly, the institute's opinion polls had limited capacity to produce findings that directly elucidated questions about political support.[154] More importantly, sufficient additional channels existed that provided the necessary information, including the Youth Research Institute that remained open until the end of the GDR. One of the luxuries afforded by redundancy is that some channels may be downgraded and others may be closed down completely without substantially limiting overall insight into the drivers of popular discontent.[155]

Information was also important during the dismantling of single-party rule. A discovery that emerges from the archives highlights the essential role of tracking popular opinion for communist governance. A week after the ouster of Honecker, the Central Committee Secretariat held a meeting on October 25, 1989.[156] Chaired by the new general secretary Egon Krenz, the conclave was attended by seven secretaries of the Central Committee: Hermann Axen, Horst Dohlus, Kurt Hager, Werner Jarowinsky, Werner Krolikowski, Ingeborg Lange, and Günter Schabowski. Guests were allowed into the meeting as specific agenda items were discussed, and they were dismissed once the secretaries advanced to the next issue. What did the top leadership deliberate on at this moment of extreme stress for the party? The meeting went through a series of what appear to

---

[152] David Priess, *The President's Book of Secrets: The Untold Story of Intelligence Briefings to America's Presidents from Kennedy to Obama* (New York: Public Affairs, 2016).

[153] Niemann argues that the IfM produced the valuable insight that not all GDR citizens were convinced of the superiority of the socialist system (Heinz Niemann, *Meinungsforschung in der DDR: Die geheimen Berichte des Instituts für Meinungsforschung an das Politbüro der SED* [Cologne: Bund-Verlag, 1993]; Heinz Niemann, *Hinterm Zaun: Politische Kultur und Meinungsforschung in der DDR—die geheimen Berichte an das Politbüro der SED* [Berlin: Edition Ost, 1995]). Honecker stated that opinion polling was not very useful, as the top leadership already knew that people needed food, clothing, and entertainment (Andert and Herzberg, *Der Sturz*, 311). Ultimately, the consumers of the institute's research did not value it.

[154] Hans Erxleben, "Das Dilemma der parteieigenen Meinungsforschung in der DDR: Einblicke aus der Innensicht eines ehemaligen SED-Meinungsforschers" (unpublished manuscript, 2015), 12.

[155] The apocryphal story of the 1979 closure coming in response to a 1972 survey showing that Ulbricht and Honecker were less popular than Brandt has no empirical support: according to an IfM insider, no such poll was ever conducted, even if the West German *Vorwärts* magazine reported otherwise. See *Vorwärts*, November 30, 1972, as referenced in Erxleben, "Das Dilemma der parteieigenen Meinungsforschung in der DDR," 11.

[156] SAPMO DY30/J/IV/213/4455 (October 25, 1989).

be trivial questions, such as the promotion of East German tourism to Albania; the issuing of diplomatic passports; the preparations for marking the 90th anniversary of the birth of progressive songwriter Ernst Busch; and exchange programs with the Soviet Union focusing on training industrial managers. And then, a crucial agenda item was announced: creation of a working group that would analyze and synthesize all letters received by the Central Committee and the Politburo. To incentivize citizens to write to the party, an official press release was to be published expressing the gratitude of the Central Committee to members of the public who provided suggestions and recommendations.[157] The Central Committee voraciously used all sources of information (letters, phone calls, and in-person visits to party offices) to generate daily bulletins on the public mood (*Stimmung der Bevölkerung*) and on the situation in the party (*Lage in der Partei*),[158] but one trend is unmistakable: despite invitations to complain, citizens were turning to the party less often, and instead they were going out into the square; within a five-day period, complaints declined three-fold.[159] As elsewhere in the communist world, unwillingness to complain was sending a signal of lack of trust in the regime. Single-party rule was coming undone.

9.3.5 Information and the End of the GDR

The end of the GDR poses two questions about information. The first is about the actions of the incumbent. A related but separate concern is how other members of the top leadership reacted to the classified reporting they received as the events of 1989 were unfolding.

Did the inaction by Honecker in the face of growing discontent and, ultimately, revolution stem from a lack of information? Although this view is intuitively appealing and has received academic currency,[160] newly available archival materials make clear that it is unwarranted. Several indicators support the conclusion that Honecker received repeated warnings about the escalation of popular discontent. The first sign of concern was the distressing trend in the voluntary transmission of information. Subnationally, complaints were declining during the second half of the 1980s, as they did elsewhere in Eastern Europe and

---

[157] SAPMO DY30/J/IV/213/4455 (October 25, 1989).

[158] SAPMO DY30/6266 (November 14, 1989); SAPMO DY30/6266 (November 27, 1989).

[159] SAPMO DY30/IV2/1/704 (November 4, 1989).

[160] Timur Kuran, "Now Out of Never: The Element of Surprise in the East European Revolution of 1989," *World Politics* 44:1 (October 1991), 7–48; Timur Kuran, *Private Truths, Public Lies: The Social Consequences of Preference Falsification* (Cambridge, MA: Harvard University Press, 1995).

China.[161] Petitions sent to the Central Committee and the State Council, however, increased.[162] Some have interpreted this to mean that citizens lost confidence in local governments but trusted the center.[163] A closer look reveals a peculiar feature of the East German categorization of petitions: in contrast to Bulgaria, requests for permanent exit from the GDR and for visits to West Germany, West Berlin, and nonsocialist countries were included in the total count of complaints. These exit requests began to increase at a double-digit rate in the early 1980s, and by the second half of 1987 they were the most frequent type of complaint to reach the Central Committee, accounting for 25.3 percent of all petitions; a year later, the share of these requests was 32.2 percent of all complaints.[164] Germans were exiting the system by applying for permits to leave the country.

The second indicator of brewing trouble is contained in the involuntarily collected information by the party, by the police, and by the Stasi. Reports were produced with various periodicity, but they all pointed to the rapid rise in discontent. Instead of limiting information transfer, in September–October 1989 the Stasi expanded the list of recipients of its reports,[165] which clearly described the political crisis in the GDR,[166] even if the Stasi's evaluations and analyses were tainted by the friend–enemy thinking (*Freund-Feind-Denken*),[167] which saw Western influence and infiltration as the root source of political opposition.[168] Prominent historians employed by the German government to analyze the Stasi materials have concluded that the MfS had a very clear understanding of the protest movement, the wave of refugees, and the rise of an organized opposition movement.[169] Minister for State Security Mielke was correct that the Stasi reported on everything and made suggestions.[170] The incapacity of Honecker to react in 1989 by using force did not reflect an insufficient supply of information by the MfS.[171] On the contrary, leading scholars working in the Stasi archives

---

[161] No comprehensive subnational data exist. For data on Karl-Marx-Stadt (Chemnitz, a city in Saxony), see Felix Mühlberg, *Bürger, Bitten und Behörden: Geschichte der Eingabe in der DDR* (Berlin: Karl Dietz Verlag, 2004), 176.

[162] SAPMO DY30 6265 (1988); SAPMO DY30 6266 (1989).

[163] Jochen Staadt, *Eingaben: Die institutionalisierte Meckerkultur in der DDR: Goldbrokat, Kaffee-Mix, Büttenreden, Ausreiseanträge und andere Schwierigkeiten mit den Untertanen* (Berlin: Arbeitspapiere des Forschungsverbundes SED-Staat, no. 24/1996), 37.

[164] SAPMO DY30 6265 (1988), 26; SAPMO DY30 6266 (1989), 3.

[165] Schiefer and Stief, eds., *Die DDR im Blick der Stasi 1989*, 54.

[166] Schiefer and Stief, eds., *Die DDR im Blick der Stasi 1989*, 41.

[167] Schiefer and Stief, eds., *Die DDR im Blick der Stasi 1989*, 57.

[168] Daniela Münkel, ed., *Die DDR im Blick der Stasi: Die geheimen Berichte an die SED-Führung Herbst 1989* (Berlin: BStU, 2014), 15.

[169] Münkel, ed., *Die DDR im Blick der Stasi Herbst 1989*, 11.

[170] Münkel, ed., *Die DDR im Blick der Stasi Herbst 1989*, 19.

[171] Münkel, ed., *Die DDR im Blick der Stasi Herbst 1989*, 19.

have concluded that the nonuse of force was the only course of action that was consistent with the intelligence that Honecker was receiving.[172]

Honecker was not the only recipient of classified information in the GDR. As in Bulgaria, others in the leadership were reading Stasi and party internal reports. Therefore, fine-grained knowledge of the rising popular dissatisfaction was widespread within the top echelon of the party-state. Beyond Honecker, none was better informed than Politburo member Egon Krenz (see Table 9.3), who, as Central Committee Secretary for Security, directly monitored the army, the Stasi, and the Ministry of the Interior. Not coincidentally, it was Egon Krenz who initiated the removal of Honecker from his position as general secretary. However, the other members of the Politburo and the Central Committee who supported replacing Honecker with Krenz in October 1989 were also operating with full knowledge that this was the best course of action in light of the available information. In parallel to Bulgaria, the palace coup was a calculated insider move.

Also as in Bulgaria, by removing the incumbent and replacing him with another insider, the party was trying to save itself. Subsequent events would show that this maneuver only gave the East German Socialist Party an extra six months in power, which was four times less than the two additional years the Bulgarian Communist Party was able to secure by removing Zhivkov in November 1989. Although the process unfolded at a different speed, in both countries the party stepped down after losing competitive elections: in Bulgaria two election cycles were needed (1990 and 1991), whereas in the GDR the party suffered a resounding loss in the first (and last) free and fair election in East German history in the spring of 1990.

9.4 Cuba

Cuba offers important insights into how a revolutionary regime, which controlled neither a communist party nor a Ministry of the Interior at the time of its seizure of power, approached the problem of collecting information necessary to solve the governance challenges that accompanied the establishment and consolidation of a new political system. Cuba demonstrates that a rebel army and citizen policing can be mobilized, at least temporarily, to carry out the information-collection tasks that are typically executed by the Ministry of the Interior and by the party in communist regimes. Once these essential institutions of communist governance are established, the role of the army and of citizen policing in

---

[172] Daniela Münkel, "Die DDR im Blick der Stasi 1989," *Aus Politik und Zeitgeschichte*, nos. 21–22 (May 2009), 26–32.

assessing and counteracting dissent declines. The theoretically relevant insight is that, despite its different initial trajectory, Cuba gradually developed a complement of mechanisms to facilitate the involuntary extraction and the voluntary provision of information on citizen discontent that were remarkably similar to those found in most other communist regimes. The Cuban example clarifies that, regardless of regime origins (revolutionary or imposed) and of the initial institutional setup, communist information gathering requires a set of standard tools: a mass-based Leninist party; a Department of State Security (usually located at the Ministry of the Interior); internal journalism; and incentives for the voluntary transmission of information.

9.4.1 Information Gathering during the Period of Regime Establishment and Consolidation

The Cuban revolution culminated in the seizure of power by Fidel Castro's rebel movement on January 1, 1959. The new political entity underwent the typical sequence of regime establishment (1959–1962), consolidation (1962–1969), and maturation (1970–onward).[173] The paucity of institutions generated a significant constraint to governance during the initial postrevolutionary period. The Ministry of the Interior was not created until June 1961, which was two months after the Bay of Pigs invasion and following Fidel's official announcement of the socialist character of the revolution.[174] The precursor of the communist party was not established until 1961, when Fidel Castro's 26th of July Movement merged with the Socialist Popular Party to form the Integrated Revolutionary Organizations (ORI). In 1962, the ORI was transformed into the United Party of the Cuban Socialist Revolution (PURSC), which eventually became the Cuban Communist Party in 1965. The party did not experience substantial growth in its initial years: it had a mere 55,000 members in 1969, which is equivalent to 0.7 percent of the population (by contrast, the Chinese Communist Party claimed 0.7 percent of the population at the time of its seizure of power).[175] This slow pace of institution building in Cuba means that during much of its initial decade in power, the leadership of the revolutionary regime had to govern without access to the information-gathering prowess of a communist party or a Department of State Security within the Ministry of the Interior.

---

[173] Dimitrov, ed., *Why Communism Did Not Collapse*, 14.

[174] "Proclama Fidel el carácter socialista de la Revolución cubana," *Granma*, April 16, 2019.

[175] The CCP had 4.2 million members at the end of September 1949, which is equivalent to 0.7 percent of the population at the time. Calculated from Zhonggong Zhongyang Zuzhi Bu, *Zhongguo gongchandang dangnei tongji ziliao huibian, 1921–2000* (Beijing: Zhonggong Zhongyang Zuzhi Bu Xinxi Guanli Zhongxin, 2002), 72–73.

The leadership tasked the military with monitoring and managing popular discontent during the initial postrevolutionary years. Weeks after the takeover of power, two entities were created under the aegis of the rebel army (*el Ejército Rebelde*): the intelligence service (*Departamento de Investigaciones del Ejército Rebelde*, or DIER) and the National Revolutionary Police (*Policía Nacional Revolucionaria*, or PNR), which was promptly merged with the intelligence service.[176] In October 1959, the rebel army was incorporated into the newly created Ministry of Defense (MINFAR) and the intelligence service was renamed DIIFAR (*Departamento de Información e Investigaciones de las Fuerzas Armadas Revolucionarias*). Like its predecessor, DIIFAR focused primarily on urgent matters of domestic counterintelligence; one section (*Sección U*) was specifically tasked with supervision of the information-gathering activities of the Committees for Defense of the Revolution (CDR),[177] which were established in September 1960, with the explicit mandate to engage in citizen policing by recruiting individuals to act as informants.[178] In June 1961, the policing and intelligence organs were transferred from the MINFAR to the newly established Ministry of the Interior (MININT). Henceforth, the intelligence and counterintelligence forces were known as the State Security Department (*Departamento de la Seguridad del Estado*, or DSE).[179] Colloquially, State Security was referred to as G-2.

The chief task of G-2 was to catalog regime enemies. In the 1960s, the capacity of the DSE was gradually strengthened to identify individual and organized dissent, especially in urban areas.[180] The authorities were concerned about the loyalty of the *ancien régime* elite, in particular, high-level bureaucrats and the remnants of the top military brass.[181] Parallel with other communist regimes, threat perceptions during the initial years of communist rule centered on the dangers posed by foreign spies; by armed bandits operating individually or in small groups; by the diffusion of counterrevolutionary propaganda; and by the deployment of sabotage and terrorism with the aim of bringing about political

[176] In addition, a system of revolutionary tribunals (*Tribunales Revolucionarios*) existed to handle counterrevolutionary crimes; these tribunals operated outside the official judicial system and were directly subordinate to Fidel. See Juan Antonio Rodríguez Menier, *Cuba por dentro: El MININT* (Miami: Ediciones Universal, 1994), 35–36.

[177] Rodríguez, *Cuba por dentro*, 38.

[178] Comités de Defensa de la Revolución, *CDR: 10 Años de Trabajo* (La Habana: Instituto Cubano de Libro, 1971), 23–33 and Lillian Guerra, *Visions of Power in Cuba: Revolution, Redemption, and Resistance, 1959–1971* (Chapel Hill: University of North Carolina Press, 2012), 207–15.

[179] Rodríguez, *Cuba por dentro*, 31–39; "Organismos de Seguridad con raíces rebeldes," *Granma*, March 26, 2009.

[180] Report from *Director General de Q.* to *Jefe de Departamento de la Seguridad del Estado* of the Cuban Ministry of the Interior, "Organizaciones Contrarrevolucionarias: Breve Historia de las Mismas" (October 19, 1964) (document made available by the *Memorial de la Denuncia*, Havana) (on file with the author).

[181] "Organizaciones Contrarrevolucionarias."

destabilization.[182] Assassination attempts against the leader justifiably emerged as a major concern as well.[183] Cuba aimed to produce enemy rosters that were as detailed as possible and could thus be used to identify those who had engaged (or were likely to engage) in behaviors that threatened state security.

The creation of a new ministry responsible for protecting state security did not mean that the MINFAR immediately relinquished this portfolio. Mass domestic threats justified the persistence of institutional fragmentation. The MINFAR, rather than the MININT, took the lead in eliminating armed guerrillas, who constituted the most significant internal threat to state security during the initial decade of communist rule. The fight against guerrillas (*la lucha contra bandidos*) began in 1959, but it intensified after the Bay of Pigs invasion and did not conclude until the "bandits" had been eliminated in 1965.[184] In 1961, the newly established State Security Department of the Ministry of the Interior created a Bands Bureau (*Buro de Bandas*),[185] which was supposed to use its full-time staff, part-time informants, and the intelligence collected through the Committees for Defense of the Revolution to identify and eliminate "bandits." However, the *Buro de Bandas* and the mostly urban CDR activists proved ill equipped to penetrate the guerrilla groups, which were hiding in inhospitable mountainous terrain and were able to secure the support of a numerically large and socially diverse network of collaborators, ranging from farmworkers and housewives to skilled mechanics and accountants.[186] The army took the lead in suppressing the *bandidos* and, as it lacked detailed information, deployed disproportionate force to eradicate the guerrilla movement.[187] For example, 8,000 troops were dispatched to the Escambray Mountains in 1963 to encircle and capture a group that had a mere 4 members.[188] Although the absolute number of bandits in Cuba was small (under

---

[182] See the stenographic record of the conversation between the Cuban and the Bulgarian ministers of the interior, Archive of the Bulgarian Ministry of the Interior (AMVR) f. 9 op. 2 a. e. 665 l. 62–92 (March 1, 1971).

[183] According to data tabulated by the *Memorial de la Denuncia* in Havana, there were 637 plots to assassinate Fidel Castro (based on a personal visit by the author to the museum, May 2019).

[184] José Angel Gárciga Blanco, *LCB: Tropa de Tomassevich* (Havana: Verde Olivo, 2002), 41.

[185] José Angel Gárciga Blanco, *LCB 1962: En el Escambray y más allá* (Havana: Verde Olivo, 2010), 69.

[186] Based on detailed statistics of the social characteristics of 251 punished collaborators of the 28 bandits captured in the province of Las Tunas (Plácido Cruz Infante, *La lucha contra bandidos en Las Tunas* [Las Tunas: Editorial Sanlope, 2008], 46–8). The Las Tunas data allow us to calculate a baseline collaborator-to-bandit ratio of 9:1; assuming that the Las Tunas ratio is representative for the entire territory of Cuba, we can estimate that there were at least 36,000 collaborators for the 3,995 bandits who operated in 1959–1965.

[187] The fact that joining a band was made a capital offense in November 1961 demonstrated the resolve of the regime to tackle this problem (on Law 988, see Gárciga, *LCB 1962*, 11). The law also penalized those assisting armed groups (see José Suárez Amador, *De Las Villas a Oriente: Combatiendo el bandidismo, 1959–1965* [Santiago de Cuba: Editorial Oriente, 2014], 118–19).

[188] Gárciga, *LCB*, 152–53.

4,000),[189] eradication required an extraordinary outlay of resources by the army. This stands in contrast to the situation in China or Bulgaria, where the problem of armed resisters was handled by the police with a higher degree of professionalism and was therefore solved with considerably less manpower.

After the guerrillas were eliminated, Cuba gradually began to move to a less violent and more stable form of government. Although forced conscription of 35,000 conscientious objectors (up to one-tenth of whom were gay men, Adventists, Jehovah's Witnesses, Protestant and Catholic priests, and peasants who had resisted collectivization) was implemented in 1965, it was discontinued in 1968.[190] Subsequently, overt expressions of discontent declined and repression was less frequent.[191] The dominant strategy for dealing with regime enemies was to offer an exit option to the most vociferous malcontents. Cuba allowed regime critics to emigrate, as powerfully illustrated by the release of the Bay of Pigs invaders in exchange for a shipment of U.S. tractors. Altogether, at least half a million Cubans left the island during the first two waves of migration (1959–1962 and 1965–1973).[192]

Once the communist party was established in 1965, it began to collect information, with the military and the CDR correspondingly declining in importance as vehicles for managing popular unrest. By the start of the 1970s, Cuba had developed the complement of institutions associated with information gathering in communist regimes.

9.4.2 Information Collection in a Mature Communist Regime: Cuba since 1970

As in other communist regimes, information about popular discontent in Cuba was provided voluntarily through citizen complaints and collected involuntarily

---

[189] Elvin Fontaine Ortiz, *Fidel y la guerra desconocida* (Havana: Editora Política, 2014), 18. Fontaine reports 299 organized groups with 3,995 members in 1959–1965. Also see AMVR f. 9 op. 2 a. e. 665 l. 62–92 (March 1, 1971).

[190] Joseph Tabhaz, "Demystifying las UMAP: The Politics of Sugar, Gender, and Religion in 1960s Cuba," *Delaware Review of Latin American Studies* 14:2 (December 31, 2013), http://www1.udel.edu/LAS/Vol14-2Tahbaz.html (accessed April 19, 2022); Abel Sierra Maduro, "'El trabajo os hará hombres': Masculinización nacional, trabajo forzado y control social en Cuba durante los años sesenta," *Cuban Studies*, no. 44 (2016), 309–41.

[191] See statistics presented during the discussions of Minister of the Interior Sergio del Valle Jiménez with his counterpart at the Bulgarian Ministry of the Interior, AMVR f. 9 op. 2 a. e. 665 l. 62–92 (March 1, 1971) and AMVR f. 9 op. 2 a. e. 871 l. 132–38 (April 10, 1971).

[192] Jorge Duany has documented that since 1959 as many as 1.4 million Cubans left for the United States and another 300,000 made it to Spain, Mexico, and other countries. The emigration waves occurred in 1959–1962, 1965–1973, 1980, 1994, and 1995–onward. See Jorge Duany, "Cuban Migration: A Postrevolution Exodus Ebbs and Flows," July 6, 2017, https://www.migrationpolicy.org/article/cuban-migration-postrevolution-exodus-ebbs-and-flows (accessed April 19, 2022).

by State Security, the party, and the media. The system making these collection efforts possible was operational by the 1970s and, aside from technological upgrading, it has not experienced any major changes in the intervening decades.

A key development is the rise of a sophisticated state security apparatus, whose structure and operational priorities can be ascertained on the basis of a memoir written by a highly placed intelligence operative (Juan Antonio Rodríguez Menier),[193] archival materials from Bulgaria on cooperation between the Bulgarian and the Cuban interior ministries, and Cuban State Security documents that have been made available by the *Memorial de la Denuncia* in Havana. Despite some initial concerns about the educational backgrounds of the MININT personnel,[194] the Department of State Security quickly built a cadre of competent full-time staff. Officers, numbering 3,000 in 1986, who engaged in running agents were known as *oficiales operativos*;[195] these Cuban statistics align very well with comparable data from Bulgaria.[196] Agents were subdivided into categories: penetration agents (*agente de penetración*); plants (*agente "sembrado"*); spy ring agents (*agente de posición*); liaison agents (*agente de enlace*); and mailbox agents (*agente "buzon"*).[197] Technical surveillance (primarily phone tapping and mail inspection) was used as well.[198] State Security was divided into counterintelligence (*Dirección General de Contrainteligencia*, or DGCI) and intelligence (*Dirección General de Inteligencia*, or DGI).[199] The main tasks of the Counterintelligence Directorate were to monitor foreigners (intelligence operatives, diplomats, specialists, and ordinary visitors), religious devotees, intellectuals, youth, and Cuban exiles returning to the island as tourists; to prevent economic sabotage; and to control other acts of individual dissent or organized opposition. The Intelligence Directorate consisted of divisions focusing on Latin America and the Caribbean; North America; the Middle East; and Eurasia

---

[193] Rodríguez, *Cuba por dentro*.
[194] "Meeting of Cuban Minister of the Interior Sergio del Valle Jiménez with His Counterpart at the Bulgarian Ministry of the Interior," AMVR f. 9 op. 2 a. e. 665 l. 62–92 (March 1, 1971).
[195] Rodríguez, *Cuba por dentro*, 58.
[196] In Bulgaria, which had a population that was 10.2 percent smaller than that in Cuba, the number of State Security officers who handled agents stood at 2,432 in 1978 (the last year for which this information is available), which was exactly one-third of the cadre of 7,290 Bulgarian State Security officers at the time (Momchil Metodiev and Mariia Dermendzhieva, *Durzhavna sigurnost: Predimstvo po nasledstvo: Profesionalni biografii na vodeshti ofitseri* [Sofia: Ciela, 2015], 911). The statistics reported by Metodiev and Dermendzhieva exclude the external intelligence directorate, which had 900 officers. Assuming that the proportion of officers who handled agents was the same for the external intelligence directorate as it was for the domestic counterintelligence divisions, a reasonable estimate would be that no more than 300 external intelligence officers handled agents in 1978, thus bringing the total to 2,732 officers.
[197] Rodríguez, *Cuba por dentro*, 64–69.
[198] Rodríguez, *Cuba por dentro*, 110–11.
[199] Comisión de Historia de los Organos de la Seguridad del Estado, Dirección Política Central, Ministerio del Interior, *30 Años: Historia de la Seguridad Cubana: Las reglas del juego* (La Habana: Ministerio del Interior, 1988).

and Australia. Information was collected through various methods, including agents who were illegals.[200]

When setting up its systems for protecting state security, Cuba received technical assistance from the Eastern Bloc. In recognition of the high quality of its work, by the 1980s the Cuban Ministry of the Interior was included in most multilateral meetings of the State Security organizations of the Eastern Bloc regimes. It maintained a vibrant schedule of visits to the Soviet Union and various Eastern European countries until the very end of the Cold War. This close integration with Eastern Europe meant that assistance could be extended on bread-and-butter issues, such as audio-video surveillance techniques and the identification of suspicious correspondence as well as more advanced tradecraft like disinformation campaigns (active measures), assassinations (sharp measures), and the deployment of illegals.[201]

A central question focuses on how information transfer operated in the Cuban case. Initially, transmission of intelligence was the realm of the MININT's *Servicios de Información*,[202] though the minister of the interior would personally draft sensitive reports to Fidel on Department of State Security letterhead.[203] By the 1970s, an Information Directorate was created within the Ministry of the Interior. It produced a daily bulletin (*el parte diario*) of no more than five pages and a unique televised newscast (*emisión televisiva*) for the top leadership.[204] As in other communist regimes, these materials aimed to anticipate and prevent the transformation of latent discontent into open acts of opposition.

The second entity that engaged in information collection was the communist party. After it was established, party congresses were held at irregular intervals in 1975, 1980, 1986, 1991, 1997, 2011, 2016, and 2021. By the time of its Second Congress in 1980, the Cuban Communist Party had 434,143 members, which is equivalent to 4.41 percent of the population. Party building continued apace. At the Sixth Congress of the Cuban Communist Party in 2011, 7.05 percent of the population belonged to the party. This is similar to the size of the CPSU at the height of its development in 1988, when its members constituted 6.83 percent of the Soviet population. Party size decreased after 2011 and stood at 6.3 percent of the population in 2021.[205] Though not as large as in the nonrevolutionary

---

[200] Rodríguez, *Cuba por dentro*, 116–17.

[201] See State Security documents covering the period from 1968 to 1975 in the Archive of the Bulgarian Ministry of the Interior (AMVR) f. 9 op. 2 a. e. 354, 538, 665, 865, 866, 868, 869, 870 (1968–1976).

[202] See report from the Director of *Servicios de Información* to the Director of the State Security Department of the Ministry of the Interior, November 3, 1961 (made available by the *Memorial de la Denuncia*, Havana) (on file with the author).

[203] See "Informe del Ministro del Interior al Primer Ministro del Gobierno Revolucionario," October 2, 1961 (made available by the *Memorial de la Denuncia*, Havana) (on file with the author).

[204] Rodríguez, *Cuba por dentro*, 142–44.

[205] *Informe Central al Octavo Congreso del Partido Comunista de Cuba* (April 17, 2021).

regimes, the size of the Cuban Communist Party is nevertheless sufficient for executing state-building projects.

The communist party has its own information-collection machinery. In 1967, it created the *Equipo Nacional de Opinión Pública* (National Group on Public Opinion), which was promptly renamed *Equipo Nacional de Opinión del Pueblo* (National Group on Popular Opinion).[206] Since 1991, it has been known as CESPO (*Centro de Estudios Sociopolíticos y de Opinión adjunto al Comité Central del Partido Comunista de Cuba*, or Center for Sociopolitical Studies and Opinion Research Associated with the Central Committee of the Cuban Communist Party).[207] Among other publications, CESPO issues a bulletin entitled *En Consulta con el Pueblo* (In Consultation with the People), which is typically printed on a monthly basis. No copies of this bulletin have become publicly available, though Cuban sources occasionally refer to it.[208] In addition, the preface to a book by Naida Orozco Sánchez, one of the compilers of the bulletin, provides valuable insight into how this serial is produced. The preface reveals that *En Consulta con el Pueblo* includes information collected via the spontaneous registration of public opinion (executed by dispatching staff to listen to conversations taking place in queues and on overcrowded public transportation); express surveys (*sondeos*); and opinion polling (*encuestas de opinión*).[209] This and other classified bulletins circulate to the top leadership to keep it apprised of public opinion.[210]

In other communist regimes, a third channel for solving the dictator's dilemma is provided by internal media, which are classified publications with restricted circulation prepared by the telegraph agency and the major print and electronic media (historically radio and TV, and now various Internet companies). Although no such publications have surfaced, there is no reason to expect that they do not exist in Cuba as well.

9.4.3 Voluntary Provision of Information

It is important to highlight Cuban understandings of the sources of political dissent. While not denying the existence of an external ideological vector, the

---

[206] Naida Orozco Sánchez, *Lo perdurable es el pueblo: Fidel Castro y la opinión pública* (La Habana: Editora Política, 2016), 5.

[207] Ariadna Pérez Valdés, "Celebra sistema de Estudios Sociopolíticos y de Opinión medio siglo de existencia," *Trabajadores*, October 19, 2017.

[208] José Raúl Gallego Ramos and Arailasy Rosabal García, "Las cartas sobre la mesa: Un estudio sobre la relación entre agenda pública y mediática en Cuba: Caso *Granma*," *Signo y Pensamiento* 32 (January–June 2013), 98–113.

[209] Orozco, *Lo perdurable es el pueblo*, 5–6.

[210] Orozco, *Lo perdurable es el pueblo*, 5–6.

Cuban regime very early on also acknowledged that there were domestic factors that generated dissent. For example, during an official visit to Sofia in March 1971, Cuban Minister of the Interior Sergio del Valle Jiménez shared his assessment that political dissent encompassed counterrevolutionary propaganda, riots, assassination attempts, sabotage, terrorist plans, and attempts to flee the country; these were individual rather than organized antiregime efforts.[211] In the view of Minister del Valle, dissent was motivated by expectations of an imminent successful assassination of Castro and, importantly, by dissatisfaction stemming from the economic difficulties experienced by average citizens.[212] By drawing a direct link between the state of the economy and political dissent, Cuban repressive organs displayed an understanding of discontent similar to that which had already become dominant throughout the Eastern Bloc.[213] By analogy, this link also suggested a solution, namely, utilizing the socialist welfare state to satisfy the expanding material expectations of the population. Therefore, citizen complaints, which were a vehicle for the voluntary transmission of information to the leadership, were highly valuable in this regard.

To incentivize citizens to complain, the Cuban media have been publishing carefully selected letters to the editor. The practice dates back to the 1970s, when *Granma* featured specialized sections like "Luz Roja" (which focused on traffic problems) and "A Vuelta de Correo" (By Return Post). Currently, several media outlets publish letters to the editor. One is *Bohemia*, which runs "Puntillazos"; the section features several short critical commentaries, typically accompanied by a photograph, on negative phenomena (noise; accumulation of uncollected trash in the streets; or the poor quality of services) that are extracted from readers' letters. Three other print media publish readers' letters: one is *Trabajadores*, the second is *La Tribuna de La Habana*, and the third is *Juventud Rebelde*. All three feature articles reminiscent in style to those that appeared in "A Vuelta de Correo" in the 1970s and 1980s: they typically include a redacted letter, a response from the entity that is criticized in the letter, and some editorial commentary. The only major outlet that publishes entire nonredacted letters is *Granma*, which is the official organ of the Cuban Communist Party.[214]

To signal Raúl Castro's openness to criticism, *Granma* introduced a new section entitled "Cartas a la Dirección" on March 14, 2008. The section prints letters to the editor containing complaints, criticisms, and suggestions. Unsurprisingly,

---

[211] AMVR f. 9 op. 2 a. e. 665 l. 62–92 (March 1, 1971).

[212] AMVR f. 9 op. 2 a. e. 665 l. 62–92 (March 1, 1971).

[213] In China, this type of understanding would not emerge until after Tiananmen Spring, when socioeconomic protests and strikes were classified as threats to state security in internal MPS documents.

[214] *Granma*, March 14, 2010, 10.

it has rapidly grown in popularity to become the most closely read portion of the Friday paper. Since March 2008, the section has appeared almost every week, featuring over 3,000 letters and more than 1,000 official responses to these letters.[215] The editorial staff of the newspaper makes a concerted effort to secure responses to every letter that is printed. Entities that fail to react within three months are named and shamed by being singled out when the newspaper prints the results of its regular six-month audit of the published letters and the official replies. Since 2013, *Granma* has also been flagging unsatisfactory pro-forma responses by publishing editorial postscripts (*coletillas*). The message sent by the official party newspaper is clear: the leadership welcomes citizen input.

What is the real utility of soliciting such letters? Other communist regimes help generate a hypothesis. Archival materials from the Soviet Union and Bulgaria demonstrate that the top leadership was regularly briefed on the content of the unpublished complaint letters, which were understood to be a "barometer of public opinion."[216] In China, overviews of letters sent to *Renmin ribao* and other media outlets have been prepared for the top leaderships since the 1950s.[217] Our working assumption is that the letters received by *Granma* have the same function and result in similar internal analysis and reporting that is aimed to apprise the top leaders of the content of voluntarily transmitted information. This is corroborated through interview data and scholarly research.[218]

The case of Cuba leads to some general reflections. When institutions outlive their utility for information gathering, they are no longer assigned such tasks. For example, the MINFAR no longer runs the totality of Cuba's state security system, although it maintains certain military intelligence functions. Likewise, the CDR has long abandoned its citizen-policing mandate and has transformed itself into a toothless parastatal organization. Instead of wielding fear, these committees currently meet with popular disdain, as illustrated in Figure 9.1, which documents the reactions of the residents of a posh Havana apartment building in 2013 to a call to meet with the local chapter of the CDR to review what the CDR had done to improve the municipal services provided to the building ("I am not coming—I will be partying," said one). Institutions adapt and fight for their survival. For the CDR, this has meant largely abandoning the

---

[215] Martin K. Dimitrov, "The Functions of Letters to the Editor in Reform-Era Cuba," *Latin American Research Review* 54:1 (2019), 1–15.

[216] Dimitrov, "Tracking Public Opinion Under Authoritarianism" and Dimitrov, "What the Party Wanted to Know."

[217] This took place both nationally (see *Neibu cankao*, no. 2698 [January 30, 1959], 18–23) and subnationally (see Sichuan Gongren Ribao Bianji Bu, *Duzhe laixin zhaibian*, no. 98 [March 3, 1986]).

[218] Personal interview with a *Juventud rebelde* journalist, Havana, June 16, 2015; Gallego and Rosabal, "Las cartas sobre la mesa."

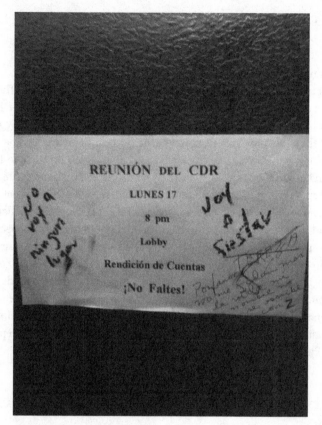

Figure 9.1 CDR in contemporary Cuba.
Source: Photo taken by the author in a residential building in Havana (June 2013).

information-collection mandate it had during the initial postrevolutionary years prior to the creation of the Ministry of the Interior.

In sum, Cuba is an unusual case, as it began as a military regime. The early years of postrevolutionary governance highlight the tradeoffs that exist when the standard complement of communist information-gathering institutions is not present. Lacking such institutions, the army and the CDR did extract intelligence, but in a crudely involuntary, repressive, and inefficient manner. Gradually, the army and the CDR were sidelined by the standard communist information-collection institutions: the party, State Security, and internal media. These institutions have persisted from the 1970s to the current day without change. The most valuable insight from the Cuban case is that communist state building may proceed from various starting points across different countries but it will eventually culminate in the same complement of institutions for the involuntary extraction and voluntary provision of information on popular discontent.

9.5 Information-Gathering Institution under Martial Law in Taiwan, 1949–1987

As the only noncommunist regime to be ruled by a Leninist party,[219] Taiwan provides an important test for the scope conditions of our theory. The relevant questions are whether institutions for the collection of information in a non-communist autocracy mirror those that can be found in communist regimes and whether they function in similar ways. This section demonstrates that involuntary extraction in Taiwan was executed through channels identical to those that existed in Eastern Europe and China: party reporting, internal journalism, and State Security surveillance. Another important parallel is the function of petitions as a mechanism for the voluntary transmission of information. These similarities notwithstanding, there are two key differences, both stemming from the fact that as a noncommunist regime, Taiwan never developed a social contract that guaranteed welfare in exchange for popular quiescence. One effect was infrequent complaints, which meant that involuntary extraction persisted as the primary mode of collection of information throughout the martial law period. The second consequnce of the absence of a social contract is that levels of violence were high, flaring up even as the regime matured, in contrast to the gradual and steady decline of repression in Eastern Europe.

9.5.1 The Party

The Guomindang (KMT) was formidable in size both on the mainland and after its retreat to Taiwan. In 1948, its membership was one-third greater than that of the CCP.[220] One-twentieth of KMT members moved to Taiwan in 1949,[221] which is equivalent to 2.7 percent of the population of the island at the time. Party building continued at a rapid pace under martial law and the KMT grew to 2,500,000 members (12.06 percent of the population) by 1987.[222] The main information-gathering tasks of the party involved intelligence work, which was carried out by the Sixth Department (Intelligence and Security), the

---

[219] Bruce Dickson, *Democratization in China and Taiwan: The Adaptability of Leninist Regimes* (New York: Oxford University Press, 1997).

[220] The KMT had 4,080,293 members in 1948, whereas the CCP had 3,065,533. On the KMT, see Li Li, *Taiwan zhengdang zhengzhi fazhan shi* (Beijing: Jiujiu Chubanshe, 2014), 30. On the CCP, see Zhonggong Zhongyang Zuzhi Bu, *Zhongguo gongchandang dangnei tongji ziliao huibian, 1921–2010* (Beijing: Dangjian Duwu Chubanshe, 2011), 7.

[221] Li, *Taiwan zhengdang zhengzhi*, 30.

[222] Dickson, *Democratization in China and Taiwan*, 61.

Second Department (Mainland Affairs), and the Third Department (Overseas Work). Domestic affairs were the prerogative of the Fourth Department (Propaganda) and the Fifth Department (Popular Movements and Activities of Mass Organizations, which was renamed the Social Department in 1972).[223] Penetration (*shentou* 滲透) of the entire territory of Taiwan was accomplished via 15,000 ordinary and 23,000 special (military and security) party cells established in 1952.[224] The task of grassroots party cells was to act as eyes and ears by engaging in social survey work and by producing regular updates on social trends.[225] Social surveys conducted by KMT cells were a form of social control; cell meetings would discuss suspicious people, events, and matters and subsequently transfer their reports to the intelligence organs.[226] Based on the aforementioned indicators, we can confidently conclude that the KMT prioritized information gathering just as the communist parties did.

9.5.2 Internal Journalism

Although internal journalistic reporting existed in Taiwan, it was limited to bulletins on international affairs produced by the Central News Agency (CNA) (*Zhongyang she* 中央社). There were two kinds of internal reference (*Zhongyang she Cankao xiaoxi* 中央社參考消息): *A Can* (A參) for the President and *B Can* (B參) for the heads of the five Yuan and for cabinet ministers. Taiwan's *Cankao xiaoxi* focused on foreign news; during his twenty-seven years working for CNA, a journalist recalls having only two reports published in this classified outlet— one on an American professor in New York City who spoke favorably about the CCP despite receiving financial support from Taiwan and another on partnering with United Way as a way to enhance the potential impact of Taiwanese cultural diplomacy in the United States by giving access to high-profile venues for Taiwanese performers.[227] This external focus stands in contrast to the intelligence briefs of Xinhua News Agency, which cover both sensitive domestic and international news—but it is similar to the function of the telegraph agency in the Soviet Union. However, in contrast to both Eastern Europe and China, there is

---

[223] Chen Tsui-lian, "Taiwan jieyan shiqi de tewu tongzhi yu baise kongbu fenwei," in Zhang Yanxian and Chen Meirong, eds., *Jieyan shiqi baise kongbu yu zhuanxing zhengyi lunwen ji* (Taipei: Wu San-lian Taiwan Shiliao Jijinhui, Taiwan Lishi Xuehui, 2009), 43–70, at 58.

[224] Chen, "Taiwan jieyan shiqi de tewu tongzhi," 59. On party cells and required attendance at cell meetings, also see Dickson, *Democratization in China and Taiwan*, 58–59.

[225] Chen, "Taiwan jieyan shiqi de tewu tongzhi," 61.

[226] Gao Minghui, *Qingzhi dang'an: Yige lao diaochayuan de zishu* (Taipei: Shangzhou Chuban, 1995), 177.

[227] Hu Zongju, *Xinwen shouwang ren: Jizhe shengya 40 nian* (Gaoxiong: Juliu, 2010), 74–75.

no evidence that the print media produced classified internal reports in Taiwan. The explanation for this is that Taiwan had a certain degree of freedom of the press, even during martial law; this was true not only for magazines but also for some newspapers.[228] The net result was that the print media did not function as peons of the KMT.

9.5.3 Classified Bulletins

Another similarity between Taiwan and the communist regimes lies in the extensive range of classified bulletins generated for the leadership by the KMT, by the intelligence services, and by the presidential administration. Within the party, the Sixth Department had a "bandit research committee" (*feiqing yanjiu weiyuanhui* 匪情研究委員會), which produced both regular overviews and specialized in-depth analyses of the political and economic situation on the mainland.[229] The precursor to the National Security Bureau (*zongtongfu jiyaoshi ziliaozu* 總統府機要室資料組) generated a daily intelligence brief entitled *Meiri qingbao zhaiyao* (每日情報摘要),[230] in addition to weekly reports on party, government, military, and social developments in the PRC (*Zhonggong zhoubao* 中共週報). The situation on the mainland received extraordinary attention. Thematic briefs titled *yanjiu zhuanbao* (研究專報, or "research report") and *zhonggong xianzhuang huibian* (中共現狀匯編, or "compilation on the current status of the CCP") were prepared on issues like Sino–Soviet relations, land reform, industry and finance, education and culture, communications, public security, the judicial system, and borderland minorities.[231] Military intelligence also published a bulletin on mainland affairs.[232] Finally, the Investigation Bureau produced briefs focusing on issues such as bandit area research;[233] communist bandit tyranny;[234] PRC spy activities and secrecy work;[235] and the international, PRC, and domestic economic situations, with detailed breakdown by industrial sector.[236] Thus, the archives reveal that the president and other members of the top KMT leadership

[228] Chin-Chuan Lee, "Sparking a Fire: The Press and the Ferment of Democratic Change in Taiwan," *Journalism Monographs*, no. 138 (1993).

[229] Yang Ruichun, *Zhongguo Guomindang dalu gongzuo zuzhi yanjiu 1950–1990* (Beijing: Jiuzhou Chubanshe, 2012), 309.

[230] KMT Archives, Chang Kai-shek Special Files (總裁批簽) 39/0127 (December 15, 1950); KMT Archives file 禾13358, bulletin nos. 62–89 (March 15–April 17, 1951).

[231] Yang, *Zhongguo Guomindang dalu gongzuo*, 307 (based on data for 1950).

[232] Chen, "Taiwan jieyan shiqi de tewu tongzhi," 55.

[233] *Feiqu yanjiu zhuanbao*, KMT Archives file 581/1580 (September 1956).

[234] *Gongfei baozheng shilu*, KMT Archives, file 581/1291, bulletin nos. 92–94 (June–August 1965).

[235] KMT Archives, file 稚00600 (November 1, 1950).

[236] *Jingji yuebao*, KMT Archives, file 554/176 (May 1955, July–August 1955, September–October 1955).

were supplied with numerous intelligence bulletins focusing on foreign, and especially on PRC, news.[237]

9.5.4 State Security

In contrast to the communist world, the apparatus for state security in Taiwan featured nearly a dozen entities with overlapping mandates. The main agencies were the National Security Bureau (*guojia anquan ju* 國家安全局); the Investigation Bureau (*diaocha ju* 調查局);[238] the Intelligence Bureau of the Ministry of Defense (*guofang bu qingbao ju* 國防部情報局); and the Garrison Command (*jingbei zongbu* 警備總部).[239] The spycraft of these numerous security entities was similar to that practiced in the communist regimes. It involved standard techniques like the use of full-time staff, part-time informants, and technical surveillance to monitor and counteract dissent. Technical surveillance methods included phone tapping, mail control, and the perlustration of telegrams. This work was carried out by several entities: the President's Office had a team of 30 who engaged in tapping the phones of individuals suspected of plotting Taiwanese independence riots; the post office relied on 170 employees who read letters in 1951 (focusing on communist psychological warfare black letters and mail from the communist area); and the Garrison Command Special Inspection Office, which confiscated suspicious correspondence, seized 120,201 letters sent from China in 1979.[240]

Agent work relied on several types of informants. Ordinary agents (*yiban bujian* 一般布建) were also referred to as eyes and ears (*ermu* 耳目) or liaisons (*tongxin yuan* 通信員). There were also key agents (*zhongdian bujian* 重點布建), who were dispatched to monitor special groups, political organizations, and the media. A third category was those involved in detective work (*zhenpo bujian* 偵破布建) or special agents (*zhuan'an bujian* 專案布建), who helped solve drug trafficking, arms dealing, and economic crimes; these agents were also used in sensitive settings such as government offices and certain media outlets. In the early 1980s, ordinary agents did not receive any monetary support but they might be given small gifts; monthly stipends of NT\$2,000–3,000 (equivalent

---

[237] Many of those intelligence streams survived the end of the martial law period and persist to the current day.

[238] The Investigation Bureau belonged to the Ministry of the Interior until 1955. Since 1955, it has been a part of the Ministry of Judicial Administration (which was renamed the Ministry of Justice in 1980).

[239] The Garrison Command had a very extensive purview that included antispy activities, riot control, and imprisonment of political activists; phone tapping, mail control, and blocking unauthorized radio broadcasts; and control of the media, among others. Chen, "Taiwan jieyan shiqi de tewu tongzhi," 53.

[240] Chen, "Taiwan jieyan shiqi de tewu tongzhi," 62.

to US$55–83) were allotted to key agents; and detection agents were awarded NT$20,000–30,000 (US$550–830 in 1981) per month, which significantly exceeded the average monthly wage of NT$15,344.[241] Both the existence of various types of informants and their differential remuneration mirror the handling of agents in the communist world.

The size of the agent network has not been determined definitively. In his memoir, Ministry of Justice Investigation Bureau (MJIB) Vice-Head Gao Minghui states that in the late 1970s, the head of the MJIB, Ruan Chengzhang, articulated the goal of having every field employee (*waiqin* 外勤) handle 30–40 agents, thus leading to a ratio of 1 agent for every 500 citizens.[242] Had this goal been realized, it would have netted 36,400 agents (the population at the time was 18.2 million). However, there were 30,000 *ermu* in 1981,[243] producing a penetration rate of 0.16 percent rather than the desired 0.2 percent. A Taiwanese scholar referencing Gao discusses a plan to have every one of the MJIB's 2,000-strong staff (not only the field officers, as stated by Gao) manage 30–40 agents; this produces an aspirational figure of 60,000–80,000 MJIB agents, a goal that was not realized.[244] An American scholar cites both the Taiwanese scholar and the original Taiwanese source to claim that there were 80,000 MJIB agents; this source proceeds to calculate a ratio of agents to adult citizens of 1:132.[245] Although other agencies also had domestic spies, the MJIB was the main entity in charge of counterintelligence. Its levels of agent penetration (0.16 percent in 1981, or 1 agent per 625 citizens, based on data provided by Gao Minghui) are consistent with those in the Soviet Union.

Apart from conducting mainland-focused intelligence activities, the state security apparatus monitored a range of domestic and international targets: communist and leftist organizations such as the Taiwan Chinese Communist Party (*Shenggongwei* 省工委) and the Taiwan Democratic Self-Government League (*Taimeng* 台盟); student groups in Taiwan and overseas;[246] dissident intellectuals (including those living in the United States);[247] pro-democracy activists, like those arrested in the 1979 Formosa Incident that involved human

[241] For stipend information, see Gao, *Qingzhi dang'an*, 169–73. The 1981 exchange rate was NT$36.01 = US$1. For 1981 average wages, see Chun-Hung Andy Lin, "Changing Wages and Employment by Skill in Taiwan, 1978–1996: The Roles of Education Policy, Trade, and Immigration" (PhD Dissertation, Iowa State University, Department of Economics, 2000), 8.

[242] Gao, *Qingzhi dang'an*, 171.

[243] Gao, *Qingzhi dang'an*, 171.

[244] Chen, "Taiwan jieyan shiqi de tewu tongzhi," 61.

[245] Sheena Chestnut Greitens, *Dictators and Their Secret Police: Coercive Institutions and State Violence* (New York: Cambridge University Press, 2016), 107.

[246] On the MIT Taiwanese spy ring, see *The Tech*, October 31, 1981, 5.

[247] On the killing of, for example, Carnegie Mellon professor Chen Wen-cheng by the Garrison Command after interrogations about his activities in the United States. in 1981, see Henry Kamm, "Taipei Irritated by Protests in the U.S.," *The New York Times*, August 9, 1981, p. 9, https://www.

rights demonstrations; aboriginal rights advocates; the Taiwanese independence (*Taidu* 台獨) movement; and the media.[248]

The information collected was used to compile blacklists of individuals who had caused problems (*hei mingdan/guanzhi mingdan* 黑名單/管制名單).[249] The roster comprised local assembly members and opposition movement followers as well as those in economic, religious, social, and cultural circles (including media personalities); blacklisted individuals living overseas were discouraged from returning to Taiwan as they could be denied entry or detained. The lists were sizable: the one maintained by the National Security Bureau had 26,000 names in 1950–1967 and the one compiled by the Personnel Department of the President's Office included 110,000 individuals in 1967.[250] There also existed a roster of those currently monitored (*guankao fenzi* 管考分子), consisting of rebels and prisoners of conscience released from prisons and labor camps (出獄的叛亂犯/生教所來的思想犯). Created by the National Security Bureau, this roster had 15,000 names in 1969–1970.[251] The list is similar to the surveillance catalogs maintained by the communist regimes in Eastern Europe and Asia.

The most consequential, albeit not widely appreciated, difference between Taiwan and the communist countries has to do with levels of repression. The exact magnitude of repression is difficult to ascertain, though it is beyond dispute that the February 28 Incident in 1947, during which 5,000–28,000 people were killed, set the stage for the White Terror, which resulted in either 29,407 trials of 140,000 people or 60,000–70,000 political trials of 200,000 people.[252] It is less clear whether, as some have claimed, repression during the period of martial law decreased steadily. The argument about a decline relies on statistics about individuals who sought compensation for wrongful sentencing during the White Terror.[253] As only some victims sought compensation, such data are not representative of overall patterns in politically motivated repression during the period. Government statistics that have been available for decades indicate

---

nytimes.com/1981/08/09/world/taipei-irritated-by-protests-in-us.html (accessed April 19, 2022). Another important case is that of Jiang Nan, who was assassinated in San Francisco in 1984 after publishing an unauthorized biography of Chiang Ching-kuo; Jiang Nan's murder parallels the killing of Bulgarian BBC journalist Georgi Markov in London in 1978 (see Khristo Khristov, *Ubiite "Skitnik": Bulgarskata i britanskata durzhavna politika po sluchaia Georgi Markov* [Sofia: Ciela, 2006]).

[248] Zhang and Chen, eds., *Jieyan shiqi baise kongbu*.

[249] Gao, *Qingzhi dang'an*, 180.

[250] Chen "Taiwan jieyan shiqi de tewu tongzhi," 63.

[251] Gao, *Qingzhi dang'an*, 227.

[252] Chen, "Taiwan jieyan shiqi de tewu tongzhi," 44; Julia C. Strauss, *State Formation in China and Taiwan: Bureaucracy, Campaign, and Performance* (New York: Cambridge University Press, 2020), 76–119.

[253] Greitens, *Dictators and Their Secret Police*, 180–84.

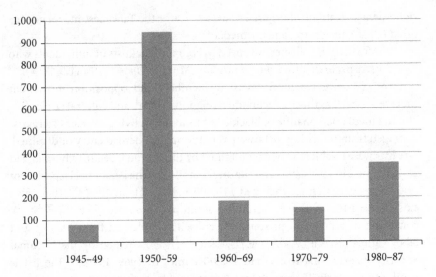

Figure 9.2 Rebellion and spy cases in Taiwan, 1945–1987 (average per year).

Source: Rebellion and spy cases (only for those sentenced by the military) from Chen Wencheng Boshi Jinian Jijinhui, Renquan Zhilu 2008 Ban Bianji Xiaozu, "Baise kongbu zhengzhi anjian gaishu," at http://docs.google.com/View?docid=dctzj6jf_1fn85k7d9 (accessed December 29, 2008).

that patterns of political persecution were cyclical (see Figures 9.2 and 9.3). Repression dropped but then rose again (in contrast to the situation in Eastern Europe) and it was at significantly higher levels than that in the Soviet Union.

What might explain these patterns of repression? Most important is that Taiwan had no social contract, so there was no expectation that violence would consistently decline in exchange for quiescence by a population whose welfare needs were met by the state. In contrast to the communist regimes, Taiwan never developed selective repression based on prophylaxis.

But a secondary factor that likely contributed to high violence may have been over-enforcement: interagency competition persisted to the extent that it gave rise to a special kind of cases in the 1960s and 1970s, namely, wrongful political prosecutions arising from rivalries among spy agencies (*tewu neidou anjian* 特務內鬥案件).[254] One point that deserves future research is whether, as some have claimed,[255] the creation of the National Security Bureau in 1955 led to the centralization of the intelligence apparatus and the coordination of the activities of its dozen or so constituent entities. There is certainly evidence that efforts were made to clarify jurisdictional overlap. For example, in 1955 Jiang Jingguo

---

[254] Chen Tsui-lian, "Qingzhi jiguan neibu douzheng suo yinqi de baise kongbu zhengzhi an," in Zhang and Chen, eds., *Jieyan shiqi baise kongbu*, 253–65.
[255] Greitens, *Dictators and Their Secret Police*.

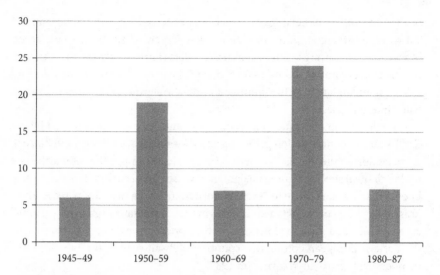

Figure 9.3 Opposition cases in Taiwan, 1945–1987 (average per year).

Sources: Qiu Pei'en, *Zhanhou Taiwan zhengzhifan de falü chuzhi* (Taipei: Taiwan Daxue Falü Yanjiusuo, 1997), 13; Chen Jiahong, *Taiwan duli yundongshi* (Taipei: Yushanshe, 2006), 95.

decided that mainland work had to be transferred from the Investigation Bureau of the Ministry of Justice to the Intelligence Bureau (情報局) of the Ministry of Defense; in turn, the Intelligence Bureau was to transfer domestic protection work to the Investigation Bureau. The goal was to have the Investigation Bureau handle domestic security and to assign mainland work to the Intelligence Bureau.[256] Despite this attempt to clarify responsibilities for external intelligence versus domestic counterintelligence, overlap and rivalries survived throughout the martial law period.[257]

A third reason for the high rate of repression might have been the deep internal and external insecurity of the regime: the distrust of locals (as revealed by the February 28 Incident and by the White Terror) and the existential threat from China were both real. Discrimination against locals persisted, as evidenced by the fact that as late as 1984, only twelve of the thirty-one positions on the Central Standing Committee were occupied by native Taiwanese (to make matters worse, the positions did not confer real power—e.g., islanders were allotted only one of the eight security sector [military and police] seats—that

[256] Li Shijie, *Diaocha ju yanjiu* (Taibei: Li Ao Chubanshe, 1988), 132.
[257] Li, *Diaocha ju yanjiu*; Chen, "Taiwan jieyan shiqi de tewu tongzhi," 43–70; and Chen, "Qingzhi jiguan neibu douzheng," 253–65.

of the head of the Judicial Yuan, which was occupied by Hung Shou-nan).[258] Taiwanese representation in the Cabinet was somewhat stronger, where seven of seventeen seats were taken by nonmainlanders (importantly, the ministries of the interior, communications, and as of 1984, justice).[259] Maintaining minority rule by mainlanders over the dominant population group of Taiwanese exacerbated internal insecurity.

Overall, we can conclude that security was an obsession, as indicated by the KMT's focus on information gathering and the presence of so many intelligence agencies during the martial law period (of course, the imposition of martial law itself demonstrates the regime's heightened sense of insecurity). It is not widely known that Taiwan's move to "soft" authoritarianism featured an increase in repression.[260] This contradicts assumptions in the "democratization from strength" argument about declining violence after the Formosa Incident.[261] In contrast to the Eastern European communist countries, Taiwan remained repressive until democratization began in earnest in 1987.

9.5.5 Voluntary Provision of Information through Petitions

As this book argues, citizen complaints are the most important channel for the transmission of information on mass preferences in nonelectoral autocracies. There existed many entities that received petitions under martial law (for simplicity, the term "petitions" is used to describe all types of citizen requests in Taiwan): the Executive Yuan, the Provincial Government, the Provincial Consultative Council (*sheng yihui* 省議會), the Legislative Yuan, and the Control Yuan.[262] Different terms were used to describe the various citizen communications: requests (*chenqing* 陳情), supplications (*qingyuan* 請願), appeals (*suyuan* 訴願), re-appeals (*zai suyuan* 再訴願), and petitions (*shuzhuang* 書狀). Requests and supplications were accepted by the Unified Reception Center of the Provincial Government, by the Provincial Consultative Council, and by the Legislative Yuan. Appeals and re-appeals were examined by the appeal boards (*suyuan hui* 訴願會); in 1981, these were located within the Executive Yuan, the Ministry of the Interior, the Ministry of Finance, the Ministry of Economic

---

[258] Edwin A. Winckler, "Institutionalization and Participation in Taiwan: From Hard to Soft Authoritarianism?" *The China Quarterly*, no. 99 (September 1984), 481–99, at 489.

[259] Winckler "Institutionalization and Participation in Taiwan," 490.

[260] Winckler "Institutionalization and Participation in Taiwan."

[261] Dan Slater and Joseph Wong, "The Strength to Concede: Ruling Parties and Democratization in Developmental Asia," *Perspectives on Politics* 11:3 (September 2013), 717–33.

[262] *Renmin chenqing anjian zhi fenxi yanjiu* (Taipei: Taiwan Sheng Zhengfu Yanjiu Fazhan Kaohe Weiyuanhui, 1979); *Renmin chenqing anjian zhi fenxi yanjiu* (Taipei: Xingzhengyuan Yanjiu Fazhan Kaohe Weiyuanhui, 1981).

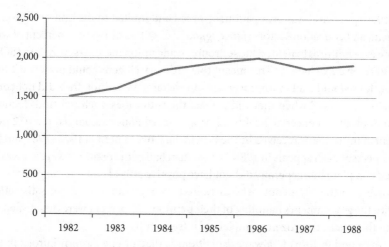

Figure 9.4 Petitions in Taiwan, 1982–1988 (per million people).

Sources: Calculated from data in Lu Zhengxun, "Woguo renmin chenqing zhidu zhi yanjiu" (MA Thesis, Chinese Culture University, 1991), 82, 104–7, 112, 120–21; *Taiwan sheng zhengfu suyuan nianbao* (Taipei: Taiwan Sheng Zhengfu Suyuan Shenyi Weiyuanhui, June 30, 1989), 27; Department of Supervisory Operations, *Standing Committees of the Control Yuan* (Taipei: Control Yuan, 2000).

Affairs, the Ministry of Education, the Taiwan Provincial Government, the Taipei City Government, and the Kaohsiung Government.[263] Petitions (書狀) were handled by the Control Yuan.

In light of the numerous options that existed for lodging petitions, it is notable how infrequently citizens complained. Composite statistics compiled for the 1982–1988 period reveal that the total volume of complaints per million people never exceeded 2,000 annually (see Figure 9.4). It is useful to put this number in comparative perspective. In China, where only petitions received by the Bureaus of Letters and Visits can be systematically tracked, complaints reached 13,862 per million people in 1979 (the peak year for petitioning between the end of the Cultural Revolution and the 1989 protests) and again rose to 10,870 at their post-1989 peak in 2003. In Bulgaria, the composite number of complaints in 1978–1989 ranged between a low of 27,777 per million people (in 1989) and a high of 75,120 per million people (in 1984). Thus, the volume of petitions in Taiwan is low by comparison with the communist regimes.

The root cause of the low volume of complaints is that the military dictatorship made no commitment to provide Eastern European–style welfare. In 1952, a mere 2 percent of the population had labor insurance.[264] Rather than universal,

---

[263] Huang Qinghe, "Woguo xianxing suyuan zhidu zhi yanjiu" (MA Thesis, Chengchi University, Department of Public Administration, 1983), 216.

[264] Joseph Wong, *Healthy Democracies: Welfare Politics in Taiwan and South Korea* (Ithaca, NY: Cornell University Press, 2004), 49.

welfare provision was occupationally based and limited to the military, government, and education sectors (*jungongjiao* 軍公教); as of 1991, 74 percent of welfare expenditures benefited those groups; trade union members from large SOEs also received welfare.[265] This meant that ordinary citizens could not expect that petitions would lead to improvements in welfare. As a result, they did not complain often—and when they did contact the authorities, their petitions focused on nonwelfare concerns: health, labor, and social issues accounted for 10.2 percent of the requests received by the Provincial Government in 1977–1987 and for 6.7 percent of all appeals in 1988.[266] Less than half of the petitions were successful and complainants generally did not have positive attitudes about the petitioning process: of the 141 people who answered a survey question about satisfaction with the government's handling of their petitions, 73 percent were dissatisfied.[267] For these reasons, citizens complained infrequently.

A second feature of Taiwanese petitions is that, unlike Eastern Europe in the second half of the 1980s or China in the lead-up to Tiananmen, there was no significant drop in the number of complaints prior to democratization. Figure 9.4 shows that petitions, though low, stayed at a constant level. Complaints did not decline because there were modest improvements in welfare provision: in the 1980s, health coverage increased from 17 percent of the population in 1980 to 25 percent by 1985 and 37.5 percent by 1988 due to farmers' insurance.[268] The limited but slowly expanding commitments to welfare are also illustrated by the size of government expenditures on life support (*shenghuo fuzhu* 生活扶助), medical assistance (*yiliao buzhu* 醫療補助), emergency relief (*jinan jiuzhu* 急難救助), and disaster relief (*zaihai jiuzhu* 災害救助), which amounted to NT$3.29 billion in 1978–1983 (when GDP equaled NT$9,655.2 billion) and it grew to NT$8.77 billion in 1984–1989 (when GDP equaled NT$18,909.8 billion).[269] However, even with these improvements, state provision of social services still fell considerably short of Eastern European–style welfare. The voluntary transmission of information through complaints never developed in Taiwan. Given the lower expectations, citizens were not disappointed with the capacity of the regime to deliver benefits. The dictatorship did not end because of welfare frustrations. In contrast, in Eastern Europe, they were a major catalyst for regime

---

[265] Dafydd Fell, *Government and Politics of Taiwan*, 2nd edition (New York: Routledge, 2018), 224–26.

[266] Calculated from Lu, "Woguo renmin chenqing zhidu," 82 and *Taiwan sheng zhengfu suyuan nianbao*, 25 and 32.

[267] *Renmin chenqing anjian* (1979), 38.

[268] Wong, *Healthy Democracies*, 43, 49, 52.

[269] Welfare expenditures calculated from Lu "Woguo renmin chenqing zhidu," 122. Nominal GDP from Bureau of Statistics of the Directorate General of Budget, Accounting and Statistics of the Republic of China, https://www1.stat.gov.tw/point.asp?index=1 (accessed April 19, 2022).

change (even if democratization cannot be attributed exclusively to the failed social contract).

At a more general level, Taiwan demonstrates that there exist striking parallels between the make-up of communist and noncommunist Leninist information states. In light of these parallels, the differences are even more surprising. As institutions serve concrete regime goals, studying them without knowledge of these goals may be misleading. Overall, the case of Taiwan compellingly shows that identical information-gathering institutions will have varying functions in different political settings.

9.6 Information Gathering in Single-Party Noncommunist Regimes and in Dominant-Party Authoritarian Regimes: Iraq (1968–2003) and Russia under Putin

Moving outside the world of Leninist regimes, we can ask how the institutional make-up of single-party autocracies is similar or different to the Leninist regimes in terms of involuntary extraction and voluntary provision. One of the two regimes examined in this section is postcommunist, thus allowing us to also assess the impact of institutional legacies on information gathering.

9.6.1 Iraq under the Ba'th Party (1968–2003)

As a noncommunist single-party dictatorship, Iraq developed an information-gathering system that diverged in some ways from those in the communist countries. Like all autocracies, Iraq entrusted its numerous intelligence agencies to monitor overt discontent.[270] The existing literature has not documented the informant saturation rate,[271] though it has established that similar to the ethnically heterogeneous communist regimes, Iraq had difficulties penetrating minorities.[272] Another similarity is the role of the party in collecting information. Like the communist parties, the Ba'th had full members, candidates, and sympathizers; the number of full members expanded from 0.25 percent of the population in 1986 to 0.9 percent in 2001 and perhaps as much as 2.2 percent in

---

[270] Joseph Sassoon, *Saddam Hussein's Ba'th Party: Inside an Authoritarian Regime* (New York: Cambridge University Press, 2012).

[271] On the recruitment of informants, see Martin K. Dimitrov and Joseph Sassoon, "State Security, Information, and Repression: A Comparison of Communist Bulgaria and Ba'thist Iraq," *Journal of Cold War Studies* 16:2 (Spring 2014), 4–31, esp. 22–30.

[272] Lisa Blaydes, *State of Repression: Iraq under Saddam Hussein* (Princeton, NJ: Princeton University Press, 2018); Lisa Blaydes, "Rebuilding the Ba'thist State: Party, Tribe, and Administrative Control in Authoritarian Iraq, 1991–1996," *Comparative Politics* 51:1 (2020), 93–115.

2002.[273] Although the density of the Ba'th networks varied across governorates, from a low of 3.9 party members to a high of 17.7 per 1,000 residents (with Baghdad having 6.8 members per 1,000 residents in 2002),[274] the party nevertheless established a presence throughout the country and extracted significant amounts of information on dissent.[275] However, as party development occurred during war,[276] the emphasis was on collecting information that could be used to wield repression.[277] In practice, this meant that the Ba'th had a capacity to monitor overt discontent but not to detect latent discontent. In terms of the voluntary transmission of information, although we know that Saddam read individual petitions,[278] there is no evidence in the scholarly record that the systematic analysis of citizen complaints was developed as a strategy for gleaning knowledge of latent dissatisfaction among the citizenry. Another difference from the communist world involves internal journalistic reporting. No study mentions its existence under the Ba'th. Overall, based on the current state of the scholarly record, we can conclude that Iraq had a fairly developed system for the involuntary extraction of information, though voluntary provision was embryonic at best.

9.6.2 Russia

In an electoral authoritarian regime like Russia, regime insiders have access to sources of information on popular discontent that did not exist under communist rule, such as reliable internal opinion polling.[279] Actual tallies of competitive voting (rather than officially announced results) present further information about support. Frequent protests and strikes also sensitize regime insiders to political and socioeconomic grievances.[280] At the same time, traditional communist-era channels for the collection of information persist. First, the security services continue to monitor the popular mood by adding

[273] Aaron M. Faust, *The Ba'thication of Iraq: Saddam Hussein's Totalitarianism* (Austin: University of Texas Press, 2015).

[274] Blaydes, *State of Repression*, 185.

[275] Among other indicia of discontent, the Ba'th monitored rumors (see Blaydes, *State of Repression*). This is an additional similarity with the communist regimes.

[276] Dina Rizk Khoury, *Iraq in Wartime: Soldiering, Martyrdom, and Remembrance* (New York: Cambridge University Press, 2013).

[277] Dimitrov and Sassoon, "State Security, Information, and Repression."

[278] Faust, *The Ba'thication of Iraq*, 78; Alissa Walter, "Petitioning Saddam: Voices from the Iraqi Archives," in Aidan Russell, ed., *Truth, Silence, and Violence in Emerging States: Histories of the Unspoken* (New York: Routledge, 2019), 127–46.

[279] Ellen Barry, "Before Voting, Russian Leaders Go to the Polls," *The New York Times*, August 17, 2011, A1, https://www.nytimes.com/2011/08/17/world/europe/17polling.html (accessed April 19, 2022).

[280] P. V. Biziukov, "Trudovye protesty v Rossii 2008–2017 gg." (Moscow: Center for Social and Labor Rights, 2018), http://trudprava.ru/expert/analytics/protestanalyt/2015 (accessed April 19, 2020).

new methods, such as the tracking of online activity and social media posts, to their arsenal of existing tools for the involuntary extraction of information about the spread of popular dissatisfaction. Second, United Russia's 2.074 million members are dispersed throughout the country (ranging from 0.6 percent to 5.3 percent of the regional population),[281] allowing the party to operate as a formidable nationwide collector of information. Social organizations like neighborhood and community councils are co-opted by the local party-state to monitor citizen discontent and to pre-empt protests.[282] Communist-era institutions such as the People's Control Committees have been revived by United Russia and tasked with conducting checks on the pricing and quality of goods and services, thus generating internal information on a key source of consumer discontent.[283] Third, internal media reporting persists.[284] Last and most important is the preservation of the voluntary transmission of information by citizens through letters (which, in keeping with the times, now arrive overwhelmingly by email). One of the main recipients is the President's Office, which handled more citizen complaints on an annual basis in the 2010s than the Central Committee of the CPSU in the 1980s.[285] Detailed analysis indicates that about 40 percent of the concerns raised in the letters to the President in 2012–2019 centered on welfare and housing issues.[286] Similar patterns can be observed in petitions directed to the St. Petersburg city government.[287] Thus, there exist remarkable continuities in the information-collection methods and in the attention paid to citizen welfare both under communism and in Putin's Russia.

---

[281] Calculated on the basis of January 2011 regional membership data for United Russia in each of the then-existing eighty-three regions of the Russian Federation, https://web.archive.org/web/201 21025025351/http://www.minjust.ru/common/img/uploaded/docs/2011.02.01_Edinaya_Rossiya_perechen.doc (accessed June 30, 2021) and regional population data from the October 2010 census (on file with the author).

[282] Natalia Forrat, *The Social Roots of Authoritarian Power: State–Society Relations and the Political Machines in the Russian Regions* (book manuscript).

[283] https://proekty.er.ru/node/6591 (accessed June 30, 2021).

[284] Ostal'skii, *Sud'ba nerezidenta.*

[285] Calculations based on *Informatsionno-statisticheskii obzor rassmotrennykh v 2019 godu obrashchenii grazhdan, organizatsii i obshchestvennykh ob'edinenii, adresovannykh Prezidentu Rossiiskoi Federatsii, a takzhe rezul'tatov rassmotreniia i priniatykh mer* (Moscow: Upravlenie Prezidenta Rosssiiskoi Federatsii po Rabote s Obrashcheniiami Grazhdan i Orgaznizatsii, 2020), 7 and Martin K. Dimitrov "Zhalbite na grazhdanite v komunisticheska Bulgariia," in Ivailo Znepolski, ed., *Da poznaem komunizma: Izsledvaniia* (Sofia: Institute for Studies of the Recent Past and Ciela Publishers, 2012), 167–226, esp. 217–21.

[286] *Informatsionno-statisticheskii obzor rassmotrennykh v 2019 godu obrashchenii,* 7.

[287] Elena Bogdanova, *Complaints to the Authorities in Russia: A Trap between Tradition and Legal Modernization* (London: Routledge, 2021), 156.

9.6.3 Summary Assessment

To sum up, postcommunist single-party regimes like Russia maintain the complement of voluntary and involuntary information-collection avenues, even though new channels have also emerged. As a noncommunist single-party regime, Iraq did not develop the full set of institutions, especially in terms of the voluntary transmission of information.[288] The main divergence between Russia and Iraq is that they paid differing degrees of attention to the masses and to assessing the reasons for their dissatisfaction, in order to counteract popular discontent prior to its transformation into overt opposition to the regime.

9.7 Information Gathering without Parties: Argentina and Chile

Argentina offers important insights into how a regime without political parties approaches the challenge of gathering information on popular discontent. Available evidence indicates that there was no voluntary transmission of information through citizen complaints during the last military dictatorship (*la última dictadura militar*) (1976–1983). Moreover, standard tools for the involuntary collection of information in the communist world, such as party reporting and internal journalism, were also absent under the junta. Involuntary collection did take place, but it was handled only by numerous security services with overlapping mandates. These entities collected low-quality information that was used to deploy poorly targeted repression against real and imaginary enemies of the dictatorship. Two counterfactuals about institutional design arise from the Argentine case. One, illustrated by a comparison with Chile under Pinochet, involves whether a clear hierarchy of enforcement agencies would have led to more precisely deployed repression. The second centers on whether

---

[288] When such institutions do develop, it happens slowly and over time (Donna J. Guy, *Creating Charismatic Bonds in Argentina: Letters to Juan and Eva Perón* [Albuquerque: University of New Mexico Press, 2016]; María del Carmen Nava Nava, *Los abajo firmantes: Cartas a los presidentes 1920–1928 & 1934–1946* [México: SEP/AGN/Editorial Patria, 1994]). One consequential difference between single-party communist regimes and noncommunist autocracies is the relative frequency of writing such letters: for example, although Mexico had a population that was five times greater than that of East Germany, the annual number of letters received by President Carlos Salinas de Gortari was almost identical to the volume of the letters that reached Erich Honecker when he was the leader of the GDR. Salinas received 432,996 letters in the first four years of his presidency (Josefina MacGregor, *México de su puño y letra: El sentir de un Pueblo en las cartas al Presidente* [México: Editorial Diana 1993], 15), whereas 2 million letters were addressed to Honecker during his eighteen years in office (Monika Deutz-Schroeder and Jochen Staadt, eds., *Teurer Genosse! Briefe an Erich Honecker* [Berlin: Transit, 1994], 6), resulting in 108,249 letters per year for Mexico and 111,111 letters per year for the GDR. The average population of Mexico in 1988–1992 was 85.6 million, whereas the GDR had an average population of 16.7 million citizens in 1971–1989.

a more diverse information-gathering setup, similar to that found in communist regimes, might have enabled a nimbler governance approach combining selective repression with targeted redistribution.

9.7.1 The Military in Charge of Information Collection

In the aftermath of the March 1976 coup, assessing and responding to dissent were the exclusive domain of the security services. Five main entities collected information and wielded repression: the three arms of the military (the army, the navy, and the air force), whose leaders collectively made up the junta; the federal police; and the National Intelligence Secretariat (*Secretaría de Inteligencia del Estado*, or SIDE), which had both intelligence and counterintelligence functions.[289] The five agencies were assisted as needed by the gendarmerie (especially in border regions) and by the federal penitentiary system (which administered prisons and collected intelligence from inmates). Collectively, these entities used their full-time staff and part-time informant networks to launch their battle against leftist subversion (*la lucha contra la subversión*).[290] A wide range of individuals became targets of the security services. Some were obvious, like leftwing organizations (the Montoneros, the Popular Revolutionary Army, and the communist party), labor union members (*gremialistas*), teachers, and students.[291] We can also understand why opposition to the junta was pronounced among progressive groups such as journalists,[292] lawyers,[293] and Jews.[294] The rationale for persecuting others, like actors, housewives (*amas de casa*), and security force personnel, is less readily apparent.[295] Overall, the list of enemies reflects the uncoordinated countersubversion initiatives of the numerous entities that constituted the security apparatus.

One obstacle to effective information gathering was created by the inappropriate qualifications for handling dissent among three of the five security agencies sharing this portfolio. The army, the navy, and the air force specialized

---

[289] Ministerio de Justicia y Derechos Humanos, *El Batallón de Inteligencia 601* (Buenos Aires: Ministerio de Justicia y Derechos Humanos, 2015), ix, 2.

[290] Ministerio de Justicia, *El Batallón de Inteligencia 601*, xi. As the governing philosophy of the regime, the battle against subversion impacted all spheres of life: see Nadia Zysman, "La militarización del ámbito educativo: La última dictadura militar argentina y su vínculo con la historia escolar, 1976–1983," *Latin American Research Review* 51:3 (2016), 47–63.

[291] For a breakdown of the categories of individuals who were disappeared, see Comisión Nacional sobre la Desaparición de Personas, *Nunca más: Informe de la Comisión Nacional sobre la Desaparición de Personas*, 10th ed. (Buenos Aires: Eudeba, 2017), 296.

[292] Rodolfo Walsh, "Carta abierta a la junta militar," March 24, 1977.

[293] Comisión Nacional, *Nunca más*, 430–34.

[294] On anti-Semitism, see Comisión Nacional, *Nunca más*, 71–77.

[295] Comisión Nacional, *Nunca más*, 296.

in military intelligence, which involved assessments of technological capacity, order of battle, armaments, training, bases, and communications systems of foreign adversaries.[296] This was quite different from focusing on an internal enemy. Poorly trained officers used crude techniques to round up subversives: for example, a quarter of those who were disappeared were detained in public places.[297] To avoid being spotted when preparing to abduct civilians in broad daylight, military officers resorted to various camouflage techniques, such as appearing plainclothes and wearing wigs (*vestidos de civil y con peluca*).[298] There was a proliferation of clandestine detention centers (*Centros Clandestinos de Detención*): at least 340 existed throughout the country,[299] with each security agency operating some of the centers. One of the largest was at the Higher School of Mechanics of the Navy (currently *Museo Sitio de Memoria ESMA*); the excessive atrocities committed at this illegal detention center attest to the incapacity of the armed forces to engage in the targeted collection of information.

Another suboptimal feature of the Argentine model is that informants were not used as a primary instrument for intelligence collection. The literature mentions the existence of police agents, confidants, and infiltrators.[300] However, the army's own manuals list three rank-ordered methods for information collection: first and foremost, interrogation of captured detainees; second, examination of captured materials; and last, analysis of captured documentation, aimed at identifying the strategy and tactics of organizations and persons to be detained in the future.[301] An information-collection doctrine that prioritized extracting information from detainees meant that the Argentine dictatorship practiced an unusually brutal form of repression. Had the security services created and carefully nurtured an informant corps, they could have deployed selective repression as an alternative strategy for handling dissent.

The sheer number of enforcers also raises concerns about coordination and the division of responsibility. The framework for coordination had been set up several months prior to the coup when army headquarters Intelligence Battalion 601 was designated as an information clearinghouse. The battalion established a meeting center (*la Central de Reunión del Batallón de Inteligencia 601*), with full-time personnel from each of the five main intelligence collectors, as well as from the gendarmerie and the penitentiary service.[302] It received intelligence

[296] Ministerio de Justicia, *El Batallón de Inteligencia 601*, 5.

[297] Comisión Nacional, *Nunca más*, 17.

[298] Ministerio de Justicia, *El Batallón de Inteligencia 601*, 6.

[299] Comisión Nacional, *Nunca más*, 55.

[300] José Luis Méndez Méndez and Pedro Etcheverry Vásquez, *Más allá del dolor* (Havana: Editorial Capitán San Luis, 2017), 367–71; Ministerio de Justicia, *El Batallón de Inteligencia 601*, 25, 37.

[301] Ministerio de Justicia, *El Batallón de Inteligencia 601*, 12.

[302] Later renamed *Central de Operaciones e Inteligencia*. See Ministerio de Defensa, *Relevamiento y análisis documental de los archivos de las Fuerzas Armadas 1976–1983* (Buenos Aires: Ministerio de Defensa, 2015), 109; Ministerio de Justicia, *El Batallón de Inteligencia 601*, 21–29.

from local information communities (*comunidades informativas*), which were established in 1975 to mirror the interagency participation design of the central meeting center.[303] To ensure functional specialization at the central level, five task forces (*Grupos de Tarea*) were established under the aegis of Battalion 601 several months before the coup; each had a specific task, such as fighting communists or leftist guerrillas.[304] On paper, intelligence gathering was streamlined and jurisdictional overlap did not exist.

In practice, problems abounded. A diplomatic cable from the U.S. embassy in Buenos Aires notes that competing jurisdictions and poor coordination (both nationally and locally) hampered intelligence work.[305] A high-level source from within Battalion 601 pointed out to the embassy officials that the security agencies (except the Navy) "refuse to send their best men" to the *Central de Reunión*, preferring to keep them in their own in-house intelligence units.[306] The lack of cooperation is also demonstrated by an admission of the head of the *Central de Reunión* that "due to lack of space" (*como en el Batallón 601 el lugar físico era escaso*), the five functionally specialized task forces continued to be located in each of the five security agencies.[307] This led to some odd choices: for example, the air force was in charge of pursuing the communist party.[308] The different agencies (and the task forces they managed) engaged in rivalries, with negative effects. As the U.S. embassy cable states, "Competition among many units put a high premium on fast action, which often meant that action was ill considered."[309] This competitive zeal among the various security agencies to detain individuals on the basis of poor information produced the unfortunate result of crudely targeted and excessive repression. Even if the numbers are in dispute (a low count of 8,960 disappeared and a high count of 22,000; tens of thousands victimized),[310] the abuses this system perpetuated are well known: torture, disappearances, and extrajudicial killings.

---

[303] Ministerio de Justicia, *El Batallón de Inteligencia 601*, 18–21; Ministerio de Defensa, *Relevamiento y análisis*, 253.

[304] Ministerio de Justicia, *El Batallón de Inteligencia 601*, 29–37.

[305] U.S. Embassy Buenos Aires, Memorandum of Conversation "Nuts and Bolts of the Government's Repression of Terrorism-Subversion," August 7, 1979, 8–9.

[306] U.S. Embassy, "Nuts and Bolts," 7–8.

[307] Ministerio de Justicia, *El Batallón de Inteligencia 601*, 24–25.

[308] Ministerio de Justicia, *El Batallón de Inteligencia 601*, 31.

[309] U.S. Embassy, "Nuts and Bolts," 6.

[310] For the low count, see Comisión Nacional, *Nunca más*, 16. For the high estimate, see Enrique Arancibia Clavel files, doc. label Carpeta V 232–238 (July 14, 1978). Also see Kathryn Sikkink, "From Pariah State to Global Protagonist: Argentina and the Struggle for International Human Rights," *Latin American Politics and Societies* 50:1 (2008), 1–29.

9.7.2   Counterfactuals: Variations in Institutional Setup and Levels of Repression and Concessions

The key features of the Argentine model of monitoring dissent during the last military dictatorship were the proliferation of security agencies and the lack of other institutions for the involuntary extraction or voluntary provision of information beyond these security agencies. There are theoretical payoffs to engaging with two counterfactuals: one involving a more streamlined state security apparatus and the other a more diverse set of information-gathering mechanisms. These counterfactuals allow us to explore how variations in institutional design may impact the frequency of the deployment of repression and concessions.

The first counterfactual is presented by the case of Chile under Pinochet (1973–1989), which was another military dictatorship governed by a junta that entrusted the armed forces with the collection of information on popular dissent. Initially, multiple branches of the military (army, navy, air force, gendarmerie) and the investigative police all collected information on dissent and engaged in extrajudicial detention, torture, and killings.[311] As in Argentina, elevated levels of repression marked the first months after the September 1973 coup. However, by June 1974, Pinochet succeeded in creating an intelligence agency (*Dirección de Inteligencia Nacional*, or DINA) that reported to him directly. The other security services continued to collect intelligence and even attempted to challenge DINA in 1975–1976,[312] but DINA (and its successor entity the *Central Nacional de Informaciones*, or CNI, which was created in 1977) maintained a role as the primary security agency in charge of assessing and counteracting dissent. Once DINA's placement at the top of the security agency hierarchy became clear, repression declined precipitously in comparison with that in 1973 (see Figure 9.5). This reduction is remarkable because, controlling for population, the level of repression during the first year of the dictatorship was higher in Chile than the low estimate of repression for the first year of the Argentine dictatorship (see Figure 9.6). The Chilean example raises the question of whether creating a clear intelligence agency hierarchy in Argentina would have had similar effects on the

---

[311] Pablo Policzer, *The Rise and Fall of Repression in Chile* (Notre Dame, IN: University of Notre Dame Press, 2009).

[312] These entities were the intelligence arms of the air force (*Dirección de Inteligencia de la Fuerza Aérea*, or DIFA), the navy (*Servicio de Inteligencia Naval*, or SIN), the army (*Dirección de Inteligencia del Ejército*, or DINE), and the gendarmerie (*Servicio de Inteligencia de Carabineros*, or SICAR). DIFA, SIN, DINE, and SICAR operated out of the same building and in 1975–1976 formed the *Comando Conjunto* (Joint Command), which unsuccessfully sought to challenge the primacy of DINA in the intelligence community. After DINA was dissolved and replaced by the CNI, the army and the gendarmerie continued to independently collect information on domestic dissent. See Comisión Nacional de Verdad y Reconciliación, *Informe de la Comisión Nacional de Verdad y Reconciliación*, vol. 2 (Santiago: Comisión Nacional de Verdad y Reconciliación, 1991), 718–32, 977–85.

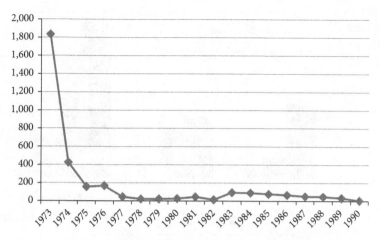

Figure 9.5 Individuals disappeared and executed in Chile, 1973–1990.

Sources: Comisión Nacional de Verdad y Reconciliación, *Informe de la Comisión Nacional de Verdad y Reconciliación*, vol. 2 (Santiago: Comisión Nacional de Verdad y Reconciliación, 1991), 1366; Corporación Nacional de Reparación y Reconciliación, *Informe de le Corporación Nacional de Reparación y Reconciliación*, 11th ed. (Santiago: Corporación Nacional de Reparación y Reconciliación, 1996), 526; Comisión Nacional sobre Prisión Política y Tortura, *Nómina de Detenidos Desaparecidos y Ejecutados Políticos, reconocidos por la Comisión Asesora para la Calificación de Detenidos Desaparecidos y Ejecutados Políticos y Víctimas de Prisión Política y Tortura* (Santiago: Comisión Nacional sobre Prísion Política y Tortura, 2010).

NB: These statistics are similar but not identical to those found in Policzer, *The Rise and Fall of Repression in Chile* (p. 89) and reproduced fully in Greitens, *Dictators and Their Secret Police* (p. 272). They incorporate data from an additional source (*Nómina de Detenidos Desaparecidos y Ejecutados Políticos* [2010]) that was not available when Policzer's study was published.

frequency of repression by improving the quality of the information collected and thus enabling more precise and selective targeting of violence.

The communist countries offer a second counterfactual. Could Argentina have relied on the party and on internal journalistic reporting as additional instruments for the involuntary collection of information? The junta suspended political parties and included journalists among the categories of individuals who were being disappeared,[313] so it foreclosed both options. Similarly, although the voluntary transmission of information through citizen letters existed in the early years of Perón's rule,[314] there is no evidence that the practice was institutionalized or survived under the junta. Would a richer set of institutions have resulted in a different type of approach? Even if the initial trajectory had been the

---

[313] Rodolfo Walsh, one of the most prominent journalists to be targeted, ran the so-called Clandestine News Agency (*Agencia de Noticias Clandestina*, or ANCLA), which dispatched 200 cables in the fifteen months of its existence (June 1976–September 1977). See Lila Pastoriza, "Homenaje a Rodolfo Walsh," *Conexiones Memoria*, no. 1 (2016), 10–14.

[314] Guy, *Creating Charismatic Bonds in Argentina*.

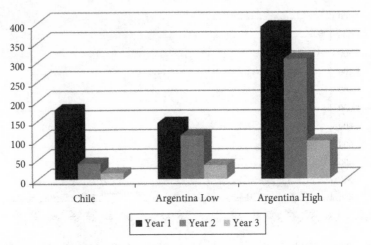

Figure 9.6 Disappearances and executions during the first three years of the military dictatorships in Chile and Argentina (per million people).

Sources: a) Chile: *Informe de la Comisión Nacional de Verdad y Reconciliación,* vol. 2, 1366; *Informe de le Corporación Nacional de Reparación y Reconciliación,* 526; *Nómina de Detenidos Desaparecidos y Ejecutados Políticos;* b) Argentina, low estimate: Comisión Nacional sobre la Desaparición de Personas, *Nunca más,* 16, 298; c) Argentina, high estimate: Enrique Arancibia Clavel files, doc. label Carpeta V 232–238 (July 14, 1978); John Dinges, *The Condor Years: How Pinochet and His Allies Brought Terrorism to Three Continents* (New York: New Press, 2004), 139.

same, the presence of such institutions would have likely paved the way for a less repressive and more redistributive (and ultimately, more durable) regime. The case of Cuba, which started out by granting the military extraordinary powers to monitor and counteract dissent, demonstrates that the creation of additional information-gathering institutions can force a gradual retreat of the armed forces from their hegemonic position of assessing and responding to popular discontent.

9.8 Conclusion

This chapter has analyzed information-gathering institutions in the complete range of autocracies: regimes without political parties; multiparty nondemocracies; and single-party dictatorships; in the last group, this chapter distinguishes among communist, noncommunist Leninist, and non-Leninist regimes. Cumulatively, the chapter outlines the scope conditions for the argument presented in the book. Only single-party communist regimes with a centrally planned economy are likely to develop complex information states where the party, State Security, and the media supply involuntarily collected and voluntarily provided complaints information that can be used to solve the dictator's dilemma by informing decisions about repression and concessions. Herein lies the communist information difference. The argument makes no assumption that communist regimes will develop such institutions at the same time or in the same sequence. But when these institutions do emerge, they deliver stability and thus help increase regime longevity—though, of course, even they cannot guarantee perpetual authoritarian rule. The issue of authoritarian durability over the long term will be discussed at greater length in the following concluding chapter.

10
Conclusion

Information and Authoritarian Regime Resilience

Autocracies need three types of sociopolitical information: military and foreign intelligence; assessments of the mood of elites; and evaluations of the level of popular discontent. As state survival depends on accurate evaluations of external risks, all regimes develop mechanisms for the collection of military and foreign intelligence. Likewise, autocrats who do not counteract the elite threat face the risk of being deposed. The mechanisms for the collection of the first two types of information are widely known: military and external intelligence services address the foreign threat, whereas coup-proofing is handled by the domestic security apparatus. The contribution of this book is to focus on the institutions that are deployed to address the popular threat. As we approach this issue, one relevant distinction can be made between overt and latent dissatisfaction: while all regimes task the security services with monitoring overt dissent, only some autocracies develop the more sophisticated institutions that are necessary to assess latent discontent prior to its transformation into overt acts of opposition to the system. Regimes that only monitor overt discontent practice highly repressive ex-post rule, whereas autocracies that track latent discontent adopt ex-ante anticipatory governance, which relies on low levels of repression. This book focuses on the complement of institutions needed for anticipatory rule and on the conditions under which regimes may transition from ex-post to ex-ante governance.

In comparing the information-collection institutions of communist regimes (which are the most durable type of dictatorship) with those of noncommunist autocracies (which have shorter lifespans), this book finds that the most sophisticated systems for assessing popular discontent emerge in single-party communist regimes. Regardless of whether they originate after a war or following a revolution, eventually all communist autocracies sideline the military from domestic information collection and develop the intelligence-gathering triumvirate consisting of State Security, the party, and internal media. Where communist regimes diverge is in their capacity to make the transition from ex-post to ex-ante governance. As ex-ante governance relies on evaluating latent discontent through voluntarily provided information, it cannot emerge unless levels of fear are low and responsiveness high. The book distinguishes between

Dictatorship and Information. Martin K. Dimitrov, Oxford University Press. © Oxford University Press 2023.
DOI: 10.1093/oso/9780197672921.003.0010

a low-repression high-redistribution socialist social contract (which features an elevated level of voluntary provision of information through complaints) and a moderate-repression moderate-redistribution market social contract with modest levels of voluntary provision through complaints. The socialist social contract emerged in Eastern Europe after the protests of the 1950s, whereas the market social contract arose in China after Tiananmen.

Regardless of which social contract is adopted, long-term regime resilience rests on repression, redistribution, and counteracting foreign influences through the promotion of indigenous cultural consumption. What differs across the two social contracts is the amount of repression and redistribution. Because it was more redistributive and less repressive, the socialist social contract ultimately led to a higher quality of governance than the market social contract. However, socialist social contracts were costly: they created unrealistic expectations of continuous improvements in the standards of living and universal welfare provision that could not be sustained under a centrally planned economy. This meant that the Eastern European regimes eventually reneged on their commitments, thus leading to the withdrawal of conditional loyalty on the part of the citizenry. Elite divisions and minority unrest then paved the way for democratization in 1989–1991. In China, the market social contract has featured welfare commitments that are more extensive than those that existed under Mao but are modest by Eastern European standards. Thus far, the model with fewer commitments and lower responsiveness appears more durable—though socioeconomic protests and minority unrest may destabilize it.

The remainder of this concluding chapter will first briefly summarize the empirical, methodological, and theoretical contributions of the book that are relevant for studies of autocracies; it will then review the key findings that pertain to research on China and Eastern Europe; and it will conclude by offering some reflections about information gathering and regime resilience in China after the arrival of COVID-19.

10.1 Contributions

10.1.1 General Empirical Contributions

Information gathering in autocracies is a black box. We have a general awareness of the existence of individual institutions (especially the secret police) and specific mechanisms that reveal dissent (in particular elections, protests, rumors, and complaints), but we do not have a clear sense of how these institutions and mechanisms operate together as a system. Moreover, we do not know how and why intelligence-gathering institutions evolve and change over time. Finally, the relative contribution of various institutions and mechanisms to generating actionable intelligence is not generally made clear in the literature. This study sheds light on these issues and clarifies how intelligence-collection agencies operate, what information they collect, and how this information is used to guide decisions about the use of repression and redistribution. This book also highlights the communist difference in information gathering, namely, although all countries monitor foreign and elite threats,[1] only communist regimes develop sophisticated institutions for the collection of information that allows for antic-ipatory ex-ante rule based on monitoring latent discontent—noncommunist regimes have cruder information-collection infrastructures that enable retro-spective ex-post governance.

By adopting a comparative perspective, this study highlights that the initial governance challenges confronted by communist regimes as different as Bulgaria and China were remarkably similar. Also similar were the institutional solutions to these challenges and their limits in terms of minority penetration. Involuntary extraction throughout the communist world relied on identical mechanisms, which were upgraded as technology evolved. One difference emerged in vol-untary provision through complaints, which was abundant under the socialist social contract but much less so under the market social contract, in which frus-trated petitioners turned to protests. Although protests are also a form of vol-untary provision, they index overt discontent and spread knowledge about it horizontally, potentially facilitating further anti-regime collective action. This is why regime insiders discourage protests and encourage complaints, which allow for the confidential vertical transmission of information about latent discontent.

10.1.2 General Methodological Contributions

When developing theories of authoritarian politics, scholars have three options: to rely on stylized facts or secondary sources; to draw on informa-tion that has been made available by the regime—research on the function of elections, protests, and liberalized media is an example of this approach; or to use materials that are meant for regime insiders rather than for public dissemi-nation. Driven by the logic that public artifacts are equivocal sources,[2] this study develops its theoretical argument on the basis of classified internal-circulation

---

[1] Those working on noncommunist regimes have argued that a fragmented security apparatus is necessary for coup-proofing: James Quinlivan, "Coup Proofing," *International Security* 24:2 (1999), 131–65; Sheena Chestnut Greitens, *Dictators and Their Secret Police: Coercive Institutions and State Violence* (New York: Cambridge University Press, 2016). In the communist world, the obverse is true: the number of intelligence agencies is reduced during periods of an elevated coup threat.

[2] Robert Barros, "On the Outside Looking In: Secrecy and the Study of Authoritarian Regimes," *Social Science Quarterly* 97:4 (December 2016), 953–73.

materials (direct sources) from China and Bulgaria, supplemented by similar documents from four Leninist regimes and by primary and secondary sources from four non-Leninist autocracies. These materials, which are analyzed via the method of archival ethnography, allow us to see how regime insiders understood their information problem. They also reveal how elections and protests, which generate knowledge of discontent both for regime insiders and for the general public, were perceived. Finally, they suggest an alternative explanation for the function of liberalized media: considering that internal media are investigative by design, the function of "investigative" reporting in the publicly accessible media is to demonstrate responsiveness to the masses rather than to satisfy the information needs of the regime. Thus, internal documents produce different explanations for the hidden dynamics in autocracies than those suggested by officially disseminated materials or by publicly observable indicators.

10.1.3 General Theoretical Contributions

A stylized fact in research on autocracies is that the dictator's dilemma cannot be solved because citizens engage in preference falsification, which involves publicly declaring support for the regime while privately being opposed to it. The central theoretical contribution of this study is to demonstrate that the dictator's dilemma can be solved—although the solution is more complex than that of the security dilemma or the elite threat, which have occupied center stage in studies of authoritarian politics. This book calls for theories of authoritarian rule to take seriously the role of the masses by studying discontent during its latent stage before it is transformed into system-destabilizing overt protests or revolutions.

There are several solutions to the dictator's dilemma. Overt expressions of discontent are, of course, free from preference falsification but they cannot emerge as an optimal solution because they hold the potential of undermining the regime as a whole while also providing information about the extent of opposition to the incumbent. For this reason, assessing discontent during its latent stage and deploying repression and concessions to prevent its transformation into overt opposition to the regime is a superior strategy for solving the dilemma. As this study demonstrates, when it is interpreted carefully and is cross-checked against the redundant intelligence generated through other channels, even involuntarily extracted information can provide detailed indicia of discontent. However, voluntarily provided information in the form of citizen complaints is more valuable for solving the dictator's dilemma as it is free from preference falsification and thus it is easier to analyze. An additional advantage of voluntary transmission of information is that it binds citizens to the regime through a social contract, whereby they exchange quiescence for material and cultural consumption.

Vertical voluntary information transmission in the form of complaints therefore directly contributes to regime resilience. Horizontal voluntary transmission in the form of protests does not.

A related finding of this study is that solving the dictator's dilemma cannot ensure the permanence of either the dictator or the regime. Information is only useful when it can be deployed effectively. This is possible only under certain optimal conditions discussed in this book. When those conditions are absent, even well-informed dictators may be deposed.

A final implication of the argument is that revolutionary cascades need not indicate that dictators are uninformed. It is both theoretically plausible and empirically demonstrable that dictators may make a rational decision not to oppose a revolutionary cascade when they know that the elites have defected, and that mass discontent cannot be counteracted through either repression or concessions. This is precisely what occurred in Eastern Europe in 1989–1991.

10.1.4 China-Specific Contributions

It is impossible to know whether and how China might be unique until we systematically compare it with another regime. The comparisons here reveal several features of the Chinese information state that are unfamiliar to scholars. First, despite the differences in their precommunist historical trajectories, levels of development, and regime origins, prior to 1989 both China and Bulgaria created identical institutions for the involuntary extraction and voluntary provision of information: the party, State Security, and the internal media. Naturally, those institutions developed at a different speed and in different sequences: for example, the threat of ideological subversion in China was not strong in the 1960s–1970s, thus delaying the upgrading of the existing state security apparatus into the Ministry of State Security until 1983, whereas Bulgaria re-organized its political police as early as 1967 to better safeguard its ideological security. Nevertheless, the existence of identical institutional complements in these otherwise remarkably different countries highlights the communist specificity of information gathering. In each state, the party emerged as both a coordinating agency and a key collector of intelligence. Second, a stylized fact is that the German Democratic Republic (GDR) was the most highly penetrated communist regime. As this book documents, China's counterintelligence penetration rate in the 2010s significantly exceeded that of the GDR at the peak of the expansion of its informant network in the 1980s. Most remarkably, the advent of the Internet, social media, and sophisticated surveillance systems led to an *increase* in the number of informants who are needed to supply the fine-grained intelligence that allows analysts to interpret the raw data collected through technological surveillance. Finally, despite the existence of identical institutions for voluntary provision, the rate of complaining in China has been extremely low since 1949 by comparison with that in Eastern Europe. It remained so in the 2000s and 2010s as well, after online complaints and mayor's mailboxes were introduced. Technology cannot compensate for low levels of responsiveness, which disincentivizes citizens to petition and directs them toward joining protests. Identical institutions have different effects under the socialist and the market social contracts.

10.1.5 Eastern Europe–Specific Contributions

As with the case of China, the specificities of the Eastern European cases become clearer in a comparative framework. Several surprising findings emerge. First, these regimes were much less repressive than is commonly thought. A virtuous feedback loop existed in terms of repression: low repression enabled the voluntary transmission of information, and, in turn, abundant information allowed for the deployment of anticipatory rule, which rested on selective repression. The lower level of repression is highlighted by the differential frequency of labor-camp detention of Muslims in the 1980s in Bulgaria and the 2010s in China (0.3 percent of the Turks vs. 10 percent of the Uyghurs). Second, the Eastern European leaders were not uninformed in 1989, thus placing the revolutions of 1989 in a new light. Finally, the existence of social contracts constrained the leaders. Such contracts developed for domestic reasons but also as a result of the competition with the West, and they gave rise to classic welfare dictatorships that combined selective repression with extensive state-supplied material and cultural consumption. While we may think that socialist welfare states were doomed to fail, the Cuban case demonstrates that these economically inefficient but politically expedient arrangements may persist for decades past 1989 (we should also note that China did not surpass Cuba in per capita GDP until 2016, after four decades of robust Chinese growth and three decades of steady Cuban decline, thus revealing how highly developed the Cuban welfare state was during the Cold War).[3] The comparison highlights that the trifecta of economic downturns, elite splits, and minority unrest facilitated democratization in Eastern Europe in the 1980s; the last two elements were not present in Cuba in 1989—by contrast, China had all three, but they were limited to the cities.

---

[3] World Development Indicators Online. GDP measured in constant 2010 U.S. dollars.

10.2 Information Gathering since 2019, Regime Resilience, and the Future of China

One question that we have not yet examined is whether COVID-19 has introduced a major rupture in information gathering. As of 2022, the available evidence indicates that the pandemic has made involuntary extraction more pervasive, as individuals have had to submit to even more intrusive surveillance for reasons of public health. AI and smart policing continue to evolve, with camera density increasing at a constant pace. Other initiatives, such as the social credit system and blacklists, are also expanding,[4] even though there are questions about how well the different bureaucratic and regional blacklists are integrated.[5] As we think about technological evolution, a historical parallel might be relevant for understanding the blacklists. Under the Qing, a system of ideological control known as *xiangyue* (乡约) emerged.[6] Through public lectures, the Board of Rites aimed to educate rural residents about proper behavior inside and outside the family. An important feature of the *xiangyue* system was the temporary public display in exposition pavilions of the names of those who had violated their filial duties or failed to maintain harmonious social relations. The names were removed once the misconduct had been corrected.[7] Public blacklists in contemporary China have an identical logic and a similar function of exerting social control through naming and shaming those who have engaged in transgressive behavior. Based on currently available information, we can say that the pandemic has not functioned as a critical juncture in information collection. The pre-existing systems persist, though they are continuously being upgraded. Perhaps the best illustration of the mélange of analog and digital practices is that community policing remains an important part of information gathering, which is why visible and secret informants have not been made redundant by COVID-19.

10.2.1 Information and Regime Resilience

As Xi Jinping was assuming power a decade ago, I argued that apart from repression, communist regime resilience rests on four types of adaptations: of the economy and welfare; of ideology; of the systems for inclusion; and of the

---

[4] Wen-Hsuan Tsai, Hsin-Hsian Wang, and Ruihua Lin, "Hobbling Big Brother: Top-Level Design and Local Discretion in China's Social Credit System," *The China Journal*, no. 86 (2021), 1–20.

[5] Séverine Arsène, "China's Social Credit System: A Chimera with Real Claws" (Paris: French Institute of International Relations, 2019).

[6] Kung-chuan Hsiao, *Rural China: Imperial Control in the Nineteenth Century* (Seattle: University of Washington Press, 1960), 184–258.

[7] Hsiao, *Rural China*, 186.

mechanisms for responsiveness and accountability.[8] Information is, of course, essential to both decisions about repression and to the finetuning of these four adaptations. What is relevant as we think about the future is that none of the adaptations are proceeding smoothly, which, in turn, fuels increased repression. This is not a model that augurs well for China.

The market social contract contains pitfalls for the regime. Under the socialist social contract in Eastern Europe, citizens expected a steady increase in standards of living as a result of economic growth and extensive price subsidies; in addition, they received a comprehensive package of welfare benefits (lifetime employment, subsidized housing, free healthcare and education, and universal pensions at age 55 for women and 60 for men); importantly, inequality was low. In China under Mao, the socialist social contract extended only to a subset of the urban population.[9] The market social contract currently in place involves elevated levels of economic growth, universal pensions (at age 50 or 55 for women and 60 for men) and health insurance, and access to free education through junior high school. Apart from extreme inequalities in wealth and vast regional and sectoral disparities in welfare provision,[10] discontent is high because of the difficulties of enforcing labor regulations, the insecurity of urban property rights (especially over housing), and the displacement of rural residents from their homes due to lucrative land redevelopment schemes supported by local governments. Trust in the party in the 2010s was declining and presumably decreased further during the initial cover-up of COVID-19 and during the 2022 lockdowns.[11] A question that will impact the future is how much longer the party-state will be able to direct welfare discontent away from Beijing toward the local governments. Should dissatisfaction turn against the central government, systemwide instability is likely to follow.

A second concern is about the firmness of the ideological foundations of the regime. It is clear that the party is committed to resisting Western influence, as reaffirmed by Xi Jinping in the centenary speech he delivered on July 1, 2021, when audiences were reminded that China had withstood "subversion, sabotage, and armed provocation" and that it would not allow foreign forces to "bully, oppress, and subjugate" it.[12] In contrast to Eastern Europe and similar to Cuba

---

[8] Martin K. Dimitrov, ed., *Why Communism Did Not Collapse: Understanding Authoritarian Regime Resilience in Asia and Europe* (New York: Cambridge University Press, 2013).

[9] Nara Dillon, *Radical Inequalities: China's Revolutionary Welfare State in Comparative Perspective* (Cambridge, MA: Harvard University Asia Center, 2015).

[10] Xian Huang, *Social Protection under Authoritarianism: Health Politics and Policy in China* (New York: Oxford University Press, 2020).

[11] Information about epidemics was considered sensitive in both the Soviet Union under Gorbachev and in China under Xi: see TsKhSD f. 89 per. 9 d. 24 (August 25, 1989) and "Dangzheng xinxixie gongzuo de jidian tihui," http://www.zk168.com/fanwen/fanwenxinde_274744 (accessed April 5, 2019).

[12] http://www.xinhuanet.com/2021-07/01/c_1127615334.htm (accessed April 19, 2022).

and North Korea, the Chinese regime benefits from a robust stock of nationalist support. In addition, exposure to Western ideas is much more limited in China today than it was in Eastern Europe during the Cold War.[13] Nevertheless, Chinese concerns about cultural security are real and parallel those that existed in the Eastern Bloc beginning in the late 1950s. Alongside the harassment of rights-based NGOs, strategies such as traditional learning (*guoxue* 国学), cultural confidence (*wenhua zixin* 文化自信), and the Sinicization of religion have been deployed to counteract Western ideological infiltration.[14] Whether promoting patriotic pride and indigenous cultural products to distract from searching for Western entertainment (and finding Western ideas) will continue to be successful in the future is an open question.[15]

Turning to the third adaptation, we also detect deficiencies in the incorporation of potential rivals. On the whole, both the rank-and-file and the ultra-rich private entrepreneurs seem to be well integrated into the communist party.[16] Similarly, intellectuals do not appear likely to go against the party: those harboring pro-democratic ideals are imprisoned, exiled, or otherwise silenced; the rest are sufficiently content with their sinecures not to risk angering the Chinese Communist Party (CCP) by expressing independent thoughts. The main challenge to the party arises from the compactly settled minorities, especially the Tibetans, the Uyghurs, and the Mongols. The official understanding is that hostile foreign forces are promoting secessionism among these minorities. Pervasive policing (including by the ubiquitous "becoming kin" [*jiedui renqin* 结对认亲] cadres), mass incarcerations, and detention in reeducation centers have resulted in a lack of open dissent in Xinjiang since 2018. A relevant point of comparison might be that the forced assimilation campaign unleashed against the Bulgarian Turks in 1984–1985 led to four years of calm—until the spring of 1989, when pent-up discontent erupted forcefully. The continued resilience of the Chinese regime would require solving the problem of minority inclusion.

Finally, responsiveness and accountability are at a crisis point. In the Chinese context, the most meaningful metric for evaluating responsiveness is the handling of citizen complaints. As this book has shown, after growing in the 1990s, the number of petitions has been declining for the past two decades. In parallel,

---

[13] On China, see U.S. Agency for Global Media, *Audience and Impact: Overview for 2019* (Washington, DC: U.S. Agency for Global Media, 2018), 15. On Eastern Europe, see *Cold War Broadcasting Impact* (Stanford, CA: Hoover Institution, 2005), 45–47.

[14] http://www.xinhuanet.com/politics/xxjxs/2019-06/19/c_1124642114.htm (accessed April 19, 2022).

[15] Margaret E. Roberts, *Censored: Distraction and Diversion Inside China's Great Wall* (Princeton, NJ: Princeton University Press, 2018).

[16] Yue Hou, *The Private Sector in Public Office: Selective Property Rights in China* (New York: Cambridge University Press, 2019); Zhu Zhang, "Wealth Without Power: The Rise of China's Super-Rich and Their Relationship to the Communist Party" (PhD Dissertation, Tulane University, Department of Political Science, 2021).

the incidence of protests has been increasing. Socioeconomic protests emerge overwhelmingly from frustrated petitions, thus demonstrating that officials handling complaints are not sufficiently responsive to citizen requests for welfare, labor protection, or redress in cases of predatory displacement from land or housing. Low responsiveness to complaints signals the breakdown of the market social contract. Moreover, the new normal under Xi Jinping is to treat both socioeconomic and political protests as threats to social stability (and, by extension, to state security). This has meant that instead of concessions, contentious acts are likely to be met with repression. Such an equilibrium cannot bode well for the future stability of the system. Improving responsiveness is imperative for incentivizing citizens to return to the complaints system and to engage in the private transmission of information rather than in public displays of dissatisfaction. The alternative would be to allow the wave of protests to continue to grow until the volcanic stability that China has experienced for at least a decade ruptures.[17]

Despite these challenges, the CCP celebrated its 100th birthday in July 2021.[18] This is an impressive achievement. As we move forward, there are two possible paths. One is suggested by the Bulgarian Communist Party, which turned 98 when democratization began in 1989 and celebrated its 100th birthday when it stepped down from power in 1991. It governed again in the mid-1990s and the 2000s, but as the result of democratic elections. In 2021, the party turned 130 years old. Renamed socialist, it is resilient; its logo features 1891 as its year of creation. Single-party rule, however, is long-gone. As the CCP looks toward the centenary of the establishment of the People's Republic of China (PRC) in 2049, it should want to be on a different pathway from the one of the Bulgarian Socialist Party. The CCP, which will be 128 years old in 2049, will most certainly still exist then, perhaps even under its current name. The question is whether the single-party system will be preserved. As we contemplate the possible futures, we should be mindful that information is essential for the survival of single-party rule. Involuntary extraction is useful for repression, yet this governance strategy is not sustainable in the long term. Voluntarily transmitted complaints information is indispensable for anticipatory ex-ante rule. The key to improving voluntary transmission is higher responsiveness to citizen concerns. As far as the management of popular discontent is concerned, this is the survival formula for the CCP.

[17] Martin King Whyte, *Myth of the Social Volcano: Perceptions of Inequality and Distributive Injustice in China* (Stanford, CA: Stanford University Press, 2010).

[18] Bruce Dickson, *The Party and the People: Chinese Politics in the 21st Century* (Princeton, NJ: Princeton University Press, 2021); Tony Saich, *From Rebel to Ruler: One Hundred Years of the Chinese Communist Party* (Cambridge, MA: Harvard University Press, 2021); David Shambaugh, *China's Leaders: From Mao to Now* (New York: Polity Press, 2021); Timothy Cheek, Klaus Mühlhahn, and Hans van de Ven, eds., *The Chinese Communist Party: A Century in Ten Lives* (New York: Cambridge University Press, 2021).

Index